PRODUCTION OF LEGAL RULES

Encyclopedia of Law and Economics, Second Edition

General Editor: Gerrit De Geest
School of Law, Washington University, St. Louis, MO, USA

1. Tort Law and Economics
Edited by Michael Faure
2. Labor and Employment Law and Economics
Edited by Kenneth G. Dau-Schmidt, Seth D. Harris and Orly Lobel
3. Criminal Law and Economics
Edited by Nuno Garoupa
4. Antitrust Law and Economics
Edited by Keith N. Hylton
5. Property Law and Economics
Edited by Boudewijn Bouckaert
6. Contract Law and Economics
Edited by Gerrit De Geest
7. Production of Legal Rules
Edited by Francesco Parisi
8. Procedural Law and Economics
Edited by Chris William Sanchirico

Future titles will include:

Regulation and Economics
Edited by Roger Van den Bergh and Alessio M. Pacces

Methodology of Law and Economics
Edited by Thomas S. Ulen

Corporate Law and Economics
Edited by Joseph A. McCahery and Erik P.M. Vermeulen

Intellectual Property Law and Economics
Edited by Ben Depoorter and Michael Meurer

For a list of all Edward Elgar published titles visit our website at
http://www.e-elgar.co.uk

Production of Legal Rules

Edited by
Francesco Parisi

Oppenheimer Wolff and Donnelly Professor of Law,
University of Minnesota, USA and
Professor of Economics, University of Bologna, Italy

ENCYCLOPEDIA OF LAW AND ECONOMICS, SECOND EDITION

Edward Elgar

Cheltenham, UK • Northampton, MA, USA

Published by
Edward Elgar Publishing Limited
The Lypiatts
15 Lansdown Road
Cheltenham
Glos GL50 2JA
UK

Edward Elgar Publishing, Inc.
William Pratt House
9 Dewey Court
Northampton
Massachusetts 01060
USA

A catalogue record for this book
is available from the British Library

Library of Congress Control Number: 2011927283

MIX
Paper from
responsible sources
FSC® C018575

ISBN 978 1 84844 032 6

Printed and bound by MPG Books Group, UK

Contents

Contributors

Enrico Baffi, University of Rome (Roma Tre), Faculty of Law, Italy
Emanuela Carbonara, University of Bologna, Department of Economics, Italy
Robert Cooter, University of California at Berkeley, School of Law, USA
Jef De Mot, Ghent University, Faculty of Law, Belgium
Laarni Escresa, University of Hamburg, Germany
Michael Faure, Erasmus University, Rotterdam, Faculty of Law and Maastricht University, Faculty of Law, Netherlands
Vincy Fon, George Washington University, Department of Economics, USA
Nita Ghei, Cato Institute, USA
Carmine Guerriero, University of Amsterdam, Department of Economics, Netherlands
Robert P. Inman, University of Pennsylvania, Wharton School of Business, USA
Louis Kaplow, Harvard Law School, USA
Jonathan Klick, University of Pennsylvania, Law School, USA and Erasmus University, Rotterdam, Faculty of Law, Netherlands
Barbara Luppi, University of Modena and Reggio Emilia, Department of Economics, Italy
Richard H. McAdams, University of Chicago, Law School, USA
Anthony Ogus, University of Manchester, Faculty of Law, UK
Francesco Parisi, University of Minnesota Law School, USA and University of Bologna, Department of Economics, Italy
Paul H. Rubin, Emory University, Department of Economics, USA
Daniel L. Rubinfeld, University of California at Berkeley, School of Law and Department of Economics, USA
Paolo Santella, Central Bank of Italy, Italy
Hans-Bernd Schäfer, Bucerius Law School, Hamburg, Germany
Duncan Snidal, Nuffield College, University of Oxford, UK
Paul B. Stephan, University of Virginia, School of Law, USA
Edward Peter Stringham, Fayetteville State University, North Carolina, USA
Alexander Thompson, Ohio State University, Department of Political Science, USA
Stefan Voigt, University of Hamburg, Department of Economics, Germany
Georg von Wangenheim, University of Kassel, Faculty of Law, Germany
Todd J. Zywicki, George Mason University, School of Law, USA

Introduction

In recent years literature in law and economics directed its attention to the study of law as a product. These contributions are of great theoretical and practical importance. This volume collects original contributions from several scholars that have been protagonists in this trend in the literature. Viewed in its entirety, this volume provides comprehensive coverage of alternative sources of law, such as legislation, judge-made law, custom, and treaty law. Individual chapters focus on the characteristics of specific instruments of legal intervention and on broader topics such as conflict of law, federalism, regulatory competition, and law and development. Selecting topics for inclusion in this volume was far from easy. The final selection hopefully strikes a good balance between the need for systematic coverage and practical relevance.

The volume is divided into five parts. Part I includes chapters on the economics of legislation and regulation. The first chapter by Stefan Voigt covers issues of constitutional design of lawmaking. The second chapter by Louis Kaplow discusses the general characteristics of legal rules. In the following chapters, Barbara Luppi and Francesco Parisi detail the optimal specificity of laws and the distinction between rules and standards, Nita Ghei discusses the optimal timing of legal intervention, and Georg von Wangenheim analyzes the production of legal rules by agencies and bureaucracies.

Part II of this volume considers judge-made law, with original contributions by Paul H. Rubin on the economics of judge-made law, Todd Zywicki and Edward Peter Stringham on the efficiency of the common law hypothesis, Jeff De Mot on the study of bias in the common law, and Carmine Guerriero on the empirical evidence regarding the effect of legal systems on economic performance.

Part III considers social norms and customary law. Topics covered in this section range from Richard McAdams' treatment of expressive law to Emanuela Carbonara, Francesco Parisi and Georg von Wangenheim's exploration of countervailing norms. Michael Faure and Laarni Escresa add a discussion of the role of social stigma in legal compliance, while Anthony Ogus and Emanuela Carbonara cover self-regulation.

Part IV considers the economics of international law, with Paul Stephan's general chapter on international law as a source of law, and specific chapters on the economics of international treaties by Vincy Fon, customary international law by Jef De Mot, Vincy Fon and Francesco Parisi, and international organizations by Alexander Thompson and Duncan Snidal.

Part V concludes this volume with an analysis of topics relating to federalism, legal harmonization and development. Contributions include Robert P. Inman and Daniel L. Rubinfeld's economics of federalism, legal harmonization by Enrico Baffi and Paolo Santella, forum shopping and the evolution of choice of law by Nita Ghei, regulatory competition by Jonathan Klick, and Robert D. Cooter and Hans-Bernd Schäfer's growth-oriented legal reforms.

This collection of original contributions by leading scholars in the field contributes to a more systematic understanding of lawmaking as a production process emphasizing the respective advantages and proper scope of application of alternative sources law. The contributions to this volume will hopefully shed new light on the important issue of the institutional design of lawmaking through the lens of economic analysis and public choice theory.

PART I

LEGISLATION AND REGULATION

1 Constitutional design of lawmaking

Stefan Voigt

1. Introduction

The economic analysis of constitutional law has not been one of the most researched topics within law and economics. The research program known as "constitutional economics" or "constitutional political economy" has primarily been developed by scholars emanating from public choice, i.e. "the application of economics to political science" (Mueller 1989, p. 1). James M. Buchanan, the most prominent proponent of constitutional economics, has described law and economics as a related subdiscipline that has remained, however, closer to orthodox economic theory because the standard efficiency norm remains central to it (Buchanan 1987a, p. 586). Scholars of constitutional economics have broadened the standard research program of economics. Standard economics is interested in the analysis of choices within rules, thus assuming rules to be exogenously given and fixed. Constitutional economics broadens this research program by analyzing the choice of rules using the standard method of economics, i.e. rational choice.

Buchanan defines constitutions in their most basic sense as "a set of rules which constrain the activities of persons and agents in the pursuits of their own ends and objectives" (Buchanan 1977, p. 292). Defined as such, quite a few rule systems could be analyzed as constitutions: a firm's partnership agreement as well as a church statute. Although such rule systems have indeed been analyzed from the point of view of constitutional economics (for a firm's constitution, see Gifford 1991 or Vanberg 1992), the rule system analyzed most often remains the constitution of the state. Two broad avenues in the economic analysis of constitutions can be conceived of: (1) The normative branch of the research program is interested in legitimizing the state and the actions of its representatives. In other words, it is interested in identifying conditions under which the outcomes of collective choices can be judged as "fair" or "efficient". (2) The positive branch of the research program is interested in explaining (a) the emergence and modification of constitutional rules and (b) the outcomes that are the consequence of (alternative) constitutional rules (for a similar demarcation of the topic, see Mueller, 1996; Voigt 2011 is an up-to-date survey of the field).

The entry is organized as follows: Section A is devoted to normative constitutional economics whereas section B deals with positive constitutional economics. The entry closes with an outlook.

A. NORMATIVE CONSTITUTIONAL ECONOMICS

2. Methodological Foundations

Normative constitutional economics has the potential to deal with a variety of questions, e.g. (1) How should societies proceed in order to bring about constitutional rules that fulfill some criterion like being "just" or "efficient"? (2) What contents should the constitutional rules have? (3) Which issues should be dealt with in the constitution – and which should be left to sub-constitutional choice? (4) What characteristics should constitutional rules have? And many more. Buchanan answers none of these questions directly but hopes to offer a conceptual frame that would make them answerable. The frame is based on social contract theory as developed most prominently by Hobbes. According to Buchanan (1987b, p. 249), the purpose of this contractarian approach is justificatory in the sense that "it offers a basis for normative evaluation. Could the observed rules that constrain the activity of ordinary politics have emerged from agreement in constitutional contract? To the extent that this question can be affirmatively answered, we have established a legitimating linkage between the individual and the state."

The value judgment that nobody's goals and values should *a priori* be more important than those of anybody else, i.e. normative individualism, is the basis of Buchanan's entire model. One implication of this norm is that societal goals cannot exist. According to this view, every single individual has the right to pursue her or his own ends within the frame of collectively agreed upon rules. Therefore, a collective evaluation criterion that compared the societal "is" with some "ought" cannot exist since there is no such thing as a societal "ought". But it is possible to derive a procedural norm from the value judgment stated. Buchanan borrowed this idea from Knut Wicksell (1896). Agreements to exchange private goods are judged as advantageous if the parties involved agree voluntarily. The agreement is supposed to be "efficient", "good" or "advantageous" because the parties involved expect to be better off with the agreement than without it. Often, the exchange activities are considered to be taking place only between two parties, the seller and the buyer. Buchanan follows Wicksell, who had demanded the same evaluation criterion for decisions that affect more than two parties, at the extreme an entire society. Rules that have consequences for every single member of a society can only be looked upon as advantageous if every single member of that society has voluntarily agreed to them. This is the Pareto criterion applied to collectivities. Deviations from the unanimity principle might occur during the decision process on the production of collective goods, but this would only be within the realm of the Buchanan model as long as the constitution itself provided for a decision rule below unanimity. Deviations from the unanimity rule would have to be based on a provision that was brought about unanimously.

3. Giving Efficiency Another Meaning

Normative constitutional economics thus re-interprets the Pareto criterion in a twofold way: it is not outcomes but rules or procedures that lead to outcomes which are evaluated using the criterion. The evaluation is not carried out by an omniscient scientist or politician but by the concerned individuals themselves: "In a sense, the political economist is concerned with 'what people want'" (Buchanan 1959, p. 137). In order to find out what people want Buchanan proposes to carry out a consensus test. The specification of this test will be crucial as to which rules can be considered legitimate. In 1959, Buchanan had factual unanimity in mind and those citizens that expect to be worse off due to some rule changes would have to be factually compensated. This test would thus be equivalent to a modified Kaldor-Hicks criterion. In the meantime, Buchanan seems to have changed his position: hypothetical consent deduced by an economist will do in order to legitimize some rule (see e.g. Buchanan 1977, 1978, 1986). This position can be criticized because a large variety of rules seem to be legitimizable depending on the assumptions of the scientist who does the process. Scientists arguing in favor of an extensive welfare state will most likely assume risk-averse individuals, while scientists who argue for cuts in the welfare budgets will assume people to be risk-neutral.

4. Critical Evaluation of Normative Constitutional Economics

The possibility of hypothetical consent crucially depends on the information assumptions. Buchanan and Tullock (1962, p. 78) introduced the veil of uncertainty in which the individual cannot make any long-term predictions about her or his future socio-economic position. John Rawls' (1971) veil of ignorance is more radical because the consenting individuals are asked to decide on proposed rules *as if* they did not have any knowledge on their individual fate. Rawls' veil is thus more demanding on the individuals. Both veils assume a rather curious asymmetry concerning certain kinds of knowledge: on the one hand, the citizens are supposed to know very little about their own socio-economic position, but on the other, they are supposed to have at their disposal a consistent theory concerning the working properties of alternative constitutional rules (Reisman 1990, pp. 23–30 describes the differences between the two conceptions of the veil).

In order to discuss the usefulness of the conceptual frame, suppose for a moment that it is impossible to legitimize a currently valid constitutional rule and that some constitutional economist has proposed an alternative rule for which she has ascertained a hypothetical consent. Further suppose that it is impossible to transform the hypothetical consent into majorities through which the constitution could be changed. Clearly, the non-legitimizable *status quo* would prevail over the legitimate constitutional rule.

B. POSITIVE CONSTITUTIONAL ECONOMICS

Positive constitutional economics can be divided into two parts: On the one hand, it is interested in explaining the outcomes that result from (alternative) rule sets. Here, constitutional rules are part of the *explanans*. On the other hand, positive constitutional economics is interested in explaining the emergence and modification of constitutional rules. In that case, constitutional rules are the *explanandum*.

B.A. CONSTITUTIONAL RULES AS EXPLANANDUM

5. Procedures for Generating Constitutional Rules

Constitutional rules can be analyzed as the outcome of certain procedures used to bring them about. Jon Elster's (1993, 1995) research program concerning constitutional economics puts a strong emphasis on hypotheses of this kind. He inquires about the consequences of time limits for constitutional conventions, about how constitutional conventions that simultaneously serve as legislature allocate their time between the two functions, about what effects providing regular information to the public concerning the progress of constitutional negotiations has and about how certain supermajorities and election rules can determine the outcome of conventions (Elster 1995, p. 30). Some of William Riker's articles (1983, 1984) can also be interpreted as an encouragement to search for hypotheses of this kind. He calls for an extension of traditional rational choice theory, pointing to the fact that in its traditional form it is incapable of taking into account dynamic and creative processes which structure the decision space of the actors.

This part of constitutional economics does not offer a general perspective on the process of constitution-making (Elster 1993, p. 174). There is, however, a large number of case studies (see, e.g., the volume edited by Goldwin and Kaufman 1988; Voigt and Wagener 2002 contains some first-hand descriptions of constitution-making processes in Central and Eastern Europe). Ginsburg et al. (2009) is a survey of both the theoretical conjectures and the available empirical evidence. They expect constitution-making processes centered around the legislature to be positively correlated with post-constitutional legislative powers, whereas constitution-making processes centered around the executive would be negatively correlated with post-constitutional legislative powers. Interestingly, the first half of the conjecture is not supported by the data, whereas the second half is. In a book-length work on the lifespan of constitutions, Elkins et al. (2009) report that public involvement in constitution-making is indeed correlated with a longer constitutional lifespan.

By and large, neither the Elster nor the Riker program has really caught the attention of constitutional economics, possibly because of huge methodological problems.

6. The Relevance of Preferences and Restrictions for Generating Constitutional Rules

Procedures are a modus of aggregating inputs and can therefore never bring about constitutional rules by themselves. It is therefore only logical to analyze whether a bunch of potentially relevant variables can explain the choice of certain constitutional rules. There are good reasons – and some empirical evidence – to assume that (1) the individual preferences of the members of constitutional conventions will directly enter into the deliberations and that (2) the preferences of all the citizens concerned will be recognized in the final document in quite diverse ways. This would mean that rent-seeking does play a role even on the constitutional level, a conjecture that is often excluded by representatives of normative constitutional economics.

McGuire and Ohsfeldt (1986, 1989a, b) have tried to explain the voting behavior of the Philadelphia delegates as well as those of the delegates to the 13 state-ratifying conventions that led to the US Constitution. Their statistical results show that merchants, western landowners, financiers, and large public-securities holders, *ceteris paribus*, supported the new constitution, whereas debtors and slave owners, *ceteris paribus*, opposed it (1989a, p. 175).

7. Explicit Constitutional Change

The two approaches towards constitutions as *explananda* just sketched are rather static. A third approach focuses on explaining the modifications of constitutions over time. Constitutional change that results in a modified document will be called explicit constitutional change here, whereas constitutional change that does not result in a modified document – i.e. change that is due to a different interpretation of formally unaltered rules – will be called implicit constitutional change.

One approach towards explaining long-run explicit constitutional change focuses on changes in the relative bargaining power of organized groups. Due to a comparative advantage in using violence (see North 1981), an autocrat is able to establish government and secure a rent from that activity. As soon as an (organized) group is convinced that its own cooperation with the autocrat is crucial for the maintenance of the rent, it will seek negotiations with the autocrat. Since the current constitution is the basis for the autocrat's ability to appropriate a rent, the opposition will strive to change it. In this approach, bargaining power is defined as the capability of inflicting costs on your opponent. The prediction of this approach is that a change in (relative) bargaining power will lead to modified constitutional rules (Voigt 1999, chapter 6).

Explicit constitutional change can be sought by interest groups who try to convince legislators to change the constitution. If constitutional change is only sought in disequilibrium, the interest group seeking change must perceive its own relevance as having changed. Boudreaux and Pritchard (1993) analyze from an economic perspective the 27 amendments that have so far been made to the US Constitution. They begin with the conjecture that a lobby group interested in constitutional change principally has two possibilities of seeking its realization: It can either lobby for a simple law or it can lobby for constitutional change. The second option is, however, more expensive. The trivial prediction of rational choice theory is that the group will choose the option with the higher expected utility. In order to be able to make predictions about the option chosen, it is therefore necessary to specify the cost and benefit categories implied. Boudreaux and Pritchard specify two categories and predict a demand for constitutional change in cases in which the costs of maintaining an interest group over time are high, and today's opposition is weak but expected to be strong in the future.

8. Implicit Constitutional Change

Implicit constitutional change has been defined as a changed constitutional interpretation that occurs even though the formal constitutional document remains unchanged. This means that the conceptual separation between choice of rules on the one hand and choice within rules on the other has been factually blurred. This possibility must be disturbing to the proponents of normative constitutional economics. To adherents of positive constitutional economics, it amounts to an analytical difficulty, because the identification of what is analyzed as the valid "constitution" either as *explanandum* or as *explanans* becomes more difficult. At the same time, the possibility of implicit constitutional change also becomes an object of inquiry. It can be asked which variables determine the scope and extent of the implicit constitutional change to be expected.

Suppose a constitution in the sense of constitutionalism exists and the government branches are legislature, executive and judiciary. If all government representatives have at their disposal a certain latitude concerning the interpretation of the constitution, it can be argued that all branches can bring about implicit constitutional change. If an independent judiciary exists, it seems plausible to assume that it has most latitude in causing implicit constitutional change because it has the power to judge the constitutional conformity of the actions of the other two government branches. It can now be argued that the judiciary is subject to a number of constraints, among which those laid down in the original constitutional document play a rather marginal role. Instead, the current preferences of the other branches are more relevant restrictions.

There are various factors that determine the latitude that justices have to bring about implicit constitutional change. Cooter and Ginsburg (1996) show that it depends on the number of chambers whose consent is needed to pass fresh legislation. The higher its number, the more difficult it will be for the other branches to correct implicit constitutional change by changing the constitutional document explicitly. They further show (ibid.) that it depends on the existence of a "dominant disciplined party". If such a party exists, it will be more difficult for the justices to bring about implicit constitutional change. Other variables that influence the amount of implicit constitutional change include the following: (1) If implicit constitutional change can only be prevented by changing the document explicitly, the necessary majority becomes a factor. The more inclusive it is, the more difficult it will be to prevent such change. (2) The possibility of referendums should be another explanatory variable. If the population at large can overturn the justices, they have an incentive not to deviate too drastically from the preferences of the median voter. (3) The extent of implicit constitutional change should be higher in common law systems than in continental law systems, because, in the first group, decisions by justices become directly applicable law.

B.B. CONSTITUTIONAL RULES AS EXPLANANS

In the previous part of this chapter, constitutional rules were analyzed as *explananda*. Such an analysis is of interest only if it can be shown that constitutional rules are themselves relevant to bringing about certain results or patterns that concern economists or social scientists in general; in other words, if constitutions matter. Possible *explananda* include fiscal policy variables (such as government revenue, expenditure, debt), governance variables (such as corruption), but also per capita income, its growth rate and factor productivity. In this area, empirical studies have proliferated over the last decade. Only a small fraction is mentioned here (Voigt 2011 is a more complete survey).

9. The Horizontal Separation of Powers in General

Brennan and Hamlin (1994) develop a "revisionist view" of the separation of powers. To make their point, they draw on standard monopoly models used in economics and distinguish between a horizontal and a vertical separation of powers. Starting out with a monopoly, the introduction of the horizontal separation amounts to two (or more) suppliers competing for demand and thus to the introduction of duopoly (or oligopoly). The equilibrium price will then be below the monopoly price and consumer rent will subsequently increase. A vertical separation of powers also entails a division of the original monopoly, albeit in a different way: Now, single functions of the process are divided; there is, for example, one monopolistic firm that produces certain goods and a second monopolistic firm that distributes it. Brennan and Hamlin call this functional separation of powers as well. The (individually) maximizing strategies of the vertically separated firms will at best lead to the monopoly price, but usually the price will be even higher and the accruing consumer rent will thus be lower than in the original monopoly. Brennan and Hamlin argue that the separation of powers doctrine as conventionally understood is equivalent to the functional separation of powers and will therefore not protect citizens from exploitation by the governed. The horizontal separation of powers could, instead, have beneficial results. In order to unfold, it needs to entail an "exit" option for citizens, as well as the absence of strong externalities between competing states.

Persson et al. (1997) argue that politicians have two possible routes to enriching themselves to the detriment of citizens, the first based on the misuse of power, the second on exploiting information advantages. The authors show that both possibilities can be reduced by implementing checks and balances between the legislature and the executive. This was one of the first models dealing with the (horizontal) separation of powers. However, it falls short of the traditional notion going back to Montesquieu, since it is based on two government branches only and does not take a third branch (the judiciary) into consideration.

10. Form of Government: Presidential versus Parliamentary Systems

The degree of separation of powers is greater in presidential than in parliamentary systems, since the head of the executive (the president) does not depend on the confidence of the legislature (parliament) to survive. Persson et al. (1997, 2000) argue that it is easier for legislatures to collude with the executive in parliamentary systems, which is why they expect more corruption and higher taxes in those systems than in presidential systems. They further argue that the majority (of both voters and legislators) in parliamentary systems can pass spending programs whose benefits are clearly targeted at themselves, implying that they are able to make themselves better off to the detriment of the minority. This is why Persson et al. (2000) predict that both taxes and government expenditures will be higher in parliamentary than in presidential systems.

Persson and Tabellini (2003) derive the following results: (1) Government spending is some 6% of GDP lower in presidential compared with parliamentary systems. (2) The size of the welfare state is some 2–3% lower in presidential systems. (3) The influence of form of government on the budget deficit is rather marginal; the binary variable explains only a small proportion of the variation in budget deficits. (4) Presidential systems seem to have lower levels of corruption. (5) There are no significant differences in the level of government efficiency between the two forms of government. (6) Presidential systems appear to be a hindrance to increased productivity, but this result is significant only at the 10% level.

These results are impressive and intriguing. Although government spending is less in presidential systems, and such systems suffer less from corruption than parliamentary systems, parliamentary systems have an advantage over presidential systems in terms of productivity, if only at a low level of significance. In a study replicating and extending the Persson and Tabellini estimates, Blume et al. (2009b) pour some water into the wine. It turns out that their results are not robust, even to minor modifications. Increasing the number of observations from 80 to 92 makes the presidential dummy insignificant in explaining variation in central government expenditure. This is also the case as soon as a slightly different delineation of presidentialism is used. If the dependent variable is changed to total (instead of central) government expenditure, the dummy also becomes insignificant. Persson and Tabellini's estimates of the effects of form of government on "graft" are based on data from 1997/98. If data for the period 1996 to 2004 are used instead (or the number of observations is increased, or a slightly different definition of presidentialism used, or a combination thereof), the dummy becomes insignificant. For total factor productivity, Persson and Tabellini did not find the presidentialism dummy significant. Interestingly, if a slightly different delineation of presidentialism or estimates of total factor productivity for 2000 (instead of 1988) are used, presidentialism becomes significantly (negatively) correlated with total factor productivity.

The differences in these results clarify an important point: to date, many of the effects supposedly induced by constitutional rules are not very robust, but crucially hinge upon the exact specification of the variables, the years considered, the control variables included, and so on. What this suggests is that further research needs to be as specific as possible in trying to identify possible transmission channels, as well as needing to take into consideration the possibility that small differences in institutional details can have far-reaching effects.

11. Unicameral versus Bicameral Systems

Presidentialism increases the separation of powers by separating the executive from the legislature; bicameralism does the same by dividing the legislature. Although bicameralism is a frequently found constitutional setting (according to Tsebelis and Money 1997, it can be found in approximately one-third of all legislatures), its economic effects remain underresearched. In their survey paper on bicameralism, Cutrone and McCarty (2006) note that it "has not received the scholarly attention that other legislative institutions have". Similarly, Bradbury and Crain (2002) find that, in contrast to the 19th century, when it was subject to heated discussion, bicameralism "receives scant attention in modern political economy".

The differential effects of unicameral and bicameral legislatures were first analyzed from an economic point of view by Buchanan and Tullock (1962, chapter 16). In their analytical frame, the optimal decision rule leads to a minimum of interdependence costs, which are defined as the sum of decision-making costs and those external costs that an actor has to bear in case his individually most preferred outcome is not the outcome of the collective choice. They conjecture that, in comparison with unicameral systems, bicameral systems have higher decision costs, and then go on to state that "[o]n the other hand, if the basis of representation can be made significantly different in the two houses, the institutions of the bicameral legislature may prove to be an effective means of securing a substantial reduction in the expected external costs of collective action without incurring as much added decision-making costs as a more inclusive rule would involve in a single house" (ibid., pp. 235 f.). The larger the majority required to reach a certain decision, the lower the external costs connected with that decision because the number of opponents is negatively correlated with the required majority. On the other hand, it will become increasingly difficult to reach a decision at all, because the decision costs are positively correlated with the required majority. One possibility for keeping external costs down is to require a supermajority (say of three-quarters or five-sixths) in the single-house system. Supermajorities in a single-house system and simple majorities in a two-house system can thus be considered as alternatives. Buchanan and Tullock conjecture that – given identical external costs – decision costs will be lower in a bicameral than in a unicameral system.

Miller and Hammond (1989) inquire into the effects of bicameralism and the executive veto, sometimes considered the third chamber, on stability in the sense of reducing the probability of cycling majorities à la Condorcet or Arrow (1951). They conclude that bicameralism and the executive veto increase stability. The stability-enhancing effect of bicameralism depends on some preference difference between the two chambers. Levmore (1992) changes the focus of the analysis somewhat when he conjectures that a bicameral system might be better than a corresponding qualified majority in a unicameral system at reducing the power of the agenda setter. Bicameral systems are often interpreted as a check against overly active legislatures.

In sum, then, it is argued that bicameralism protects minorities, reduces cycling, and curbs the power of the agenda setter.

12. Direct Democratic versus Representative Institutions

Representatives of normative constitutional economics ask on what rules the members of a society could agree behind a veil of uncertainty. If they agree on a democratic constitution, they would further have to specify whether and to what extent they want to combine representative with direct democratic elements. In order to make an informed decision, the citizens would be interested in knowing whether there are systematic relationships between these institutions and the patterns that they are interested in.

In real-world societies of a size too large to efficiently vote directly on all issues, representative and direct democracy are complementary institutions. In these societies, a different degree of direct democratic institutions is combined with representative institutions. With regard to direct democratic institutions, referendums are usually distinguished from initiatives. The constitution can prescribe the use of referendums for passing certain types of legislation, in which case agenda-setting power remains with parliament, but citizen consent is required. Initiatives, in contrast, allow citizens to become agenda setters: the citizens propose a piece of legislation that will then be decided upon, given that they manage to secure a certain quorum of votes in favor of the initiative. Initiatives can be aimed at different levels of legislation (constitutional versus ordinary legislation), and their scope can vary immensely (e.g. some constitutions prohibit initiatives on budget-relevant issues).

Matsusaka (1995, 2004) estimates the effects of the right to an initiative on fiscal policy among all US states except Alaska. States with the right to an initiative have lower expenditures and lower revenues than states without that institution. With regard to Switzerland, Feld and Kirchgässner (2001) deal with the effects of a mandatory fiscal referendum on the same variables. They find that in cantons with the mandatory referendum, both expenditure and revenue are lower by about 7% to 11% compared with cantons without mandatory referendums. Matsusaka (2004, chapter 4) also deals with the question of whether initiatives have any effect on the distribution of government spending between the state and the local level and finds that initiative states spend 13% less per capita at the state level than noninitiative states, but that initiative states spend 4% more on the local level.

Finally, do direct democratic institutions have any discernible effect on productivity and thus on per capita income? Feld and Savioz (1997) find that per capita GDP in cantons with extended democracy rights is some 5% higher than in cantons without such rights. Frey and co-authors argue that one should not look only at the outcomes that direct democratic institutions produce, but also at the political processes they induce (e.g. Frey and Stutzer 2006). Kirchgässner and Frey (1990) speculate that the readiness of voters to incur information costs would, *ceteris paribus*, be higher in democracies with direct democratic institutions, because the voters participate more directly in the decisions (ibid., p.63).

Blume et al. (2009a) is the first cross-country study to analyze the economic effects of direct democracy and their findings only partially confirm the previous results. They do find a significant influence by direct democratic institutions on fiscal policy variables and government efficiency, but no significant correlation between direct democratic institutions and productivity or happiness. Institutional detail matters a great deal: while mandatory referendums appear to constrain government spending, initiatives seem to increase it. The actual use of direct democratic institutions often has more significant effects than their potential use, implying that – contrary to what economists would expect – the direct effect of direct democratic institutions is more relevant than its indirect effect. It is also noteworthy that the effects are usually stronger in countries with weaker democracies.

13. Individual Rights and Economic Growth

Many constitutions contain an elaborate catalogue of basic rights, which are often separated into positive or negative rights. Negative rights can further be delineated into rights establishing *freedom from* state or third-party interference (such as torture, imprisonment without trial, etc.) and *freedom to* do something (assemble with others, criticize the government in public, etc.). Examples of positive rights are rights to food, housing, paid jobs, and so forth. Negative rights create a protected domain that not even the state is allowed to trespass. For democratically organized states, this implies that negative rights limit the possible scope of majority decision making: if rights are really basic, even large majorities are bound by them and cannot simply ignore them. Negative rights can thus protect minorities against current majorities and can be thought of as "veto rights", as they give their holders the right to behave in a certain way, even if a huge majority would like the right holders to behave differently.

When it comes to basic rights, the congruence between formally granted rights and their actual enforcement is especially crucial. It is even plausible to assume that the degree of factual enforcement is a function of other constitutional characteristics. For example, a greater separation of powers – be it horizontal, vertical, or a combination thereof – would appear conducive to a high degree of factual enforcement. In the literature, basic rights are usually sorted into three categories: (1) economic rights, which include primarily private property rights broadly defined; (2) civil and political rights, which include unrestricted travel, the possibility of participating in political life, freedom from government censorship, and so forth, although it is not uncommon for political rights to be explicitly separated from civil rights; and (3) social or emancipatory rights, which endow the individual with positive rights vis-à-vis the state. Blume and Voigt (2007) propose a fourth category, namely, basic human rights, which includes the absence of torture, the absence of political killings, the absence of people who disappear, etc.

There is a sizable literature inquiring into whether economic rights have a significant effect on economic growth, Knack and Keefer (1995) being a pathbreaker on this topic. Their paper, for the first time, uses data from the International Country Risk Guide and Business Environment Risk Intelligence as proxies for the security of property rights and finds that the security of these rights is significant for explaining both investment and growth. Around the same time, the Economic Freedom Index first appeared (Gwartney et al. 1996), as did the Index of Economic Freedom, which was produced jointly by the Heritage Foundation and the *Wall Street Journal*. These data sets gave rise to an entire cottage industry, focusing on the interrelations between various aspects of economic freedom and prosperity.

Two follow-up questions suggest themselves. (1) What about the effects of constitutional entrenchment on other variables, such as government spending or corruption? After all, a long list of positive rights means that resources will be needed for their implementation. This should be reflected in the structure of the budget and – most likely – also in the overall level of government spending. (2) What factors determine whether constitutionally guaranteed rights will be factually enforced?

C. OUTLOOK

John Neville Keynes proposed a tripartite division of political economy, introducing the "art of political economy" besides the more standard positive and normative branches. This art deals with the possibilities of reducing differences between "is" and "ought" (Keynes 1955). It almost suggests conceiving of an "art of constitutional political economy" analogously. This art would itself have to have a positive foundation: Knowledge about the potential to modify constitutions intentionally is primordial for such a third branch. If one thinks that constitutional economics is potentially relevant for real-world constitution writers, then one must be disappointed with the degree to which insights from this research program have entered into the newly written constitutions of Central and Eastern Europe. In order to become more relevant, it seems essential to work on the third branch.

A central presumption of both the branches presented in Sections 2 and 3 is that constitutional rules constrain human behavior and that they can therefore be relevant to explaining it. Representatives of the New Institutional Economics would broaden this presumption and claim that institutions in general constrain human behavior. It thus almost represents a plea for the integration of constitutional economics into the New Institutional Economics. Whereas Brennan and Hamlin (1995) argue that one can conceptualize the "new institutionalism" as a subordinate research program, one can also argue exactly the other way round: If one does not start with the assumption that constitutional design is possible to a large extent and if one is furthermore critical of the assumed hierarchy of rules, and rather points to the complex interdependence between informal constraints and formal rules (North 1990) or between internal and external institutions (Kiwit and Voigt 1995), one would tend to conceptualize constitutional economics as part of the New Institutional Economics.

Bibliography

Arrow. K. (1951), *Social choice and individual values*, New York: Chapman and Hall.

Blume, L., Müller, J., and Voigt, S. (2009a), "The Economic Effects of Direct Democracy – A First Global Assessment", *Public Choice* 140: 431–61.

Blume, L., Müller, J., Voigt, S., and Wolf, C. (2009b), "The Economic Effects of Constitutions: Replicating – and Extending – Persson and Tabellini", *Public Choice*, 139: 197–225.

Blume, L., and Voigt, S. (2007), "The Economic Effects of Human Rights", *Kyklos*, 60(4): 509–38.

Boudreaux, Donald J. and Pritchard, A.C. (1993), "Rewriting the Constitution: An Economic Analysis of the Constitutional Amendment Process", *Fordham Law Review*, 62: 111–62.

Bradbury, J.C., and Crain, W.M. (2002), "Bicameral Legislatures and Fiscal Policy", *Southern Economic Journal*, 68(3): 646–59.

Brennan, Geoffrey and Hamlin, Alan (1994), "A Revisionist View of the Separation of Powers", *Journal of Theoretical Politics*, 6(3): 345–68.

Brennan, Geoffrey and Hamlin, Alan (1995), "Constitutional Political Economy: The Political Philosophy of Homo Economicus?", *Journal of Political Philosophy*, 3(3): 280–303.

Buchanan, James M. (1959), "Positive Economics, Welfare Economics, and Political Economy", *Journal of Law and Economics*, 2: 124–38.

Buchanan, James M. (1977), *Freedom in Constitutional Contract – Perspectives of a Political Economist*, College Station, TX and London: Texas A&M University Press.

Buchanan, James (1978), "A Contractarian Perspective on Anarchy", in J. Roland Pennock and John W. Chapman (eds.), *Anarchism*, New York, New York University Press, 29–42

Buchanan, James (1986), "Political Economy and Social Philosophy", in James Buchanan (ed.), *Liberty, Market and State – Political Economy in the 1980s*, Brighton, Sussex: Wheatsheaf Books, 261–74.

Buchanan, James M. (1987a), "Constitutional Economics", in J. Eatwell, M. Milgate and P. Newman (eds.), *The New Palgrave – A Dictionary of Economics*, London and Basingstoke: Macmillan, vol. 1: 585–8.

Buchanan, James M. (1987b), "The Constitution of Economic Policy", *American Economic Review*, 77: 243–50.

Buchanan, James M. and Tullock, Gordon (1962), *The Calculus of Consent – Logical Foundations of Constitutional Democracy*, Ann Arbor, MI: University of Michigan Press.

Cooter, Robert D. and Ginsburg, Tom (1996), "Comparative Judicial Discretion: An Empirical Test of Economic Models", *International Review of Law and Economics*, 16(3): 295–313.

Cutrone, M., and McCarty, N. (2006), "Does Bicameralism Matter?" in B. Weingast and D. Wittman (eds.), *Oxford Handbook of Political Economy*, Oxford: Oxford University Press, 180–95.

Elkins, Z., Ginsburg, T. and Melton, J. (2009), *The Endurance of National Constitutions*, Cambridge: Cambridge University Press.

Elster, Jon (1993), "Constitution-Making in Eastern Europe: Rebuilding the Boat in the Open Sea", *Public Administration*, 71(1/2): 169–217.

Elster, Jon (1995), "Forces and Mechanisms in the Constitution-Making Process", *Duke Law Journal*, 45: 364–96.

Feld, L.P. and Kirchgässner, G. (2001), "The Political Economy of Direct Legislation: Direct Democracy and Local Decision-Making", *Economic Policy*, 33, 329–63.

Feld, L. P. and Savioz, M. (1997), "Direct Democracy Matters for Economic Performance: An Empirical Investigation", *Kyklos,* 50(4), 507–38.

Frey. B. and Stutzer, A. (2006), "Direct Democracy: Designing a Living Constitution", in R. Congleton (ed.), *Democratic Constitutional Design and Public Policy – Analysis and Evidence*, Cambridge, MA: MIT Press, 39–80.

Gifford, Adam (1991), "A Constitutional Interpretation of the Firm", *Public Choice*, 68: 91–106.

Ginsburg, T., Elkins, Z. and Blount, J. (2009), "Does the Process of Constitution-Making Matter?", *Annual Review of Law and Science*, 5: 5.1–5.23.

Goldwin, Robert A. and Kaufman, Art (eds.) (1988), *Constitution-Makers on Constitution-Making*, Washington, DC: American Enterprise Institute.

Gwartney, James, Lawson, Robert and Block, Walter (1996), *Economic Freedom of the World: 1975–1995*, Vancouver et al.: The Fraser Institute et al.

Keynes, John Neville (1955), *The Scope and Method of Political Economy*, New York: Kelley.

Kirchgässner, G. and Frey, B. (1990), "Volksabstimmung und direkte Demokratie: Ein Beitrag zur Verfassungsdiskussion", in H.D. Klingmann and M. Kaase (eds.), *Wahlen und Wähler – Analysen aus Anlaß der Bundestagswahl*, Opladen: Westdeutscher Verlag, 42–69.

Kiwit, Daniel and Voigt, Stefan (1995), "Überlegungen zum institutionellen Wandel unter Berücksichtigung des Verhältnisses interner und externer Institutionen", *ORDO*, 46: 117–47.

Knack, S. and Keefer, P. (1995), "Institutions and Economic Performance: Cross-Country Tests Using Alternative Institutional Measures", *Economics and Politics*, 7(3), 207–27.

Levmore, Saul (1992), "Bicameralism: When are Two Decisions Better than One?", *International Review of Law and Economics*, 12: 145–62.

Matsusaka, J. (1995), "Fiscal Effects of the Voter Initiative: Evidence from the last 30 Years", *Journal of Political Economy*, 102(2): 587–623.

Matsusaka, J. (2004), *For the Many or the Few. The Initiative, Public Policy, and American Democracy*, Chicago: The University of Chicago Press.

McGuire, Robert A. and Ohsfeldt, Robert L. (1986), "An Economic Model of Voting Behavior over Specific Issues at the Constitutional Convention of 1787", *Journal of Economic History*, 46(1): 79–111.

McGuire, Robert A. and Ohsfeldt, Robert L. (1989a), "Self-Interest, Agency Theory, and Political Voting Behavior: The Ratification of the United States Constitution", *American Economic Review*, 79(1): 219–34.

McGuire, Robert A. and Ohsfeldt, Robert L. (1989b), "Public Choice Analysis and the Ratification of the Constitution", in Bernard Grofman and Donald Wittman (eds.), *The Federalist Papers and the New Institutionalism*, New York: Agathon, 175–204.

Miller, Gary J. and Hammond, Thomas H. (1989), "Stability and Efficiency in a Separation-of-Powers Constitutional System", in B. Grofman and D. Wittman (eds.), *The Federalist Papers and the New Institutionalism,* New York: Agathon Press, 85–99.

Mueller, Dennis C. (1989), *Public Choice II*, Cambridge: Cambridge University Press.

Mueller, D. (1996), *Constitutional Democracy*, New York: Oxford University Press.

North, Douglass C. (1981), *Structure and Change in Economic History*, New York: Norton.

North, Douglass C. (1990), *Institutions, Institutional Change and Economic Performance*, Cambridge: Cambridge University Press.

Persson, T., Roland, G. and Tabellini, G. (1997), "Separation of Powers and Political Accountability", *Quarterly Journal of Economics*, 112: 310–27.

Persson, T., Roland, G. and Tabellini, G. (2000), "Comparative Politics and Public Finance", *Journal of Political Economy*, 108(6): 1121–61.

Persson, T. and Tabellini, G. (2003), *The Economic Effects of Constitutions*, Cambridge, MA: MIT Press.

Rawls, John (1971), *A Theory of Justice*, Cambridge, MA: Belknap.

Reisman, David (1990), *The Political Economy of James Buchanan*, College Station, TX: Texas A & M University Press.

Riker, William H. (1983), "Political Theory and the Art of Heresthetics", in A. Finifter (ed.), *Political Science: the State of the Discipline*, Washington, DC: American Political Science Association, 47–67.

Riker, William H. (1984), "The Heresthetics of Constitution-Making: The Presidency in 1787, with Comments on Determinism and Rational Choice", *American Political Science Review*, 78: 1–16.

Tsebelis, G. (2000), "Veto Players and Institutional Analysis", *Governance*, 13(4), 441–74.

Tsebelis, G. and Money, J. (1997), *Bicameralism*, Cambridge: Cambridge University Press.

Vanberg, Viktor J. (1992), "Organizations as Constitutional Systems", *Constitutional Political Economy,* 3(2): 223–53.

Voigt, S. (1999), *Explaining Constitutional Change – A Positive Economics Approach*, Cheltenham, UK and Northampton, MA, USA: Edward Elgar.

Voigt, S. (2011), "Positive Constitutional Economics II: A Survey of Recent Developments", *Public Choice*, 146(1–2): 205–56.

Voigt, S. and Wagener, H.-J. (2002), *Constitutions, Markets and Law – Recent Experiences in Transition Economies*, Cheltenham, UK and Northampton, MA, USA: Edward Elgar.

Wicksell, Knut (1896), *Finanztheoretische Untersuchungen*, Jena: Fischer.

2 General characteristics of rules

*Louis Kaplow**

1. Introduction

Legal rules serve many functions: channeling behavior (for example, tort law, environmental law, criminal law), providing background rules (much of contract, commercial and corporate law), and defining obligations and eligibility for benefits (tax law, social welfare provisions). This chapter, following existing research, focuses on the first type of law. The relevance (or irrelevance) of the analysis to other types of law will usually be apparent, and some comments about the differences in contexts will be noted.

The most commonly noted characteristic of rules concerns the degree of precision, detail, or complexity they embody: how finely are different sorts of behavior to be distinguished? Such matters may arise in defining the scope of a legal command, providing for exceptions, adjusting sanctions based upon aggravating and mitigating circumstances, and so on. A related aspect of legal commands concerns *when* a given level of detail is provided – at the time of promulgation ('rules') or subsequent to individuals' actions, in the context of adjudication ('standards'). These aspects of rules are considered from a perspective that focuses upon information costs and dissemination: different sorts of legal commands involve differing costs of formulation and application by private parties (deciding upon their own conduct) and adjudicators, and the character of laws also influences how well parties actually will understand them and conform their conduct accordingly. This approach is used to illuminate choices about the degree of precision (or complexity) with which legal commands are formulated and between rules and standards. These subjects, in turn, encompass related questions involving the role of precedent, the evolution of the law over time, legal uncertainty and accuracy in adjudication.

After outlining the main ideas concerning these topics, this chapter addresses the separate problem of how changes in the law should apply to prior behavior or preexisting investments – issues of retroactivity and transition – and considers some other aspects of rules that have been addressed in the economic analysis of law.

* I am grateful for comments from Steven Shavell and the referees, research assistance from Enrique Arana, Judson Berkey and Jerry Fang, and support from the John M. Olin Center for Law, Economics and Business at Harvard Law School.

A. PRECISION OF THE LAW

2. Precision of the Law: The Problem

The precision of a legal command is taken here to refer to the degree of detail or differentiation involved. For example, an environmental regulation is more precise if more types of pollutants or sources of pollution are distinguished. A negligence regime is more precise if the standard of care is more finely tailored to different types of actors in different contexts. A damages scheme is more precise the greater the extent to which damages are designed to reflect the particular harm done to a particular victim.

The greater the degree of precision, the greater will be the costs of formulating legal commands and applying them in adjudication and of parties interpreting them for purposes of deciding how to conform behavior to the law. But it does not follow that the costs of precision – any more than costs of litigation or of pollution control – should be minimized: the simplest rules might permit all acts, require equal reduction of pollutants regardless of their toxicity, or require the same speed limits on all roads. Rather, the degree of precision should be optimized, which makes an economic analysis particularly useful.

Before proceeding, it is worth noting that greater precision in legal commands – higher levels of detail, more distinctions recognized in rules and exceptions – is a primary source of legal complexity, which is broadly condemned. The subject of the next section, whether a legal command is formulated as a rule or a standard (the latter leaving more open to subsequent adjudication and thus being more difficult to interpret), also may bear on what is often described as legal complexity. A number of other sources of complexity could be considered, but they have received little attention in the literature. Most obviously, poorly drafted laws and legal opinions will be more confusing; it will be more costly to extract less information. Although this problem is often serious, analysis of it is straightforward. More subtle are problems like those confronted under tax laws wherein parties may devise complicated schemes to circumvent simple legal commands. In this setting, complexity may be unavoidable. Moreover, it is possible that greater complexity will reduce costs: if a more complex regime successfully discourages transactional manipulations, parties might in the end spend less in learning the intricacies of legal rules and in making convoluted arrangements.

3. Effects of Precision on Legal Costs and on Behavior

The presentation here follows most closely the model in Kaplow (1995a) (see also Ehrlich and Posner, 1974; Diver, 1983). First, we can consider the effects of precision on legal costs. It is straightforward that greater precision tends to increase them: more detailed laws tend to be more costly for the government to promulgate, for parties to interpret, and for enforcers to apply. The second factor – private interpretation costs – involves some subtlety, because parties will incur such costs only if they find it in their interest to do so. For example, extremely complex details may be ignored by almost everyone.

Second, more precise commands – those that differentiate behavior more precisely – will generally result in better behavior. If pollutants are differentiated and subject to particularized sanctions, rather than grouped together and subject to a single sanction (reflecting, say, the average harm they cause), there will be two beneficial results. Activities that are more harmful will be subject to higher sanctions than otherwise, which will efficiently deter additional undesirable activity. Similarly, less harmful activities will face lower sanctions, avoiding inefficient overdeterrence.

These behavioral benefits are related to private legal costs, because the benefits can arise only if private actors expend the resources necessary to learn whether their particular activity is of a more or less harmful type, and thus subject to a higher or lower sanction. If the cost of determining the relevant sanction – which may involve learning about the content of legal commands or about the nature of one's own activity (such as by testing the chemical content of discharges) – is too high, individuals will not learn about the legal rules. Individuals with rather low benefits may simply forgo activities, even though there is some chance that they may be subject to low sanctions or no sanction, in which case their activities would be worth undertaking. Individuals with high benefits may simply act, even though there is some chance that they may face a very high sanction, in which case they will regret their decision. Individuals with intermediate benefits, however, will tend to acquire information and then to act accordingly – that is, to proceed if the sanction is low and abstain if the sanction is high.

Given the nature of this problem, it is natural to ask whether private parties' incentives to acquire information will be socially appropriate. It turns out that in the simplest case, in which liability is strict and there are no predictable errors in adjudication, private and social incentives are aligned (for the familiar reason that private actors bear all the social costs of their activities, here including the cost of acquiring information). More generally – if there is legal error, if individuals may misestimate the value of information, if information facilitates circumvention of legal sanctions, or if a negligence regime governs – private incentives may be excessive or inadequate (see Shavell, 1988a; Kaplow, 1990; Kaplow and Shavell, 1992).

Having stated how parties will behave and what costs will be incurred when laws are more detailed, it is possible to characterize when greater precision is desirable. At the broadest level, the lower the information costs and the greater the variation in harm caused by different individuals' actions, the larger will be the net benefit of precision in legal commands. To offer more insight, it is helpful to consider some special cases.

First, suppose that formulation costs are low (perhaps because a single rule will apply to a large number of actions) and that adjudication costs are low (perhaps because harm occurs only with a low probability or because violations are enforced with a low probability/high sanction strategy, as suggested by Becker, 1968). In this case, more precise laws tend to be desirable as long as information is not prohibitively costly for actors to obtain. The reason is that the actors have the option of not obtaining information. Those who do make expenditures to become informed will be only those for whom the expected behavioral benefit is large – individuals whose acts will be significantly desirable if they are not in fact very harmful, but significantly undesirable if they are of the more harmful type. For example, consider a complex rule scheme that regulates routes over which hazardous substances may be transported. Most drivers – those who never or rarely carry significant amounts of such substances – will ignore the rules. Those who regularly transport hazardous materials, however, will undertake the necessary effort to learn the rules and conform their behavior. Their information costs may be high, but the benefits from better controlling their activity will be even larger.

One implication of this analysis is that the existence of high total compliance expenditures is not an unambiguous sign of excessively detailed or complex rules. Low total expenditures may indicate that few individuals bother to learn the details of the law, in which case any additional formulation or adjudication costs would largely be wasted. High total expenditures, on the other hand, reflect that many individuals contemplate actions the desirability of which is contingent upon the type of their act; in this case, saving compliance costs by eliminating the law's precision may be a mistake because significant behavioral benefits will be sacrificed. Another implication of the analysis is that widespread noncompliance need not indicate that rules are unduly complex; as long as the few for whom the rules are most important do learn the details, the benefits of precision will be achieved at little cost with regard to others.

As a second case, suppose that private information costs are low (perhaps most individuals already know the details of their actions and how they might be sanctioned), but that the cost of differentiating acts in adjudication would be high (because it is hard for the state to learn the details of individuals' behavior). In this case, more refined legal commands may or may not be desirable. For example, additional costs may be repeatedly incurred in adjudication, even though few individuals' behavior would be affected as a result of greater detail in the law. The distinction between this case and the forgoing one is that the state must make additional expenditures on adjudication even when the *ex ante* benefit of improved behavior would be small, because the state will not know when this is true; by contrast, when only *ex ante* information costs are high, private parties will incur them selectively.

4. Relationship of the Precision of the Law to the Accuracy of Adjudication

The precision of the law has a direct connection to the accuracy of adjudication, a topic explored in Kaplow (1994a) and Kaplow and Shavell (1994, 1996a). The former subject can be taken to refer to the precision of the law on the books and the latter question to the precision with which the law actually is applied. At the time they act, individuals will be induced to become more informed about the details of their situation only if, in a subsequent adjudication, their behavior will in fact be differentiated from that of others. If, instead, individuals' acts will be assigned to different legal categories largely at random, or if no effort will be made to refine the classification of acts, the situation is much as if the law itself did not make the refined distinctions in the first place. Many topics of procedure – discovery, the use of experts, evidentiary rules, summary judgment, juries, appeals, burdens of proof – and many substantive rules – notably, concerning which categories of damages may be established and whether damages are determined by individualized evidence or by standardized tables – may thus be illuminated by analysis similar to that presented here. A central concern when assessing these features of adjudication is parties' incentives in litigation to make expenditures on their own behalf: it often may be the case that parties, if freely permitted to undertake further efforts in litigation, will spend excessively because the private benefits from favorably influencing the outcome will exceed any social benefits from enhanced precision in applying legal rules.

5. Related Issues and Literature

The preceding discussion may be extended in a number of ways. Spier (1994) incorporates *settlement* bargaining. The interesting complication is that application of a more precise rule in adjudication may make information that is possessed by only one party relevant to the outcome. By thereby creating a situation involving asymmetric information, settlement becomes less likely. Thus, greater precision may be accompanied by increased litigation costs.

Kaplow (1995a) briefly considers *costly sanctions* – monetary payments made by risk-averse individuals and nonmonetary sanctions. Few generalizations are possible. For risk-averse actors who do not become informed, greater differentiation may increase risk-bearing costs, although, as noted in Kaplow and Shavell (1996a), more precise damage awards may reduce the risks borne by uninsured victims.

Kaplow (1990) examines the case in which some individuals know how the law differentiates among acts but others do not. In this case, there is no general deterrence rationale favoring lower sanctions for *individuals who mistakenly commit violations*, but reducing their sanctions may be optimal when sanctions are socially costly, because the lower rate of compliance by mistaken individuals results in sanctions being imposed more often.

Kaplow (1995a) extends the analysis to regimes of *self-reporting*, as is common with much environmental and safety regulation, as well as with many forms of taxation. Self-reporting tends to be efficient when individuals' information costs are much lower than the government's; increasing precision in a self-reporting regime has the confounding effect of inducing some individuals to acquire information, not to determine how better to behave, but solely to determine how best to report their conduct.

Most applied work on complexity and compliance costs is in the field of *taxation*. Empirical work is extensive: see, for example, Long and Swingen (1987), Arthur D. Little (1988), Slemrod (1989), Blumenthal and Slemrod (1992). Analysis of the benefits of precision in the tax context is qualitatively different from that presented here, because the benefits of fine-tuning taxpayers' payments typically involve matters of distributive equity and minimizing adverse incentive effects of taxation rather than of optimally controlling harm-causing behavior (see, for example, Yitzhaki, 1979; Kaplow, 1994c, 1996). The most obvious simplifying devices in the United States income tax code are the standard deduction (which taxpayers may take instead of itemizing particular deductions) and the use of floors (which forbid small amounts of deductions); they are analyzed in Kaplow (1994b) and Slemrod and Yitzhaki (1994).

The discussion here, like much analysis in law and economics, emphasizes the role of legal commands in providing incentives to govern parties' behavior *ex ante*. Modifications to the analysis would be required when adjudication concerns *future behavior*, as in the granting of licenses, enjoining harm-causing behavior, incarcerating dangerous individuals, or determining eligibility for government benefits. In particular, the benefit of precision in adjudication will be greater than otherwise, because the outcome will affect future activity directly (perhaps in addition to influencing *ex ante* incentives), and concerns about whether individuals will learn the relevant details of the law may be less relevant.

Finally, it is worth noting that the benefits of more detailed rules are relevant to wholly *private ordering*, as in contractual arrangements (contingencies can be distinguished more precisely, and provisions may provide reasonably complete specifications or be more open-ended) or in the internal organization of firms. As a result, work on the economics of contracting and organizations, wholly apart from analysis of the law, can illuminate issues concerning the design of legal rules, and conversely.

B. RULES VERSUS STANDARDS

6. Rules versus Standards: The Problem

The choice between rules and standards has long received attention from legal commentators and, more recently, has been addressed from an economic perspective. The presentation here will follow Kaplow (1992a); a number of the points, particularly concerning the effects of rules and standards on legal costs and on behavior, can also be found in the prior economic analyses by Ehrlich and Posner (1974) and Diver (1983).

An initial obstacle in analyzing rules and standards involves matters of definition. Usage varies greatly (which is no surprise since most dictionaries offer definitions of each term that use the other), and logically distinct issues are often combined or confused. For purposes of economic analysis, it is useful to define the difference between rules and standards as involving exclusively the distinction between whether the law is given content *ex ante* or *ex post*. Thus, a rule might list hazardous substances that may not be released into the water supply, whereas a standard may only proscribe releases of hazardous substances, leaving the determination of which substances are hazardous to adjudication, after releases have occurred.

This distinction between rules and standards is obviously one of degree, although it often is convenient to discuss it as an all-or-nothing choice. A law is more rule-like the greater the extent to which it provides advance guidance: it may, for example, provide a partial list or state criteria to be used, either of which will ease the application of the legal norm to particular behavior. Moreover, even a given formal specification will have a different character depending upon what is understood about the mode of adjudication and upon what other information is available in advance. For example, if everyone knows that an adjudicator is likely to rely upon a recent government study that indicates the degree of danger posed by potentially hazardous substances, the situation will be almost the same as that under a rule that incorporated the study's results. For present purposes, such a situation will be viewed as essentially rule-like, as the economic analysis depends upon the extent to which content – as understood by private parties and adjudicators – has actually been provided in advance, not upon the wording of legal commands. (It thus can be seen that the generation and dissemination of information, even when not explicitly embodied in a legal rule, is an important aspect of the law.)

Finally, it is important to distinguish the question of the degree to which content is determined *ex ante* from the preceding subject, which concerns the degree of precision with which a law is formulated or applied. Often, commentators assume that standards are inherently more precise or subtle than rules because standards leave open the possibility of considering all possible factors, whereas rules, no matter how detailed, provide a definitive resolution that is not open to reconsideration. But this assumption implicitly contemplates that adjudicators will devote virtually unlimited resources in applying standards. Such an outcome is irrational, implausible, and inconsistent with the actual operation of legal systems. For example, tax codes and many safety regulations are far more detailed and context-dependent than, say, the results that would be produced by a jury that was presented with the open-ended question of what tax payment or safety regime was appropriate. As a result of law, custom, or the application of common sense, an adjudicator may well consider far less than all conceivably relevant factors. In an ordinary negligence dispute involving modest stakes, parties will not commission numerous expert studies; nor will the adjudicator commit substantial time to consider all possibilities.

Thus, it is a matter of choice how much detail will be incorporated in rules and standards, and it is hardly the case that rule-like systems tend to be particularly simple and standard-like schemes extremely precise in actual operation. The main point for present purposes is that the question of how much refinement is optimal when formulating and applying the law – legal precision – is logically and, to a great extent, practically distinct from the question whether a given degree of precision is best specified in advance (rules) or left to adjudication (standards). In the end, one can combine the following analysis of rules versus standards with the preceding analysis of the optimal precision of the law to determine what sort of legal command is best.

7. Effects of Rules and Standards on Legal Costs and on Behavior

Rules are defined as legal commands that provide greater specification in advance. Hence, the initial cost of formulating rules will be greater than the cost of formulating standards. It will be necessary, for example, to undertake studies to determine which substances are hazardous and to determine appropriate thresholds of safety if a rule listing hazardous substances is to be promulgated. Such efforts can be avoided (for the moment) under a standard that merely proscribes the release of hazardous substances and leaves their determination to subsequent proceedings.

On the other hand, rules will be cheaper for private parties to interpret when deciding upon their own conduct and for adjudicators to apply to past behavior. Precisely because more has been determined in advance, there will be less need for parties to conduct their own studies and to predict legal outcomes and for adjudicators to devote effort to determine whether a violation should be deemed to have occurred. If a rule specifies which substances may be discharged, actors and adjudicators need merely consult the list to apply a rule, whereas substantial inquiry may be necessary under a standard.

The same reasoning concerning the ease of application suggests that rules will tend to produce behavior more in conformity with legal norms than would equivalent standards. Because parties will be able to learn the governing norms more cheaply and accurately in advance, they will tend to behave more in accord with such norms. (This raises the question, explored in Kaplow and Shavell (1992) and noted above, whether private parties' incentives to learn about the law will be socially appropriate.) When guidance is easier to obtain, fewer parties will be deterred from behavior that actually is not objectionable, because they will have greater confidence that such behavior will not be subject to legal sanctions. More parties will be deterred from truly undesirable behavior because they are less likely to proceed in the mistaken belief that the prospect of being sanctioned is remote. It is important to observe that the desirable effect of rules on behavior may hold even when standards turn out to be more precise in actual adjudication, for any refinement embodied in the application of standards will influence behavior only to the extent parties are able to predict the relevant details in advance, and often parties will not make such precise predictions. (The point that details tend to be helpful only when parties find it in their interest to learn them was emphasized in the preceding section on the precision of legal rules.)

Combining these effects, one can see that rules tend to be preferable when particular activities are frequent, and standards do best when behavior varies so greatly that any particular scenario is relatively rare. The reason is that the added cost of rules, at the formulation stage, is borne once, whereas the relative benefits of rules – lower costs and greater compliance for private actors and lower costs of adjudication – may arise often or almost never, as the case may be. Thus, for dry cleaning and automotive fluids, it would be best to specify permitted disposal techniques in advance, for the many small establishments would be unlikely to be able to determine the effects on their own and, even if they could, the costs of each obtaining information on the matter would be great; also, redundant costs would be incurred in inevitable enforcement proceedings. But in the case of substances that are rarely used, it may not be worthwhile to specify the range of permitted and prohibited disposal techniques in advance, because most scenarios involving potentially hazardous action may never arise.

In this regard, it should be noted that the frequency of activity may be great even if reported adjudications in a field are few. For example, rules might lead countless individuals to comply with the law at very low cost. Even when compliance is imperfect (or when harm nonetheless arises and is subject to a regime of strict liability), there may be little adjudication despite frequent activity, because the probability of harm is low, detection of harm is unlikely, or most legal disputes are quickly settled. Conversely, disputes may appear to be frequent but not indicate that conditions are favorable to the use of rules. For example, there are many negligence disputes but some types may involve unique situations that, *ex ante*, were unlikely ever to arise.

Finally, the costs and benefits of rules and standards are important for determining the optimal effort to devote to formulating rules and to applying rules and standards in adjudication. All else equal, the greater the frequency of the behavior to be governed, the more valuable it will be to formulate the law with greater care. Conversely, to the extent that an adjudication is relevant to only a single case, it will not be very valuable to expend substantial resources to consider myriad factors in order to reach a precise determination – unless a precedent is to be set, as discussed below. That individuals may have difficulty predicting refined decisions with any accuracy will strengthen this point. These considerations reinforce the previous observation that, in fact, rules often will be more precise and subtle than standards, taking into account how the latter will actually be applied.

8. Precedent, Other Legal Interpretations, and the Evolution of Legal Commands

Precedent may be seen as the (perhaps partial) conversion of a standard into a rule. Whether after accumulated experience or as a result of hearing a single case, a tribunal may issue a statement that will govern future adjudication. At that point, and to that extent, a rule will have been established. Similarly, even less authoritative legal interpretations, ranging from discussions in judicial opinions to public statements of enforcement agencies, will tend to guide future behavior and adjudications to some degree. Once the analysis of standards – the state of affairs before the precedent – and of rules – after the precedent – is understood, the study of precedent (and other legal interpretations) is straightforward. A few particular factors, however, deserve some elaboration.

It is worth asking why the use of precedent is superior to an earlier announcement of rules. After all, the primary burden of using a rule, incurring additional formulation costs, is ultimately borne when the precedent is established. But in the interim, before the precedent is announced, the benefits – of cheaper and better guidance of behavior and simpler adjudication – are forgone. This point is particularly striking when an important, open legal question is identified many years or decades before a precedent is finally announced. The primary advantage of delay is that more information may be collected in the interim – information about the optimal legal command or about the importance of resolving an issue. But many precedents are announced with little more information than existed initially. Moreover, the most efficient way to collect information may be to commission a study in the first place rather than to wait until a case happens to appear before the relevant tribunal (when all that is then learned is the single data point from that case or perhaps a handful of data points). Also, once more information does become available through whatever means, it is not clear why the legal system should not make an announcement immediately rather than waiting still further.

It should be noted that making initial legal commands more rule-like does not imply that they cannot be changed if new information becomes available. The prospect of change does reduce the benefit of rules, but it does not follow that there will be no benefit from providing guidance in the interim. Indeed, many detailed regimes that are designed by regulatory agencies have a more rule-like character, with occasional revision, and detailed statutes, such as tax codes, are made precise but often revised later. (And, of course, precedents themselves are extended, narrowed, and reversed.) With standards, change may occur implicitly, but the prospect of change will accordingly increase the cost and difficulty of prediction. Substantial developments that call for significantly different legal commands may be apparent, making prediction under standards easier, but also presenting a clear case for adjusting rules. It is hardly the case that operative legal commands in heavily rule-governed domains (like tax and environmental regulation) and the interpretation of important precedents change slowly compared, say, to applications of the negligence rule.

For prior economic analyses of precedent, emphasizing that the body of precedent can be analogized to a capital stock that depreciates over time, see Landes and Posner (1976) and Posner (1992). See also Landes and Posner's (1994) discussion of the related subject of anticipatory adjudication, in which a party may seek a legal decision before undertaking an activity, so as to avoid the need to wait for a precedent.

9. Related Issues and Literature

Other law and economics work that is addressed directly to the subjects considered herein includes Ogus (1981) (discussing rules formulated in quantitative terms), and Ogus (1992) (emphasizing private actors' greater ability to predict rules than standards).

The choice between rules and standards is closely related to the problem of *legal uncertainty*. Indeed, if rules are defined as the extent to which legal commands are given content *ex ante* and thus the ease with which private parties can predict how the law will apply to their conduct, legal uncertainty might be viewed as simply a measure of the extent to which a legal command is standard-like. Uncertainty about the negligence rule has received the greatest attention in the literature (see Calfee and Craswell, 1984; Craswell and Calfee, 1986, and Shavell, 1987). Because the negligence rule has an all-or-nothing (discontinuous) character – taking slightly more care will exonerate an actor from what otherwise would be significant liability – uncertainty about the legal standard may tend to produce excessive care (although it is also possible that great uncertainty will produce too little care). The suggestion that malpractice liability results in overly defensive medicine is one example. For empirical evidence, see Kessler and McClellan (1996). Kahan (1989) shows that these issues would not arise if negligent actors were not responsible for all the harm they caused, but only for the incremental increase in harm due to their negligence. Also, in considering legal uncertainty, it would be appropriate to extend the present analysis and that in prior work on the negligence rule to take explicit account of risk-bearing costs.

As noted when addressing legal precision, the discussion here focuses on the role of law in providing incentives to control parties' *ex ante* behavior. When *future behavior* (licenses, injunctions, incarceration, benefit eligibility) is involved, the analysis will differ. Indeed, the difference between *ex ante* and *ex post* formulation may be moot, as a definitive resolution will in any event precede the relevant effect of a legal decision. There are, nonetheless, similar questions about the benefits of wholesale decision making, as in stating a rule for a class of cases rather than adjudicating the same question repeatedly. And the forgoing analysis remains applicable to the extent adjudication will influence *ex ante* incentives in addition to regulating future behavior (such as in the case of incarceration).

There are other functions of law as well. Much of *contract law* and related fields is concerned with providing rules of form or background rules that leave parties free to transact as they wish (see, for example, Baird and Weisberg, 1982). Because the purpose of such law is different – law is largely facilitating rather than constraining – the analysis would have to be different. Nonetheless, it seems that in contexts where transactions are frequent, the benefit of greater *ex ante* formulation – through rules – would be larger.

Yet another concern with some bodies of law is to constrain *fraud*. In some instances (notably, tax evasion) greater specificity in advance might be problematic because parties will better be able to evade legal norms. Both uncertainty and complexity, discussed previously, may be desirable precisely because parties will be less able to predict the law.

Apart from normative analysis, one can inquire into *lawyers' and legal institutions' incentives to formulate legal commands*. In this regard, conflicts between private and social interest may be noted. For example, lower legal costs save social resources but may reduce the demand for lawyers (see, for example, White, 1992). And legislation might be designed with an eye to attracting campaign contributions rather than serving the public interest (see, for example, Doernberg and McChesney, 1987). Regulators may be more concerned with their own costs in formulating and applying rules than in private costs (see, for example, Diver, 1983).

Finally, the present discussion may be situated in the large literatures in the areas of *legal philosophy* and *public choice* which examine the rule of law and in particular address the use of rules to constrain official discretion. For a reasonably comprehensive treatment of rules that attends to functional concerns, see Schauer (1991).

C. CHANGES IN LEGAL RULES: TRANSITIONS AND RETROACTIVITY

10. Transitions and Retroactivity: The Problem

Transition rules, including a determination of whether a law is to apply retroactively, concern not the form and content of substantive legal commands but instead how the problem of legal change is to be addressed. The most common problem of legal change concerns the fact that investments and other actions often have effects in the future, at which time the governing legal regime may be different. Changes in the law will affect, positively or negatively as the case may be, the returns from prior actions. This raises the question whether losses from legal change should be compensated or otherwise mitigated (as through grandfather provisions that exempt prior investments or phase-ins that implement the change only gradually) and, analogously, whether gains from legal change should be subject to windfall taxation or otherwise reduced.

As first analyzed carefully in the context of tax reform by Graetz (1977), these problems arise even when new legislation is nominally prospective. For example, if a tax subsidy is repealed, a prior investment that benefited on a continuing basis from the subsidy will become less valuable even if none of the prior subsidy payments must be returned to the government. The possibility of explicit retroactivity does, however, expand the potential scope for transition issues: even completed transactions might subsequently be rewarded or penalized when laws change.

The general problem of transition, analyzed in Hale (1927), Samuels (1974), and Kaplow (1986, 1987, 1992b), arises much more widely and with more common elements than is usually appreciated. Basically, whenever there is uncertainty concerning government policy – about statutory change, new regulation or deregulation, court decisions, government spending priorities, takings of private property for public use, tariffs, and so on – the resolution of the uncertainty will create winners and losers. Thus, all government action (unless fully anticipated), government inaction (that is not fully anticipated – that is, when change had a positive probability that was not realized), and even changes in the prospect for action in the future, will tend to affect the value of prior investments. The potentially affected investments include physical and financial assets, investments in human capital, and choices of location and occupation, among others.

As this general description suggests, an important aspect of the transition problem concerns the *ex ante* choice of private actors – individuals and firms – under uncertainty. The prospect of legal change (like that of any other change) will affect both investment incentives and the imposition of risk, and these incentive effects and risk-bearing costs will in turn be influenced by whether transition relief is anticipated and provided. The immediately following analysis considers the question of optimal government transition policy, taking as given the actual change in the law that might occur and its desirability. The focus is on how transition relief affects the behavior and wellbeing of private parties and, accordingly, its effect on social welfare. Subsequent discussion will take up concerns about possible government misbehavior in changing the law and how different transition policies may influence government activity.

11. Effects of Transitions and Transition Relief on Private Actors' Incentives and on Risk-bearing Costs

Begin by considering the case in which private actors are risk-neutral (which may be approximately true for large, widely owned enterprises that are the subject of much legal regulation). Suppose that there is some prospect, say, a 50 percent chance, of an adverse legal change: a firm's product might be banned if it turns out that the product is dangerous. Anticipating such a possibility – and assuming for the moment that there will be no compensation, exemption, or other relief to those investing prior to the transition – private parties will invest less than they would otherwise. Half the time they will earn some positive return and the other half of the time they will earn no return (and, indeed, they may lose their initial investment).

Now suppose instead that investors anticipate that there will be complete transition relief, say, full compensation. In this case, investors expect a positive return for sure, so they are more likely to invest – or to invest at a larger scale – than if there were to be no relief. As Blume, Rubinfeld and Shapiro (1984) first showed formally in the takings context, the prospect of such relief induces inefficient overinvestment. The key point is that a private loss in such instances corresponds to a real social loss. If a product is too dangerous and must be banned, sunk investments that are valuable only for producing such a product will be of no subsequent social value. Hence, insulating investors from such risks is inefficient, just as it would be inefficient to insulate investors from the prospect that their products might become obsolete or lose out to better products of competitors. As noted by Hale (1927), Samuels (1974), Graetz (1977), and Kaplow (1986, 1987, 1992b), from the perspective of investors, the risk of future government action is similar to various market risks and natural risks (earthquakes, hurricanes). Private decisions are efficient when actors bear the full costs and benefits of their actions. Transition relief thus does not correct an externality; it creates one.

This analysis of transition relief may be extended to determine when retroactive application of legal changes is efficient (see Kaplow, 1986, 1987, 1992b). If a product is banned because it is discovered to be dangerous, it is probably the case that past production of the product resulted in danger as well. Thus, imposing retrospective liability will tend to be efficient, in order for investors *ex ante* to have had the proper incentives to take safety into account. By contrast, if a pollutant is to be regulated because it damages a newly introduced crop strain, there is no reason to impose retrospective liability, for the decision to regulate the pollutant does not suggest that the pollutant previously caused some social harm. To generalize, when the government discovers new information about conditions that have long been in existence, retroactive application in some form will often be necessary to provide the right *ex ante* incentives, but when there is a change in circumstances that makes future use undesirable without affecting the desirability of past conduct, retroactivity will be inefficient.

Similar reasoning suggests that transition relief is inefficient even when private actors are risk averse (see Kaplow, 1986, 1987, 1992b). In this case, relief has the advantage of reducing risk-bearing costs. But private arrangements – diversified ownership, insurance, contractual risk allocations, and the like – also may be available. Moreover, these mechanisms have systematic advantages over transition relief. First, they often are implemented in ways that preserve incentives, in full or in part. For example, insurance premiums are greater the more assets are covered, so investors contemplating expansion in the face of some risk will bear the expected loss *ex ante* through higher insurance payments. In other cases, private risk mitigation is partial precisely to preserve incentives; absent other market imperfections (notably, adverse selection), private risk-sharing arrangements tend to be efficient. Transition relief generally lacks these features. Second, even if transition relief were only partial, private parties would undertake actions to further mitigate risk; such actions may worsen their incentives (moral hazard), but some of the resulting cost would be borne by the government. Again the analogy to market risks can be made: just as government relief (as in the case of disaster relief) tends to be inefficient for ordinary risks (see Arnott and Stiglitz, 1991; Kaplow, 1991), so government relief against government-created risks tends to be inefficient with regard to private investment and risk-mitigation incentives.

12. Related Issues

The analysis assumes that transition policy will be *anticipated* by investors and actually *implemented* by the government. To the extent such policy is embodied in constitutional provisions or strong norms that guide legal reform, the assumption is plausible. More generally, a government is unlikely to succeed in the long run in getting investors to expect one transition policy while often implementing another. Problems of credible commitment may make it difficult to establish a desired transition policy. To consider a familiar analogy, some governments regularly offer *ex post* relief when natural disasters strike, which has the effect of encouraging individuals to, say, invest excessively in building on flood plains. A possible solution to this political commitment problem is for the government either to regulate such activity (limiting investment in high-risk areas) or to compel the purchase of insurance in advance at actuarially fair rates (the insurance premiums would discourage excessive investment and the fact that victims have paid for compensation in advance would eliminate the pressure for *ex post* relief).

Most of the discussion here, like most in various literatures that address transition issues – ranging from tax reform to deregulation – emphasizes the case in which investors suffer transition *losses*. But it was noted at the outset that transition *gains* arise with similar frequency. The analysis of both possibilities is symmetric: just as providing relief for losses will encourage overinvestment, imposing windfall taxes on gains (or otherwise reducing them) will produce underinvestment. Few if any windfall gains – or losses – are really pure windfalls. It tends to be best for investors to bear all the gains and losses they cause, with any risk mitigation being contractually arranged to provide for the most effective limitation of adverse incentive effects.

Another question of transition policy concerns the *means* of relief. One can compensate losers (and tax winners) in whole or in part, grandfather prior investors (that is, provide some exemption from new rules), or curtail the new policy (as by delay or phase-in or implementing reform only partially). With regard to *ex ante* incentives and mitigation of risk, all of these approaches are similar, to the extent that they provide the same degree of effective relief. (For example, a phase-in that reduces gains and losses by half has effects like that of 50 percent compensation and 50 percent windfall taxation.) With regard to future behavior, however, compensation and windfall taxation are generally superior to other forms of relief. Grandfathering, for example, might exempt existing producers of dangerous products, allowing the danger to continue (but perhaps not to grow); delaying implementation would similarly permit some future harm. By contrast, immediate elimination of the danger accompanied by compensation would avoid this difficulty.

As in the discussion of rule formulation, the present analysis is most applicable to *laws that regulate behavior*. Contract rules that serve as defaults are quite different. If a default rule is changed, it may well be that the prior rule should govern preexisting contracts, for parties may have failed to make special provision in their contracts precisely because they knew they could rely upon background rules. On the other hand, if a default is changed because new analysis suggests that most parties have a different preference than previously suspected, and if many contracts are silent simply because of the cost of making special provision, it could be best to apply the new default to preexisting agreements.

13. Effects on Government Behavior of Requiring Transition Relief

The forgoing analysis takes as given a particular legal change, assumes that it is well conceived, and asks how transition relief affects private behavior. But it cannot be assumed that government always acts appropriately, and transition relief may affect the behavior of government.

One familiar argument is that transition relief – in particular, requiring compensation – *provides the government with proper incentives* because then government bears the full costs of its actions. One can make the analogy to tort liability when both injurers' and victims' behavior affects accident costs. For analysis of this tort problem, see Shavell (1980), and for application to the transition context see Kaplow (1986, 1987); for a similar discussion, see

Blume, Rubinfeld and Shapiro (1984). No liability – or schemes that provide no compensation when injurers behave well, a negligence-type rule, or that deny compensation when victims behave improperly, contributory or comparative negligence rules – is best for victims' incentives (like investors' incentives, above), whereas full liability – strict or otherwise – is best for injurers' incentives. If one can assume that the government (the 'injurer') always behaves properly, then a regime that denies compensation is best for the incentives of investors (the 'victims'). But if one cannot make this assumption about government behavior, one may wish to impose liability on the government – for example, by requiring compensation. Unless some tribunal can determine when the government or investors misbehaved, which is likely to be very difficult in most transition contexts (and which involves courts second-guessing legislative, executive, agency, or their own actions), it must be recognized that any solution will be a compromise: if some relief is required, government's incentives may improve but investors' incentives will be worse.

This argument, however, is incomplete (see Kaplow, 1986, 1987). The implicit assumption is that the government, like a private investor, receives the benefits from its actions. But the benefits of most government action – banning hazardous products, improving tort rules, building highways – are received by private citizens. Thus, making the legislature or an agency pay for transition losses (in addition to paying for direct costs, as in building a highway) when few if any of the benefits are directly received might systematically skew decisions against any change. Once benefits as well as costs are considered, it is not obvious that even a highly imperfect government is generally biased in favor of change when no compensation or other relief is required. For any bias – whether for or against change – to exist, there must be some *asymmetry* in the government's treatment of costs and benefits. Some theories of government action (see Downs, 1957 and Olson, 1965) suggest that the most effective political interest groups are those on whom gains or losses are concentrated. Other theories are concerned with the majority exploiting the minority. Still others (see Niskanen, 1971) emphasize bureaucrats' desire to enhance their budget or prestige. Thus, whether requiring compensation would make government behavior better or worse depends upon which theories of government behavior are most plausible, whether it is the benefits or the costs that are more concentrated, and other factors (see also Quinn and Trebilcock, 1982).

Another concern with government behavior involves the problem of pure *expropriation* (see Kaplow, 1987). It is familiar from public economics that the most efficient government tax is a one-time capital levy, in which capital (more broadly, savings, assets in any form) is taken and the government promises never to repeat the action. As long as the expropriation is wholly unanticipated, there will be no adverse *ex ante* incentive effects; likewise, if it will never be repeated, there will be no future distortions in behavior. Levmore (1993) offers this as a basis for a more favorable view toward retroactive taxation. But it has long been recognized that governments would find it difficult to engage in such inconsistent behavior. Rather, there needs to be some commitment – whether through constitutional means or long-established norms – that the government will not expropriate, and governments that deviate from such a path will be unlikely to be able to provide investors with confidence for the future.

In principle, expropriation can be distinguished from other government action. As noted when addressing private incentives, it is efficient for investors to anticipate and respond to the prospect that new information or changed circumstances will affect what government regulation is optimal, just as new developments will influence the market directly in ways that investors should take into account. Anticipating expropriation, however, is inefficient *ex ante*. The benefit arises from transferring resources to the government, not from providing proper incentives for private behavior. To be sure, some taxation is required, to fund public goods and services and to accomplish redistribution. Particularly with regard to redistribution, it would improve efficiency if taxpayers did not anticipate having to pay taxes, as such anticipation results in distortion of behavior. But this problem is largely unavoidable.

Successful economies seem to have succeeded, for the most part, in avoiding expropriation. The mechanism by which this is accomplished is not that clear; no system prohibits taxation or legal changes, and constitutional or other strong compensation requirements are limited. (For example, in the United States, the government must compensate a landowner whose building is taken for a highway, but a high capital income or wealth tax is not legally proscribed.) The development of strong norms seems to play a greater role in successful economies, but such norms cannot succeed unless the relevant audience can understand which legal reforms are improper in the relevant respect.

A variant of the expropriation problem arises when the government is involved with ordinary *contractual behavior* and related activity. In fact, most governments accomplish many of their purposes – building roads, procuring military equipment, hiring employees – through ordinary market transactions. (In some countries, state enterprises are common; these too, however, often use ordinary contractual means of paying workers and purchasing other necessary inputs.) Moreover, most governments, despite the availability of sovereign immunity from private suits, voluntarily subject themselves to a legal regime under which their contracts have a binding effect similar to that of private contracts. This avoids problems of opportunism, both large and small.

Some commentators have analogized legislation and other government law-making to government contracts (see, for example, Graetz, 1977; Kaplow, 1986, 1987; Ramseyer and Nakazato, 1989; Logue, 1996). Thus, sometimes the government uses subsidies to induce certain behavior rather than explicit contracts under which it pays for a promise to undertake certain activity. If the subsidy is terminated, this might be viewed as a breach of an implicit contract. Of course, subsidies are routinely terminated. When governments use ongoing subsidies to encourage an activity rather than entering into a long-term contract to pay for a given amount of the activity, they are choosing to use a more flexible mechanism, allowing the possibility of change without compensation. To impose a norm or constitutional requirement that all law be treated as if it were a binding contract would not add to the government's options; it would eliminate one. (Actually, it may have no effect at all, as laws could simply be written to expire unless extended or with some other loophole providing the government a way to avoid any binding obligation.)

14. Additional Issues

Transition relief is sometimes favored because it may make it politically feasible to implement desirable reform. For example, efficient deregulation might be opposed by protected incumbents, who could be bought out with compensation (see Tullock, 1978; see also Usher, 1995, addressing compensation for takings). The problem is that, *ex ante*, special interest groups would have a greater incentive to seek inefficient rules, knowing that even if the rules were subsequently repealed, they would benefit from transition relief (see Kitch, 1977; Quinn and Trebilcock, 1982; McKenzie, 1986; Kaplow, 1987, 1992b). Thus, it is not obvious that a policy of buying out such political opposition would in the long run produce better or worse laws and lead to more or less resources being wasted on rent-seeking activity.

Another problem concerns changes in political power that may produce legal changes that do not reflect real changes in information or circumstances (although legal reforms may reflect shifts in perceptions or in value judgments). Small changes in beliefs may produce large legal changes (as when an opposition party gains a few percentage points in support and comes into power), and such change may be frequent. *Ex ante* behavior that is desirable from the perspective of one party's policies may be undesirable from the perspective of the other's. Use of transition relief will tend to cause investors to put more weight on the status quo, something unlikely to be favored by a subsequent regime seeking change. Analysis of social welfare in such instances is difficult.

15. Literature

The first careful analysis of many issues concerning legal transitions appears to be Hale (1927). For a general analysis of changing legal rules in a variety of contexts, see Kaplow (1986, 1987, 1992b).

Most writing by legal academics on the subject focuses on takings or on tax reform. With respect to takings, Michelman (1967) offers an important early analysis, although it does not take the economic approach as far as subsequent work. Baxter and Altree (1972) advance a 'first-in-time' approach to address the problem of airport noise; they are among the first to pursue directly the problem of the adverse incentive effects of compensation. Blume, Rubinfeld and Shapiro (1984) analyze incentive effects of compensation in a formal model and Blume and Rubinfeld (1984) consider risk, although these authors do not integrate the two analyses or systematically consider private risk mitigation. Kaplow (1986, 1987) discusses takings in the context of analyzing the transition problem more generally. For additional work, with emphasis on the problem of the government's incentives, see, for example, Fischel and Shapiro (1989) and Hermalin (1995). For an empirical analysis of the effect of requiring compensation on government behavior, see Cordes and Weisbrod (1979).

Feldstein (1976a, 1976b) and Graetz (1977) offer the first substantial treatments of tax transitions, followed by Kaplow (1986, 1987, 1992b), who more explicitly analyzes effects of relief on investors' incentives and private risk mitigation, compares alternative transition mechanisms, and addresses institutional problems with government decision making. This latter problem is also considered by Ramseyer and Nakazato (1989) and Logue (1996), who are both favorable toward relief because of concerns about government misbehavior. Levmore (1993) is more favorable to (uncompensated) retroactivity, because of the possibility of an efficient capital levy. The particular problem of transition to a consumption tax is addressed in Graetz (1979), Kaplow (1986, 1987, 1995b), Sarkar and Zodrow (1993) and Bradford (1996).

Another subject receiving increased attention is deregulation and other regulatory changes (see Quinn and Trebilcock, 1982; Kolbe, Tye and Myers, 1993; Kaplow, 1993).

D. ADDITIONAL TOPICS

16. Additional Topics

There are a number of other dimensions along which many legal rules vary that are sufficiently general to warrant independent study. Because these subjects are addressed in other fields within law and economics, the present discussion will be brief. Each of the topics considered involves the general question of whether laws should identify certain conduct as permitted or prohibited or should instead impose fines, provide for private liability, or use other means of aligning private and social interests so as to induce parties to make efficient choices on their own.

Strict Liability versus Negligence

The choice between strict liability and negligence has received much attention. Similar issues arise involving defenses based upon victim behavior. And other areas of law present analogous questions: namely, is a party responsible for all harm caused, or is the party responsible only if behavior was improper (and, then, only to the extent of any additional harm caused by the inappropriate action)? The latter type of law requires both defining a norm of behavior (which may be done *ex ante*, as a rule, or *ex post*, as a standard, and which may be done in a simple or precise manner), and both types of law require provisions governing the measurement of harm. This sort of choice involves many of the issues considered here, as well as concerns for the frequency of litigation, victims' incentives, and other factors (see Brown, 1973; Shavell, 1980, and Schäfer and Schönenberger, 2000, on strict liability versus negligence in tort).

Property versus Liability Rules

The distinction between property and liability rules involves remedies: if one party wishes to infringe the legal rights of another, must the acting party first obtain permission (or else be subject to extreme sanctions and the possibility of injunction, if feasible) – a property rule – or may the party simply act and pay damages – a liability rule? This scheme is first explored in detail by Calabresi and Melamed (1972) and has subsequently been expanded in Kaplow and Shavell (1996b). Other relevant work includes Ellickson (1973), Polinsky (1979, 1980) and Krier and Schwab (1995). The problem of bargaining under asymmetric information has attracted disproportionate attention, beginning with Samuelson (1985) and followed, for example, by Farrell (1987), Shavell (1988b), Johnston (1995), Ayres and Talley (1995a, 1995b) and Kaplow and Shavell (1995, 1996b). See Krauss (2000) on property versus liability rules.

Bibliography

Arthur D. Little (1988), *Development of Methodology for Estimating the Taxpayer Paperwork Burden, Final Report to the Department of the Treasury*, Washington, DC, Internal Revenue Service.

Baird, Douglas G. and Weisberg, Robert (1982), 'Rules, Standards and the Battle of the Forms: A Reassessment of §2–207', **68** *Virginia Law Review*, 1217–62.

Baxter, William F. and Altree, Lillian R. (1972), 'Legal Aspects of Airport Noise', **15** *Journal of Law and Economics*, 1–113.

Blume, Lawrence and Rubinfeld, Daniel L. (1984), 'Compensation for Takings: An Economic Analysis', **72** *California Law Review*, 569–628.

Blume, Lawrence, Rubinfeld, Daniel L. and Shapiro, Perry (1984), 'The Taking of Land: When Should Compensation be Paid?', **99** *Quarterly Journal of Economics*, 71–92.

Blumenthal, Marsha and Slemrod, Joel B. (1992), 'The Compliance Cost of the U.S. Individual Income Tax System: A Second Look After Tax Reform', **45** *National Tax Journal*, 185–202.

Bouckaert, Boudewijn and Schäfer, Hans-Bernd (1995), 'Mistake of Law and the Economics of Legal Information', in Bouckaert, Boudewijn and De Geest, Gerrit (eds), *Essays in Law and Economics II: Contract Law, Regulation, and Reflections on Law and Economics*, Antwerpen, Maklu, 217–45.

Bradford, David F. (1996), 'Consumption Taxes: Some Fundamental Transition Issues', in Boskin, Michael J. (ed.), *Frontiers of Tax Reform*, Stanford, CA, Hoover Institution Press.

Calfee, John E. and Craswell, Richard (1984), 'Some Effects of Uncertainty on Compliance with Legal Standards', **70** *Virginia Law Review*, 965–1003.

Cordes, Joseph J. and Weisbrod, Burton A. (1979), 'Governmental Behavior in Response to Compensation Requirements', **11** *Journal of Public Economics*, 47–58.

Coulange, Pierre (1990a), 'La Production de Droit (The Production of Legal Rules)', **3** *Journal des Economistes et des Etudes Humaines*, 277–302.

Coulange, Pierre (1990b), *Analyse Économique de la Production de Droit* (Economic Analysis of the Production of Legal Rules), PhD, Aix-en-Provence, Université d'Aix-Marseille III, Faculté d'Economie Appliquée.

Craswell, Richard and Calfee, John E. (1986), 'Deterrence and Uncertain Legal Standards', **2** *Journal of Law, Economics and Organization*, 279–303.

Diver, Colin S. (1983), 'The Optimal Precision of Administrative Rules', **93** *Yale Law Journal*, 65–109.

Doernberg, Richard L. and McChesney, Fred S. (1987), 'On the Accelerating Rate and Decreasing Durability of Tax Reform', **71** *Minnesota Law Review*, 913–62.

Ehrlich, Isaac and Posner, Richard A. (1974), 'An Economic Analysis of Legal Rulemaking', **3** *Journal of Legal Studies*, 257–86.

Feldstein, Martin (1976a), 'On the Theory of Tax Reform', **6** *Journal of Public Economics*, 77–104.

Feldstein, Martin (1976b), 'Compensation in Tax Reform', **29** *National Tax Journal*, 123–30.

Fisch, Jill E. (1997), 'Retroactivity and Legal Change: An Equilibrium Approach', **110** *Harvard Law Review*, 1055–123.

Fischel, William A. and Shapiro, Perry (1989), 'A Constitutional Choice Model of Compensation for Takings', **9** *International Review of Law and Economics*, 115–28.

Graetz, Michael J. (1977), 'Legal Transitions: The Case of Retroactivity in Income Tax Revision', **126** *University of Pennsylvania Law Review*, 47–87.

Graetz, Michael J. (1979), 'Implementing a Progressive Consumption Tax', **92** *Harvard Law Review*, 1575–661.

Graetz, Michael J. (1985), 'Retroactivity Revisited', **98** *Harvard Law Review*, 1820–41.

Hale, Robert L. (1927), 'Value and Vested Rights', **27** *Columbia Law Review*, 523–29.

Hermalin, Benjamin E. (1995), 'An Economic Analysis of Takings', **11** *Journal of Law, Economics and Organization*, 64–86.

Hutter, Michael (1989), *Die Produktion von Recht: Eine selb streferentielle Theorie der Wirtschaft, angewandt auf den Fall des Arzneimittelpatentrechts* (The Production of Law. A Selfreferential Theory of the Economy, applied to the Case of Pharmaceutical Patent Law), Tübingen, J.C.B. Mohr.

Kahan, Marcel (1989), 'Causation and Incentives to Take Care Under the Negligence Rule', **18** *Journal of Legal Studies*, 427–47.

Kaplow, Louis (1986), 'An Economic Analysis of Legal Transitions', **99** *Harvard Law Review*, 509–617.

Kaplow, Louis (1987), 'Optimal Transition Policy: Replacing Horizontal Equity with an Ex Ante Incentives Perspective', dissertation accepted by Harvard University Department of Economics, Cambridge, MA.

Kaplow, Louis (1990), 'Optimal Deterrence, Uninformed Individuals, and Acquiring Information about Whether Acts are Subject to Sanctions', **6** *Journal of Law, Economics and Organization*, 93–128.

Kaplow, Louis (1992a), 'Rules versus Standards: An Economic Analysis', **42** *Duke Law Journal*, 557–629.

Kaplow, Louis (1992b), 'Government Relief for Risk Associated with Government Action', **94** *Scandinavian Journal of Economics*, 525–41.

Kaplow, Louis (1993), 'An Ex Ante Perspective on Deregulation, Viewed ex post', **15** *Resource and Energy Economics*, 153–73.

Kaplow, Louis (1994a), 'The Value of Accuracy in Adjudication: An Economic Analysis', **23** *Journal of Legal Studies*, 307–401.

Kaplow, Louis (1994b), 'The Standard Deduction and Floors in the Income Tax', **50** *Tax Law Review*, 1–31.

Kaplow, Louis (1994c), 'Accuracy, Complexity, and the Income Tax', Working Paper No. 4631, Cambridge, MA, National Bureau of Economic Research.

Kaplow, Louis (1995a), 'A Model of the Optimal Complexity of Legal Rules', **11** *Journal of Law, Economics and Organization*, 150–63.

Kaplow, Louis (1995b), 'Recovery of Pre-Enactment Basis under a Consumption Tax: The USA Tax System', **68** *Tax Notes*, 1109–18.
Kaplow, Louis (1996), 'How Tax Complexity and Enforcement Affect the Equity and Efficiency of the Income Tax', **49** *National Tax Journal*, 135–50.
Kaplow, Louis and Shavell, Steven (1992), 'Private versus Socially Optimal Provision of Ex Ante Legal Advice', **8** *Journal of Law, Economics and Organization*, 306–20.
Kaplow, Louis and Shavell, Steven (1994), 'Accuracy in the Determination of Liability', **37** *Journal of Law and Economics*, 1–15.
Kaplow, Louis and Shavell, Steven (1996a), 'Accuracy in the Assessment of Damages', **39** *Journal of Law and Economics*, 191–210.
Kessler, Daniel and McClellan, Mark (1996), 'Do Doctors Practice Defensive Medicine?', **111** *Quarterly Journal of Economics*, 352–90.
Kitch, Edmund W. (1977), 'Can We Buy Our Way Out of Harmful Regulation?', in Martin, Donald L. and Schwartz, Warren F. (eds), *Deregulating American Industry: Legal and Economic Problems*, Lexington, MA, Lexington Books.
Kolbe, A. Lawrence, Tye, William B. and Myers, Stewart C. (1993), *Regulatory Risk: Economic Principles and Applications to Natural Gas Pipelines and Other Industries*, Boston, Kluwer Academic Press.
Landes, William M. and Posner, Richard A. (1976), 'Legal Precedent: A Theoretical and Empirical Analysis', **19** *Journal of Law and Economics*, 249–307.
Landes, William M. and Posner, Richard A. (1994), 'The Economics of Anticipatory Adjudication', **23** *Journal of Legal Studies*, 683–719.
Levmore, Saul (1993), 'The Case for Retroactive Taxation', **22** *Journal of Legal Studies*, 265–307.
Logue, Kyle D. (1996), 'Tax Treatments, Opportunistic Retroactivity, and the Benefits of Government Precommitment', **94** *Michigan Law Review*, 1129–96.
Long, Susan B. and Swingen, Judyth A. (1987), 'An Approach to the Measurement of Tax Law Complexity', **8** *Journal of the American Tax Association*, 22–36.
MacKaay, Ejan (1979), 'Les Notions Floues ou l'Economie de l'Imprécision (Fuzzy Concepts or the Economics of Imprecision)', **12** *Langages*, 33–50.
MacKaay, Ejan (1980), 'Le Nozione "Fluide" Ovvero l'Economia Dell'Imprecisione (Fuzzy Concepts or the Economics of Imprecision)', *Informatica e Diritto*, 253–74.
McKenzie, Richard B. (1986), 'Tax/Compensation Schemes: Misleading Advice in a Rent-Seeking Society', **48** *Public Choice*, 189–94.
Michelman, Frank I. (1967), 'Property, Utility and Fairness: Comments on the Ethical Foundations of "Just Compensation" Law', **80** *Harvard Law Review*, 1165–258.
Munzer, Stephen R. (1977), 'Retroactive Law', **6** *Journal of Legal Studies*, 373–97.
Ogus, Anthony I. (1981), 'Quantitative Rules and Judicial Decision Making', in Burrows, Paul and Veljanovski, Cento G. (eds), *The Economic Approach to Law*, London, Butterworths, 210–25.
Ogus, Anthony I. (1992), 'Information, Error Costs and Regulation', **12** *International Review of Law and Economics*, 411–21.
Posner, Richard A. (1992), *Economic Analysis of Law* (4th edn), Boston, Little, Brown and Company.
Quinn, John and Trebilcock, Michael J. (1982), 'Compensation, Transition Costs, and Regulatory Change', **32** *University of Toronto Law Journal*, 117–75.
Ramseyer, J. Mark and Nakazato, Minoru (1989), 'Tax Transitions and the Protection Racket: A Reply to Professors Graetz and Kaplow', **75** *Virginia Law Review*, 1155–75.
Russell, A.M. and Rickard, J.A. (1987), 'A Model of Tax Evasion Incorporating Income Variation and Retroactive Penalities', **26** *Australian Economic Papers*, 254–64.
Samuels, Warren J. (1974), 'Commentary: An Economic Perspective on the Compensation Problem', **21** *Wayne Law Review*, 113–34.
Sarkar, Shounak and Zodrow, George R. (1993), 'Transitional Issues in Moving to a Direct Consumption Tax', **46** *National Tax Journal*, 359–76.
Schauer, Frederick (1991), *Playing by the Rules: A Philosophical Examination of Rule-Based Decisionmaking in Law and in Life*, New York, Oxford University Press.
Schwartz, Gary T. (1983), 'New Products, Old Products, Evolving Law, Retroactive Law', **58** *New York University Law Review*, 796–852.

Shavell, Steven (1988a), 'Legal Advice about Contemplated Acts: The Decision to Obtain Advice, Its Social Desirability, and the Protection of Confidentiality', **17** *Journal of Legal Studies*, 123–50.

Shavell, Steven (1988b), 'Property Rights and the Rule of Liability in a Simple Bargaining Model', unpublished manuscript, on file with the Harvard Law School Library, Cambridge, MA.

Skogh, Göran (1985), 'Rättssäkerhet I Marknadsekonomin (Legal Certainty in the Market Economy)', in Segerstedt, Tetal (ed.), *Rättssäkerhet och Demokrati*, Bergen Ratio, förlag.

Slemrod, Joel B. (1989), 'Complexity, Compliance Costs, and Tax Evasion', in Roth, Jeffrey A. and Scholz, John T. (eds), *Taxpayer Compliance, Volume 2: Social Science Perspectives*, Philadelphia, University of Pennsylvania Press.

Slemrod, Joel B. and Yitzhaki, Shlomo (1994), 'Analyzing the Standard Deduction as a Presumptive Tax', **1** *International Tax and Public Finance*, 25–34.

Slot, P.J. (1983), *Regelen en Ontregelen: Oratie Leiden* (Regulating and De-regulating), Kluwer, Deventer.

Spier, Kathryn E. (1994), 'Settlement Bargaining and the Design of Damage Awards', **10** *Journal of Law, Economics and Organization*, 84–95.

Tullock, Gordon (1978), 'Achieving Deregulation – A Public Choice Perspective', **2** *Regulation*, 50–4.

Usher, Dan (1995), 'Victimization, Rent-Seeking and Just Compensation', **83** *Public Choice*, 1–20.

Walz, W. Rainer (1988), 'Rechtssicherheit und Risikozuweisung bei Steuerrechtsänderungen – Verbotene Rückwirkung, gebotene Übergangsregelung, richterliche Vertragsanpassung' (Legal Certainty and Risk Allocation for Changes in Tax Law – Illegal Retroaction, Transitional Rules), *Recht und Risiko*, 252–86.

White, Michelle J. (1992), 'Legal Complexity and Lawyers' Benefit from Litigation', **12** *International Review of Law and Economics*, 381–395.

Yitzhaki, Shlomo (1979), 'A Note on Optimal Taxation and Administrative Costs', **69** *American Economic Review*, 475–80.

Other References

Arnott, Richard and Stiglitz, Joseph E. (1991), 'Moral Hazard and Nonmarket Institutions: Dysfunctional Crowding Out or Peer Monitoring?', **81** *American Economic Review*, 179–90.

Ayres, Ian and Talley, Eric (1995a), 'Solomonic Bargaining: Dividing a Legal Entitlement to Facilitate a Coasean Trade', **104** *Yale Law Journal*, 1027–117.

Ayres, Ian and Talley, Eric (1995b), 'Distinguishing Between Consensual and Nonconsensual Advantages of Liability Rules', **105** *Yale Law Journal*, 235–53.

Becker, Gary S. (1968), 'Crime and Punishment: An Economic Approach', **76** *Journal of Political Economy*, 169–217.

Brown, John (1973), 'Toward an Economic Theory of Liability', **2** *Journal of Legal Studies*, 323–50.

Calabresi, Guido and Melamed, A. Douglas (1972), 'Property Rules, Liability Rules, and Inalienability: One View of the Cathedral', **85** *Harvard Law Review*, 1089–128.

Downs, Anthony (1957), *An Economic Theory of Democracy*, New York, Harper.

Ellickson, Robert C. (1973), 'Alternatives to Zoning: Covenants, Nuisance Rules, and Fines as Land Use Controls', **40** *University of Chicago Law Review*, 681–781.

Farrell, Joseph (1987), 'Information and the Coase Theorem', **1** *Journal of Economic Perspectives*, 113–29.

Johnston, Jason Scott (1995), 'Bargaining under Rules versus Standards', **11** *Journal of Law, Economics and Organization*, 256–81.

Kaplow, Louis (1991), 'Incentives and Government Relief for Risk', **4** *Journal of Risk and Uncertainty*, 167–75.

Kaplow, Louis and Shavell, Steven (1995), 'Do Liability Rules Facilitate Bargaining? A Reply to Ayres and Talley', **105** *Yale Law Journal*, 221–33.

Kaplow, Louis and Shavell, Steven (1996b), 'Property Rules versus Liability Rules: An Economic Analysis', **109** *Harvard Law Review*, 713–90.

Krauss, Michael I. (2000), 'Property Rules vs. Liability Rules', in Bouckaert, Boudewijn and De Geest, Gerrit (eds), *Encyclopedia of Law and Economics, Volume II: Civil Law and Economics*, Cheltenham, UK and Northampton, MA, USA: Edward Elgar, 782–94.

Krier, James E. and Schwab, Stewart J. (1995), 'Property Rules and Liability Rules: The Cathedral in Another Light', **70** *New York University Law Review*, 440–83.

Niskanen, William A. (1971), *Bureaucracy and Representative Government*, Chicago, Aldine, Atherton.

Olson, Mancur (1965), *The Logic of Collective Action; Public Goods and the Theory of Groups*, Cambridge, MA, Harvard University Press.

Polinsky, A. Mitchell (1979), 'Controlling Externalities and Protecting Entitlements: Property Right, Liability Rule, and Tax-Subsidy Approaches', **8** *Journal of Legal Studies*, 1–48.

Polinsky, A. Mitchell (1980), 'Resolving Nuisance Disputes: The Simple Economics of Injunctive and Damage Remedies', **32** *Stanford Law Review*, 1075–112.

Samuelson, William (1985), 'A Comment on the Coase Theorem', in Roth, Alvin E. (ed.), *Game-Theoretic Models of Bargaining*, New York, Cambridge University Press.

Schäfer, Hans-Bernd and Schönenberger, Andreas (2000), 'Strict Liabilitiy versus Negligence', in Bouckaert, Boudewijn and De Geest, Gerrit (eds), *Encyclopedia of Law and Economics, Volume II: Civil Law and Economics*, Cheltenham, UK and Northampton, MA, USA: Edward Elgar, 597–624.

Shavell, Steven (1980), 'Strict Liability Versus Negligence', **9** *Journal of Legal Studies*, 1–25.

Shavell, Steven (1987), *Economic Analysis of Accident Law*, Cambridge, MA, Harvard University Press.

3 Rules versus standards

Barbara Luppi and Francesco Parisi

Just like contracts, laws are of necessity incomplete. Lawmakers cannot effectively foresee all the particular circumstances to which their laws could apply. Incompleteness of law is not only a matter of unavoidable necessity. At times, incomplete laws can be purposefully enacted as a way to delay the decision-making process, transferring to the judiciary some of the tasks otherwise carried out *ex ante* by the legislature. Lawmakers can choose the level of incompleteness of the laws that they write by formulating laws with different degrees of specificity. The law and economics literature refers to the choice of specificity of legal rules as a choice between "rules" (laws with high levels of specificity) and "standards" (laws with low levels of specificity). The present study concerns the functionality of these rules or standards, the consequences of their incorporation into laws, and their significance from an economic perspective.

A "standard" is the legal or social criterion that adjudicators use to judge actions under particular circumstances. Standards provide a greater degree of flexibility to judges and allow them to consider fact-specific circumstantial evidence, such as whether a driver's behavior was the "reason" for an accident. While a standard like "reasonableness" can be subjective, judicial precedent may provide some guidelines for adjudication (Kaplow, 1992).

A "rule," conversely, provides a definitive criterion for the resolution of a legal issue. Rules contain a higher degree of specificity and often bright-line tests. For instance, a rule establishes a maximum blood alcohol content for drivers. An individual who drives while above the legal limit has broken the law regardless of the surrounding circumstances. With greater specificity comes less flexibility, often at the expense of an optimal fit between the coverage of a rule and the regulated conduct.

When legislators choose between rules and standards, they must consider whether the law should be given content *ex ante* or *ex post* and calculate the costs associated with each option (Kaplow, 1992). For instance, rules require a higher degree of specificity during conception to provide a concrete framework for judicial decision making (Schwartz and Scott, 1995). The *ex ante* calculation that lawmakers must perform requires research, an upfront cost that often exceeds the cost for developing a less specific standard. Standards, however, are more difficult to interpret, since they require determinations of the law's content to be made *ex post*. Hence, in the event of an accident in which a driver was intoxicated, a bright-line rule would automatically assign fault to that tortfeasor. Conversely, when adjudicators must determine comparative causation, they have to consider the facts and circumstances at the time of the accident, and decide whether to impose liability. Standards provide a more fact-specific determination, but remain erratic in application over time. Thus, rules are typically optimal *ex ante*, and standards are better *ex post*.

1. The Problem of Judicial Interpretation

The optimal degree of specificity of laws has been a subject of debate for centuries. As pointed out by Parisi and Fon (2009), legal theorists have long attempted to formulate principles that guide judges in interpreting incomplete legal precepts. In 350 BC (or BCE), the Greek philosopher Aristotle realized the unavoidable incompleteness of laws. He pushed the logic of original intent to suggest that, in the process of legislative interpretation, judges should fill the gaps in incomplete legislation by discovering how the original lawmakers would have specified the rule in light of the specific facts, had they foreseen the problem and dealt with it explicitly. Jeremy Bentham (1776) approaches the question of optimal specificity of laws by creating a two-tiered system; the public learns the general rules, while judges evaluate specific cases with some leeway in interpreting the *ex ante* rules. In Bentham's world, judicial discretion could well coexist with detailed and fully specified *ex ante* rules, because judges would have some adjudicatory flexibility when applying the *ex ante* rule to the case (see e.g. Dan-Cohen, 1984; and Parisi, 1992).

The understanding of incompleteness of law as a legislative choice variable in itself has shifted attention to the question of the optimal specificity of laws. Within the margins of reasonable foresight, lawmakers have some choice over the degree of legal rules' specificity. Laws that are not fully specified upfront impose greater implementation and decision-making costs upon judicial and administrative bodies at a later stage. The optimal degree of specificity of law thus critically depends on the relative costs and political advantages of lawmaking by different branches of government. The evaluation of comparative advantages in lawmaking necessarily rests on the full understanding of the public choice implications of alternative allocations of lawmaking power.

Ehrlich and Posner (1973) conjecture that when the rule is statutory and the conduct to be regulated is politically controversial, the cost of promulgating a rule is highest. The formulation of a statutory rule requires negotiation among the legislators. The analysis of transaction costs in other contexts suggests that the costs of legislative negotiation are likely to be substantial due to the number of legislators whose agreement must be secured, and will be even higher when the proposed rule is controversial. Transaction costs increase with the number of parties whose agreement is necessary for the transaction to occur. The presence of so many parameters that affect the choice of optimal degree of detail of legal rules led Diver (1983: 76) to conclude that, while some laws may better serve their purpose as rules and others as standards, "[g]eneralizations about optimal-rule precision are inherently suspect."

Under-inclusion and Over-inclusion Problems

As pointed out by Parisi and Fon (2009), from an efficiency perspective, there are both under- and over-inclusive effects that occur when deciding to implement a rule in specific circumstances that were not specifically envisioned by the lawmaker. Ehrlich and Posner note that coupling a rule with a standard can solve the problem of under-inclusion. For example, it can thus be made unlawful to drive more than 70 miles per hour *or* to drive at any speed that is unreasonably fast given the particular circumstances of the case. While adding a standard to a rule can remedy under-inclusion, it can also diminish the benefits of legislating with rules, namely the low cost for adjudicators in determining when an individual has violated the rule.

When implementing a rule or a standard, there are also over-inclusive effects. The problem of over-inclusion is frequently dealt with by allowing enforcement officials to waive *ex post* the application of the rule or standard (e.g. speeding violations can be excused in case of emergency, etc.). Theoretically, a rule could be formulated with sufficient level of detail to contemplate all the possible exceptions, excuses and justifications. In practice, however, it may be less possible to envision *ex ante* all possible contingencies, or too costly to allow case-by-case exceptions to be made at the enforcement level.

The problems of over-inclusion and under-inclusion are more serious the greater the heterogeneity of the regulated conduct, and the faster the rate of change of the regulated environment. Kaplow (1992) suggests that even an activity that may appear homogeneous and objectively ascertainable, such as speeding, contains overriding elements of heterogeneity. The reasonableness of speeding depends on the particular circumstances of the case. A single speed limit, or even a number of speed limits set contingently in consideration of particular circumstances, would by necessity lead to occasional under-inclusiveness or over-inclusiveness. Social losses can occur when parties are deterred from undertaking socially desirable actions in the belief that they may be sanctioned by a seemingly over-inclusive standard or when parties participate in undesirable behavior not explicitly covered by an overly detailed, yet under-inclusive, rule (Kaplow, 1992). These costs fluctuate depending on the relative value and externalities produced by the regulated or unconstrained activity. In this context, Ehrlich and Posner suggest that minimizing the social-loss function with respect to potential under-inclusion and over-inclusion costs maximizes efficiency and they predict that rules will be more common in areas of homogeneous conduct.

2. Rules, Standards, and the Social Cost of Lawmaking and Adjudication

Law and economics scholars have often considered the criteria for determining the optimal degree of specificity of legal rules. Scholars who have entered the debate have used instruments from optimal decision theory, public choice theory, and constitutional political economy, with differing and often antithetical results. "Standards" are generally considered to provide judges and administrative agencies with more discretion when adjudicating specific cases, whereas rules provide a more rigid framework taking discretion away from the adjudicating body.

There are, of course, costs and benefits to governing with rules or with standards, and such costs should be taken into account in choosing the optimal specificity of a law. Those variables that bear on the choice of optimal degree of specificity of legal rules include the law's intended objective, the frequency of the application of the legal rule, the total cost of lawmaking, the net social welfare, and the cost of legal advice.

The law's intended objective is important because if the law's purpose is deterrence of specific conduct, criminal or otherwise, rules are typically preferable (Diver, 1983: 77). This is because laws written with deterrence in mind send clear signals to the population at large that certain conduct will yield certain consequences, regardless of extraneous or mitigating factors. Where deterrence is not the primary goal, standards are often more appropriate (Diver, 1983: 77). When crimes have already been committed, for example, lawmakers may prefer to equip adjudicators and enforcers with specific standards that permit the consideration of extraneous or mitigating factors. Rules and standards may come together in this way so that rules efficiently govern conduct and standards govern punishment (see Dan-Cohen, 1984; and Parisi, 1992).

It is important to consider the frequency of a law's application in determining optimal specificity so that lawmakers can strike the right balance between promulgation and enforcement costs. If a law is frequently applied, enforcement costs will tend to be higher than promulgation costs. This necessarily means that rules will be more efficient than standards when the law is frequently applied. Since legislators must absorb promulgation costs only once, standards have the potential to cost significantly more because adjudicators accrue enforcement costs each time there is a violation (Kaplow, 1992: 577). Rules are also more efficient when individuals frequently engage in the regulated activity, since rules are then easier to learn, which may increase compliance.

The total cost of lawmaking is another factor that economists weigh heavily in determining the optimal specificity of legal rules. Ehrlich and Posner have advanced the notion that total cost (including promulgation and enforcement costs) should ultimately control a legislature's determination. Rules require a high degree of specificity and therefore have higher promulgation costs, which may include detailed research (Kaplow, 1992: 570). Standards, on the other hand, will be costlier to enforce for adjudicators, draining more resources from the judicial system (Kaplow, 1992: 577). Adjudicators must give content to standards, which is a key factor in high enforcement costs (Kaplow, 1992: 570).

Economists concerned about net social welfare tend to favor rules because they guarantee greater certainty, consistency, and predictability to private parties (Sullivan, 1992). Sullivan argues that rules promote judicial economies by minimizing the need for a detailed consideration of facts and circumstances each time a law is applied (Sullivan, 1992: 63).

The cost of legal advice is a final factor in determining the optimal specificity of legal rules. The cost of consulting with an attorney to determine whether certain conduct violates a standard is higher than it is for rules (Kaplow, 1992: 571). Attorneys will convey a more concrete understanding of the consequences of an actor's conduct where rules are concerned because they are easier to apply *ex ante*. Given the cheaper cost factor, more individuals are likely to become informed in a rule-dominated regime (Kaplow, 1992: 574).

Rules, Standards and Information Costs

Economists note that there are information costs associated with promulgating and enforcing rules and standards, particularly with regard to compliance with rules and standards. Under rules, informed individuals can fully identify the content of the law since legal provisions are fully articulated upfront and, as a result, individuals may more easily conform their behavior to the law. Rules are precise and it is easier to conform conduct to a precise rule. A precise definition of "reasonable" conduct under a reasonableness standard has been ellusive; hence, legal actors must resort to potentially expensive research that may not produce definitive answers, increasing the cost for the individual. Furthermore, standards are given content and substance only after individuals act, which increases the difficulty of pre-action decision making and decreases consistency amongst actors. On the other hand, when individuals can clearly determine the application of rules to their potential acts, their conduct is more likely to reflect the previously promulgated rules. Under rules, individuals are more likely to be informed, and under standards, individuals are likely to be relatively uninformed. Kaplow suggests that uninformed individuals act based on their best guess about how the law will apply to their contemplated conduct, whereas informed individuals act based on their actual knowledge of the law.

Lawmaking as a Production Function: The Optimal Scale Problem

The lawmaking process can be thought as a production process that imposes on the lawmaker the requirement to incur both fixed and variable costs. In this sense, the creation of the law requires the lawmaker to invest in the fixed cost required for the production of legal order. Lawmakers choose the level of fixed capital to allocate in the promulgation of a law. By choosing their fixed cost investment, lawmakers indeed choose the level of specificity of legal rules (Parisi and Ghei, 2005). The greater the law's specificity, the more costly it is to promulgate. However, less flexibility results in a less intensive fact-finding process, reducing implementation costs by courts and administrative agencies. Thus, increasing the fixed investment (i.e. the degree of specificity) lowers the variable implementation costs of adjudication.

The choice of a well-specified rule is likely to require a larger upfront investment, but has lower operating costs later. Enacting a rule requires a large outlay in the initial acquisition of information, but because the rule is simple to understand and apply, the operating costs are low. A standard requires a smaller initial investment, as it requires less information and legislative detail to enact. However, it requires larger outlays in its enforcement, in that it costs more for individuals to acquire information about a standard and requires greater implementation and interpretation efforts by the courts.

Kaplow suggests that regulation is sometimes served better with a rule, and at other times is better served with a standard, depending on frequency of application of the relevant law. For legal issues that arise frequently, in settings with common characteristics, a law with a greater level of specificity (e.g. a 65 mph speed limit) would be preferable to a more generic legal standard of conduct (e.g. drive at a reasonable speed). Because learning about a rule is less costly, individuals may spend less in learning about the law and may be better guided by a rule, since the law's content can be readily ascertained (Kaplow, 1992).

Conversely, where legal issues rarely arise and the circumstances are varied, designing a rule that accounts for every relevant contingency would be wasteful, as most of such hypothetical circumstances would never arise in actual cases. Designing a negligence rule that could take into account each unique situation *ex ante* would be prohibitively expensive, if not impossible (Kaplow, 1992). Since rules have a higher fixed cost than standards, whereas standards generally have a higher variable cost, Kaplow shows that when frequency is low, a general standard is preferable.

Fon and Parisi (2007) model the choice of optimal specificity of laws, denoted by s, as a function of the frequency of application of the law, denoted by N and a number of exogenous parameters, such as obsolescence, denoted by o, the degree of specialization of the court c, the complexity of the environment k and coordination cost using existing legislation h. Lawmakers choose the specificity level to maximize the net total value of the legislation, measured as the average value of the law V net of the production cost function of lawmakers. The production cost of legislation is the sum of a fixed cost component, denoted by F, and a variable cost component, denoted by C. Analytically, the objective function of lawmakers takes the following form:

$$max_s \; NV(s,o) - F(s,h,k) - NC(s,c,k)$$

The degree of specificity s impacts positively on the value of the law: the more specifically detailed is the legal issue, the more informative it is and the greater is the value of legislation. At the same time, the more detailed the law, the higher the fixed costs F incurred by the lawmaker in promulgating the law, and the lower the marginal cost of implementation and adjudication of the law, C. The frequency of application of the law N impacts on the net social value of legislation: the higher the application frequency, the higher is the value of the law and the higher are the implementation costs of the law.

Fon and Parisi (2007) show that the frequency of application of a law is a crucial determinant of the optimal level of specificity. Consistently with Kaplow (1992), rules (i.e. laws that are well-specified) are more efficient than standards, when that legal issue arises often in settings characterized by common traits. The reason is that a higher upfront fixed cost of promulgation will consistently reduce the adjudication cost required for implementation. Additionally, the more specific the law, the easier it will be for individuals to learn the law. Conversely, standards are more efficient than rules, when that legal issue occurs rarely or in settings with varied traits. In these circumstances, in fact, it would be very expensive to design a law that would fit every relevant contingency in a complex environment.

Addressing the lawmaking problem of the specificity level of legislation allows us to identify and characterize the different patterns of lawmaking that arise under different legal, social and economic conditions. According to the analysis developed, legal systems respond to exogenous changes, for example in the level of complexity of the legal and social environment or in the coordination cost of existing legislation. In the presence of different environments, lawmakers adopt varying patterns of lawmaking, aiming to maximize the value of a legal intervention. To clarify the importance of exogenous parameters for optimal specificity, consider the degree of specialization of the courts. The optimal level of law specificity increases if applied by more specialized courts (i.e. for higher c). This is the case in most civil law jurisdictions, that are characterized by specialized sections that are called upon to deal with a given set of legal issues. Conversely, the coordination costs of existing legislation have a negative impact on optimal specificity. The cost of revising legislation in civil law systems is higher than in common law systems, since codification is designed to provide a comprehensive set of rules and principles. In these circumstances, the revision of legislation in civil law countries appears to be more difficult, requiring the work of committees of experts, thereby inducing a lower optimal level of specificity and a more frequent use of standards.

The model provides the basis for further consideration of likely departures from such optimal lawmaking patterns due to specific public choice failures.

The Obsolescence Problem

Lawmakers promulgate a law characterized by a certain level of specificity that maximizes the net value of legislation, designed in the light of the social, economic and technological characteristics of the environment. However, the optimal level of specificity chosen for legislation is not constant over time, due to changing circumstances that evolve over time and reflect social, economic and technological changes. Lawmakers should face additional regulation costs when revising legislation to realign the law with the evolution of the external environment. For example, the development of air bags and anti-lock brakes on vehicles altered the relative costs of accident avoidance. Such changes and advances can even render rules obsolete. Posner and Ehrlich (1973) suggest that more detailed rules require more frequent and more costly changes. In the analytical framework developed by Fon and Parisi (2007), obsolescence is modeled as an exogenous parameter, o, that measures environmental volatility, i.e. the rate at which the environment changes. According to the economic analysis, the optimal specificity level decreases, the more volatile the environment.

Standards, however, are less affected by changing circumstances. Since they indicate only the types of circumstances that are relevant and not particular, specific circumstances, their flexibility allows an adjudicating official to consider innovations in technology and changing economic and social circumstances. The reasonableness standard directs the decision maker to determine *ex post* what behavior by the parties would have minimized the sum of the expected accident costs and the accident avoidance costs. This concept can be followed despite changes in the optimal course of conduct over time. The optimal rule maker, then, would use more specific rules when there is a stable environment, and general standards when there is a high rate of change.

Since detailed rules are more sensitive to changes in the regulated environment, they are more prone to obsolescence. Ehrlich and Posner (1973) note that detailed, judge-made rules of liability, derived from the standards and characteristics of the nineteenth century, have given way to detailed traffic and other safety codes that, through the doctrine of negligence *per se*, operate as rules of tort liability as well as standards. The rise in the rate of economic and technological change over time has increased the cost of the judicial process. While the judicial process is not well-suited to the rapid alteration of rules, a general standard can accommodate more change. However, the first adjudication under a standard constitutes a precedent for future enforcement proceedings and almost transforms the standard into a rule (Kaplow, 1992).

Environmental volatility impacts on the optimal specificity of legislation. At the same time, both environmental volatility and legislation specificity will affect the optimal timing of legal intervention.[1] Lawmakers choose when to intervene and revise legislation and legal rules. Hence, the obsolence rate, optimal legislation specificity and optimal timing of legal interventions are intertwined. Parisi and Ghei (2005) draw an analogy between the lawmaking process and the production process. In the analysis developed by the authors, lawmakers invest in the fixed production of capital and choose the timing of replacement of obsolete capital. The social planner chooses the degree of specificity and the timing of legal intervention, which are critical control variables, to maximize the net present value of legislation. Parisi and Ghei (2005) characterize the optimal balance of timing and specificity as a function of exogenous parameters, such as the expected frequency of application of the legal rule; the degree of uncertainty in the regulated environment; the extent to which lawmaking costs are irreversible (i.e., sunk); and the time preference rate of the social planner.

Lawmaking under Uncertainty

As pointed out by Parisi, Fon and Ghei (2004), an important dimension of the optimal-specificity problem concerns the conditions of uncertainty that surround the enactment of any law. The fundamental premise of recent law and economics research is that lawmaking can be likened to an investment, where the process of lawmaking imposes a present cost in the expectation of future benefits (Dixit and Pindyck, 1994). The creation of legal rules often imposes initial lawmaking costs that are at least partially sunk. The sunk and irreversible nature of lawmaking costs has important implications for the understanding of optimal lawmaking. Models of optimal lawmaking that ignore the option value of delaying legal intervention will be often be biased towards excessive legal innovation. As in any investment decision, the choice of the timing of the investment is crucial. Lawmakers need to choose the timing of legal intervention. Given uncertainty about future returns, investment can be postponed to acquire more information. The same logic may explain the use of narrowly tailored decisions and dicta, when judicial precedents are issues surrounded by uncertainty. But delays in legal intervention often come at a cost, given the foregone benefits of investment in the immediate future.

As the emerging investment theory literature has amply shown (see e.g. Pindyck, 1991), contrary to what traditional investment theory once suggested,

---

[1] See Gersen and Posner (2008) and Luppi and Parisi (2009) for a discussion of the optimal choice of timing rules in legislation.

legal intervention is not necessarily warranted by the fact that intervention can generate a net increase in present value. As option-pricing theory (McDonald and Siegel, 1985; Pindyck, 1991) has revealed, the optimal choice of an investment under uncertainty is not that generated by net present value calculations, but the one that takes into account the full value of the option to invest. As shown by Parisi, Fon and Ghei (2004), in the presence of uncertainty and sunk investment costs, a lawmaker is faced with a wedge between the economies obtainable with the implementation of a specified rule and the value of the option to await legal intervention.[2] The dual optimization problem facing the lawmaker, then, is that of determining the optimal level of specificity and timing of intervention, taking into consideration the above factors.

3. Conclusion: Policy Implications

As discussed above, the use of rules versus standards has broad implications for judicial interpretation and the cost and benefits of lawmaking. As a policy matter, Schäfer (2001) suggests that the use of rules rather than standards has the advantage of reducing corruption, concentrating human capital, and cutting down court delays caused by complex decisions. Schäfer's conclusions are based primarily on the idea that rule-based systems are preferable in developing countries. Using China as an example, Schäfer declares that efforts there to find the optimal degree of specificity of laws are unsuccessful because the judiciary is composed of largely untrained or unqualified personnel. Adjudicators apply the standards haphazardly and so frequently that no clear signals are sent to the public. Schäfer's argument depends critically on the tenuous premise that legislatures are inherently less corrupt and better informed than the judiciary (perhaps since the legislature is elected on a regular basis, whereas much of the judiciary is appointed and can enjoy lifetime tenure). Additionally, regulated environments in developing countries may be more volatile than those in industrialized countries. Volatility of the external environment creates an increased opportunity for obsolescence of legal rules. This in turn would render standards preferable to specific rules and prevent the legislature from constantly having to incur the cost of legislative amendment to modify previous legal enactments after each new development in the external environment.

---

[2] Parisi and Ghei (2005) have also tackled the issue of optimal timing of lawmaking using the insights of option pricing theory. Parisi and Ghei observe that the choice of optimal timing in lawmaking should be derived considering the option-like characteristics of lawmaking decisions. The authors show that the net present value methodology is inappropriate for dealing with lawmaking decisions under uncertainty, illustrating the different results obtained taking account of the option value of deferring legal intervention, showing how the resulting lawmaking rules depend on various parameters of the regulated environment.

References

Aristotle (350 BC). *Nicomachean Ethics*, bk. V. §10, in Roger Crisp (ed. and trans.), *Nicomachean Ethics*. New York: Cambridge University Press, 2000.

Bentham, J. (1776). "A fragment on Government", in J.H. Burns and H.L.A. Hart (eds.), *A Comment on the Commentaries and a Fragment on Government*. London: University of London Athlone Press, 1977.

Dan-Cohen, M. (1984). "Decision Rules and Conduct Rules: On Acoustic Separation in Criminal Law". *Harvard Law Review*, 97: 625.

Diver, C.S. (1983). "The Optimal Precision of Administrative Rules". *Yale Law Journal*, 93: 65–109.

Dixit, A.K. and Pindyck, R.S. (1994). *Investment under Uncertainty*. Princeton, NJ: Princeton University Press.

Ehrlich, I. and Posner, R.A. (1973). "An Economic Analysis of Legal Rulemaking". *Journal of Legal Studies*, 11 (January): 257–86.

Fon, V. and Parisi , F. (2007). "On the Optimal Specificity of Legal Rules". *Journal of Institutional Economics*, 3 (3): 147–64.

Gersen, J.E. and Posner, E.A. (2007). "Timing Rules and Legal Institutions". *Harvard Law Review*, 121: 543–89.

Kaplow, L. (1992). "Rules versus Standards: An Economic Analysis". *Duke Law Journal*, 42: 557–629.

Luppi, B. and Parisi, F. (2009). "Optimal Timing of Legal Intervention: The Role of Timing Rules". *Harvard Law Review Forum*, 122: 1–14.

McDonald, R. and Siegel, D.R. (1985). "Investment and Valuation of Firms when there is an Option to Shut Down". *International Law Review*, 26(2): 331–49.

Parisi, F. (1992). *Liability for Negligence and Judicial Discretion* (2nd ed.). Berkeley: California University Press (IAS Series).

Parisi, F. and Fon, V. (2009). *The Economics of Lawmaking*. Oxford: Oxford University Press.

Parisi, F., Fon, V. and Ghei, N. (2004). "The Value of Waiting in Lawmaking". *European Journal of Law and Economics*, 18: 131–48.

Parisi, F. and Ghei, N. (2005) "Legislate Today or Wait Until Tomorrow? An Investment Approach to Lawmaking". *Journal of Public Finance and Public Choice*, 23: 19–42.

Pindyck, R.S. (1991). "Irreversibility, Uncertainty and Investment". *Journal of Economic Literature*, 29: 1110–48.

Posner, R.A. (1989). "Legislation and its Interpretation: A Primer". *Nebraska Law Review*, 68: 432–53.

Schäfer, H. (2001). "Rules versus Standards in Developing Countries: Should Poor Countries Have a More Rule Based Legal System?" Unpublished manuscript from University of California at Berkeley.

Schwartz, A. and Scott, R.E. (1995). "The Political Economy of Private Legislatures". *University of Pennsylvania Law Review*, 143: 595–654.

Sullivan, K.M. (1992). "The Justices of Rules and Standards". *Harvard Law Review*, 106: 22–123.

4 The optimal timing of lawmaking

Nita Ghei

Introduction

In a dynamic society, laws will need to change as economic relationships change, as technological innovations take place, as social customs evolve. Old laws, broadly defined to include legislation, custom, and judge-made law, become increasingly inefficient in the new environment. The question then is: what is the optimal timing of lawmaking?

Customary law, by definition, changes by an endogenous process, and will not be addressed here. The focus of the discussion will be legislation, where the element of choice is substantial, and the agency problem consequently a matter of importance. In common law jurisdictions, judge-made law remains an important source of law making. While judges have far less discretion than legislators in the matter of the hearing of a case, they do exercise some control over the scope of the decision rendered, and therefore have some control of the timing of lawmaking. Nonetheless, legislation remains the type of lawmaking where timing matters the most, and will be the focus of the discussion here, including the inherent agency problems and the timing rules that emerge to address these issues.

The process of lawmaking is analogous to investment (Parisi, Fon and Ghei 2004; Parisi and Ghei 2005). More specifically, lawmaking shares three critical characteristics with investments in physical assets: irreversibility in investment (sunk costs); uncertainty about future returns; and discretion with respect to the timing of investment. Once enacted, the costs sunk into legislation cannot be recovered if it turns out the legislation proves to be ineffective or worse. In fact, repeal comes with additional costs.

The ability to delay an irreversible investment profoundly affects the logic of whether and when to invest (see e.g. Pindyck 1991; Dixit and Pindyck 1994). In particular, ignoring the value of the option in the optimization calculation will result in the investment being undertaken too soon.

The application of the traditional net present value rule would dictate investment when the present expected value of the investment, the legal rule in this case, is equal to or greater than the cost of enacting the legislation. This rule, however, fails to take into account the value of the option when the costs of the legal intervention are irreversible and the innovation can be postponed. Parisi, Fon and Ghei (2004) and Parisi and Ghei (2005) use formal dynamic models from the investment literature model to explore the problems of lawmaking under uncertainty and to illustrate the effects of the option to delay legal intervention on the optimal timing of lawmaking. Both these studies use the construct of a benevolent planner, and discuss the political agency problem as an extension. Gerson and Posner (2007) focus on how timing rules address the agency problems in legal institutions; Luppi and Parisi (2009) compute the option value of these timing rules, and suggest different forms of legislation consistent with these parameters. Some of the earliest work in the area was by Heiner (1986), on judicially driven innovation and the general wisdom in the political economy of regulation stressing the importance of stability and certainty in the legal system. Nonetheless, over time, the focus for timing of lawmaking has come to be legislation, where this element is of critical importance.

Much like investment in an asset, adoption of a new law requires a direct investment cost (I). The value of the law (V) is given by the present discounted value of the law's future benefits. These benefits could include an immediate short-run payoff (δ), and a long-run benefit, which is uncertain. Parisi, Fon and Ghei (2004), in the formal model, conceptualize the long-run value of the law, V, as a stochastic process that follows a Brownian motion, with α as the growth rate, and σ as the volatility measure of the law. Lawmaking can yield immediate benefits, first, by replacing rules that were outmoded or inefficient. Alternatively, if the activity was previously unregulated, the clarity provided by the rule could provide some advantage in encouraging exchange. Waiting to legislate would mean forgoing these benefits of legal intervention, and it is therefore appropriate to think of these as a cost of waiting to legislate.

Implementing legislation is costly, as well, and none of these costs can be recovered if the enacted rule proves to be inefficient or otherwise undesirable. There are the direct legislative and political costs, including publication and notice costs. The process of rulemaking through private legislatures, as discussed by Schwartz and Scott (1995), should also be considered in this context. There are the costs of disseminating information (Kaplow 1992) and of acquiring information about the new law (Ehrlich and Posner 1973). There are substantial learning costs for all agents, including the courts, enforcement agencies and private individuals. There might be adjustment costs if the legal innovation results in changes to the existing set of legal entitlements. There will also be institutional costs associated with the discontinuation of an existing rule, including sunk costs by enforcement agencies. These costs cannot be recovered once the new law is promulgated. The irreversibility of lawmaking costs requires lawmakers to be sensitive to uncertainty over future costs and benefits from the new rule, and changes in the environment that might render the rule obsolete. Any model of optimal lawmaking that fails to consider the option value of waiting is necessarily assuming that the legal system can avoid sunk costs and abrogate and enact law with sunk expenditures.

The Basic Problem

The lawmaker is risk neutral and benevolent. The external environment changes at a stochastic rate. The lawmaker can choose the optimal legislative instrument and control the timing of legal intervention. The new law is always more efficient. The lawmaker always has the option of waiting until another period to change the law. The lawmaker's task, therefore, is determining the optimal timing of legal intervention.

The problem is formulated as a binary dynamic programming problem (Parisi, Fon and Ghei 2004). At each time, t, the legislature can adopt the new law, or postpone the legal intervention. The net present value of the optimal payoff of the law-adopting opportunity is $P_t\,(V_t)$. If the legislature chooses to terminate the wait, the termination payoff will be $V_t - 1$. On the other hand, if the legislature chooses to wait, there is no immediate payoff in the current period. There is, however, a value to waiting, given by expected future (optimal) adoption payoff in the next period, discounted to the present period: $\frac{1}{1+\alpha+\delta}E\left[P_{t+1}\left(V_{t+1}\right)\right]$. The optimal payoff value for $P_t\,(V_t)$ is equal to the larger of the two. Due to the stochastic nature of the problem, the precise timing of adoption cannot be found. It is possible, however, to formulate the problem in terms of finding a threshold value for the payoff, V^*, such that it is optimal to innovate whenever $V \geq V^*$ and cash in the option. When the value falls below this critical level, an optimizing lawmaker will maintain the status quo and delay legal innovation, that is, keep the option.

There are four variables that will impact the decision about timing of lawmaking. First, the extent to which the costs are irreversible. The value of waiting should increase with the extent of irreversibility. As discussed above, costs associated with legal innovations are peculiarly likely to be irreversible. In the real world, with agency problems, as will be discussed below, reputational and other considerations are an additional sunk cost that lawmakers need to take into account in the decision-making process. The second variable that matters is the extent of uncertainty in the system. The greater the uncertainty, the greater the cost of giving up the option of waiting. Waiting allows the lawmaker to acquire more information, and preserve the opportunity of undertaking legal innovation based on this information in the future. This is particularly true when it comes to information technology, which has evolved, and continues to evolve, rapidly, and regulators struggle to keep up with innovations in technology. The third factor that matters is the value of the law over time. The greater the expected value of the law, the greater should be the value of waiting. On the other hand, the greater the short-term benefits of legal innovation, the lower is the net value of waiting. Thus, if an immediate ban could prevent an endangered species from extinction, for example, the gain could outweigh the value of waiting.

The general problem facing the lawmaker is that of choosing the right moment to switch to a new law. On one extreme, the lawmaker could change the law in response to each change in the environment; on the other, he or she could never change the law. The former would be cost prohibitive; the latter would result in laws that would be obsolete and inefficient. In between these extremes, there should be a range where the benefits of an innovation exceed the sunk costs.

The importance of the option in the context of law is that, by waiting, the lawmaker preserves the opportunity to make the innovation in the future. The lawmaking opportunity is always available, and is comparable to a perpetual option with no expiration date. When a lawmaker chooses to legislate, this option is killed. Legal innovation should be undertaken only when the expected value of lawmaking exceeds the lawmaking costs by an amount equal to the value of keeping the option alive. In the presence of uncertainty, this result modifies considerably the criterion that suggests proceeding with legal innovation any time the present value of the expected benefits of legal innovation exceed the expected costs.[1]

Extensions

Sequential Lawmaking

Many lawmaking exercises in the real world are not the one time legal intervention discussed above, but instead, involve sequential multistage intervention, such as regulatory programs that are implemented in stages, or international treaties that require ratification and subsequent harmonization in a process that can sometime take decades (such as the General Agreement on Tariffs and Trade (GATT), which commenced after the end of the Second World War, and is still under way in the form of the Doha Round). Under plausible assumptions, the sequential lawmaking problem will result in the effects of uncertainty and irreversibility having increased importance. The longer it takes for a legal enactment to come into force, the greater is the uncertainty regarding the value of the innovation at the time of entry into force of the final law, and therefore an even higher expected discounted benefit from legal innovation will be necessary to justify that innovation.

Benefits from Experimentation

Even unsuccessful legal innovation can occasionally generate informational benefits, since it discloses the intrinsic value of the attempted legal solutions and reduces the risk of similar legislative errors in the future. Legislative errors

---

1 Majd and Pindyck (1987) address a similar problem, where a firm invests continuously until the project is completed. The analogy with a multistage legal intervention is obvious.

may indeed provide valuable information about the net benefits (or lack thereof) of alternate legal rules. Thus, for example, collectivization of land did not help productivity of land in the then Soviet Union (Ghei 2009) – which provides valuable information for property rights rules.

The informational value of past legislative errors reduces uncertainty over the value of future legal innovation alternatives. The value of learning from experimentation offsets, to some extent, the value of waiting. With learning, the test for optimal timing becomes more permissive. There are two relevant types of learning. First, if the underlying learning evolves stochastically, the value of learning is given by the opportunity to observe the unknown reality. To the extent that this "learning" is only obtainable in conjunction with actual legal innovation, delaying intervention would preclude the acquisition of such benefits. Second, learning can be independent of any stochastic uncertainty. The identity of the best legal rule might be unknown, but the rule itself does not evolve over time. If so, there is no gain from waiting, and in fact, there is an opportunity cost to delaying experimentation.

Specificity of Legal Rules

The specificity of legal rules is an issue that is very much interrelated with that of timing, even though the two have been treated as essentially independent in the literature. Ehrlich and Posner (1973) were the first to discuss the problem of the optimal degree of specificity of legal rules. Schwartz and Scott (1995) modeled rulemaking in the context of a private legislature as a single-shot multistate game. However, Kaplow (1992) points out that it is possible to have a complex rule and simple standard.

The problem of optimal specificity can be reassessed in a dynamic fashion. The more specific the law is, the more expensive it is going to be to enact. On the other hand, a well-specified rule, though it requires a larger upfront investment, will have lower operating costs. A simple rule will have lower enactment costs, but higher implementation costs. Thus, the sunk costs are very different depending on the degree of specificity of a law. The option value of delaying legal intervention will vary in the presence of uncertainty and sunk costs, and economies of scale – all factors a lawmaker needs to take into account in the decision-making process.

The Political Agency Problem

The formal model above assumed a benevolent planner. In the real world, of course, as the rich public choice literature has examined, there are significant agency problems (see e.g. Mueller 2003) when it comes to political institutions, in that a small number of legislators and a somewhat larger, but still small, number of judges and regulators have the authority to act on behalf of voters.

There is no reason, a priori, to believe that the agent's goals will always be identical to that of the principal.

Gerson and Posner (2007) identify the following relationships where agency problems dominate: "between voters and legislators, between Congress as a whole and committee members, and between legislators and bureaucrats."

Gerson and Posner analyze the vast panoply of timing rules that exist in the context of the principal–agent relationships that dominate political institutions. They categorize timing rules into four types: delay rules, rapidity rules, coordination rules, and trigger rules. Delay rules slow action. Rapidity rules specify a time period and mandate action within that time period. Coordination rules specify when an action must take place. The timing might be arbitrary, but helpful in that the decision-making body would otherwise have trouble coordinating on its own. Trigger rules "use the timing of legislative action to trigger some other feature of the legislative process."

They then proceed to consider the problem of the optimal timing of legislation in an uncertain environment. The choice of legislation is immediate legislation, where the public good is created in time period 1, to take effect in the same time period. The benefit B is created with probability p. The cost C_H and legislative cost k are certain. The value of the action is $pB - C_H - k$.

Alternatively, the legislature can choose to wait, and pass the law in period 2 only if the public good will create the benefit B. The cost is lower, C_L, because people can anticipate the deferred legislation. Both the cost and benefit are incurred with probability p, but they must be discounted by d where $d < 1$. The value of the deferred legislation is $dp(B - C_L - k)$.

Immediate legislation dominates the higher the value of p, the lower the cost of enactment and adjustment, and the higher the discount rate.

The legislature can also pass anticipatory legislation in period 1, to take effect in period 2, such that legislative costs are incurred with certainty and without discounting; the benefits of the public good are discounted and probabilistic. The legislature can also pass conditional legislation in period 1 that provides that the public good will be created in period 2 if and only if B turns out to be greater than C_L, avoiding the cost of repeal.

What is the impact of timing rules? Delay rules would seem to increase the probability of deferred legislation – but they can also increase the probability of anticipatory and conditional legislation. So delay rules can cause the legislature to act too quickly, and add to the inefficiency of the system. Rapidity rules may also force the legislature to act quickly when it might be inclined to delay.

Timing rules could have two different functions. They might reduce agency costs, in that they reduce the advantages of interest groups in the legislative process. It takes time for groups to mobilize, and the general public will take longer than organized special interest groups. Therefore, delay rules help larger, less organized groups to be heard. Or delay rules could create new problems.

If the public is largely passive, delay rules make it easier for interest groups to monitor legislators and enhance their influence in the process. The same can be said for rapidity rules.

Nonetheless, Gerson and Posner find that timing rules work to facilitate the

> monitoring of agents by principals and reduce the ability of ill-motivated agents to make policy decisions that violate the policy preferences of political principals. . . . [W]ithin the legislature timing rules may ensure that committees develop relevant expertise without also using that expertise to excessively self-serving ends. Outside the legislature, timing rules can allow a diffuse and disorganized public to combat the influence of private interest groups on legislation and to monitor legislative behavior more carefully.

They do issue a warning that

> [m]any timing rules create new agency problems, generating risk of undesirable behavior by political actors in future periods. And, because many timing rules are chosen by potentially ill-motivated legislators, there is no reason to believe timing rules will always serve the good.

Luppi and Parisi (2009) extend the framework to seven timing rules, and calculate the option values. Immediate legislation also causes an obsolescence problem. Deferred legislation creates an option to defer, and citizens have time to adapt. The value of this option needs to be included in the optimization exercise. Anticipatory legislation is similar to deferred legislation, but it has the possibility of repeal. The timing rule offers an option of exit through repeal, and the value of this option is the difference between the net present value of the anticipatory legislation and the value of immediate legislation. Conditional legislation, where the law comes into effect only if B exceeds C_L, offers an option of exit without repeal. All these options need to be factored into the optimization problem in view of the irreversibility problem discussed above.

Luppi and Parisi also consider three other cases that Gerson and Posner do not: sunset legislation, delayed legislation, and revisable legislation. Sunset legislation offers the option of preordered exit. Delayed legislation is a commonly used legislative strategy when law is enacted with an option to delay entry into force, to allow adaptation and behavioral changes. Revisable legislation has an option to revise, so the lawmaker has the benefit of a rule in place while taking into account the possibility of changes in the future.

The dynamic pattern of cost structure will affect the optimal choice of legal rules. As legislative costs increase, the value of the option to delay decreases, and makes immediate legislation more attractive. There are also reputational and other costs to be kept in mind, as well as the agency problems mentioned.

In the real world, the socially optimal timing of lawmaking can often diverge from what is optimal for the legislator, in view of the agency problems that exist.

Timing rules go some way toward correcting the problem, but they can also add to the problem. Even abstracting from the agency problem, in an uncertain world, when investment is irreversible, using a simple net present value rule, without taking into account the value of waiting, will result in rushing into lawmaking too soon.

References

Dixit, Avinash, and Robert S. Pindyck (1994), *Investment under Uncertainty*, Princeton NJ: Princeton University Press.

Ehrlich, Isaac, and Richard A. Posner (1973), "An Economic Analysis of Rulemaking", *Journal of Legal Studies*, 11: 257–86.

Gerson, Jacob E., and Eric A. Posner (2007), "Timing Rules and Legal Institutions", *Harvard Law Review*, 121: 543–89.

Ghei, Nita (2009), "Institutional Arrangements, Property Rights, and the Endogenity of Comparative Advantage", *Transnational Law and Contemporary Problems*, 18: 617–55.

Heiner, Ronald A. (1986), "Imperfect Decisions and the Law: On the Evolution of Legal Precedent and Rule", *Journal of Legal Studies*, 15: 227–61.

Kaplow, Louis (1992), "Rules v. Standards: An Economic Analysis", *Duke Law Journal*, 42: 557–629.

Luppi, Barbara, and Francesco Parisi (2009), "Optimal Timing of Legal Intervention: The Role of Timing Rules", *Harvard Law Review Forum*, 122: 18–31.

Majd, Suman, and Robert S. Pindyck (1987), "Time to Build, Option Value and Investment Decisions", *Journal of Financial Economics*, 18: 7–27.

Mueller, Dennis (2003), *Public Choice III*, New York: Cambridge University Press.

Parisi, Francesco, Vincy Fon and Nita Ghei (2004), "The Value of Waiting in Lawmaking", *European Journal of Law and Economics*, 18: 131–48

Parisi, Francesco and Nita Ghei (2005), "Legislate Today or Wait Until Tomorrow? An Investment Approach to Lawmaking", *Journal of Public Finance and Public Choice*, 23: 19–41.

Pindyck, Robert S. (1991), "Irreversibility, Uncertainty and Investment", *Journal of Economic Literature*, 29: 1110–48.

Schwartz, Alan and Robert E. Scott, "The Political Economy of Private Legislatures", *University of Pennsylvania Law Review*, 595–654.

5 Production of legal rules by agencies and bureaucracies

Georg von Wangenheim[*]

1. Introduction

The central question posed in the literature on the production of rules by agencies is how the discretion of law-making agencies can be curbed. The political preferences of bureaucracies are most often taken to be exogenously given. These may be the personal political preferences of the director of a single agency or may reflect the influence of interest groups. The influence of interest groups on rule-making agencies has been studied in a descriptive way by Furlong (1997) and Furlong and Kerwin (2005), but is rarely modeled explicitly in this literature. Based on more or less complete answers to the central question, explanations are given for why a legislator may want to delegate law-making power to bureaucracies and how control of this delegated power is to be organized. The key normative question is how much delegation there ought to be. However, answers given to this question barely rely on the positive analyses mentioned herein.

Current positive law-and-economics analyses of how agencies and bureaucracies (the terms are used as synonyms here) produce legal rules differ substantially from approaches applied to other law-making institutions. These analyses do not follow the Public Choice approach commonly used to explain the production of legal rules by legislators, nor do they follow the evolutionary approaches mostly used to explain production of rules by the court system. Theories dealing with bureaucratic law-making do not therefore derive one utility-maximizing position of bureaucratic decision makers (which are hardly ever modeled as multiple individuals); nor do these theories rely on the assumption that inefficient legal rules are challenged more often than efficient ones (so that, on average, legal rules tend to evolve towards an efficient state). Only where the study of production of rules by the legislator concentrates on the consequences of more than one institution needed to pass a law do strong similarities arise with approaches to bureaucratic rule production. There

[*] I am indebted to two anonymous referees who drew my attention to parts of the literature which had escaped my notice for the first edition of this *Encyclopedia*. All remaining errors are, of course, mine.

are no such similarities between theories of bureaucratic rule making and the evolutionary approach.

Comparing the literature on decision-making by agencies and bureaucracies with research on the production of legal rules by the legislator on the one side, and rule production by the judiciary on the other, not only demonstrates how the approaches to very similar problems differ, but also underlines a problem which seems to be purely semantic: bureaucratic rule-making and bureaucratic adjudication are analytically distinct, as are legislative rule-making and judicial adjudication. If bureaucratic decisions are rule-making, Public Choice theory suggests itself for tackling bureaucratic rule making; if they are adjudication, an evolutionary approach seems to be more appropriate. The problem arises in much of the theoretical literature and holds true for many empirical studies. Single bureaucratic decisions or entire classes of bureaucratic decisions are often analyzed without giving any thought as to whether these decisions are rule making or adjudication.

The reason for the reluctance to distinguish between rule-making and adjudication may be that the distinction is not as clear in American administrative law (see, for example, Rugge, 1987) as it would seem to be from the Administrative Procedures Act (5 USC §551 (4)–(7)). This lack of clarity may be a problem in other jurisdictions as well. As a result, very few authors in the field reviewed here mention the distinction at all (for example, Lupia and McCubbins, 1994b). It is therefore often not possible to restrict this review to the literature on bureaucratic rule-making; research with regard to decisions made in single cases has to be referred to in many places. Likewise, some of the literature reviewed here may overlap with the literature discussed in the articles on regulation of contracts and on environmental regulation. Yet the emphasis of this chapter will be different: it deals with the 'production of legal rules by agencies and bureaucracies', that is with the rule-making activities of agencies and bureaucracies. I will, however, avoid making too many references to scholarly works on bureaucracies in general, if there is no specific relation to rule-making (for an overview of this literature with special reference to Public Choice arguments, see Benson, 1995).

The chapter is organized as follows: Sections 2 and 3, respectively, review the literature that describes how procedural rules, by framing the production of substantive rules by agencies, facilitate the control of agencies by their principal, that is, the legislator, and writings comparing the different ways in which the legislator is able to control a rule-making agency. The following two sections, 4 and 5, concentrate on the literature breaking down the legislator into its different institutions, including the courts in the analysis of constraints on bureaucratic rule production. Section 4 deals with econometric studies, while Section 5 presents the spatial approach to the topic. Section 6 surveys works that ask normatively whether there ought to be delegation of rule production to agencies and bureaucracies at all. Section 7 reviews the few inquiries there have been into the interior process of agencies which produce rules, and Section 8 concludes.

2. Curbing Bureaucratic Discretion by Procedural Rules

Two distinct phenomena bring about bureaucratic discretion: one, the inability of legislative institutions to perfectly control the activities of bureaucracies at reasonable costs; the other, the need for cooperation among more than one legislative institution, to sanction an agency or to replace bureaucratic rules by new statutory rules. Although a clear distinction between these phenomena cannot be maintained in reviewing all publications, the first phenomenon is dealt with in this and the next section; the second, in Sections 4 and 5.

As stressed by McCubbins, Noll and Weingast (1987) ('McNollgast'), the principal–agent relationship between legislators and bureaucracies cannot be dealt with appropriately by mere reference to general principal–agent models of the Laffont-Tirole-Holmström-Milgrom type. The reason is that *ex post* sanctions, which are imposed after the bureaucracy deviates from the political preferences of the politicians, are far too limited, in view of low probabilities of detection, high monitoring costs, and the costs which legislators themselves must bear to impose sanctions (additional workload, political backlash for poorly working agencies, further deterioration of the agency's work). Note however, that Mitnick (1975) emphasizes that one has to be careful about the short- and long-run costs and benefits of control here: strict control by the principal may run up more costs than benefits in the short run, but be profitable in the long run because agents become 'educated' by control, and strict control may result in the self-selection of 'good' agents. In McCubbins, Noll and Weingast (1989), the authors extend the reasons for the inappropriateness of the general principal–agent model to embrace the phenomenon to be discussed extensively in Section 5 of this chapter: the need for coordination among several institutions if control of bureaucratic rule production is to be exercised by the shadow of overriding statutory legislation.

McNollgast argue that the remaining, large problems of compliance may be partly solved by procedural rules. In this respect, procedural rules governing the agency's soliciting of information and the consequences of not doing so properly are most important: they may ensure that agencies base their decisions on large sets of information which would also be sufficient for legislative control. Soliciting information can only be successful if those who are better informed have enough incentives to disclose their information. This is, of course, the case if the stakes of affected groups in an issue are high or the issue is highly controversial. These variables, however, fail to be within the control of the legislator. The legislator is, thus, forced to concentrate on enacting procedural rules that modify the costs and the effectiveness of providing information to the bureaucracy.

McNollgast study such procedural rules. Public disclosure requirements facilitate the political intervention of interest groups at early stages in the rule-making process, even earlier than in the legislative process. Thus, political intervention of interest groups may allow *ex ante* control of bureaucratic rule production. Elaborate rules of procedure result in high costs of rent-seeking and, accordingly, favor those groups that have large resources to spend on representation. On the other hand, budget subsidies for poorly represented groups favor these groups, instead. Next, the discretion of an agency is limited by evidentiary standards, which refer to how evidence must be processed to come to a decision. Burden-of-proof rules may favor or hamper groups which base arguments on unclear cause–effect relationships. Further, '*ex parte*' rules serve to prohibit direct informal communication between private parties and an agency during the formal rule-making process. These rules variously provide for sanctions against prohibited *ex parte* communications, which run the gamut up to, at the extreme, imposing a final decision against the infringing group. *Ex parte* rules enable politicians to participate in the rule-making process, at least as brokers of communication. Also, politicians may exert direct pressure on agencies. For all these procedural rules to enable politicians to exert *ex ante* control, a judicial remedy for their infringement must be sufficiently likely to occur. This can be achieved by decentralized enforcement of these rules if private parties are able to sue at low costs.

McNollgast not only examine ways in which procedural rules and interest groups interact to curb decision-making by bureaucrats and agencies, but also argue that politicians are not constrained to granting a policy which is currently favorable to some interest groups. McNollgast suggest politicians are able to ensure, for the future, that changes of legal (agency-made) rules are favorable to the interest groups that constitute the original coalition. This 'autopilot' for future decisions relieves the enacting coalition of the problem that future political majorities might favor other interest groups. DeShazo and Freeman (2005) extend the argument to competing agencies, which may be used to interfere with an agency's rule-making in a similar way to lobbying interest groups. The problem of the 'slack' of future legislators as opposed to regulatory slack in rule-making is particularly stressed by Horn and Shepsle (1989) and by Steunenberg (1992). They emphasize that there is a trade-off between these two kinds of slack, because constraints on either the agency or future legislators require freedom to act by the other institution. DeShazo and Freeman (2003) draw their readers' attention to a related problem which one might label 'committee slack', that is to the possible deviation of the agency-controlling committees' preferences from the legislator's preferences.

McNollgast allow, against the thrust of their argument, that the control of agencies exercised by the interest groups may evolve in an unexpected direction, or be impeded altogether, if the interest groups that are engaged in the original deal with the legislator cease to exist. Macey (1992) discounts the importance of this caveat for three reasons, all related to the design of a newly formed agency, and thus strengthening the thrust of McNollgast's argument: First, when interest groups agree with the legislator to institute a regulatory agency, the agreement is likely to cover institutional rules about which parties may influence the future agency's decisions and the ways influence can be exerted. For example, the influence of poorly organized groups may be secured by facilitating access for individuals with an interest to agency hearings or judicial review of agency decisions. Levine (1992) criticizes this argument on the basis that, while one may predict that liberalized standing will increase the degree of interference by the courts with regulatory drift, one is unable to predict easily the direction of this interference. This argument apparently neglects the results of evolutionary approaches to the common law (compare the literature following Rubin, 1977 and Priest, 1977), where predictions on the directions of judicial rule-making are certainly possible, even if the court system is not systematically biased in some direction. If the court system is known to be biased, it is obvious that one may predict in what direction judge-made law will evolve.

Second, limiting the jurisdiction of a newly installed agency to the regulation of a small number of industries, or even to parts of a single industry, assures that the agency will recruit its expertise in this specialized field, mainly from the same industry or part of an industry. As a result, opinions held by the agency and industry will usually concur. Accordingly, at least regulation in favor of the regulated industry is stable over time.

Third, when agencies compete for jurisdiction with each other, they seek out the support of constituents and hence will not deviate from the preferences of their constituency. The agency and its constituent interest group(s) thus mutually support each other in order to further their own *raison d'être* and improve their chances of survival over time. This mutual support, together with the procedural rules mentioned above, serves as an 'autopilot' for rule-making by the agency. A similar argument had already been put forward by Benson (1981, 1983a and 1983b), although Benson did not state the argument in terms of curbing regulative drift. Benson focuses on the size of the bureau and the problem of over-regulation. Johnson and Libecap (1994) drive home the argument that the rank-and-file bureaucrats are interested in the duration of their agency to the point that they become an influential interest group, shaping long-run trends in bureaucratic institutions. With particular reference to the third argument (mutual support of regulator and regulated industry), Macey (1992) rejects Shepsle's (1992) view (also expressed by Horn and Shepsle, 1989 and by Steunenberg, 1992) that more emphasis should be placed on the trade-off between regulatory and legislative slack. Macey claims that there is no such trade-off, but interest groups with political clout, which participate in the original, political decision to set up an agency, retain their political power through this mutual support and continue to exert a similar influence on the legislator as well as on the agency.

Although both of the McNollgast papers give case studies as empirical examples of their theory (see Basinger, 2003, for another, historical case study), Robinson (1989) casts severe doubts on the empirical relevance of McNollgast's argument. McNollgast argue that procedural provisions serve mainly as a curb on the discretion of agencies. Robinson points out that while most of the examples cited by McNollgast do not support their theory, the examples introduced by Robinson himself provide even less support. He contends, however, that McNollgast's approach could be very useful. If the empirical relevance of the argument was shown, it could substantially change and advance the understanding of the legal-administrative process.

In a related study, Rose-Ackermann (1995) compares how procedural rules enable interested (third) parties to control and interfere with bureaucratic rule-making in Germany and the US. In contrast to the situation in the US, in Germany individual citizens have little chance to control rule production by bureaucracies; this control only extends to applications of the rules. Rule-making by bureaucracies in Germany is typically under the influence of well-organized interest groups, in the same informal way as is statutory legislation in both countries. Only in the US do procedural rules give the power to control bureaucratic rule-making to interested parties which are not otherwise politically powerful in the legislative process.

Hamilton and Schroeder (1994) call into question this entire line of reasoning. They ask why agencies would follow procedural rules more strictly than substantive rules. Though they do not enter into a theoretical discussion of this point of view, they provide some empirical evidence that procedural rules are, in fact, circumvented. Agencies leave substantive rules incomplete and fill the gaps with extensive directives, guidance documents and policy memoranda, which fail to be rules in a formal sense and are not subject to formal rule-making procedures that require the participation of interest groups, in particular of those groups that are protected by procedural rules.

DeMesquita and Stephenson (2007) point out the risk that bureaucratic discretion may be over-controlled if oversight is restricted to observable activity by the bureaucracy, but the quality of bureaucratic actions also depends on unobservable activity. In the same vein as the multi-tasking problem modeled by Holmström and Milgrom (1991), they assume a partly benevolent regulator who inefficiently replaces observable with unobservable activity if controlled too tightly.

Jason MacDonald (2010) varies the approach by investigating the effect on agencies' behavior of limitation riders, which allow the legislator to forbid agencies to spend money on specific uses for a certain length of time.

3. Police-Patrol Control versus Fire-Alarm Control

An issue closely related to the question of how procedural rules give control over bureaucratic rule-making to third parties is the question of how legislators can best control agencies. The problem posed is whether legislators take a random sample of bureaucratic activity (including its rule-making activity) in the same manner in which a police patrol randomly inspects the streets; or whether legislators look at bureaucratic decisions only if and when someone protests vehemently against a particular decision in the same way in which the fire department takes action only after someone sounds a fire alarm. I refer to this question as the optimal-type-of-control problem.

The leading articles that discuss the optimal-type-of-control problem (for an overview of the consequential literature until 1990, see Ogul and Rockmann, 1990) are McCubbins and Schwartz (1984) and Weingast (1984). These articles argue that, in general, Congress prefers fire-alarm to police-patrol oversight, because the costs of the monitoring activities are partly transferred from Congress itself to interested groups and individuals. However, citizens harmed by violations of legislative goals are not always represented by well-organized groups and, accordingly, are unable to sound alarms loud enough to obtain redress of grievances. The authors answer this criticism by referring to arguments like those in the previous section: disadvantaged groups often have public spokesmen; problems of collective action are overcome by legislation which favors the organization of interest groups, particularly those affected by collective action problems; extensive constituent service by congress(wo)men opens up review procedures.

In the optimal-type-of-control literature, there is no discussion of the social costs of fire-alarm oversight, but one might speculate that it is socially cheaper. With fire-alarm oversight, individuals, who are affected by bureaucratic rule-making and will notice it anyway, detect regulatory slack; with police-patrol oversight, legislators must fund specialized individuals to scrutinize bureaucratic decisions for which they have little inherent regard. The argument might, however, be weakened if one takes into account a problem like dispersed damages in tort law: the adverse effects of regulatory slack may be so dispersed that sounding a fire alarm is too costly for anyone other than specialists hired to search for regulatory slack. This assumption, once again to some extent, harks back to the argument in the previous section.

It is, however, unclear whether asymmetric degrees of organization among opposing interest groups can be completely offset by procedural rules. Hopenhayn and Lohmann (1996) study the results of asymmetric access to review procedures for a particular kind of fire-alarm oversight, where an agency's decision can be (partly) controlled before there are adverse effects on social welfare. A fire alarm can be sounded either (i) only if the agency has allowed some regulated activity, even though the activity decreases social welfare or (ii) in addition to this condition, also if the agency prohibits a regulated activity, even though the activity would increase social welfare. If political institutions rely on this kind of fire-alarm oversight, fewer activities will be allowed in case (i) than in case (ii). Hence, there may be adverse social welfare effects due to reliance on fire-alarm oversight, as opposed to some symmetric oversight system, possibly a police-patrol system.

Aberbach (1990) questions the theoretical findings of McCubbins and Schwartz (1984) and Weingast (1984) on factual grounds. They argue that Congress prefers fire-alarm to police-patrol oversight; he offers empirical evidence that Congress has increasingly used police-patrol oversight instead of only fire-alarm oversight. Ogul and Rockmann (1990) explain this finding by pointing to the greater resources employed by Congress (in particular more staff) to scrutinize agencies, where fewer resources are allocated to new legislative activity because congress(wo)men have, in general, fewer opportunities to obtain name recognition through new legislation.

Lupia and McCubbins (1994a and 1994b) develop formal models of both police-patrol and fire-alarm oversight. They explore under what conditions each kind of control is superior to no oversight from the viewpoint of Congress-as-principal. The hardly surprising conditions they derive for police-patrol oversight being superior to no oversight are: large differences between an agency's and legislators' preferences; and low costs of oversight. Fire-alarm oversight is superior to no oversight when high penalties are imposed for false fire alarms, or where the preferences of legislators and of interested groups or individuals that may raise the fire alarm are close to each other. Figueiredo et al. (1999) develop a variation of the model in which they allow both for fire-alarm monitors with or without own interests and for monitors with information which is better than the principal's, but still incomplete.

Due to the disparate structure of their two models, Lupia and McCubbins fail to compare the two kinds of oversight with one another. After making exactly this point (Bawn, 1994), Bawn (1997) constructs another formal model to carry out this comparison. This model again mainly restates the arguments of McCubbins and Schwartz (1984) in a formal way. By emphasizing that marginal costs of oversight are lower for members of the committee with jurisdiction over the agency than for other members of the chamber, she adds, however, the insight that the latter will prefer more fire-alarm-like or (as Bawn calls it in a slightly broader sense) statutory control. Bawn provides some empirical evidence for her hypothesis by comparing the likelihood that floor amendments to EPA rules increase statutory control for sponsors that are members of the committee with jurisdiction and non-members. Balla (2000) casts doubts on these results by controlling for the distance between the sponsor's and the median committee member's preferences. In all his regressions, the latter difference in preferences has a statistically significant effect on the likelihood of (co-)sponsorship, while committee membership does not.

Both Lindsay (1976) and Holmström and Milgrom (1991) express fundamental doubts as to whether an optimal degree of control over agencies can be defined merely by taking into account the direct costs of control. They stress that agents that have multiple tasks, which the principal can monitor to different degrees, tend to carry out only tasks for which they will get credit, namely those tasks which the principal can monitor. Such agents neglect the tasks which the principal cannot monitor. By distorting the allocation of the agent's efforts, additional oversight may thus lead to indirect costs. As there is no common denominator in which to measure the net benefits reaped in the public sector, such as profits, the problem they discuss is particularly relevant to government bureaucracies.

4. Who Controls Bureaucratic Discretion: Econometric Approaches

While the literature discussed so far concentrates on how to overcome bureaucratic discretion by assuming a dichotomy between agencies and the legislature (as a unitary actor), many authors also ask who exactly controls the bureaucracy: whether it is a particular institution among several engaged in the legislative process or none of these, but an independent judiciary. Two strands of literature, only loosely intertwined, must be distinguished: econometric studies (discussed in this section) and theoretical arguments, based on sequential games, which describe strategic choices made between policies, represented by different points in a given policy space (discussed in Section 5.)

Among the econometric approaches surveyed here, some authors ask which of several possible institutions controls an agency. Other authors test whether a particular institution controls an agency's decisions or not. A typical and prominent example of the first type of approach is Moe (1985) (also compare Moe, 1987). He takes the National Labor Relations Board (NLRB) as an example of an agency which could be influenced by the political preferences of the President, of Congress, or of the courts. His analysis clearly shows that all these institutions are important (changes in political orientation have a significant impact on the decisions of the NLRB), but the President has the strongest impact on the NLRB. The NLRB is not a prominent example of rule production by agencies, because its decisions are nearly all adjudicatory. Notwithstanding this limitation, Moe's paper may well be labeled as path-breaking: it lays the ground for later econometric studies to inquire which institutions wield the most power over agencies that make rules.

Beck (1987) employs a model that is less ambitious in comparing the power wielded over agencies by different institutions, but more directly focused on rule production. He studies to what extent the US President is able to influence rule-making within the Federal Reserve. In particular, he tests whether the monetary policy of the Federal Reserve supports a political business cycle favorable to incumbent Presidents. His findings are that the Fed does not actively support such cycles by inducing political monetary cycles, but that it passively accepts such cycles induced by fiscal policy. Accordingly, Beck asserts that the President of the US exerts a certain, but limited degree of power to control the Fed.

Probably the most extensive and detailed econometric study of bureaucratic rule production has been conducted by Magat, Krupnick and Harrington (1986, p.8). Their book aims at clarifying which factors influence bureaucratic decisions with regard to rule-making. They test fourteen hypotheses derived from different theoretical approaches to bureaucratic rule-making. Unfortunately, few of the results of the study are statistically significant, but most parameters do have the sign to be expected from the theoretical argument. The same caveat holds for the work of Hamilton and Schroeder (1994), who study how much an agency will resort to 'informal' rule-making (in the form of directives, guidance documents and policy memoranda issued by an agency) in order to avoid the control of formalized rule-making procedures.

Drawing on studies of the Food and Drug Administration (FDA), Olson (1995 and 1996) does not so much consider which political institutions exert power in controlling agencies; rather she contrasts different approaches to predicting bureaucratic behavior. In particular, she compares capture theory (agencies are controlled by the industries they are supposed to regulate), public interest theory (agencies are the benevolent pursuers of social welfare), and Congressional control theory (legislative institutions, modeled by Olson as a unitary actor, control agencies). She finds that the behavior of one and the same agency is best explained by different theories or even by different combinations of theories for different industries which are regulated. Accordingly, she suggests that unless subsequent empirical studies focus on the micro-level trade-offs which face regulators, it is impossible to get a clear answer as to what are the important incentives in bureaucratic rule production. In order to formulate better explanations or even predictions of bureaucratic behavior, future research must be more sensitive to different regulatory actions and their specific constraints and trade-offs for the regulator.

Hammond and Knott (1996) reject completely econometric analyses of which institutions control the bureaucracy, based on the correlation between, on the one hand, changes in preferences of an institution, and, on the other hand, changes in policy of the agency. As they point out, it is impossible for one institution to control an agency without the cooperation of the other institutions. Thus, future empirical work on political control should incorporate the interplay of the preferences of the controlling institutions. These authors do not develop, however, an operational measure of the power wielded by institutions over agencies, although they consider such a measure to be indispensable in conducting empirical studies. Comparing the policy orientation of agencies' monitors to the orientation and the likelihood of re-election of the government-controlling party installing the monitor, Holburn and Vanden Bergh (2006) find empirical support for the hypothesis that procedural rules aim to control agencies in the medium run.

Furlong (1997) and McKay and Yackee (2007) offer empirical studies concentrating on the effectiveness of rent-seekers' efforts to influence administrative rule-making. McKay and Yackee (2007) also find that the activity of one lobbying group fails to provoke counter-activity by opposing interest groups in a statistically significant way.

5. Who Controls Bureaucratic Discretion: Spatial Approaches

The literature reviewed in Sections 2 and 3 explained the discretion exercised by bureaucrats by highlighting the superior information which agencies possess and explored the ways in which control of the bureaucracy is achieved. The literature discussed in this section takes a game-theoretic approach. This approach is based on preferences in a given policy space to show that bureaucratic discretion exists even without asymmetric information. The basic idea developed in this body of literature is that an agency can be sanctioned, for example, by new legislation that overrules the decisions of an agency or interferes with the resources of the agency, only if more than one of the institutions agree to apply sanctions. If n institutions are needed to sanction an agency and every institution has single-peaked preferences in the policy space, Pareto sets of dimension $n - 1$ or less result. Within these Pareto sets, the agency is free to act because every change in policy makes at least one institution better off; accordingly, this 'winning' institution will be reluctant to sanction the agency. As legislative procedures become more complex than simple acceptance by all relevant institutions, the models are formed as sequential games. In these games, institutions can veto, accept or amend proposals from institutions with the right to take the initiative, according to (a simplified version of) the constitution.

The starting point for this discussion is a paper by Weingast (1981), in which he develops a spatial policy model (of one and two policy dimensions) that explains the bounds of agencies' decisions on regulation. Based on three examples (airlines, telecommunications, and nuclear power), he studies the interplay between possibly more than one Congressional (sub)committee; interest groups which form the clientele of both the (sub)committee(s) and the agency controlled by the (sub)committee(s); and sometimes (namely if he makes appointments to the agency himself) the President. Weingast shows how this interplay restricts the range of discretion of the agency. Using the same approach, Weingast and Moran (1983) explain why there is scant evidence of Congressional oversight. They put forward this approach as an alternative to the dominant view in the literature at the time that this lack of evidence is due to major imperfections in the oversight exercised by Congress, due to Congress's lack of information. This approach argues, alternatively, that Congressional oversight is near perfect; accordingly, agencies do not even attempt to deviate from the preferences of the legislature. Weingast and Moran demonstrate that their theory explains better than an imperfect-oversight theory why Congress was extraordinarily active in its oversight of the Federal Trade Commission (FTC) in 1979–80, after a turnover in the members of the appropriate Senate subcommittee. The FTC temporarily lacked sufficient information on new constraints imposed on its discretion by new Senate subcommittee members, and the FTC deviated involuntarily from the preferences of the subcommittee. Finally, Weingast and Moran test their theory econometrically. Their econometric analysis is challenged by Muris (1986) and successfully defended by Weingast and Moran (1986). Econometric support for their theory is also offered in a paper by Faith et al. (1982). They reject the claim of Katzman (1980) (who relies exclusively on a non-statistical analysis of interviews conducted with members of the FTC) that the decisions of the FTC are independent of Congressional influence and of efforts to maximize the budget of the Commission. Instead, they offer compelling econometric evidence that both the House and the Senate have a substantial impact on the selection of cases by the FTC, though the impact of the Senate seems to vanish after sweeping reforms of the FTC were carried out in 1970.

In ensuing years, the approach of Weingast has been criticized, mainly for its simplifying assumptions on Congressional legislative procedures (see, for example, Moe, 1987). Complicating assumptions, however, were only introduced into the model in the early 1990s. Two papers, by Ferejohn and Shipan (1990) and Gely and Spiller (1990), written independently of each other, incorporate into the model: judicial review of administrative decisions, as well as Presidential veto of Congressional override of both decisions of agencies and judicial review of decisions of agencies. The preferences of agencies are assumed to be identical to those of the President (this flaw is overcome by Steunenberg, 1992). Ferejohn and Shipan allow for an override of a Presidential veto by a two-thirds majority in Congress, which is modeled as a unicameral legislative body. In a different vein, Gely and Spiller abstract from the opportunity to override a Presidential veto but treat the House and the Senate as two different (unitary) agents and extend the model to a two-dimensional policy space. A final important difference between the two models is that judicial control is restricted to replacing the agency's issuance of new rules by the *status quo ante* in the paper of Ferejohn and Shipan. In a variation on the model of Gely and Spiller, the courts act as a kind of super-agency able to replace the agency's choice of a new rule with whatever policy the courts prefer most (subject to the threat of new legislation).

Ferejohn and Shipan deduce that the next (namely judicial) step in the control of policy-making by agencies restricts the power of agencies, and makes agencies more responsive to the preferences of the current (not the originally enacting) legislature. In a comment on this article, Spitzer (1990) studies some cases in which agencies have preferences which differ from those of the President. In another comment, Rose-Ackermann (1990) expresses the criticism that it is unclear why Congress should allow its own committee to deviate as much from Congress's own preferences as is assumed in the Ferejohn and Shipan paper and, more closely related to the general approach adopted by Ferejohn and Shipan, that it might substantially increase the agency's and the court's discretion and influence to abandon the assumption of costless Congressional action.

The paper by Gely and Spiller yields the same result with respect to judicial control over an agency: the reduction in the discretion of an agency is substantially greater if courts are able to impose the policy they most prefer. Allowing the President to have preferences different from those of an agency forces Gely and Spiller to introduce a second dimension in the policy space. Only then can they demonstrate how an increase in the number of institutions that must cooperate to enact a statute increases the dimension of the Pareto set which defines the discretion of an agency. They apply their model to two cases decided by the Supreme Court. The examples show how the ruling of an agency changes after and due to a change in the preferences of the legislature. Tiller and Spiller (1999) introduce differential costs and benefits of alternative administrative instruments both for the agency making the decision and for the court, or other institution, reviewing it. As a consequence, they can show not only that the choice of the policy is a strategic decision, but also the selection of the instrument to implement it.

Formalizing the presentation of the spatial approach, thus far most often based on a graphical exposition, Hammond and Knott (1996) show that any number of dimensions of the policy space and a complete model of US institutions are tractable with this approach. They set forth a formal model. They include all five institutions most relevant to American legislation: the House, the Senate, the relevant committees of both (some multi-person institutions are even divided into their members) and the President. They include two alternative procedures of legislation: a majority of House and Senate and approval by the President, as well as a two thirds majority of the House and Senate. The judiciary is added in an informal way, which may be more appropriate than the alternative approaches chosen by Ferejohn and Shipan (1990) and Gely and Spiller (1990). The power of the judiciary is reduced to stretch the set of legal policies constraining the agency in the direction preferred by the judiciary. And Hammond and Knott include in their model the President's ability or inability to fire an agency director. Complicating the assumptions in the analysis does not provide new insights into how, in theory, bureaucratic discretion changes when additional institutions are included in the model. But they offer the insight that the results of less comprehensive models are not due to their simplifying assumptions. Hammond and Knott, however, stress the conclusion that it is impossible to give a clear answer to the question of who really controls an agency; control is exerted by the interplay of institutions. Thus, they reject empirical studies on the power of controlling institutions if such studies are based on correlations between changes in the preferences of the allegedly controlling institutions and agency policy.

A general problem in the literature is, of course, that the information requirements about the preferences of other agents are as strong as they are for most models of sequential games. One should not overemphasize this problem, though, because spatial approaches to bureaucratic discretion have to be seen as a complement to the literature that bases the explanation of bureaucratic discretion on incomplete information.

While earlier articles which take spatial approaches (this section) or optimal-type-of-control approaches (Section 3) to bureaucratic discretion merely refer to the other approach, only Epstein and O'Halloran (1995, 1999) integrate both spatial and optimal-type-of-control approaches in one formal model. These authors assume that only interest groups and the agency are completely informed about the state of the world and hence know what policy they prefer most. The legislator (modeled as a unitary actor and thus re-simplified as compared to the newer spatial literature) only knows its most preferred policy as a function of the true state of the world. When an agency proposes a policy change to the legislator, the legislator may accept or reject the proposal, but not amend it. From the legislator's perfect knowledge of the preferences of the other actors, the rule proposed by the agency, and the reaction of the interest groups (which sound a fire alarm or not), the legislator is able to deduce a piece of information about the true state of the world and react accordingly. The most important result derived from this model is that the legislator can deduce the most information from the reaction of an interest group if the legislators' most preferred policy lies between those of the agency and the interest group. Less information can be deduced if the interest groups' most preferred policy is at the center. No information can be deduced if the agency's most preferred policy is at the center. The reaction of more interest groups increases the information deduced by the legislator only if the interests of the additional groups differ more than, and in the same direction as, the preferences of the legislators differ from the most preferred policy of the agency.

The model of Epstein and O'Halloran (1995, 1999) is seminal in spawning a large lineage of follow-up publications. Sloof (2000) extends the influence of the interest group to sending a signal not only to the agency after delegation, but also to the legislator before the decision to delegate. Eric Posner (2001) combines the asymmetric-information spatial model with the procedural rule (see Section 2) of requiring a cost-benefit analysis. He shows that this may reduce the principal's lack of information if the signal emanating from the agency's cost-benefit analysis is precise, that is, if it is more costly, the more the signal favors inefficient action. Huber and Shipan (2002) vary the model to allow for the costs of restricting the agency's discretionary range. Bendor and Meirowitz (2004) generalize the assumptions to show that many results do not depend on the relatively restrictive framework in Epstein and O'Halloran (1995, 1999) and Huber and Shipan (2002). Holburn and Vanden Bergh (2004) discuss in a formal model and an empirical analysis whether and under which conditions interest groups would aim to influence the agency rather than the legislator or the executive.

Bennedsen and Feldman (2006) introduce interest groups' efforts to influence the agency's rule-making. Assuming a single and unitary interest group, they show that due to lobbying at the bureaucratic level, legislators' willingness to delegate increases if the interest group's preferences are close enough to the legislator's and declines otherwise. As a consequence, the interest group's influence grows with the legislator's uncertainty about the state of the world if the interest group's preferences are close enough to the legislator's. Grajzl (2011) develops a similar model from a property rights perspective in which either the legislator (in case of non-delegation) or the bureaucracy (in case of delegation) reaps benefits from a single interest group willing to transfer resources to the competent rule-making authority. Eom and Sweeny (2009) allow for competing interest groups in a similar model. They model how groups with conflicting interests make proposals for regulations. They find that these proposals become less polarized and eventually converge, if either of the interest groups becomes more effective at influencing the rule-making agency, because more effectiveness implies larger lobbying costs for both groups. They apply their model to incentive-rate proposals made by stakeholders of California energy efficiency programs.

Somewhat deviating from the standard spatial approach, Lehmann (2002) develops a model in which an agency's monitor may not neglect to act against an agency running astray (type I errors), but may also commit errors of type II, that is raise the alarm although the agency is perfectly on track. They provide conditions under which a court filtering the monitor's alarm should employ extremely high or extremely low evidentiary standards, to completely avoid either type I or type II errors.

6. Ought there to be Delegation of Rule-Making Power to Agencies and Bureaucracies?

While the literature discussed thus far looks at the positive questions of how bureaucratic discretion in rule production can best be controlled by the legislature (Sections 2 and 3) and which particular institution controls agencies (Sections 4 and 5), other authors ask more fundamentally whether there ought to be delegation of rule-making to the bureaucracy from the point of view of the legislature or society. Since answers to the positive questions mentioned above are mostly based on fire-alarm control by the same interest groups which influence the legislation, most authors neglect the problems discussed by the capture theory of regulation. They do not even perceive them as problems, if capture works in favor of the same groups in both legislation and bureaucratic rule-making. This is not the case for the normative question discussed in this section.

Imperfect control of agencies can only be used as an argument against having delegation of rule-making authority from the legislator to the bureaucracy for three reasons: (1) a bureaucrat (agency director) has political preferences that differ from those of the legislator; (2) a bureaucrat (agency director) exploits his superior knowledge for his own non-political advantage, as described by Niskanen (1971 and 1975) (also compare Migué and Belanger, 1974); (3) an agency gets captured by the regulated industry more often than the legislator. The first reason vanishes if the legislator can choose the bureaucrat. The second reason either coincides with the third or does not systematically interfere with the content of rules produced by agencies, except for the case where some rules allow collusion of an agency with the regulated industry or firm and consequential rent-sharing, while other rules do not allow this. An example of such a case is discussed by Laffont and Tirole (1990). They conclude that for the case of price regulation, it might be reasonable not to delegate to the agency the decision between (average) cost-plus pricing and marginal-cost pricing with a transfer to the firm(s) covering the fixed costs.

The third reason is discussed more extensively. Contradicting Page (1981), Wiley (1986) argues (and the argument is reinforced in Wiley, 1988) that there is no general evidence that regulated entities have a disproportionate influence upon regulatory agencies. Accordingly, the decision to delegate regulatory rule-making to an agency ought to be based mainly on the agency's advantages and disadvantages in dealing with specific rule production as compared to the legislator himself. This argument is refuted by Spitzer (1988), who claims with reference to Fiorina (1977, pp. 15–29) that rule making by agencies is more prone to capture by interest groups than rule-making by the legislator because the latter uses the agency to shirk responsibility for the costs imposed by regulation, while claiming credit for the benefits at the same time (also compare Vaubel, 1991, who applies the same argument to the European legislative institutions;

and Moe, 1989). Wiley (1988) points to the many other reasons for a legislator to delegate specific rule-making to a bureaucracy in order to reduce the importance of the argument of Spitzer (1988). Referring to better responsiveness of the law to specific local conditions, Mashaw (1985) supports this pro-delegation position. Bawn (1995) compares the costs and benefits faced by the legislator from delegation of rule-making in a formal model. She shows that the legislator will balance marginal costs incurred as a result of a loss of control through the delegation with marginal benefits reaped as a result of the better fit between agency decisions and specific cases. Her model uses quite specific functional forms, but can be generalized easily. Cooter (2000, chapter 4) provides simple formal models on the topic in his textbook on the economics of constitutions and constitutional law.

Spulber and Besanko (1992) argue that a problem similar to capture may arise from the way the regulator and the regulated firm or industry interact. If the former is able to commit to some environmental quality standard, that is, if the regulator is a Stackelberg leader, then it is sufficient to choose an agency director with political preferences similar to those of the legislator. However, if the regulator is unable to commit to a specific environmental quality standard, but is likely to adapt the standard to the firm's or industry's activities (levels of output and levels of pollution), that is, if the relationship between regulator and regulated industry or firm is Nash, then an optimizing legislator will choose an agency director with preferences deviating from its own and will enact statutory limits to bureaucratic standard setting. The answer which Spulber and Besanko give to the question as to whether or not statutory limits ought to be imposed on regulatory discretion depends upon whether the relationship between the regulator and the regulated firm or industry is Stackelberg or Nash. In addition, their answer to the question *in what direction* these limits should be erected also depends on the circumstances of the specific case. As stressed by Arvan (1992), the ambiguities can only be cleared up by empirical studies. The results of Spulber and Besanko (1992) are ambiguous even though they abstract from important aspects influencing the degree of *ex ante* statutory constraints on regulatory agencies, such as judicial review, problems of incomplete information on the technology (legislators have to know the technology up to one parameter which does not influence complementarity or substitutiveness of pollution abatement and production costs), and incomplete knowledge of the preferences of other political actors (Ross, 1992).

If non-delegation is assumed to be the only alternative, the question whether there ought to be a delegation of rule-making power to agencies and bureaucracies is only incompletely answered. In his structural approach to law, Cooter (1996a, also 1994a and 1996b) argues that, among rule-making bodies, agencies should make as few rules as possible because they do not follow social norms to the extent that courts do or at least ought to do. Following social norms which evolve from efficient incentive structures (that is, social settings in which spillovers to groups not engaged in the social formation of the norms do not exist nor do evolutionary traps resulting from non-convexities exist) is better than rules issued by law-makers such as legislators or regulatory agencies and bureaucracies (that is, constructivist law-makers in a Hayekian sense).

Kaplow (1992), too, deals with the role of the courts in the question of whether to delegate rule-making authority to agencies. Yet he does not see rule production by the courts as an alternative to rule production by agencies. Rather, he emphasizes that non-delegation is only possible if the legislator includes overly general clauses in statutes. Thus, courts are forced to deduce concrete standards from the general clauses and do so necessarily after the regulated firm or industry has acted, whereas rules set by agencies are promulgated before a regulated firm or industry acts. Regulation by *ex post* standards is inferior to (bureaucratic) regulation by rules if and only if the costs measured per case of formulating *ex ante* rules, which are readily applicable, outweigh the costs which result from less precise standards. Thus, if and only if the law under review is relevant to frequent behavior of a clearly distinguishable type, bureaucratic regulation through rules will be superior to regulation by standards which courts interpret from statutes.

With the same problem in mind, Fiorina (1982 and 1986) tries to develop a model that shows how legislative decisions to delegate rule interpretation (and thereby the making of new, less abstract rules) to the courts or to an agency depend on the substantive preferences of the legislators. Unfortunately, all his results depend on incorrect graphical representations of the expected utilities of legislators and, in the 1982 article, also on the assumption of bell-shaped utility functions of legislators (compare also Nichols, 1982). Accordingly, the results are not reported here.

Finally, Rubin and Cohen (1985) mention a third alternative to delegation of rule-making to agencies. Law (in particular, regulatory statutes) should be made more concrete and enforced by private firms and not by state agencies for several reasons: the legislator (the state) must merely formulate policies on a general, aggregate level and does not have to deal with specific technologies. These technologies can be decided upon by the private law enforcer who signs a contract to pay some (positive or negative) per-unit tax on the aggregate level of pollution or safety or other regulatory targets. Then, he may require firms to abide by a standard or to pay a fee sufficient to cover the tax. Hence, which technology is used becomes a decision subject to market forces. The private enforcer has stronger (monetary) incentives than an agency. The rules governing the relationship between the firms and the enforcer become more efficient, because evolutionary theory of efficient common law is applicable, since both sides have long-lasting economic stakes in these rules. Rubin and Cohen's basic idea is to make existing substantive regulation a property right (entitlement) of the private enforcement agency, and the absence of some regulation a property right of the regulated industry. The property right becomes valuable for the enforcer, since he is paid some money for avoiding (statistical) damages (for example, saved statistical lives) and the enforcer is made liable for (statistical) damages. Property rights thus clearly defined will be reallocated in a Pareto-optimal way by Coasean bargaining.

7. The Rule-Production Process Itself

Little has been written in the law-and-economics literature on how rules are actually produced by agencies and bureaucracies, although taking this approach might substantially clarify the relevance of different arguments with respect to control of bureaucratic rule production by the legislator and its branches. One of the few examples of this approach is the paper by McCubbins and Page (1986). They conclude that decentralized incentives within agencies are too flexible for congress(wo)men who want close control over an agency and, perhaps more importantly, that incentives in an agency are such that agencies do not strive for positive overall results, but for countable 'beans' (for example, a ban on dioxin instead of the improvement of public health). If research were to take these insights into account, the models constructed to predict the degree and relevance of bureaucratic discretion would gain in explanatory power.

In developing concise models of bureaucratic rule production, law-and-economics scholars might have to take a close look at general descriptions of the rule-making process, such as the book by Kerwin (1992) and case studies such as those of Fox (1987) and McGarity (1991). And more descriptive studies of this kind might be needed. Kerwin thoroughly describes the legal background and actual process of rule-making at the federal level in the US. Though he does not have a consistent theoretical approach, let alone rely on economic theory, his study is very helpful as a starter and as background knowledge for any scholar not wholly familiar with US institutions. On the basis of three cases, Fox describes how decision-making in the FTC changes with the chairman of the Commission. McGarity studies the effects of having different types of employees working for regulatory agencies. He contrasts the 'techno-bureaucratic rationality' for rule-making of one group of employees with the 'comprehensive analytical rationality' of another. The former group, professionals who typically have technical or legal training, draft rules without paying much attention to economic trade-offs. The latter group, young economists trained in an anti-regulative atmosphere, entered agencies during the 1970s. McGarity uses the term 'comprehensive' to stress that the ideal pursued by this second group is an open-ended decision-making process based on the quantitative comparison of all possible routes to a goal, which in turn may be defined as quantitative cost-benefit analysis. Based on a large number of case studies, he discusses different institutional settings within bureaucracies which may promote or hinder the relevance of cost-benefit analysis to bureaucratic rule-making. Yet McGarity notes that at first, many of the analysts with thorough microeconomic training went too far in replacing the pro-regulation biases of techno-bureaucrats with anti-regulation biases. In his opinion, the different but equally strong biases of the young economists neither furthered their goals nor overcame traditional and still-dominant engineering-and-legal orientations to bureaucratic rule-making. Were case studies such as those of Fox and McGarity to be turned into models of bureaucratic behavior (adding the preference dimension to the constraints thus far discussed in the literature), much would be gained in understanding, predicting, and evaluating rule production by agencies.

An early theoretical approach, which unfortunately did not find many followers, is the study conducted by Breton and Winetrobe (1982). They argue that the lack of economic discussion of what happens inside bureaucracies (both public and private!) is due to a seeming absence of property rights and competition in bureaucratic interactions. Introducing a theory of trust as an instrument which backs inter-temporal contracts, they succeed in establishing an analogy with a pure barter economy. Concentrating on Schumpeterian competition instead of neoclassical price competition, they even construct market-like 'networks' within bureaucracies. By combining trust and Schumpeterian competition, they can explain not only many of the alleged inefficiencies in bureaucracies, but also the existence of particularly efficient bureaucratic organizations which replace market exchanges to a greater degree than transaction cost arguments are able to justify. Unfortunately, it seems that it would be difficult to apply this innovative theory to rule production by public bureaucracies. Johnson and Libecap (1994) make further progress (based on more standard, neoclassical assumptions) toward understanding what happens inside bureaucracies but, like Breton and Winetrobe, they do not concentrate on rule-making.

Notwithstanding these problems with positive approaches, some articles and books deal with normative questions of how rules ought to be made by agencies and on what arguments decisions of agencies should be based. For example, Breyer (1985) emphasizes that, of course, it would be most appropriate to base regulation entirely on simple economic models, but that this is often impossible because the resulting policies would lack practicability. Still, economic models ought to be used to organize regulators' analyses and focus their attention on the relevant questions (McGarity, 1991 is clearly supportive of this point).

Ribstein and Kobayashi (1996a and 1996b) discuss a different kind of rule production by agencies. These authors look at agencies which only draft rules which a legislator may subsequently enact or amend. In particular, they discuss the effects and the efficiency of the National Conference of Commissioners on Uniform State Laws (NCCUSL), which provides fully formulated drafts of statutes to state legislatures. They claim that this procedure may have advantages over enacting federal laws, but that it is clearly worse than free competition among diverse state laws, which would result in an evolution towards the most efficient laws (for example, other jurisdictions copy provisions out of the corporations code of Delaware because many firms choose to incorporate in that jurisdiction). These authors allow that model codes facilitate competition between jurisdictions and overall law-making by exploiting economies of scale. Yet they point out that private institutions such as the American Bar Association draft model laws more dispassionately. It is claimed that agencies like the NCCUSL are too easily influenced by interest groups. The reviewer comments that the reference which these authors make to capture theory is relevant only if the agencies have a monopoly of the supply of model laws, for if they do not, private institutions are free to provide *additional* competing drafts.

Closely related to the inquiry into how rules are actually produced by agencies and bureaucracies is the question of how long the process of such rule-making takes. Over the 1990s and 2000s, discussions about the duration of administrative procedure emerged in several countries, independently of whether the procedure is mainly legislative or mainly adjudicatory in the respective countries (see Balla and Wright, 2003, for the US and von Wangenheim, 2005, for Germany). For rule-making by agencies, more empirical insights on the actual duration exist (Balla and Wright, 2003; Kerwin, 1992; Kerwin and Furlong 1992) than for adjudication by agencies (Ziekow et al., 2005), and economic theory is scarce (see Hafner, 1999 and 2000, and von Wangenheim, 2005, with respect to adjudication).

8. Conclusion

Both the positive and the normative literature on the rule production by agencies and bureaucracies are still incomplete, and further work is necessary and seems to be promising. Substantial progress has been made in the positive literature concerning the constraints of regulatory rule production. Yet it is still particularly difficult to derive a complete microeconomic model which describes or predicts the rule-producing behavior of agencies because the political preferences of agencies and bureaucracies have hardly been discussed outside capture theory. Capture theory suffers from weak econometric support and, if taken seriously, would make obsolete many of the problems posed in the literature based on positive political theory. Bureaucratic preferences obviously are not determined by a single individual but are the result of a decision-making process *within* a bureaucracy. Models of this process would substantially facilitate understanding and prediction of the rule-making behavior of agencies.

On the normative side, due to the lack of complete positive theories on bureaucratic decision-making constrained by legislative and judicial oversight, arguments often do not seem to be too strong because normative conclusions cannot be based on a clear relationship between institutional settings and their welfare effects. Hence, much of this literature must be based on ideological premises concerning the behavior of agencies and bureaucracies.

Bibliography

Aberbach, Joel (1990), *Keeping a Watchful Eye*, Washington: Brookings Institution.

Arvan, Lanny (1992), 'Delegation, Commitment, and the Regulatory Mandate: Comments', **8** *Journal of Law, Economics, and Organization*, 159–64.

Bagnoli, Mark and McKee, Michael (1991), 'Controlling the Game: Political Sponsors and Bureaus', **7** *Journal of Law, Economics, and Organization*, 229–47.

Bainbridge, Stephen M. (1991), 'The Short Life and Resurrection of SEC Rule 19c–4', **69** *Washington University Law Quarterly*, 565–634.

Bainbridge, Stephen M. (1995), 'Incorporating State Law Fiduciary Duties into the Federal Insider Trading Prohibition', **52** *Washington and Lee Law Review*, 1189–298.

Balla, Steven J. (2000), 'Legislative Organization and Congressional Review of Agency Regulations,' **16** *Journal of Law, Economics, and Organization*, 424–48.

Balla, Steven J. and Wright, John R. (2003), 'Consensual Rule Making and the Time it Takes to Develop Rules', in Krause, George A. and Meier, Kenneth J. (eds), *Politics, Policy, and Organizations – Frontiers in the Scientific Study of Bureaucracy*, Ann Arbor: University of Michigan Press.

Basinger, Scott J. (2003), 'Regulating Slavery: Deckstacking and Credible Commitment in the Fugitive Slave Act of 1850', **19** *Journal of Law, Economics, and Organization*, 307–42.

Bauer, Michael W. (2002), 'Limitations to Agency Control in European Union Policy-Making: The Commission and the Poverty Programmes', **40** *Journal of Common Market Studies*, 381–400.

Bawn, Kathleen (1994), 'Bureaucratic Accountability for Regulatory Decisions: Comment on Lupia and McCubbins', **57** *Law and Contemporary Problems*, 139–42.

Bawn, Kathleen (1995), 'Political Control versus Expertise: Congressional Choices about Administrative Procedures', **89** *American Political Science Review*, 62–73.

Bawn, Kathleen (1997), 'Choosing Strategies to Control the Bureaucracy: Statutory Constraints, Oversight, and the Committee System', **13** *Journal of Law, Economics, and Organization*, 101–26.

Beck, Nathaniel (1987), 'Elections and the Fed: Is there a National Monetary Cycle?', **31** *American Journal of Political Science*, 194–216.

Bendor, Jonathan and Meirowitz, Adam (2004), 'Spatial Models of Delegation' **98** *American Political Science Review*, 293–310.

Bennedsen, Morten and Feldman, Sven E. (2006), 'Lobbying Bureaucrats', **108** *Scandinavian Journal of Economics*, 643–68.

Benson, Bruce L. (1981), 'Why are Congressional Committees Dominated by "High Demand" Legislators?', **48** *Southern Economic Journal*, 68–77.

Benson, Bruce L. (1983a), 'The Economic Theory of Regulation as an Explanation of Policies toward Bank Mergers and Holding Company Acquisitions', **28** *Antitrust Bulletin*, 839–62.

Benson, Bruce L. (1983b), 'High Demand Legislative Committees and Bureaucratic Output', **11** *Public Finance Quarterly*, 259–81.

Benson, Bruce L. (1989), 'Further Thoughts on Rent Seeking, Bureaucratic Output, and the Price of Complements', **63** *Public Choice*, 279–81.

Benson, Bruce L. (1990), *The Enterprise of Law: Justice without the State*, San Francisco: Pacific Research Institute for Public Policy.

Benson, Bruce L. (1994), 'Third Thoughts on Contracting Out', **11** *Journal of Libertarian Studies*, 44–78.

Benson, Bruce L. (1995), 'Understanding Bureaucratic Behavior: Implications from the Public Choice Literature', **13** *Journal of Public Finance and Public Choice/Economia delle Scelte Pubbliche*, 89–117.

Benson, Bruce L. and Greenhut, Melvin L. (1986), 'Interest Groups, Bureaucrats and Antitrust: An Explanation of the Antitrust Paradox', in Grieson, Ronald E. (ed.), *Antitrust and Regulation*, Lexington, MA: Lexington Books, 53–90.

Benson, Bruce L., Greenhut, Melvin L. and Holcombe, Randall (1987), 'Interest Groups and the Antitrust Paradox', **6** *Cato Journal*, 801–17.

Benson, Bruce L. and Mitchell, Jean (1988), 'Rent Seekers Who Demand Government Production: Bureaucratic Output and the Price of Complements', **56** *Public Choice*, 3–16.

Benson, Bruce L., Rasmussen, David W. and Sollars, David L. (1995), 'Police Bureaucrats, their Incentives, and the War on Drugs', **83** *Public Choice*, 21–45.

Bos, P.V.F. (1994), 'Van Ontvoogding naar Ontgoocheling of van Interstatelijkheid naar Communautaire Dimensie? (From Guardianship to Illusion or from a State to a Community Perspective)', **69** *Nederlands Juristen Blad*, 906–11.

Bressman, Lisa Schultz (2007), 'Procedures as Politics in Administrative Law', **107** *Columbia Law Review,* 1749–821.

Breton, Albert and Winetrobe, Ronald (1982), *The Logic of Bureaucratic Conduct*, Cambridge: Cambridge University Press.

Breyer, Stephen G. (1985), 'Economists and Economic Regulation', **47** *University of Pittsburgh Law Review*, 205–18.

Centner, Terence J. (1995), 'Organically-produced Food Products: Regulations from the European Union and the United States Set the Stage for Imports', **7(4)** *Journal of International Food and Agribusiness Marketing*, 41–58.

Centner, Terence J. and Lathrop, K.W. (1996), 'Differentiating Food Products: Organic Labeling Provisions Facilitate Consumer Choice', **1** *Drake Agricultural Law Review*, 30–50.

Cooter, Robert D. (1994a), 'Structural Adjudication and the New Law Merchant: A Model of Decentralized Law', **14** *International Review of Law and Economics*, 215–31.

Cooter, Robert D. (1994b), 'Decentralized Law for a Complex Economy', **23** *Southwestern Law Review, Hayek Symposium*, 443–51.

Cooter, Robert D. (1996a), 'Decentralized Law for a Complex Economy: The Structural Approach to Adjudicating the New Law Merchant', **144** *University of Pennsylvania Law Review*, 1643–96.

Cooter, Robert D. (1996b), 'The Theory of Market Modernization of Law', **16** *International Review of Law and Economics*, 141–72.

Cooter, Robert D. (2000), *The Strategic Constitution*, Princeton, NJ: Princeton University Press.

DeMesquita, Ethan Bueno and Stephenson, Matthew C. (2007), 'Regulatory Quality under Imperfect Oversight', **101** *American Political Science Review,* 605–20.

DeShazo, J.R. and Freeman, Jody (2003), 'The Congressional Competition to Control Delegated Power', **81** *Texas Law Review*, 1443–519.

DeShazo, J.R. and Freeman, Jody (2005), 'Public Agencies as Lobbyists', **105** *Columbia Law Review*, 2217–309.

Eckert, Ross D. (1981), 'The Life Cycle of Regulatory Commissioners', **24** *Journal of Law and Economics*, 113–20.

Eijlander, P. (1996), 'Regulering van de Kwaliteit van Zorginstellingen (Regulating the Quality of Care Organizations)', in Gestel, R.A.J. van et al. (eds), *Markt en Wet*, Deventer: W.E.J. Tjeenk Willink, 209–19.

Eom, Jiyong and Sweeny, James L. (2009), 'A Theory of Interest Group Proposals in Agency Rulemaking', Working Paper, available at SSRN: http://ssrn.com/abstract=1401536.

Epstein, David and O'Halloran, Sharyn (1995), 'Theory of Strategic Oversight: Congress, Lobbyists, and the Bureaucracy', **11** *Journal of Law, Economics, and Organization*, 227–55.

Epstein, David and O'Halloran, Sharyn (1999), *Delegating Powers: A Transaction Cost Politics Approach to Policy Making under Separate Powers*, New York: Cambridge University Press.

Faith, Roger L., Leavens, Donald R. and Tollison, Roger D. (1982), 'Antitrust Pork Barrel', **25** *Journal of Law and Economics*, 329–42.

Ferejohn, John A. (1987), 'On a Structuring Principle for Administrative Agencies', in McCubbins, Mathew D. and Sullivan, Terry (eds), *Congress: Structure and Policy*, Cambridge: Cambridge University Press.

Ferejohn, John A. and Shipan, Charles (1990), 'Congressional Influence on Bureaucracy', **6(S)** *Journal of Law, Economics, and Organization*, 1–20.

Figueiredo, Rui J.P. de; Spiller, Pablo T. and Urbiztondo, Santiago (1999), 'An Informational Perspective on Administrative Procedures', **15** *Journal of Law, Economics, and Organization*, 283–305.

Fiorina, Morris P. (1977), *Congress: Keystone of the Washington Establishment*, New Haven, CT: Yale University Press.

Fiorina, Morris P. (1982), 'Legislative Choice of Regulatory Forms: Legal Process or Administrative Process?', **39** *Public Choice*, 33–66.

Fiorina, Morris P. (1986), 'Legislator Uncertainty, Legislative Control, and the Delegation of Legislative Power', **2** *Journal of Law, Economics, and Organization*, 33–51.

Fox, Eleanor M. (1987), 'Chairman Miller, the Federal Trade Commission, Economics, and Rashomon', **50(4)** *Law and Contemporary Problems*, 33–55.

Frech, H. Edward III and Samprone, Joseph C., Jr (1980), 'The Welfare Loss of Excess Nonprice Competition: The Case of Property-Liability Insurance Regulation', **13** *Journal of Law and Economics*, 429–40.

Fuchs, Edward Paul and Anderson, James E. (1987), 'Institutionalizing Cost-Benefit Analysis in Regulatory Agencies', in Nagel, Stuart S. (ed.), *Research in Public Policy Analysis and Management, Volume 4*, Greenwich, CT: JAI Press, 187–211.

Furlong, Scott R. (1997), 'Interest Group Influence on Rule Making', **29** *Administration and Society*, 325–47.

Furlong, Scott R. and Kerwin, Cornelius M. (2005), 'Interest Group Participation in Rule Making: A Decade of Change', **15** *Journal of Public Administration Research Theory*, 353–70.

Gailmard, Sean (2002), 'Expertise, Subversion, and Bureaucratic Discretion', **18** *Journal of Law, Economics, and Organization*, 536–55.

Gely, Rafael and Spiller, Pablo T. (1990), 'A Rational Choice Theory of Supreme Court Statutory Decisions with Applications to the State Farm and Grove City Cases', **6** *Journal of Law, Economics, and Organization*, 263–300.

Golden, Marissa Martino (1998), 'Interest Groups in the Rule-Making Process: Who Participates? Whose Voices Get Heard?', **8** *Journal of Public Administration Research and Theory*, 245–70.

Graham, John D. (2007), 'The Evolving Regulatory Role of the U.S. Office of Management and Budget', **1** *Review of Environmental Economics and Policy* 171–91.

Grajzl, Peter (2011), 'A Property Rights Approach to Legislative Delegation', **12(2)** *Economics of Government*, 177–200.

Greenhut, Melvin L. and Benson, Bruce L. (1989), *American Antitrust Law in Theory and in Practice*, Aldershot: Avebury.

Grier, Kevin (1984), 'The Political Economy of Monetary Policy', Ph.D. dissertation.

Hafner, Mathias (1999), 'Das optionale Anzeigeverfahren nach §231a BlmSchG (The optional notification procedure of Sec. 231a of the Federal Emission Control Act)', in Schmidtchen, Dieter and Schmidt-Trenz, Hans-Jörg (eds), *Vom Hoheitsstaat zum Konsensualstaat – Ökonomische Analyse der Flexibilisierung von Genehmigungsverfahren*, Baden-Baden: Nomos Verlagsgesellschaft, 127–47.

Hafner, Mathias (2000), *Behördliche Diagnosefehler im Genehmigungsverfahren: Eine ökonomische Analyse immissionsschutzrechtlicher Eröffnungskontrollen und ihrer Reform (Administrative Diagnostic Errors in Licensing Procedures: An Economic Analysis of Disclosure Controls in Emission Control Law and their Reform)*, Wiesbaden: Gabler.

Hahn, Robert W. (2000), 'State and Federal Regulatory Reform: A Comparative Analysis', **29** *Journal of Legal Studies*, 873–912.

Hall, Richard L. and Miler, Kristina C. (2008), 'What Happens after the Alarm? Interest Group Subsidies to Legislative Overseers', **70** *Journal of Politics*, 990–1005.

Hamilton, James T. and Schroeder, Christopher H. (1994), 'Strategic Regulators and the Choice of Rulemaking Procedures: The Selection of Formal vs. Informal Rules in Regulating Hazardous Waste', **57** *Law and Contemporary Problems*, 111–60.

Hammond, Thomas H. and Knott, Jack H. (1996), 'Who Controls the Bureaucracy?: Presidential Power, Congressional Dominance, Legal Constraints and Bureaucratic Autonomy in a Model of Multi-Institutional Policy-Making', **12** *Journal of Law, Economics, and Organization*, 119–66.

Hatzis, Aristides N. (1998), 'Mancur Olson, Jr (1932–1998)', **1** *Episteme and Koinonia*, 195–202.

Hatzis, Aristides N. (1999), 'Rent-Seeking and Vested Interests', in O'Hara, Phillip (ed.), *Encyclopedia of Political Economy*, London: Routledge, 947–77.

Hazlett, Thomas W. and Viani, Bruno E. (2005), 'Legislators v. Regulators: The Case of Low Power FM Radio', **7** *Business and Politics*, 1–31.

Holburn, Guy L.F. and Vanden Bergh, Richard G. (2004), 'Influencing Agencies through Pivotal Political Institutions', **20** *Journal of Law, Economics, and Organization*, 459–83.

Holburn, Guy L.F. and Vanden Bergh, Richard G. (2006), 'Consumer capture of regulatory institutions: The Creation of Public Utility Consumer Advocates in the United States', **126** *Public Choice*, 45–73.

Holmström, Bengt and Milgrom, Paul R. (1991), 'Multitask Principal-Agent Analysis: Incentive Contracts, Asset Ownership, and Job Design', **7** *Journal of Law, Economics, and Organization*, 24–52.

Hopenhayn, Hugo and Lohmann, Susanne (1996), 'Fire Alarm Signals and the Political Oversight of Regulatory Agencies', **12** *Journal of Law, Economics, and Organization*, 196–213.

Horn, Murray J. (1995), *The Political Economy of Public Administration – Institutional Choice in the Public Sector*, Cambridge: Cambridge University Press.

Horn, Murray J. and Shepsle, Kenneth A. (1989), 'Commentary: Administrative Process and Organizational Form as Legislative Responses to Agency Costs', **75** *Virginia Law Review*, 499–508.

Huber, John D. and Shipan, Charles R. (2002), *Deliberate Discretion? The Institutional Foundations of Bureaucratic Autonomy*, New York: Cambridge University Press.

Immergut, Ellen M. (2006), 'Institutional Constraints on Policy', in Moran, Michael, Rein, Martin and Goodin, Robert (eds) *The Oxford Handbook of Public Policy*, Oxford: Oxford University Press, 557–71.

Jensen, Christian B. (2007), 'Implementing Europe', **8** *European Union Politics*, 451–77.

Johnson, Ronald N. and Libecap, Gary D. (1994), *The Federal Civil Service System and the Problem of Bureaucracy*, Chicago: University of Chicago Press.

Kaplow, Louis (1992), 'Rules versus Standards: An Economic Analysis', **42** *Duke Law Journal*, 557–629.

Kaplow, Louis (1995), 'A Model of the Optimal Complexity of Legal Rules', **11** *Journal of Law, Economics, and Organization*, 150–63.

Katzmann, Robert A. (1980), *Regulatory Bureaucracy: The Federal Trade Commission and Antitrust Policy*, Cambridge, MA: MIT Press.

Kerwin, Cornelius (1992), *Rulemaking: How Government Agencies Write Law and Make Policy*, Washington, DC: Congressional Quarterly Press, 2nd edn, 1999.

Kerwin, Cornelius M. and Furlong, Scott R. (1992), 'Time and Rulemaking: An Empirical Test of Theory', **2** *Journal of Public Administration Research and Theory*, 113–38.

Kobayashi, Bruce H. and Ribstein, Larry E. (1996), 'Evolution and Spontaneous Uniformity: Evidence from the Evolution of the Limited Liability Company', **34** *Economic Inquiry*, 464–83.

Laffont, Jean-Jacques and Tirole, Jean (1990), 'The Politics of Government Decision Making: Regulatory Institutions', **6** *Journal of Law, Economics, and Organization*, 1–31.

Landy, Marc K., Roberts, Mark J. and Thomas, Stephen R. (1990), *The Environmental Protection Agency: Asking the Wrong Questions*, Oxford: Oxford University Press.

Lehmann, Markus A. (2002), 'Error Minimization and Deterrence in Agency Control', **21** *International Review of Law and Economics*, 373–91.

Lemieux, Vincent (1991), *Les Relations de Pouvoir dans les Lois – Comparaison entre les Gouvernements du Québec de 1944 à 1985* (Power Relations in Laws – Comparison between Quebec Governments from 1944 to 1985), Sainte-Foy: Presses de l'Université Laval.

Levine, Michael E. (1992), 'Organizational Design and Political Control of Administrative Agencies: Comment', **8** *Journal of Law, Economics, and Organization*, 119–25.

Lewis, Tracy and Poitevin, Michel (1997), 'Disclosure of Information in Regulatory Proceedings', **13** *Journal of Law, Economics, and Organization*, 50–73.

Lindsay, Cotton M. (1976), 'A Theory of Government Enterprise', **84** *Journal of Political Economy*, 1061–77.

Lupia, Arthur and McCubbins, Mathew D. (1994a), 'Learning from Oversight: Fire Alarms and Police Patrols Reconstructed', **10** *Journal of Law, Economics, and Organization*, 96–125.

Lupia, Arthur and McCubbins, Mathew D. (1994b), 'Designing Bureaucratic Accountability', **57** *Law and Contemporary Problems*, 91–126.

MacDonald, Jason A. (2010), 'Limitation Riders and Congressional Influence over Bureaucratic Policy Decisions', **104** *American Political Science Review*, 766–82.

Macey, Jonathan R. (1992), 'Organizational Design and Political Control of Administrative Agencies', **8** *Journal of Law, Economics, and Organization*, 93–110.

MacKay, Robert J., Miller, James C., III and Yandle, Bruce (1987a), 'Public Choice and Regulation: An Overview', in MacKay, Robert J., Miller, James C., III and Yandle, Bruce (eds), *Public Choice and Regulation: A View from Inside the Federal Trade Commission*, Stanford, CA: Hoover Institute Press, Stanford University, 3–12.

MacKay, Robert J., Miller, James C., III and Yandle, Bruce (eds) (1987b), *Public Choice and Regulation: A View from Inside the Federal Trade Commission*, Stanford, CA: Hoover Institute Press, Stanford University.

Magat, Wesley A., Krupnick, A. and Harrington, W. (1986), *Rules in the Making: A Statistical Analysis of Regulatory Agency Behavior*, Washington: Resources for the Future.

Mashaw, Jerry L. (1985), 'Prodelegation: Why Administrators should Make Political Decisions', **1** *Journal of Law, Economics, and Organization*, 81–100.

McCubbins, Mathew D., Noll, Roger G. and Weingast, Barry R. (1987), 'Administrative Procedures as Instruments of Political Control', **3** *Journal of Law, Economics and Organization*, 243–77.

McCubbins, Mathew D., Noll, Roger G. and Weingast, Barry R. (1989), 'Structure and Process, Politics and Policy: Administrative Arrangements and the Political Control of Agencies', **75** *Virginia Law Review*, 431–82.

McCubbins, Mathew D., Noll, Roger G. and Weingast, Barry R. (1999), 'The Political Origins of the Administrative Procedures Act', **15** *Journal of Law, Economics, and Organization*, 180–217.

McCubbins, Mathew D. and Page, Talbot (1986), 'The Congressional Foundations of Agency Performance', **51** *Public Choice*, 173–90.

McCubbins, Mathew D. and Page, Talbot (1987), 'A Theory of Congressional Delegation', in McCubbins, Mathew D. and Sullivan, Terry (eds), *Congress: Structure and Policy*, Cambridge: Cambridge University Press.

McCubbins, Mathew D. and Schwartz, T. (1984), 'Congressional Oversight Overlooked: Policy Patrols vs. Fire Alarms', **28** *American Journal of Political Science*, 165–79.

McGarity, Thomas O. (1991), *Reinventing Rationality - The Role of Regulatory Analysis in the Federal Bureaucracy*, Cambridge: Cambridge University Press.

McKay, Amy and Yackee, Susan Webb (2007), 'Interest Group Competition on Federal Agency Rules', **35** *American Politics Research*, 336–57.

Migué, Jean-Luc and Belanger, Gerard (1974), 'Towards a General Theory of Managerial Discretion', **17** *Public Choice*, 27–43.

Miller, James C., III (1989), *The Economist as Reformer: Revamping the FTC, 1981*, Washington: American Enterprise Institute for Public Policy Research.

Mitnick, Barry M. (1975), 'The Theory of Agency: The Political Paradox and Regulatory Behaviour', **24** *Public Choice*, 27–47.

Mitnick, Barry M. (1980), *Political-Economy of Regulation*, New York: Columbia University Press.

Moe, Terry M. (1985), 'Control and Feedback in Economic Regulation: The Case of the NLRB', **79** *American Political Science Review*, 1094–117.

Moe, Terry M. (1987), 'An Assessment of the Positive Theory of Congressional Dominance', **12** *Legislative Studies Quarterly*, 475–520.

Moe, Terry M. (1989), 'The Politics of Bureaucratic Structure', in Chubb, John and Peterson, Paul (eds), *Can the Government Govern?*, Washington: Brookings Institution.

Moe, Terry M. (2005), 'Political Control and the Power of the Agent', **22** *Journal of Law, Economics, and Organization*, 1–29.

Muris, Timothy J. (1986), 'Regulatory Policymaking at the Federal Trade Commission: The Extent of Congressional Control', **94** *Journal of Political Economy*, 884–9.

Nichols, Albert L. (1982), 'Legislative Choice of Regulatory Forms: A Comment on Fiorina', **39** *Public Choice*, 67–71.

Nicolaides, Phedon (2004), 'The Political Economy of Multi-tiered Regulation in Europe', **42** *Journal of Common Market Studies*, 599–618.

Niskanen, William A. (1971), *Bureaucracy and Representive Government*, Chicago: Aldine-Atherton.

Niskanen, William A. (1975), 'Bureaucrats and Politicians', **18** *Journal of Law and Economics*, 617–43.

Nixon, David C., Howard, Robert M. and DeWitt, Jeff R. (2002), 'With Friends Like These: Rule-Making Comment Submissions to the Securities and Exchange Commission', **12** *Journal of Public Administration Research and Theory*, 59–76.

Noll, R. (1971), *Reforming Regulation: An Evaluation of the Ash Council Proposals*, Washington: Brookings Institution.

O'Connell, Anne Joseph (2008), 'Political Cycles of Rulemaking: An Empirical Portrait of the Modern Administrative State', **94** *Virginia Law Review*, 889–986.

Ogul, Morris S. and Rockmann, Bert A. (1990), 'Overseeing Oversight: New Departures and an Old Problem', **15** *Legislative Studies Quarterly*, 5–24.

Ogus, Anthony I. (1995), 'Economics and Law Reform: Thirty Years of Law Commission Endeavor', **11** *Law Quarterly Review*, 407–20.

Olson, Mary (1995), 'Regulatory Agency Discretion among Competing Industries: Inside the FDA', **11** *Journal of Law, Economics, and Organization*, 379–408.

Olson, Mary (1996), 'Substitution in Regulatory Agencies: FDA Enforcement Alternatives', **12** *Journal of Law, Economics, and Organization*, 376–407.

Page, William H. (1981), 'Antitrust, Federalism, and the Regulatory Process: A Reconstruction and Critique of the State Action Exemption after Midcal Aluminium', **61** *Boston University Law Review*, 1099–138.

Parisi, Francesco (1995), 'Public Choice Theory and International Institutions: One More Comment on Richard Falk', **1** *International Legal Theory*, 45–8.

Parisi, Francesco (1997), *The Market of Votes: Coasian Bargaining in an Arrovian Setting*, George Mason University Law and Economics Working Paper Series, No. 97-05.

Parisi, Francesco (1998a), *A Property-Right Theory of Democratic Voting*, George Mason University Law and Economics Working Paper Series, No. 98-04.

Parisi, Francesco (1998b), 'The Market for Votes: Coasian Bargaining in an Arrovian Setting', **6** *George Mason Law Review*, 745–66.

Posner, Eric A. (2001), 'Controlling Agencies with Cost-Benefit Analysis: A Positive Political Theory Perspective', **68** *The University of Chicago Law Review*, 1137–99.

Posner, Richard A. (1972), 'The Behavior of Administrative Agencies', **1** *Journal of Legal Studies*, 305–47.

Prendergast, Canice (2003), 'The Limits of Bureaucratic Efficiency', **111** *Journal of Political Economy*, 929–58.

Provopoulos, George and Zambaras, Athanassios (1991), 'Testing for Causality Between Government Spending and Taxation', **68** *Public Choice*, 277–82.

Raadschelders, Jos C.N. (2008), 'Understanding Government: Four Intellectual Traditions in the Study of Public Administration', **86** *Public Administration*, 925–49.

Rasmussen, David W. and Benson, Bruce L. (eds) (1994), *The Economic Anatomy of a Drug War: Criminal Justice in the Commons*, Lanham, MD: Rowman and Littlefield.

Ribstein, Larry E. and Kobayashi, Bruce H. (1996a), 'An Economic Analysis of Uniform State Laws', **25** *Journal of Legal Studies*, 131–99.

Ribstein, Larry E. and Kobayashi, Bruce H. (1996b), 'Uniform Laws, Model Laws and Limited Liability Companies', **66** *University of Colorado Law Review*, 947–99.

Robinson, Glen O. (1989), 'Commentary: Political Uses of Structure and Process', **75** *Virginia Law Review*, 483–98.

Rose, Jonathan (1985a), 'Executive Oversight of Rulemaking in Arizona: The Governor's Regulatory Review Counsel – the First Three Years', *Arizona State Law Journal*, 425–91.

Rose, Jonathan (1985b), 'Nonlawyer Practice before Federal Administrative Agencies Should be Encouraged', **37** *Administrative Law Review*, 363–73.

Rose-Ackerman, Susan (1978), *Corruption*, New York: Academic Press.

Rose-Ackerman, Susan (1979), *Political Corruption*, New York: Academic Press.

Rose-Ackerman, Susan (1990), 'Comment (on Ferejohn and Shipan's "Congressional Influence (on Bureaucracy)"', **6(S)** *Journal of Law, Economics, and Organization*, 21–7.

Rose-Ackerman, Susan (1995), *Controlling Environmental Policy*, New Haven, CN and London: Yale University Press.

Ross, Stephen F. (1992), 'Delegation, Commitment, and the Regulatory Mandate: Comment', **8** *Journal of Law, Economics, and Organization*, 155–8.
Rubin, Paul H. and Cohen, Mark A. (1985), 'Private Enforcement of Public Policy', **3(1)** *Yale Journal on Regulation*, 167–93.
Rugge, Dale R. (1987), 'Judicial Review of Environmental Protection Agency Rule Promulgation – Clean Air Act State Implementation Plan Requirement', **27** *Natural Resources Journal*, 723–37.
Schauer, Frederick and Zeckhauser, Richard (2009), 'The Trouble with Cases', *NBER Working Paper Series, Working Paper 15279*.
Schmidt, P. (2002), 'Pursuing Regulatory Relief: Strategic Participation and Litigation in U.S. OSHA Rulemaking', **4** *Business and Politics*, 71–89.
Shepsle, Kenneth A. (1992), 'Organizational Design and Political Control of Administrative Agencies: A Comment: Bureaucratic Drift, Coalition Drift, and Time Consistency', **8** *Journal of Law, Economics, and Organization*, 111–18.
Shipan, Charles R. (2004), 'Regulatory Regimes, Agency Actions, and the Conditional Nature of Congressional Influence', **98** *American Political Science Review*, 467–80.
Simon, Herbert A., Smith, D.W. and Thompson, Victor A. (1950/1991), *Public Administration*, New York: Alfred A. Knopf, 2nd edn, 1991.
Sloof, Randolph (2000), 'Interest Group Lobbying and the Delegation of Policy Authority', **12** *Economics and Politics*, 247–74.
Smith, Janet Kiholm (1982a), 'Production of Licensing Legislation: An Economic Analysis of Interstate Differences', **11** *Journal of Legal Studies*, 117–37.
Smith, Janet Kiholm (1982b), 'An Analysis of State Regulations Governing Liquor Store Licensees', **25** *Journal of Law and Economics*, 301–20.
Snyder, Susan K. and Weingast, Barry R. (2000), 'The American System of Shared Powers: The President, Congress and the NLRB', **16** *Journal of Law, Economics, and Organization*, 269–305.
Spence, David B. (1999), 'Managing Delegation Ex Ante: Using Law to Steer Administrative Agencies', **28** *Journal of Legal Studies*, 413–59.
Spence, David B. and Cross, Frank B. (2000), 'A Public Choice Case for the Administrative State', **89** *Georgetown Law Journal*, 97–142.
Spiller, Pablo T. and Tiller, Emerson H. (1997), 'Decision Costs and the Strategic Design of Administrative Process and Judicial Review', **16** *Journal of Legal Studies*, 347–70.
Spitzer, Matthew L. (1988), 'Antitrust Federalism and Rational Choice Political Economy: A Critique of Capture Theory', **61** *Southern California Law Review*, 1293–326.
Spitzer, Matthew L. (1990), 'Extensions of Ferejohn and Shipan's Model of Administrative Agency Behavior', **6(S)** *Journal of Law, Economics, and Organization*, 29–43.
Spulber, Daniel F. and Besanko, David A. (1992), 'Delegation, Commitment, and the Regulatory Mandate', **8** *Journal of Law, Economics, and Organization*, 126–54.
Stalon, Charles G. (1986), 'Analysis and Synthesis in Quasi-Judicial Multimember Regulatory Agencies', in Saltzman, Sidney and Schuler, Richard E. (eds), *The Future of Electrical Energy: A Regional Perspective*, New York: Greenwood Press, 330–39.
Stephenson, Matthew C. (2008), 'Evidentiary Standards and Information Acquisition in Public Law', **10** *American Law and Economics Review*, 351–87.
Steunenberg, Bernard (1992), 'Congress, Bureaucracy, and Regulatory Policy Making', **8** *Journal of Law, Economics, and Organization*, 673–94.
Tiller, Emerson H. and Spiller, Pablo T. (1999), 'Strategic Instruments: Legal Structures and Political Games in Administrative Law', **15** *Journal of Law, Economics, and Organization*, 349–77.
Van Damme, E.E.C. (1996), 'Marktwerking en Herregulering (Markets and Re-regulation)', in Gestel, R.A.J. van et al. (eds), *Markt en Wet*, Deventer: W.E.J. Tjeenk Willink, 19–43.
Vaubel, Roland (1991), 'A Public Choice View of International Organizations', in Vaubel, Roland and Willet, Thomas D. (eds), *The Political Economy of International Organizations*, Boulder, CO: Westview Press, 27–45.
Voigt, Stefan and Salzberger, Eli M. (2002), 'Choosing Not To Choose: When Politicians Choose To Delegate Powers', **55** *KYKLOS*, 289–310.
Volden, Craig (2002), 'Delegating Power to Bureaucracies: Evidence from the States', **18** *Journal of Law, Economics, and Organization*, 187–220.

Waline, M. (1965), 'Quelques Facteurs Sociologiques de l'Evolution Actuelle du Droit (Some Sociological Factors in the Contemporary Evolution of Law)', in Dubuisson, Bernard et al. (eds.), *Mélanges Offerts à René Savatier*, Brussels: De Boeck & Larcier.

Wangenheim, Georg von (2005), 'Should Non-Expert Courts Control Expert Administrations?' in Marciano, Alain and Josselin, Jean-Michel (eds), *Law and the State: A Political Economy Approach*, Cheltenham, UK and Northampton, MA, USA: Edward Elgar 310–32.

Weingast, Barry R. (1981), 'Regulation, Reregulation, and Deregulation: The Political Foundations of Agency Clientele Relationships', **44** *Law and Contemporary Problems*, 147–77.

Weingast, Barry R. (1984), 'The Congressional-Bureaucratic System: A Principal Agent Perspective (with Applications to the SEC)', **44** *Public Choice*, 147–91.

Weingast, Barry R. and Moran, Mark J. (1983), 'Bureaucratic Discretion or Congressional Control? Regulatory Policymaking by the Federal Trade Commission', **91** *Journal of Political Economy*, 765–800. Reprinted in Mackay, Robert J., Miller, James C., III and Yandle, Bruce (eds) (1987), *Public Choice and Regulation: A View form Inside the Federal Trade Commission*, Stanford, CA: Hoover Institution Press, 30–62.

Weingast, Barry R. and Moran, Mark J. (1986), 'Congress and Regulatory Agency Choice: Reply', **94** *Journal of Political Economy*, 890–94.

Wiley, John Shepard, Jr (1986), 'A Capture Theory of Antitrust Federalism', **99** *Harvard Law Review*, 713–89.

Wiley, John Shepard, Jr (1988), 'A Capture Theory of Antitrust Federalism: Reply to Professors Page and Spitzer', **61** *Southern California Law Review*, 1327–41.

Zarkin, Michael J. (2003), 'Telecommunications Policy Learning: The Case of the FCC's Computer Inquiries', **27** *Telecommunications Policy*, 283–99.

Ziekow, Jan, Oertel, Martin-Peter and Windoffer, Alexander (2005), *Dauer von Zulassungsverfahren: eine empirische Untersuchung zu Implementation und Wirkungsgrad von Regelungen zur Verfahrensbeschleunigung*, Cologne: Heymann.

Other References

Holmström, Bengt and Milgrom, Paul (1991), 'Multitask Principal-Agent Analyses: Incentive Contracts, Asset Ownership, and Job Design', **7** *Journal of Law, Economics and Organization*, 24–52.

Priest, George L. (1977), 'The Common Law Process and the Selection of Efficient Rules', **6** *Journal of Legal Studies*, 65–82.

Rubin, Paul H. (1977), 'Why is the Common Law Efficient?', **6** *Journal of Legal Studies*, 51–63.

PART II

JUDGE-MADE LAW

6 Judge-made law

Paul H. Rubin

At the heart of economic analysis of law is a mystery that is also an embarrassment: how to explain judicial behavior in economic terms ... Posner (1993, p. 2)

1. Introduction

As the quotation from Posner indicates, explanation of the behavior of judges is one of the most important but also most difficult problems facing law and economics scholars. This is because judicial opinions are the result of utility-maximizing behavior and economists are unable to specify the details of judges' (or anyone else's) utility functions. Consequently, it has proven difficult to develop a theory that explains why judges make the decisions that we observe, though, as we discuss below, many have tried. Because of the difficulty of explaining decisions in terms of utility functions, there have also been attempts to use evolutionary models to explain outcomes. In these models, the form of law is due to factors involving wealth-maximizing behavior of actors in the legal process such as litigants or attorneys, and judges play a minor role.

The structure of this chapter is as follows: I first consider briefly arguments regarding the efficiency of common law. I then discuss utility-maximizing models of judicial behavior. I next consider the evolutionary models. The final section discusses models of multi-judge behavior.

2. Efficiency of Common Law

A basic question for law and economics is the efficiency of law. Hayek (1960, 1973), although writing before the law and economics movement and writing from another perspective, had argued that common or judge-made law was better than statute law (see Christiansen, 1990, for an attempt to reconcile Hayekian arguments with law and economics). More recently, Posner (1992) has of course argued often and forcefully that the common law is efficient. His arguments are based on examination of particular legal doctrines. The difficulty of this method is that often the conclusion regarding the efficiency of a particular rule depends on unmeasured transactions costs of various sorts; if Posner's intuition about relative magnitudes of costs is incorrect, then doctrines he claims are efficient may not be so. Nonetheless, his analysis has been the intellectual spark behind the growth of law and economics, and questions of efficiency of the sort he was the first to raise have dominated the literature. Much of this literature may be considered as detailed attempts to answer the positive efficiency question first posed by Posner, and much of the rest aims at deriving normative conclusions as to what is efficient.

Others are less certain that common law is efficient. Tullock (1971, 1980) has long argued that the English common law process is less efficient than Continental processes. Rizzo (1980a, 1980b) argues from an Austrian perspective that the amount of information needed for judges to achieve efficiency is excessive, although Rubin (1980) in a critique argues that Rizzo's criticism might apply to efficiency in all of economics, not merely in law and economics. Aranson (1992) argues that it is impossible for judges to seek efficiency because the calculations required are equivalent to those required to make central planning work. Hadfield (1992b) has argued that because judges see only a biased sample of potential cases, depending on the rules in existence, it is impossible for judges to move towards efficiency, even if they desire to do so.

Much of the literature in law and economics consists of attempts to examine particular legal doctrines and attempts to determine if they are efficient. (Much of my own work is of this type; see for example Rubin, 1983.) This method of analysis is fundamentally different from efficiency analysis in other branches of economics. There, a process (market competition) is postulated and it is shown that the process leads to efficient outcomes. Economists do not generally examine consumers to see if they are equating ratios of marginal utilities to prices, or firms to see if they are charging marginal cost. Rather, the process by which outcomes are generated is shown to lead to efficiency. It is for this reason that many economists are uncomfortable with the efficiency arguments of law and economics. Nonetheless, because this is the standard method in law and economics, any analysis of the efficiency of any particular body of law can be considered as evidence for or against Posner's hypothesis. If some law is found efficient, then this is evidence for the hypothesis. If some law is found inefficient, or if there are proposals for reform, then this is evidence against the hypothesis. In this sense, all of law and economics is aimed at testing this fundamental hypothesis.

Scholars are of course aware of this difficulty, and have sought to identify a process that would lead to efficiency. The two candidates are utility maximization by judges and evolutionary models. I discuss each. As we will see, there is no definitive demonstration in the literature of a mechanism that would lead to efficiency. This has led many to conclude that the law is not so efficient as Posner believes.

3. Utility Maximization

The first argument regarding utility maximization by judges was in Posner (1992, first edition, 1973). The argument (elaborated in Posner, 1993) is that judges are so insulated from personal factors and from interest group and other pressures that the only remaining decision factor is efficiency. The only other candidate is income redistribution, and judges lack the tools needed for such redistribution. This explanation was and is not terribly convincing to economists because it ultimately relies on judicial tastes for efficiency and economists prefer not to explain behavior on this basis.

There have been some attempts to model judicial utility functions in terms of economically relevant and observable variables. The first such effort was by Higgins and Rubin (1980). They argued that promotion to a higher position was an element of judicial utility functions, that promotion was more likely if the judge was reversed less, and that the value of promotion was reduced as the judge became older. However, in their sample they were unable to find any relation between age or any other factor and reversal, and only a weak relation between reversal and promotion.

In two articles, Cohen continued to examine promotion possibilities for federal judges. His argument was that if the Justice Department recommended a judge, then promotion was more likely. In Cohen (1991) he examined voting on the constitutionality of the US Sentencing Commission and found that judges voting for constitutionality were more likely to be promoted; the Justice Department favored this position. In Cohen (1992) he found that judges who imposed more severe antitrust sanctions, again in line with the desires of the Department, were more likely to be promoted. Thus, there is evidence for normal utility maximization by judges. The problem is that it is difficult to see how these results generalize to explain other types of decisions, including common law decisions. Macey (1994) has argued that many rules of procedure are aimed at maximizing judicial utility – for example by emphasizing procedure, where judges have a comparative advantage, over substance, where they do not.

Landes and Posner (1980) examined differences between state court judges and federal court judges. Their hypothesis was that since federal judges are paid more and have life tenure, we would expect higher quality people to occupy these positions and write better opinions. Their measures of quality had to do with citations to opinions as discussed in Landes and Posner (1976) and with use of opinions in legal casebooks. Except for the last measure, they found little difference. Other variables such as age and the political party appointing the judge also had little influence. Ashenfelter, Eisenberg and Schwab (1995) examined the extent to which judicial decisions are influenced by the political party appointing the judge and other elements of the judges' personal background. They find little or no influence. Thus, if we believe that these characteristics influence the judges' utility function, this may be taken as an argument that this aspect of utility has little impact.

It is apparent that there is little evidence regarding the effect of utility maximization on the mass of case outcomes. This is clearly an area for future research.

4. Evolutionary Models

The evolutionary models are attempts to explain judicial behavior without resort to utility functions. Initially, these models aimed at explaining Posner's putative observation that the common law was efficient. It is fair to say that the models failed in this endeavor, perhaps because the law is not so efficient as Posner argued. Nonetheless, these models have had an important impact on the literature because they have called attention to forces other than judicial preferences in explaining the law. The evolutionary models are ultimately based on the model of the litigation process first set forth by Landes (1971).

The first paper applying an evolutionary model to the common law was Rubin (1977). Following Landes (1971) Rubin argued that most cases are settled, rather than litigated, and that it is only litigated cases that can lead to legal change. Cases are settled when the expected value to the plaintiff of a case is less than the expected cost to the defendant, which is generally true if stakes are symmetric. However, inefficient laws can sometimes create asymmetric stakes because the inefficiency means that there are deadweight losses that cannot be bargained away in the settlement process. That is, an inefficient rule creates a loss to one party that is greater than the gain to the other because of future stakes in similar type cases. Thus, litigation becomes more likely when rules are inefficient, and so inefficient rules are subject to greater selection pressure, and more likely to be overturned. (Note that this model, like many of its successors, depends on parties having ongoing interests in disputes of a certain sort, rather than merely in the matter at hand.)

Following this initial contribution were several extensions and modifications. Priest (1977) argued that inefficient rules generated larger stakes and so were more likely to be litigated, again subjecting them to increased selection pressure. Goodman (1979) argued that efficient precedents were worth more to parties who would benefit than inefficient precedents were worth to their beneficiaries, and that parties to whom a decision was worth more would spend more litigating and so would be more likely to win. In other words, efficient precedents were more likely to win in litigation and survive than were inefficient precedents. Katz (1988) expanded on this notion in the context of presenting a model of litigation expenditures. Terrebonne (1981) also presented a model of efficient legal evolution.

Other scholars began critically examining these models. Landes and Posner (1979) in a symposium paper published in the *Journal of Legal Studies* argued that the earlier models had erred by modeling precedent as an all or nothing issue, when the proper question was whether a precedent was stronger or weaker. That is, litigation might strengthen or weaken a precedent without overturning it completely. Thus a party with an interest in overturning an inefficient precedent would also have to consider the possibility that litigation could strengthen as well as weaken the precedent. This consideration greatly weakens the evolutionary pressures for efficiency. Parsons (1983) combined Priest's point (that inefficient precedents would lead to increasing litigation) with the Landes and Posner point (that precedents that were litigated might become entrenched) to argue that there is a tendency for the common law to become 'reckless' – to favor rules that inefficiently lead to increased accidents.

Cooter et al. (1979) presented a model in which movement towards efficiency could only occur if judges sought such a movement. In a more elaborate examination of the issue, Cooter and Kornhauser (1980) present a complex evolutionary model in which there are some tendencies towards efficiency, but in which both efficient and inefficient rules will be observed at any time. This model, and alternative definitions and implications of efficiency, are discussed in Kornhauser (1980). Von Wangenheim (1993) presents a model with similar results.

Hirshleifer (1982), building on Rubin's discussion of inefficiency when stakes in precedent are asymmetric, provided what may be the most useful and influential criticism of the evolutionary models. Recall that in the original Rubin (1977) model and in some others, including Goodman (1979) and Landes and Posner (1979), evolutionary forces moved the law towards efficiency only if the party with an interest in efficiency had an ongoing interest in the form of the law. Hirshleifer generalized this point to show that the law could come to favor whichever party could most easily organize and mobilize resources for litigation of unfavorable precedents. This movement would be independent of efficiency. Rubin (1982) uses this point to argue that common law was more like statute law than many want to admit: interest groups could use either common or statute law to achieve their goals. He argued that the apparent efficiency of the common law was because most common law was developed at a time when organization of interest groups was expensive, and that more recently both common and statute law have been subject to interest group pressures. Crew and Twight (1990) expanded on this point and found common law less subject to rent seeking than statute law. Rowley and Brough (1987) find that contract and property might be expected to be efficient, but not tort. Bailey and Rubin (1994) have extended this theme in a formal model of the influence of interest groups on the law, and Rubin and Bailey (1994) have shown that plaintiffs' attorneys have been responsible for the shape of modern tort law, using an evolutionary mechanism to shape the law. An interesting question worthy of future exploration is the extent to which other interest groups have found litigating for precedent worthwhile.

Heiner (1986) explains stare decisis and other features of the law as a result of human imperfect decision making. Because attempts to achieve optimality in each decision might lead to erroneous decisions in many cases, it may be more efficient to rely on rather simple rules that minimize the potential costs of error.

An interesting set of hypotheses regarding legal evolution is in Roe (1996). Roe argues that the notion of evolution towards efficiency is an important determinant of legal form, but it is not the only determinant. He incorporates three subsidiary notions into an efficiency framework – the importance of initial conditions (borrowed from chaos theory), path dependence and evolutionary accidents. The result of these processes would be that laws would be well but not perfectly adapted. However, while these notions are interesting, as Roe himself admits, they do not as of yet provide refutable hypotheses. It would be interesting to see if these propositions can be generalized to provide some implications.

What can we say about the evolutionary models? They have not succeeded in the original task of providing an explanation for common law efficiency. However, by demonstrating the difficulty of achieving this goal, they have helped understand when the law may be efficient and when it is likely not to be efficient. Moreover, an important component of the evolutionary models was their focus on the litigation decision as driving legal evolution. Other models of legal evolution, both economic and non-economic, either leave mechanisms for evolution unspecified or assume that the preferences of judges are the driving forces. The economic models were the first to focus on the motives of litigants, realizing that judges can decide only those cases that come before them.

As Elliott (1985, p.71), in an important study of the history of evolutionary models, indicates: 'Moreover, the economic school of evolution has broadened our view of the legal system to include the role of litigants, as well as judges, in making law.' The literature associated with Priest and Klein (1984) on selectivity bias in case selection is a result of the focus on litigants' decisions, which has come out of the evolutionary models; for a discussion, see Priest (1980). (For an analysis of theories of legal evolution from 1880–1940 (which thus omits analysis of the economic theories), see Hovenkamp, 1985.)

Aranson (1986) summarizes the assumptions of several of the evolutionary models. He shows that many combinations of assumptions have not been examined, and thus provides clues for further research. There is much useful research to be done on evolutionary models of legal change.

More recently, Gennaioli and Shleifer (2007, 2008) have extended this model. They find that under some circumstances legal evolution is beneficial even when judges are biased, because evolution increases the precision of the law and reduces the effects of biases.

5. Multi-Judge Interactions

Matters become more complex when more than one judge is involved in a decision or sequence of decisions. Multiple judges may be involved because a judicial panel may consist of more than one judge; because different judges may hear similar cases at different times; or because the appellate process may involve judges at different levels of a judicial hierarchy hearing the same case.

One issue that appears when panels of judges hear a matter is the potential for inconsistency. Easterbrook (1982) was the first to point out that the Arrow theorem (which shows that there is no way of aggregating preferences that is not subject to some flaw, and that, for example, majority voting can lead to cycles: A defeats B, B defeats C, C defeats A) also applies to judicial voting; see also Easterbrook (1984).

Kornhauser has written extensively on issues that arise in multi-judge settings, both alone and with Sager. Kornhauser and Sager (1986) apply the Condorcet Jury Theorem to the context of judicial panels and show that increasing the number of judges on a panel will increase the accuracy of the outcome. In addition, they argue that multi-judge panels can act consistently (in the sense of avoiding cycles), but that multi-judge panels may act incoherently, in the sense that the pattern of decision will not satisfy community principles of coherent explanation.

In two related papers, Kornhauser (1992a, 1992b) investigated several additional characteristics of collegial courts. He emphasized the dichotomous nature of common law adjudication. He argued further that judges had to respect the results rather than the rules or rationales of prior decisions. In this context, he showed that, except under implausible conditions, a legal system will be path dependent; that is, the state of the law at any time will be a result of the order in which the court has heard disputes. This path dependence, however, will not lead to inconsistency if the legal system observes strict stare decisis.

Next, Kornhauser observed that common law practice incorporates two distinct ways of aggregating judgments of multiple judges: courts may resolve matters on a case-by-case or on an issue-by-issue basis. Kornhauser shows that there is a 'doctrinal paradox' in that these two methods may lead to different outcomes. He shows that the doctrinal paradox is distinct from the Condorcet paradox. Kornhauser and Sager (1993) extend the analysis of the doctrinal paradox in several ways. They observe, for instance, that in actual practice each judge decides how to aggregate the votes of other members on the court and that this may affect the outcome.

Kornhauser (1995) considers the hierarchical structure of courts systems. It explains many of the features of the US judicial system through a simple production model. Kornhauser assumes that judges in the system form a team, in that they all want the same goal, the maximization of the 'number of correct answers subject to its resource constraint'. Then the structure of the production function explains the pattern of precedent observed and the specialization of trial courts to fact finding and appellate courts to review of law. Other features, such as the lack of specialization of courts by subject matter, are not explained by the model.

Miceli and Cosgel (1994) and Rasmusen (1994) have argued that judges' behavior is based on a tradeoff between writing decisions they prefer and the possibility of reversal, either by higher courts or by future judges. O'Hara (1993) analyzes why appellate judges choose to follow precedents in the absence of any formal rule mandating adherence to precedent. She explains this behavior as the result of a repeated game between different appellate judges, each of whom follows the precedents established by his or her colleagues' decisions in order to avoid triggering a 'punishment' phase. In this punishment phase the precedents established by the errant judge's decisions are ignored by his or her colleagues. Shavell (1995) argues that the structure of the appellate process is a low cost method of error correction, since only a subset of cases are examined for error through an appeal.

Bibliography

Alexander, Janet Cooper (1994), 'Judges' Self Interest and Procedural Rules: Comment', **23** *Journal of Legal Studies*, 647–65.

Alpa, Guido, Pulitini, Francesco, Rodota, Stefano and Romani, Franco (1982), *Interpretazione Giuridica e Analisi Economica* (Legal Interpretation and Economic Analysis), Milano: Giuffrè.

Aranson, Peter H. (1986), 'Economic Efficiency and the Common Law: A Critical Survey', in Graf von der Schulenburg, J.-Matthias and Skogh, Göran (eds), *Law and Economics and the Economics of Legal Regulation*, Dordrecht: Kluwer, 51–84.

Aranson, Peter H. (1992), 'The Common Law as Central Economic Planning', **3** *Constitutional Political Economy*, 289–317.

Armitage, Thomas C. (1985), 'Economic Efficiency as a Legal Norm', **7** *Research in Law and Economics*, 1–27.

Ashenfelter, Orley, Eisenberg, Theodore and Schwab, Stewart J. (1995), 'Politics and the Judiciary: The Influence of Judicial Background on Case Outcomes', **24** *Journal of Legal Studies*, 257–81.

Backhaus, Jürgen G. (1989), 'Efficient Statute Law', in Faure, Michael and Van den Bergh, Roger (eds), *Essays in Law and Economics: Corporations, Accident Prevention and Compensation for Losses*, Antwerp: Maklu, 23–32.

Bailey, Martin J. and Rubin, Paul H. (1994), 'A Positive Theory of Legal Change', **14** *International Review of Law and Economics*, 467–77.

Benson, Bruce L. (1990), *The Enterprise of Law: Justice Without the State*, San Francisco: Pacific Research Institute for Public Policy.

Benson, Bruce L. (1992), 'Market Failure versus Government Failure in the Production of Adjudication', in Bowman, Gary, Hakim, Simon and Seidenstat, Paul (eds), *Privatizing the United States Justice System: Police, Adjudication, and Corrections Services from the Private Sector*, Jefferson, NC: McFarland & Co., 203–25.

Benson, Bruce L. (1995), 'An Exploration of the Impact of Modern Arbitration Statutes on the Development of Arbitration in the United States', **11** *Journal of Law, Economics, and Organization*, 479–501.

Benson, Bruce L. (1996), 'Uncertainty, the Race for Property Rights, and Rent Dissipation due to Judicial Changes in Product Liability Tort Law', **8** *Cultural Dynamics*, 333–51.

Benson, Bruce L. and Wollan, Laurin A., Jr (1991), 'Increasing Judicial Responsibility can Reduce Prison Overcrowding', in Tipp, Stacey L. (ed.), *America's Prisons: Opposing Viewpoints*, San Diego, CA: Greenhaven Press, 139–44.

Blume, Lawrence E. and Rubinfeld, Daniel L. (1982), 'The Dynamics of the Legal Process', **11** *Journal of Legal Studies*, 405–20.

Bruce, Christopher J. (1984), 'Testing the Hypothesis of Common Law Efficiency: The Doctrine of Informed Consent', **6** *Research in Law and Economics*, 227–65.

Bruce, Christopher J. (1988), 'The Adjudication of Labor Disputes as a Private Good', **8** *International Review of Law and Economics*, 3–19.

Buchanan, James M. (1978), 'Law and the Invisible Hand', in Siegan, Bernard H. (ed.), *The Interaction of Economics and the Law*, Lexington, MA: Lexington Books.

Carrington, Paul D. (1979), 'Adjudication as a Private Good: A Comment', **8** *Journal of Legal Studies*, 303–17.

Che, Yeon Koo and Yi, Jong Goo (1993), 'The Role of Precedents in Repeated Litigation', **9** *Journal of Law, Economics and Organization*, 399–424.

Christiansen, Gregory B. (1990), 'Law as a Discovery Procedure', **9** *Cato Journal*, 497–530.

Chubb, Larry L. (1989), 'Economic Analysis in the Courts: Limits and Constraints', **64** *Indiana Law Journal*, 769–801.

Clark, Robert C. (1981), 'The Interdisciplinary Study of "Legal Evolution"', **90** *Yale Law Journal*, 1238–74.

Cohen, George M. (1985), 'Posnerian Jurisprudence and Economic Analysis of Law: The View from the Bench', **133** *University of Pennsylvania Law Review*, 1117–66.

Cohen, Mark A. (1991), 'Explaining Judicial Behavior or What's "Unconstitutional" about the Sentencing Commission?', **7** *Journal of Law, Economics, and Organization*, 183–99.

Cohen, Mark A. (1992), 'The Motives of Judges: Empirical Evidence from Antitrust Sentencing', **12** *International Review of Law and Economics*, 13–30.

Cooter, Robert D. (1983), 'The Objectives of Private and Public Judges', **41** *Public Choice*, 107–32.

Cooter, Robert D. (1987), 'Liberty, Efficiency, and Law', **50 (4)** *Law and Contemporary Problems*, 141–63.

Cooter, Robert D. (1990), 'The Structural Approach to Adjudicating Social Norms: Evolution of the Common Law Reconsidered', Working Paper, School of Law, University of California at Berkeley.

Cooter, Robert (1992), 'The Minimax Constitution as Democracy', **12 (2)** *International Review of Law and Economics*, 292–4.

Cooter, Robert D. and Kornhauser, Lewis A. (1980), 'Can Litigation Improve the Law without the Help of Judges?', **9** *Journal of Legal Studies*, 139–63.

Cooter, Robert D., Kornhauser, Lewis A. and Lane, D. (1979), 'Liability Rules, Limited Information, and the Role of Precedent', **10** *Bell Journal of Economics*, 366–73.

Cooter, Robert D. and Rubinfeld, Daniel L. (1989), 'Economic Analysis of Legal Disputes and their Resolution', **27 (3)** *Journal of Economic Literature*, 1067–97.

Cramton, Roger C. (1959), 'The Supreme Court and the Decline of State Power', **2** *Journal of Law and Economics*, 175–89.

Crew, Michael A. and Twight, Charlotte (1990), 'On the Efficiency of Law: A Public Choice Perspective', **66** *Public Choice*, 15–136.

Culp, Jerome M. (1987), 'Judex Economicus', **50 (4)** *Law and Contemporary Problems*, 95–140.

Davis, Otto A. (1979), 'Public and Private Characteristics of a Legal Process: A Comment', **8** *Journal of Legal Studies*, 285–93.

Daynard, Richard A. (1971), 'Use of Social Policy in Judicial Decision-Making', **56** *Cornell Law Review*, 919–50.

De Alessi, Louis (1985), 'Property Rights and the Judiciary', **4** *Cato Journal*, 805–11. Reprinted in Dorn, James A. and Manne, Henry G. (eds) (1987), *Economic Liberties and the Judiciary*, Fairfax, VA: George Mason University Press, 175–81.

Denzau, Arthur (1979), 'Litigation Expenditures as Private Determinants of Judicial Decisions: A Comment', **8** *Journal of Legal Studies*, 295–302.

Dicke, Hugo and Hartung, Hans (1986), 'Externe Kosten von Rechtsvorschriften (External Effects of Legal Rules)', in *Möglichkeiten und Grenzen der ökonomischen Gesetzesanalyse*, Tübingen: J.C.B. Mohr, 123 ff.

Easterbrook, Frank H. (1982), 'Ways of Criticizing the Court', **95** *Harvard Law Review*, 802–32.

Easterbrook, Frank H. (1984), 'The Supreme Court, 1983 Term, Foreword: The Court and the Economic System', **98** *Harvard Law Review*, 4–60.

Easterbrook, Frank H. (1992), 'Some Tasks in Understanding Law through the Lens of Public Choice: General Panel Commentary', **12** *International Review of Law and Economics*, 284–8.

Eisenberg, Melvin Aron (1988), *The Nature of the Common Law*, Cambridge, MA: Harvard University Press.

Ellickson, Robert C. (1989), 'A Hypothesis of Wealth-Maximizing Norms: Evidence from the Whaling Industry', **5** *Journal of Law, Economics, and Organization*, 83–97.

Elliott, E. Donald (1985), 'The Evolutionary Tradition in Jurisprudence', **85** *Columbia Law Review*, 38–94.
Epstein, Richard A. (1980), 'The Static Conception of the Common Law', **9** *Journal of Legal Studies*, 253–75.
Epstein, Richard A. (1982), 'The Social Consequences of Common Law Rules', **95** *Harvard Law Review*, 1717–51.
Epstein, Richard A. (1987), 'Judicial Review: Reckoning on Two Kinds of Error', in Dorn, James A. and Manne, Henry G. (eds), *Economic Liberties and the Judiciary*, Fairfax, VA: George Mason University Press, 39–46.
Fox, Eleanor M. (1986), 'The Politics of Law and Economics in Judicial Decision Making: Antitrust as a Window', **61** *New York University Law Review*, 554–88.
Friedman, David (1979), 'Private Creation and Enforcement of Law: A Historical Case', **8** *Journal of Legal Studies*, 399–415.
Gennaioli, Nicola and Andrei Shleifer (2007), 'The Evolution of Law', **115** *Journal of Political Economy*, 43–68.
Gennaioli, Nicola and Andrei Shleifer (2008), 'Judicial Fact Discretion,' **37** Journal of Legal Studies, 1–35.
Gerhart, Peter M. (1982), 'The Supreme Court and Antitrust Analysis: The (Near) Triumph of the Chicago School', **1982** *Supreme Court Review*, 319–49.
Golbert, J.P. and Lowenstein, Paul (1982), 'The Court and the Marketplace: Who Should Regulate Whom?', **34** *Baylor Law Review*, 39–65.
Goldberg, Victor P. (ed.) (1979), 'Discussion by Seminar Participants', **8** *Journal of Legal Studies*, 323–98.
Goodman, John C. (1979), 'An Economic Theory of the Evolution of the Common Law', **7** *Journal of Legal Studies*, 393–406.
Greenwalt, Kent (1977), 'Policy, Rights and Judicial Decision', **11** *Georgia Law Review*, 991–1053.
Hadfield, Gillian K. (1992a), 'Incomplete Contracts and Statutes: Commentary', **12** *International Review of Law and Economics*, 257–9.
Hadfield, Gillian K. (1992b), 'Biases in the Evolution of Legal Rules,' **80** *Georgetown Law Journal*, 583–616.
Harris, Peter (1985), 'Difficult Cases and the Display of Authority', **1** *Journal of Law, Economics, and Organization*, 209–21.
Hayek, Friedrich A. (1960), *The Constitution of Liberty*, Chicago: University of Chicago Press.
Hayek, Friedrich A. (1973), *Law, Legislation, and Liberty*, **1** *Rules and Order*, Chicago: University of Chicago Press.
Hazard, Geoffrey C., Jr (1979), 'Adjudication as a Private Good: A Comment', **8** *Journal of Legal Studies*, 319–21.
Heiner, Ronald A. (1986), 'Imperfect Decisions and the Law: On the Evolution of Legal Precedent and Rules', **15** *Journal of Legal Studies*, 227–61.
Higgins, Richard S. and Rubin, Paul H. (1980), 'Judicial Discretion', **9** *Journal of Legal Studies*, 129–38.
Hirshleifer, Jack (1982), 'Evolutionary Models in Economics and Law', **4** *Research in Law and Economics*, 1–60.
Holmes, Oliver Wendell (1880), *The Common Law*, Boston, MA: Little Brown.
Hovenkamp, Herbert (1985), 'Evolutionary Models in Jurisprudence,' **64** *Texas Law Review*, 645–85.
Kaplow, Louis (1987), 'Antitrust, Law and Economics, and the Courts', **50 (4)** *Law and Contemporary Problems*, 181–216.
Katz, Avery (1988), 'Judicial Decisionmaking and Litigation Expenditure', **8** *International Review of Law and Economics*, 127–43.
Kennedy, Duncan (1981), 'Cost-Reduction Theory as Legitimation', **90** *Yale Law Journal*, 1275–83.
Kenny, Paul (1982), 'Economic Analysis and Efficiency in the Common Law', in Cranston, Ross and Schick, Anne (eds), *Law and Economics*, Canberra: Australian National University, 42–58.
Kobayashi, Bruce H. and Lott, John R., Jr (1994), 'Judicial Reputation and the Efficiency of the Common Law', mimeo, George Mason University.

Kornhauser, Lewis A. (1980), 'A Guide to the Perplexed Claims of Efficiency in the Law', **8** *Hofstra Law Review*, 591–639.

Kornhauser, Lewis A. (1989a), 'An Economic Perspective of Stare Decisis', **65** *Chicago-Kent Law Review*, 63–92.

Kornhauser, Lewis A. (1989b), 'Response to Macey', **65** *Chicago-Kent Law Review*, 115–22.

Kornhauser, Lewis A. (1992a), 'Modeling Collegial Courts I: Path Dependence', **12** *International Review of Law and Economics*, 169–85.

Kornhauser, Lewis A. (1992b), 'Modeling Collegial Courts. II: Legal Doctrine', **8** *Journal of Law, Economics and Organization*, 441–70.

Kornhauser, Lewis (1995), 'Adjudication by a Resource-Constrained Team: Hierarchy and Precedent in a Judicial System', **68** *Southern California Law Review*, 1605–30.

Kornhauser, Lewis (1996), 'Notes on the Logic of Legal Change', in David Braybrooke (ed.), *Social Rules: Origin, Character, Logic, Change*, Boulder, CO: Westview Press.

Kornhauser, Lewis, Cooter, Robert and Lane, D. (1979), 'Liability Rules, Limited Information, and the Role of Precedent', **10** *Bell Journal of Economics*, 366–81.

Kornhauser, Lewis and Sager, L. (1986), 'Unpacking the Court', **96** *Yale Law Journal*, 82–117.

Kornhauser, Lewis A. and Sager, Lawrence G. (1993), 'The One and the Many: Adjudication in Collegial Courts', **81** *California Law Review*, 1–59.

Kübler, Friedrich (1990), 'Effizienz als Rechtsprinzip – Überlegungen zum rechtspraktischen Gebrauch ökonomischer Argumente (Efficiency as Legal Principle – Considerations for the Legal Practice Use of Economic Arguments)', in Baur, Jürgen F., Hopt, Klaus J. and Mailänder, Peter K. (eds), *Festschrift für Ernst Steindorff*, Berlin: de Gruyter, 687–704.

Landes, William M. (1971), 'An Economic Analysis of the Courts', **14** *Journal of Law and Economics*, 61–107.

Landes, William M. and Posner, Richard A. (1976), 'Legal Precedent: A Theoretical and Empirical Analysis', **19** *Journal of Law and Economics*, 249–307.

Landes, William M. and Posner, Richard A. (1979), 'Adjudication as a Private Good', **8** *Journal of Legal Studies*, 235–84.

Landes, William and Posner, Richard (1980), 'Legal Change, Judicial Behavior, and the Diversity Jurisdiction', **9** *Journal of Legal Studies*, 367–86.

Landes, William and Posner, Richard (1987), *The Economic Structure of Tort Law*, Cambridge, MA: Harvard University Press.

Latin, Howard (1987), 'Legal and Economic Considerations in the Decisions of Judge Breyer', **50 (4)** *Law and Contemporary Problems*, 57–86.

Liebeler, Wesley J. (1985), 'A Property Rights Approach to Judicial Decision Making', **4** *Cato Journal*, 783–804. Reprinted in Dorn, James A. and Manne, Henry G. (eds) (1987), *Economic Liberties and the Judiciary*, Fairfax, VA: George Mason University Press, 153–74.

Liebermann, Yehoshua (1986), 'Economic Efficiency and Making of the Law: The Case of Transaction Costs in Jewish Law', **15** *Journal of Legal Studies*, 387–404.

Linder, Douglas O. (1989), 'Some Doubts Concerning the Selection Hypothesis of George Priest', **37** *University of Kansas Law Review*, 319–47.

Macey, Jonathan R. (1989), 'The Internal and External Costs and Benefits of Stare Decisis', **65** *Chicago-Kent Law Review*, 93–113.

Macey, Jonathan R. (1994), 'Judicial Preferences, Public Choice, and the Rules of Procedure', **23** *Journal of Legal Studies*, 627–46.

Magat, Wesley A. (1987), 'Howard Latin's Analysis of the Legal and Economic Considerations in the Decisions of Judge Breyer', **50** *Law and Contemporary Problems*, 87–93.

McNollgast (1992), 'The Theory of Interpretive Canon and Legislative Behavior: Commentary', **12** *International Review of Law and Economics*, 235–38.

Mendelson, Wallace (1961), 'The Politics of Judicial Supremacy', **4** *Journal of Law and Economics*, 175–85.

Miceli, Thomas J. and Cosgel, Metin M. (1994), 'Reputation and Judicial Decision-Making', **23** *Journal of Economic Behavior and Organization*, 31–51.

Michelman, Frank I. (1978), 'Norms and Normativity in the Economic Theory of Law', **62** *Minnesota Law Review*, 1015–48.

Miller, Geoffrey P. (1989), 'Comment: Some Thoughts on the Equilibrium Hypothesis', **69** *Boston University Law Review*, 561–8.
O'Hara, Erin (1993), 'Social Constraint or Implicit Collusion?: Toward a Game Theoretic Analysis of Stare Decisis', **24** *Seton Hall Law Review*, 736–78.
Parsons, Wes (Student Contribution) (1983), 'The Inefficient Common Law', **92** *Yale Law Journal*, 863–87.
Polinsky, A. Mitchell and Rubinfeld, Daniel L. (1988), 'The Deterrent Effects of Settlements and Trials', **8** *International Review of Law and Economics*, 109–16.
Pollock, Stewart G. (1988), 'Economic Analysis at Work in Judicial Decision-Making', *Annual Survey of American Law*, 133–6.
Posner, Richard A. (1980), 'The Ethical and Political Basis of the Efficiency Norm in Common Law Adjudication', **8** *Hofstra Law Review*, 487–507.
Posner, Richard A. (1981a), 'A Reply to Some Recent Criticisms of the Efficiency Theory of the Common Law', **9** *Hofstra Law Review*, 775–94.
Posner, Richard A. (1981b), 'The Present Situation in Legal Scholarship', **90** *Yale Law Journal*, 1113–30.
Posner, Richard A. (1985), *The Federal Courts: Crisis and Reform*, Cambridge, MA: Harvard University Press.
Posner, Richard A. (1992), *Economic Analysis of Law,* 4th edn, Boston, MA: Little, Brown.
Posner, Richard A. (1993), 'What do Judges Maximize? (The Same Thing Everybody Else Does)', **3** *Supreme Court Economic Review*, 1–41.
Priest, George L. (1977), 'The Common Law Process and the Selection of Efficient Rules', **6** *Journal of Legal Studies*, 65–82.
Priest, George L. (1980), 'Selective Characteristics of Litigation', **9** *Journal of Legal Studies*, 399–421.
Priest, George L. (1981), 'The New Scientism in Legal Scholarship: A Comment on Clark and Posner', **90** *Yale Law Journal*, 1284–95.
Priest, George (1985), 'The Invention of Enterprise Liability: A Critical History of the Intellectual Foundations of Modern Tort Law', **14** *Journal of Legal Studies*, 461–528.
Priest, George L. (1987), 'Measuring Legal Change', **3** *Journal of Law, Economics, and Organization*, 193–225.
Priest, George L. and Klein, Benjamin (1984), 'The Selection of Disputes for Litigation', **13** *Journal of Legal Studies,* 1–55.
Rasmusen, Eric (1994), 'Judicial Legitimacy as a Repeated Game', **10** *Journal of Law, Economics and Organization*, 63–83.
Richter, Rudolf (1987), 'The Efficiency of the Common Law: A New Institutional Economics Perspective: Comment', in Pethig, Rudiger and Schlieper, Ulrich (eds), *Efficiency, Institutions, and Economic Policy: Proceedings of a Workshop Held by the Sonderforschungsbereich 5 at the University of Mannheim*, June 1986, New York: Springer, 123–5.
Rizzo, Mario J. (1979), 'Uncertainty, Subjectivity and the Economic Analysis of Law', in Rizzo, Mario J. (ed.), *Time, Uncertainty and Disequilibrium*, Lexington, MA: Lexington Books, 71–89.
Rizzo, Mario J. (1980a), 'The Mirage of Efficiency', **8** *Hofstra Law Review*, 641–58.
Rizzo, Mario J. (1980b), 'Law Amid Flux: The Economics of Negligence and Strict Liability in Tort', **9** *Journal of Legal Studies*, 291–318.
Rizzo, Mario J. (ed.) (1980c), 'Symposium: Change in the Common Law: Legal and Economic Perspectives. A Symposium Sponsored by The Institute for Humane Studies and the Liberty Fund', **9** *Journal of Legal Studies*, 189–427.
Rizzo, Mario J. (1980d), 'Can There be a Principle of Explanation in Common Law Decisions? A Comment on Priest', **9** *Journal of Legal Studies*, 423–7.
Rizzo, Mario J. (1985), 'Rules versus Cost-Benefit Analysis in the Common Law', **4** *Cato Journal*, 865–84. Reprinted in Dorn, James A. and Manne, Henry G. (eds) (1987), *Economic Liberties and the Judiciary,* Fairfax, VA: George Mason University Press, 1987, 225–44.
Rizzo, Mario J. and Arnold, Frank S. (1987), 'An Economic Framework for Statutory Interpretation', **50** *Law and Contemporary Problems*, 165–80.
Roberts, Neal A. (1980), 'Beaches: The Efficiency of the Common Law and Other Fairy Tales', **28** *UCLA Law Review*, 169–96.

Roe, Mark J. (1996), 'Chaos and Evolution in Law and Economics', **109** *Harvard Law Review*, 641–68.
Romano, Roberta (1992), 'Judicial Choice of Legal Doctrines: Comment', **8** *Journal of Law, Economics and Organization*, 47–58.
Rose-Ackerman, Susan (1987), 'Tullock and the Inefficiency of the Common Law', in Rowley, Charles K. (ed.), *Democracy and Public Choice: Essays in Honor of Gordon Tullock*, Oxford: Blackwell, 181–5.
Rowley, Charles K. (1987), 'Comment: A Public Choice Perspective on Judicial Pragmactivism', in Dorn, James A. and Manne, Henry G. (eds), *Economic Liberties and the Judiciary*, Fairfax, VA: George Mason University Press, 219–24.
Rowley, Charles K. and Brough, Wayne (1987), 'The Efficiency of the Common Law: A New Institutional Economics Perspective', in Pethig, Rudiger and Schlieper, Ulrich (eds), *Efficiency, Institutions, and Economic Policy: Proceedings of a Workshop Held by the Sonderforschungsbereich 5 at the University of Mannheim*, New York: Springer, 103–21.
Rubin, Paul H. (1977), 'Why is the Common Law Efficient?', **6** *Journal of Legal Studies*, 51–63.
Rubin, Paul H. (1980), 'Decision Making and the Efficiency of Law: A Comment on Rizzo', **9** *Journal of Legal Studies*, 319–34.
Rubin, Paul H. (1982), 'Common Law and Statute Law', **11** *Journal of Legal Studies*, 205–23.
Rubin, Paul H. (1983), *Business Firms and the Common Law. The Evolution of Efficient Rules*, New York, Praeger.
Rubin, Paul H. and Bailey, Martin J. (1994), 'The Role of Lawyers in Changing the Law', **23** *Journal of Legal Studies*, 807–31.
Sajó, András (1981), 'A Gazdaság jogi Szabályozásának egy Lehetséges útja (A Possible Way of Legal Regulation of the Economy)', **4** *Jogtudományi Közlöny*, 297–308.
Sajó, András (1987), 'A jog a Gazdaság Szabályozástechnikái Közt (Law as One of the Regulating Means of the Economy)', **3** *Jogtudományi Közlöny*, 126–32.
Samuels, Warren J. and Mercuro, Nicholas (1984), 'Posnerian Law and Economics on the Bench', **4** *International Review of Law and Economics*, 107–30.
Samuels, Warren J. and Mercuro, Nicholas (1986), 'Wealth Maximization and Judicial Decision-Making: The Issues Further Clarified', **6** *International Review of Law and Economics*, 133–7.
Schäfer, Hans-Bernd (1989), 'Allokationseffizienz als Grundprinzip des Zivilrechts (Allocative Efficiency as Basic Principle of Civil Law)', in Ott, Claus and Schäfer, Hans-Bernd (eds), *Allokationseffizienz in der Rechtsordnung*, Berlin: Springer, 1–24.
Scheppele, Kim Lane (1988), *Legal Secrets, Equality and Efficiency in the Common Law*, Chicago: University of Chicago Press.
Schwartz, Edward P. (1992), 'Policy, Precedent, and Power: A Positive Theory of Supreme Court Decision Making', **8** *Journal of Law, Economics and Organization*, 219–52.
Shapiro, Martin (1972), 'Toward a Theory of Stare Decisis', **1** *Journal of Legal Studies*, 125–34.
Shavell, Steven (1995), 'The Appeals Process as a Means of Error Correction', **24** *Journal of Legal Studies*, 379–425.
Shepsle, Kenneth A. (1992), 'Congress is a "They", not an "It": Legislative Intent as Oxymoron', **12** *International Review of Law and Economics*, 239–56.
Simpson, A.W.B. (1979), 'The Horwitz Thesis and the History of Contracts', **46** *University of Chicago Law Review*, 533–601.
Sinder, Janet (1987), 'Economists as Judges: A Selective, Annotated Bibliography', **50 (4)** *Law and Contemporary Problems*, 279–86.
Smith, Steven D. (1984), 'Rhetoric and Rationality in the Law of Negligence', **69** *Minnesota Law Review*, 277–323.
Spiller, Pablo T. and Spitzer, Matthew L. (1992), 'Judicial Choice of Legal Doctrines', **8** *Journal of Law, Economics and Organization*, 8–46.
Spitzer, Matthew L. (1992), 'Jurisprudence and Formal Models', **12** *International Review of Law and Economics*, 295–6.
Sunstein, Cass R. (1992), 'Public Choice, Endogenous Preferences', **12** *International Review of Law and Economics*, 289–91.

Terrebonne, R. Peter (1981), 'A Strictly Evolutionary Model of Common Law', **10** *Journal of Legal Studies*, 397–407.

Tullock, Gordon (1971), *The Logic of the Law*, New York: Basic Books.

Tullock, Gordon (1980), *Trials on Trial: The Pure Theory of Legal Procedure*, New York: Columbia University Press.

Varat, Jonathan D. (1986), 'Review Essay: Economic Ideology and the Federal Judicial Task (Review of The Federal Courts: Crisis and Reform by Richard A. Posner)', **74** *California Law Review*, 649–74.

Veljanovski, Cento G. (1985), 'The Role of Economics in the Common Law', **7** *Research in Law and Economics*, 41–64.

Von Wangenheim, Georg (1993), 'The Evolution of Judge Made Law', **13** *International Review of Law and Economics*, 381–411.

Wald, Patricia M. (1987), 'Limits on the Use of Economic Analysis in Judicial Decisionmaking', **50 (4)** *Law and Contemporary Problems*, 225–44.

Whichard, Willis P. (1987), 'A Common Law Judge's View of the Appropriate Use of Economics in Common Law Adjudication', **50 (4)** *Law and Contemporary Problems*, 253–63.

Williams, Stephen F. (1980), 'The Static Conception of the Common Law: A Comment', **9** *Journal of Legal Studies*, 277–89.

Wilson, James G. (1986), 'Justice Diffused: A Comparison of Edmund Burke's Conservatism with the Views of Five Conservative, Academic Judges', **40** *University of Miami Law Review*, 913–75.

Wittman, Donald (1989), 'Why Democracies Produce Efficient Results', **97** *Journal of Political Economy*, 1395–424.

X (1987), 'Note: Judge Frank H. Easterbrook: A Faithful Adherent of the Law and Economics Approach Advocates by Professor Frank H. Easterbrook', **50 (4)** *Law and Contemporary Problems*, 265–77.

7 Common law and economic efficiency

Todd J. Zywicki and Edward Peter Stringham

1. Introduction

From its inception, a foundational claim of law and economics is that the common law tends to the promotion of economic efficiency (Posner 2007). Much of the traditional law and economics research agenda has been concerned with positive analysis testing the efficiency properties of rules across different common law doctrinal areas. The strength of this claim has been tempered over time, however, as some leading law and economics scholars have argued that the efficiency-enhancing attributes of the common law have weakened over time and that during the 20th century the common law has increasingly produced rules that promote wealth redistribution instead of efficiency. Nonetheless, the application of economics to determine the efficiency-promoting tendencies of various legal rules remains a defining research agenda for law and economics.

Since the articulation of the efficiency of the common law hypothesis, analysts have been concerned with a corollary question: if the common law does tend to efficiency, what is the mechanism or mechanisms that produce that result? The question is especially puzzling in light of the general absence from judicial opinions of any express stated concern with promoting efficiency or any obvious expertise or concern of judges to further efficiency. Here we focus not on the postulated efficiency-enhancing properties of particular legal rules, but rather this corollary question of the common law process itself and whether that process tends to the promotion of efficiency-enhancing rules. The analysis here is structural in nature: we observe the properties of the rule-generating system to determine whether the system's design tends to promote efficiency-enhancing rules (Cooter 1996; Pritchard and Zywicki 1999; Zywicki 2006). Useful prior surveys of some of the literature discussed here can be found in Rubin (2005a), Parisi (2004), Aranson (1986), and Kornhauser (1980).

For purposes of explication, we can conceive of the production of common law rules as the interaction of supply and demand dynamics. Litigants demand judicial decisions by bringing cases for judges to decide. Judges supply legal rules according to their preferences (whatever those may be) as constrained by the set of incentives that they confront. This supply and demand heuristic can help to illuminate the rule-generating properties of the system to assess the mechanisms that produce efficient law. After reviewing the arguments about why the common law may or may not have incentives to be efficient, we conclude with a discussion about why judges may be unable to identify, much less implement, economically efficient legal rules. This set of arguments questions whether efficiency as defined by Kaldor-Hicks efficiency or wealth maximization should be the goal of judges or a legal system.

2. Do Judges Seek Efficient Rules?

Posner's initial foray into a positive explanation for the tendency of the common law to promote efficient rules postulated that this tendency arose from the preferences of common law judges for efficient rules (Posner 1979). These preferences may arise either because judges affirmatively choose to prefer efficiency as a normative value over alternative values (such as wealth redistribution or some measure of social egalitarianism) or alternatively because, even if judges theoretically prefer the pursuit of other normative values, they nonetheless pursue wealth maximization as the most practical goal to accomplish, as if by an implicit process of elimination, where judges find other goals to be unattainable in light of the constraints of the judicial process. (For a discussion and summary of critiques of Posner's early hypothesis, see Zywicki 2003.)

One possible explanation for the preference of judges for economic efficiency as compared to other social values is that utilitarianism is a dominant philosophical preference of judges. Because of the difficulty of measuring utility directly, Posner argues that judges instead seek to maximize economic efficiency, defined as wealth maximization. Under this standard, also referred to as Kaldor-Hicks efficiency, efficiency is attained when the net willingness to pay associated with different outcomes is maximized (Posner 1980a, p.491; 1980b, p.243; 2007). Posner, for example, has argued that during the formative period of the common law, English judges implicitly adopted the utilitarian philosophy of 19th century English liberalism and thus implicitly sought wealth maximization (Posner 1979). To the extent that the common law has deviated from its orientation toward economic efficiency, a common claim, this presumably could be explained by a change in the philosophical orientation of judges during the 20th century toward a heightened focus on redistributive and social engineering goals of the law and away from a traditional concern for utilitarianism and classical liberal values (Priest 1991, 1985, 1987a, 1987b; Tullock 1997). Explaining changes in the orientation of the common law toward or away from efficiency by changes in judicial ideology is highly contestable. First, it assumes that earlier judges were largely moral utilitarians, as opposed to promoting some notion of "justice" or rights (O'Driscoll 1980; Claeys 2010; Cordato 1992), or imposed no systematic moral philosophy on the common law, but simply tried to apply existing precedent to the best of their ability (as implied by Hayek 1978 or Leoni 1991). Moreover, as a theory of preferences or tastes, the theory is difficult to verify as a testable hypothesis. On the other hand, there is a substantial body of literature that finds a relationship between judges' ideology and case outcomes in many areas of the law, which suggests some plausibility to the thesis (see Stearns and Zywicki 2009, chapter 7, for a summary).

Posner has also articulated a weaker version of the argument. Rather than judges professing an affirmative preference for efficiency over other moral values, he suggests that even if judges prefer other values (such as redistribution) to efficiency, they will still be led to promote efficiency because these other values are unattainable as a practical matter because of the limitations of the judicial process. Unlike redistributive goals, which are highly contested as a social matter, there is a broad consensus that efficiency is a desirable social goal, even if it is not the only social goal. Thus, everything else being equal, most people (including judges) prefer rules that result in more rather than less wealth for society. Moreover, judges have limited tools to engage in effective and consistent wealth redistribution: because most common law rules are default rules that parties can alter by contract or relative price adjustments, while judges can alter the distribution between the parties in any given case, they lack the power to engage in systematic wealth redistribution such as a legislature can do through tax, spending, and regulatory powers. Because common law judges "cannot do much . . . to alter the slices of the pie that the various groups in society receive, they might as well concentrate on increasing its size." But this explanation of judicial preferences also runs afoul of the concern about its untestable and potentially tautological nature. Moreover, this theory cannot explain the apparent trend of recent years for the common law to depart in many areas from the promotion of efficiency to the apparent motivation to satisfy other social goals, such as redistribution and the apparent growth in the number of judges dedicated to the promotion of redistributive goals for law (Krier 1974). In short, even if judges are constrained in their ability to engage in systematic wealth redistribution, they nonetheless appear to have increased their desire and efforts to do so, which seems to contradict the hypothesis of pursuing efficiency by default.

3. A Demand-Side Analysis of Common Law Efficiency

In response to the theoretical and empirical imitations of the original "judicial tastes" model of efficiency in the common law, scholars instead proposed various "demand" theories of the evolution of the common law that argue that there will be a tendency toward the promotion of efficient common law rules through an invisible hand process of selective relitigation of judicial precedents. In these models, a tendency toward efficiency will be observed regardless of judicial tastes or preferences for efficiency.

Zywicki (2003) argues that the process of litigation and common law rule production can be conceived of as a demand for judicial rule outputs, just as public choice theorists have modeled the process by which interest groups lobby (or bid) for favorable legislation or regulation (or to avoid unfavorable legislation or regulation). Zywicki argues that, as with standard models of the legislation process (Tullock 1967), parties will invest in the process of legal change in order to procure favorable judicial rules, and that, in equilibrium, parties will be willing to invest up to the expected present value of the stream of economic rents to be generated by the beneficial legal precedent (or to preserve a beneficial precedent) in securing that precedent. Zywicki thus offers a stylized demand function to illustrate the process of legal change in these expected present value terms, where the demand (D) for legal change is a function of two variables: (1) the expected total value of wealth to be transferred by the law in question (V), and (2) the expected durability or longevity of the favorable legal rule to the favored party, in terms of the expected length of time over which the valuable law will produce benefits to the parties (L):

$$D = (VL)$$

where D = demand for a particular legal rule, V = the annual value of the amounts to be transferred, and L = the expected longevity of the law and the number of periods over which wealth will be transferred.

Zywicki thus argues that, where the value of a given rule increases (in terms of the amount of wealth to be transferred per period) or the expected durability of the rule increases (in terms of its protection from being overruled or reversed), parties will be willing to invest greater amounts in litigation. As a corollary to this observation, it follows that parties who are repeat players will be more willing to invest in the promotion of favorable rules than those who are not repeat players. A favorable legal rule can thus be analogized to a sort of capital investment, in which an upfront investment in litigation to gain a favorable rule may be amortized by a subsequent stream of economic rents to the party benefited by that rule.

As with standard public choice analysis of the legislative process, there is a second-order collective action problem that arises in terms of the ability of parties to effectively organize in order to litigate strategically in order to bring about legal change. Thus, even if a group will gain a substantial benefit or incur a substantial cost from a legal rule change, they face the additional problem of organizing in order to bring about the desired rule changes.

Paul Rubin provided a demand-side model of the evolution of efficiency in the common law that is consistent with this model and which he argues tended to the production of efficient common law rules, at least during the formative periods of the common law (Rubin 1977). Rubin argues that at least to some extent the ability of one party or the other to prevail in a given case will be a reflection of the amount of money that they are willing to expend in litigating the case. Higher stakes in any given case will tend to produce larger investments in lawyers and litigation expenses. But the potential for precedent to be created by a case further raises the stakes, as a precedent increases the stakes in future cases as well as the current case. Thus, parties who have a particular stake in precedent, such as repeat players, will be willing to invest more in litigation than those who have lower interests, such as non-repeat players.

Rubin suggests that the evolution of legal rules can thus be divided into three categories depending on whether the litigants are repeat players. When both parties are repeat players then they both have a continuing interest in future precedent and they will both be expected to fully and vigorously litigate actions, such that their investments will essentially cancel out. In such cases, Rubin predicts that we will tend to see a tendency toward efficiency-enhancing rules. When neither party is a repeat player with an interest in precedent beyond the current case, and thus where parties have relatively equal stakes, we would expect to see no systematic bias in the law toward one party or the other and might instead observe either random drift or a slight tendency toward efficient rules. Finally, where one party is a repeat player and the other is not, we would expect to see a tendency for the law to favor the repeat player at the expense of the other party. This may come about either because the repeat player has a greater incentive to litigate certain cases more aggressively or alternatively because the repeat player has an incentive to avoid litigating unfavorable cases that might be expected to produce unfavorable outcomes, such as by settling a case before it results in an unfavorable judgment and precedent.

Rubin argues that this model explains trends in the common law over time. He argues that in the early nineteenth century (and presumably before), rule-making (both common law and statutory) was dominated by individual actors acting independently, rather than by organized special interests acting collectively (Rubin 1982). These interests generally were not repeat players and even if they were, they were unlikely to be consistently found on one side of a dispute. For example, small independent businesses were unlikely systematically to be plaintiffs or defendants in contract, tort, or property cases. Rubin argues that the 19th century brought about the development of large-scale manufacturing enterprises that produced repeat players with systematically biased preferences in favor of liability-limiting legal rules on issues such as nuisance and tort law (such as for workplace accidents). In the latter half of the 20th century, by contrast, a new interest group arose: trial lawyers who had an interest in expanding legal liability rules. Thus, with respect to mass torts and other similar issues, even though injured individuals are not repeat players, the lawyers who represent them often are, and thus are willing to engage in litigation and other activities in order to expand the reach of liability under law (Bailey and Rubin 1994; Rubin and Bailey 1994). Moreover, changes in communications technology and changes in legal procedure both have made it easier for interest groups (such as lawyers) to organize more effectively to promote legal change (Rubin and Bailey 1994), as well as raising the stakes in current and future cases by making it easier to aggregate plaintiffs' claims and launch expensive litigation (Zywicki 2000).

George Priest (1977) offered a complementary story to Rubin's demand-side model. Priest argues that inefficient rules will tend to produce more societal conflict which, because litigation only arises when parties' expectations clash, will lead to more litigation involving those rules than efficient rules. He postulates that even if judges reverse precedents at a stochastic rate, the tendency for inefficient rules to arise more frequently in litigation will lead to them being disproportionately overruled relative to efficient precedents (which are tested less often). This largely random process will thus lead to a tendency for inefficient rules to be tested, and thus corrected, more often than efficient rules. Of course, to the extent that other factors tend to promote efficiency as well (such as a preference by judges or parties for efficient rules), this will amplify the tendency toward efficiency.

Various refinements of these models have been offered over time. Goodman (1978) argued that efficient precedents were worth more to parties who would benefit than inefficient precedents were to their beneficiaries, and thus litigants would be willing to invest greater amounts in the pursuit of efficient precedents than inefficient precedents, producing a tendency toward efficiency. While this assumption may be true (although contestable), Goodman does not consider the potential for collective action problems to undermine the ability of parties to effectively litigate in favor of efficient rules if the benefits are widely dispersed and are received by parties other than the litigating party as discussed below. Combining the tools of economics and evolutionary biology, Terrebonne (1981) presented an evolutionary model of the common law that concludes that, where legal rules are inefficient, both plaintiffs and defendants adopt behavioral strategies that lead to a high rate of litigation, and when rules are efficient, they adopt strategies that lead to low rates of litigation. As a result, when rules are efficient, the evolutionary stable strategy for both plaintiffs and defendants is to avoid litigation and take appropriate care instead and, when rules are inefficient, the evolutionary stable strategy is to not take the mandated care and instead to litigate. This leads, via a Priest mechanism of more frequent litigation of inefficient rules, to the elimination of inefficient rules and the preservation of efficient rules, except in the narrow situation when litigation costs exceed the costs of the inefficient rule to the potential litigant, and thus the inefficient rule is not actually litigated. Landes and Posner (1979) extended the original models by noting that relitigation of precedent might not result only in overturning precedent, but repeated relitigation and reaffirmation of a precedent might actually strengthen and entrench the precedent.

Others have argued that there is no theoretical reason to believe that the common law will tend to the production of either efficient or inefficient rules. Cooter and Kornhauser (1980) argue that invisible hand evolutionary models of efficiency in the common law can provide at best a very weak tendency toward efficiency in the common law, but that the most likely result is an unstable cycle of efficient and inefficient rules and a chronic coexistence of both. They conclude that a strong tendency toward stable efficiency in the common law requires the affirmative commitment of judges. Wangenheim (1993) similarly concludes that cycles of efficiency and inefficiency are more likely than stable efficiency. He argues that judges follow a sort of herd behavior, which leads them to follow one another's opinion, regardless of whether they trend toward or away from efficiency. Thus, he predicts the generations of broad cycles of efficiency and inefficiency as judges follow one another. He does suggest, however, that there may be a systematic tendency toward inefficiency in a dynamic sense that results from the unusually difficult collective action problems faced by innovators, who will have an especially difficult time identifying one another and organizing to have their views heard. Drawing on evolutionary biology and evolutionary game theory, Hirshleifer (1982) argues that evolutionary models provide little reason to believe that there will be any strong tendency toward efficiency in economics or law. He also stresses that a complicating factor in the context of law is the public goods nature of more efficient law, which raises substantial collective action problems in organizing to litigate for more efficient law.

Others have argued that the common law might be predicted to actually exhibit a tendency toward inefficiency. A student comment in the *Yale Law Journal* (Comment 1983) observes that in theory the combination of the tendency of inefficient rules to be litigated more often (as described by Priest), together with the phenomenon described by Landes and Posner that repeated reaffirmation of rules in litigation might entrench inefficient rules, could perversely lead the common law to favor rules that inefficiently lead to more accidents and greater social costs. He argues that these "reckless" rules will be both deeper rooted (because repeatedly reaffirmed), but also more sophisticated and well-developed intellectually; thus they will cast a larger shadow and bear more weight as persuasive authority. Thus reckless principles will gradually displace efficient principles which are less frequently litigated and less developed. Thus, he argues, reckless rules will come to dominate the common law and he further speculates that the growth in legislation displacing the common law in the 20th century might result from a perceived need to correct reckless common law doctrines. Hathaway (2001) similarly argues that the use of *stare decisis* in the common law could lead to lock-in or path dependency in the common law, potentially preserving inefficient precedents (or precedents that are originally efficient but which become inefficient as social conditions change) as much as efficient ones. She argues that judges should be alert to situations where the costs of path dependency are especially high and should relax the binding force of precedent in those situations. Stearns notes that this problem of path dependency gives rise to the problem of strategic litigation as parties seek to engage in "path manipulation" in order to gain favorable precedents (Stearns 1995). He argues that judges use procedural rules such as the standing requirement in order to reduce this threat of strategic path manipulation.

These contrarian theorists thus provide several theoretical arguments as to why the mechanisms of common law adjudication should not lead to the production of efficient rules. On the other hand, these articles do not seem to rebut the central empirical phenomenon to be explained: the apparent tendency of the common law to produce efficient rules over time, even if that tendency is weaker than in prior eras. While some of these authors provide some isolated examples where the phenomena they describe arguably explain inefficient rules, they do not seem to rebut the central claim of common law efficiency that the original generation of scholars sought to explain. Thus, it is not always clear whether they reject the premise that the common law tends toward efficiency or whether they accept the proposition but not the models that have been offered to explain it.

4. A Supply-Side Model of Common Law Efficiency

Todd Zywicki (2003) has supplemented the models developed by Rubin and Priest with a supply-side analysis that explains what he characterizes as the rise and fall of efficiency in the common law. Rather than focusing on judicial preferences, as Posner's original model did, Zywicki instead points to the constraints imposed upon judges. Like the Rubin-Priest demand-side models, Zywicki suggests that the preferences of judges are largely irrelevant to the efficiency of the common law if the demand and supply structure provides meaningful constraints on judges from indulging their preferences. But Zywicki focuses on the incentives of judges rather than litigants and, in particular, traces changes in legal institutions over time that he argues explains the strong tendency toward efficiency in the common law during its classical period and the more recent susceptibility to rent-seeking litigation of the modern era.

In particular, Zywicki focuses on the polycentric legal order that characterized the English legal system during the formative centuries of the English common law system, when England had in many areas a competitive and non-coercive legal order. During the Middle Ages multiple courts with overlapping jurisdictions existed side-by-side throughout England (and Europe generally; see Berman 1983), including: ecclesiastical (church) courts, law merchant courts, local courts, the Chancery Court, and three different common law courts, the King's Bench, the Court of Common Pleas, and the Exchequer Courts. For many legal matters, a litigant could bring her case in several different courts. For instance, church courts had jurisdiction over all matters related to testamentary succession, but, if the deceased owed a debt at the time of his death, this suggested the possibility of jurisdiction in other courts as well.

Judges were paid in part from the litigant filing fees, thus providing competitive incentives respecting the scope of jurisdiction and expansion of judicial dockets. This encouraged judges to compete for litigants. Depending on the institutional context, competition could provoke judges to compete either by offering pro-plaintiff or pro-efficiency law. As Adam Smith (1976, pp. 241–2), writing in the 18th century, observed, the competition of the Middle Ages generally encouraged the production of efficient law:

> The present admirable constitution of the courts of justice in England was, perhaps, originally in a great measure, formed by this emulation, which anciently took place between their respective judges; each judge endeavouring to give, in his own court, the speediest and most effectual remedy, which the law would admit, for every sort of injustice.

Smith also noted that requiring judges to compete for fees motivated them to work harder and more efficiently, thereby removing incentives for judges to shirk or to indulge their personal preferences. Zywicki claims that this judicial competition helped drive the early common law toward efficiency as courts competed to provide the law and procedures most appropriate to parties' needs (see also Rowley 1989). Choice of court was either implicitly or explicitly made ex ante (at the outset of the contract), which would be expected to lead parties to prefer efficient rules that minimized transaction costs (Stringham and Zywicki 2010). Moreover, many of these competing courts (most notably the law merchant and ecclesiastical courts) provided law that was rooted in principles of reciprocity derived from merchant custom or religious belief. Reciprocity tends to promote efficient legal rules as well, as parties who don't know ex ante whether they are likely to be the plaintiff or defendant in a subsequent dispute will tend to favor fair and cost-minimizing rules. Many of these substantive and procedural rules entered the common law and equity courts during the mid-19th century. In fact, many of the doctrines which are often identified as demonstrating the efficiency of the common law, especially contract law, were originally created in these non-common law courts and incorporated into the common law by judges such as Mansfield.

Zywicki further explains that the polycentric legal order in which the common law emerged as a result of judicial competition, spurred in part by the judges' own financial incentives, produced an additional beneficial effect. The regime allowed dissatisfied parties to opt out of inefficient legal regimes and into more efficient ones. For instance, merchants rarely resorted to common law courts, opting instead for law merchant courts, thus limiting the reach of sometimes archaic common law rules in commercial transactions. Zywicki also explains that the coercive element necessary for judicial rent-seeking was largely absent, giving potentially burdened parties an exit option. For parties to successfully rent-seek via litigation it is necessary for beneficiaries of wealth transfers to be able to involuntarily capture the wealth of otherwise unwilling parties to provide the transfer. In this sense, choice among competing courts can be thought of as a radical form of federalism, providing a heightened version of the exit and matching (Tiebout) functions of federalism.

Easy exit provided by a polycentric legal system enabled parties to avoid being the source of involuntary transfers. Authors such as Benson (1990) describe how many of these courts did not involve compulsion, but judgments were enforced by threat of ostracism and reputational sanctions. Zywicki argues that, in the United States, the legal regime of competing courts that prevailed prior to *Erie Railroad v Tompkins* served a similar function of reducing the opportunities for rent-seeking via litigation by enabling out-of-state corporate defendants to avoid the clutches of state legislatures and judges responding to incentives to transfer wealth from out-of-state defendants (often corporations) to in-state plaintiffs. Federal courts were generally considered to be less susceptible to these parochial political forces than state courts. Over time, however, the common law became more monopolized to which Zywicki attributes the subsequent tendency toward inefficient common law rules in the 20th century. The reduced ability of litigants to choose their court or to exit inefficient courts dampened the incentives for judges to be responsive to parties' needs, raised the agency costs associated with judicial decision-making, and increased the incentives and opportunities for rent-seeking litigation. Under a monopolized system, judges have a much greater ability to infuse ideology, such as redistributive goals, into their judicial opinions and to respond to pressures for rent-seeking litigation.

In a recent article, Daniel Klerman has explored some of the historical facts that underlie these conclusions (Klerman 2007). Contrary to the argument of Adam Smith and Zywicki, Klerman argues that inter-jurisdictional competition actually spurred the development of pro-plaintiff rules rather than efficiency-enhancing rules, at least in the common law courts of the King's/Queen's Bench, Common Pleas, and Exchequer. Klerman observes that statutes enacted in 1799 and 1825 shifted judges to a salary-based compensation system, stripping them of their right to collect fees from litigants. Klerman claims that this reform led to a gradual elimination of the pro-plaintiff bias in the common law courts and to the adoption of a variety of pro-defendant rules instead. Although highly illuminating with respect to those areas under his scope, Klerman's analysis is limited just to cases in the Royal courts and ignores others, such as the law merchant, ecclesiastical, and Staple Courts (Stringham and Zywicki 2010). He also notes that the pro-plaintiff bias of the common law court was constrained to some extent by the Chancery, to which disputes could be removed, and which frequently served to restrain some of the rule-bound decision-making of the Royal courts that produced problematic results. Other scholars have raised doubts about the importance and autonomy of the law merchant courts, but as noted by Benson (2010) and Stringham and Zywicki (2010), inferences drawn from these findings are highly overstated.

5. Public Choice Critiques of the Common Law

As the foregoing discussion suggests, interest groups have the potential to influence both the judiciary and legislatures, although the nature of such influence might differ from institution to institution. In his article, "Does Interest Group Theory Justify More Intrusive Judicial Review?", Elhauge (1991) claims that judicial processes are subject to the same sorts of interest-group pressures as are legislatures. In particular, those groups seeking to change the law through litigation (as in Rubin's model of legal evolution) will confront many of the same collective action problems as groups seeking change (or to prevent change) through the legislative process. Discrete well-organized groups, for instance, will tend to be more effective in organizing strategic litigation in much the same manner that they will in organizing for effective lobbying. Well-organized groups may also be able to bring about settlements that prevent "bad" cases from establishing undesirable precedents (Stearns and Zywicki 2009) or seek to influence judicial appointments or elections (Zywicki 2000; Rubin 2005b).

This analysis suggests that it might not be enough for a group to be a repeat player to effect legal change. If the group members are heterogeneous, dispersed, or otherwise difficult to organize, they might be unable to monitor contributions effectively to ensure sufficient resources to bring about doctrinal change. As noted, Paul Rubin and Martin Bailey (1994) have argued that one reason trial lawyers have been effective in changing tort law in recent decades has been their considerable ability to organize and to engage in strategic litigation through organizations such as the American Association for Justice (formerly the Association of Trial Lawyers of America).

Thomas Merrill (1997a, 1997b) has argued that although it is true that interest groups influence both judges and legislatures, the pattern of influence is not identical and, most notably, the demand curve for legal change differs in these two contexts. Merrill claims that, in general, interest groups seeking to lobby the legislature probably have to spend substantially more money to gain influence than do those seeking to effect legal change judicially. Specifically, he claims that the marginal return on each dollar invested in legislative lobbying is likely to decline much more slowly than for investments in litigation. Simply put, politicians always need more money for reelection. In contrast, Merrill claims that the marginal return from increased financial investments in litigation will likely fall off very rapidly. Thus, Merrill argues, even if some groups are likely to outspend in absolute terms, the *relative* difference in terms of the influence is likely to be much smaller in adjudication than in legislative lobbying.

Adam Pritchard and Todd Zywicki (1999) have argued that in addition to the difference in the demand function that Merrill identifies, there might also be a difference in the relevant supply curves of legal change. The authors begin with the public choice premise that legislators generally seek election and reelection. In contrast, the judicial utility function is more elusive. Nonetheless, an important component appears to include the opportunity for judges to infuse their legal policy preferences in the cases that they decide. The authors further claim that judges are likely motivated by the desire for status and prestige. In the case of judges, the authors posit that status is substantially derived from perceptions of practicing lawyers and commentators in the academy and media. Thus, if lawyers and legal commentators have any sort of consistent ideological preferences, judges may tend to issue opinions that reflect those views.

Pritchard and Zywicki also suggest that judges might be biased in the direction of trying to enhance judicial power by absorbing a broad range of social issues under their jurisdictional umbrella. Moreover, the authors note, judges might not be entirely insulated from interest group pressures. Judges are obviously less susceptible than legislatures to influence produced by various forms of financial contribution. Instead, interest groups "appeal to judges' interest in status, power, and ideological voting, rather than pecuniary gains or political support" (Pritchard and Zywicki 1999, p. 499). Interest group tools include strategic litigation, filing amicus briefs in pending cases, or organizing judicial rallies. Those seeking judicial influence also might write scholarly or popular articles. Thus, in earlier eras when judges were drawn from a commercial class of lawyers, they were favorably disposed to business interests. Today, however, judges often reflect intellectual class values and seek the esteem of academics and journalists, which are often hostile toward commercial interests and more interested in social issues. Thus, while legislators are likely to be more responsive to those groups that can offer electoral and financial support, judges might be more receptive to those groups whose expressed views find reflection in the opinions they produce.

One implication of Pritchard and Zywicki's model is that it suggests that different interest groups will have a comparative advantage in pursuing their competing interests in different forums and will rationally allocate their resources and efforts to influence policy accordingly. The analysis thus implicates the demand function of interest group litigants and the supply functions of judges and legislators. Legal change can be produced in several different institutional arenas: most commonly courts and legislatures, as well as regulation by executive or independent agencies. In some situations, however, formal constitutional processes are used (Boudreaux and Pritchard 1993; Crain and Tollison 1979), including initiative, referendum, and other direct democratic means. (For an overview, see Stearns and Zywicki 2009). In some areas of law, "private legislatures" exist, such as the American Law Institute which drafts the various Restatements of the Law, or the National Conference of Commissioners on Uniform State Laws which drafts and revises the Uniform Commercial Code and other uniform laws. State legislatures often then adopt these restatements or uniform codes as binding law (Schwartz and Scott 1995). Pritchard and Zywicki argue that interest groups will allocate their lobbying efforts among these various institutional decision-makers in the manner designed to maximize the marginal return from their lobbying activity, a calculation that implicates the interaction of the demand function of various interest groups on one side and the supply of legal rules by judges, legislators, private legislators, or constitutional processes on the other. Rubin, Curran, and Curran (2001) and Osborne (2002) propose similar models of interest groups deciding whether to use litigation or legislative lobbying as a method for rent-seeking. Crew and Twight (1990) provide a comparative analysis of rent-seeking in the common law and legislative processes.

A related problem is that of forum shopping to advance rent-seeking goals. As noted in the discussion on the polycentric and competing legal systems of the Middle Ages, forum shopping can promote economic efficiency by enabling parties to contract for law that closely matches their expectations, encourages judges to compete for cases by being responsive to the parties' needs, and discourages rent-seeking litigation by enabling those who otherwise would be forced to provide wealth transfers to avoid doing so by exit. This benevolent forum-shopping competition can arise where the parties agree *ex ante* to the body of law that will govern any disputes that arise under the contract, encouraging the parties to agree to be governed by the law that minimizes the transaction costs of entering into and performing the contract (Zywicki 2006). On the other hand, where court choice is unilateral, such as by allowing a plaintiff to file a case without the defendant's implicit or explicit agreement, this can give rise to malign forum shopping, as plaintiffs can involuntarily drag defendants into jurisdictions favorable to the plaintiff. In this situation, judges competing for cases will do so by aggressively promoting pro-plaintiff law in order to attract cases to their jurisdiction (Zywicki 2006; DiIanni 2010; Stringham and Zywicki 2010). Fon and Parisi (2003) provide a similar insight: since plaintiffs decide in which court to file, those with marginal cases will file cases with judges who favor rules that expand liability. This creates a problem of adverse selection, as judges who favor expanded liability will have more cases filed in their court, providing them with more cases on which to imprint their stamp on the law. As a result, those judges will also have greater long-run influence on the path of the law as well. Fon and Parisi observe that this theoretical model of strategic forum shopping is consistent with an observed trend in the law over time toward more expansive liability. In other situations, whether the results of forum shopping will be benign or malign will be ambiguous as an a priori matter, rendering the inquiry empirical in nature (Zywicki 2006).

6. The Common Law as a Rent-Seeking System

Scholars have also explored the implications of public choice theory for evaluating the relative merits of the adversary process within common law systems and the inquisitorial process within civil law systems. Gordon Tullock argues that the adversarial feature of common law adjudication is fundamentally a rent-seeking, or rent-dissipating, system (Tullock 1997, 2005). As applied to a civil lawsuit, for example, Tullock assumes that the parties are exclusively concerned with the distributional consequences determined by which party prevails. Tullock posits that the parties within adversarial systems can increase their likelihood of prevailing by investing additional financial resources, thus transforming the litigation process into something akin to a rent-seeking game. Tullock likens the resulting litigation to an arms race in which each party has an incentive to expend increasing amounts, with the risk that the overall process might dissipate the entire value of the dispute through lawyers' fees and other costs.

Tullock assumes that within each dispute one side's claim is consistent with revealing the truth to the factfinder, while the other side's expenditures primarily obstruct discovery of the truth. He further assumes that the most important normative criterion for comparing the adversarial and inquisitorial adjudicatory processes is the joint minimization of administrative and error costs (i.e. the highest level of accuracy at the lowest possible cost). Tullock contends that expenditures that obstruct the search for truth – or that would not arise but for the other side's tactical obfuscation of the truth – provide no social benefit. Within the inquisitorial system, the judges rather than the parties generally control the expenditure of resources in the quest for truth. Because inquisitorial judges internalize most of the costs of the litigation process, Tullock posits that they therefore lack incentives to expend resources in a manner that obstructs the quest for outcomes consistent with the truth. Tullock concludes that, as compared with the adversarial systems, inquisitorial systems eliminate, or at least significantly reduce, incentives for rent dissipation. From a social perspective, Tullock maintains not only that the adversarial system is more expensive than the inquisitorial system, but also that the increased expense is unjustified given that, as compared with the common law system, the inquisitorial system produces more accurate judgments at lower cost.

Zywicki (2008) has evaluated Tullock's claim of the superiority of the inquisitorial system by noting that the efficacy of a legal system can be evaluated according to two criteria: administrative costs and error costs. The most efficient dispute resolution system can be recognized as that which minimizes these joint costs. Zywicki notes that, in part for the reasons Tullock identifies, the administrative costs of dispute resolution in the adversary system is almost certainly higher than for the inquisitorial system. Thus, to the extent that the higher administrative costs of the adversary system can be justified, it must be on the basis that the error costs associated with the adversary system are sufficiently reduced so as to justify these higher administrative costs. Surveying available experimental and empirical literature, Zywicki finds some scholarly agreement that the adversary system produces more accurate decisions than the inquisitorial system in cases where relevant evidence is difficult or expensive to locate. In more routine cases, there is no noticeable difference in accuracy between the two systems. Finally, Tullock's argument rests in part on the assumption that judges in the inquisitorial system will act efficiently and diligently in pursuing the truth, an assumption that seems untenable in light of the absence of any obvious incentives for judges to engage in an energetic pursuit of the truth. Judges bear the full cost of additional work expended to increase the marginal accuracy of their decisions, while externalizing much of the cost of errors on the parties and the public. Many adverse decisions are not appealed and, among those that are, judges are rarely reversed on appeal (Higgins and Rubin 1980). Moreover, there is an information asymmetry between trial court judges and appellate judges with respect to the facts of any given case. This may suggest substantial agency slack for judges which might permit them to engage in some degree of shirking. Parisi (2002) also compares the dynamics of rent-seeking and rent-dissipation in the adversarial and inquisitorial systems.

Zywicki (2003) argues that, in addition to the ability of parties to exit inefficient jurisdictions, there are various institutional elements of a legal system that can make the system more or less resistant to rent-seeking litigation. In particular, Zywicki notes the double-edged sword nature of a regime of strong *stare decisis* regarding judicial precedent in contrast with a regime of more flexible precedent, such as the view that prevailed in the formative centuries of the common law, where precedents do not become established at once, but rather only when a succession of several independent judges agree upon the proper resolution of the issue. Precedent in this view is treated as inherently persuasive rather than binding, with the degree of persuasiveness growing marginally with each affirmation of agreement. While strict *stare decisis* can theoretically increase the predictability of the law (although this is not clear, as Zywicki 1996 and Leoni 1991 note) and reduce the administrative costs associated with relitigating issues until established as precedent, this comes at the cost of potentially encouraging greater rent-seeking litigation. Where one case establishes a binding precedent with just one favorable decision (as under *stare decisis*), this provides a target for interest groups to shoot at in seeking to establish a favorable precedent. By contrast, where precedent is established only after the independent agreement of several different judges, this opportunity and the incentive to engage in rent-seeking litigation are less likely to be successful, more expensive to establish, and less valuable as a prize, thereby reducing both the incentives to engage in rent-seeking litigation and the value of the prize to be obtained. Zywicki argues that once rent-seeking costs are taken into account, the optimal level of adherence to precedent may be less than the strict rules of *stare decisis*, but instead may be some more moderate form of adherence to precedent similar to that in the earlier ages of the common law.

Oman (2009) argues that another feature of the common law that makes it more resistant to rent-seeking than civil law is that it generally operates (with some exceptions) according to a conceptual framework that applies general abstract categories of doctrine to a wide range of specific subject-matter disputes (such as the doctrines of consideration or negligence), rather than providing different rules and doctrines for specific subject areas (such as fundamentally distinct liability rules for cars versus trains or different standards of negligence for lawyers versus doctors). This requirement of generality and abstractness of principle, Oman argues, makes it more difficult for interest groups to manipulate the path of the law by carving out unique favorable rules for themselves, thereby insulating the common law from rent-seeking to some extent (see also Zywicki 2003). With legislation, or by implication civil law systems, discrete rules for particular categories of goods and services are more common, perhaps exposing those systems to greater rent-seeking pressures.

Luppi and Parisi (2009) offer a similar analysis of precedent and *stare decisis*, describing a tradeoff between the costs of judicial error and legal certainty. Like Zywicki (2003), they implicitly assume that a system of weaker precedent may be more likely to promote correct (or efficient) rules if a decision must be agreed to by several different judges deciding independently before maturing into a binding precedent, as opposed to enabling a single decision to establish the law. In this sense, although they do not expressly develop the argument, both Zywicki and Luppi and Parisi may be implicitly invoking the logic of the Condorcet Jury Theorem by suggesting that the agreement of multiple judges is more likely to generate a correct outcome than just one. Fon, Parisi, and DePoorter (2005) contrast the regime of *stare decisis* under the common law with the weaker form of precedent that prevails in the civil law system that resembles the older common law rule, such as the Louisiana doctrine of *jurisprudence constante* ("settled jurisprudence") or the German concept of "permanent adjudication." As noted by Fon and Parisi (2006), under the doctrine of *jurisprudence constante*, caselaw decisions are persuasive in nature and the force of judicial decisions derives from "a consolidated trend of decisions" on point, not a single decision. Luppi and Parisi (2010) also note that because one source of rent-seeking in Tullock's model of the adversary system is the ability of parties to externalize some of their costs on their rivals, this problem can be mitigated by adopting the British "loser pays" approach that requires the losing party to pay the attorneys' fees and expenses of the prevailing party, thereby forcing parties to internalize a greater share of the costs of meritless litigation.

One implication of Zywicki's model is that strict adherence to *stare decisis* has the potential to increase the stability of both efficient and inefficient precedents, including those that result from rent-seeking litigation. Moreover, stronger *stare decisis* doctrine increases the societal costs of rent-producing precedents by making overruling more difficult, and thus simultaneously increases the value of the "prize" ex ante by increasing the precedent's lifespan. Zywicki contends that to the extent that rent-seeking litigation dynamics approximate those in legislatures in favoring well-organized discrete groups, the result may be to increase the production and maintenance of inefficient precedents relative to efficient precedents. Zywicki posits therefore that interest groups might prefer a more costly common law ex ante that produces more stable rules (and hence longer payouts) ex post and that this is most likely to hold for those groups that are better suited than their competitors to engage in judicial rent-seeking.

Tullock also argues that the civil law system of lawmaking is superior to the common law system. This claim is susceptible to economic testing. If Tullock is correct that the civil law is a better and more efficient system of rule generation than the common law, then countries that have adopted the civil law system should be wealthier than those that have adopted the common law system. Based on this criterion, Tullock's expressed preference for the civil law is difficult to justify. Mahoney (2001), for example, finds that current countries with common law legal origins tend to have more economic freedom and tend to be wealthier. The underlying causal explanation for these observed relationships, whether freedom or legal origins matter most, remains open. Several possible mechanisms about the importance of legal origins have been postulated: first, a "political" theory that points to a general preference for private ordering in the common law versus the civil law; second, an "adaptability" theory that points to the flexibility of the common law system to respond to societal and economic changes more rapidly and sensibly than the civil law (Beck et al. 2003). Others have explained the relationship by pointing to differences in norms and social trust among countries, which may hold some correlation with the development of the common law system (Coffee 2001). Some authors argue that the rights of financial investors are stronger in common law countries, leading to greater levels of investment and economic growth (Levine 1998, Laporta et al. 1997, 1998).

On the other hand, authors such as Rajan and Zingales (2003) and Mussachio (2008) point out that many of the correlations between legal origins and current economic outcomes may be specious. For example, although in today's world well-developed financial markets happen to be in countries with common law origins, this was not always the case. Mussachio (2008, p. 80) concludes, "there is too much variation over time in terms of bond market size, creditor protections, and court enforcement of bond contracts to assume that the adoption of a legal system can constrain future financial development." If one looks to the world's first two successful stock markets in 17th century Amsterdam (not in a common law country) and 18th century London (in a common law country), the fact that government did not enforce most contracts, yet markets developed, indicates that limited government intervention and successful self-policing were far more important than any positive legal action (Stringham 2002, 2003). Such findings lend support to Zywicki's (2003) hypothesis that if one wants to understand the legal order in a country, one must look to more than just government courts.

7. Austrian Critique and Theory of Efficiency in the Common Law

Beginning with Hayek (1978) there has been an alternative model of efficiency in the common law deriving primarily from the Austrian economic theory. Austrian theories of the common law are grounded in significantly different assumptions and methodologies than those that drive the standard neoclassical model of efficiency in the common law (Zywicki and Sanders 2008). In particular, those writing in the Austrian tradition stress the substantial knowledge problems that confront judges seeking to even determine, much less to implement, their preferred vision of an efficient common law rule. In this sense, judges seeking to promote the economic efficiency of the law are in a similar position to a Soviet-style central planner seeking to allocate resources in an efficient manner. Austrians also emphasize the subjective nature of individual cost and choice and the challenges this provides for any judge seeking to ascertain the efficient rule in any scenario. Austrian economists also stress the dynamism and constantly changing nature of the economy and society, thereby highlighting law's primacy in providing a stable rule-bound framework within which people can coordinate their individual plans. Austrian economists also recognize the radical uncertainty that confronts a judge seeking to improve the efficiency of the law by tweaking the details of any particular rule. This fails to take account of the delicate intertwining of any particular rule with the myriad of other rules that comprise the legal system such that an adjustment to any particular rule may have profound implications for other rules within the legal system. For instance, a movement from contributory to comparative negligence may have implications not only for other elements of the tort system (such as liability rules or damages), but also contract law, procedure, and remedies. For Hayek, therefore, the relevant level of analysis and selection for evaluating the law is at the level of the legal *system* or collection of relevant rules rather than at the level of any particular rule studied in isolation (Zywicki and Sanders 2008). Given this complexity, when confronted with an ambiguous case, Hayek argues that the task of the judge should be to try to determine the individual rule that provides the best fit or coherence with the existing overall rule structure, rather than seeking to determine the best rule in isolation, which could disrupt the smooth functioning of the overall rule structure and thereby undermine predictability and coordination.

Hayek (1978) argued that the classical common law was a spontaneous order system in which the doctrines and principles of the law were emergent properties of individual judges deciding individual cases (Leoni (1991) argued that the classical Roman Law had similar spontaneous order properties). Hayek analogized the common law process to the spontaneous order of markets: just as the prices for various goods and services that emerge from the "market" are really the byproduct of millions of individual consumer decisions, he argues that the legal principles that emerged under the classical common law reflected the decentralized decisions of many litigants and judges acting independently over time. Thus, just as no single person sets the price of apples, no single person makes the body of law that comprises contract or tort law, or even the concepts that lie within them, such as consideration, negligence, or strict liability. This decentralized process of lawmaking has two key elements that support a general preference for the common law over centralized legislative rule-making or the quasi-legislative rule-making of a Posnerian judge seeking to maximize social efficiency. First, it draws on the local and decentralized knowledge of many judges and litigants resolving many cases in concrete factual disputes that arise from particular conflicts, rather than a judge essentially articulating a rule for the economy. Second, because rules emerge from the interaction of many judges not just one, there is no central decision-maker for interested parties to capture which reduces the opportunity and incentive for rent-seeking litigation. This combination of the benefits of decentralization and the use of local knowledge and insulation from rent-seeking litigation was reinforced by the common law's traditional reliance on custom as a source of legal principles, which manifests these characteristics in an even more robust manner than the traditional common law itself (Zywicki 2003; Pritchard and Zywicki 1999; Parisi 1995).

Working within this tradition, O'Driscoll (1980), Rizzo (1980b), Aranson (1992), and Zywicki and Sanders (2008) focus on the challenges that a Posnerian judge would confront in seeking even to identify, much less to implement, economically efficient legal rules. To consciously determine the efficient legal rule or allocation of rights in any given case presents challenges very similar to that of a Soviet-style economic central planner, a feat that was shown to be impossible during the so-called Socialist calculation debate of the 1920s. Given the inherent limitations of the litigation process on the ability of judges to acquire and assess the information necessary to determine the efficiency properties of any particular rule, and limits on their ability to acquire feedback necessary to fine-tune their rules, judges will have even greater difficulty in engaging economic planning than a central planning board. Hadfield (1992) makes a similar but more narrowly focused argument, that even if judges sought to improve the operation of the law through conscious effort, they would be unable to do so coherently because the cases that come to trial are a small and non-random sample of all of the interactions in society and the economy that are governed by legal rules. In order to assess the full efficiency implications of any decision, however, judges must possess information about all of the non-litigant parties who are affected by the decision but are not before the court. It is far from obvious how judges could possibly obtain the necessary information to conduct this inquiry. Given this radical ignorance, judges cannot have any reasonable expectation that they will improve the efficiency of the law.

An important difference between Austrian and neoclassical theories of efficiency in the common law is that of the nature of law and legal rules. An ideal Posnerian judge presumably would seek to ascertain the efficient rules and allocation of rights at any given time, using an explicit or implicit cost-benefit analysis of the marginal impacts of alternative rules. As optimal rules governing behavior and use changed, judges presumably would be encouraged to reallocate rights and responsibilities to reflect this new reality. This model implicitly assumes that at any given time the rest of the world is in equilibrium, enabling judges to estimate with confidence the costs and benefits of different allocations of rights and to reallocate those rights when necessary. Legal rules operate within and fine-tune this system of equilibrium relationships.

In the Austrian theory, by contrast, the world is in a state of constant disequilibrium as billions of consumers around the world seek to constantly adjust to millions of constant and simultaneous interactions that disrupt relationships and produce conflict among individuals (Zywicki and Sanders 2008). Equilibrium, Hayek (1981) argues, cannot describe the world in the abstract, but is rather a relationship that describes the ability of individuals to mesh their particular plans at any given time and to form expectations about how parties will perform in the future. In this view, the primary purpose of the law is not to try to impose rules that promote overall efficiency, but instead to provide a stable institutional framework that will enable individuals to plan and coordinate their affairs in a world of constant "flux" (Rizzo 1980a, 1987). Economic efficiency arises as a byproduct of enabling individuals to plan and coordinate their affairs, not by direct design. In this vision of the relationship between law and economics, there is a premium on the legal system providing a set of clear, stable rules that enable people to predict one another's behavior, rather than on judicial tinkering and fine-tuning fine points of law, which might not only be impossible (because of the knowledge problem of central planning) but undesirable and welfare-reducing if such tinkering makes it more difficult for parties to predict the law and conform their behavior to it. As Hayek (1978), Epstein (1980), and Zywicki (1998) observe, clear and stable rules create boundaries for property rights and other legal obligations enable individuals to use their local knowledge and to adapt their behavior to the ever-changing world that surrounds them. Adding a constantly changing legal system – even one animated by a search for more efficient rules – to this chaotic world could create uncertainty and undermine the ability of individuals to coordinate their plans in the face of the constant need for adaptation. For example, once these larger concerns of clarity and stability are considered, strict liability might be more conducive to social coordination and wealth production than a more fine-tuned but complex rule such as negligence, or equitable remedies such as injunctions or specific performance might be more predictable and clear than damages.

A final challenge for a Posnerian judge is dealing with the presence of subjective value. Posner justifies wealth maximization as a desirable normative value as being a proxy for ethical utilitarianism, and one that is arguably more workable in practice than utilitarianism. But wealth maximization is an imperfect proxy at best, and the divergence between the two yardsticks widens if subjective value is taken seriously. Some economists argue that the only reliable evidence of whether an exchange is efficient is the voluntary consent of the parties to the transaction, and the only conceptually permissible framework for assessing social efficiency is Pareto optimality in which all exchanges are carried out (Buchanan 1969, 1981, 1959, 1987, 1982).

The wealth-maximization framework relies on Kaldor-Hicks efficiency, which relies on hypothetical compensation rather than actual agreed-upon compensation as the yardstick for efficiency. If subjective value is important, however, then judges may have no idea how much people value outcomes, so this conceptual move from Pareto optimality to Kaldor-Hicks efficiency is not defensible (Stringham and White 2004; Stringham 2001; Zywicki 1996). Indeed, attempting to measure net willingness to pay at most only makes sense with a given legal system and allocation of rights, and if one changes a legal system, one changes net willingness to pay associated with different outcomes. As Scitovsky (1951) and others (Rizzo 1980b) have pointed out, as one changes the distribution of property rights, the economically "efficient" outcome can change, leading to a non-commensurability of different regimes, even within the same system under two hypothetically different property right allocations. In addition, the assumption that one can assume away the relevance of wealth effects is untenable to the extent that wealth distributions change individual budget constraints (and hence the willingness to pay) and because of the diminishing marginal utility of wealth (Rizzo 1980b).

Instead, in order to promote economic efficiency, it arguably follows that the role of the judges and the law should be to establish a clear, predictable legal framework that encourages consensual exchanges with a minimum of judicial intervention beyond enforcing consensual contracts (Aranson 1990). Acknowledging the presence of subjective value suggests that where possible the law should seek to promote voluntary market-based exchanges, such as by the use of property rules versus liability rules in many situations or a broader use of injunctive remedies that promote subsequent bargaining rather than damages as remedies. De Alessi and Staaf (1991) argue that not only does the presence of subjective cost make determining Kaldor-Hicks efficiency infeasible with any degree of confidence, but it also creates a conflict with Arrow's (1963)

General Possibility Theorem by implicitly assuming that all actors in society share the same preference ordering as the litigants before the court or even the average litigant. Following Buchanan (1954), they argue instead that the virtue of the common law is not in its promotion of Kaldor-Hicks efficiency, but rather that it provides parties with a stable institutional framework of default rules and then parties voluntarily contract around those rules, thereby respecting subjective cost by promoting unanimity and Arrovian values. With respect to non-consensual transactions such as torts, where consensual transactions are not always present, Zywicki (1996) suggests that the protection of subjective value might be furthered by reliance on juries applying their intuitions about the degree of subjective value present in any given case. Inherently, however, non-consensual interactions present challenges for any economic theory of law that seeks to take subjective cost seriously.

References

Aranson, Peter H. 1992. "The Common Law as Central Economic Planning". *Constitutional Political Economy* 3(3): 289–319.

Aranson, Peter H. 1986. "Economic Efficiency and the Common Law: A Critical Survey", in J.-Matthias Graf von der Schulenburg and G. Skogh (eds.), *Law and Economics and the Economics of Regulation*, Boston: Kluwer Academic Publishers, 51–84.

Arrow, Kenneth J. 1963. *Social Choice and Individual Values*. 2nd edition. New York: John Wiley & Sons.

Bailey, Martin J. and Paul H. Rubin. 1994. "A Positive Theory of Legal Change". *International Review of Law and Economics* 14: 467–77.

Beck, Thorsten, Asli Demirgüç-Kunt and Ross Levine. 2003. "Law and Finance: Why does Legal Origin Matter?", *Journal of Comparative Economics* 31: 653–75.

Benson, Bruce. 2010. "The Law Merchant's Story: How Romantic Is It?", in Gralf Calliess and Peer Zumbansen, (eds.), *Law, Economics and Evolutionary Theory*, Cheltenham, UK and Northampton, MA, USA Edward Elgar, 68–87.

Benson, Bruce. 1990. *The Enterprise of Law*. San Francisco: Pacific Research Institute for Public Policy.

Berman, Harold. 1983. *Law and Revolution: The Formation of the Western Legal Tradition*. Cambridge, MA: Harvard University Press.

Boudreaux, Donald J. and A.C. Pritchard. 1993. "Rewriting the Constitution: An Economic Analysis of the Constitutional Amendment Process". *Fordham Law Review* 62(1): 111–62.

Buchanan, James M. 1987. "Rights, Efficiency, and Exchange: The Irrelevance of Transaction Cost". Reprinted in Robert D. Tollison and Viktor J. Vanberg (eds.), *Economics: Between Predictive Science and Moral Philosophy* College Station, TX: Texas A&M University Press, 153–68.

Buchanan, James M. 1982. "Order Defined in the Process of its Emergence". *Literature of Liberty* 5(4): 5–18.

Buchanan, James M. 1981. "Introduction: L.S.E. Cost Theory in Retrospect", in James M. Buchanan and G.F. Thirlby (eds.), *L.S.E. Essays on Cost*. New York: New York University Press.

Buchanan, James M. 1969. *Cost and Choice: An Inquiry in Economic Theory*. Chicago and London: The University of Chicago Press.

Buchanan, James M. 1959. "Positive Economics, Welfare Economics, and Political Economy". *Journal of Law and Economics* 2: 124–38.

Buchanan, James M. 1954. "Social Choice, Democracy, and Free Markets". *Journal of Political Economy* 62: 114–23.

Claeys, Eric R. 2010. "Jefferson Meets Coase: Land-Use Torts, Law and Economics, and Natural Property Rights". *Notre Dame Law Review* 85(4): 101–64.

Coffee, John C., Jr. 2001. "Do Norms Matter? A Cross-Country Evaluation". *University of Pennsylvania Law Review* 149: 2151–77.

Comment. 1983. "The Inefficient Common Law". *Yale Law Journal* 92: 862–87.
Cooter, Robert D. 1996. "Decentralized Law for a Complex Economy: The Structural Approach to Adjudicating the New Law Merchant". *University of Pennsylvania Law Review* 144: 1643–96.
Cooter, Robert and Lewis Kornhauser. 1980. "Can Litigation Improve the Law Without the Help of Judges?" *Journal of Legal Studies* 9: 139–63.
Cordato, Roy E. 1992. *Welfare Economics and Externaltieis in an Open Ended Universe: A Modern Austrian Perspective*. Boston, MA: Kluwer Academic Publishers.
Crain, W. Mark and Robert D. Tollison. 1979. "Constitutional Change in an Interest-Group Perspective". *Journal of Legal Studies* 8(1): 165–76.
Crew, Michael A. and Charlotte Twight. 1990. "On the Efficiency of Law: A Public Choice Perspective". *Public Choice* 66(1): 15–36.
De Alessi, Louis and Robert J. Staaf. 1991. "The Common Law Process: Efficiency or Order?" *Constitutional Political Economy* 2(1): 107–26.
DiIanni, Isaac. 2010. "The Role of Competition in the Market for Adjudication". *Supreme Court Economic Review* 18: 203–31.
Elhauge, Einer R. 1991. "Does Interest Group Theory Justify More Intrusive Judicial Review?" *Yale Law Journal* 101(1): 31–110.
Epstein, Richard A. 1980. "The Static Conception of the Common Law". *Journal of Legal Studies* 9: 253–75.
Fon, Vincy and Francesco Parisi. 2006. "Judicial Precedents in Civil Law Systems: A Dynamic Analysis". *International Review of Law and Economics* 26: 519–35.
Fon, Vincy and Francesco Parisi. 2003. "Litigation and the Evolution of Legal Remedies: A Dynamic Model". *Public Choice* 116: 419–33.
Fon, Vincy, Franceso Parisi, and Ben DePoorter. 2005. "Litigation, Judicial Path-Dependence, and Legal Change". *European Journal of Law and Economics* 20: 43–56.
Goodman, John C. 1978. "An Economic Theory of the Evolution of Common Law". *Journal of Legal Studies* 7: 393–406.
Hadfield, Gillian K. 1992. "Bias in the Evolution of Legal Rules". *Georgetown Law Journal* 80: 583–616.
Hathaway, Oona A. 2001. "Path Dependence in the Law: The Course and Pattern of Legal Change in a Common Law System". *Iowa Law Review* 86: 601–65.
Hayek, F.A. von 1981. "Economics and Knowledge", in James M. Buchanan and G.F. Thirlby (eds). *L.S.E. Essays on Cost*, New York: New York University Press, 31–50.
Hayek, F.A. 1978. *Law, Legislation, and Liberty: Rules and Order*, vol. 1. Chicago, IL: University of Chicago Press.
Higgins, Richard S. and Paul H. Rubin. 1980. "Judicial Discretion". *Journal of Legal Studies* 9: 129–38.
Hirshleifer, Jack. 1982. *Research in Law and Economics: Evolutionary Models in Economics in Law*, 4 Greenwich, CT: JAI Press, 1–60.
Klerman, Daniel. 2007. "Jurisdictional Competition and the Evolution of the Common Law". *University of Chicago Law Review* 74: 1179–226.
Kornhauser, Lewis A. 1980. "A Guide to the Perplexed Claims of Efficiency in the Law". *Hofstra Law Review* 8: 591–639.
Krier, James E. 1974. Book Review. *University of Pennsylvania Law Review* 122: 1664–706.
Landes, William M. and Richard A. Posner. 1979. "Adjudication as a Private Good". *Journal of Legal Studies* 9: 235–84.
La Porta, Rafael, Florencio Lopez-de-Silanes, Andrei Shleifer, and Robert W. Vishny. 1998. "Law and Finance". *Journal of Political Economy* 106: 1113–55.
La Porta, Rafael, Florencio Lopez-de-Silanes, Andrei Shleifer, and Robert W. Vishny. 1997. "Legal Determinants of External Finance". *Journal of Finance* 52: 1131–50.
Leoni, Bruno. 1991. *Freedom and the Law*, 3rd edition. Indianapolis, IN: Liberty Fund.
Levine, Ross. 1998. "The Legal Environment, Banks, and Long-Run Economic Growth". *Journal of Money, Credit and Banking* 30: 596–613.
Luppi, Barbara and Francesco Parisi. 2010. "Litigation and Legal Evolution: Does Procedure Matter?" University of Minnesota Law School, Legal Studies Research Paper Series, Research Paper No. 10–09.

Luppi, Barbara and Francesco Parisi. 2009. "Judicial Creativity and Judicial Errors: An Organizational Perspective". University of Minnesota Law School, Legal Studies Research Paper Series, Research Paper No. 09–09.
Mahoney, Paul G. 2001. "The Common Law and Economic Growth: Hayek Might be Right". *Journal of Legal Studies* 30: 503–25.
Merrill, Thomas W. 1997a. "Does Public Choice Theory Justify Judicial Activism After All?" *Harvard Journal of Law and Public Policy* 21: 219–30.
Merrill, Thomas W. 1997b. "Institutional Choice and Political Faith". *Law and Social Inquiry* 22: 959–98.
Musacchio, Aldo. 2008. "Can Civil Law Countries Get Good Institutions? Lessons from the History of Creditor Rights and Bond Markets in Brazil". *Journal of Economic History* 68(1): 80–108.
O'Driscoll, Gerald P. 1998. "Justice, Efficiency, and the Economic Analysis of Law: A Comment on Fried". *Journal of Legal Studies* 9: 355–66.
Oman, Nathan B. 2009. "A Pragmatic Defense of Contract Law". *Georgetown Law Journal* 98(1): 77–116.
Osborne, Evan. 2002. "What's Yours is Mine: Rent-Seeking and the Common Law". *Public Choice* 111(3/4): 399–415.
Parisi, Francesco. 2004. "The Efficiency of the Common Law Hypothesis", in Charles K. Rowley and Friedrich Schneider (eds.), *Encyclopedia of Public Choice* New York: Kluwer Academic Publishers, 195–8.
Parisi, Francesco. 2002. "Rent-Seeking through Litigation: Adversarial and Inquisitorial Systems Compared". *International Review of Law and Economics* 22(2): 193–216.
Parisi, Francesco. 1995. "Toward a Theory of Spontaneous Law". *Constitutional Political Economy* 6: 211–31.
Posner, Richard A. 2007. *Economic Analysis of Law*, 7th edition, New York: Aspen Publishing.
Posner, Richard A. 1980a. "The Ethical and Political Basis of the Efficiency Norm in Common Law Adjudication". *Hofstra Law Review* 8: 487–507.
Posner, Richard A. 1980b. "The Value of Wealth: A Comment on Dworkin and Kronman". *Journal of Legal Studies* 9: 243–52.
Posner, Richard A. 1979. "Utilitarianism, Economics, and Legal Theory". *Journal of Legal Studies* 8: 103–40.
Priest, George L. 1991. "The Modern Expansion of Tort Liability: Its Sources, its Effects, and its Reform". *Journal of Economic Perspectives* 5(3): 31–50.
Priest, George L. 1987a. "The Current Insurance Crisis and Modern Tort Law". *Yale Law Journal* 96(7): 1521–90.
Priest, George L. 1987b. "Puzzles of the Tort Crisis". *Ohio State Law Journal* 48: 497–502.
Priest, George L. 1985. "The Invention of Enterprise Liability: A Critical History of the Intellectual Foundations of Modern Tort Law". *Journal of Legal Studies* 14(3): 461–527.
Priest, George L. 1977. "The Common Law Process and the Selection of Efficient Rules". *Journal of Legal Studies* 6(1): 65–82.
Pritchard, A.C. and Todd J. Zywicki. 1999. "Finding the Constitution: An Economic Analysis of Tradition's Role in Constitutional Decision-Making". *North Carolina Law Review* 77: 409–521.
Rajan, Raghuram and Luigi Zingales. 2003. "The Great Reversals: The Politics of Financial Development in the 20th Century". *Journal of Financial Economics* 69: 5–50.
Rizzo, Mario J. 1987. "Rules versus Cost-Benefit Analysis in the Common Law", in James A. Dorn and Henry G. Manne (eds.), *Economic Liberties and the Judiciary*. Fairfax, VA: George Mason University Press, 225–44.
Rizzo, Mario J. 1980a. "Law amid Flux: The Economics of Negligence and Strict Liability in Tort". *Journal of Legal Studies* 9: 291–318.
Rizzo, Mario J. 1980b. "The Mirage of Efficiency". *Hofstra Law Review* 8: 641–58.
Rowley, Charles K. 1989. "Common Law in Public Choice Perspective: A Theoretical and Institutional Critique". *Hamline Law Review* 12(2): 355–84.
Rubin, Paul H. 2005a. "Why was the Common Law Efficient?", in Francesco Parisi and Charles H. Rowley (eds.), *The Origins of Law and Economics: Essays by the Founding Fathers*. Cheltenham, UK and Northampton, MA, USA: Edward Elgar Publishing, 383–95.
Rubin, Paul H. 2005b. "Public Choice and Tort Reform". *Public Choice* 124(1): 223–36.
Rubin, Paul H. 1982. "Common Law and Statute Law". *Journal of Legal Studies* 11(2): 205–23.

Rubin, Paul H. 1977. "Why is the Common Law Efficient?" *Journal of Legal Studies* 6: 51–63.
Rubin, Paul H. and Martin J. Bailey. 1994. "The Role of Lawyers in Changing the Law". *Journal of Legal Studies* 23: 807–31.
Rubin, Paul H., Christopher Curran, and John F. Curran. 2001. "Litigation versus Legislation: Forum Shopping by Rent Seekers". *Public Choice* 107(3/4): 295–310.
Schwartz, Alan and Robert E. Scott. 1995. "Political Economy of Private Legislatures". *University of Pennsylvania Law Review* 143: 595–654.
Scitovsky, Tibor. 1951. "The State of Welfare Economics". *American Economic Review* 41: 303–15.
Smith, Adam. 1976. *An Inquiry into the Nature and Causes of the Wealth of Nations*. Edward Cannan, ed. Chicago, IL: University of Chicago Press.
Stearns, Maxwell L. 1995. "Standing Back from the Forest: Justiciability and Social Choice". *California Law Review* 83(6): 1309–414.
Stearns, Maxwell L. and Todd J. Zywicki. 2009. *Public Choice Concepts and Applications in Law*. St Paul, MN: West Publishing.
Stringham, Edward Peter. 2003. "The Extralegal Development of Securities Trading in Seventeenth Century Amsterdam". *Quarterly Review of Economics and Finance*: 43(2): 321–44.
Stringham, Edward Peter. 2002. "The Emergence of the London Stock Exchange as a Self-Policing Club". *Journal of Private Enterprise*: 17(2): 1–19.
Stringham, Edward Peter. 2001. "Kaldor-Hicks Efficiency and the Problem of Central Planning". *Quarterly Journal of Austrian Economics* 4(2): 41–50.
Stringham, Edward Peter, and Mark White. 2004. "Economic Analysis of Tort Law: Austrian and Kantian Perspectives", in Margaret Oppenheimer and Nicholas Mercuro,(eds.), *Law and Economics: Alternative Economic Approaches to Legal and Regulatory Issues*. New York: M.E. Sharpe, 374–92.
Stringham, Edward Peter and Todd J. Zywicki. 2010. "Rivalship and Superior Dispatch: An Analysis of Competing Courts in Medieval and Early Modern England". Working Paper, George Mason University School of Law. May 30.
Terrebonne, R. Peter. 1981. "A Strictly Evolutionary Model of Common Law". *Journal of Legal Studies* 10: 397–407.
Tullock, Gordon. 2005. "Technology: The Anglo-Saxons versus the Rest of the World", in Charles K. Rowley (ed.), *The Selected Works of Gordon Tullock*. Indianapolis: Liberty Fund, 291–308.
Tullock, Gordon. 1997. *The Case against the Common Law*, vol. 1, Blackstone Commentaries Series. Durham, NC: Carolina Academic Press.
Tullock, Gordon. 1967. "The Welfare Cost of Tariffs, Monopoly, and Theft". *Western Economic Journal* 5: 224–32.
Wangenheim, Georg von. 1993. "The Evolution of Judge-Made Law". *International Review of Law and Economics* 13: 381–411.
Zywicki, Todd J. 2008. "Spontaneous Order and the Common Law: Gordon Tullock's Critique". *Public Choice* 135: 35–53.
Zywicki, Todd J. 2006. "Is Forum-Shopping Corrupting America's Bankruptcy Courts?" *Georgetown Law Journal* 94: 1141–95.
Zywicki, Todd J. 2003. "The Rule of Law, Freedom, and Prosperity". *Supreme Court Economic Review*: 10: 1–26.
Zywicki, Todd J. 2000. "Public Choice and Tort Reform". George Mason University School of Law Law & Economics Research Paper No. 00–36 (October 2000).
Zywicki, Todd J. 1998. "Epstein & Polanyi on Simple Rules, Complex Systems, and Decentralization". *Constitutional Political Economy* 9: 143–50.
Zywicki, Todd J. 1996. "A Unanimity-Reinforcing Model of Efficiency in the Common Law: An Institutional Comparison of Common Law and Legislative Solutions to Large-Number Externality Problems". *Case Western Reserve Law Review* 46(4): 961–1031.
Zywicki, Todd J. and Anthony B. Sanders. 2008. "Posner, Hayek, and the Economic Analysis of Law". *Iowa Law Review* 93: 559–604.

8 Bias in the common law

Jef De Mot[*]

1. Introduction

According to the efficiency of the common law hypothesis, common law rules (i.e. judge-made law) attempt to allocate resources efficiently, typically in a Pareto or Kaldor-Hicks efficient way. The common law process enjoys a comparative advantage over legislation in the creation of efficient law. Initially, the arguments in favor of the efficiency hypothesis were based on examination of particular legal doctrines (see Posner, 1973; Ehrlich and Posner, 1974). Because conclusions regarding the efficiency of a particular rule depend on intuition about the relative magnitudes of costs, many economists were uncomfortable with the efficiency argument (see Rubin, 2005a). Some of them have – more in line with the standard method in economics – sought to identify *a process* that would explain Posner's obervation that the common law was efficient. Several models of efficient legal evolution were created (e.g. Rubin, 1977; Priest, 1977). The essence of these models is that inefficient laws will be litigated more frequently than efficient laws because the former impose larger costs on victims. Consequently, inefficient laws will come before the court for re-examination more often, resulting in a trend toward efficiency. Other scholars soon began to critically examine these models. For example, Landes and Posner (1979) argued that litigation might strengthen or weaken a precedent without overturning it completely and showed that this consideration weakens the evolutionary pressures for efficiency. Hirshleifer (1982) showed that the law could come to favor whichever party can most easily organize and mobilize resources for litigation of unfavorable precedents and that this movement would be independent of efficiency. Zywicki (2003) added a "supply side" (i.e. competition between several court systems) to the existing "demand side" (i.e. litigants demanding efficient rules) evolutionary models. He argued that when competition is lacking, only weak or even non-existing tendencies for efficiency will exist.[1] Some of the criticizing models reveal the possibility of

* University of Ghent, Postdoctoral Researcher, Research Foundation – Flanders (FWO).

[1] For extensive reviews of the early evolutionary models and critical analyses of these models, I refer to the chapters by Paul Rubin and Todd Zywicki and Edward Stringham.

an evolutionary bias in the production of legal rules by courts (e.g. Rubin and Bailey, 1994; Bailey and Rubin, 1994; Whitman, 2000; Fon and Parisi, 2003; Fon, Parisi and Depoorter, 2005; Hylton, 2006; Gennaioli and Shleifer, 2007a and 2007b; Miceli, 2009; Depoorter, 2010; Miceli, 2010; Luppi and Parisi, forthcoming). They mainly focus on mechanisms that may bias legal evolution toward expansion or contraction. These models are the center of attention in this chapter. In the following sections, we will look at the different sources of evolutionary bias: the long-term interests of tort lawyers (Section 2), judicial bias (Section 3), judicial path dependence (Section 4), Asymmetric information (Section 5) and the feedback effect of settlements (Section 6).

2. The Long-term Interests of Tort Lawyers

Rubin and Bailey (1994) argue that the shape of tort law, and more specifically modern product liability law, can be explained by the long-term interests of tort lawyers. They provide several reasons why the interests of attorneys in precedent will generally be larger than the interest of manufacturers and insurance companies. The costs of a firm's liability raise the prices of the goods and services the firm sells. Firms only have a transitional interest in changes in liability (unless the transition is so extreme as to bankrupt the firm). Customers also lack an interest. The cost borne by any one customer is usually small, and problems of organizing consumer groups would prevail. Next, while plaintiff's attorneys are potentially interested in all products, a defendant's attorney is interested in only one product and its history. Consequently, a plaintiff's attorney is much more interested in the stated grounds of the decision than is the defendant. Also, there are limits to the ability of firms in different industries to join together to organize for the purpose of litigation, since different types of manufacturers have different interests (see Epstein, 1988). Even for firms within the same industry, successfully organizing may be difficult. When a manufacturer is sued, other manufacturers may be ambivalent about the outcome: a loss will change the legal rule in an unfavorable direction, but it will also harm the reputation of a competitor. Of course there are some issues of interest to all businesses, such as the locus of lawsuits (businesses favor federal rather than state jurisdiction), procedural rules (e.g. limits on class actions), and the amount and form of damages (e.g. all firms may be interested in severely limiting punitive damage payments) (see also Rubin, 2005b). Next, there may be agency problems between businesses and their attorneys. Defense attorneys gain when the law becomes more complex and when liability suits become more likely. Such problems need not exist between plaintiffs' attorneys and their clients. If the sum of expected values of litigation is positive, then the fee may be adjusted so that the client will also prefer litigation. With respect to insurance companies, their interests are mixed at best. In the short run, they may lose from product liability litigation, but, in the long run, they would expect to gain business from a more costly products liability system (see also Viscusi, 1991). Rubin and Bailey argue that tort lawyers are organized in exactly the way one would expect an interest group interested in shaping the law to be organized. The Association of Trial Lawyers of America (ATLA) provides several private goods to its members which are exactly related to its law-changing mission (e.g. information about techniques, data and methods of litigation). The pooling of information that occurs through the auspices of the ATLA both increases the chances of each lawyer winning a particular case and helps create precedents favorable to other lawyers working in the same area (see Rubin, 2005b).

Rubin and Bailey argue that the forces they identify will lead to increased damages payments, reduced consideration given to private agreements, and increased uncertainty and unpredictability in the law. All of these benefit lawyers by increasing the amount of litigation. This can explain the replacement of contract by tort in the context of products liability and other examples of courts' unwillingness to enforce freely agreed on contract terms (e.g. the treatment of "unconscionability"), the weakened use of custom as a defense in cases where there is a contractual relationship between potential injurers and potential victims, the movement toward allowing payments for non-pecuniary losses, the replacement of contributory negligence with comparative negligence and the replacement of the rule of no contribution among joint tortfeasors with a rule of contribution. The authors also discuss some statistical evidence in support of their hypothesis. First, states with more attorneys per capita were likely to adopt comparative negligence sooner, with the number of lawyers leading the decision to adopt (see Curran, 1992). Second, after re-examining some results from Landes and Posner (1987), Rubin and Bailey find that states with more lawyers per capita were likely to reject privity sooner. Third, lawyers have benefited from the legal changes. The Association of Trial Lawyers of America was founded in 1946 and grew considerably in the next decades. Pashigian (1977) found that real earnings of lawyers increased markedly from the middle 1950s and that the increase in demand for lawyers cannot be explained by government regulation. According to Rubin and Bailey, the demand for lawyers will continue to grow as long as plaintiffs' attorneys are successful in continuing to change legal doctrine.

3. Judicial Bias

3.1. Judicial Bias and Plaintiff Case Selection

Fon and Parisi (2003) provide an adverse selection model of legal evolution to explain the gradual expansion of legal remedies, and the resulting tendency of legal systems to grant ever-increasing levels of relief for plaintiffs' claims. The main assumptions of the model are the following. The parties face symmetric stakes and cases are filed whenever the expected value from the case is positive.

Plaintiffs thus decide whether to file suit based on the likelihood of success in a specific court. The expected value of a case depends on the current state of the law. For some marginal cases, which are generally outside the domain of past rules and emerge out of novel or borderline cases, expected value is also affected by the ideological views of the judge. Judges are assumed to have different policy perspectives and different propensities to expand the scope of legal remedies and causes of action. Although judges recognize the binding force of past precedents, their policy views can affect outcomes in new or borderline cases. Litigants form rational estimates of likely decisions. Plaintiffs (and their lawyers) have estimates of judges' biases and take these ideological components into account when evaluating the expected value of their cases. From these assumptions, it follows that conservative and liberal judges are asymmetrically predisposed toward marginal cases. When given an opportunity to do so, all judges, both liberal and conservative, would push the threshold of liability closer to their ideal point. However, liberal judges have a greater opportunity to create pro-plaintiff precedents than conservative judges have to create pro-defendant precedents. Given rational choices by plaintiffs, marginal cases that are not supported by current case law are unlikely to be brought before a conservative court, but may be filed before a liberal court. The marginal cases, once adjudicated, may then affect the future state of the law. Subsequent cases are adjudicated according to new standards set forth by past marginal precedents. The biased flow of precedents in favor of plaintiffs will over time affect the interpretive standards of future judges, liberal or conservative. In the long run, this changes the liability threshold necessary for a plaintiff to obtain judicial relief. Whether the liability threshold will stabilize at a given point depends on whether ideology is absolute or is itself shifting over time. If liberal judges do not become more liberal, at some point no new precedents will be set. If ideology is not absolute, the interpretive standards of liberal judges may become more liberal over time and this will lead to an ongoing monotonic increase of remedial protection in the legal system.

Although Fon and Parisi mainly focus on expansion of legal remedies, they stress that their model is agnostic on the actual direction of legal evolution. Depending on the initial environmental conditions, the adverse selection mechanism may bias legal evolution toward expansion or contraction. In the case where defendants have better control of the jurisdiction, a gradual shrinking of remedial protection may be observed.

Luppi and Parisi (2010) discuss some effects of anonymous judicial decision-making, including the effect of the possibility of adverse selection on the selection of disputes brought for litigation. More anonymous decision-making will thwart adverse case selection and weaken the tendency of legal remedies to expand in number and scope of application. All else equal, adverse case selection should be weaker in civil law jurisdictions than in common law jurisdictions.

The reason is that several decision drafting practices in civil law jurisdictions make it difficult to discern the ideology of individual judges. While signed opinions and concurring and dissenting opinions characterize common law adjudication in appellate and supreme court cases, in most civil law countries panel decisions are generally taken on a simple majority vote and dissenting and concurring opinions are generally not admitted.

3.2. Judicial Bias without Plaintiff Case Selection

Some articles have modeled the impact of judicial bias on legal change, without relying on an adverse selection mechanism. Whitman (2000) provides a model of self-interested decision-making by judges. In the model, an endless succession of cases arise in sequence within a certain area of the law. For each new case, a judge is selected at random from a pool of judges. This judge takes as the relevant precedent the rule announced by the last judge to decide such a case. The current judge must decide whether to follow the precedent or to announce an alternative rule, which will then constitute the precedent faced by the next judge. If a judge chooses to break from precedent, she experiences "preference satisfaction" (see Kuran, 1990) and reaps a reputational gain if the next judge upholds her decision or a reputational loss otherwise. Judges are taken to be expected utility maximizers. There are two rules competing for the attention of judges. A certain proportion of judges favor rule 1, the others favor rule 2. When a substantial majority of judges favor one rule over the other, the division of opinion is said to be low. When the two rules command more or less equal support among judges, there is greater division of opinion. The ratio of the greatest potential gain from breaking precedent to the total utility at stake in the gamble of breaking precedent is treated as a measure of the strength of a judge's activist impulses. Whitman finds that if division of opinion among judges is low relative to the strength of judges' activist tendencies, then the system will converge on a single rule. The reason is that even activist judges who disagree with a precedent will follow the precedent anyway, for fear of rejection by subsequent judges. If division of opinion is high, however, oscillation between the two rules will take place. Whitman also revises his model by adding a third, compromise rule into the mix. No judge considers it the best rule, but all judges consider it better than the alternative. Whitman finds that the legal system is most likely to converge on the compromise rule when opinion is divided. Note that the judges need not explicitly agree to announce only the compromise rule. The compromise emerges out of a decentralized process of judge-by-judge decision-making and does not need an external enforcement mechanism.

Gennaioli and Schleifer (2007a and 2007b) assume that judges are principally efficiency-seeking, but that they may be biased in favor of one or the other side in a dispute. They examine the direction of legal change when judges are bound by precedent (in which case legal change can only occur if judges distinguish their decision from existing precedent) and when judges are not bound by precedent (they can change the law directly by overruling previous decisions). In the first case, judicial bias distorts the law away from efficiency, but it can improve the precision of law in the long run. In the second case, they find that selective litigation cannot counteract the detrimental effect of judicial bias when the bias is strong enough. Miceli (2010) criticizes this result, however, because Gennaioli and Shleifer assume that the divergence of beliefs by litigants about trial is unrelated to the nature of judicial bias. This treatment of the impact of selective litigation does not allow a careful examination of its interaction with judicial bias in determining the direction of legal change.

Miceli (2010) focuses on the interaction between judicial bias and the (Rubin-Priest) selective litigation effect.[2] He considers a unilateral care accident model in which potential injurers and victims interact a fixed number of times over a given time interval and each interaction is a potential accident. Injurers choose a level of care in anticipation of each interaction. There are two rules for allocating liability: strict liability and no liability. Initially, both rules exist within the population of legal rules in some arbitrary proportion. Each potential accident involves just one of these rules. Both parties know with certainty the prevailing rule that applies to their particular interaction. Judges have biases (either pro-plaintiff or pro-defendant) and are imperfectly bound by precedent, so they will occasionally overturn laws based on their preferences. The probability that a judge will overrule a precedent is exogenously determined. Since there are only two rules, overruling means replacing strict liability with no liability and vice versa. Consequently, as time unfolds, the process of litigation will cause the distribution of legal rules to evolve as cases come before the court to be adjudicated. One of Miceli's main goals is to find the ultimate distribution of legal rules (more formally, the steady state equilibrium distribution).[3] Miceli finds that the ultimate proportion of strict liability rules depends on the relative number of trials that arise under each of the two rules, and on the distribution of judicial bias. Logically, a larger fraction of pro-defendant judges leads to a smaller ultimate proportion of strict liability rules. Likewise, a larger relative number of trials under strict liability leads to a smaller ultimate proportion of strict liability rules.[4] Intuitively, the more often a rule comes to trial, the more

---

[2] The analysis in Miceli (2010) builds further on Miceli (2009). That is why we will only discuss the former article.

[3] Note that the equilibrium distribution of rules is a description of the overall state of the legal system at a point in time, as seen by an outsider. The equilibrium does not have any relevance to litigants, who know the particular rule in place in their jurisdiction. The model can best be seen as a way of describing how an aggregate index of the legal system emerges from individual optimizing behavior.

[4] Note that the number of trials may be larger or smaller under strict liability compared to no liability. Strict liability leads to fewer accidents, but results in a higher probability of trial given an accident (since strict liability makes trials more valuable).

chances it has to be overturned by a judge and replaced by another rule. The strength of precedent affects the rate of legal change (how long it takes to reach the steady state), but not the long-run distribution of legal rules. Only in some special cases will the law converge to a single rule (to strict liability when all judges are pro-plaintiff and to no liability when all judges are pro-defendant). Generally, the common law will embody multiple rules, reflecting the biases of judges and the selection of cases for trial.

4. Judicial Path Dependence

Fon, Parisi and Depoorter (2005) examine the effect of judicial path dependence on the consolidation and contraction of liability rules and legal remedies. They highlight the importance of an often overlooked condition for the emergence of a relevant legal dispute: cases that may lead to litigation must have a positive expected net return. This condition may create a bias in the evolution of case law. This result does not, in contrast to the one in Fon and Parisi (2003), rest on judges' ideological decision-making but complements the results reached in the earlier literature. The authors use the following assumptions. First, a judge does not consider himself bound by a single decision in a single previous instance, but considerable authoritative force stems from a consolidated trend of decisions on a certain point (*jurisprudence constante*; see e.g. Lambert and Wasserman, 1929; Dennis, 1993; Dainow 1974; MacCormick and Summers, 1997). Consequently, if the rate of positive judgments with respect to some new legal issue or interpretation of existing causes of action falls above a critical institutionally determined threshold, the recognition of such legal claims in future disputes will be facilitated by the presence of legal authority. Positive precedents are assumed to have equal weight with negative precedents. Second, potential litigants form rational estimates of the probability of success in litigation and take them into account when evaluating the expected value of their cases. The expectations of the parties are unbiased, but have some margin of error (which explains why some disputes are litigated). Third, the plaintiff obtains a judicial award (W) when he wins in court and suffers a prejudice (L) in case of a verdict in favor of the defendant. The prejudice can be seen as an immediate cost imposed on plaintiffs or any other liability imposed by the court in case of unsuccessful action by court sanctions or defendants' counterclaims, or as the net present value of the loss from litigation in similar cases in the future (as in Rubin, 1977). Plaintiffs also face direct litigation costs (C). Fourth, plaintiffs are rational in deciding whether to pursue litigation. Thus, the expected net judicial award should be positive and should exceed the settlement amount offered by the defendant. Based on these assumptions, the process of legal evolution can be described as follows. With relatively high win-loss ratios (W/L), cases can be rationally filed even when the probability of success is small. Consequently, a large number of negative precedents may be produced. When the percentage of positive precedents falls below the level of support that the legal system considers necessary before widespread judicial recognition occurs, an initial wave of filing may be followed by a gradual implosion. Conversely, a small fraction of early favorable decisions could lead to wider acceptance and eventually be consolidated into a binding doctrine. It's easy to see that an increase in the win-loss ratio and a decrease in litigation costs, given a fixed win-loss ratio, increase the scope for gradual contraction of remedies, since they render smaller probability cases worthy of pursuit. A change in the institutional weight of past precedents may have a substantial impact on the stability of remedies and on the direction of the process of legal evolution. For example, an increase in the level of case consistency required for an emerging jurisprudential trend to become binding case law may reduce the likelihood of gradual consolidation and undermine conditions for legal stability.

Building further on this framework, Luppi and Parisi (forthcoming) study the effect of the American and the English rule of cost allocation on the path of evolution of judge-made law. Under the American rule, each party is responsible for paying his own litigation costs. Under the English rule, the losing party pays (at least some) of the legal expenses of his winning counterpart. Since the American and the English rule affect the typology of cases filed for litigation, they will have different effects on legal evolution. Under the American rule, some cases with small probability of success are filed, although they would not be filed under the English rule. The reason is that the American rule allows losing plaintiffs to impose an uncompensated externality on the defendant. Over time, these low probability cases may result in the accumulation of negative precedent and lead to a decreased likelihood of success for similar cases in the future. This can generate bubbles of litigation and the possibility of contractionary trends under the American rule that would not be observed under the English rule. Conversely, some low-stake cases with a higher probability of success will be filed under the English rule, but not under the American rule. The filing and adjudication of these cases will expedite the consolidation of judge-made rules (when the higher probability of success hinges upon a question of law). The higher probability of success means that a larger flow of positive precedents will be generated, with a resulting path dependence in the evolution of case law.

5. Asymmetric Information

Hylton (2006) provides a general model that includes both the Priest-Klein model (see Priest and Klein, 1984) and asymmetric information models (e.g. Bebchuk, 1984)[5] as special cases. His model shows that an *apparent* bias in the legal standard can occur and trends can develop favoring the better informed

[5] To simplify the analysis, Hylton (2006) dispenses with modeling strategic behavior.

litigant (i.e. the litigant who makes a superior prediction of the case outcome) whose case is also meritorious. The model points out that the direction of the law is influenced by the "litigation likelihood ratio" of innocent to guilty litigants. In the Priest-Klein case, a challenge (of a practice as negligent) is most likely to go to judgment if the standard's application to the particular practice is highly uncertain. Given that the rational components of the litigant's predictions are the same, the plaintiff and the defendant appear equally likely to win and the litigation likelihood ratio is thus equal to one. Consequently, the law is equally likely to move in a direction favoring plaintiffs as it is to move in a direction favoring defendants (see also Priest, 1980). In cases involving asymmetric information, the relative frequency of litigation favors the party who is informed and has the strongest case. The reason is that informed and non-meritorious parties (e.g. guilty defendants) tend to settle, which leaves a relatively large share of informed and meritorious litigants in the pool of cases litigated all the way to judgment. In the asymmetric information setting, existing legal rules are thus shaped by the information provided by innocent litigants in court. To make it more concrete, Hylton considers the example of a medical malpractice claim. Suppose the doctor is far better informed than the plaintiff as to the doctor's potential compliance with the legal standard (negligence). A priori, the negligence standard is somewhat ambiguous. The model implies that, over time, the negligence standard in medical malpractice is infused disproportionately by the information provided by innocent doctors. The case law will be "informationally biased": it tends largely to identify specific types of non-negligent conduct.

Hylton describes his model as one of "short-run evolution" because it focuses on short-run changes in the information content of the legal standard. However, the informational bias could lead to "rule evolution" over time, as the information embodied in legal rules alters the nature of the rule itself. Returning to the medical malpractice example, negligence determinations are made predominantly by referring to the custom of the profession. The emergence and resilience of the custom rule may be because the case law, summing up so many specific types of conduct deemed to be non-negligent, has generated the custom rule to supplant the (relatively ambiguous) negligence test.

The information biasing that occurs in Hylton's model seems consistent with the common law efficiency hypothesis: the party in a legal dispute who is likely to be in the best position to improve the efficiency of a legal rule is the party that is both informed and meritorious. However, as Hylton explains, the model does not suggest an unambiguous trend toward efficient legal rules.

6. The Feedback Effect of Civil Settlements

Depoorter (2010) highlights the influence that civil settlements have on legal change when (1) settlement outcomes do not simply reflect the expected outcome at trial and (2) information on settlements is not confined to the parties involved in the settlement. Regarding the first condition, if settlement outcomes simply reflect the expected outcome of trial, then settlements are not relevant as a source of law. However, it is now widely understood that various factors unrelated to the substantive merits of a legal dispute often influence negotiated outcomes (e.g. Mnookin and Kornhauser, 1979). These non-legal factors include the ability to bear litigation costs, diverse attitudes toward risk, asymmetric information, the principal–agent relationship between an attorney and his or her client, cognitive limitations and a party's sensitivity to the negative public attention that a lawsuit generates. Such factors may cause the terms of private settlement agreements to be below, but also above, legally available awards. Consequently, settlement trends may provide remarkable departures from the conventional expectation of the available legal remedies. Regarding the second condition, Depoorter argues that despite the widespread use of non-disclosure agreements, information on settlements is available to those legal professionals for whom such information is most valuable. Information on settlements is distributed through various channels, reaching actors both inside and outside legal communities. The channels include specialized reporters, professional interest organizations, mass media coverage and the oral culture in legal communities. An incentive analysis of the parties involved leads Depoorter to conclude that information on novel settlements featuring high awards and novel remedies is especially widely distributed. For example, special interest groups focus on extravagant settlements that are most likely to induce legislative action, media reports highlight spectacular tort awards and professional organizations bring attention to novel settlements that are strategically important to lawyers.

In view of these observations, Depoorter argues that novel civil settlements have a feedback effect on the path of the law. First, individual settlement concessions make it more difficult for similarly situated defendants to deflect forthcoming claims. Ambitious trial lawyers will use innovative settlements as benchmarks, making plaintiffs in future cases more reluctant to accept settlements below what others have agreed to in prior, analogous cases. Second, settlements may frame the normative outlook on particular claims, due to their non-coercive nature. A novel legal claim is less likely to be perceived as outrageous if such a claim has been gratified by a prior concession in a settlement agreement. Judges may interpret settlement precedents as expressive statements regarding the appropriateness of compensation. A defendant who is unwilling to settle when the settlement proposal is comparable to concessions made by other defendants in similar cases risks receiving little sympathy from a judge or jury in subsequent proceedings. Prior settlement concessions may thus create sustained pressure towards higher awards and novel remedies, resulting in a gradual expansion of the legal system. Depoorter stresses, however, that in some instances, defendants might be able to drive down legally available awards over time. For example, in concentrated industries where tort settlements are handled by a few select lawyers or defense firms, we can expect that selective use will be made of information on settlements that are below the going rate at trial. The feedback effect does not work to the exclusive benefit of claimants and trial lawyers.

7. Conclusion

The law and economics literature has provided several reasons why judge-made law may become biased over time: the long-term interests of tort lawyers, judicial bias (with or without plaintiff case selection), judicial path dependence, asymmetric information and the feedback effect of settlement. Most of this literature is quite recent. There is still room for exponential growth in this field of academic research. Future studies could use empirical data to validate the predictions of the various models and to discover their relative importance. Theoretical extensions could examine the effect of a combination of adverse selection and asymmetric stakes, could study the interaction between ideological judicial intervention and path dependence in judicial action, could analyze the effect of complex doctrines of stare decisis and percolation theories, could examine in greater detail the influence of short-term information biasing on the long-term pressure toward inefficient rules when some parties are better able to devote resources to litigate in favor of their preferred rules etc.

Bibliography

Bailey, M. and Rubin, P. (1994). "A Positive Theory of Legal Change". *International Review of Law and Economics* 14(4): 467–77.

Bebchuk, L.A. (1984), "Litigatation and Settlement under Imperfect Information". *Rand Journal of Economics* 15(3): 404–15.

Cooter, R. and Kornhauser, L. (1980). "Can Litigation Improve the Law without the Help of Judges?" *Journal of Legal Studies* 9(1): 139–63.

Curran, C. (1992). "The Spread of Comparative Negligence in the United States". *International Review of Law and Economics* 12: 317–32.

Dainow, Joseph (ed.) (1974), *The Role of Judicial Decisions and Doctrine in Civil Law and Mixed Jurisdictions*, Baton Rouge, LA: LSU Press.

Dennis, James L. (1993). "The John Tucker, Jr. Lecture in Civil Law: Interpretation and Application of the Civil Code and the Evaluation of Judicial Precedent". *Louisiana Law Review* 54: 1–18.

Depoorter, Ben W.F. (2010). "Law in the Shadow of Bargaining: The Feedback Effect of Civil Settlements". *Cornell Law Review* 95: 957–87.

Ehrlich, I. and Posner, R.A. (1974). "An Economic Analysis of Legal Rulemaking". *Journal of Legal Studies* 3: 257–86.

Epstein, Richard A. (1988) "The Political Economy of Product Liability Reform". *American Economic Review* 78: 311–15.

Fon, V. and Parisi, F. (2003). "Litigation and the Evolution of Legal Remedies: A Dynamic Model". *Public Choice* 116(3–4): 419–33.

Fon, V., F. Parisi and B. Depoorter (2005). "Litigation, Judicial Path Dependence, and Legal Change". *European Journal of Law and Economics* 20: 43–56.

Gennaioli, N. and A. Shleifer (2007a). "The Evolution of the Common Law". *Journal of Political Economy* 115: 43–68.

Gennaioli, N. and A. Shleifer (2007b). "Overruling and the Instability of Law". *Journal of Comparative Economics* 35: 309–28.

Goodman, J. (1979). "An Economic Theory of the Evolution of the Common Law". *Journal of Legal Studies* 7(2): 393–406.
Hadfield, G. (1992). "Biases in the Evolution of Legal Rules". *Georgetown Law Journal* 80: 583–616.
Hirshleifer, J. (1982). "Evolutionary Models in Economics and Law", in P. Rubin and R. Zerbe (eds.), *Research in Law and Economics*, Greenwich, CT: JAI Press.
Hylton, K. (2006). "Information, Litigation, and Common Law Evolution". *American Law and Economics Review* 8: 33–61.
Kuran, T. (1990). "Private and Public Preferences". *Economics and Philosophy* 6: 1–26.
Lambert, E. and M.J. Wasserman (1929). "The Case Method in Canada and the Possibilities of its Adaptation to the Civil Law". *Yale Law Journal* 39:1–21.
Landes, William M. and Richard A. Posner (1979). "Adjudication as a Private Good". *Journal of Legal Studies* 8: 235–84.
Landes, William M. and Richard A. Posner (1987). *The Economic Structure of Tort Law*. Cambridge, MA: Harvard University Press.
Luppi, B. and F. Parisi (2010). "Judicial Creativity and Judicial Errors: An Organizational Perspective". *Journal of Institutional Economics* 6: 91–98.
Luppi, B. and F. Parisi (forthcoming). "Litigation and Legal Evolution: Does Procedure Matter?" *Public Choice*.
MacCormick, Neil D. and Robert S. Summers (eds) (1997). *Interpreting Precedent*. Aldershot: Ashgate Publishing.
Miceli, T. (2009). "Legal Change: Selective Litigation, Judicial Bias, and Precedent". *Journal of Legal Studies* 38: 157–68.
Miceli, T. (2010). "Legal Change and the Social Value of Lawsuits". *International Review of Law and Economics* 30: 203–8.
Mnookin, Robert H. and L. Kornhauser (1979). "Bargaining in the Shadow of the Law: The Case of Divorce". *Yale Law Journal* 88: 950–97.
Pashigian, B.P. (1977). "The Market for Lawyers: The Determinants of the Demand for and Supply of Lawyers". *Journal of Law and Economics* 20: 53–86.
Posner, R. (1973). *Economic Analysis of Law*, 1st edition. Boston: Little, Brown.
Priest, G. (1977). "The Common Law Process and the Selection of Efficient Rules". *Journal of Legal Studies* 6(1): 65–82.
Priest, G. (1980). "Selective Characteristics of Litigation". *Journal of Legal Studies* 9: 399–421.
Priest, G. and Klein, B. (1984). "The Selection of Disputes for Litigation". *Journal of Legal Studies* 13: 1–55.
Rubin, P. (1977). "Why is the Common Law Efficient?" *Journal of Legal Studies* 6(1): 51–63.
Rubin, P. (2005a). "Micro and Macro Legal Efficiency: Supply and Demand". *Supreme Court Economic Review* 13: 19–34.
Rubin, P. (2005b). "Public Choice and Tort Reform". *Public Choice* 124 (1): 223–36.
Rubin, P. and Bailey, M. (1994). "The Role of Lawyers in Changing the Law". *Journal of Legal Studies* 23(2): 807–31.
Terrebonne, R. (1981). "A Strictly Evolutionary Model of Common Law". *Journal of Legal Studies* 10(2): 397–408.
Tullock, G. (1997). *The Case against the Common Law*. Durham, NC: Carolina Academic Press.
Viscusi, W. Kip (1991). "The Dimensions of the Product Liability Crisis". *Journal of Legal Studies* 20(1): 147–77.
Whitman, D. (2000). "Evolution of the Common Law and the Emergence of Compromise". *Journal of Legal Studies* 29: 753–81.
Zywicki, T. (2003). "The Rise and Fall of Efficiency in the Common Law: A Supply-Side Analysis". *Northwestern Law Review* 97(4): 1551–63.

9 Legal traditions and economic performance: theory and evidence

Carmine Guerriero[*]

> A legal tradition . . . is not a set of rules of law . . . rather it is a set of deeply rooted, historically conditioned attitudes about . . . the proper organization and operation of a legal system. The legal tradition relates the legal system to the culture of which it is a partial expression. (Merryman, 1969, p.2)

1. Introduction: A Primer on Legal Traditions

The law and the economy are profoundly influenced, in much of the world, by either the civil or the common law legal tradition. A legal tradition or origin is a bundle of well-defined institutions governing either the creation of the law or the procedural style of dispute adjudication, and sharing a common "historical background, [a common] characteristic mode of thought in legal matters [and a common] ideology" (Zweigert and Kötz, 1998, p.68). Common law originated in thirteenth century England, and has been transplanted through colonization to England's ex-colonies.[1] Civil law has its roots in Roman law, and has been imported through the Napoleonic codes to Italy, Belgium, the Netherlands, Spain and Portugal. These last four powers, along with France, spread it to the Near East, Latin America, Northern Africa and Indochina. Structurally the two traditions operate in different ways: while common law accords a key role to precedents and allows more procedural discretion to lower adjudicating courts, civil law relies on legal codes and bright-line adjudication rules (Zweigert and Kötz, 1998).

Building on the wide differences between the French civil law and the English common law,[2] Rafael La Porta, Florencio Lopez-de-Silanes, Andrei Shleifer, and Robert Vishny (or LLSV) proposed, in two influential papers (LLSV, 1997 and 1998), the idea that the exogenous transplantation process brought not only

* I am grateful to Toke Aidt, Giuseppe Dari-Mattiacci, and Francesco Parisi for valuable discussions on earlier drafts.

1 These are the United States, Canada, Australia, and many countries in Africa and Asia.

2 While the Austrian and Russian empires designed legal systems that were quite similar to the French, Germany, Switzerland and the Scandinavian countries embraced judge-made law along with bright-line adjudication rules (David et al., 1995). However, this variation is of little relevance because Scandinavian countries did not have colonies and Germany had a strong influence only on China, Japan, Korea and Taiwan.

specific laws and regulations, but also a more "general style of the legal system", as well as human capital from the mother-country.[3] Consequently, even if the original transplanted laws adapted to local circumstances and to technological progress, the basic legal institutions, with their ideological content and their impact on the judiciary, remained unaltered, continuing to shape the quality of the new laws. Accordingly, the "legal origins" movement has provided evidence suggesting that, compared to the countries to which the French civil law was originally transplanted, those that initially received common law show:

> (a) better investor protection, which in turn is associated with improved financial development . . . , (b) lighter government ownership and regulation, which are in turn associated with less corruption, better functioning labor markets, and smaller unofficial economies, and (c) less formalized and more independent judicial systems, which are in turn associated with more secure property rights and better contract enforcement. (La Porta, Lopez-de-Silanes and Shleifer (or LLS), 2008, p. 298)

Yet, increasingly, recent legal studies have criticized the "legal origins" assumption that transplanted legal infrastructures remain unchanged over time, noticing, in the first place, the growing importance of legislation in common law countries (Roe, 2004 and 2006). Inspired by this crucial observation, Guerriero (2010) has recorded: (1) the law-making institution in place at independence and in 2000 in 156 "transplanted" countries, i.e. countries that received their initial legal order externally; (2) the four most relevant adjudication institutions in place in 98 of these 156 countries at the same points in time.[4] Contrary to the "legal origins" hypothesis, 26 countries have reformed their law-making institution and 91 their law-making and/or at least one of their adjudication procedures.[5] This pattern casts two fundamental doubts on the "legal origins" approach. First, how can we give a causal interpretation to the impact of institutions which were not even in place? Second, even if we take into account the observed reforms, how can we defend the exogeneity assumption if the evolution of legal systems is driven by primitive forces that also affect the economic performances we want to explain? Before discussing these points at length, along with the other challenges to the "legal origins" theory in Section 4, I will summarize the theoretical works comparing civil and common law in

---

[3] Ethiopia, Japan and Thailand voluntarily chose their legal order with the intention of modernizing their economy (David et al., 1995): excluding these countries does not affect the gist of the present discussion.

[4] The adjudication rules distinguishing the French civil law from common law are: (1) an extensive supreme court review of lower courts' decisions; (2) a judgment based on law and not also on equity; (3) inquisitorial dispute resolution; (4) the requirement of written evidence (see Merryman, 1969; Zweigert and Kötz, 1998).

[5] Of the 145 countries common to LLS (2008), 26 changed their law-making institution and 88 at least one rule.

Section 2. Also, in Section 3, I will review the conclusions of those empirical papers that have looked at the effect of the initially transplanted legal tradition – that is, legal origin. Finally, in Section 5, I will argue that future studies should carefully consider the evolution of legal institutions.

2. The Putative Primacy of Common Law: Theory

Many academics have been using the diversity of the rules sustaining the two traditions and the historical narrative about their origins to put forward two grounds for the alleged superiority of common law: (1) historical events in England and in France have built into the common law a stronger emphasis on the independence of the judiciary in resolving private disputes and a deeper respect for private ordering; (2) judge-made law makes common law more adaptable to the contracting needs of the economy. I will first illustrate the strengths and weaknesses of these two points and, then, discuss a new synthetic theory.

2.1 A Historical Common Law Emphasis on Private Ordering?

Several legal historians, including Dawson (1960) and Berman (1983), make sense of the divergence between French and English law through the following interpretation of the medieval history of the two countries. In the twelfth century, the French crown, struggling to control the Ile de France, adopted the bureaucratic system of the Roman Church as a way to unify the country. Over the centuries, the power of the judges increased because they started to buy their office from the crown and, not surprisingly, the revolutionaries, seeing such judicial independence as an expression of the loathed monarchic order, proclaimed legislation to be the sole source of law. Napoleon enshrined this idea in his codes, turning the judiciary into a bureaucracy employed and controlled by the State. Twelfth century England, instead, developed jury trials and established, in the 1215 Magna Carta, the idea that the crown could not take the life or property of the nobles without due process. Such judicial independence was continuously challenged, and the courts of royal prerogative, subordinate to the crown, grew in importance in the sixteenth century. This struggle ended only with the 1688 Glorious Revolution, when the independence of the English judges from the crown was finally established. In particular, judges gained lifetime appointment in the 1701 Act of Settlement and, shortly after, the power to review administrative acts.

Informed by this reconstruction, Glaeser and Shleifer (2002) contend that the development of a system of adjudication by lay juries in England and one of adjudication by professional judges in France were conscious choices reflecting the different political power of the English and French barons.

> The former were concerned about the powerful English king's ability to interfere in adjudication and bargained for trial by local, lay juries, a right enshrined in Magna

> Carta. The relatively weak French crown, by contrast, was less a threat than other barons. French barons accordingly desired a centralized adjudication system controlled by royal judges who would not be easily captured by local interests. (Klerman and Mahoney, 2007, p.279)

The post-revolutionary facts just reinforced these structural dissimilarities, reinforcing a stronger emphasis on judicial independence and on the protection of private property and ordering into the common law.

Even if fascinating, this economic justification of the medieval facts has been proved wrong due to the inaccurate selection of sources. Building on more recent historical accounts (Holt, 1992; Macnair, 1999), Klerman and Mahoney (2007) conclude that a system of adjudication by lay juries was initially favored, in England, due to low literacy levels and later enforced, contrary to Glaeser and Shleifer's (2002) view, in order to place the judicial power in the hands of the crown.[6] Moreover, during the Middle Ages, not only did both French and English judiciaries have *de facto* power to make law through precedent, but French judges enjoyed a greater independence exactly because their office was a heritable property shielded from the crown. Hence, the only permanent and consequential divergence between the legal orders in England and in France originated from the different fortunes of the judiciary in the aftermath of their respective revolutions. Crucially, the idiosyncratic nature of these shocks also throws doubt on the corollary of Glaeser and Shleifer's (2002) "coercion" theory, which LLS (2008) have christened "the legal origins theory". According to the latter, given that all legal systems seek to simultaneously address the problems of disorder and state abuse (see also Djankov et al., 2003a), the long-lasting legacy of the two differing medieval experiences is that French civil law has remained a system of social control that is relatively more concerned with disorder and less with state abuse. Hence, in the spirit of Hayek (1960), the common law will always solve the private disorder-public abuse trade-off by shoring up markets, and the civil law will always even it out by restricting markets or even replacing them with state commands.[7] Next, I turn to comment on the more serious argument dealing with the adaptability of common law.

---

[6] Also, as clarified by Roe (2007), not only should the jury system be considered an adjudication procedure weaker than that based on expert judges, but it was not even transferred to the majority of the colonies.

[7] LLS (2008) acknowledge that the "legal origins" theory admits state control as an efficient response to disorder when common-law solutions fail to sustain markets. Accordingly, Glaeser and Shleifer (2003) interpret the early twentieth century rise of the regulatory state in the USA as a defense from the subversion of the justice system by large corporations. Recently, Knittel (2006) and Benmelech and Moskowitz (2010) have shown that the regulatory expansion was, instead, a response to sector-specific technological needs.

2.2 *The Adaptability of Common Law?*

As seen above, the key institution differentiating the two legal traditions is the law-making rule, which constitutes the mechanism aggregating citizens' preferences over the harshness of punishment. While common law relies on case law – that is, the precedents of appellate courts guide subsequent adjudication by courts of the same or lower standing and can be changed by appellate judges only with a costly effort at justification, civil law is grounded on acts of legislation by the democratically elected representatives of the people – i.e. statute law.

Three main properties of judge-made law have been identified as justifying its superior adaptability to social and economic changes: (1) the evolutionary properties of overruled precedents; (2) the ability of appellate judges to introduce new information into the law by distinguishing the existing precedent; (3) the tendency of inefficient rules to be more often evaluated by the law-maker under case law. In order to clarify each of these, I present in the following a simplified version of the model of law-making recently proposed by Fernandez and Ponzetto (2008) and Guerriero (2010). Although the comparative merits of statute and case law have been debated for centuries,[8] these works represent the first attempt to formalize this comparison. Moreover, these papers have the merit of encompassing, for the first time, three key stylized facts about law-making: (1) there are systematic differences across cultural and economic groups in their preferences regarding the harshness of punishment for deviant actions (see Herrmann, Thöni and Gächter, 2008); (2) statute law can be seen as the product of the bargaining interaction between the legislator – that is, the government, the legislature or the president – and the lobbies interested in favoring special interests (Grossman and Helpman, 1994); (3) appellate judges change the law to reflect their own preferences (Posner, 1973; Gennaioli and Shleifer, 2007a and b).[9]

The regulation problem Consider a two-tier legal system concerned with the regulation of a harmful act: at the upper tier, the law-maker – i.e., either the Legislator or an appellate judge – decides the prevailing law, at the lower tier, adjudicating courts rule accordingly. At adjudication, lower courts observe only one of two signals – $a \in [0,1]$ and $u \in [0,1]$ – on the defendant's culpability. The signals are independently and uniformly distributed in the population of cases

---

[8] While Hobbes (1681) and Bentham (1891) exalted the democratic nature of legislation, Cardozo (1921) and Hayek (1960) emphasized the evolutionary properties of judge-made law.

[9] Klein (2002) documents that US appellate courts overrule precedents incompatible with their political orientation, follow only those prior court decisions that are compatible with their own ideologies, and do not revise their past votes after the court they sit on has established a new legal rule they had voted against.

and such that the defendant should be convicted if $a + u \geq 1$. Since only a is observable: (1) under institution $i \in \{s,c\}$, the law-maker needs just to find the level of a – call it A^i – such that the defendant is convicted if and only if $a \geq A^i$; (2) the probability of a false positive is $(1/2)(1 - A^i)^2$ and that of a false negative is $(1/2)(A^i)^2$.[10] The cost of the former (latter) equals the foregone utility from acting net of the expected harm (the expected harm less the foregone utility), and the relative cost of a false positive is λ.

The population is equally split into two groups $j \in \{L,H\}$ caring only about the minimization of statistical errors, which they weigh differently and according to the "perceived" relative cost of a false positive β_j. In particular, the ex post loss of welfare with respect to the first best for a type j citizen is $\Lambda_j(A^i) = (1/2)\ \{\Gamma(\beta_j)(1 - A^i)^2 + [1 - \Gamma(\beta_j)](A^i)^2\}$, where the relative weight function is $\Gamma(x) \equiv x(1 + x)^{-1}$.[11] While the unconcerned group L has $\beta_L = \lambda\pi$ and thus prefers the lenient rule $\hat{A}_L = \lambda\pi(1 + \lambda\pi)^{-1}$, the concerned group has $\beta_H = \lambda\pi^{-1}$ and would rather have more convictions or $\hat{A}_H = \lambda(\pi + \lambda)^{-1}$. Hence, $\pi \in (1,\infty)$ should be correctly considered as a measure of preference heterogeneity – i.e. the extent of disagreement about the perceived harm associated with the action among citizens belonging to groups with different ethnic, religious or political ideologies. In a forward-looking society – i.e. one concerned only with future efficiency, the optimal law-making institution should minimize the expected loss of social welfare $(1/2)\mathrm{E}(\Lambda_L(A^i) + \Lambda_H(A^i))$ which is proportional to $(1/2(A^i - E(\hat{A}_j)) = (1/2)\mathrm{V}(\hat{A}^i) + (1/2)(\mathrm{E}(\hat{A}^i) - \tilde{A})^2$. Also, the socially optimal law should be a certain threshold $\tilde{A} = E(\hat{A}_j) = (1/2)\hat{A}_L + (1/2)\hat{A}_H$, which is the statistical compromise between the divergent visions of the world held by the two groups.

Statute law As noticed before, statute law can be seen as essentially shaped by the activity of lobbies that provide contributions to elected officials in order to move A^s toward the preferences of the special interest they represent. Following Grossman and Helpman (1994), Fernandez and Ponzetto (2008) capture this interaction assuming that A^s is chosen by a Legislator minimizing $(1/2)[A^s - (1 - \mu)\tilde{A} - \mu A_j^{\,2}]$ where μ is a measure of the quality of the political process and $l \in \{L,H\}$ is an exogenously formed lobby. Hence, there is no average bias in the expected threshold but statute law still delivers a loss due

---

[10] Indeed, a false positive (negative) happens for $a \geq A^i$ and $a < 1 - u$ ($a < A^i$ and $a \geq 1 - u$).

[11] Under complete information, the defendant is optimally convicted in half the cases.

to the uncertainty over the bias, which is proportional to $(\mu^2/2)V(A_j) = (\mu^2/8)(\hat{A}_L - \hat{A}_H)^2$ and thus higher the less democratic policy-making is – i.e., the higher μ is.

Case law As proposed by Posner (1973), *stare decisis* only binds in so far as it is costly for judges to change the precedent.[12] Building on this intuition, Fernandez and Ponzetto (2008) suppose that a judge, inheriting a rule $A^{c,t-1}$ and setting $A^{c,t} \neq A^{c,t-1}$, can introduce any change in the law provided that she incurs a persuasive effort whose cost rises with the relevance of the doctrine of *stare decisis* $K > 0$ and the magnitude of the legal revision. Indeed, the further away a decision drifts from precedent the harder is the justification work of an appellate judge, who clearly needs to illustrate the novel aspects of the case and the legal arguments that shield the ruling from the scrutiny by both the legal doctrine and extra-judicial institutions.[13] Hence, a type j judge minimizes both the loss she bears as part of group j when $A^{c,t}$ differs from $\hat{A}_j$ and that of justifying an $A^{c,t}$ far from $A^{c,t-1}$ – i.e. $(1/2)(A^{c,t}(j) - \hat{A}_i)^2 + (K/2)(A^{c,t}(j) - \hat{A}^{c,t-1})^2$. There is a unique optimal threshold $\Gamma(K)A^{c,t-1} + [1 - \Gamma(K)]\,\hat{A}_j$ and, consequently, case law follows a first order auto-regressive process converging upon the distribution with mean $\tilde{A}$ and variance $V(\hat{A}_j)(1 + 2K)^{-1}$. Thus, leaving aside convergence, the only expected loss of social welfare under case law is given by the uncertainty over future overrulings which is proportional to $V(\hat{A}_j)[2(1 + 2K)]^{-1}$.

The optimal law-making institution All in all, in Fernandez and Ponzetto's (2008) view, while statute law possibly brings with it the cost of a rule biased by the imperfection of the political process, case law always comes at the cost of a rule distorted by a combination of judicial activism and imperfect *stare decisis*. Yet, whenever a society is sufficiently able to enforce *stare decisis* – i.e., when $(1 + 2K)^{-1} < \mu^2$ or $K > (1 - \mu^2)/2\,\mu^2$, case law is bound to outperform statute law, due to the disciplining effect of scrutiny by differently biased judges.

The effective existence of the evolutionary properties paraded by Fernandez and Ponzetto (2008) has been heavily challenged by recent theoretical and empirical contributions. Starting with the former, Baker and Mezzetti (2010)

---

[12] Ruling after economic choices are sunk, courts have a temptation to be excessively lenient – from an ex-ante point of view. Starting from this observation, Anderlini, Felli and Riboni (2010) rationalize *stare decisis* as a disciplinary device prompting courts to consider also the benefits of tougher current ruling on future rulings.

[13] Gennaioli and Shleifer (2007b) question this assumption, contending that overruling costs should be considered as fixed. In this case, for a low level of preference heterogeneity π the first appellate judge ruling will stick forever and, for a sufficiently high level of preference heterogeneity, case law will bounce between $\hat{A}_L$ and $\hat{A}_H$. In any case, the evolutionary properties of case law will be lost and statutes will always constitute a better option.

posit that appellate judges design opinions to maximize the new information arising in future disputes. This incentive promotes rulings that are broad at the beginning and then more refined later; yet, in general, judge-made law never reaches optimality because the refinement stops because of hearing and adjudication error costs. The same result is obtained by Anderlini, Felli and Riboni (2010) in another dynamic model where time-inconsistent judges are forced by *stare decisis* to consider the effect of their ruling on the decisions of future time-inconsistent colleagues. Since *stare decisis* is unable to nullify short-termism, case law is bound to be inefficient. Crucially, this legacy of impossibility results is increasingly supported by empirical evidence. Looking at the evolution of legal doctrine governing construction disputes in the USA over the period of 1970–2005, Niblett, Posner and Shleifer (forthcoming) find little evidence of either convergence or evolution toward efficiency. Also, Hefeker and Neugart (2009) show that divergent rulings by discretionary appellate judges lead governments to be more actively involved in labor market reforms in common law countries.

This highly pessimistic assessment of the quality of legal evolution under overruling has urged Gennaioli and Shleifer (2007a) to discuss the idea that, in reality, the real central property of case law is to allow appellate judges to introduce new information by identifying the existing precedent. Responding to factual circumstances – i.e. in the model discussed above, information on the initially unobserved μ, distinguishing refines and improves the law on average without, however, assuring convergence upon the efficient legal rule.[14] This aspect is also related to another long strand of literature, started with the seminal works of Priest (1977), Rubin (1977) and Cooter and Kornhauser (1980), claiming that another informational advantage of case law is the tendency of inefficient rules to be more often evaluated by the law-maker. Miceli (2009) evaluates this claim in the environment presented above and concludes that this selective litigation property could lead to the efficient rule being achieved only when the margin of judicial bias is not too great.[15] Should the latter not be the case, judge-made law inexorably tends to float off from efficiency.

2.3 *Endogenous Legal Traditions*

A completely new perspective on the issue has recently been offered by Guerriero (2010), who has pointed out that, regardless of the specific hypotheses on the

---

[14] In a two-periods version of the model discussed above, Gennaioli and Shleifer (2007a) assume that appellate judges choose thresholds $\underline{B}$ and $\overline{B}$ such that the defendant is convicted if and only if $a < \hat{A}^c$ and $b \geq B$ or $a \geq \hat{A}^c$ and $b \geq \overline{B}$. Fernandez and Ponzetto (forthcoming) attack this set-up, affirming that, in reality, appellate judges can always implement the optimal two-dimensional rule $B = 1 - a$ as soon as u becomes observable.

[15] Luppi and Parisi (2010) reach a similar conclusion, putting a stronger focus on adjudication procedures.

incentives moving appellate judges, it is a peculiar feature of statute law that shapes the comparison between the two institutions. Indeed, growing empirical evidence has proved the inconsistency of the exogenous lobbying model assumption that all groups are equally willing to participate in policy-making (Wright, 1996). Hence, it makes sense to think, as advised by a recent work on endogenous lobbying (Felli and Merlo, 2006), that in the above model: (1) the Legislator has as an outside option the optimal rule $\tilde{A}$ and chooses one among the possible coalitions of the cultural groups; (2) the winning coalition has to pay a fixed "collective action" cost.[16] Clearly, when the cultural distance between groups is limited, statute law will prevail over case law because the "collective action" costs will discourage side contracts and the prevailing rule will be unbiased and certain.[17] In a sufficiently polarized society the Legislator will, instead, favor one of the two coalitions and select a rule further away from the optimal rule the less democratic the political process is. In the last scenario, statute law could outperform case law only when the political process is sufficiently efficient – i.e. when μ is sufficiently small with respect to K.[18] The model also shows that the use of limited discretion by lower adjudicating courts curbs the volatility costs associated with judge-made law and makes statute law volatile. Thus, a pure common (civil) law tradition where case (statute) law is used along with flexible (bright-line) adjudication rules will endogenously arise. The model's message – common law is optimal in relatively heterogeneous and/or less democratic societies – stands: (1) when there is also a third unbiased group; (2) when the Legislator is elected among citizen-candidates; (3) where appellate judges are corruptible or forward looking; (4) under both overruling and distinguishing, whether the cost of changing the precedent is fixed or variable; (5) when the institutional choice is taken by a corruptible Constitutional table. This last point gives a positive characterization to the model's normative results, and it is simply driven by the fact that, even when one group is penalized by one rule, she will be compensated by the other exactly because optimal institutions deliver a higher expected long-run social welfare.

---

16 Formally, the Legislator maximizes now a function $-(1/2)(1-\mu)(A^s - E(\hat{A}_j)^2) + \mu W_l(A^s,\tilde{A})$, where $W_l(A^s,\tilde{A}) = (1/4)\Sigma_{j\in l}[(\tilde{A} - \hat{A}_j)^2 - (A^s - \hat{A}_j)^2] - \Psi$ is the sum of the maximum individually rational side contracts each lobby j in the generic coalition $l\in\{\{\phi\},\{L,\},\{H\},\{L,H\}\}$ is willing to pay less the fixed "collective action" fee Ψ.

17 To see this, notice that each coalition's willingness to pay increases with the extent of disagreement between groups $\bar{A} - A$, which, in turn, rises with the degree of polarization π.

18 Unlike Fernandez and Ponzetto (2008), this model focuses on the expected long-run losses of social welfare only and makes the very reasonable point that, in a world where the disagreement among citizens is limited, special interests would not bear "collective action" costs in order to distract the Legislator from the maximization of social welfare.

As discussed below, Guerriero (2010) confirms the model's empirical implications using data on 156 transplanted countries. This evidence represents one of the key criticisms of the "legal origins" theory. Before analyzing this result, I will review the most interesting empirical exercises looking at the impact of legal origins, as coded by LLSV (1997), on prevailing laws. I will not discuss the related strand of literature investigating the relation among these regulations and economic outcomes. A clear survey of these papers is given by LLS (2008), who also out point correctly that two-stage approaches, using the initial transplantation as an instrument, are unreliable because it is virtually impossible to include in the second stage all the relevant omitted variables related to legal traditions.

3. The Putative Primacy of Common Law: Evidence

The available studies, which are all cross-country, can be divided into three categories depending on whether legal origins are related to: (1) investor protection; (2) government regulation or ownership of economic activities; (3) the characteristics of the judiciary and of the government. Some of these rules are "laws on the books", others are mixtures of procedural and substantive rules. This choice has "advantages and problems" (LLS, 2008).[19]

Starting from investor protection, LSSV (1997 and 1998) document that the laws in the countries they assign to the common law group are more protective of outsider shareholders and senior creditors than those in the countries whose legal origin is civil law. Also, LLSV show that, in accordance with the basic agency theory of corporate law (e.g., Shleifer and Wolfenzon, 2002), legal investor protection from expropriation by corporate insiders promotes financial development. Following these two influential works, several studies have: (1) devised improved indexes of shareholder protection;[20] (2) found qualitatively similar differences between the two legal origins groups, looking however at different proxies of the efficiency of financial markets, such as: ownership dispersion (La Porta, Lopez-de-Silanes and Shleifer, 1999), dividend payouts (La Porta et al., 2000), Tobin's Q (La Porta et al., 2002), the voting premium (Dyck and Zingales, 2004), external finance (Beck, Demirguc-Kunt and Ross, 2005), the size and the perceived quality of private debt markets (Djankov et al., 2007 and 2008a), the ratio of stock market capitalization to GDP and the

---

19 This methodology could lead to inconsistent estimates if the indicators are not equally informative about the underlying concept or do not measure a single dimension (Rosenthal and Voeten, 2007).

20 While La Porta, Lopez-de-Silanes and Shleifer (2006) have focused on a measure of shareholder protection through securities laws in offerings of new issues, Djankov et al. (2008b) have analyzed the existing remedies against self-dealing by corporate insiders through corporate law.

pace of public offering activity (Djankov et al., 2008b), first lead investments (Cumming, Schmidt and Walz, 2010), and tax aggressiveness (Atwood et al., 2010). Other contributions have proposed different channels through which legal origins may shape finance: while Amin (2008) shows that firms in countries with a common law legal origin perceive the government as less helpful for doing business, Julio and Yook (2009) document that firms in the same group face a stronger political uncertainty which, in turn, depresses corporate investments.

Turning to market regulation, Djankov et al. (2002) calculate that: (1) the number of procedures and the administrative costs that a start-up must bear before it can operate legally are significantly higher in countries that are part of the French civil law group; (2) such proxies of entry regulation are correlated with more dramatic corruption, a larger unofficial economy, and a poorer quality of public or private goods. Looking at labor market regulation, Botero et al. (2004) obtain qualitatively similar patterns. Finally, the estimates discussed by Djankov et al. (2003c) (La Porta, Lopez-de-Silanes and Shleifer, 2002) reveal that government ownership of the media (banks) is significantly higher in countries whose legal origin is civil law. The latter also rely more heavily on military conscription (Mulligan and Shleifer, 2005a and 2005b).

A smaller body of literature has been interested in the characteristics of the judiciary and the government. While La Porta et al. (1999) focus on summary measures of government intervention and public sector efficiency, Djankov et al. (2003b) build a synthetic index of the formalism of adjudication procedures, linking it to the time it takes to evict a non-paying tenant or to collect a bounced check. Also, La Porta et al. (2004) try to characterize the interplay between judicial independence, as proxied by Supreme Court judicial tenure and case law, and the quality of contract enforcement, and Djankov et al. (2010) study the relation between the rules of financial and conflict disclosure by members of Parliament and the extent of corruption. The basic message coming from these four papers is that the countries that received at independence institutions typical of the common law have less formalized adjudication, longer constitutional tenure of Supreme Court judges, greater recognition of case law as a source of law, and major disclosure by politicians.[21] Berkowitz and Clay (2005, 2006) observe similar patterns, though exploiting the fact that ten US states were initially settled by France, Spain or Mexico. In recent decades, these states have granted less independence to their judiciary, and used different judicial budgeting procedures. Kim (2009) reaches similar conclusions focusing on Virginia and Massachusetts only.

---

[21] Ben-Bassat and Dahan (2008), however, report that common law countries place less emphasis on constitutional commitments to the right to social security, education, health, housing and workers' welfare.

4. Criticisms: Legal Origins and Dynamics

Based on the evidence summarized above, LLS (2008) conclude that "compared to French civil law, common law countries have less formalized contract enforcement, [a stronger judicial independence], and greater recognition of case law as a source of law . . .; these characteristics of legal systems predict both the efficiency of contract enforcement . . . and the security of property rights. [Also] civil law countries are more likely to address social problems through government ownership and mandates" (LLS, 2008, p.309–10). In the following, I will clarify how weak this conclusion is, basing my argumentation on the two main groups of criticisms dealing with the "legal origins" project's empirical approach. While the first complains of the omission of other relevant determinants of policy-making, the second shows the inconsistency of LLSV's original (1997) codification.

4.1 Omitted Variables and Observational Equivalence

The first immediate objection to the evidence summarized in Section 3 is the existence of omitted variables: since legal origins are an expression of colonial history, how can we claim that the effect of differences among colonizers' strategies is not misattributed to differences in their legal systems? As acknowledged by LLS (2008), three key colonizers' characteristics may possibly be confused with legal origins: their culture, their politics and their history.

Starting from culture, while Stulz and Williamson (2003) suggest that the hostility of some religions to lending on interest may be more relevant in determining creditor protection, Licht, Goldschmidt and Schwartz (2005) claim that cultural attitudes toward individualism could predict legal rules supporting a free market better than legal origins. LLS (2008) have replied to these alternative theories showing that neither of the two proxies for culture makes much of a dent in the explanatory power of legal origins. A more devastating attack has been launched by Klerman et al. (2009), who have noticed that, although common law countries have experienced higher growth rates since 1960, this advantage disappears when one controls for the dominant pre-independence colonial power or for human capital in 1960. The latter was significantly higher in the countries aggregated by LLSV (1997) into the common law group (Rostowski and Stacescu, 2006). Agbory, Fedderkez and Viegi (2010) confirm this idea, looking at sub-Saharan regions.

Another challenge to the "legal origins" literature has been posed by political economy theories of policy-making. A first body of literature (Pagano and Volpin, 2005 and 2006; Roe, 2006; Perotti and Von Thadden, 2006) has advanced the hypothesis that following the major crises of the twentieth century, many powerful Continental European families that controlled firms and/or labor formed alliances with the aim of drawing up self-protecting regulations. Rich capitalistic families obtained rules shielding their private benefits to the detriment of outside shareholders; organized labor got social security and worker protection laws. Also, these families and labor joined forces against product market competition, pushing for stricter regulation of entry. Hence, clusters of countries with weak shareholder protection, strong protection of labor and high regulation of entry formed, alongside clusters of countries with the opposite characteristics. In this perspective, using the civil law legal origin just picks up the role of proportional representation (Pagano and Volpin, 2005 and 2006), socialist politics (Roe, 2006) and social democracy (Perotti and Von Thadden, 2006) in favoring the rise of the "insiders". Even though appealing, this political account fails to explain the differences between civil and common law countries when tested in samples bigger than those studied in the original papers (see LLS, 2008).[22] Instead, a stronger point has been made by more recent contributions that look at the political mechanisms transmitting colonial origins into economic development. Acemoglu and Johnson (2005) find that, once one takes into consideration the European colonization strategy as shaped by the settler mortality rate and the population density before colonization, legal origins have no first-order effect on long-run economic growth, investment, and financial development. A possible explanation for this pattern is that individuals often find ways of altering the terms of their formal and informal contracts to avoid the adverse effects of weak contracting institutions, but find it harder to mitigate the risk of expropriation in this way.[23] Two recent papers confirm this view, looking to well-defined study cases. Henry and Miller (2009), in the first place, show that the income levels of Barbados and Jamaica, two countries assigned by LLSV (1997) to the common law group, significantly diverged over just 40 years because of the quality of macroeconomics policies alone.[24] Similarly, looking at US states, Arruñada, Williamson and Zanarone (2009) discover that, once the impact of intra-state special political interests is controlled for, a state's legal origin has no significant effect on courts' output.

The last line of attack has claimed that if one looks at historical data the correlations discussed in Section 3 vanish. Rajan and Zingales (2003) open this body of research, presenting evidence showing that in 1913 French civil

---

22 Along the same lines, looking at a panel of 85 countries over the period 1975–2004, Gourevitch, Pinto and Weymouth (2009) find evidence that, contrary to the political economy view, not only are legal origins relevant but also left-leaning governments are more likely to be associated with higher stock market capitalization. LLS (2008) document that the legal origins theory continues to work outside democracies.

23 Similarly, Bloom and Echeverri-Gent (2010) find that, in a panel of 197 countries over 34 years, the consideration of regulatory resources leaves almost no role to legal origins in explaining financial market development (see also the evidence on public enforcement in Jackson and Roe, 2009; Nee and Opper, 2009).

24 A similar exercise is carried out, focusing on the last two decades in India, by Armour and Lele (2009).

law countries had more developed financial markets than did common law countries. Yet, as proved by LLS (2008), their conclusions rest mainly on several questionable data construction assumptions. More compelling, however, is historical evidence on the quality of prevailing regulations. Sgard (2006) builds an original database of 51 bankruptcy laws, ranging over 15 European countries and more than a hundred years: i.e. between 1808 and 1914. There are two key conclusions of the analysis of these data: (1) over the entire period, all legal traditions except English law strongly protected creditors' rights; (2) the evolution of financial regulation was influenced crucially by continent-wide trends and not by legal origins (similar conclusions are reached by: Lamoreaux and Rosenthal, 2005; Deakin, 2009; Serpoul, 2009; Roe and Siegel, 2009; Musacchio, 2010). This expanding literature on the evolution of legal traditions has paved the way to a more fundamental criticism of the legal origins theory.

4.2 Codification Failures and Endogenous Legal Traditions

As seen above, increasingly legal studies have criticized the basic assumption of the legal origins theory that transplanted legal infrastructures remained unchanged over time (Roe, 2004 and 2006). Starting from this crucial observation, Guerriero (2010) has recorded: (1) the law-making institution in place at independence and in 2000 in 156 transplanted countries; (2) the four most relevant adjudication institutions in place in 98 of these 156 countries at the same points in time and listed in footnote 4 above.[25] Consistent with the theoretical account given in Section 2.3, instrumental variables estimates reveal that, in countries in which statute (case) law was transplanted, reforms toward case (statute) law were more likely the broader (smaller) was the long-run cultural heterogeneity as proxied by: (1) the genetic distance between the plurality ethnic group in the country which chose the law-making institution and the one in the transplanted country; (2) the ethnic fractionalization in the transplanted country.[26] Also, moves toward common law – i.e. case law and flexible adjudication rules – in countries on which statute law was imposed are

---

[25] Apart from attempts to understand the extent of transplantation (Berkowitz, Pistor and Richard, 2003), Guerriero (2010) is the first economics work that has taken up the largely unheard request by legal scholars that "robust micro-based assessments of rules and legal institutions should prevail over macro generalizations and 'cherry-picking' theories" (Garoupa and Gomez Liguerre, forthcoming). A complementary effort has recently been made to obtain more accurate measures of the prevailing regulations (Graff, 2008; Spamann, 2010).

[26] Recently, Dari-Mattiacci and Guerriero (2010) have been studying the evolution of law-making in ancient Rome to confirm this pattern in a case in which more than one switch can be observed. Between the fifth century BC and the fifth century AD Rome went through two momentous law-making reforms.

found where the long-run quality of the political process is poorest.[27] Hence, the distribution of the key institutions shaping the functioning of actual legal systems is neither fixed nor randomly given. Instead, it is the outcome of a unique historical shock and of the welfare-maximizing effort of the society as a whole. This evidence constitutes a decisive critique of the legal origins literature. Not only is the evolution of legal traditions driven by factors affecting those economic outcomes we want to explain (see Alesina et al., 2003; Persson and Tabellini, 2009), but the LLSV's (1997) classification is also plagued by several inconsistencies.

In the first place, the authors do not notice the evolution of transplanted law-making institutions.[28] In the second place, among countries for which data on the adjudication rules are available, 54% (39%) of the observations coded by LLSV (1997) as having an English (French) law origin have reshaped their legal order in such a way as to be nearer to a pure civil law (common law) legal system. In other words, these countries have reformed the fundamental structures of their legal order in a direction showing a *de facto* interest in aggregating the citizenry preferences with rules different from those transplanted.

5. Conclusions: A New Legal Origins Literature

This chapter has discussed the main achievements and failures of the legal origins literature. From a theoretical point of view, the legal origins project has been challenged on two grounds: (1) more careful historical analyses have refuted the medieval-grounded (Klerman and Mahoney, 2007) primacy of common law in protecting private contracting and ordering; (2) consistent with recent evidence (Niblett, Posner and Shleifer, forthcoming), a growing series of models has clarified that the evolutionary efficiency of case law is far from obvious (Gennaioli and Shleifer, 2007a; Anderlini, Felli and Riboni, 2010; Baker and Mezzetti, 2010). On empirical grounds, the evidence on legal origins has been proved inconsistent because of its codification. The latter, which is based essentially on colonial origins, raises two main issues: (1) the correlation between the LLSV (1997) groups and economic development reveals a correlation between specific features of colonization, such as human capital and the public enforcement of property rights, and economic development; (2)

[27] These results also cast doubt on the literature on legal formalism (Djankov at al., 2003b) which sees the higher number of bright-line rules in civil law as driving less efficient adjudication. The pattern speaks, instead, of an optimal choice driven by the preference aggregation properties of statute law.

[28] Also three non-Scandinavian countries coded as having some form of civil law origin (three countries assigned to the English law group) were instead using case (statute) law over the whole independence period.

econometricians cannot give a causal interpretation to legal institutions that, for the vast majority, were not even in place.

Driven by this raging storm of criticism, I close by highlighting two avenues for further research. The first obvious need for the new legal origins literature is a structural and evidence-based theory of precedent and statute formation and evolution, bringing together the preference and information aggregation role of law-making institutions.[29] Second, the empirical literature on comparative legal and economic systems should not only consider all the different institutions characterizing the two traditions, but also the fact that the design of these arrangements is driven by long-lasting cultural features which affect also the economic performances we are interested in: Guerriero (2011) constitutes a first contribution along this line. Such an exercise will help to deal with two immediate policy issues: (1) understanding whether, as claimed by Acemoglu and Johnson (2005) and contrary to the incomplete markets intuition, contracting institutions, as driven by prevailing legal institutions, have no first-order effect on long-run economic growth, investment, and financial development;[30] (2) avoiding the implementation of ineffective or even harmful restructuring based on the results obtained by the old legal origins literature.[31] All in all, the new legal origins literature constitutes a crucial challenge for law and economics scholars to be met by both in-depth theoretical effort and solid statistical work.

References

Acemoglu, Daron, and Simon Johnson. 2005. "Unbundling Institutions." *Journal of Political Economy*, 113: 949–95.

Agbory, Julius A., Johannes W. Fedderkez, Nicola Viegi. 2010. "Does Colonial Origin Really Matter for Economic Growth in sub-Saharan Africa?" Unpublished.

---

29 A first attempt along these lines has been undetaken by Dari-Mattiacci, Deffains and Lovat (forthcoming), who study the relationship between litigation rates and the balance between case law and legislation.

30 Should the groups weigh preferences aggregation against technological efficiency – i.e. the distance $(A^i - A^*)^2$ – the analysis in Guerriero (2010) would still hold and for negligible switching costs, we should observe no differences between the two traditions, provided that the performance proxies we use capture both preferences and technological efficiency. Yet, those employed in the existing literature measure only the second dimension. Based on the latter, at low level of π statute law outperforms case law because it produces certain and unbiased rules. If, instead, π is sufficiently high and only the long-run bias (both the long-run bias and volatility) of the law affects performances, case (statute) law is welfare maximizing (provided that democracy is sufficiently strong) because unbiased (certain). Looking at a cross section of transplanted countries, Guerriero (2011) confirms this prediction.

31 The World Bank "doing business" project reports yearly advances in regulatory reforms identified as key by the old legal origins literature – for example, reducing the steps necessary to open a new business, to obtain a new license or to employ a worker. See http://www.doingbusiness.org/Documents/FullReport/2009.

Alesina, Alberto, Arnaud Devleeschauwer, William Easterly, Sergio Kurlat, and Romain Wacziarg. 2003. "Fractionalization." *Journal of Economic Growth*, 8: 155–94.
Amin, Mohammad. 2008. "Helpful Governments." Unpublished.
Anderlini, Luca, Leonardo Felli, and Alessandro Riboni. 2010. "Why Stare Decisis?" Unpublished.
Armour, John, and Priya Lele. 2009. "Law, Finance, and Politics: The Case of India." *Law and Society Review*, 43: 491–526.
Arruñada, Benito, Dean Williamson, and Giorgio Zanarone. 2009. "The Influence of Interest Groups on Institutions: Evidence from the American State Courts." Unpublished.
Atwood, Tedd J., Michael S. Drake, James N. Myers, and Linda A. Myers. 2010. "The Cross-country Determinants of Corporate Tax Aggressiveness." Unpublished.
Baker, Scott, and Claudio Mezzetti. 2010. "A Theory of Rational Jurisprudence." Unpublished.
Beck, Thorsten, Asli Demirguc-Kunt, and Ross Levine. 2005. "Law and Firms' Access to Finance." *American Law and Economics Review*, 7: 211–52.
Ben-Bassat, Avi, and Momi Dahan. 2008. "Social Rights in the Constitution and in Practice." *Journal of Comparative Economics*, 36: 103–19.
Benmelech, Efraim, and Tobias J. Moskowitz. 2010. "The Political Economy of Financial Regulation: Evidence from U.S. State Usury Laws in the 19th Century." *Journal of Finance*, 65: 1029–73.
Bentham, Jeremy. 1891. *A Fragment on Government*. Cambridge, UK: Cambridge University Press.
Berkowitz, Daniel, and Karen B. Clay. 2005. "American Civil Law Origins: Implications for State Constitutions." *American Law and Economics Review*, 7: 62–84.
Berkowitz, Daniel, and Karen B. Clay. 2006. "The Effect of Judicial Independence on Courts: Evidence from the American States." *Journal of Legal Studies*, 35: 399–440.
Berkowitz, Daniel, Katharina Pistor, and Jean-Francois Richard. 2003. "Economic Development, Legality, and the Transplant Effect." *European Economic Review*, 47: 165–95.
Berman, Harold J. 1983. *Law and Revolution: The Formation of the Western Legal Tradition*. Cambridge, MA and London: Harvard University Press.
Bloom, Benjamin, and John Echeverri-Gent. 2010. "Do Competitive Politics Produce Competitive Markets? Politics of Financial Market Development." Unpublished.
Botero, Juan C., Simeon Djankov, Rafael La Porta, Florencio Lopez-de-Silanes, and Andrei Shleifer. 2004. "The Regulation of Labor." *Quarterly Journal of Economics*, 119: 1339–82.
Cardozo, Benjamin, N. 1921. *The Nature of the Judicial Process*. New Haven, CT: Yale University Press.
Cooter, Robert, and Lewis Kornhauser. 1980. "Can Litigation Improve the Law without the Help of Judges?" *Journal Legal Studies*, 9: 139–63.
Cumming, Douglas, Daniel Schmidt, and Uwe Walz. 2010. "Legality and Venture Capital Governance around the World." *Journal of Business Venturing*, 25: 54–72.
Dari-Mattiacci, Giuseppe, Bruno Deffains, and Bruno Lovat. Forthcoming. "The Dynamics of the Legal System." *Journal of Economic Behavior and Organization*.
Dari-Mattiacci, Giuseppe, and Carmine Guerriero. 2010. "Fiat Lex: Law-making, Politics, and Cultural Heterogeneity in Ancient Rome." Unpublished.
David, René, et al., eds. 1995. *International Encyclopedia of Comparative Law*. Vol. 1, *National Reports*. New York: Oceana Publications Incorporation.
Dawson, John P. 1960. *A History of Lay Judges*. Cambridge, MA and London: Harvard University Press.
Deakin, Simon. 2009. "Legal Origin, Juridical Form and Industrialisation in Historical Perspective: The Case of the Employment Contract and the Joint-Stock Company." *Socio-Economic Review*, 7: 35–65.
Djankov, Simeon, Edward Glaeser, Rafael La Porta, Florencio Lopez-de-Silanes, and Andrei Shleifer. 2003a. "The New Comparative Economics." *Journal of Comparative Economics*, 31: 595–619.
Djankov, Simeon, Oliver D. Hart, Caralee McLiesh, and Andrei Shleifer. 2008a. "Debt Enforcement around the World." *Journal of Political Economy*, 116: 1105–49.
Djankov, Simeon, Rafael La Porta, Florencio Lopez-de-Silanes, and Andrei Shleifer. 2002. "The Regulation of Entry." *Quarterly Journal of Economics*, 117: 1–37.

Djankov, Simeon, Rafael La Porta, Florencio Lopez-de-Silanes, and Andrei Shleifer. 2003b. "Courts." *Quarterly Journal of Economics*, 118: 453–517.
Djankov, Simeon, Rafael La Porta, Florencio Lopez-de-Silanes, and Andrei Shleifer. 2008b. "The Law and Economics of Self-Dealing." *Journal of Financial Economics*, 88: 430–65.
Djankov, Simeon, Rafael La Porta, Florencio Lopez-de-Silanes, and Andrei Shleifer. 2010. "Disclosure by Politicians." *American Economic Journal: Applied Economics*, 2: 179–209.
Djankov, Simeon, Caralee McLiesh, Tatiana Nenova, and Andrei Shleifer. 2003c. "Who Owns the Media?" *Journal of Law and Economics*, 46: 341–81.
Djankov, Simeon, Caralee McLiesh, and Andrei Shleifer. 2007. "Private Credit in 129 Countries." *Journal of Financial Economics*, 84: 299–329.
Dyck, Alexander, and Luigi Zingales. 2004. "Private Benefits of Control: An International Comparison." *Journal of Finance*, 59: 537–600.
Felli, Leonardo, and Antonio Merlo. 2006. "Endogenous Lobbying." *Journal of the European Economic Association*, 4: 180–215.
Fernandez, Patricio, A., and Giacomo A. M. Ponzetto. 2008. "Case Law vs. Statute Law: an Evolutionary Comparison." *Journal of Legal Studies*, 37: 379–430.
Fernandez, Patricio, A., and Giacomo A. M. Ponzetto. Forthcoming. "Stare Decisis: Rhetoric and Substance." *Journal of Law, Economics and Organization*.
Garoupa, Nuno, and Carlos Gomez Liguerre. Forthcoming. "The Syndrome of the Efficiency of the Common Law." *Boston University Journal of International Law*.
Gennaioli, Nicola, and Andrei Shleifer. 2007a. "The Evolution of Common Law." *Journal of Political Economy*, 115: 43–68.
Gennaioli, Nicola, and Andrei Shleifer. 2007b. "Overruling and the Instability of Law." *Journal of Comparative Economics*, 35: 309–28.
Glaeser, Edward, and Andrei Shleifer. 2002. "Legal Origins." *Quarterly Journal of Economics*, 117: 1193–229.
Glaeser, Edward L., and Andrei Shleifer. 2003. "The Rise of the Regulatory State." *Journal of Economic Literature*, 41: 401–25.
Gourevitch, Peter, Pablo M. Pinto, and Stephen Weymouth. 2009. "The Politics of Stock Market Development." Unpublished.
Graff, Michael. 2008. "Law and Finance: Common-law and Civil-law Countries Compared – An Empirical Critique." *Economica*, 75: 60–83.
Grossman, Gene, and Elhanan Helpman. 1994. "Protection for Sale." *American Economic Review*, 84: 833–50.
Guerriero, Carmine. 2010. "Democracy, Judicial Attitudes and Heterogeneity: The Civil Versus Common Law Tradition." ACLE Working Papers, 2010–10.
Guerriero, Carmine. 2011. "Endogenous Legal Traditions and Economic Outcomes." Unpublished.
Hayek, Friedrich, A. 1960. *The Constitution of Liberty*. South Bend, IN: Gateway.
Hefeker, Carsten, and Michael Neugart. 2009. "Labor Market Regulation and the Legal System." Unpublished.
Henry, Peter Blair, and Conrad Miller. 2009. "Institutions versus Policies: A Tale of Two Islands." *American Economic Review*, 99: 261–267.
Herrmann, Benedikt, Christian Thöni, and Simon Gächter. 2008. "Antisocial Punishment Across Societies." *Science*, 319: 1362–7.
Hobbes, Thomas. 1681. *A Dialogue between a Philosopher and a Student of the Common Laws of England*. New York: Oxford University Press.
Holt, James Clarke. 1992. *Magna Carta*. Cambridge and New York: Cambridge University Press.
Jackson, Howell, and Mark J. Roe. 2009. "Public and Private Enforcement of Securities Laws: Resource-based Evidence." *Journal of Financial Economics*, 93: 207–38.
Julio, Brandon, and Youngsuk Yook. 2009. "Political Uncertainty and Corporate Investment Cycles." Unpublished.
Kim, Sukkoo. 2009. "Institutions and U.S. Regional Development: A Study of Massachussetts and Virginia." *Journal of Institutional Economics*, 5: 181–205.
Klein, David E. 2002. *Making Law in the United States Courts of Appeals*. Cambridge: Cambridge University Press.

Klerman, Daniel, and Paul G. Mahoney. 2007. "Legal Origin?" *Journal of Comparative Economics*, 35: 278–93.
Klerman, Daniel, Paul G. Mahoney, Holger Spamann, and Mark Weinstein. 2009. "Legal Origin and Economic Growth." Unpublished.
Knittel, Christopher R. 2006. "The Adoption of State Electricity Regulation: The Role of Interest Groups." *Journal of Industrial Economics*, 54: 201–22.
Lamoreaux, Naomi R., and Jean-Laurent Rosenthal. 2005. "Legal Regime and Contractual Flexibility: A Comparison of Business's Organizational Choices in France and the United States during the Era of Industrialization." *American Law and Economics Review*, 7: 28–61.
La Porta, Rafael, Florencio Lopez-de-Silanes, Cristian Pop-Eleches, and Andrei Shleifer. 2004. "Judicial Checks and Balances." *Journal of Political Economy*, 112: 445–70.
La Porta, Rafael, Florencio Lopez-de-Silanes, and Andrei Shleifer. 1999. "Corporate Ownership around the World." *Journal of Finance*, 54: 471–517.
La Porta, Rafael, Florencio Lopez-de-Silanes, and Andrei Shleifer. 2002. "Government Ownership of Banks." *Journal of Finance*, 57: 265–301.
La Porta, Rafael, Florencio Lopez-de-Silanes, and Andrei Shleifer. 2006. "What Works in Securities Laws?" *Journal of Finance*, 61: 1–32.
La Porta, Rafael, Florencio Lopez-de-Silanes, and Andrei Shleifer. 2008. "The Economic Consequences of Legal Origins." *Journal of Economic Literature*, 46: 285–332.
La Porta, Rafael, Florencio Lopez-de-Silanes, Andrei Shleifer, and Robert W. Vishny. 1997. "Legal Determinants of External Finance." *Journal of Finance*, 52: 1131–50.
La Porta, Rafael, Florencio Lopez-de-Silanes, Andrei Shleifer, and Robert W. Vishny. 1998. "Law and Finance." *Journal of Political Economy*, 106: 1113–55.
La Porta, Rafael, Florencio Lopez-de-Silanes, Andrei Shleifer, and Robert W. Vishny. 1999. "The Quality of Government." *Journal of Law, Economics and Organization*, 15: 222–79.
La Porta, Rafael, Florencio Lopez-de-Silanes, Andrei Shleifer, and Robert W. Vishny. 2000. "Agency Problems and Dividend Policies around the World." *Journal of Finance*, 55: 1–33.
La Porta, Rafael, Florencio Lopez-de-Silanes, Andrei Shleifer, and Robert W. Vishny. 2002. "Investor Protection and Corporate Valuation." *Journal of Finance*, 57: 1147–70.
Licht, Amir N., Chanan Goldschmidt, and Shalom H. Schwartz. 2005. "Culture, Law, and Corporate Governance." *International Review of Law and Economics*, 25: 229–55.
Luppi, Barbara, and Francesco Parisi. 2010. "Litigation and Legal Evolution: Does Procedure Matter?" Unpublished.
Macnair, Mike. 1999. "Vicinage and the Antecedents of the Jury." *Law and History Review*, 17: 537–90.
Merryman, John H. 1969. *The Civil Law Tradition*. Stanford, CA: Stanford University Press.
Miceli, Thomas J. 2009. "Legal Change: Selective Litigation, Judicial Bias, and Precedent." *Journal of Legal Studies*, 38: 157–68.
Mulligan, Casey B., and Andrei Shleifer. 2005a. "Conscription as Regulation." *American Law and Economics Review*, 7: 85–111.
Mulligan, Casey B., and Andrei Shleifer. 2005b. "The Extent of the Market and the Supply of Regulation." *Quarterly Journal of Economics*, 120: 1445–73.
Musacchio, Aldo. 2010. "Law and Finance C. 1900." NBER working paper no. 16216.
Nee, Victor, and Sonja Opper. 2009. "Bureaucracy and Financial Markets." *Kyklos*, 62: 293–315.
Niblett, Anthony, Richard A. Posner, and Andrei Shleifer. Forthcoming. "The Evolution of a Legal Rule." *Journal of Legal Studies*.
Pagano, Marco, and Paolo F. Volpin. 2005. "The Political Economy of Corporate Governance." *American Economic Review*, 95: 1005–30.
Pagano, Marco, and Paolo F. Volpin. 2006. "Shareholder Protection, Stock Market Development, and Politics." *Journal of the European Economic Association*, 4: 315–41.
Perotti, Enrico C., and Ernst-Ludwig Von Thadden. 2006. "The Political Economy of Corporate Control and Labor Rents." *Journal of Political Economy*, 114: 145–74.
Persson, Torsten, and Guido Tabellini. 2009. "Democratic capital: The Nexus of Political and Economic Change." *American Economic Journal: Macroeconomics*, 1: 88–126.
Posner, Richard A. 1973. *The Economic Analysis of Law*. New York: Aspen Publishers.

Priest, George L. 1977. "The Common Law Process and the Selection of Efficient Rules." *Journal of Legal Studies*, 6: 65–82.

Rajan, Raghuram G., and Luigi Zingales. 2003. "The Great Reversals: The Politics of Financial Development in the Twentieth Century." *Journal of Financial Economics*, 69: 5–50.

Roe, Mark, J. 2004. *Convergence and Persistence in Corporate Governance*. Cambridge: Cambridge University Press.

Roe, Mark, J. 2006. "Legal Origins, Politics, and Modern Stock Markets." *Harvard Law Review*, 120: 460–527.

Roe, Mark, J. 2007. "Juries and the Political Economy of Legal Origin." *Journal of Comparative Economics*, 35: 294–308.

Roe, Mark J., and Jordan I. Siegel. 2009. "Finance and Politics: A Review Essay based on Kenneth Dam's Analysis of Legal Traditions in The Law-Growth Nexus." *Journal of Economic Literature*, 47: 781–800.

Rosenthal, Howard, and Erik Voeten. 2007. "Measuring Legal Systems." *Journal of Comparative Economics*, 35: 711–28.

Rostowski, Jacek, and Bogdan Stacescu. 2006. "The Wig and the Pith Helmet – The Impact of 'Legal School' and Colonial Institutions on Economic Performance." Center for Social and Economic Research Network Studies and Analyses, 300.

Rubin, Paul H. 1977. "Why is the Common Law Efficient?" *Journal of Legal Studies*, 6: 51–63.

Serpoul, Frédéric. 2009. "Shareholder Protection and Stock Market Development in France (1852–2007)." Unpublished.

Sgard, Jérôme. 2006. "Do Legal Origins Matter? The Case of Bankruptcy Laws in Europe: 1808–1914." *European Review of Economic History*, 10: 389–419.

Shleifer, Andrei, and Daniel Wolfenzon. 2002. "Investor Protection and Equity Markets." *Journal of Financial Economics*, 66: 3–27.

Spamann, Holger. 2010. "The 'Anti-director Rights Index' Revisited." *The Review of Financial Studies*, 23: 467–86.

Stulz, René M., and Rohan Williamson. 2003. "Culture, Openness, and Finance." *Journal of Financial Economics*, 70: 313–49.

Wright, John R. 1996. *Interest Groups and Congress*. New York: Allyn and Bacon.

Zweigert, Konrad, and Hein Kötz. 1998. *Introduction to Comparative Law*, 3rd edition. Oxford and New York: Oxford University Press.

PART III

SOCIAL NORMS AND CUSTOMS

10 The focal point theory of expressive law

Richard H. McAdams

1. Introduction

A common claim about law is that it influences behavior "expressively." At the most general level, the claim is that law's behavioral influence is not entirely limited to the effect of legal sanctions (deterrence and incapacitation). The residual effect is termed "expressive." Unfortunately, the expressive effect is often left at this vague level, with no specific theory of how it works. But some theorists offer expressive mechanisms of law's influence. One possibility is that law communicates information, as by revealing the law-makers' information about public attitudes or the risks of regulated behavior (see Geisinger 2002; McAdams 2000a; Dharmapala and McAdams 2003). Another theory is that law changes preferences (see Cooter 1998, 2000b; Dau-Schmidt 1990). This chapter addresses a third expressive theory: that in certain circumstances law facilitates coordination by supplying a focal point (see e.g. Cooter 2000a; Garrett and Weingast 1993; Hadfield and Weingast 2010a, 2010b; McAdams 2000b). To some degree, these different theories – sanctions, information, preference change, focal point – may be seen as rival hypotheses for how law influences behavior. But there is no reason why law cannot have all these effects, some being expressive, which work in an additive way.

The focal point theory might also be termed a "coordination theory" of expressive law. Game theory shows how individuals often have a common interest in coordinating their behavior. In these situations, if anything makes mutually salient a particular way of coordinating behavior, we frequently observe self-fulfilling expectations that the salient behavior – the focal point – will occur. One can construct focal points with "cheap talk" and law is one of the ways to do so. Merely by pointing out one way for individuals to coordinate, the law nudges their behavior toward compliance.

An obvious example is a law that tells everyone to drive on the right side of the road. The state's announcement may be self-enforcing because everyone has an incentive to do what everyone else is doing – to coordinate – so as to avoid a collision. And the announcement makes everyone expect everyone else to drive on the right (below, I discuss whether we know why this is). But this example involves a *pure* coordination game because there is no conflict over whether to drive on the left or the right side. If law's focal point power exists solely in games without conflict, then it is very limited, even trivial, because law almost always addresses conflict. Indeed, this criticism is broader than law. If focal points generally matter only in games of pure coordination, then they are a mere curiosity and not, as Roger Myerson (2004: 92) calls them, "one of the great fundamental ideas of social philosophy."

Myerson is correct, however, because focal points also influence behavior in what Thomas Schelling (1960) called "mixed motive" games, where there exists both conflict and common interests. Individuals often have a common interest in coordinating their behavior even when some of their other interests conflict. The literature has explored two main categories: (1) games where the players need to coordinate their *primary* behavior (e.g. McAdams 2000b; McAdams and Nadler 2005) and (2) games where the players need to coordinate their *enforcement* behavior that sanctions some other individual's primary behavior (e.g. Hadfield and Weingast 2010a, 2010b; McAdams 2005). Primary behavior might be driving, smoking, recognition of property boundaries, or finance, each of which has an element of coordination despite conflict, modeled by a game like Hawk-Dove, as explained below. Secondary or enforcement behavior might enforce decentralized social norms, private organizational rules, or any other kind of informal order, where the enforcers are more likely to succeed in sustaining the order if they coordinate their enforcement on the same understanding of the rule being enforced, even though they may each prefer a different conception.

This chapter reviews and extends the literature on focal point theory of law. Section 2 describes the general theory of focal points and the specific theory of law as a focal point. Section 3 describes some of the experimental literature supporting the claim. Section 4 shows how the literature has applied the theory to specific areas of law: constitutional law, international law, everyday disputing, and the enforcement of custom. Section 5 contends that the focal point power is so fundamental that it is necessary to explain the operation of legal sanctions. Section 6 concludes.

2. Theory

2.1. Focal Point Theory – Generally

Game theory attempts to predict behavior by deriving equilibria from the players' beliefs, preferences, and opportunities. The payoffs for each outcome capture the players' preferences. Sometimes the payoffs and other variables rationally constrain the possible outcomes to a single equilibrium. In single-equilibrium situations, game theory predicts that rational players will play the strategies that produce that one outcome; here, we can also say that the payoffs create expectations that the sole equilibrium outcome will occur. Yet sometimes the payoffs fail to constrain the outcomes and there are multiple equilibria consistent with rationality. Here, we cannot say that the payoffs determine a unique set of expectations about how the game will be played. When payoffs do not uniquely determine behavior, then influences *other than payoffs* can.

Schelling (1960) famously labeled these non-payoff influences "focal points." He introduced the concept with pure coordination games. If you ask two separated people to name the same positive number as the other without communicating, there are an infinite number of ways to match answers. Yet when Schelling (pp. 55–6) posed the problem to his Yale colleagues and students, 40 percent named the same number – the number one. One might be tempted to say there is a purely rational process that produces this selection, but Schelling's next example better illustrates the cultural contingency of focal points. Schelling modified the number problem by asking individuals what amount of money they would name if, by matching their answer with someone else trying to match them, *they would each win that amount of money*. Again, random matching should almost never occur, while matching at the amount of 1 dollar would produce almost no monetary return. Instead, a plurality of 29 percent of his respondents named 1 million dollars (though respondents knew they would not actually receive the money). It is difficult to imagine a culturally neutral explanation of this result. Indeed, psychological research finds that people from different cultures have different perceptual styles, rendering different objects "focal" in their visual field and visual recall. See Nisbett et al. (2001).

An equilibrium is focal because it differs in some salient way from the other equilibria for reasons not captured in the model. As Schelling (p. 96) puts it, some "symbolic or connotative characteristics that transcend the mathematical structure of the game" will tend to draw attention to one solution, making it "stick out" from the others. And human beings have learned that, when faced with just this sort of problem, the best way to proceed is to pick the salient or prominent possibility. Schelling (p. 57) summarizes: "Finding . . . a key – any key that is mutually recognized as the key becomes the key – may depend on imagination more than on logic; it may depend on analogy, precedent, accidental arrangement, symmetry, aesthetic or geometric configuration, casuistic reasoning, and who the parties are and what they know about each other."

Schelling asserts that what is true of the pure coordination game is also true of the mixed motive games. We can see his point by introducing a slight degree of conflict in the above examples. Suppose we tell two individuals that they will receive a monetary payoff if they "match" in naming a positive number and nothing if they fail to match. But suppose we tell both individuals that one of them – Player *A* – will receive $100 if they match on an odd number and $99 if they match on an even number, while the other – Player *B* – will receive $100 for an even numbered match and $99 for an odd numbered match. The conflict here is trivial compared to the common interest in coordination, so we should not necessarily expect it to prevent coordination at the focal equilibrium. If the number one is sufficiently salient, *B* will be better off naming that number and getting a high probability of $99 than naming a non-focal even number and most likely receiving nothing. Although the size of the focal point effect is a contingent and empirical matter (see the experimental discussion below), there is no reason a priori to think that it disappears entirely as the magnitude of the conflict grows.

Where nothing in the feature of a situation makes a particular solution focal, Schelling contended that *third party expression* can make an outcome focal and thereby influence behavior. When a third party suggests or demands that the individuals coordinate in a particular way, she makes that outcome salient in a way that tends to create self-fulfilling expectations that the recommended or demanded behavior will occur. The third party expression can influence behavior even though it is "cheap talk" and does not change the payoffs or signal pre-existing information.

Schelling offers a paradigmatic example: the coordination of driving by a bystander. Imagine that a failed traffic light causes a traffic jam:

> The bystander who jumps into an intersection and begins to direct traffic at an impromptu traffic jam is conceded the power to discriminate among cars by being able to offer a sufficient increase in efficiency to benefit even the cars most discriminated against; his directions have only the power of suggestion, but coordination requires the common acceptance of some source of suggestion. (p. 144)

The situation involves mixed motives: there is conflict because each driver wishes to proceed before the other, but a mutual interest in coordinating to avoid a collision. Yet it seems likely that there will be some, even substantial, compliance with the Bystander's hand signals. The Bystander does not threaten to chase down and punish drivers who ignore her hand signals, nor does she possess the indicia of legitimacy that sociologists and psychologists attribute to law. Nonetheless, given a need to coordinate, the Bystander's ability to make salient one of the multiple equilibria gives her, as Schelling puts it, a genuine "power of suggestion."

2.2. *The Focal Point Theory of Expressive Law – Generally*

The focal point theory of expressive law claims that law can work like Schelling's bystander in the intersection, by using cheap talk to make salient a particular outcome. The theory claims that economists err in treating sanctions as strictly necessary to change behavior in the presence of multiple equilibria. Legal expression is one of the factors *other than payoffs* that can influence behavior.

Yet the scope of the theory is limited. McAdams and Nadler (2005) specify four conditions: (1) The situation the law addresses includes an element of coordination – the most important limit, addressed extensively below; (2) the law is sufficiently public; (3) the law is sufficiently clear, and; (4) there are no other competing focal points. The necessary conditions for the focal effect obviously do not always hold. First, law may address situations of pure conflict, where there is no element of coordination. For example, there is no element of coordination in a one-shot Prisoners' Dilemma. Second, the publicity of the law usually depends on media coverage or advertisement. Law cannot create a focal point if the content of the law is generally unknown. Third, the content of the law is often unclear, especially to non-lawyers. Law cannot align expectations unless it is sufficiently clear that most individuals have the same interpretation of it, that is, believe it "points to" the same outcome. Finally, even if the rule is clear, law may face competition from factors that make another outcome salient. Most commonly, the law might attempt to change an existing norm that, as precedent for past behavior, continues to make salient the behavior that adheres to the norm.

Nevertheless, the necessary conditions frequently do hold. Indeed, law might be the form of third party expression for which these conditions are most likely to hold, making law a society's general purpose mechanism for constructing a focal point. First, law frequently addresses disputes that often contain an element of coordination, as addressed extensively below in section 4. Second, there is often great publicity for legal rules from either media coverage or direct government advertising, as by public service announcements or the posting of signs. In any event, while it is true that law will have no focal point effect if it is not generally known, it is also true that law will have no sanction (or legitimacy) effect among those who are not aware of its existence. Third, though many laws are opaque, some are fairly simple, for example, the right of way goes to the driver with the green light or "no smoking" in restaurants. Finally, law often avoids having to compete with other stronger focal points, as where expectations are not fully settled.

3. The Experimental Literature on Legal Focal Points

An experimental literature generally supports the focal point theory. Several papers demonstrate the basic idea that focal points influence behavior in games of coordination (see e.g. Bacharach and Bernasconi 1997; Bosch-Domènech and Vriend 2008; Mehta et al. 1992, 1994a, 1994b). The Mehta et al. papers show that individuals do not just thoughtlessly choose the salient solution, but reason about what is likely to be mutually understood as the salient solution. Bosch-Domènech and Vriend (2008) demonstrate that focal points can even cause players to reach non-equilibrium and Pareto-dominated outcomes.

Considerable research demonstrates that cheap talk can create a focal point. When two players need to coordinate and one can send a message to the other identifying one of multiple equilibria, the expressed equilibrium tends to result. For reviews, see Crawford (1998); Valley et al. (2002). Other experiments establish specifically that *third party* expression can influence behavior in coordination situations. See Brandts and Holt (1992); Brandts and MacLeod (1995); Croson and Marks (2001); McAdams and Nadler (2005; 2008); Schotter and Sopher (2003); Van Huyck, Gillette, and Battalio (1992); Wilson and Rhodes (1997).

Most of these experiments involve pure coordination games, which heightens the possible importance of Crawford et al. (2008), who find that focal point influence can collapse as one moves from a pure coordination game to an asymmetric coordination game. Crawford et al. make an equilibrium focal by using a more salient label for the strategies that produce that equilibrium. They identify a pair of labels (e.g., among Chicago subjects, the Sears Tower versus AT&T Tower) that successfully produces coordination in the pure form of the game and then show that the same labels fail to produce coordination when they introduced even slightly asymmetric payoffs (creating a slight degree of conflict between the players over which equilibrium is best). Yet the Crawford et al. results are not uniform. In two conditions of their second experiment (AM1 and AL1 of the "pie games" results reported in Table 5 on p. 1455), the focal point continues to influence behavior despite payoff asymmetries. As the authors state (p. 1454): "label salience remains powerful, even in the presence of very large payoff asymmetries." Thus, on the evidence presented, the provocative title of the article – "The Power of Focal Points is Limited" – is not generalizable. Apparently, some focal points work in the face of conflict and some don't. More data are needed.

In any event, there are additional experiments finding focal point power in mixed motive games. One example is McAdams and Nadler (2005), who randomly assigned subjects to play the game in Figure 10.1. The subjects were not given the labels "hawk" or "dove," but that is the game (Hawk-Dove) these monetary payoffs produce (where strategy 1 is Hawk and strategy 2 is Dove). The two equilibria are C1/R2 and C2/R1 (where payoffs are underlined). The game creates conflict because player 1 prefers the R2/C1 equilibrium, while player 2 prefers the R1/C2 equilibrium. Yet the players also share an interest in avoiding the R2/C2 outcome.

	Player 2	
Player 1	C1	C2
R1	1, 1	<u>0</u>, <u>2</u>
R2	<u>2</u>, <u>0</u>	–1,–1

Figure 10.1 A Hawk-Dove Game

McAdams and Nadler compared the participants' interactions with and without third party cheap talk. Thus, in the control, there was no expression. The expressive condition consisted of one of two messages describing the two equilibria: either "R1/C2" or "C1/R2," delivered in one of two ways: (1) by engaging a mechanical device (spinning a spinner) that would randomly point to a space containing one message or the other (where each message took up exactly half of the space to which the spinner could point); or (2) by keeping one subject – a "leader" – out of the Hawk-Dove interaction and assigning him or her instead the task of writing one message or the other on a blackboard. All messages were in plain view of all the participants in the decision-making process, so there was common knowledge that each individual observed the message.

Because of the conflict, a subject who receives a message to play Dove (and receive 0) would prefer that both parties ignore the message and instead play the mixed strategy equilibrium (and receive 0.5). Nonetheless, expression influenced the behavior of the subjects in the expected direction. The R player was significantly more likely to play strategy 2 (Dove) when the message included R2, compared to the no-expression control, while the C player was significantly more likely to play strategy 1 (Hawk) when the message included C1, compared to the control. The opposite message had the opposite effects (also significant). McAdams and Nadler found a stronger effect when a human leader delivered the message, but even the mechanical device produced a significant effect on behavior.

Other experiments more explicitly introduce law. One way is to test whether behavior changes when the experimenters introduce a rule enforced by *non-deterrent* sanctions (see Bohnet and Cooter 2001 and Tyran and Feld 2006). If the rule's only effect is the deterrence generated by the fines enforcing the rule, then non-deterrent sanctions should have no effect on behavior. But these studies find that the expression of a rule affects behavior. For example, Tyran and Feld (2006) have players in a three-person voluntary contributions game vote for or against a rule requiring a certain level of contribution, and find that the creation of a rule increases contributions even though the sanctions enforcing the rule are non-deterrent. Based on the material payoffs, there is only one equilibrium to the game, but one can explain the results as a focal point by noting that non-material payoffs (which typically produce results other than the sole Nash equilibrium) can create multiple equilibria and a need to coordinate among them.

Similarly, Galbiati and Vertova (2008) run experiments with public goods games (where each subject decides whether to contribute some part of his or her monetary endowment, provided by the experimenter, to the group, where it will be multiplied and then allocated back in equal shares to each member of the group). The efficient outcome is for everyone to allocate all of their endowment, but the only Nash equilibrium is to give nothing. Despite this prediction, public goods experiments typically find that some individuals will contribute. Usually, however, if the game is repeated, the contribution rates fall towards zero. One possibility for explaining why there are any contributions is that, because of non-self-interested or non-material motivations the experiment cannot exclude, some people act as *reciprocators*. For reciprocators, the public goods game involves coordination. A reciprocator may be torn between returning the high contribution levels from other reciprocators (who start out expecting high contributions) and the zero contribution levels from selfish players taking advantage of the reciprocators. Anticipating the non-contributors, and given risk aversion, reciprocators may begin with modest contributions. So reciprocators struggle to coordinate with each other on single contribution level, while selfish players drag that level towards zero.

If reciprocators need to coordinate around a particular contribution level, then they would be influenced by the third party construction of a focal point. The Galbiati and Vertova (2008) experiment captures this dynamic. When the experimenters included in the instructions a statement that a specific "minimum contribution" of 80 percent of the per round endowment "is required," contributions rose significantly compared to the control that imposed no such obligation, even though there was still no monetary incentive to contribute in either condition. Galbiati and Vertova also created a monetary incentive for correctly predicting what amounts the other players would contribute. They determined that the effect of the high "minimum contribution" requirement was to increase the subjects' estimate of how much others would give. For reciprocators, this belief would motivate increased contributions. Galbiati and Vertova infer that the 80 percent obligation operated as a focal point for such players, creating self-fulfilling expectations that others would give close to 80 percent. See also McAdams and Nadler (2008).

In sum, the experimental evidence supports the idea that legal expression influences behavior by creating a focal point for coordination.

4. Applications: The Scope of Focal Point Theory

Theorists have discussed several important examples of the coordinating power of legal focal points, primarily in legal contexts where the threat of sanctions does not exist to explain compliance. Most of the existing discussion concerns the need to coordinate primary behavior, where the underlying game is one of coordination. Sections 4.1, 4.2, and 4.3 discuss constitutional law, international law, and the possibility of law's margin of focal point influence in everyday disputes. By contrast, section 4.4 discusses the enforcement of informal order, where the underlying primary conduct may not present a game of coordination, but those enforcing the informal rules may need to coordinate their sanctions.

4.1. The Focal Power of Constitutional Law

Some constitutional law is enforceable like other law, as where a private party resists a private claim of defamation by asserting free speech limits to the tort.

But when disputes arise directly between private citizens and the government or between different branches of government, it is artificial to speak of legal sanctions enforcing constitutional rights. In these contexts, one must wonder why the executive or legislative branches would heed judicial declarations of unconstitutionality, given that the courts have no legal means of enforcing their judgments except through agents of the executive and no way of funding itself except through agents of the legislature. Stephenson (2003) frames the general question by asking why the parts of government with "the money and guns" listen to the part with neither? One can go a step further and ask, in what sense the legislature has any money to allocate or the chief executive has any arms to wield except for the *expectation* that lower level actors will carry out legislative directives on the budget and executive directive on coercion.

The answer is that legal actors, as salient speakers, can provide a focal point around which the parties coordinate. The first step is to see that constitutions address coordination problems, as a significant political science literature suggests. Hardin (1989, 1999, 2006) characterizes constitutions as arising from a bargain between powerful interest groups who wish to form a state. He models the situation as a multi-player Battle of the Sexes game because the players are always better off "matching" their strategies, by agreeing to the same structure of government, than they are if they fail to agree. In Elster's (2007) model, political parties expect to alternate control of government and thus find themselves in an iterated Prisoners' Dilemma (PD) game where each party will benefit if both parties adhere to certain restraints of power when in office. Despite the conflict between parties, there is a strong element of coordination because, to achieve cooperation in the iterated PD game, the parties must agree on the boundaries of governmental powers.

Weingast (1997) focuses on democratic constitutions. He claims that the stability of democracy depends on "the people" being willing to challenge official action that transgresses democratic principles, as by a politician attempting to stay in office after being defeated in a lawful election. He models the problem as a complex game where citizen groups can maintain democratic rule only if they challenge the official jointly. Each group prefers to challenge the official if the other group does the same, because only joint action will work, but would rather acquiesce if the other group acquiesces, because unilateral action is costly as well as ineffective. It is therefore essential that citizen groups coordinate their efforts to challenge government officials around a "social consensus" of state authority. In a large diverse society, that consensus is unlikely to arise in a decentralized fashion, so the constitution is the means by which some actors create a consensus. See also Ordeshook (1992, 2002); Posner (2001); Posner and Vermeule (2008).

In these theories, a constitutional text works by making focal the forms of governmental behavior the constitution demands. Writing down the allocation of power in a particular structure of government makes that allocation salient and creates self-fulfilling expectations that the various players will demand at least as much power as granted in the writing, forcing players who wish to avoid chaos to cede that much power. Strauss (1996) observes that the theory directs courts to give serious weight to constitutional text. We see the tool of writing used not only in nation states, but by organizations that enact by-laws that constrain the powers of different actors in the organization. Even pirates used written constitutions to limit the power of their captains and quartermasters (see Leeson 2007, 2009).

4.2 The Focal Power of International Law

Because there is no overarching sovereign among nations, international relations are understood as a form of anarchy, a state of nature. Various scholars, notably Goldsmith and Posner (1999, 2005), have made the same points about international treaties as those just covered regarding constitutions: First, the interaction of states frequently presents a game involving coordination. Second, a written arrangement or adjudication between states may influence their behavior by virtue of creating a focal point and thereby creating self-fulfilling expectations of how to behave.

Garrett and Weingast (1993) provide perhaps the first model of this sort, viewing international law as arising in an iterated PD game. They make the same analytic move as Elster does with constitutional law, emphasizing an element of coordination *within* the PD game because there is more than one way to cooperate. All states are better off when everyone complies with one form of cooperation than when all states defect or try to cooperate in different ways. Thus, they view a treaty as a potentially self-enforcing agreement that specifies what form their cooperation will take.

McAdams (2005) uses coordination games and focal points to explain the puzzle of successful international adjudication despite the substantial lack of sanctions. If disputing states have an interest in coordinating – as where the worst outcome for each is a Hawk/Hawk conflict – then the arbiter can influence their behavior by making one equilibrium a focal point (the one where the party the arbiter declares to be the loser gives in to the arbiter's declared winner). Ginsburg and McAdams (2004) use this theory to explain international adjudication, including the puzzling fact that 68 percent of the decisions of the International Court of Justice ("ICJ") produce prompt compliance, despite the fact that the ICJ cannot credibly threaten sanctions. Ginsburg and McAdams claim that the compliance rate is high because nations tend to bring to the ICJ those disputes for which a focal point will resolve their dispute. They also claim to explain the observed low compliance in cases lacking mutual consent to the adjudication, i.e. where the ICJ overrules one party's jurisdictional objection and later rules against the same party on the merits. If one party seeks to avoid

IC jurisdiction, that party may not regard the dispute as a game involving coordination, in which case there is no room for a focal point.

Another international example is standard setting (see Drezner 2007). When international parties seek to standardize weights and measures, communications protocols for air traffic control, the right of way among vessels in international waters, the international exchange of mailed and telephonic communications, or the exchange of fingerprints by police departments, they are solving a coordination problem. If the states were indifferent between different standards, the problem would be purely one of coordination. More likely, the states disagree over which standard is best, each preferring its own national standard. But despite this disagreement, the great benefit from "matching" standards with others means that the worst outcome is often to fail to coordinate. A legal agreement setting a standard works by creating a focal point.

Finally, the effort to harmonize domestic regulations and legal rules is itself a type of standard setting. Here the "standard" is the private domestic law of say, contracts, securities, or antitrust. The greater the divergences between nations, the more difficult it is to transact across national borders. Policy convergence and harmonization save transaction costs when private firms seek to do business internationally. At the same time, a state incurs costs in switching from one legal standard to another. When two or more nations would benefit from policy convergence or harmonization, but each would prefer that other nations shift to their legal standard, the result is a Battle of the Sexes game. Again, once the legal agreement is made, it works as a focal point and there is no incentive to deviate.

4.3. The Focal Power of Law in Everyday Disputes

The above examples are relatively clear because much of the compliance we observe with international or constitutional law does not appear to be the result of sanctions. McAdams (2005) and McAdams and Nadler (2005, 2008) argue that, even where sanctions exist, law's focal point power may have some independent influence on behavior. They focus on disputes, which can frequently be modeled by the Hawk-Dove game in those cases where the worst outcome for both sides is the "total conflict" that results when the parties fail to resolve the dispute.

One example is traffic, which involves priority "disputes" between drivers. For example, two stopped drivers on perpendicular streets seek to make turns that cut across the path of the other. Or where drivers are in merging lanes, each seeks to get ahead of the other. Or drivers traveling in opposite directions approach a one-lane bridge that each wishes to cross first. In all these cases, each driver wants to proceed ahead of the other, but there is a common interest in coordinating to avoid a collision (and to avoid the outcome where both wait for the other to proceed). In traffic situations, the state may generate much of the compliance that it achieves merely by expression. Traffic signals, for example, are much like the randomizing device (a spinner) that McAdams and

Nadler (2005) used experimentally to express one or the other equilibrium to a Hawk-Dove game. If a driver approaches an intersection for the first time, sees a "yield" sign, and knows there is no such sign for the other road or lane, the driver is more likely to expect a collision if he fails to yield. If the drivers in the other lane can see that the first driver's yield sign applies only to his road or lane, the inference that the *other* drivers will not yield is particularly strong. Even without the fear of state sanctions or respect for state legitimacy, the driver complies with the yield sign to avoid a collision.

Many disputes have the same structure because disputants may share an interest in avoiding the outcome of "all-out" conflict (unlike a Prisoners' Dilemma). The most pervasive reason to avoid winning at all costs is the potential for violence. However unlikely, violence is a background risk of disputing. Besides American news reports of a shooting over something trivial, like breaking in line or talking in the movie theatre, much of the violence in ostensibly ordered societies involves individuals engaged in "self-help" remedies against someone whom they regard as having infringed on their rights (see Black 1983; Merry 1991; Nisbett and Cohen 1996). Less dramatically, a second result of continued conflict is a heated shouting match or exchange of profane insults. The parties may regard this outcome as the worst possible result of a dispute, particularly when people know each other socially – such as neighbors or co-workers – because the exchange may terminate their relationship.

Thus, for example, suppose two individuals want to sit in the same public area for a time and one wishes to smoke a cigarette and the other wishes not to be exposed to cigarette smoke. Or two neighbors dispute the exact location of their property line and one wants to plant a tree on the contested land while the other wants that no tree be planted. It is likely that the smoker and non-smoker will each think it better to give in to the other side that to have a physical brawl. Thus, the smoker wants to give in if the non-smoker will insist, but to insist if the non-smoker will give in; so too for the non-smoker. In these cases, there are two equilibria: where the smoker defers and non-smoker insists and vice versa. Similarly, the neighbors may not care enough about a sliver of property to think it worth committing or suffering an assault. Here, too, there are multiple equilibria, each being where one party gives in to the other.

Whether the concern is avoiding violence or embarrassment, these are situations where a legally constructed focal point will generate compliance. A law that is sufficiently publicized – say, by a "smoking prohibited" sign – can influence expectations by making focal the outcome where the non-smoker insists and the smoker gives in. In the designated no-smoking area, the law "waves on" the non-smoker and the smoker believes it is more likely he will insist. In a designated smoking area, the law (or other designator) creates the opposite expectations. The same is true of a legal rule or ruling that clearly awards the disputed property to one of the claimants. Law can create self-fulfilling expectations of what the players will do, generating compliance independently of sanctions or legitimacy.

4.4 The Focal Point Power to Clarify Customary Rules

Hadfield and Weingast (2010a, 2010b) emphasize an entirely different coordination problem, not the one that arises between branches of government, nations, drivers, or disputants, but one that arises between mutual *enforcers* of informal order. Informal order arises without law and may determine how people solve coordination problems. But ambiguity in informal order can prevent coordination in some cases As Postema (1982: 178) explains, while "the standard situations needing coordination are provided for," "[t]here may . . . be substantial differences of opinion in the community regarding what the convention requires in some specific instances." The inevitability of ambiguity is an old idea in language and law. One example is the inevitable incompleteness of contracts, which Garrett and Weingast (1993) use to explain why international tribunals are needed to supplement the meaning of treaties. McAdams (2005) discusses two forms of ambiguity in informal order: "fuzziness" – when the conditions for conventional rules are not precisely defined – and "potential incompleteness" – where there is uncertainty whether the precisely defined convention is subject to some exception for novel circumstances.

Hadfield and Weingast (2010a, 2010b) discuss the example of trade. A trading culture may informally sanction contractual cheating, but the ban on cheating may be effective only because third parties – not the cheater or the cheater's victim – boycott the cheater. (Note this model is similar to Weingast's model of democratic government, where the citizens can hold politicians in check only if they coordinate their sanctioning.) McAdams (2005) discusses the example of property. For example, Sugden (1986) describes property as a convention that emerges informally when individuals play strategies based on who currently possesses a valued resource. But McAdams (2005) argues that, without centralized articulation of rules, individuals will encounter some cases where it is difficult to decide who is currently in possession and other cases with uncertainty whether something other than current possession matters.

Without common expectations, players fail to coordinate. Legal expression is one salient means of clarifying an existing custom, removing ambiguity in how it applies to a particular situation. Clarifying the custom means providing a supplement to the customary rule. If the legal supplement is salient, it is a focal point. Even without possessing sanctions (or legitimacy), the legal clarification can align the disputant's expectations and change behavior.

5. The Focal Point Theory of Legal Sanctions

In mature legal systems, one may lapse into thinking that sanctions are independent and exogenous. But why does it change the expected payoffs of a behavior when a legislature or administrative agency promulgates penalties for the behavior? Why should one fear sanctions when the court announces a judgment of damages or a sentence of imprisonment? To ask these questions is really to ask why enforcement agents who actually impose sanctions obey officials who pronounce the law. Here, there is a potential for infinite regress. One can say that the sheriff fears that, if he refuses to carry out a court order to seize property, then the court will hold him in contempt. One could then say that the sheriff fears being held in contempt because, if he is, the bailiff will seize him. But why will the bailiff do that? Who does *he* fear? Obviously, the bailiff does not comply because the individual who issues the legal pronouncement – the judge – will personally, physically enforce it.

So the problem arises at each level – the legal pronouncement that *Y* is to sanction *Z* does not ensure that *Y* fears sanctions for failing to sanction *Z*. The pronouncement that *X* is to sanction *Y* for failing to sanction *Z* does not ensure that *X* fears sanctions for failing to sanction *Y*. And so on. As Mailath et al. (2001: 3) put it: "Words written on a piece of paper don't alter the laws of physics." Thus, the law against theft doesn't "affect what physical activities (such as attempts to lock an individual in a cell) individuals are capable of. . . . [M]y struggle to keep from being locked in a cage by you will result in an outcome that is determined by our relative strengths and martial arts abilities, but not by the existence or nonexistence of a law" (p. 3).

The path out of this puzzle is the power of expectations in a coordination situation. A mob boss (or guerilla leader or pirate captain) may not be the best physical fighter in his organization, but has power by virtue of everyone expecting everyone else to obey his orders. Any one person expects other mob members to kill him if he defies the boss's orders just because he would expect the boss to respond by ordering his death and would expect others will follow the boss's order. Wherever there is effective leadership, these interlocking expectations exist that one must obey the leader because the leader controls the group and the group has more power than any one individual.

Why does this leadership situation occur? Again, the basic answer is coordination. As Schelling (1960: 91) says, "The coordination game probably lies behind the stability of institutions and traditions and perhaps the phenomenon of leadership itself." The first level of coordination is merely that there is some advantage for the group to have different people doing different tasks at different times. Carrying out illegal activities, fighting a war, sailing a ship, all require careful coordination of the labor of multiple individuals. Frequently, the best action to take depends on circumstances that are changing rapidly, making time of the essence. For this reason, coordination is unlikely to occur in a decentralized, bottoms-up fashion. Even though everyone in the mob or guerilla army benefits from coordinating an attack on rival forces, it will not naturally occur that everyone decides on his own to implement the individual parts of the best overall strategy of attack. Instead, an individual needs to give orders. The group requires a leader.

Now we reach the second level of coordination: who will the leader be? If everyone has an opinion he is willing to express about how the group should proceed, upon which expression will everyone coordinate? To solve this problem, the group needs to designate a particular speaker whose expression, being the focus of everyone's attention, will be salient. But there are too many volunteers to lead. Here the situation is like a Battle of the Sexes game: possibly every individual would like to be the boss (commander, captain, etc.), but if each holds out to be the leader, then the result is chaos. Because there are gains from coordination – for example, the profits of criminal organization – each person gains more from being in a mob where someone else is boss than from the chaos where everyone claims to be the boss and no one is.

The critical point is that, once the group selects a boss, this person is like the Bystander Example in the introduction: his instructions create self-fulfilling expectations of compliance. The same is true of legal actors. First, society has basic needs for coordination that it accomplishes through law. Building roads, fighting crime, regulating pollution, waging war, all require coordination. Second, to solve the basic coordination problem, societies will in some way select a political and legal leader or, more likely, an array of them. This selection will render focal the orders of that individual. Once in place, the orders of legislators or judges are obeyed merely because everyone expects everyone else to obey them (and everyone expects everyone to expect everyone to obey them, etc.). Given those expectations, the legal actor can use expression to influence the enforcers who impose sanctions. Like the mob boss, everyone comes to expect that everyone else (or enough to make it matter) will obey the executive's order or the judge's decree. The legal actors have the power, by expression, to create self-fulfilling expectations that their demanded behavior will occur.

To return to game theory, where legal sanctions work, it is not by changing the payoffs for given actions, but by changing expectations about what actions will be taken. The act of stealing always pays x if no one subsequently seizes the thief's property and always pays y when someone later seizes the thief's property. Law does not affect these functions. Instead, because the political and legal leaders – legislators and judges – declare that the thief's property will be seized, the law changes the expectations about whether one's property will be seized if one steals. This is the foundation of legal sanctions.

6. Conclusion

The need for coordination is ubiquitous. When coordination is required, law can influence behavior merely by making the outcome it demands focal. The articulation of legal rules can also facilitate coordination among enforcers of informal customs and norms. Ultimately, the coordination provided by leaders underlies the actual infliction of legal sanctions.

References

Bacharach, Michael, and Michele Bernasconi, "The Variable Frame Theory of Focal Points: An Experimental Study", 19 *Games and Economic Behavior* 1 1–45 (1997).

Black, Donald, "Crime as Social Control", 48 *American Sociological Review* 34–45 (1983).

Bohnet, Iris and Robert Cooter, "Expressive Law: Framing of Equilibrium Selection?" Unpublished manuscript 2001.

Bosch-Domènech, Antoni and Nicolaas J. Vriend, *On the Role of Non-equilibrium Focal Points as Coordination Devices* (2008).

Brandts, J. and C. A. Holt, "An Experimental Test of Equilibrium Dominance in Signaling Games", 82 *American Economic Review* 1350–65 (1992).

Brandts, J. and W. B. MacLeod, "Equilibrium Selection in Experimental Games with Recommended Play", 11 *Games and Economic Behavior* 36–63 (1995).

Cooter, Robert D., "Expressive Law and Economics," 27 *Journal of Legal Studies* 585–608 (1998).

Cooter, Robert D., "Three Effects of Social Norms on Law: Expression, Deterrence, and Internalization," 79 *Oregon Law Review* 1–22 (2000a).

Cooter, Robert D., "Do Good Laws Make Good Citizens?" 86 *Virginia Law Review* 1577–1601 (2000b).

Crawford, Vincent, "A Survey of Experiments on Communication via Cheap Talk", 78 *Journal of Economic Theory* 286–98 (1998).

Crawford, Vincent P., Uri Gneezy, and Yuval Rottenstreich, "The Power of Focal Points Is Limited: Even Minute Payoff Asymmetry May Yield Large Coordination Failures", 98(4) *American Economic Review* 1443–58 (2008).

Croson, Rachel and M. Marks, "The Effect of Recommended Contributions in the Voluntary Provision of Public Goods", 39 *Economic Inquiry* 238–49 (2001).

Dau-Schmidt, Kenneth, "An Economic Analysis of the Criminal Law as a Preference Shaping Policy", *Duke Law Journal* 1–38 (1990).

Dharmapala, Dhammika and Richard H. McAdams, "The Condorcet Jury Theorem and the Expressive Function of Law: A Theory of Informative Law," 5 *American Law and Economics Review* 1–31 (2003).

Drezner, Daniel W., *All Politics is Global: Explaining International Regulatory Regimes* (2007).

Elster, Jon, "Unwritten Constitutional Norms," Unpublished manuscript 2007.

Galbiati, Roberto and Pietro Vertova, "How Laws Affect Behavior," Unpublished manuscript 2008.

Garrett, Geoffrey and Barry R. Weingast, "Ideas, Interests, and Institutions: Constructing the European Community's Internal Market," in *Ideas and Foreign Policy: Beliefs, Institutions, and Political Change* (J. Goldstein and R.O. Keohane, eds. 1993).

Geisinger, Alex "A Belief-Change Theory of Expressive Law," 88 *Iowa Law Review* 35–73 (2002).

Ginsburg, Tom and Richard H. McAdams, "Adjudicating in Anarchy: An Expressive Theory of International Dispute Resolution," 45 *William & Mary Law Review* 1229–339 (2004).

Goldsmith, Jack L. and Eric A. Posner, "A Theory of Customary International Law," 66 *University of Chicago Law Review* 1113 (1999).

Goldsmith, Jack L. and Eric A. Posner, *The Limits of International Law* (2005).

Hadfield, Gillian K. and Barry R. Weingast, "What is Law? A Coordination Model of the Characteristics of Legal Order," USC Legal Studies Research Paper No. 10-20 (2010a).

Hadfield, Gillian K. and Barry R. Weingast, *Endogenous Institutions: Law as a Coordinating Device* (2010b).

Hardin, Russell, "Why a Constitution?," in *The Federalist Papers and the New Institutionalism* (Bernard Grofman and Donald Wittman eds., 1989).

Hardin, Russell, *Liberalism, Constitutionalism, and Democracy* (1999).

Hardin, Russell, "Constitutionalism," in *The Oxford Handbook of Political Economy* 289–311 (Barry R. Weingast and Donald A. Wittman eds., 2006).

Leeson, Peter T., "An-arrgh-chy: The Law and Economics of Pirate Organization," 115 *Journal of Political Economy* 1049–84 (2007).
Leeson, Peter T., "The Calculus of Piratical Consent: The Myth of the Myth of Social Contract," 139(3–4) *Public Choice* 443–59 (2009).
Mailath, George J., Stephen Morris, and Andrew Postlewaite, "Laws and Authority," Working Paper 2001.
Mailath, George J., Stephen Morris and Andrew Postlewaithe, "Maintaining Authority," Working Paper 2007.
McAdams, Richard H., "An Attitudinal Theory of Expressive Law," 79 *Oregon Law Review* 339–90 (2000a).
McAdams, Richard H., "A Focal Point Theory of Expressive Law," 86 *Virginia Law Review* 1649–729 (2000b).
McAdams, Richard H., "The Expressive Power of Adjudication," *University of Illinois Law Review* 1043–121 (2005).
McAdams, Richard H. and Janice Nadler, "Testing the Focal Point Theory of Legal Compliance: The Effect of Third-Party Expression in an Experimental Hawk/Dove Game," 2 *Journal of Empirical Legal Studies* 87–123 (2005).
McAdams, Richard H. and Janice Nadler, "Coordinating in the Shadow of the Law: Two Contextualized Tests of the Focal Point Theory of Legal Compliance," 42 *Law and Society Review* 865–98 (2008).
Mehta, Judith, Chris Starmer and Robert Sugden, "An Experimental Investigation of Focal Points in Coordination and Bargaining: Some Preliminary Results," in *Decision Making Under Risk and Uncertainty: New Models and Empirical Findings* 211 (John Geweke ed., 1992).
Mehta, Judith, Chris Starmer and Robert Sugden, "Focal Points in Pure Coordination Games: An Experimental Investigation," 36 *Theory and Decision* 163–85 (1994a).
Mehta, Judith, Chris Starmer and Robert Sugden, "The Nature of Salience: An Experimental Investigation of Pure Coordination Games," 84 *American Economic Review* 658–73 (1994b).
Merry, Sally Engle, *Urban Danger* 175–86 (1981).
Myerson, Roger B., "Justice, Institutions, and Multiple Equilibria," 5 *Chicago Journal of International Law* 91 (2004).
Nisbett, Richard E. and Dov Cohen, *Culture of Honor* (1996).
Nisbett, Richard E., Kaiping Peng, Incheol Choi, and Ara Norenzayan, "Culture and Systems of Thought: Holistic Versus Analytic Cognition," 108(2) *Psychological Review* 291–310 (2001).
Ordeshook, Peter C., "Constitutional Stability," 3 *Constitutional Political Economy* 137–75 (1992).
Ordeshook, Peter C., "Are 'Western' Constitutions Relevant to Anything Other than the Countries They Serve?", 13 *Constitutional Political Economy* 3 3–11 (2002).
Posner, Eric A., "Strategies of Constitutional Scholarship", 26 *Law and Social Inquiry* 529–46 (2001).
Posner, Eric A. and Adrian Vermeule, "Constitutional Showdowns," 156 *University of Pennsylvania Law Review* 991 (2008).
Postema, Gerald J., "Coordination and Convention at the Foundation of Law," 11 *Journal of Legal Studies* 165–203 (1982).
Schelling, Thomas C., *The Strategy of Conflict* (1960).
Schotter, A. and B. Sopher, "Social Learning and Coordination Conventions in Intergenerational Games: An Experimental Study," 111 *Journal of Political Economy* 4987–529 (2003).
Stephenson, Matthew C. "'When the Devil Turns . . .': The Political Foundations of Independent Judicial Review," 32 *Journal of Legal Studies* 59–89 (2003).
Strauss, David A., "Common Law Constitutional Interpretation," 63 *University of Chicago Law Review* 877–935 (1996).
Sugden, Robert, *The Economics of Rights, Cooperation, and Welfare* (1986).
Sunstein, Cass, "On the Expressive Function of Law," 144 *University of Pennsylvania Law Review* 2021–53 (1996).
Tyran, Jean-Robert and Lars P. Feld, "Achieving Compliance When Legal Sanctions are Non-Deterrent," 108 *Scandinavian Journal of Economics* 135–56 (2006).

Valley, K., L. Thompson, R. Gibbons and M. Bazerman, "How Communication Improves Efficiency in Bargaining Games," 38 *Games and Economic Behavior* 127–55 (2002).
Van Huyck, J. B., A. B. Gillette and R. C. Battalio, "Credible Assignments in Coordination Games," 4 *Games and Economic Behavior* 606–26 (1992).
Wilson, R. K. and C. M. Rhodes, "Leadership and Credibility in N-Person Coordination Games," 41 *Journal of Conflict Resolution* 767–91 (1997).
Weingast, Barry R., "The Political Foundations of Democracy and the Rule of Law," 91 *American Political Science Review* 245–63 (1997).

11 Countervailing norms

Emanuela Carbonara, Francesco Parisi and Georg von Wangenheim

1. Introduction

There are some circumstances in which social norms counteract legal norms, reduce their effect and even produce results that are opposite to those intended by the lawmaker. In this sense, we say that social norms may be "countervailing". Then, legal intervention that does not take into account existing social norms may not only be ineffective but may even have a negative impact. For instance, a law introducing a new sanction may either be less effective than expected or even cause an increase in the sanctioned behavior.

Such results contradict the predictions of traditional law and economics theories. According to such theories, the law is "an obligation backed by a sanction" (Raz, 1980). Economic analysts characterize legal sanctions as a price. Individuals consider sanctions as an external incentive and make decisions regarding legally relevant behavior by means of standard cost and benefits analysis. Alternatively, expressive-law theories argue that individuals tend to internalize the obligations expressed by the law, so that legal norms become social norms.

Both theories predict a unique outcome of lawmaking: stricter laws and larger sanctions reduce the prevalence of the regulated behavior. Conversely, more lenient laws and smaller sanctions increase its frequency.

Such a conclusion has recently been challenged by experimental evidence. Gneezy and Rustichini (2000) tested the effects of the introduction of a fine for latecomers on parents' behavior in several day-care centers. In a field experiment, they found that the introduction of a fine produced an increase in the number of children picked up late by parents. According to the traditional economic model, since the fine increases the price of coming late, fewer parents should do so. Similarly, according to expressive-law theories, the fine should represent the obligation for parents to collect their children on time and should therefore induce parents to be timely. There could be several explanations for this phenomenon; the fine could have been interpreted as a price by parents who recognized it as a new service offered by the center. Alternatively, paying an additional fee may have assuaged the guilt associated with lateness. Whatever the real motivation, the main point is that the new rule contradicted both traditional and expressive-law theories.

This result, albeit striking, is not the only one highlighting the unintended results of legal rules. Stuntz (2000) considers how criminal law can be self-defeating if it is not aligned with general values and norms. He illustrates how laws against vice crimes (gambling, drinking during the Prohibition) and highly divisive "moral" crimes (e.g. slavery) raised fierce opposition and generated disobedience rather than obedience. In these cases, opposition was made even stronger by the perception that these policies were biased against specific ethnic groups and social classes and this corroded the legitimacy of the law.

Empirical evidence showed that the enactment of restrictive copyright laws had unintended effects on the amount of peer-to-peer file sharing over the internet. After music companies started suing people for illegal downloading, in the summer 2003, the number of downloads increased significantly (Depoorter and Vanneste, 2005; Oksanen and Välimäki, 2007). Moreover, there is experimental evidence indicating that legal sanctioning of file sharing produces a backlash effect on behavior; exclusive reliance on punishment might be unfortunate if sanctions have a countervailing effect (Depoorter, Parisi and Vanneste, 2005).

Understanding both responses to legal rules is therefore crucial, in order to explain the huge variety of different and unexpected results of legal innovation. A regulator introducing new rules assessed on the basis of a wrong or incomplete model of human behavior may lead to outcomes far from the social optimum.

Human behavior is affected by a series of factors that go beyond the mere extrinsic incentives of sanctions and rewards. These factors include individual values and social norms and constitute the intrinsic motivation of behavior. Intrinsic and extrinsic motivations interact in a variety of ways. If the law reflects generally accepted values, then intrinsic motivation and extrinsic incentives push individual behavior in the same direction and the law produces the expected results. This occurs also when the law has a high expressive value, i.e. if the obligation contained in the law is internalized quickly by individuals. If, on the other hand, the law clashes with social norms, and intrinsic motivation exerts a stronger influence on individual behavior, then social norms may have a countervailing effect. Finally, the same type of extrinsic incentives introduced by the law may have a framing effect on behavior, determining the direction of the interaction with social norms. Particularly, designing incentives in the form of sanctions for violators rather than rewards for compliers may make a difference on how the law is perceived and may determine obedience or backlash.

An analysis of the effects of legal innovation must necessarily consider the interplay between social norms and the law. Particularly, we need to study how social norms are formed and enforced. Then we need to briefly characterize the expressive function of the law, to understand under which conditions the law comports with social norms. This will help us understand when legal innovation may lead to a backlash due to countervailing social norms.

2. The Origins and Evolution of Social Norms

Social norms are defined as conventions accompanied by normative expectations (Sugden, 1989; Bicchieri, 2006). A convention is a pattern of behavior followed by the majority in a given social group (Young, 1993). Breaking such a pattern may result in substantial costs. Given that everybody else follows the convention, an individual following a different behavior most likely prevents coordination, thus imposing a cost on others. The classic example of this is choosing which side of the road to drive on, left or right. If one driver starts to drive on the left while everybody else drives on the right, an accident will almost surely happen. Hence, each person expects others to follow a convention and observing lack of compliance provokes anger and resentment and possibly leads to a social sanction. Such expectations, which might lead to anger and sanctions, are termed "normative expectations", because they trigger the enforcement that transforms a behavior followed by a majority into a norm.

The enforcement of social sanctions follows two distinct channels. The first channel we described above and termed second-party and third-party enforcement. The direct victims of disobedience implement second-party enforcement, while other individuals who may be harmed indirectly apply third-party enforcement strategies, such as public disapproval, ostracism, or even physical punishment. The second channel is more subtle and can be termed "first-party enforcement" and, in this case, punishment is applied by violators themselves: since individuals dislike being disapproved of, they suffer a (psychological) cost (guilt).

How is a convention (and then, possibly, a social norm) established? The process closely resembles a bandwagon effect, that is, a situation in which a given behavior becomes more attractive the more people follow the same behavior (Leibenstein, 1950). A bandwagon effect presupposes the existence of a threshold number of followers, above which following the convention becomes optimal. In other words, a bandwagon effect implies that the number of followers needs to reach a critical mass.

Becoming the object of resentment and social sanctions reduces the individual's utility from breaking with convention, while obedience to social customs yields extra utility, as people feel they are approved and are part of a community. This mechanism of expectations and social sanctions can pull individual behavior in socially undesirable directions. The literature establishes that people do not necessarily enact the most efficient social norm when more than one is available (Sugden, 2004). Once the number of people following a social norm reaches a given threshold, more and more people will be encouraged to follow it, regardless of whether such a norm is just and efficient. The possible inefficiency and unjustness of social norms can be found also in Cesare Beccaria's words "human conventions [...] are expressly formulated or simply assumed in view of common necessity and utility" (Cesare Beccaria, 1764).

Conventions typically spread because of past experience (the last time I encountered another driver, he kept to his side of the road), common background and ideas, and by analogy. There is, therefore, a strong path dependency in the adoption of a convention (Sugden, 1989). Individuals choose behavior based on what they did or what they saw others doing in similar past circumstances. They take decisions following a backward-looking, myopic approach, the exact opposite of a forward-looking, rational expectations approach. Forward-looking individuals are able to spot the convention that maximizes total surplus among the many possible conventions upon which they may converge. On the contrary, backward-looking agents are not able to assess the effect of their choices on total surplus and can adopt and maintain the wrong convention. Similarly, conventions and social norms can be unjust. One should consider the many social conventions turned into very strict social norms that have limited the freedom, restricted the rights and diminished the dignity of women and ethnic minorities (Carbonara and Pasotti, 2010).

This is one of the reasons why a lawmaker may choose to enact laws that do not align with pre-existing social norms, in an attempt to correct those which are inefficient or unjust. We will state other possible explanations below, after describing how the law can bend moral and social values.

3. The Expressive Power of the Law

According to expressive law theories, the law can influence behavior independently of the sanction it imposes (McAdams, 2000a). Expressive-law scholars have provided several examples of how the law can change individual preferences and tastes and, in some cases, affect social norms and values. For instance, the ban on public smoking reduced the number of young black Americans who smoke by changing the social meaning of smoking from rebellion to dirtiness and foolishness (Sunstein, 1996). Then, the lawmaker can use the law to provoke changes in the social meaning of behavior (Lessig, 1995 and 1996).

The law can also create focal points that help people solve coordination problems in environments characterized by a multiplicity of equilibria (McAdams, 2000a). Driving conventions, once again, provide a good example. People can either drive on the right-hand or on the left-hand side of the road. Without a coordinating device, some individuals may choose to drive on the right, some on the left and several collisions may ensue. By stating that drivers should keep to the right, the law may solve the coordination problem, since now people receive an indication of the correct behavior and form expectations on the actions followed by others. This may have the effect of changing previous equilibria, as people may change their behavior and become unwilling to follow tradition. Then, expressive law may contribute to changing existing social norms. To illustrate how that could happen, McAdams presents the example of a community in which smokers traditionally follow very aggressive strategies towards non-smokers, to affirm their perceived right to smoke in public. A law prohibiting smoking in public places may change not only the behavior of non-smokers, who now have a basis for questioning whether the strategies followed in the past will continue to apply in the future, but also the expectations of smokers about non-smokers' reaction. Before the enactment of the law they expected passive behavior, but now they may believe that non-smokers feel entitled to react strongly to their smoking in prohibited public places. If non-smokers fight against smoking in public places in sufficiently high numbers, "they will establish a [...] convention against smoking" (McAdams, 2000a) and the law will be enforced by second-party sanctions. Moreover, laws enacted through a democratic process are generally positively correlated with "popular attitudes" (McAdams, 2000b) and thus provide a signal of those attitudes, changing one's beliefs about what others will think. Given that individual preferences are affected by what others approve or disapprove of, the law can influence behavior even without a legal sanction.

Through expression, the law can also induce individuals to internalize the values it embodies (Cooter, 1998 and 2000). This distinguishes expressive-law theories from traditional theories focused on the role of law as an instrument for creating external incentives, such as taxes, sanctions and rewards. According to expressive-law theories, internalized rules may trigger private enforcement mechanisms and change observed patterns of behavior, even in the absence of other external incentives. As mentioned above, private enforcement mechanisms include first-party, second-party and third-party enforcement. First-party enforcement implies that legal rules are also able to affect behavior through "internalization." To explain how the internalization process takes place, Cooter refers to social psychological research that suggests that the majority of citizens obey laws out of internal respect for the law in general (see Tyler, 1990). Citizens have a preference for obeying the law, so that the (psychological) cost of performing a given action increases after that particular action is prohibited by the law. Thus people are induced to refrain from that action.

Legal rules differ in their expressive power. Laws with a strong expressive power are laws that citizens are willing to pay a lot to obey. In general, even if literature on this specific issue is almost non-existent, it seems that the expressive power of a law is inversely related to the degree of forcefulness of the social values the law tries to bend. Therefore, the alignment of legal precepts and decisions of authorities with current social norms and values has a positive influence on whether people comply with law, even when it is not in their self-interest to do so (Tyler, 1990 addresses this issue with respect to law;

and Tyler and Huo, 2002 do so with respect to the decisions of authorities). Legitimacy is undermined when the content of the law departs from social norms, be they based on moral, ethical, or merely cultural values. Tyler (1990) and Sunshine and Tyler (2003) provide support for the argument that the public's perceptions of legitimacy impact people's compliance with the law.

4. Why Do Laws Clash With Social Norms?

We have just seen that the expressive power of the law is stronger the closer the content of the law to existing social norms. Whenever the law differs from current values, we might observe a backlash when society tries to correct the law and align it with social norms. The effects of the law therefore depend on the social "reaction" triggered by legal innovation, whereas social reaction is likely to be proportional to the degree of consistency of the new law with prior social values.

The question then becomes why lawmakers and norm entrepreneurs (i.e. individuals interested in changing the law; see Sunstein, 1996; Ellickson, 2001) enact laws that depart from the values and norms shared by the majority of the citizenry. As we argued in Section 2, social norms can be unjust and/or inefficient. A welfare-maximizing lawmaker may exert a paternalistic role, in the attempt to change "wrong" social norms. This happened when more severe rape laws were passed in an attempt to change the behavior of men (and women) who may have acted according to the belief that "no sometimes means yes". Similarly, there are numerous attempts to reduce drunk driving by enacting more restrictive laws and penalties (Kahan, 2000).

Sometimes, however, new laws may reflect the values held by the majority at the moment of enactment, values that may then change (possibly as a result of legal innovation itself), leading to a misalignment between the content of the law and the new social norm. Stuntz (2000) uses Prohibition as an enlightening example of this principle.

The majority of the U.S. population approved of laws enacted in 1919 that banned the use of alcohol in the United States. Alcohol was a perceived cause of many social problems; such problems predominantly affected the poor. Many factory workers struggled with alcoholism and spent all their wages on alcohol, left their families with hardly anything to eat and were often physically abusive. That is why the white, protestant majority saw Prohibition as a paternalistic way to tackle a problem affecting mainly poor neighborhoods, generally populated by immigrants (typically Italian and Irish Catholics). This explains why Prohibition passed notwithstanding strong opposition by rich lobbies. In 1933, Prohibition was repealed and an overwhelming majority approved repeal (Kyvig, 1979). What explains such a dramatic shift in social preferences? According to scholars, the way Prohibition was enforced had a negative impact on its legitimacy. Alcoholism permeated society, both poor and rich neighborhoods alike. However, the police chose to target only poor neighborhoods. The reason is rather straightforward, even without resorting to arguments of social favoritism. Scarce police forces were allocated where the problems of alcohol abuse were more severe. However, ethnic minorities in poor neighborhoods felt persecuted; while alcohol consumption was criminal for them, it was not for rich Anglo-Saxon protestants. This eroded the power of the law in those communities, eliciting an enormous rise in the phenomenon (additionally, the price of alcohol had increased significantly, making alcohol manufacturing and distribution attractive to criminal organizations).

When the expressive power of a law vanishes completely, the lawmaker faces two possibilities: either increase sanctions considerably (which is costly) or lift the legal ban altogether. In the early 1930s, America was suffering through the Great Depression and it could not afford the costs of a war against the consumption of alcohol. Alternatively, it may have been that the majority of citizens could not bear to see a large number of white immigrants in jail for selling beer. Whatever the reason, an overwhelming majority supported the abandonment of Prohibition. This illustrates how a legislature might enact laws which depart from social values regardless of the fact that they are elected to represent their constituents. The same dynamics were observed when laws punishing crack consumption were passed in the United States in the 1980s and 1990s (Tonry, 1995). In that case, enforcement targeted poor, black neighborhoods, where crack use rose to incredible heights as enforcement grew. Unlike Prohibition, however, lawmakers responded to the backlash by dramatically raising penalties, because drug abuse presents even more serious social implications.

Finally, laws departing from existing social norms may be enacted in situations of serious danger for the population or in times of war. For example, following the terrorist attack on the World Trade Center in New York on September 11, 2001, the US Congress passed the Patriot Act, which limited personal freedom and constitutional rights. Such law raised considerable criticism as it was deemed to excessively weaken the protection of civil liberties (Carbonara et al., 2010).

5. Social Norms and Legal Backlash

We now explicitly consider the case of laws that do not align with pre-existing moral norms and social beliefs. By inducing civil disobedience, such laws might reinforce social values contrary to law, producing a countervailing effect.

Particularly, when the law is perceived as too strong, people tend to approve disobedience and try to stop enforcement of an "unjust law". In addition to that, they might publicly protest and engage in civil disobedience. When the law is more lenient than socially desired, people tend to show reprobation when confronted with an infringement of the (weak) law. They might even try themselves to apply the larger penalty they believe appropriate. Hence social reaction may reinforce or undermine the effect of legal intervention, depending on whether the law is too strict or too weak compared to the social norms.

Kahan (2000) considers the case in which a law is passed that tries to change an existing social norm. Modern sexual assault laws were passed that attempted to change the "no sometimes means yes" social norm. Those laws eliminated the physical resistance requirement traditionally needed to prove that intercourse was non-consensual. Such legal innovation has been highly ineffective, since prosecutors have been reluctant to charge men who disregarded verbal protestations and juries have rarely convicted them (Schulhofer, 1998). Kahan (2000) calls this the "sticky-norm problem": social norms so rooted in common behavior that enforcers are reluctant to apply laws contrary to such norms. Enforcers face a tradeoff between their desire to do their civic duty by correctly applying the laws of the state and their aversion to enforcing rules that punish what is socially accepted behavior. He then argues that the sticky-norm problem affects laws that punish far more severely than enforcers believe is right. In such cases, in fact, their aversion to punish too severely will dominate their disposition to apply the law, and they will refuse to proceed.

The decision of some enforcers may affect other enforcers, who may follow suit. This "cascade effect" may also be driven by the legal system itself: if the enforcer is a judge, then her decision will constitute a precedent in common-law countries and this may bias future decisions toward the non-application of the controversial rule. Such an effect may occur in civil-law countries too, where judges base their interpretation of the law on precedent decisions (especially those by Supreme Courts).

As a result, legal innovation that departs too much from current social norms is incapable of reducing incidences of the prohibited actions. Kahan (2000) argues that it might even increase incidence. In fact, not applying the law (for instance, acquitting a defendant accused of raping a woman who protested but did not physically resist) reasserts the norm the law was trying to change, perpetuating and even encouraging the crime.

The solution to the sticky-norm problem then is to proceed with "gentle nudges" in lawmaking. If the increase in severity is limited in size, enforcers will apply the law, eroding the social norm, as individuals will refrain from the sanctioned behavior if they observe consistent punishment. "Hard shoves" (meaning sudden and conspicuous increases in severity) are therefore counterproductive.

Carbonara, Parisi and von Wangenheim (2008a) explicitly analyze the effect of the enactment of the law on social norms and their evolution. They assume that people behave according to prevailing social norms (Sugden, 1989; Sunstein, 1996; Cooter, 1998, 2000). There is an initial distribution of individual beliefs about the appropriateness of a given behavior, and social norms reflect such distribution (to continue with the previous example, if the majority believes that "no sometimes means yes", then rape when a woman protested but did not physically resist will not be the object of social sanctions and will generally be tolerated).

How does the initial distribution of beliefs originate a social norm? Individuals in society interact and exchange opinions, influencing each other's beliefs (Bikhchandani, Hirschleifer and Welch, 1992 and 1998). Depending on the number of people holding a given belief and on the strength with which each belief is held and publicly defended, other individuals may be influenced. Then, some of the beliefs in society will function as "attractors". If a sufficiently high number of individuals end up sharing the same belief, that belief will become a social norm. If the majority converges on a unique belief, then society will hold a shared social norm. If, however, individuals cluster around different beliefs, multiple social norms will coexist. It may even happen that a polarized society results from such a process, with people clustering around opposite social norms.

In this evolving scenario, in which people converge on social norms through interaction and mutual influence, the law exerts a twofold impact. On one hand, it is capable of attracting individual opinions towards the value embodied in the law (expressive function). On the other hand, it could repel those who hold strong contrary beliefs (countervailing effect).

If the second effect is strong enough, legal innovation can generate a social norm different from the norms embodied in the law. It may also generate social divide even in the face of a previously balanced society. Social divide is particularly problematic, since it provides grounds for discrimination, segregation or other forms of social conflict and violence (Carbonara and Pasotti, 2010). Social divide more likely occurs when individuals feel very strongly about discrepancies between their beliefs and the values embedded in the new law, which act as a powerful "repellent" for those whose beliefs are different enough, but as an effective attractor for those whose views are similar enough.

So far, we have considered how the law influences social norms. The analysis can be pushed forward to include the impact of the law on individual behavior. There are multiple determinants of behavior, each possibly exerting a different force. First of all, behavior is affected by external incentives, like the monetary gains from performing an action (or, more generally, the utility derived from it) and the sanction imposed by the law. Generally, in this respect, a higher sanction would increase the relative price of the sanctioned activity, leading to a substitution toward other non-sanctioned activities. The prevalence of a given action in the society also affects behavior: if many people perform it, no matter whether it is illegal or contrary to social norms, "wrongdoers" feel more comfortable. Finally, last but not least, behavior is influenced by social norms, which, as argued above, are not passive and react to legal innovation. When the expressive effect of the newly enacted law is strong enough, it might bend existing social norms. As mentioned above, a powerful social norm and one of the main constituents of individual intrinsic motivation is the desire to obey the law (Cooter, 2000). Enacting strict laws that severely punish a given behavior clearly signals that the state considers of primary importance deterring citizens from performing the sanctioned action, and this tends to reduce prevalence. Conversely, a new law that is markedly contrary to current social values or more restrictive than what people would support triggers opposition, in the form of both open protest and civil disobedience and might bend social norms in the opposite direction.

Carbonara, Parisi and von Wangenheim (2010) study how these influences affect behavior. They find that negative reactions by a sufficiently high number of individuals may result in a reinforcement of other individuals' dislike of the law, with countervailing effects. Such a result is even more likely if the expressive power of the law is not very strong and the behavior is relatively common. Then, the situation after legal change is characterized by high protest and an increased rate of violations compared to the initial situation.

From this, the following intuition results. When legal innovation is not far from pre-existing social values, sanctions and the expressive effect of the law move preferences in the same direction, forcing internalization. Conversely, when the law departs from current social values, the expressive and reaction effects pull behavior in opposite directions. The final outcome and the ability of the legislator to achieve her intended goal depends on the relative magnitude of external incentives, of expressive and reaction effects. In the following, we will provide an account of the results of our economic models. Thus, legal innovation may have the undesired consequence of increasing prevalence of the behavior it intends to ban. This result is similar to Kahan (2000), but is obtained through a completely new and more general mechanism. While in Kahan it was only a matter of enforcement, in Carbonara et al. (2010) the new law is enforced, notwithstanding possible disapproval. Hence, the countervailing effect is obtained in the face of opposing extrinsic incentives and not because such incentives are blocked by enforcers. It is therefore a much stronger result, obtained in a framework that seems more suitable to describe recent cases of countervailing effects, like the increase in music downloading presented above.

To see how the model works, consider a simple setting in which individuals decide whether to obey the law according to the magnitude of the sanction, the strength of the expressive power and expressed opinion (approval or disapproval) about a specific law. As it would be realistic to assume, individuals are more prone to obey the higher the sanction and the stronger the expressive power of the new law. The new element in the analysis is the effect of expressed opinion on compliance. The more individuals engage in social protest against the law, the less likely it is that people will obey the new law, since protest represents the public expression of dissent, which reveals that the law clashes with the values shared by those who protest. A very high level of protest shows that the new law does not reflect social norms. Conversely, if many people express an opinion in favor of the new law, there would be no countervailing effect.

The more severe the law, the higher the likelihood that the law will be disapproved of and that protest will be high. In fact, consider an individual who believes that downloading music from the internet, infringing the copyright, is wrong (so that she would approve a law sanctioning such conduct) and that somebody downloading one song should be fined $10 (about ten times the price of a song purchased legally). Now assume that the law prescribes a fine equal to $2000. Our individual would disapprove of the excessive harshness of the law and empathize with the "wrongdoer", notwithstanding her initial belief that illegal downloading should be punished.

To understand how the various forces illustrated above can impact behavior, consider the following simple model, introduced in Carbonara, Parisi and von Wangenheim (2008b). Define c as the percentage of people violating the law, and p as the level of protest. As explained above, c is an increasing function of protest, $c'(p)>0$. Now assume that a new legal standard is introduced, which increases the sanction imposed on violators from S_A to S_B. The function $c(p)$ is drawn for a given sanction. Since a higher sanction reduces the incentive to violate the law, there will be fewer violators for all levels of protest. Hence, $c(p)$ shifts downwards, as in Figure 11.1, where the increase from S_A to S_B moves the

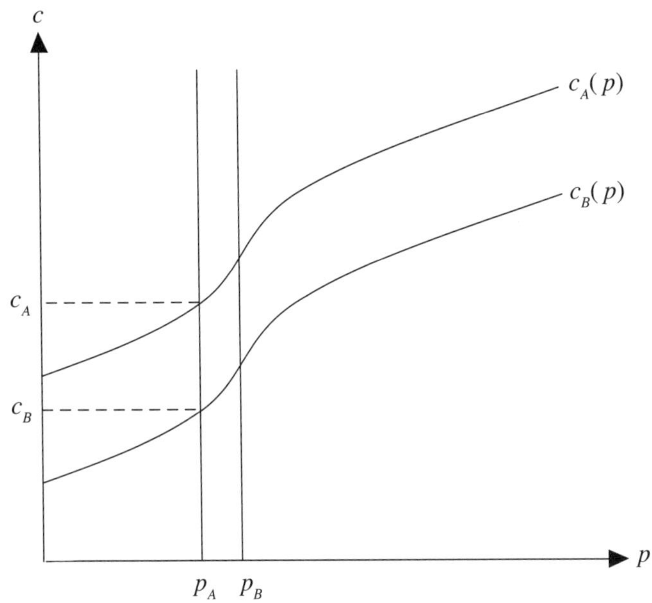

Figure 11.1 A more restrictive law with strong expressive power: the law has the desired effects

curve $c(p)$ from $c_A(p)$ to $c_B(p)$. The increase in the sanction also has the effect of raising protest, from p_A to p_B. However, protest is directly influenced by the expressive power of the law, so that a law with a high expressive power will inhibit protest and generate a moderate increase in p. This is the case depicted in Figure 11.1, where the shift in protest is not high enough to compensate for the effect of extrinsic incentives and the new rate of violations, c_B, is lower than the initial rate, c_A. Then, when the law has a strong expressive power, the combined impact of incentives and internalization will dominate and the increase in the severity of the law counterbalances the effect of protest and increases legal compliance. The enactment of a law backed by an enforceable sanction thus reduces the rate of violations, as normally expected.

Conversely, when the expressive power of the law is limited, the combined effect of incentives and internalization may not be sufficient to dominate the impact of protest. Figure 11.2 considers again the same increase in the sanction from S_A to S_B, which causes $c(p)$ to shift from $c_A(p)$ to $c'_B(p)$. However, this time the expressive effect is low, so that social reaction predominates and protest increases from p_A to p_B', much more so than in Figure 11.1. Then, protest more than compensates for the incentives determined by the stronger sanction, and the new rate of violations, c_B', is now larger than the initial rate,

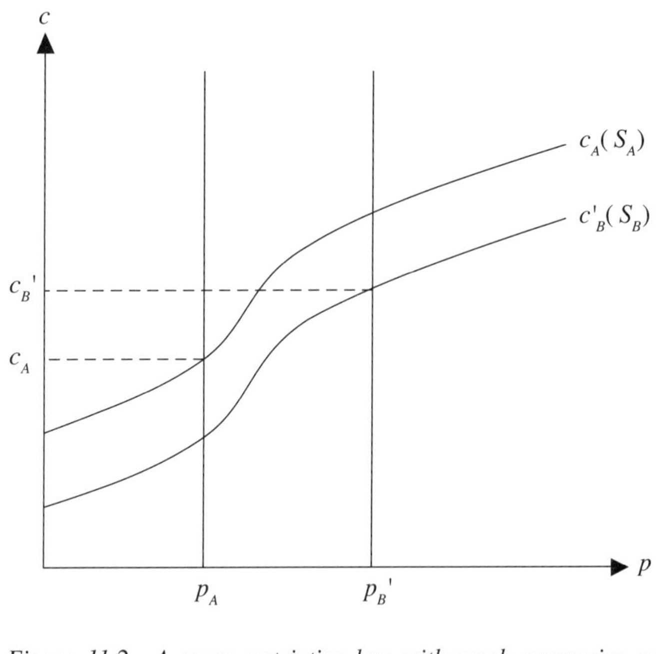

Figure 11.2 A more restrictive law with weak expressive power: countervailing effects

c_A. Adding incentives by exacerbating legal sanctions may be counterproductive in this case.

Such an unintended effect of legal intervention would thus lead to a compliance paradox, where an increase in the strictness of the law leads to more violations, defeating the goals pursued by the lawmaker. That is why the law, in this case, is self-defeating.

Finally, one should also consider the case in which a very lenient law is passed. For instance, a behavior that was previously banned now becomes legal (the obvious example in this case is abortion, legalized in the US in 1973 by the Supreme Court's decision *Roe v Wade*). This case too is likely to raise strong protest. In contrast to the above, however, protest in this case would signal disapproval of the now legal behavior and would inhibit it. The countervailing effect now would consist in a decrease in the prevalence of the behavior, notwithstanding liberalization. In the case of abortion, for instance, *Roe* and the recent battle over partial birth abortion played out in *Gonzales v Carhart* (2007) has sparked a political battle and still provokes much protest by pro-life groups. Protest ranges from open expression of dissent to violent assaults on women trying to access abortion services, doctors and abortion clinics. There is empirical evidence that such anti-abortion activities have had a significant impact on both the supply of and demand for abortion services in the US (Kahane, 2000).

6. Faster Social Reaction and Social Outrage

We have seen above that any time the law has limited expressive power and social reaction is strong, the compliance paradox is more likely to occur. However, the model illustrated above implies that, in order to observe countervailing effects, the upsurge in protest has to be extreme and persistent in time. Generally, although legal innovation may provoke social reaction, protest tends to subside over time. Moreover, an extreme social reaction, of the kind needed for countervailing effects to materialize, is exceptional, and a theory capable of explaining only exceptional cases is of little use to the lawmaker. Therefore, we shall now present alternative explanations for the countervailing effects, explanations that do not require persistent increases in protest (this section follows Carbonara et al., 2010).

In general, protest is not triggered solely by the "absolute strictness" of the law but also by the relative change. Increasing a sanction from one year in jail to ten years in prison likely sparks much more protest than an increase from one to two years. The fact that protest is not influenced only by the absolute sanction S but also by the relative change $\Delta S = S_B - S_A$, causes protest to rise more than it would if only the absolute level S affected it. Protest may then subside over time, but if the initial rise is large enough, it might stabilize at a high enough rate to justify an increase in violations. Countervailing effects are therefore explained also by "social outrage", an initial, strong reaction that generally fades away over time. Due to such reaction, protest changes much faster than behavior, which facilitates the insurgence of countervailing effects (as Figure 11.2 shows).

A social reaction may occur much faster than a change in behavior. Also, when changes in the law are announced some time before actual enactment, it can hardly produce any deterrent effect on current behavior until it is in force. It can, however, trigger protest if it diverges from current social norms. When the new law eventually comes into force, the regulated behavior may be so prevalent that society converges toward an equilibrium with more violations than before the enactment of the law.

7. Choosing Optimal Instruments of Legal Innovation

The analysis in the previous sections shows that, when designing new laws, lawmakers should take into account several, often contrasting factors. Particularly, they should balance extrinsic incentives, internalization and reaction effects. First of all, the existence of a compliance paradox indicates that laws intending to induce substantial shifts from current norms may have to proceed in a gradual fashion. Moving the law in the desired direction in small, consecutive steps allows for the gradual adaptation of individual values to the values expressed in the law, and avoids countervailing effects, since the disobedience rate will be small at every step. The compliance paradox suggests another interesting solution. Legal deterrence could be increased by reducing the strictness of the law. This would induce approval of the law and reveal that society condemns the regulated behavior, thus discouraging it and magnifying the deterrence effect. When gradual adjustments are not possible (e.g. due to the discrete nature of legal change or where they are not viable on political grounds), legal instruments other than sanctions may be required to obtain the desired result. In some circumstances, taxes might be a better option, as they are perceived as a "price" that individuals are free to pay if they want to indulge in a given, socially costly, behavior (like polluting). However, taxes may also be unacceptable in some circumstances. It may be then be possible to induce the desired behavior by means of positive incentives (i.e. rewards and prizes).

Typically, the literature has shown the equivalence of positive and negative (i.e. sanctions) incentives (Fudenberg and Tirole, 1992). The reward of a non-violation may be seen as equivalent (in incentive terms) to the sanctioning of a violation. Experimental studies have, however, found that rewards and sanctions are perceived differently by people (Kahneman and Twersky, 1979). Reaction to incentives is sensitive to framing, and in some contexts individuals are much more motivated if they face the perspective of receiving a prize for good performance rather than a sanction for bad behavior. In a contracting environment, for instance, it has been shown that the introduction of a penalty clause in the contract significantly increases the incidence of contract breach and decreases the productivity of specific investments (Fehr and Rockenbach, 2003). Moreover, this equivalence may be lost when the expressive and countervailing effects are taken into account. While positive and negative incentives may have similar expressive effects, they may have opposite countervailing effects. The giving of a reward is in fact less likely to trigger reaction than the imposition of a punishment.

It would, however, be hard to maintain that criminal law should be enforced by rewarding those who do not commit crimes rather than punishing criminals. Perhaps criminal law is not the best environment in which to test positive incentives. However, many other legal fields, such as torts and contracts, may benefit from such a perspective. Previous literature has stressed that positive incentives are much more expensive to provide than negative ones (Dari-Mattiacci and De Geest, 2010). If a policymaker is willing to motivate individuals with prizes, they have to reward all those who behave correctly and do so repeatedly to avoid misbehavior once the prize has been received. With a sanction, the threat of applying it if deviations from correct behavior are detected is sufficient to guarantee compliance. A "dictator with one bullet" is enough to subdue an entire country. However, this argument should be amended to take into account the costs of the enforcement of sanctions. Even if, in equilibrium, no one will be sanctioned when negative incentives are designed properly, it is true that the policymaker will have to invest in "sanctioning capacity" (e.g. building prisons) and that the threat of the sanction will have to be credible (meaning that there will have to be a conspicuous investment in detection capacity, which is likely to be very costly).

Once these costs are taken into account, the difference in efficiency between positive and negative incentives may be considerably reduced. In circumstances in which countervailing effects are important, rewards may become socially preferable and more effective in taming certain types of socially undesirable behavior. It is interesting to notice that the balance between prizes and sanctions was explored back in 1767 by the Italian philosopher Giacinto Dragonetti, in his *Essay On Virtues and Rewards*, which was a response to the far more famous *Essay on Crimes and Punishments* by Cesare Beccaria (1764).

Finally, the analysis of countervailing norms sheds new light on the debate between the magnitude and the probability of a fine, a debate dating back to Becker (1968). As is well known in the literature, the same expected fine can be generated with infinite combinations of probability versus magnitude of a sanction. Given that increasing the probability of a sanction entails high costs and that increasing the magnitude of the fine is not as costly, the conclusion supported in the past is that the tradeoff between probability and magnitude should be resolved by setting the maximum fine as high as possible and reducing the probability of application. In the light of our results, the choice of probability and magnitude combinations may have different effects with respect to countervailing norms. This might change quite substantially the policy recommendations made in the literature inspired by Becker's model.

Bibliography

Bar-Gill, Oren and Alon Harel (2001). "Crime Rates and Expected Sanctions: The Economics of Deterrence Revisited." *Journal of Legal Studies* 30: 485–501.

Beccaria, Cesare (1764). *An Essay on Crime and Punishment* (second American edition), translated from the French by Edward D. Ingraham. Philadelphia: Philip H. Nicklin, 1819.

Becker, Gary S. (1968). "Crime and Punishment: An Economic Approach." *Journal of Political Economy* 76: 169–217.

Beetham, David (1991). *The Legitimation of Power*. Atlantic Highlands, NJ: Humanities Press International.

Bergstrom, Theodore C. (2002). "Evolution of Social Behavior: Individual and Group Selection." *Constitutional Political Economy* 13: 149–72.

Bernstein, Lisa (1992). "Opting Out of the Legal System: Extralegal Contractual Relations in the Diamond Industry." *Journal of Legal Studies* 21: 115–57.

Bicchieri, Cristina (2006). *The Grammar of Society: The Nature and Dynamics of Social Norms*, New York: Cambridge University Press.

Bikhchandani, Sushil, David Hirschleifer, and Ivo Welch (1992). "A Theory of Fads, Fashion, Custom and Cultural Change as Informational Cascades." *Journal of Political Economy* 58: 211–21.

Bikhchandani, Sushil, David Hirschleifer, and Ivo Welch (1998). "Learning from the Behavior of Others: Conformity, Fads, and Informational Cascades." *The Journal of Economic Perspectives* 12: 151–70.

Binmore, Kenneth G. and Larry Samuelson (1994). "An Economist's Perspective on the Evolution of Norms." *Journal of Institutional and Theoretical Economics* 150: 45–63.

Bohnet, Iris and Robert Cooter (2001). "Expressive Law: Framing or Equilibrium Selection?", Berkeley Olin Program in Law & Economics, Working Paper Series (No. 36).

Bohnet, Iris, Bruno S. Frey and Steffen Huck (2001). "More Order with Less Law: On Contract Enforcement, Trust and Crowding." *American Political Science Review* 95: 131–44.

Borck, Rainald (2004). "Stricter Enforcement may Increase Tax Evasion." *European Journal of Political Economy* 20: 725–37.

Boyd, Robert and Peter J. Richerson (1994). "The Evolution of Norms: An Anthropological View." *Journal of Institutional and Theoretical Economics* 150: 72–86.

Carbonara, Emanuela and Piero Pasotti (2010). "Social Dynamics and Minority Protection." *International Review of Law and Economics* 40: 317–28.

Carbonara, Emanuela, Francesco Parisi, and Georg von Wangenheim (2008a). "Lawmakers as Norm Entrepreneurs." *Review of Law and Economics* 4: 779–99.

Carbonara, Emanuela, Francesco Parisi, and Georg von Wangenheim (2008b). "Legal Innovation and the Compliance Paradox." *Minnesota Journal of Law, Science and Technology*, 9(2): 837–60.

Carbonara, Emanuela, Francesco Parisi, and Georg von Wangenheim (2010). "Unjust Laws and Illegal Norms." Minnesota Legal Studies Research Paper No. 08-03.

Cooter, Robert (1998). "Expressive Law and Economics." *Journal of Legal Studies* 27: 585–608.

Cooter, Robert (2000). "Do Good Laws Make Good Citizens? An Economic Analysis of Internalized Norms." *Virginia Law Review* 86: 1577–601.

Dari-Mattiacci, Giuseppe and Gerrit De Geest (2010). "Carrots, Sticks and the Multiplication Effect." *Journal of Law, Economics and Organization* 26: 365–84.

Dau-Schmidt, Kenneth G. (1990). "An Economic Analysis of the Criminal Law as a Preference-Shaping Policy." *Duke Law Journal* 1990 (1), 1–38.

Depoorter, Ben and Vanneste, Sven (2005). "Norms and Enforcement: The Case against Copyright Litigation." *Oregon Law Review* 84: 1127–80.

Depoorter, Ben, Francesco Parisi, and Sven Vanneste (2005). "Problems with the Enforcement of Copyright Law: Is There a Social Norm Backlash?" *International Journal of the Economics of Business* 12: 361–9.
Dharmapala, Dhammika and Richard H. McAdams (2003). "The Condorcet Jury Theorem and the Expressive Function of Law: A Theory of Informative Law." *American Law and Economics Review* 5: 1–31.
Dragonetti, Giacinto (1767). *Traite des Vertus et Des Recompenses*. Naples: Gravier, 1767 (Paris 1768).
Ellickson, Robert C. (1991). *Order without Law: How Neighbors Settle Disputes*. Cambridge, MA: Harvard University Press.
Ellickson, Robert C. (1998). "Law and Economics Discovers Social Norms." *Journal of Legal Studies* 27: 537–52.
Ellickson, Robert (2001). "The Market for Social Norms." *American Law and Economics Review* 3: 1–49.
Ellison, Glenn and Drew Fudenberg (1993). "Rules of Thumb for Social Learning." *Journal of Political Economy* 101: 612–43.
Ellison, Glenn and Drew Fudenberg (1995). "Word-of-Mouth Communication and Social Learning." *Quarterly Journal of Economics* 110: 93–125.
Fehr, Ernst and Urs Fischbacher (2004). "Third-Party Punishment and Social Norms." *Evolution and Human Behavior* 25: 63–87.
Fehr, Ernst and Simon Gächter (2000). "Cooperation and Punishment in Public Goods Experiments." *American Economic Review* 90: 980–94.
Fehr, Ernst and Bettina Rockenbach (2003). "Detrimental Effects of Sanctions on Human Altruism." *Nature* 422: 137–40.
Festinger, Leon (1957). *A Theory of Cognitive Dissonance*, Evanston, IL: Row, Peterson.
Flieth, Burkhard and Foster, John (2002). "Interactive Expectations." *Journal of Evolutionary Economics* 12: 375–95.
Flieth, Burkhard and Georg von Wangenheim (1996). "Interactive Opinion Formation in a Multi-Opinion Model." *Papers on Economics and Evolution*, No. 9604. Max-Planck Institut zur Erforschung von Wirtschaftssystemen.
Frank, Robert H. (1987). "If Homo Economicus could Choose his Utility Function, would he want One with a Conscience?" *American Economic Review* 77: 593–604.
Frey, Bruno S. and Felix Oberholzer-Gee (1997). "The Costs of Price Incentives: An Empirical Analysis of Motivation Crowding Out." *American Economic Review* 87: 746–55.
Frey, Bruno S., Felix Oberholzer-Gee, and Reiner Eichenberger (1996). "The Old Lady Visits your Backyard: A Tale of Morals and Markets." *Journal of Political Economy* 104: 1297–313.
Fudenberg, Drew and Jean Tirole (1991). *Game Theory*, Cambridge, MA, Cambridge University Press.
Fuller, Lon L. (1969). *The Morality of Law*. New Haven, CT, Yale University Press.
Fuller, Lon L. (1981). *The Principles of Social Order*. Durham, NC: Duke University Press.
Gauthier, David (1986). *Morals by Agreement*. Oxford: Clarendon Press.
Geisinger, Alex (1988). "A Belief Change Theory of Expressive Law." *Iowa Law Review* 88: 35–73.
Gersen, Jacob E. and Eric A. Posner (2007). "Timing Rules and Legal Institutions." *Harvard Law Review* 121: 543–89.
Gneezy, Uri and A. Rustichini (2000). "A Fine is a Price." *Journal of Legal Studies* 29(1) 1–17.
Gneezy, Uri and Aldo Rustichini (2003). "Incentives, Punishment and Behavior" in Colin Camerer, George Loewenstein and Matthew Rabin (eds.), *Behavioral Economics*. Princeton, NJ: Princeton University Press.
Güth, Werner and Hartmut Kliemt (2000). "Evolutionarily Stable Co-operative Commitments." *Theory and Decision* 49: 197–221.
Hardin, Russell (2000). "Law and Social Norms in the Large." *Virginia Law Review* 86: 1821–37.
Harel, Alon and Alon Klement (2007). "The Economics of Stigma: Why More Detection of Crime May Result in Less Stigmatization." *Journal of Legal Studies* 36: 355–77.

Jolls, Christine, Cass R. Sunstein, and Richard H. Thaler (1998). "A Behavioral Approach to Law and Economics", *Stanford Law Review* 50: 1471–550.
Jost, Peter-J. (2001). "Crime, Coordination, and Punishment. An Economic Analysis." *International Review of Law and Economics* 21: 23–46.
Kahan, Dan, M. (1997). "Social Influence, Social Meaning, and Deterrence." *Virginia Law Review* 83: 349–95.
Kahan, Dan M. (1998). "Social Meaning and the Economic Analysis of Crime." *Journal of Legal Studies* 27: 609–22.
Kahan, Dan M. (2000). "Gentle Nudges v. Hard Shoves: Solving the Sticky Norms Problem." *University of Chicago Law Review* 67: 607–46.
Kahane, Leo H. (2000). "Anti-Abortion Activities and the Market for Abortion Services. Protest as a Disincentive." *American Journal of Economics and Sociology* 59: 463–85.
Kahneman, Daniel and Amos Tversky (1979). "Prospect Theory: An Analysis of Decision under Risk." *Econometrica* 47: 263–91.
Korobkin, Russell B. and Thomas S. Ulen (2000). "Law and Behavioral Science: Removing the Rationality Assumption from Law and Economics." *California Law Review* 88: 1051–44.
Kuran, Timor (1989). "Sparks and Prairie Fires: A Theory of Unanticipated Political Revolution." *Public Choice* 61: 41–74.
Kuran, Timor (1995). *Private Truths, Public Lies: The Social Consequences of Preference Falsification*, Cambridge, MA: Harvard University Press.
Kyvig, David E. (1979). *Repealing National Prohibition*. Chicago, IL: The University of Chicago Press.
Leibenstein, Harvey (1950). "Bandwagon, Snob, and Veblen Effects in the Theory of Consumer Demand." *Quarterly Journal of Economics*, 64: 183–207.
Lessig, Lawrence (1995). "The Regulation of Social Meaning." *University of Chicago Law Review* 62: 943–1045.
Lessig, Lawrence (1996). "Social Meaning and Social Norms." *University of Pennsylvania Law Review* 144: 2181–9.
Lessig, Lawrence (1998). "The New Chicago School." *Journal of Legal Studies*, 27: 661–91.
McAdams, Richard H. (1995). "Cooperation and Conflict: The Economics of Group Status Production and Race Discrimination." *Harvard Law Review* 108: 1003–84.
McAdams, Richard H. (1997). "The Origin, Development, and Regulation of Norms." *Michigan Law Review* 96: 338–433.
McAdams, Richard H. (2000a). "A Focal Point Theory of Expressive Law." *Virginia Law Review* 86: 1649–744.
McAdams, Richard H. (2000b). "An Attitudinal Theory of Expressive Law." *Virginia Law Review* 79: 339–90.
McAdams, Richard H. and Janice Nadler (2005). "Testing the Focal Point Theory of Legal Compliance: The Effect of Third-Party Expression in an Experimental Hawk/Dove Game." *Journal of Empirical Legal Studies* 2: 87–123.
Oksanen, Ville and Mikko Välimäki (2007). "Theory of Deterrence and Individual Behavior: Can Lawsuits Control File Sharing on the Internet?" *Review of Law and Economics* 3: Article 4.
Parisi, Francesco (1997). "The Economics of Customary Law: Lessons from Evolutionary Socio-Biology" in B. Bouckaert and G. De Geest (eds.), *The Production of Law: Essays in Law and Economics*. Antwerp: Maklu.
Parisi, Francesco (1998). "Customary Law," in P. Newman (ed.) *The New Palgrave Dictionary of Economics and the Law*. London and New York: Macmillan.
Parisi, Francesco (2000). "Spontaneous Emergence of Law: Customary Law," in B. Bouckaert and G. De Geest (eds.), *Encyclopedia of Law and Economics*. Cheltenham, UK and Northampton, MA, USA: Edward Elgar Publishing.
Parisi, Francesco and Georg von Wangenheim (2006). "Legislation and Countervailing Effects from Social Norms," in C. Schubert and G. von Wangenheim (eds.), *Evolution and Design of Institutions*. London: Routledge, 25–55.

Picker, Randal C. (1997). "Simple Games in a Complex World: A Generative Approach to the Adoption of Norms." *University of Chicago Law Review* 62: 1225.

Polinsky, A. Mitchell and Steven Shavell (2000a). "The Economic Theory of Public Enforcement of Law." *Journal of Economic Literature* 38: 45–76.

Polinsky, A. Mitchell and Steven Shavell (2000b). "The Fairness of Sanctions: Some Implications for Optimal Enforcement Policy." *American Law and Economics Review* 2: 223–37.

Posner, Eric A. (1996a). "Law, Economics, and Inefficient Norms." *University of Pennsylvania Law Review* 144: 1697–744.

Posner, Eric A. (1996b). "The Regulation of Groups: The Influence of Legal and Nonlegal Sanctions on Collective Action." *University of Chicago Law Review* 63: 133–97.

Posner, Eric (1998). "Symbols, Signals, and the Social Norms in Politics and the Law." *Journal of Legal Studies,* 27: 765–98.

Posner, Eric (2000). *Law and Social Norms*. Cambridge, MA: Harvard University Press.

Posner, Richard A. (1998). "Social Norms, Social Meaning, and Economic Analysis of Law: A Comment." *Journal of Legal Studies*: 27: 553–65.

Raz, Joseph (1980). *The Concept of a Legal System* (2nd edition), Oxford: Clarendon Press.

Robinson, Paul H. (2000). "Why Does the Criminal Law Care What the Layperson Thinks is Just – Coercive versus Normative Crime Control." *Virginia Law Review* 86: 1839–69.

Schelling, Thomas C. (1978). *Micromotives and Macrobehavior*. New York: Norton.

Schnabl, Hermann (1991). "Agenda-Diffusion and Innovation." *Journal of Evolutionary Economics* 1: 65–85.

Schotter, Andrew (1981). *Economic Theory of Social Institutions*. Cambridge, MA: Harvard University Press.

Schulhofer, Stephen J. (1998). *Unwanted Sex: The Culture of Intimidation and the Failure of Law*. Cambridge, MA: Harvard University Press.

Scott, Kenneth E. (1994). "Bounded Rationality and Social Norms." *Journal of Institutional and Theoretical Economics* 150: 315–19.

Scott, Robert E. (2000). "The Limits of Behavioral Theories of Law and Social Norms." *Virginia Law Review* 86: 1603–47.

Sen, Amartya (1977). "Rational Fools: A Critique of the Behavioral Foundations of Economic Theory." *Philosophy and Public Affairs* 6: 317–45.

Stuntz, William J. (2000). "Self-Defeating Crimes." *Virginia Law Review* 86: 1871–99.

Sugden, Robert (1989). "Spontaneous Order." *Journal of Economic Perspectives* 3(4): 85–97.

Sugden, Robert (2004). *The Economics of Rights, Co-operation and Welfare* (2nd edition). Basingstoke: Palgrave Macmillan.

Sunshine, Jason and Tom R. Tyler (2003). "The Role Of Procedural Justice And Legitimacy in Shaping Public Support for Policing." *Law and Society Review* 37: 555–89.

Sunstein, Cass R. (1996). "On the Expressive Function of Law." *University of Pennsylvania Law Review* 144: 2021–53.

Sunstein, Cass R. (2000). "Deliberative Trouble? Why Groups Go to Extremes?" *Yale Law Journal* 110: 71–119.

Thoreau, Henry David (1849). "Civil Disobedience," in Joseph Wood Krutch (ed.), *Walden and Other Writings by Henry David Thoreau*. New York: Bantam Books, 1981.

Tonry, Michael (1995). *Malign Neglect – Race, Crime and Punishment in America*, New York: Oxford University Press.

Tyler, Tom R. (1990). *Why People Obey the Law,* New Haven, CT: Yale.

Tyler, Tom R. (1994). "Psychological Models of the Justice Motive." *Journal of Personality and Social Psychology* 67, 850–63.

Tyler, Tom R. and Yuen J. Huo (2002). *Trust in the Law*. New York: Russell-Sage.

Ullmann-Margalit, Edna (1977). *The Emergence of Norms*. Oxford: Clarendon Press.

Vanberg, Viktor J. (1993). "Rational Choice, Rule–Following and Institutions: An Evolutionary Perspective," in Bo Gustafson, Christian Knudsen, and Uskali Maki (eds.), *Rationality, Institutions and Economic Methodology*. London: Routledge, 171–200.

von Wangenheim, Georg (1993). "The Evolution of Judge-Made Law." *International Review of Law and Economics* 13: 381–411.
Walker, Nigel and Catherine Marsh (1984). "Do Sentences Affect Public Disapproval." *British Journal of Criminology* 24: 27–48.
Wax, Amy (2000). "Expressive Law and Oppressive Norms: A Comment on Richard Mcadams's 'A Focal Point Theory Of Expressive Law.'" *Virginia Law Review* 86: 1731–79.
Weber, Max (1968). *Economy and Society*, edited by G. Roth and C. Wittich. Berkeley, CA: University of California Press.
Young, H. Peyton (1993). "The Evolution of Conventions." *Econometrica* 61(1): 57–84.
Zasu, Yoshinobu (2007). "Sanctions by Social Norms and the Law: Substitutes or Complements?" *Journal of Legal Studies* 36: 379–96.
Zwiebach, Burton (1975). *Civility and Disobedience*. Cambridge, Cambridge University Press.

12 Social stigma

Michael Faure[*] *and Laarni Escresa*

1. Introduction

The law and economics literature has for many years now pointed out that incentives guiding the behavior of individuals can not only emerge from formal rules of law, but also from social norms. An important focus in that respect is on stigma, namely that a particular behavior which would violate (social) norms would impose a negative label (stigma) upon the perpetrator of the norm. The basic idea is that fear of this negative labeling would provide ex ante incentives to individuals to avoid the stigma.

This idea also has a strong intuitive appeal. Individuals care about their reputation in social interaction. Moreover, a loss of reputation can also impose serious costs upon individuals.

It is the role of reputation and the mirror image of this, the loss of reputation or stigma, which are the focus of this chapter. Attention to stigma has of course not only been paid in the law and economics literature. Erving Goffman wrote a seminal work called *Stigma* where he qualified those who have been shamed as "discredible", referring to the fact that an alienation of an offender takes place as a result of the stigma (Goffman, 1963, 41–2).

The law and economics literature has increasingly paid attention inter alia to the question of how reputation is created and what particular aspects of social interaction can contribute to a stigmatizing effect in case of the violation of social norms.

There is one particular domain in the law which has as a particular feature that it is supposed to stigmatize the perpetrator and hence intentionally stigmatizes deviant behavior in order to provide incentives for compliance. This is the domain of the criminal law. The question that has been addressed in the literature is what it is that makes the criminal law have such a stigmatizing effect and how, to put it differently, can criminal law (via its stigmatizing effect) contribute to compliance with social norms.

In addition to this – largely theoretical, but to some extent empirical – literature, the question has also been asked how the notion of stigma in

[*] Michael Faure is grateful to Liu Jing (Maastricht University) for useful research assistance.

criminal law fits into the well-known economic theories of crime. Stigma could impose additional costs on the perpetrator which could hence amount to an additional penalty, in addition to the sanction which is formally imposed through the criminal legal system (e.g. a fine or non-monetary sanction, such as imprisonment). The question arises under what conditions a conviction through a criminal court could have such a stigmatizing effect and hence what the role of this stigma might be within the economic model of crime.

In recent years some have taken the idea of the stigmatizing effect of criminal law further and have suggested that an important function of the criminal law should be the "naming and shaming" of perpetrators, which would serve a variety of functions (such as punishment, retribution and deterrence, but to some extent also reintegration and restoration). This raises questions as to whether such "naming and shaming" can be effective as an instrument of crime control. There are increasingly empirical studies, from criminologists, among others looking at this phenomenon.

In sum, this chapter will review the way in which stigma can also be seen as a source of norms, providing incentives for compliant behavior. A crucial question in that respect is of course what affects stigma and to what extent the law itself (e.g. by criminalizing particular behavior) may contribute to this stigmatizing effect. The chapter touches upon this topic by reviewing both the empirical as well as the theoretical literature. Particular attention will also be paid to legal and criminological literature that addresses the question of whether intentionally imposing stigma (via naming and shaming of perpetrators) may contribute to the goals of crime control policy.

The chapter is structured as follows: after this introduction (Section 1), the way in which stigma is created will be sketched in the light of the literature on social norms (Section 2). Next particular attention is paid to the role of stigma in criminal law (Section 3) by addressing under what conditions (the expressive value of) criminal law can (theoretically) contribute to creating stigma and providing incentives for compliance with (social) norms.

The later sections will address stigma from a law and economics perspective, focusing in Section 4 on the way in which stigma fits into the (traditional) economic analysis of crime. Section 5 will provide some policy considerations and more particularly review the literature on stigma as an instrument of "naming and shaming". Section 6 concludes.

2. Stigma and Social Norms

The word stigma refers to an identifying mark of disgrace, and its etymology derives from the Greek and Latin word meaning a mark made on the skin by puncturing or through burning with a hot metal rod. Social stigma, on the other hand, as referred to in this chapter, is the sanction, usually informal, ranging from mere disapproval to social ostracization imposed on an individual by second parties for violating a particular social norm or for possessing an attribute or a characteristic that is considered to be devalued in a particular context and time (Crocker et al., 1998; Link and Phelan, 2001; Posner, 2000). Referring to social stigma as a type of sanction avoids the problem of arriving at a description that is merely tautological.

There are two challenges that had to be encountered in the law and economics analysis of social stigma. The first concerns the nature of the sanction. Unlike formal monetary sanctions, which the courts and formal law enforcement agencies typically base on the actual harm or damage, the metric of social stigma, while it may at times also be based on the harm, is largely determined through a social process. Hence, there are some acts where the ensuing physical harm may be low but the social stigma is high.[1] On the other hand, Rasmusen's seminal article (1996) on stigma and crime arises from an unobservable characteristic, the individual's marginal productivity of labor that is important in an employment relationship. The ensuing stigma is correlated with the difference in the average wage between the convicted and the unconvicted groups of the population. Social stigma, on the other hand, is more general than economic stigma and the attribute with which individuals are judged is related to the individual's worthiness in embarking on or maintaining social partnerships. Thus, according to Link and Phelan, any study on social stigma is necessarily multidisciplinary.

To the extent that a social norm can be defined as the expected average behavior of individuals (Ellickson, 2001), one can claim that social stigma, that is, the informal sanction imposed on an individual, is based on deviation from the average behavior or trait of the population.[2] Cooter (1998) also emphasizes the number of individuals following a rule considered to be a social norm. Similarly, what attributes or characteristics should constitute an average trait that an average person should possess in a society is also determined by a social process. Defining social stigma as a deviation from the average necessarily implies that its existence and size depend to a large extent on the strategic behavior of individuals and hence, the game-theoretic tools of economic analysis and equilibrium conditions would help shed light through providing a positive analysis and deriving conditions under which social stigma may be present.

The second challenge concerns the nature of the institution imposing the sanction. Unlike the courts and other formal law enforcement agencies that impose formal monetary sanctions, social stigma is imposed by a loose grouping of individuals that lack the time, the specialized knowledge or the skills to

---

1 This is the case for instance for so-called victimless crimes such as prostitution, drug use, abortion, and sodomy which in some jurisdictions are criminalized.

2 Social stigma can then be formalized as $\Omega = f(x_i - \bar{x})$, where x_i denotes the individual's level of activity or attribute and $\bar{x}$ denotes the average activity or attribute.

discern and assign blame. Given these characteristics, they are more likely to possess cognitive biases and rely on heuristics to simplify the time-consuming and complicated tasks involved in imposing a sanction. Empirical studies of jury behavior, for instance, point to the existence of cognitive biases (see Devine, et al., 2007 for a survey). It is therefore also necessary to have a theory of how individuals acquire and process information in ascertaining social distance.

Another issue concerns why second parties may have an incentive to stigmatize an individual. There are two reasons provided in the literature. The first is that the cost of imposing social stigma is assumed to be very low or close to zero (see Rasmusen, 1996). Another reason is that the offending individual has certain characteristics that are important for maintaining and establishing economic and social partnerships and that were unknown or hidden to second parties, but that have been revealed by the commission of a particular act.

While the particular sanction is imposed by second parties, the law and the social planner play a role in determining the social stigma by influencing the social distance. This occurs, first, by affecting expectations about the average behavior or attribute that serves as the standard with which the rest of society compares an offending individual. In this particular case, monetary sanctions indirectly influence social stigma, since higher fines have an impact on the average expected level of activity in a society. In some contexts, when the stigma is based on an unobservable attribute that is correlated with the act, the substantive issues of law may aid in making the relationship between the two clearer and more precise. To the extent that the rest of society tends to rely on heuristics, the law may also facilitate measures like the creation of categories or groups that lead toward greater cognitive efficiency.

2.1 Stigma, Norms and the Role of Information

There are two reasons cited in the literature as to why individuals obey social norms. The first concerns the intrinsic or personal motivation of individuals (Frey and Jegen, 2000; Cooter, 1998; McAdams,1997; Sunstein, 1996).[3] The second reason is that individuals are concerned about how society perceives them and hence are concerned about the reputational cost of violating a social norm (McAdams, 1997; Posner, 1998).

There are two sources of informational ambiguity with respect to defining and identifying a social norm that is crucial in the imposition of social stigma as a sanction for the norm violator. The first concerns the *announcement*; the process

---

3 McAdams refers to it as *esteem*. Sunstein calls it self-conception. This explains some empirical puzzles that can not be adequately explained by the standard classical theory of price incentives. Among them are the blood donation experiment (Mellström and Johannesson, 2008) and the kindergarten experiment (Gneezy and Rustichini, 2000a). In these cases, increasing the price of of an activity may even result in crowding out the intrinsic motivation of individuals.

by which people become aware of what constitutes an act that is sanctionable by the norm, given that it is informal and, in most cases, unwritten. The second has to do with *communicating* that a particular act is now considered wrong by the sanctioning community. When the law coincides with the social norm, then there is little or no informational problem. However, when this is not the case, a picture of how this information is transmitted over individuals should also be provided and the channels of transmission of information are to be identified.

According to McAdams, there are three conditions for norms that can signal the existence of reputation: consensus, detection and publicity. First, there should be agreement within the population about the esteem worthiness of a particular behavior and this could exist when there are venues for group discussion and exit. There should also be means to detect a violation and who violates in order to impose a good or bad reputational benefit and, finally, the information should be well known within the relevant population. All three conditions pertain to the crucial role of information with respect to the announcement of the norm, monitoring and enforcement.

According to Cooter, the net cost of an individual in following a norm depends on the proportion of people observing or violating it. When there is a small proportion of violators, the expected payoff of a norm violator is relatively higher than that of a norm follower. This being the case, more people will be encouraged to violate the norm, increasing the proportion of norm violators, which will lead to a decrease in the expected payoff. This will continue until the point is reached when an individual would be indifferent between following or violating the norm.[4] In this context, a norm serves as a focal point to coordinate people's expectations and behavior.[5] In this case, norms serve to move the people's expectations of the average and influence social stigma.

On the other hand, Ellickson describes the process of norm change and the role played by norm agents.[6] Change agents, whose income or wealth are most affected by an exogenous shock, are the first to offer a competing norm. Then norm entrepreneurs, individuals who also enjoy a tangible benefit and who possess technical skills and knowledge regarding the norm, are in the best position to gauge the efficiency or suitability of the emergent norm. Their choice gets communicated to the public and provides a clue to the welfare-enhancing capacity of the norm. This process continues in a nonlinear fashion that further sways the tide towards the adoption of the new norm, a process that could best be described as a *cascade*. According to Ellickson, it is optimal for an individual,

---

4 This defines the equilibrium position. This equilibrium may be stable or unstable depending on the shapes of the cost and benefit curves.

5 "To succeed in creating focal points, legal expression must enlist the natural sense of justice among citizens." See Cooter (1998) p.596.

6 See Ellickson (2001).

after observing the actions of those ahead of him, to follow the behavior of the preceding individual without considering the information himself.

The implicit assumption is the existence of bounded rationality on the part of individuals who follow the norm and who, at the same time, impose a sanction upon violators. Since an individual is boundedly rational,[7] he relies on heuristics, such as observing what others do as a convenient approximation for the real population statistic of the average. In this context, monetary fines, although not the direct means by which people impose stigma, play a role in shaping expectations of the average.

2.2 Stigma and the Signaling of Unobservable Attributes

The seminal article on stigma (Rasmusen, 1996) is based on a characteristic that is crucial in an employment relationship. This attribute is unobservable by the firm and a criminal conviction sends a signal to the employer about the true type of the individual concerned. In the moral hazard problem, a criminal has lower marginal productivity than a non-criminal. Committing a crime becomes more tempting when the difference between the wage of the convicted and the average of the non-convicted population is small. In the adverse selection case, the incentive to commit a crime becomes dependent on the proportion of the criminal type in the population.

On the other hand, social stigma is more general than economic stigma and the reason for imposing it concerns not only economic partnerships but social partnerships. Thus, unobservable attributes that are considered as important in social partnerships serve as the basis for the imposition of the social stigma. Benabou and Tirole (2006) identified an individual's intrinsic cost or level of personal motivation as one basis. More pro-socially oriented individuals suffer greater intrinsic cost when violating a norm or a law, which makes them more suitable partners. Given that all individuals face the same monetary sanctions and in a situation where they all get the same monetary benefits, the only explanation for why some individuals obey or violate a law or a norm is the differences in their intrinsic cost. Thus, individuals reveal their true pro-social or anti-social orientation when they commit an act.

However, the mapping between the act and the type does not necessarily involve a one-to-one correspondence, but is filtered through the lens of society, as well as the cognitive limitations of the individuals or groups of individuals imposing the stigma. This issue has been explored by Escresa and Palestini (2010), who posit that the existence of social stigma is rooted in the

---

7 Individuals face computational limitations when faced with a decision. They cannot compute the utility they will get for every expected contingency and they have physical and mental limitations. See, for instance, Kahneman (2003) and Simon (1991).

judgment heuristics adopted by the rest of society as a way of simplifying the complicated and time-consuming task of imposing social stigma, in particular, where individuals employ heuristics in order to simplify the task of attributing causality (Sloman, 2005; Pearl, 2000) and classification (Kahneman, 2003).

Empirical studies have shown that most individuals tend to overemphasize the role of individual attributes or personality predispositions as the underlying reason for the commission of an act and give less weight to external or situational factors which may have contributed to its occurrence.[8] This particular cognitive bias is known in the psychological literature as the fundamental attribution error.[9]

Attribution theory seeks to provide an understanding of how people make causal inferences concerning the information they possess. It provides an explanation of how people attribute the observable behavior of others and what they perceive to be its underlying cause.[10] It is concerned with how the "man on the street" provides casual answers to these questions and, for this reason, it is sometimes referred to as "naive psychology". According to Nisbett and Ross (1980), the person and his disposition is the most cognitively available and representative heuristic. Since the act and the actor are immediately perceivable, it is easy to establish a causal link between the two.

In imposing the informal sanction, however, it is not enough for society to learn about the individual's personality type or attributes. The rest of society compares the individual's disposition or type to the average of the population. If the individual type is believed to have the same attributes as the average person, then there exists no stigma.

This implies that the rest of society can make a rational and logical ranking of individual types along different multidimensional aspects. For instance, an individual type can be thought of as a vector, since a person can be classified as good or bad with respect to his profession, or to his role in the family and community. On the other hand, criminal law may collapse social stigma into a scalar value, being a good or bad person. However, in a situation where this is too costly for the individual, the rest of society instead resorts to assigning a heuristic attribute to the target attribute (Kahneman and Frederick, 2002)

---

8 The classic experiment is Jones and Harris. See also Morris, Larrick and Su (1999).

9 See also Morris and Larrick, (1995) for a review of how people try to explain other individuals' behavior. This is also known as inference discounting (Kelley, 1967). Succeeding studies tried to understand under what conditions this bias could exist, taking into account judgmental uncertainty, ability and motivation (Devine, 1989) and individual accountability (Tetlock, 1985). The conclusion is that there is a strong initial tendency to explain the observed behavior of others in terms of individual disposition and to discount situational factors (Kelley, 1967), especially when the acts committed deviate from widely accepted social norms (Jones and Davis, 1965). Although this particular bias tends to be adjusted as additional information is provided, the rigidity does not completely disappear.

10 For a general view of causal attribution, see Sloman (2005) and Pearl (2000).

which is more salient to the observer. This attribute substitution becomes more apparent in the context of groups, since the characteristics of the group become more associated with the individual.

Experiments in psychology have shown that when individuals think of a set, or a group, to the extent that the group is homogeneous enough to have a prototype, this information becomes more accessible to them (Posner and Keele, 1968; and Rosch and Mervis, 1975). The prototype heuristic is the attribution of the average salient features of the group to the individual. Thus, when an individual becomes convicted of a crime, his individual type becomes associated with the average characteristics of the set of the convicted. Hence, the conditions under which social stigma exists as an additional sanction in law can be described by a separating equilibrium, wherein the expectations of the rest of society with regard to the type of individuals who will violate the legal standard is also the best strategy for that particular individual.

Apart from cognitive limitations, the mapping between the attribute and the act is also dependent on social norms. According to Sunstein (1996), norms provide a system or a code by which to interpret the wrongness or goodness of a particular act. Individuals play specific roles in society and they form their expectations on how they should and ought to behave based on their respective roles.[11]

In this respect, the substantive issues of law play a more crucial role than monetary sanctions. Lessig (1995) posits that law affects social norms mainly through how society interprets these acts. Thus, the law is concerned with the regulation of an act's social meaning. Social meaning is a semiotic resource that can guide or constrain individual behavior. It can be constructed and history provides a wealth of cases where the government or other groups have used it to pursue a certain objective. In eighteenth century England, for instance, criminal penalties were meted out to individuals who dressed outside their designated class.[12]

One method involves directly changing the social meaning of the act and the other operates indirectly through a change in the frequency with which an act is observed in society. Semiotic technique proceeds by changing the social meaning of an act directly by "tying" it to or associating it with another act or institution that possesses the intended social meaning. The previous example works this way. Criminal acts carry stigma and tying improper dressing to

---

[11] Doctors, for instance, have sworn to save lives and protect the health of their patients and society therefore expects a doctor to perform this role. Similarly, bankers and financial advisors are expected to take care of the wealth and assets of their clients. Social norms, that is, the behavior and rules of conduct that are followed by the majority, are therefore very role-specific.

[12] Lessig (1995, 956).

crime carries with it the same association. Ambiguation, on the other hand, assigns to an act a second meaning that undermines its original meaning. While tying aims at clarification of an act, the latter intends to blur its present social meaning.

Behavioral technique changes social meaning indirectly by changing the frequency with which the performance of a particular act is observed and, in the process, expectations and its meaning change. Inducing certain behavior over time will eventually affect these meanings. A law that inhibits an individual from performing an act that will result in the construction or reinforcement of a social meaning changes expectations and, hence, achieves deterrence. The other technique works the opposite way by encouraging the ritualistic performance of an act in order to change social meaning.

3. Stigma and Criminal Law

Criminal law is often regarded as the branch of law that has the greatest capacity to stigmatize certain behavior (see, for instance, Shoham and Rahav, 1982). According to Hart, "what distinguishes a criminal from a civil sanction and all that distinguishes it, is the judgment of *community condemnation* which accompanies and justifies its imposition".[13] This captures succinctly what is echoed by many in the field regarding the stigmatizing aspect that is unique to criminal law.[14]

The previous section showed under what conditions social stigma exists as an additional sanction. This section describes the institutional properties of criminal law and explores the extent to which the creation of such conditions is facilitated. Since social stigma is based on a measure of social distance, or the deviation of a criminal act or attribute from the average expectations of society, criminal law serves to reduce the uncertainty involved in the process of its determination. This involves recognizing the complex relationships between cognition on the one hand and institutions (see Knight and North, 1997).

3.1 Punishment

3.1.1 Avoid crowding out of intrinsic incentives or personal motivation

Punishment under criminal law may be suited to avoid the crowding out of personal or intrinsic motivation. Although personal motivation is commonly studied in the literature within the context of conferring honor and encouraging voluntary and pro-social activities such as blood donation and voting during elections, the same mechanism applies to conferring dishonor and shame on

---

[13] Hart (1958); emphasis added.

[14] This may also be subject to debate as some tort scholars claim that civil sanctions also carry social stigma.

anti-social activities. Transposing the analogy to criminal law, most people do not refrain from committing a criminal act because they want to avoid high monetary fines or being imprisoned. They have internalized the law. If, for instance, murder were to be decriminalized, we probably wouldn't see a significant rise in intentional killings.[15] Although these are factors that enter their decision-making, most individuals do not commit a crime because they have internalized the norm of non-performance of a criminal act. Hence, the state does not spend too many resources enforcing the crime of murder because the norm of not killing another person has been internalized.[16]

Criminalizing a certain act that is not perceived negatively within certain groups could stoke the intrinsic motivation and lead to more acts of this nature being committed instead of a decrease being observed.[17] If criminal penalties were low, then the personal motivation of doing it could crowd out the prevailing price effect and hence lead to a backfiring of monetary incentives.[18] Gneezy and Rustichini (2000b) attributed the increase in late pickups of children by their parents when a fine was introduced to the fact that the fine was not high enough. Criminal law avoids this by imposing a very high fine, coupled with the possibility of imprisonment intended to punish the offender. This would ensure that, when a certain act is criminalized, the backfiring of incentives associated with low fines in a situation where personal or intrinsic motivation is already at play would not occur.

3.1.2 Inducing norm cascade With regard to the origin and evolution of social norms, a punitive sanction ensures that change agents – individuals who derive a direct monetary benefit from changing or maintaining a certain social norm – would be deterred from carrying out the act. Change agents have a crucial role to play in norm cascades.[19] To the extent that a social norm is observed largely because a sizable proportion of the population also observes it, the higher is the population ratio that observes a norm, the more likely it is that it will be selected as the prevailing norm to regulate a certain behavior. However, in order for a new norm to emerge, there should be a number of

---

15 See Cooter, 2000. In effect, most of the acts that are governed by criminal law have been internalized by most individuals in the population.

16 The role of religion in socialization and the fact that most religions forbid the killing of an individual have contributed toward the internalization of this norm.

17 This is what happened when proposals for the criminalization of file-sharing through the internet surfaced during the 1990s (David, 2010). The number of file downloads made through non-authorized sources increased during this period. Prior to the proposal, a norm of sharing had already developed among internet users, who treated the exchange of digital music and software as fostering a certain altruistic and communitarian spirit (Feldman and Nadler, 2006).

18 See also Gneezy and Rustichini (2000b).

19 See also Ellickson (2001) and Sunstein (1996).

individuals who would be willing to commit to enforcing it. They are called norm entrepreneurs. Commitment to and enforcement of a norm is not costless and change agents – persons who enjoy direct material or non-material benefit from it – are in the best position to supply a new norm.

When an exogenous shock changes the costs and benefits of a particular act among individuals, a number of different norms usually arise and compete with each other to regulate the particular behavior. Punishment ensures that a number of individuals would be deterred from performing a certain act to a sufficient extent to create or destroy a new norm. Some of the critics of criminalization claim that society would suffer from overdeterrence, as it would also discourage efficient transactions. However, if the aim of society is to affect or influence social norms and its observance depends on the proportion of people committing and enforcing it, then criminalization may also serve this goal by sufficiently deterring norm entrepreneurs.

3.2 Substantive Issues

Individuals are aware that their choices and their actions convey a particular meaning to society. Communities try to encourage or suppress the meaning of a particular act through laws and it appears that criminal law has been a suitable vehicle to carry out this societal objective (Kahan, 1998). Once an act has been criminalized, the meaning of the act becomes obscured, since it becomes associated with crimes that are traditionally considered heinous and abominable such as theft and murder. Criminals are also perceived to be individuals possessing a range of negative characteristics from being grossly negligent, amoral, wicked, and evil. This is bolstered by the requirement of intent or mens rea in the act. A certain stigma is then created, however small and ambiguous at the start of the criminalization process.

In this respect, criminalization can be considered as a semiotic technique to change a particular meaning that works either by *tying* or by *ambiguation*.[20] However, most newly criminalized acts are morally neutral and do not carry such negative connotations. In the case of insider trading, there is already a general and within group perception that the act is wrong and making it criminal only clarifies the extent of the wrongness. In contrast, in the case of criminalizing file-sharing, within the small cybernet community, this act is considered to be altruistic and to be fostering a norm of free exchange. Criminalizing provides an alternative way of interpreting the act, blurring the original meaning.

As more people are deterred, so the criminalized act becomes a rarity. People's expectations regarding the criminalized act change by changing people's behavioral patterns. While it might take a long time for criminal law

---

20 See Lessig (1995).

to change the frequency of an act through stigma, this phenomenon becomes more apparent with decriminalization. With the decriminalization of sexually related offenses such as sodomy, people have become more open over displaying their sexual preferences and as it has become more and more commonplace, people's expectations regarding the act and the individuals behind the act have also changed.

Punishment also carries a signification[21] that society wishes to condemn this act in a way that is different from merely imposing compensatory fines. Aside from this, the process of criminal adjudication that starts with a public debate in the legislature ensures that consensus, one of the main requirements for norm creation, is achieved.

To summarize, criminal law has another value aside from deterrence and it has to do with changing or constructing social meanings of a certain act, affecting social norms and inducing stigma. However, for this to work, it seems that there is a key pervading assumption that either has been left out or has been implicit throughout. This assumption, which we think should be recognized and made more explicit, concerns bounded rationality on the part of individuals in distinguishing what constitutes a wrongful act.[22]

3.3 High Standard of Proof

Choosing to obey a law or not, or choosing which of the competing norms to follow based on the individual cost-benefit calculus, is a difficult and challenging task. At the theoretical level, this is already a challenging task. In real life situations, individuals can not be expected to act like the perfectly rational decision-maker because of constraints they face with respect to processing information and in formulating and solving problems.[23] Individuals are "boundedly rational" and rely on heuristics[24] to aid and facilitate everyday decision-making.

An exogenous shock or structural change might make a certain act more harmful and if a huge part of the harm is externalized, a benevolent government could regulate behavior. From the economic point of view, criminalization is different from other forms of regulation because it does not price behavior and there are a number of economic justifications why this should and should not be the case.[25] An individual could not make this calculation for herself, but when she becomes aware that a certain act is criminalized, then the act joins

---

21 Kahan (1998).

22 This would also make it easier to reconcile with economic rationality.

23 See Kahneman (2003) and Fox and Tversky (1995).

24 Heuristics are "rules of thumb," educated guesses, intuitive judgments or simply common sense.

25 For an excellent discussion, see Bowles, Faure and Garoupa (2008).

the ranks of other acts that are bad and very harmful and, hence, she reaches the conclusion that the particular act is just as bad. Consequently, persons who commit it are tagged as criminals and, hence, deserve to be ostracized and stigmatized. This is called representative heuristics.[26]

Merely enacting a law may not be sufficient for an individual to become aware of the criminalized act and what exactly constitutes it. Prosecution and conviction transpires in the public sphere and engages the attention of individuals. Awareness becomes complete when there is conviction. Since the intensity of the stigma accorded to the individual depends on how far his action has deviated from what an individual person would normally do, then proof beyond reasonable doubt ensures that the stigma will be high.

3.4 Informational Asymmetry and the High Legal Standard

Individuals are heterogeneous regarding to what extent they are intrinsically motivated. Some individuals are very personally motivated and will follow a rule even if there is no fine or punishment for its violation simply because they derive positive utility from doing so. Individuals who are more intrinsically motivated make good economic partners or good members of a group, as the transaction and enforcement cost of engaging in a productive activity with them is lower. However, the individual type is known only to the person and is unobservable to the others. On the other hand, acts by individuals are observable. Society can make inferences with regard to a person's individual type based on whether or not he or she carried out a particular act. In our case, this is based on whether or not he or she committed a criminal act. Thus, committing or not committing a crime sends a signal of the individual type.

Thus, in order to be considered as a good signal of type, criminal standards should be set in such a way that it would be cheap enough for the high type to pass up the opportunity and tempting enough for the low type to seize it. Committing a crime is a signal that a person is of low type and it is through this mechanism that criminal law could invoke stigma or disrepute. If the standard also includes acts that confer honor or provide no clue to the type of the individual, the standard becomes a fuzzy signal and would not be welfare enhancing.

3.5 Bounded Rationality and Cognitive Biases in Ascertaining Harmful and Wrongful Behavior

When there is perfect information and people face no computational limitations in processing them, then distinguishing a harmful activity would not be a problem for society. Similarly, proving causality between an act and the

26. Note that this is related to Lessig's semiotic technique. In fact, Lessig's tools for changing social meanings, for example, semiotic and behavioral technique could be considered as a subset of heuristics.

ensuing harm would be easy. Criminal law appears to be a heuristic device that allows individuals to choose the act that maximizes both individual utility and social welfare. When individuals learn that an act had been criminalized, and since all crimes are extremely harmful, he circumvents the process of complex computation, he now regards the act as extremely harmful.

4. Stigma and Crime

4.1 Belief in the Stigmatizing Effects of Criminal Law

Having sketched out in the previous section how the creation of stigma interrelates with crime and criminal law, we will now elaborate further on this issue by reviewing some of the economic literature that points to the fact that criminal law, but more particularly a conviction through the criminal procedure, leads to a "shaming" which imposes an additional cost (supplementary to any legal consequences such as a fine) upon the offender. The way in which this stigma is imposed (or that reputation is harmed) and the conditions under which this takes place has been the subject of many studies.

Lawyers traditionally stress that an important difference between criminal law and remedies of a different nature (administrative or civil) is that the criminal sanction has the capacity to "shame" the offender: the criminal conviction conveys condemnation and disgrace (Hedman, 1991, 896). This stigmatizing effect is indeed considered to be unique to criminal law. A recent European directive (2008/99 of 19 November 2008, OJ, L328/28 of 6.12.2008) (forcing Member States to introduce criminal penalties on the violation of legislation implementing European environmental law) expresses this as follows:

> Experience has shown that the existing systems of penalties have not been sufficient to achieve complete compliance with the laws for the protection of the environment. Such compliance can and should be strengthened by the availability of criminal penalties, which demonstrate a social disapproval of a qualitatively different nature compared to administrative penalties or a compensation mechanism under civil law.

This quote shows that policy makers attach importance to the idea that criminal law stigmatizes and that they attach a positive value to it. The most straightforward reason is that stigma increases the costs of crime: in fact, it supplements the legal sanction with social sanction and thus increases the total sanction (see Cooter, 2000, 15). Stigma does therefore fit into the traditional economic theory of crime, since it adds to deterrence.

4.2 Economic Perspective on Stigma

This point, that criminal law creates a social stigma, has been stressed in many studies. Economists stress that the benefit of stigma (from a criminal policy perspective) is that it shares with fines the advantage of deterring the criminal without creating real costs (Rasmusen, 1996, 536). At least, there are no real costs for society; for the offender who is stigmatized, the costs can be substantial. Stigma may consist of economic stigma (e.g. a reduction in future income resulting from a criminal record) and social stigma (manifested in increased difficulties in social interaction) (Rasmusen, 1996). Stigmatization is in principle, considered as an effective means of reducing crime and could thus be used by government in a crime policy (Funk, 2004). However, the extent to which stigmatization is actually able to impose additional costs on the offender, as the literature generally holds, depends very much on the specific context of the case, the offence and the offender (see Massaro, 1991). Economists have spent a lot of effort attempting to identify the circumstances that could explain why stigmatization may work better in some contexts than in others. This has resulted in a large number of empirical studies that attempt to quantify the reputational losses resulting from a conviction or, more broadly, the additional costs that go beyond the formal sanction resulting from a criminal conviction.

More particularly, the basic story of why corporations suffer a (reputational) loss beyond the formal sanction which is imposed is presented in the seminal papers by Klein and Leffler (1981) and Shapiro (1983). According to these models, a reputational penalty is imposed upon a firm that is, for example, convicted of fraud. Since customers or other related parties (such as employees) feel cheated by the convicted firm, they will either refuse to deal with the offending corporation or change their willingness to pay and hence only pay a lower price for the product or service offered by the offender. Related parties, so this theoretical literature holds, hence will impose a reputational penalty upon the offending corporation. The reason is the breach of trust by the offender (see also Cannas, Masala and Micocci, 2009). The literature concerning these reputation models has also been summarized by Engelen and Van Essen (2011, 3–5).

However, Karpoff and Lott have shown that a criminal conviction only imposes this reputational penalty in case the offence is one that harms parties that are related to the offender (such as customers or employees). If damage would, on the other hand, be inflicted upon third parties that do not stand in a relationship with the offender, the reputational penalty would not be imposed (Karpoff and Lott, 1993, but also Alexander, 1999 and Engelen and Van Essen, 2010). Alexander showed convincingly in an empirical study that when corporations are convicted of crimes causing damage to related parties, a significant reputational penalty will be inflicted, as can be shown in stock-price declines (Alexander, 1999, 491). She advances various reasons why corporations suffer these so-called market place losses (the term is from Recca, 2004, 879), arguing *inter alia* that a reputational penalty is imposed when consumer expectations are not met (Alexander, 1999, 492–6). This can be supported, for example, by studies showing losses in shareholder wealth after defective product recalls (Jarrell and Peltzman, 1985), but also by studies concerning poisoning by Tylenol (Mitchell, 1989) or airline crashes (Mitchell and Maloney, 1989), all subsequently leading to losses in shareholder wealth. The evidence shows that the same reputational penalty would not be inflicted in case of a conviction for offences which would cause harm to unrelated (third) parties (see the evidence presented by Alexander, 1999, but also Engelen and Van Essen, 2011, 5).

4.3 Quantifying Stigma

Many empirical papers have subsequently attempted to quantify the reputational losses that either individuals (but mostly firms) suffer as a result of a criminal conviction (an excellent overview of this empirical research is provided in Engelen and Van Essen, 2011, 5–15). A problem with some of the research is that some studies measure the total monetary costs resulting from a criminal conviction, without distinguishing between the court-imposed penalty and the reputational losses. However, some studies do make this distinction. Alexander, for example, finds that the reputational penalty (measured in a decline of stock prices) was over four times the average court-imposed penalty (but all for cases where related parties were affected by the crime; see Alexander, 1999, 507). A recent study by Armour, Mayer and Polo (2010) finds that in the case of announcement of enforcement by the UK's financial services authority and the London stock exchange, the reputational sanction (in the sense of the stock price impact) was on average nine times larger than the financial penalties imposed by the authority. However, they also found that these reputational losses are confined to misconduct that directly affects parties who trade with the firm (customers and investors). The announcement of a fine for wrongdoing that affects third parties has only a weakly positive effect on stock prices.

Various other studies examine the reputational losses resulting from sanctions following corporate fraud (hence leading to harm for related parties). One of the first and often quoted studies in this respect is by Karpoff and Lott (1993) who found that the equity loss for fraud consisted of 90% reputational penalties and only approximately 10% expected legal penalties. Engelen recently showed a negative stock price effect of –1.5% on the day of a newspaper announcement of an illegal insider trading practice (Engelen, 2009). Evidence of a reputational effect due to internal fraud events is also presented by Cannas, Masala and Micocci (2009) and in a Dutch study by Van den Broek, Kemp, Verschoor and Devries (2010). Violation of anti-monopoly law in the Netherlands leads on average to a loss of market value of 2.3%, where the reputation effect was again substantially higher than the legal penalty. The size of the reputational penalty can, however, depend very much on context and more particularly on the question of how fraud is perceived within the particular cultural context in which the fraudulent event occurred. Recently, Tanimura and Okamoto compared the reputational losses (in terms of market values) of Japanese firms involved in corporate scandals with similar results in US studies. On the one hand, they provide empirical evidence of substantial reputational losses suffered by firms involved in corporate scandals and, moreover, they show that these losses were comparatively larger in Japan than for similar incidents in the US, because in Japan social shame was a more powerful regulator than in the US (Tanimura and Okamoto, 2010).

Other studies also show the basic point made in the Karpoff and Lott (1993) paper, namely, that these reputational losses will only occur when the offence could harm related parties, but not when only third parties are involved. A typical example is environmental harm. Karpoff, Lott and Wehrley (2005) show that firms accused of environmental violations do suffer a loss in market value. However, they argue that these losses are of similar magnitude to the legal penalties imposed. Hence, the loss in market value results only from the legal penalty and not from reputational penalties. A similar result was found in a study by Jones and Rubin: a reputation effect (in the sense of residual losses beyond the legal penalty imposed) can only be found if the offences cause harm to persons directly affected by the firm's conduct. Environmental incidents do not lead to any significant reputational penalty (Jones and Rubin, 2001). This does not, of course, mean that there may not be other negative effects resulting from a conviction for environmental violations. Decker, for example, showed that corporations that had been convicted for environmental offenses had more difficulties obtaining an environmental permit in the future (Decker, 2003).

Although most studies concerning reputational losses focus on corporations, some also attempt to measure the total costs resulting from a conviction for individuals. Individuals can obviously suffer substantial costs in addition to the formal penalty imposed. Depending upon the nature of the sanction (fine or imprisonment), the sanction could involve not only lost income (during the period of imprisonment), but also reduced legitimate earnings in the future. The issue has been empirically tested in a well-known study by Lott (1992). His study, looking at the effects of drug conviction, shows a total penalty which is much larger than the combination of fines and the foregone income costs of imprisonment. The reduction of legitimate earnings once the convict returns to the labour force accounts for between 35 and 96% of the total pecuniary penalty (Lott, 1993, 160). For individuals too, the loss of reputation resulting from a criminal conviction could substantially increase the total monetary penalty.

After having discussed some of the empirical evidence presented in economic studies concerning the (measurable) reputational effects of a criminal conviction (showing that there is economic support for the assumption that stigma imposed by a conviction does lead to additional costs), we will now ask how these studies can be used at the policy level.

5. Naming and Shaming

5.1 Reputational versus Formal Penalties

A first question that could be asked is how the insight from the previous studies (that the stigma inflicted through criminal law imposes real costs on the convicted) could be used in crime policy (as, for example, suggested by Funk, 2004). One consequence is that, according to Alexander, but also many other scholars, the fact that reputational damage will occur (especially when the offence causes harm to related parties) should be taken into account when fixing the optimal formal penalty to be imposed by courts. The studies presented in Section 4 show that, in some cases, reputational penalties can be between four to ten times as high as the formal penalty (fine) imposed by the court. One consequence may be that if this were disregarded, the formal sanction would be relatively too high (a point strongly advocated by Fischel and Sykes, 1996): they argue that a duplication of criminal and reputational penalties for corporate misconduct would lead to overdeterrence. Also, Alexander argues that a practical implication of the importance of reputational losses is that the judicial system could achieve socially optimal deterrence by setting penalties for corporate crimes against customers and other related parties at a substantial discount. Not doing so would lead to overdeterrence (Alexander, 1999, 490). Recca (2004) criticizes the federal sentencing guidelines for not taking into account reputational or "market place losses", which would thus lead to overdeterrence.

However, many scholars also point to the fact that the "shaming" effect of criminal law may equally drive a stigmatized ex-convict towards recidivism. To remedy that problem, Funk (2004) argues that harsher punishment should be imposed on repeat offenders. Harel and Clement (2007) also show the paradoxical result that increasing the rate of detection could actually reduce the effect of stigmatization. Their reasoning is that when more people are detected, more will belong to the category of "stigmatized", as a result of which the group of stigmatized will increase and stigmatization may lose its effectiveness.

5.2 Usefulness of "Shaming" Sanctions

A second question at the policy level is whether these studies showing that criminal law leads to reputational losses should lead to the consequence that the courts should impose shaming sanctions, thus adding to the reputational loss. This idea, which gains increasing popularity in some legal circles, is sometimes referred to as "naming and shaming". The concept of "reintegrative shaming" has been introduced in the work of the well-known criminologist John Braithwaite (1989). Braithwaite introduced the notion of "reintegrative shaming", which should reaffirm the morality of the offender and restore the offender in society. A "disintegrative" shaming would only label convicts as outcasts and lead to recidivism.

Many examples can now be found of laws which allow judges to "shame" a convict. A well-known example is "Megan's law", which prescribes that residents be warned about sexual offenders moving into an area. This encourages stigmatization of sexual offenders (see Funk, 2004, 716). Other examples include offenders wearing signs announcing their crimes in busy public areas, advertising offenses in local newspapers or placing stickers on offenders' cars publicizing their convictions for drunk driving (Anonymous, 2003, 2187–88). Some scholars are enthusiastic about this "shaming" and hold that it can be a low-cost alternative to imprisonment. In particular, those (criminal lawyers) who wish to fight prison sanctions have suggested naming and shaming as a useful alternative (see, for example, Kahan, 1996). A literature overview shows that the deterrent effect of this shaming approach is open to debate (Anonymous, 2189–94). Some argue that shaming may be useful, more particularly in cases where fines cannot be used, given that many offenders will be judgement proof (Shavell, 1985). Shaming penalties may have the advantage that they reinforce the community's norms against criminality and hence also have a general deterrent effect on individuals other than the shamed offender (Kahan, 1996). Others are more critical, arguing that in the US, shaming penalties will not deter, since the cultural prerequisites for effective shaming are lacking (Massaro, 1991).

One danger of shaming is that it may alienate the offender from existing communities, pushing him towards criminal subcultures and hence increase the danger of recidivism (Anonymous, 2003, 2201).

Some (more particularly, Posner, 1985, 1228) especially doubt that shaming will deter corporate crime because "a corporation can act only through individuals, and there is a constant turnover of these individuals". Buell (2006), on the other hand, argues that entity criminal liability can have a "blaming function". Law should, in his view, therefore be constructed to convey blame on the entity.

5.3 Shaming via Administrative Sanctions?

At the beginning of Section 4, we mentioned that the literature stresses that criminal law in particular would have a stigmatizing effect and that other legal remedies would lack such an effect. However, increasingly, administrative agencies also wish to impose shaming sanctions or, to put it differently, they impose a (financial) penalty, but deliberately publicize their action, knowing that this will lead to an additional reputational sanction. See, in this respect, for example the behaviour of the UK's financial services authority and the London stock exchange, who can decide to announce enforcement when they have levied a penalty (see Armour, Mayer and Polo, 2010). Also the Netherlands anti-monopoly commission often publicizes their actions on purpose, with a view to creating a stigmatizing effect and hence adding to the total penalty as a result of reputational losses (Van den Broek, Kemp, Verschoor and Devries, 2010). Increasingly, also, administrative agencies choose to "blacklist" perpetrators.

We mentioned earlier that some stress that an advantage of stigma is that it can lead to additional deterrence at no cost to society. This is, however, not entirely correct. Naming and shaming can lead to substantial error costs. Unjustly qualifying a perpetrator (more particularly a corporation) as a violator could lead, as the numbers show, to substantial costs, which can only be corrected if the announcement later is shown to be wrong. Faure, Ogus and Philipsen (2009, 176) have held that it would be inappropriate to use naming and shaming in the context of an administrative decision, unless the latter is followed by a definitive ruling by a court. The reason is that error costs can escalate if the agency has reached an incorrect decision, and reversing it on appeal will not significantly reduce the harm arising from adverse publicity. Hence, so they argue, stigmatizing sanctions should only be used in the criminal process, which can reduce the risk of wrongful convictions (Faure, Ogus and Philipsen, 2009, 179).

As can be seen, this advice is apparently not followed in practice, since often administrative agencies intentionally use shaming strategies. In particular cases, this may lead to substantial risks for administrative agencies. For example, the behaviour of the Dutch anti-competition authority (NMA), which published the names of suspected violators, was held by a civil court to be careless, as a result of which the administrative agency was held liable for the resulting damage (Pijnacker-Hordijk, 2006). Naming and shaming strategies could hence entail substantial liability risks for an agency.

Finally, we should mention a study that looks at the question of how the reputational harm of a defiant corporation should be measured in the legal system, based on stock market data (de Villiers, 2009).

6. Concluding Remarks

The law and economics literature on social norms has flourished over the last decades. However, not much attention has been paid to the particular informal sanction that is associated with norm violation, social stigma. On the other hand, economic stigma enjoys a much more focused attention in the literature (see for instance, Rasmusen, 1996; Funk, 2004; and Harel and Clement, 2007). This chapter aims to gather together the related literature within law and economics in order to provide us with a better understanding of social stigma, a subject that is widely discussed in other social sciences. We first identified the conceptual problems that inhibit or prevent further research in law and economic studies and then looked at the literature that addressed and helped clarify these issues. Thus, apart from serving as a review, this chapter is also an exploration of the possible research agenda for the future, as it looks at the gaps that need to be filled.

To conclude, this chapter looks at the law and economics literature on social stigma and, owing to the literature's focus on economic stigma, this chapter pieces together the literature that may contribute to its positive and normative analysis. Thus, it draws from different strands of the literature. This is not surprising, as the social process behind social stigma is underscored and hence, its study inevitably involves a multidisciplinary approach. In the process, the chapter shows that there are gaps that have to be filled in order to arrive at a more cohesive analysis and, as such, is a promising field for future research.

Bibliography

Akerlof, G., and Kranton, R. (2005), "Identity and the Economics of Organization", *Journal of Economic Perspectives*, **19**, 9–32.

Alexander, C.R. (1999), "On the Nature of the Reputational Penalty for Corporate Crime: Evidence", *Journal of Law and Economics*, **42**, 489–526.

Anonymous (2003), "Shame, Stigma, and Crime: Evaluating the Efficacy of Shaming Sanctions and Criminal Law", *Harvard Law Review*, **116**, 2186–207.

Armour, J., Mayer, C. and Polo, A. (2010), "Regulatory Sanctions and Reputational Damage", Oxford Legal Studies Research Paper No. 62/2010, available at http://ssrn.com/abstract=1678028.

Benabou, R. and Tirole, J. (2006), "Incentives and Prosocial Behavior", *American Economic Review*, **96**, 1652–78.

Bowles, R., Faure, M. and Garoupa, N. (2008), "The Scope of Criminal Law and Criminal Sanctions: An Economic View and Policy Implications", *Journal of Law and Society*, **35**, 389–416.

Braithwaite, J. (1989), *Crime, Shame and Reintegration*, New York: Cambridge University Press.

Buell, S. (2006), "The Blaming Function of Entity Criminal Liability", *Indiana Law Journal*, **81**, 473–537.

Cannas, G., Masala, G. and Micocci, M. (2009), "Quantifying Reputational Effects for Publicly Traded Financial Institutions", *Journal of Financial Transformation*, **27**, 76–81.

Carbonara, E., Parisi, F. and von Wangenheim, G. (2008), 'Lawmakers as Norm Entrepreneurs', *Review of Law and Economics*, **4**, 779–99.

Cooter, R. (1998), "Expressive Law and Economics", *Journal of Legal Studies*, **27**, 585–608.

Cooter, R. (2000), "Three Effects of Social Norms on Law: Expression, Deterrence, and Internalization", *Oregon Law Review*, **79**, 1–22.

Crocker, J., Major, B., and Steele, C. (1998), "Social Stigma", in S. Fiske, D. Gilbert, and G. Lindzey (eds.), *Handbook of Social Psychology*, Boston: McGraw-Hill, pp.504–53.

David, M. (2010), *Peer to Peer and the Music Industry: The Criminalization of Sharing*, Thousand Oaks, CA: Sage Publications.

Decker, C.H. (2003), "Corporate Environmentalism and Environmental Statutory Permitting", *Journal of Legal Studies*, **46**, 103–29.

de Villiers, M. (2009), "Quantitative Proof of Reputational Harm", University of New South Wales Faculty of Law Research Series Working Paper 25, available at http://law.bepress.com/unswwps/flrps09/art25.

Devine, D., Clayton L., Dunford B., Seying R., and Pryce, J. (2007), "Jury Decision Making: 45 Years of Empirical Research on Deliberating Groups", *Psychology, Public Policy and Law*, **7**, 622–727.

Devine, P. (1989), "Overattribution Effect: The Role of Confidence and Attributional Complexity", *Social Psychology Quarterly* **24**, 149–58.

Ellickson, R. (2001), "The Market for Social Norms", *American Law and Economics Review*, **3**, 1–49.

Engelen, P.J. (2009), "The Reputational Penalty for Illegal Insider Trading", paper presented at the Academy of Management Conference, Chicago, August 2009.

Engelen, P.J. and Van Essen, M. (2011), "Reputational Penalties on Financial Markets to Induce Corporate Responsibility", in W. Vandekerckhove, J. Leys, B. Scholtens, S. Signori and H. Schäfer (eds.), *Responsible Investment In Times of Turmoil*, Heidelberg: Springer.

Escresa, L. and Palestini A. (2010), "Social Stigma, Heuristics and Criminal Law", paper presented at the Annual Conference of the European Association of Law and Economics, Paris, 23–5 September.

Faure, M., Ogus, A. and Philipsen, N. (2009), "Curbing Consumer Financial Losses: the Economics of Regulatory Enforcement', *Law and Policy*, **31**, 161–91.

Feldman, Y. and Nadler, J. (2006), "The Law and Norms of File Sharing", *San Diego Law Review*, **43**, 577–618.

Fischel, D.R. and Sykes, A.L. (1996), "Corporate Crime", *Journal of Legal Studies*, **25**, 319–49.

Fox, C. and Tversky, A. (1995), "Ambiguity Aversion and Comparative Ignorance", *Quarterly Journal of Economics*, **110**, 585–603.

Frey, B. and Jegen, R. (2000), "Motivation and Human Behavior", in P. Taylor (ed.), *Risk, Trust and Welfare*, London: Macmillan Press, pp. 31–50.

Funk, P. (2004), "On the Effective Use of Stigma as a Crime-Deterrent", *European Economic Review*, **48**, 715–28.

Gneezy, U. and Rustichini, A. (2000a), "A Fine is a Price", *Journal of Legal Studies*, **29**, 1–17.

Gneezy, U. and Rustichini A. (2000b), "Pay Enough or Don't Pay At All", *Quarterly Journal of Economics*, **115**, 791–810.

Goffman, E. (1963), *Stigma: Notes on the Management of Spoiled Identity*, New Jersey: Prentice-Hall.

Harel, A. and Clement, A. (2007), "The Economics of Stigma: Why More Detection of Crime may Result in Less Stigmatization", *Journal of Legal Studies*, **36**, 355–77.

Hart, H. (1958), "The Aims of Criminal Law", *Law and Contemporary Problems*, **23**, 401–41.

Hedman, S. (1991), "Expressive Functions of Criminal Sanctions in Environmental Law", *The George Washington Law Review*, **59**, 889–99.

Jarrell, G. and Peltzman, S. (1985), "The Impact of Product Recalls on the Wealth of Sellers", *Journal of Political Economy*, **93**, 512–36.

Jones, E. and Davis, K. (1965), "A Theory of Correspondent Inferences: From Acts to Dispositions", in L. Berkowitz (ed.), *Advances in Experimental Psychology*, New York: Academic Press, pp. 219–66.

Jones, K. and Rubin, P. (2001), "Effects of Harmful Environmental Events on Reputations of Firms", in M. Hirschey, K. John and A. Makhija (eds.), *Advances in Financial Economics vol. 6*, Amsterdam: Elsevier Science, pp. 161–82.

Kahan, D. (1996), "What Do Alternative Sanctions Mean?", *University of Chicago Law Review*, **63**, 591–653.

Kahan, D. (1998), "Social Meaning and the Economic Analysis of Crime", *Journal of Legal Studies*, **27**, 609–22.

Kahneman, D. (2003), "Maps of Bounded Rationality: Psychology for Behavioral Economics", *American Economic Review*, **80**, 237–51.

Kahneman, D. and Frederick S. (2002), "Representativeness Revisited: Attribute Substitution in Intuitive Judgment", in T. Gilovich, D. Griffin, and D. Kahneman, (eds.), *Heuristics and Biases: The Psychology of Intuitive Thought*, New York: Cambridge University Press, pp. 49–81.

Karpoff, J. and Lott, J. (1993), "The Reputational Penalty Firms Bear from Committing Criminal Fraud", *Journal of Law and Economics*, **26**, 757–802.

Karpoff, J., Lott, J. and Wehrley, E. (2005), "The Reputational Penalties for Environmental Violations: Empirical Evidence", *Journal of Law and Economics*, **48**, 653–75.

Kelley, H. (1967), "The Process of Causal Attribution", *American Psychologist*, **28**, 107–28.

Klein, B. and Leffler, K. (1981), "The Role of Market Forces in Assuring Contractual Performance", *Journal of Political Economy*, **89**, 615–41.

Knight, J. and North, D. (1997), "Explaining Economic Change: The Interplay between Cognition and Institutions", *Legal Theory* , **3**, 211–26.

Lessig, L. (1995), "The Regulation of Social Meaning", *The University of Chicago Law Review*, **62**, 943–1045.

Link, B. and Phelan, J. (2001), "Conceptualizing Stigma", *Annual Review of Sociology*, **27**, 363–85.

Lott, J. (1992), "An Attempt at Measuring the Total Monetary Penalty from Drug Convictions: The Importance of an Individual's Reputation", *Journal of Legal Studies*, **21**, 159–87.

Massaro, T. (1991), "Shame, Culture, and American Criminal Law", *Michigan Law Review*, **89**, 1880–944.
McAdams, R. (1997), "The Origin, Development, and Regulation of Norms", *Michigan Law Review*, 96, 338–433.
Mellström, C. and Magnus, J. (2008), "Crowding Out in Blood Donation: Was Titmuss Right?", *Journal of European Economic Association*, **6**, 845–63.
Mitchell, N. (1989), "The Impact of External Parties on Brand-Name Capital: The 1982 Tylenol Poisonings and Subsequent Cases", *Economic Inquiry*, **27**, 601–18.
Mitchell, N. and Maloney, M. (1989), "Crisis in the Cockpit? The Rule of Market Forces in Promoting Air Travel Safety", *Journal of Law and Economics*, **32**, 329–55.
Morris, M., and Larrick, R. (1995), "When One Casts Doubt on Another: A Normative Analysis of Discounting in Causal Attribution", *Psychological Review* **102**, 331–55.
Nisbett, R. and Ross, L. (1980), *Human Inference: Strategies and Shortcomings of Social Judgment*, New Jersey: Prentice-Hall.
Parisi, F. and von Wangenheim, G. (2006), "Legislation and Countervailing Effects from Social Norms", in C. Schubert and G. von Wangenheim (eds.), *The Evolution and Design of Institutions*. New York: Routledge, pp. 25–55.
Pearl, J. (2000), *Causality: Models, Reasoning and Inference*, New York: Cambridge University Press.
Peltzman, S. (1981), "The Effects of FTC Advertising Regulation", *Journal of Law and Economics*, **24**, 403–48.
Pijnacker-Hordijk, E. (2006), "Private Handhaving als Alternatief voor Overheidshandhaving, Mede in het Licht van Overheids-Aansprakelijkheid", *Overheid en Aansprakelijkheid*, **1–2**, 31–41.
Posner, E. (1998), "Symbols, Signals, and Social Norms in Politics and the Law", *Journal of Legal Studies*, **27**, 765–98.
Posner, E. (2000), *Law and Social Norms*, Cambridge MA: Harvard University Press.
Posner, M. and Keele, S. (1968), "On the Genesis of Abstract Ideas", *Journal of Experimental Psychology*, **77**, 353–63.
Posner, R. (1985), "An Economic Theory of the Criminal Law", *Columbia Law Review*, **85**, 1193–231.
Posner, R. and Rasmusen, E. (1999), "Creating and Enforcing Norms, with Special Reference to Sanctions", *International Review of Law and Economics*, **19**, 369–82.
Rasmusen, E. (1996), "Stigma and Self-fulfilling Expectations of Criminality", *Journal of Law and Economics*, **39**, 519–43.
Recca, D. (2004), "Reputational Penalties for Corporations and the Federal Sentencing Guidelines", *Columbia Business Law Review*, **3**, 879–97.
Rosch, E. and Mervis, C. (1975), "Family Resemblances: Studies in the Internal Structure of Categories", *Cognitive Psychology*, **7**, 573–605.
Shapiro, C. (1983), "Premiums for High-Quality Products as Returns to Reputations", *Quarterly Journal of Economics*, **98**, 659–79.
Shavell, S. (1985), "Criminal Law and the Optimal Use of Nonmonetary Sanctions as a Deterrent", *Columbia Law Review*, **85**, 1232–62.
Shoham, G. and Rahav, G. (1982), *The Mark of Cain: The Stigma Theory of Crime and Social Deviance*, Queensland: University of Queensland Press.
Simon, H. (1991), "Bounded Rationality and Organizational Learning", *Organization Science*, **2**,125–34.
Sloman, S. (2005), *Causal Models: How People Think about the World and its Alternatives*, New York: Oxford University Press.
Sunstein, C., (1996), "Social Norms and Social Roles", *Columbia Law Review*, **96**, 903–68.
Sunstein, C. (2005), "Moral Heuristics", *Behavioral and Brain Sciences*, **28**, 531–73.
Tanimura, J. and Okamoto, M. (2010), "Reputational Losses in Japan: Evidence from Corporate Scandals", July 2010, available electronically at http://ssrn.com/abstract=1591025.
Tetlock, P. (1985), "Accountability: A Social Check on the Fundamental Attribution Error", *Social Psychology Quarterly*, **48**, 227–36.
Van den Broek, S., Kemp, R., Verschoor, W. and Devries, A. (2010), "Reputatieschade als Handhavingsinstrument", *Economisch Statistische Berichten*, 19 February, 122–4.

13 Self-regulation

Anthony Ogus and Emanuela Carbonara

1. Introduction

Self-regulation, understood narrowly as law formulated by private agencies to govern professional and trading activities, has been rigorously criticised by lawyers and economists alike. From a legal perspective, it is seen as an example of modern "corporatism", the acquisition of power by groups which are not accountable to the body politic through the conventional constitutional channels (Schmitter, 1985). The capacity of such groups to make rules governing the activities of members of an association or profession may itself constitute an abuse if they lack democratic legitimacy (Page, 1986). The potential for abuse may become intolerable if, and to the extent that, the rules affect third parties (Cane, 1987). Further, if the group's functions cover policy formulation, interpretation of the rules, adjudication and enforcement (including the imposition of sanctions) as well as rule making, this conflicts with basic notions of separation of powers (Harden and Lewis, 1986). For their part, economists have traditionally focused on how self-regulatory powers may be exercised to impede competition on the supply side of the market. Barriers to entry may be created, thereby raising prices and conferring rents on incumbent practitioners; standards governing practice may be devised more to confer utility on suppliers than to meet consumer preferences (Shaked and Sutton, 1981a). And the prospect of gaining such advantages may lure groups into spending resources to persuade legislatures to grant them self-regulatory powers – a social deadweight loss (Tullock, 1967).

While criticisms such as these may be appropriate in some circumstances, they are based on a very incomplete picture of self-regulation. The modern law and economics literature has been concerned to explore a much broader conception of the phenomenon and in so doing to identify institutional arrangements which may escape, or meet, the traditional criticisms and which thereby may be conducive to allocatively efficient outcomes. A survey of this literature must necessarily begin with an investigation of the nature of self-regulation.

2. The Nature of Self-Regulation

In its most literal sense, and as used in psychology (Carver and Scheier, 1981), self-regulation means acting according to one's own volition, and not as a response to an external constraint. Thus interpreted, the concept would cover an infinite number of self-imposed behavioural standards, including those determined internally by the management of a firm. Although the latter may have no legal significance, they are not irrelevant to discussions of regulatory systems (Bardach and Kagan, 1982; Cheit, 1990). The internal standards are designed to ensure quality of the kind which will meet consumer preferences.

On the assumptions of competition between suppliers, adequate information possessed by consumers and an absence of externalities, there is no need to render the standards legally enforceable.

When used in a legal context, the "self" in "self-regulation" is not used in the literal sense. Rather it connotes some degree of collective constraint, other than that directly emanating from government, to engender outcomes which would not be reached by individual market behaviour alone (Black, 1996). It is also normally taken to imply "a fairly well established and generally recognised set of rules, whether customary or reduced to writing, in accordance with which the activity is regulated" (Cane, 1987).

There is, nevertheless, a multitude of institutional arrangements which fall somewhere between government regulation on the one hand and individual, unconstrained behaviour on the other and which can therefore be treated as self-regulation (Rees, 1988; Cheit, 1990). The possibilities can be considered on two spectra depicting, respectively, degrees of autonomy from government and legal force (Page, 1986; Baggott, 1989). The first ranges from, at one extreme, rules private to firms, groups or organisations to, at the other, those approved by a government minister or some independent public authority; in between, representatives of the public interest may participate in, but not conclusively determine, the decision-making. The second encompasses varying degrees of legal force. The rules may be: formally binding, non-compliance leading to public law or private law sanctions; codes of practice which presumptively apply unless an alleged offender can show that some alternative conduct was capable of satisfactorily meeting the regulatory goals; norms the breach of which leads to non-legal sanctions, such as ostracism; or standards, compliance with which is purely voluntary.

In recent years, self-regulation has increasingly been regarded as a means of improving regulation, by both national governments and international organisations, like the EU and the OECD (Hutter, 2001; OECD, 2002). Self-regulation might help ease the burden of state regulation and (it will be argued later) may be more efficient, since it can make better use of local information and has more effective instruments to guarantee enforcement. This poses the crucial issue of the optimal relationship between centralised (or government) regulation and self-regulation. The distinction between centralised and self-regulation is not so clear cut, since many schemes based on self-regulation imply some kind of control by the government (Ogus, 1995; Black, 1996).

Moreover, self-regulation is often regarded as problematic, since the divergence between public interest and the objectives of the self-regulating entities may entail a pro-regulatee bias (see Section 4). Bartle and Vass (2007) suggest that the correct relationship between government and self-regulation should be based on a subsidiarity principle, implying that regulation should be made at the closest possible level to the regulatee, as long as the gains from decentralisation outweigh the cost of the pro-regulatee bias. Such process of deregulation should however be "embedded" within the regulatory state, which would scrutinise the outcomes of the self-regulatory process and guarantee that the procedures adopted by the self-regulated entity are not contrary to the public interest (Moran, 2003, gives an account of self-regulation along state-controlled lines in the UK).

In the remainder of the chapter we will analyse self-regulation from this perspective, paying special attention to the costs and benefits of delegated regulation. However, before that, we need to discuss the purest form of self-regulation, which occurs in the complete absence of any form of state intervention.

3. Spontaneous Private Legal Ordering

In its most complete sense, and thus at one end of the spectra described above, self-regulation involves a system of private ordering, without any form of state intervention; that is, without any imposition of rules by those with political power. Systems of private ordering are the basis for phenomena of spontaneous emergence of law and are sustained by extra-legal (or social) sanctions. We will not deal with spontaneous emergence of law, as this would be beyond the scope of the chapter. For a valuable overview of the literature, see Klein (1997).

Economic explanations of how informal systems emerge are epitomised by studies of primitive societies (Benson, 1988). The basis is reciprocity: individuals recognise the benefits they will derive from behaving in accordance with others' expectations. Such reciprocity may be reflected in individual agreements, but, as standards of behaviour, will spread to other members of a group as property rights when the benefits of doing so exceed the costs of defining those rights. While originally disputes may be resolved by force, individuals will normally find non-violent methods (for example, arbitration or mediation) to be cheaper; and ostracism from the group will generally be an adequate sanction for non-compliance.

Analysis of this kind has been used to explain other historical self-ordering arrangements, including: the Maghribi Traders (Greif, 1989); the Law Merchant (Benson, 1989; Milgrom, North and Weingast, 1990); medieval Iceland (Friedman, 1979); and the mining camps in the American West (Anderson and Hill, 1979; Umbeck, 1981). In more modern contexts, equivalent systems can emerge within groups to reduce the costs of drafting commitments and of establishing and activating enforcement systems (Charny, 1990). The expectation is that such cost savings will be significant where the group is small enough for informal control – generally requiring continuing face-to-face interaction – but where also power is broadly dispersed (Ellickson, 1993). Illustrative studies are those on diamond traders (Bernstein, 1992) and neighbour disputes (Ellickson, 1991).

Within a broader social setting decentralised law-making encounters the problem that some individuals will tend to free-ride on the enforcement of others. This may be only partly solved by the internalisation of norms, and thus public institutions (courts) are necessary to identify situations requiring state-imposed incentives (Cooter, 1996). Nevertheless, informal systems also occur in international trading environments (Benson, 1992; see also Schanze, 1988).

Here there is an increased need to accommodate the system to inter-group interaction. The co-existence of groups creates incentives for each to compete to attract or hold members and a form of mutual insurance emerges to prevent individuals taking advantage of other individuals and then escaping to another group (Benson, 1993).

A not insignificant part of the literature addresses the normative issue of choice between public and private ordering. Some (for example, Friedman, 1973; Rothbard, 1973; Benson, 1990) reveal a hostility to almost all instances of state-imposed law, arguing from public choice theory that it is predominantly motivated by pressure for wealth transfers and undermines the incentives of the reciprocity-based system of property rights. But, apart from the important reminder that the consequences of government failure may be more severe than market failure, it is not clear that these contributions add much to the debate which has taken place within the mainstream of law and economics (Katz, 1996), and which has its origin in the Coase Theorem (Coase, 1960). The ability of consensual bargaining to achieve efficient outcomes is a function of transactions costs, thus suggesting that the normative question of when private ordering should prevail should be determined by an analysis of how those costs impact on any given situation. Self-regulation may, therefore, be an appropriate solution where bargaining, at low cost, can occur between risk-creators and those affected; occupational health and safety provides a familiar example (Rees, 1988; Ogus, 1995; though for reservations, see Baldwin, 1987).

Much of the older literature on spontaneous order, surveyed above, is based on the implicit assumption that private (informal) legal systems emerge spontaneously, in response to the need to fill some regulatory void. However, such a view misses a crucial evolutionary issue.

Private legal systems are characterised by network effects: the benefits from membership increase with the number of participants. Such benefits are therefore likely to be limited in the early stages of the formation of the new network. Enforcement, on the other hand, is very costly. It is therefore difficult for newly formed private legal systems to assure compliance with the rules. With lack of enforcement, free-riding is possibly very frequent, where members enjoy the benefits from the network but then cheat on the rules. Individuals would then hardly be motivated to join the network in the first place, and the private legal system may not form. This is the "paradox of spontaneous formation" (Aviram, 2003 and 2004). Such paradox can be overcome by finding ways to exploit an existing network, with a functioning enforcement system, building the new private legal system on it. This would explain why many spontaneous institutions rely on the enforcement power of religious networks, to evolve into private legal systems joined by the vast majority of a social group. This is a fascinating theory, supported by prominent historical examples. Like all "chicken and egg" problems, however, it fails to explain how the first enforcing institution developed, the one that allowed, in a chain effect, all other social institutions to establish themselves.

The analysis in Buskens (2002) provides a possible response to such a paradox. He studies trust relationships in social networks, finding that trustworthiness is influenced by "the social context". The social context registers and publicises information regarding the past behaviour of members of the social group. It also offers the possibility of sanctioning free-riding and cheating through second- and third-party sanctions. Given that interaction in social groups is typically repeated in time, sanctions have not only the immediate benefit of reducing the incentives to cheat for current cheaters, but they also signal to future wrongdoers that the threat of punishment is credible. That is why third parties, who are not directly hit by wrongdoing, are willing to enforce sanctions, since they may obtain future benefits in terms of a reduction in the probability of being the victims of criminal acts.

4. Self-Regulation as Delegation of State Law-Making Powers

In the previous section, we examined systems of private ordering which emerge independently of state intervention. As a legal phenomenon, self-regulation is more usually analysed as a deliberate delegation of the state's law-making powers to an agency, the membership of which wholly or mainly comprises representatives of the firms or individuals whose activities are being regulated.

Public interest arguments for such delegation can be derived from principal–agent theory (Tuohy and Wolfson, 1978). Once the principal (normally, the legislature) has decided that an activity ought to be regulated on grounds of market failure, for example externalities or information asymmetries, the question arises what form of regulation is appropriate. That can be assessed by reference to such variables as the costs of information upon which the rule-making decisions are to be based and those of monitoring compliance and enforcing the rules. The principal may rationally conclude that these costs would be minimised if the tasks of rule-formulation, monitoring, adjudication and enforcement were to be conferred on a self-regulatory agency (hereafter SRA) (Trebilcock, 1983; Cane, 1987). Since SRAs typically command a greater degree of expertise and technical knowledge of practices and innovatory possibilities within the relevant area than the principal, information costs for the formulation and interpretation of standards are lower.

Delegation to SRAs should thus reduce the principal's costs of regulation; to what extent will they confer benefits of the kind which regulation is supposed to foster? Take a situation in which the quality of products or services cannot be observed by consumers prior to purchase. Although individual firms will be motivated to provide signals of quality (for example, product warranties), this may be very costly or – where the characteristics of quality are not easily definable – not feasible. It then becomes in the joint interest of the suppliers, as represented by the SRA, to maintain quality by self-regulation (Gehrig and Jost, 1995). And since, in such circumstances, attempts by consumers themselves to measure quality will also be costly and/or futile, such regulation will confer a benefit on them by obviating the need for measurement (Barzel, 1982), as are the costs to the regulatees of dealing with regulators, given that such interaction is likely to be fostered by mutual trust. This aspect is particularly important where, as with advertising, it is difficult to define the desired behaviour with precision and an adversarial relationship between regulator and regulatee is likely to be counterproductive (Baggott and Harrison, 1986). In addition, to the extent that the processes of, and rules issued by, SRAs are less formalised than those of public regulatory regimes, there are likely to be savings in the costs (including those attributable to delay) of amending rules. Finally, once such a regime of self-regulation has been established, individual suppliers have an incentive to supply (at lower cost) lower quality, but since the reputation of other firms will be affected by defaulters, the SRA will be motivated to enforce the standards. On the basis of this analysis, it has been predicted that viable self-regulatory regimes will emerge where monitoring costs for the SRA are low, the number of local markets is small, and customers are relatively mobile as between suppliers (Gehrig and Jost, 1995).

At the same time, there is every reason to expect that SRAs will use their law-making power to benefit their members in ways which are not consistent with the public interest (Horowitz, 1980). As has been formally demonstrated (Shaked and Sutton, 1981a), the self-regulatory rules may create barriers to entry and thus confer significant rents on incumbent practitioners. The latter include non-financial benefits, for example, a quiet life, as well as monetary income (Lees, 1966).

Most obviously, rent may be obtained where the SRA has the power to issue licences and therefore to determine the qualifications of those who engage in the activity (Moore, 1961). But there are also a variety of other ways in which "quality" standards may be used to promote the interests of the regulatees, rather than those of the public. For example, most professional associations have, at some time or another, prohibited their members from advertising, ostensibly on the ground that "touting" for business is incompatible with the ethical nature of professional practice (OECD, 1985). As we have seen, such bans can eliminate wasteful consumer searches on elusive quality characteristics (Barzel, 1982), but they can also inhibit comparative price shopping, thus generating monopoly rents for practitioners (Trebilcock, 1982).

Secondly, restrictions can be imposed on the legal form used by professional firms (for example, insisting on partnerships and prohibiting corporations) or on the participation of professionals from other disciplines in the firm (OECD, 1985). Both forms of control can add to client costs insofar as they inhibit productive efficiency of the firm (Evans, 1980) and, in some cases, make it necessary for consumers to deal with two or more firms, rather than one (Quinn, 1982). The quality imposed by SRAs may exceed that which presumptively will meet consumers' preferences and not be justified by externalities; and the excessive cost will be borne by consumers (Trebilcock, 1983). Other welfare losses can arise from the tendency of SRAs to discourage diversity and experimentation (Ostry, 1978; White, 1979).

We are thus left with a trade-off between the inherent pro-industry bias of self-regulation and the improvement in the quality of law-making due to the superior knowledge of the (local) regulators. When is the trade-off resolved in favour of self-regulation and when would it be preferable to leave regulation in the hands of a central authority? Self-regulation yields higher social welfare than government regulation when uncertainty is strong, when the divergence of interests between producers and consumers is small, and when the government attaches a high weight to consumer surplus in the social welfare function (Grajzl and Murrell, 2007). In all these cases, in fact, the trade-off between the pro-industry bias and the increased quality of regulation is dominated by the gains due to more efficient regulation. When there is high uncertainty regarding the characteristics of a given industry, local agents are better equipped to react faster to changes, enacting better rules. Likewise, when producers and consumers have similar preferences, a pro-industry bias cannot be welfare reducing. Finally, when consumers represent a large weight in the government's objective function, the producers' lobby is not very strong and it can hardly persuade the government to move away from the social optimum.

These results could explain the tendency of decentralised regulatory regimes to prevail in common-law countries, whereas centralised regulation is widespread in civil-law countries (case law produces more institutional uncertainty and the centralised character of civil law implies a greater efficiency of centralised institutions, such as governmental regulation). Furthermore, different regulatory regimes prevailed in different historical periods. For example, in the United States, during the Progressive Era, centralised regulation was extensively implemented, whereas self-regulation (although often government supervised) was more common during the New Deal Scholars agree that the Progressive Era was a period of relative economic stability (low uncertainty), in which interest groups had acquired a strong power and inequality was rising. Conversely, the New Deal followed a period of dramatic economic turmoil, uncertainty was high and the need to protect industries against the risk of bankruptcy led the government to attach a very low relative weight to consumer protection (Eisner, 2000).

In sectors in which corruption and coercion can undermine law enforcement and regulation, laissez-faire may guarantee a better outcome in terms of social welfare (Glaeser and Shleifer, 2003; Nunez, 2010). That is why self-regulation may be preferable to government regulation in securing compliance with safety standards (Baniak and Grajzl, 2009).

If regulation is the object of bargaining between the industry and the governmental regulators, the quality of self-regulation will depend on the relative bargaining power between the regulator and the industry and on the magnitude of the regulatory threat. If the regulator has more bargaining power and there is a high probability that tight government regulation will be imposed on the industry, then the first-best regulatory standard may be implemented through self-regulation. Conversely, if the industry has more bargaining power, then self-regulation results in the implementation of a standard that is lower than the first-best level. In such a case, the voluntarily regulated level might be increased through the use of a subsidy. In the absence of a subsidy, the self-regulated standard will also be lower than the level that might have been imposed legislatively (Segerson and Miceli, 1998, 1999).

5. Preemptive Self-Regulation

So far we have suggested several reasons why self-regulation may be preferable to other regulatory regimes. There are, however, serious implications of the pro-industry bias of self-regulation. Several authors have shown how minimum quality standards can raise welfare when products are vertically differentiated and buyers fully internalise the benefits of quality. By increasing the lowest quality level in the market, the regulator can intensify price competition to the benefit of consumers (Ronnen, 1991; Crampes and Hollander, 1995; Scarpa, 1998). However, in an industry in which firms can commit to a quality level before minimum quality standards are implemented, the centralised regulator will be induced to set a more lenient standard and social welfare will fall (Lutz, Lyon and Maxwell, 2000). By acting first and self-regulating quality, the industry plays the role of a Stackelberg leader, influencing the regulator's choice of the standard and inducing a more lenient regulation (a lower quality standard). This is particularly true in those industries in which self-regulation complements government regulation. Maxwell, Lyon and Hackett (2000) extend the analysis of pre-emptive self-regulation, imagining a scenario in which, in addition to firms and the public regulator, a third player is active in the regulatory game, namely consumers. They consider a three-stage game with pollution externalities. In the first stage, all firms in an industry jointly choose a level of abatement. In the second stage, consumers decide whether to lobby to increase abatement standards (lobbying is costly). In the third stage, firms compete à la Cournot. In such a setting, by engaging in pre-emptive self-regulation, firms increase consumer surplus, thus reducing consumers' incentives to lobby for tighter regulation. In fact, lobbying is costly and the higher the level of voluntary abatement, the lower the benefit from lobbying. It is therefore more likely that such benefit becomes smaller than the (fixed) cost of lobbying and consumers' entry in the "influence game" will not occur. Once again, pre-emptive self-regulation produces weaker standards than is socially optimal. Interestingly, however, given the lobbying costs, self-regulation represents a Pareto improvement over the status quo. A testable implication of this analysis is that an increased threat of consumer lobbying (which occurs when consumers value regulation highly) raises both the industry willingness to implement self-regulation and the level of voluntary abatement. The massive cuts in toxic chemical releases experienced in the United States in the past twenty years may therefore be due to the active role of consumers. The empirical evidence presented by Maxwell et al. (2000), in fact, shows that states with higher initial levels of toxic emissions and better organised environmental groups reduced pollution more rapidly. Given the typical assumption of decreasing marginal benefits from pollution for firms and increasing marginal costs for consumers, in this situation reducing pollution entails relatively low marginal costs for firms and relatively large marginal benefits for consumers. Then the threat of mandatory regulation is strong, while the marginal cost of self-regulation is small; and it is optimal for firms to engage in self-regulation.

The literature on regulatory pre-emption just illustrated may explain the adoption of higher standards than current regulation as an attempt to avoid tighter centralised regulation. Denicolò (2008) presents an interesting alternative hypothesis. There is evidence that, sometimes, self-regulation triggers tighter regulation rather than pre-empting it (see the 1992 California's Air Resources Board case and DuPont's lobbying for a tighter regulation of the use of chlorofluorocarbons in the mid-1980s). Then, another possible explanation for the adoption of tighter standards is that "overcompliance" may be used as a signal to the governmental regulator that stricter regulation should be imposed on the whole industry. Why would a firm prefer tighter regulation? The idea is that the firms that overcomply are characterised by relatively low costs of compliance (for example, because they own innovative technological knowledge). If the central regulator is not perfectly informed about the costs of compliance, it may infer that complying is not too costly and therefore decide to increase the standard. Then, more efficient firms would gain by raising their (less efficient) rivals' costs.

6. The Enforcement of Self-Regulation

So far, we have neglected a crucial point: the standards implemented through self-regulation need to be enforced. Differently from governmental regulation, whose enforcement costs are borne by taxpayers, in case of voluntary self-regulation, the enforcement costs are typically sustained by the members of the voluntary regulatory agreement. In a self-regulation regime, monitoring and enforcement costs are reduced. Decentralised enforcement usually benefits from a more efficient detection technology and is better suited to levy sanctions on non-compliant parties (Bailey, 1999; Nyborg, 2000; Brouhle et al., 2005; McEvoy and Stranlund, 2010). Thus, a more efficient use of resources should ensue. Finally, decentralised enforcement simply requires the observability of the fraudulent behaviour, given the more informal nature of local sanctioning procedures, whereas centralised enforcement requires that a third party verify the presence of frauds, i.e. it requires both observability and verifiability of deceit (Mayer and Neven, 1991). However, when enforcement costs are borne by the self-regulating agents, it is more difficult for self-regulation to be implemented in the first place. If self-regulation is indeed implemented, however, the number of firms in the industry which agree to participate in the self-regulatory agreement is higher than if enforcement were costless or if the costs were borne by the government (McEvoy and Stranlund, 2010). The intuition for this result is relatively straightforward. Since the enforcement costs are shared among the participants, more firms are needed to make the self-regulatory agreement profitable. Thus, if an agreement is formed at all, it will involve a higher number of firms.

Participation in self-regulating groups and enforcement raise two crucial issues in self-regulation: free-riding and the credibility and severity of internal punishment. If an industry can avoid centralised regulation by forming a voluntary agreement with less than full participation, firms that do not join can reap the benefits from avoiding the superimposed regulation without having to bear the costs of self-regulation (Dawson and Segerson, 2008). Although this is a problem concerning mainly the types of self-regulation that require an investment by the participants (such as, for instance, pollution abatement schemes), it nevertheless raises very important concerns about the feasibility and stability of the self-regulating agreements. Such concerns seem to be supported by empirical evidence. For instance, the European Environmental Agency (EEA) notes that small and medium enterprises typically display a high degree of free-riding (EEA, 1997).

As for punishments, Mayer and Neven (1991) consider the possibility of errors in sanctioning and argue that the severity of punishments should be mitigated to take into account the possibility of punishing innocent firms. Moreover, when a self-regulating group or industry sanctions one of its members, it publicly reveals that the latter has breached the rules the group had agreed upon. This may lead consumers to update their beliefs on the behaviour of all firms, reducing the perceived quality (this is especially true in the case of experience and credence goods). Then, a self-regulated group may have weak incentives to punish, for fear of ruining its reputation and damaging its honest members. Sanctioning "might be a negative signal about the average quality of remaining members" and "a sign that the fraudulent member thought that vigilance was low enough for there to be a reasonable chance of getting away with it" (Vickers, 1991).

7. Rent-Seeking Theories of Self-Regulation

In the light of public choice theory, rent-seeking explanations of regulation are, of course, commonplace (Tollison, 1982). If rule-making remains with the legislature or an independent agency, interest groups representing the regulatees have the task of exerting influence on those institutions and diverting them away from public interest goals or other, competing private interest claims. Of course, delegation of the regulatory powers to SRAs relieves the groups of this task and the relative absence of accountability and external constraints maximises the possibilities of rent-seeking – "with self-regulation, regulatory capture is there from the outset" (Kay, 1988). Governments are motivated to maintain or extend the use of self-regulation because, while they may derive political benefits from measures which appear to benefit consumers and others, the costs are not revealed in any public accounts (Trebilcock, 1983).

And it is difficult for the cost-bearers both to determine the amount of wealth transfers and to coordinate their activities in opposing them (Van den Bergh and Faure, 1991). Although, as we shall see in the next section, there is considerable empirical evidence to support this theory of self-regulation, it has not gone unchallenged. Dingwall and Fenn argue that it cannot explain the persistence and stability of entry restriction; other forces must be at work to prevent pressure from potential entrants building up to an intolerable level (Dingwall and Fenn, 1987). Such forces may lead to the emergence of illegal (or "informal") markets (De Soto, 1989), or of reasonably close, but unregulated, substitutes (Fisher, 1997). Indeed, it may be an inherent feature of regulation that it cannot control every margin of adjustable behaviour, and thus rents are dissipated as firms seek to trade on these uncontrollable margins (Cheung, 1974).

Weingast also finds it hard to reconcile the theory with the fact that many of the self-imposed restrictions can dissipate rents or seem designed to increase a perception of quality maintenance at the expense of greater rents (Weingast, 1980). Drawing on Arrow's public interest analysis (Arrow, 1963), he sees self-regulation as performing a symbolic informational function: as a consequence of the uncertainties as to both quality in the unregulated market and the effects of regulation, there is a tendency for SRAs to adopt policies which improve observable features of the activity and give the appearance of service uniformity.

8. Sector-Specific Studies

Some studies of self-regulatory systems support the notion of spontaneous, private ordering described above. For example, there are incentives for banks voluntarily to become members of private protective and certifying agencies (Gorton and Mullineaux, 1987; Gehrig and Jost, 1995), and for voluntary "best practice" auditing and other standards to be diffused among different SRAs (Belcher, 1996). The global financial crisis of 2008 has seriously questioned the effectiveness of self-regulation and auditing in financial markets and in the banking sector (Rajan, 2005; Canova, 2009; Emeseh et al., 2009; Zamagni, 2009). The debate on the merits of adopting a regime of self-regulation in financial markets nevertheless remains vibrant. De Marzo et al. (2005) have shown that self-regulation generally results in a lower degree of market transparency, because agents have the incentive to misrepresent cash flows to customers. Government supervision is then required to induce stricter enforcement and greater transparency. Stefanadis (2003), on the other hand, argues that self-regulation yields higher social welfare than government regulation in markets characterised by high rates of innovation (as financial markets are). This is because self-regulation eliminates certification-related delays in the adoption of financial innovations. It is important to notice, however, that pure self-regulation might not be enough to guarantee market discipline even in the presence of innovation. An appropriate form of "co"-regulation is required, where the threat of government intervention compels agents to pursue social optimal goals to avoid external regulations. Many scholars agree that the financial crisis in 2008 has been due to either ineffective or non-existent government regulation, whereas financial innovation has been devoted to sustain returns on riskier and riskier assets (Greenlaw et al., 2008; Reinhart and Rogoff, 2009; Duffie, 2010).

In the advertising industry, self-regulation has emerged as the suppliers have perceived the benefit to be obtained from acquiring public creditability for their products and from creating an image of professional responsibility (Baggott and Harrison, 1986, Schwartz et al., 2010). But these researchers also highlight the problem of enforcement: SRAs begin to adopt an aggressive stance only where there was perceived to be a threat of intervention by public agencies. The same phenomenon has been observed with the self-regulation of commodity exchanges (Pirrong, 1995; see also Page, 1987; Fishman, 1993; Black, 1997). Investigations of occupational health and safety systems, as they have increasingly shifted towards decentralised standard-setting by local arrangements between employers and employees, suggest this has been effective when the systems can be related to nationally established standards and are supported by knowledge that the arrangements will be enforced (Dawson et al., 1988). But there has been a decline in protection against risks created by small or non-unionised firms (Baldwin, 1987; Smith and Tombs, 1995).

An important field which has attracted a lot of attention recently is consumer protection. Several modes of consumer regulation are currently adopted in the industrialised world: centralised agencies, third-party institutions (e.g. ombudsmen) and regimes of self-regulation, the latter often aided by consumer associations. Self-regulation is efficient when there is a culture of proactive complaints by consumer associations and wrongdoing is easily detectable (Faure, Ogus and Philipsen, 2009; Hadfield, 2001).

Also the regulation of the cyberspace is presenting new challenges (Price and Verhulst, 2005; Tambini et al., 2008). During the 1990s, self-regulation was strongly advocated. Recent years have, however, seen a shift towards regimes of "co"-regulation of the internet (see, for instance, the 2007 European Commission's Audio Visual Media Services Directive), in which self-regulatory structures are required to coordinate with centralised regulatory institutions (especially in matters regarding public order, like crimes related to pornography and gambling).

Cybersecurity is another important field in which the debate of government versus private (self-) regulation has been very lively. As in the case of internet regulation, cybersecurity is a field in which the market may be unable to produce a solution. There is in fact a relevant free-riding problem, since computer users bear the full cost of protection, while the benefits are shared by the entire network. This might therefore call for centralised regulation. However, computer networks are globalised, extending far beyond the jurisdiction not only of all nations but also of all federations of states (Grady and Parisi, 2006). A complex system, in which some issues are left to self-regulation, whereas most critical ones are regulated through international cooperation, may therefore be the best way to deal with cybersecurity (Trachtman, 2006).

Beginning with the pioneering work of Friedman and Kuznets (1945), published at the end of the Second World War, most attention has been given to regimes governing the professions (for a valuable survey of studies relating to the medical professions, see Gravelle, 1985). Typically, the regimes involve SRAs having the power to issue licences and therefore the ability to restrict entry (see Kessel, 1970, for a study on how control by the SRA was used for the benefit of members of the profession). The prediction that this will enable incumbent practitioners to earn rents is difficult to substantiate because it is necessary to disentangle supra-competitive profits from higher earnings which represent legitimate compensation for higher educational costs and greater responsibilities. Nevertheless, when such variables are controlled for, researchers have found strong evidence of rents being earned by eyeglass suppliers (Benham and Benham, 1975), dry cleaners (Plott, 1965), lawyers (Holen, 1965; Lees, 1966; Domberger and Sherr, 1989; Curran, 1993) and dentists (Holen, 1965; Shepard, 1978; Wilson, 1987). Studies on other medical professions (Holen, 1965; White, 1979; Wilson, 1987; Curran, 1993) and architects (Button and Fleming, 1992) are less conclusive.

In a general study, Maurizi found that there was a significant correlation between licensing regimes and monetary returns for about half of the systems examined (Maurizi, 1974). Exacerbation of shortages in the supply of practitioners (Hogan, 1979), maldistribution of such supply (Holen, 1965; Boulier, 1980; Pashigian, 1980) and poorer quality of service (Caroll and Gaston, 1979) are other welfare effects found to have resulted from licensing regimes.

Ongoing professional standards, established by SRAs, have also enabled them to protect anti-competitive practices: for example, fee regulation and restrictions on advertising which limit price competition (Benham, 1972; Office of Fair Trading, 1982; Domberger and Sherr, 1989; Van den Bergh and Faure, 1991); and "professional ethics" which serve the well-being of practitioners rather than their clients and mask prohibitions on cost-saving innovation (Gravelle, 1985; Trautwein and Rönnau, 1993).

Kleiner (2006) presents a comprehensive survey on the effect of professional licensing. He finds little evidence of a positive relation between licensing and the quality of the services provided. He also analyses the impact of licensing on earnings, finding that professionals enjoy much higher earning premia in the US than in Europe. A possible explanation may be the relative wage rigidity characterising Europe, which may cause licensing to produce effects more through reduced employment than through prices, whereas the opposite seems to hold for the US. Overall, Kleiner concludes that the costs of licensing greatly outweigh the benefits. Therefore a different system may be preferable, i.e. certification, which provides many of the advantages of licensing but leads to more competition and lower entry barriers.

9. Competitive Self-Regulation

The above discussion suggests that, on certain key assumptions, systems of spontaneous private legal ordering can generate efficient outcomes, but that state-delegated systems of self-regulation can lead to adverse welfare effects.

The crucial factor which distinguishes the two systems is that the act of state delegation normally involves conferring on the SRA a monopoly power to legally constrain supply in the relevant market. We have seen (Baggott and Harrison, 1986; Pirrong, 1995) that the threat of state intervention may, to some extent, mitigate the harmful effects of monopolisation. A useful analogy may here be drawn with the theory of contestable markets which indicates that, under certain conditions, efficient pricing and production can be forced upon a monopolistic supplier by the threat of competition, just as much as by actual competition (Baumol, Panzar and Willig, 1982). But the necessary conditions – notably the ability of the entrant costlessly to leave the market – are rarely met in practice (Waterson, 1988).

Similarly, on cost grounds, SRAs may not regard the threat of state intervention as credible.

An alternative solution to the problem presents itself: if the principal objection to SRAs is that they are able to exploit their monopolistic control of supply so as to enable practitioners to earn rents, then why not force SRAs to compete with one another, so that the rents will be eliminated (Kay and Vickers, 1990; Ogus, 1995)? Such competition would obviously prevent SRAs creating barriers to entry. But it should also constrain SRAs to formulate standards which meet consumer preferences at lowest cost since, assuming consumers have adequate information to make appropriate comparisons, they will choose the combination of price and self-regulatory standards which most closely corresponds to those preferences.

Competition of this kind is inherent in systems of private ordering: suppliers compete to attract consumers by the quality (as well as the price) of their products and services. Quality is, to some extent at least, a consequence of standards and other forms of control imposed internally by the management of a firm. The standards may reflect public regulatory requirements, but more often they are voluntary, representing the firm's response to assumed consumer demand and, in some cases, incorporating industry-wide practices. To signal to consumers the relationship between standards and quality, some form of voluntary accreditation or certification can be used (Bardach and Kagan, 1982).

Suppliers who aim at different quality standards, and have difficulty in communicating that fact to consumers, will have an incentive to establish a rival certification system. Competing self-regulatory regimes may thus emerge. Thus envisaged, competitive self-regulation is, in essence, no different from competition between national public regulatory regimes (Bratton et al., 1997). If there is mutual recognition of national standards and freedom of trade, consumers can choose between the different quality standards imposed by the national systems in accordance with their own preferences. Provided that they are informed as to the relevant national compliance certificate, competition between national regulatory regimes should induce standard-setters to meet those preferences (Kay and Vickers, 1990).

The policy implication of this analysis is that where the public interest arguments for the state delegating its regulatory powers are strong (see above), it should not grant monopoly power but rather enable two or more SRAs within a given supplier group to formulate alternative regimes (Ogus, 1995; for the effects of competition between professionals and para-professionals, see Shaked and Sutton, 1981b). Although there is a risk of cartelisation, most industries are sufficiently heterogeneous for this purpose. An alternative is to retain the monopoly but force different SRAs to compete ex ante to acquire the right to control supply by self-regulation. Competing applicants would be required to include their self-regulatory rules as part of the bid; and, as with other public franchises (Demsetz, 1968), the competition should force applicants to offer regimes consistent with the public interest.

There are, nevertheless, potential problems with these solutions. Consumers – more precisely marginal consumers (Schwartz and Wilde, 1979) – must be able to attribute general quality characteristics to certificates generated by the competing self-regulatory regimes; otherwise there will be a "race to the bottom" (Akerlof, 1970). Secondly, there must be no significant externalities arising from their purchasing behaviour. The importance of information asymmetries and externalities and, in relation to the franchising solution, the need to scrutinize competing bids suggest that in many areas some residual form of state intervention will be optimal. It remains to consider this issue more generally.

10. Mixed Systems

As was indicated in the discussion of the nature of self-regulation, there is a wide range of possible institutional arrangements between public regulation on the one hand and pure private ordering on the other. In an effort to realise many of the benefits of self-regulation, but controlling the costs which result from SRA rent-seeking, some jurisdictions have adopted what has been referred to as "coregulation" (Grabosky and Braithwaite, 1986): SRAs regulate with some oversight or ratification by government, or officials representing the public interest (see for example Page, 1987). The main problem is that of informational asymmetry between the public agency and the SRA. The latter can withhold vital information unless there is confidence that it will be used to reach regulatory solutions which favour its members (Quirk, 1981). Typically, also, the SRA retains monopolistic control of enforcement.

In an important contribution to the literature, Ayres and Braithwaite argue, instead, for "enforced self-regulation" (Ayres and Braithwaite, 1992; see also Braithwaite, 1982). Under this model, a public agency negotiates with individual firms regulations that are particularised to each firm, with the threat of an imposition of less tailored standards if it fails to cooperate. While the firm may thus formulate the rules, they are enforced by the public agency. The advantages are clear: as with other privately ordered systems, the rules are tailored to match the firm's circumstances and are less costly to adapt; there are incentives to identify least-cost solutions, which should encourage regulatory innovation; and firms would be more committed to the rules than if imposed externally. Moreover, the very fact of individualisation avoids the monopoly problem. On the other hand, the administrative costs would be high. This suggests that, for such a regime to be cost-effective, the firm must be large and the activity to be regulated must be one in which efficiency requires significantly differentiated standards (Latin, 1985).

Finally, an important case of "mixed regulation" is "co"-regulation, described in Section 2 and investigated thoroughly by, among others, Bartle and Vass (2007).

11. Morally Motivated Self-Regulation and Corporate Social Responsibility

Self-regulation can be motivated by self-interest. In the literature surveyed above, firms resort to self-regulation to increase profits, be that through pre-emption of tougher regulation or through increasing rivals' costs.

Self-regulation can be motivated also by altruistic moral concerns. Consider, for example, a setting in which economic agents (private individuals and firms) face opportunities to free-ride on the self-regulation of other agents they interact with. In such a setting, self-regulation should be defined in a broad sense as the voluntary (private) provision of a public good. According to whether agents are private individuals or firms, the nature of the public good may change and thus the type of self-regulation. For instance, individuals may engage in the abatement of environmental externalities, they may contribute to community projects or they may purchase products only if they are produced in factories that do not exploit child labour. Similarly, firms may self-regulate by abating production externalities, treating workers well and employing sustainable inputs in the production process (i.e., roughly speaking, by following principles of Corporate Social Responsibility). Baron (2010) shows that the stronger the altruistic component in the individual utility function, the higher the incentives to adopt self-regulation. However, the extent of self-regulation is influenced by various factors, among which are the sensitivity of altruism to "closeness" and the incentives to free-ride on more altruistic trading partners. Some people, in fact, tend to be very altruistic within their kin group, but do not cooperate with agents outside their group. This is a first type of free-riding and can occur also among people with preferences characterised by the same degree of altruism. When preferences are not homogeneous, so that there is moral heterogeneity in the society, a second type of altruism can arise, in which those with weaker preferences for altruism free-ride on the cooperative behaviour of those with stronger preferences for altruism.

When agents choose to self-regulate, besides performing individual altruistic actions, they can also form voluntary organisations. Such organisations reinforce the scope of self-regulation, enhancing public good provision. Baron (2010) distinguishes between two types of voluntary organisations: enforcing organisations and informational organisations. Enforcing organisations have the capability to adopt strategies that raise the costs of non-contributing. Such costs could consist either in a loss of reputation due to public exposure in case of non-compliance, in the application of social sanctions, or in the exertion of social pressure. Examples of such organisations could be NGOs monitoring working conditions in factories or reporting cases of environmental abuse. Informational organisations lack enforcement capabilities; they simply provide information, allowing agents to interact with others with similar preferences. Such organisations provide social labels (labelling organisations) or monitor the conduct of a trading partner (certification organisations). Enforcing organisations enhance cooperation in the presence of the first type of free-riding, since they extend altruistic behaviour towards individuals not immediately close to the kin group. Conversely, labelling and certification organisations are most effective in tackling the second type of free-riding. For instance, social labelling allows agents to interact with others with similar preferences, reducing the risk of meeting less altruistic individuals and to be subject to free-riding. By joining a social label organisation that is especially tailored to the needs of a given group of individuals, agents can credibly reveal their type to others. Consider, for example, a "green club", where consumers are sure they can buy from retailers that meet green standards. This enhances cooperation every time altruism is reciprocal, i.e. every time the propensity to cooperation is positively related to the expectation of reciprocation by the counterpart. A similar effect of risk reduction is achieved by certification organisations that expose the past behaviour of trading partners.

It is immediate to extend these results to Corporate Social Responsibility (CSR) practices. CSR firms are in fact instruments through which both entrepreneurs and private citizens fulfil their altruistic preferences. The creation of a CSR firm expands the opportunities for cooperation for both social entrepreneurs and consumers/shareholders interested in social giving. To see how this occurs, consider an altruistic investor, who has the opportunity to buy shares in the capital market and to use the financial returns on those shares to (privately) provide public goods. A CSR firm can be defined as a firm involved in the provision of public goods. Individual and corporate altruism are substitutes, hence CSR practices crowd out private altruism. Generally speaking, however, they are imperfect substitutes. Then there will be individuals who draw a greater utility from corporate than from their private altruism. Such individuals will buy shares of CSR firms, reducing their private contributions to public goods accordingly. Conversely, those who prefer private giving hold no shares in CSR firms. CSR firms thus represent institutions through which citizens (in the role of investors) expand their self-regulation (Baron, 2007, 2008). Needless to say, if corporate altruism were a perfect substitute for private altruism, CSR would have no reason to exist.

This theory can also explain why perfectly rational entrepreneurs sacrifice profits in the social interest (Friedman, 1970; Baron, 2001; Reinhardt, Stavins and Vietor, 2008). If citizens derive social satisfaction from corporate altruism, they will invest in CSR firms even if such firms do not maximise profits. Then, in a society characterised by heterogeneous individuals, there will be firms that maximise profits and CSR firms, which redistribute profits to social causes.

If CSR is a self-regulation device in the sense of Baron (2010), then not only does it help private citizens to expand their set of cooperative actions, but CSR firms themselves may act opportunistically, facing incentives to free-ride. Such incentives will be reduced by enforcing institutions and by the informative action of labelling and certification organisations (the activity of NGOs is very important in this respect; see Lyon and Maxwell, 2008, for an illustration in the field of environmental CSR). Interestingly, CSR firms are subject to another important disciplining force: competition. Empirical evidence points to the existence of a negative relation between measures of market concentration and the extent of CSR activities (Fernández-Kranz and Santalo, 2010). This is taken as evidence that firms engaging in CSR do not suffer a reduction in profits and that CSR is "a way to either better differentiate, gain access to new markets, or achieve a better fit between the firm's products and services and consumer preferences in some unique market niches" (Fernández-Kranz and Santalo, 2010, p. 454). Then, most forms of CSR would not be altruistic (where altruistic CSR sacrifices profits for the social interest) but would rather be "strategic" (Baron, 2001): companies that "do well by doing good". According to such a view, CSR firms are for-profit institutions that specialise in the provisions of goods and services that allow consumers to expand the set of their altruistic actions.

Bibliography

Adelstein, Richard P. (1992), "Charles E. Lindblom", in Samuels, Warren J. (ed.), *New Horizons in Economic Thought: Appraisals of Leading Economists*, Aldershot, UK and Brookfield, US, Edward Elgar, 202–26.

Anderson, Terry L. and Hill, Peter J. (1979), "American Experiment in Anarcho-Capitalism: The Not so Wild, Wild West", *Journal of Liberation Studies*, 3: 9–19.

Aviram, Amitai (2003), "Regulation by Networks", *Brigham Young University Law Review*, 4: 1179–238.

Aviram, Amitai (2004), "The Paradox of Spontaneous Formations of Private Legal Systems", *Yale Law and Policy Review*, 22: 1–68.

Bailey, Patricia M. (1999), "The Creation and Enforcement of Environmental Agreements", *European Environmental Law Review*, 8(6), 169–79.

Baniak, Andrzej and Grajzl, Peter (2009), "Industry Self-Regulation, Subversion of Public Institutions, and Social Control of Torts", *International Review of Law and Economics*, 29: 360–74.

Baron, David P. (2001), "Private Politics, Corporate Social Responsibility, and Integrated Strategy", *Journal of Economics and Management Strategy*, 10: 7–45.

Baron, David P. (2007), "Corporate Social Responsibility and Social Entrepreneurship", *Journal of Economics and Management Strategy*, 16(3): 683–717.

Baron, David P. (2008), "Managerial Contracting and Corporate Social Responsibility", *Journal of Public Economics*, 92(1–2): 268–88.

Baron, David P. (2010), "Morally Motivated Self-Regulation", *American Economic Review*, 100: 1299–329.

Bartle, Ian and Vass, Peter (2007), "Self-Regulation within the Regulatory State", *Administration*, 85: 885–905.

Barzel, Yoram (1982), "Measurement Costs and the Organisation of Markets", *Journal of Law and Economics*, 25: 27–48.
Belcher, Alice (1996), "The Invention, Innovation and Diffusion of Self-Regulation in Corporate Governance", *Northern Ireland Law Quarterly*, 47: 322–34.
Benham, Lee (1972), "The Effect of Advertising on the Price of Eyeglasses", *Journal of Law and Economics*, 15: 337–52.
Benham, Lee and Benham, Alexandra (1975), "Regulating through the Professions: A Perspective on Information Control", *Journal of Law and Economics*, 18: 421–47.
Benson, Bruce L (1988), "Legal Evolution in Primitive Societies", *Journal of Institutional and Theoretical Economics*, 144: 772–88.
Benson, Bruce L. (1989), "The Spontaneous Evolution of Commercial Law", *Southern Economic Journal*, 55: 644–61.
Benson, Bruce L. (1990), *The Enterprise of Law: Justice without the State*, San Francisco: Pacific Research Institute for Public Policy.
Benson, Bruce L. (1992), "Customary Law as a Social Contract: International Commercial Law", *Constitutional Political Economy*, 3: 1–27.
Benson, Bruce L. (1993), "The Impetus for Recognizing Private Property and Adopting Ethical Behavior in a Market Economy: Natural Law, Government Law, or Evolving Self-Interest", *Review of Austrian Economics*, 6: 43–80.
Bernstein, Lisa (1992), "Opting Out of the Legal System: Extralegal Contractual Relations in the Diamond Industry", *Journal of Legal Studies*, 21: 115–58.
Blair, Roger D. and Rubin, Stephen (eds), *Regulating the Professions: A Public-Policy Symposium*, Lexington, MA, Lexington Books.
Boulier, B.L. (1980), "An Empirical Examination of the Influence of Licensure and Licensure Reform on the Geographical Distribution of Dentists", in Rottenberg, Simon (ed.), *Occupational Licensure and Licensure Regulation*, Washington, DC: American Enterprise Institute, 73–97.
Braithwaite, John (1982), "Enforced Self Regulation: A New Strategy for Corporate Crime", *Michigan Law Review*, 80: 1466–507.
Brouhle, Keith, Griffiths, Charles and Wolverton, Ann (2005), "The Use of Voluntary Approaches for Environmental Policymaking in the U.S.", in Croci, Edoardo (ed.) *The Handbook of Environmental Voluntary Agreements*, Dordrecht and New York: Springer.
Buskens, Vincent (2002), *Social Networks and Trust*, Boston, MA: Kluwer Academic Publisher.
Button, Kenneth and Fleming, Michael (1992), "The Effects of Regulatory Reform on the Architectural Profession in the United Kingdom", *International Review of Law and Economics*, 12: 95–116.
Canova, Timothy A. (2009) "Financial Market Failure as a Crisis in the Rule of Law: From Market Fundamentalism to a New Keynesian Regulatory Model", *Harvard Law and Policy Review*, 3: 369–96.
Caroll, Sidney L. and Gaston, Robert J. (1979), "State Occupational Licensing Provisions and Quality of Service: The Real Estate Business", *Research in Law and Economics*, 1: 1–13.
Charny, David (1990), "Nonlegal Sanctions in Commercial Relationships", *Harvard Law Review*, 104: 373–467.
Cheit, Ross E. (1990), *Setting Safety Standards: Regulation in the Public and Private Sectors*, Berkeley, CA: University of California Press.
Cheung, Steven N.S. (1974), "A Theory of Price Control", *Journal of Law and Economics*, 17: 53–72.
Cooter, Robert D. (1996), "Decentralized Law for a Complex Economy: The Structural Approach to Adjudicating the New Law Merchant", *University of Pennsylvania Law Review*, 144: 1643–96.
Crampes, Claude and Hollander, Abraham (1995),"Duopoly and Quality Standards", *European Economic Review*, 39: 71–82.
Curran, Christopher (1993), "The American Experience with Self-Regulation in the Medical and Legal Professions", in Faure, Michael, Finsinger, Jörg, Siegers, Hacques and Van den Bergh, Roger (eds), *Regulation of Professions: A Law and Economics Approach to the Regulation of Attorneys and Physicians in the US, Belgium, Netherlands, Germany and the UK*, Antwerp: Maklu, 47–87.

Dawson, Na Li and Segerson, Kathleen (2008), "Voluntary Agreements with Industries: Participation Incentives with Industry-wide Targets", *Land Economics*, 84: 97–114.

DeMarzo, Peter, Fishman, Michael and Hagerty, Kathleen (2005), "Self Regulation and Government Oversight", *Review of Economic Studies*, 72: 687–706.

Denicolò, Vincenzo (2008), "A Signaling Model of Environmental Overcompliance", *Journal of Economic Behavior and Organization*, 68: 293–303.

De Soto, Hernando (1989), *The Other Path: The Invisible Revolution in the Third World*, New York: Harper and Row.

Dingwall, Robert and Fenn, Paul (1987), "A Respectable Profession? Sociological and Economic Perspectives on the Regulation of Professional Services", *International Review of Law and Economics*, 7: 55–64.

Domberger, Simon and Sherr, Avrom (1989), "The Impact of Competition on Pricing and Quality of Legal Services", *International Review of Law and Economics*, 9: 41–56.

Duffie, Darrell (2010), "The Failure Mechanics of Dealer Banks", *Journal of Economic Perspectives*, 24(1): 51–72.

Eisner, Marc Allen (2000), Regulatory politics in transition (2nd ed.), Baltimore, MD: Johns Hopkins University Press.

Ellickson, Robert C. (1991), *Order without Law: How Neighbours Settle Disputes*, Cambridge, MA: Harvard University Press.

Ellickson, Robert C. (1993), "Property in Land", *Yale Law Journal*, 102: 1315–400.

Emeseh, Engobo, Ako, Rhuks Temitope, Okonmah, Patrick and Obokoh, Lawrence Ogechukwu (2009), "Corporations, CSR and Self Regulation: What Lessons from the Global Financial Crisis?", *German Law Journal*, 11(2): 230–59.

European Environmental Agency (EEA) (1997), "Environmental Agreements: Environmental Effectiveness", Environmental Issue Series, 3, vol. 1–2. Copenhagen.

Evans, Robert G. (1980), "Professionals and the Production Function: Can Competition Policy Improve Efficiency in the Licensed Professions?", in Rottenberg, Simon (ed.), *Occupational Licensure and Regulation,* Washington, DC: American Enterprise Institute.

Faure, Michael, Ogus, Anthony and Philipsen, Niels (2009), "Curbing Consumer Financial Losses: The Economics of Regulatory Enforcement", *Law and Policy*, 31(2): 161–91.

Fernández-Kranz, Daniel and Santaló, Juan (2010), "When Necessity Becomes a Virtue: The Effect of Product Market Competition on Corporate Social Responsibility", *Journal of Economic Management and Strategy*, 19(2): 453–87.

Friedman, David (1973), *The Machinery of Freedom: Guide to Radical Capitalism*, New York: Harper and Row.

Friedman, David (1979), "Private Creation and Enforcement of Law: A Historical Case", *Journal of Legal Studies*, 8: 399–415.

Friedman, Milton (1970), "The Social Responsibility of Business is to Increase Profits", *New York Times Magazine*, September 13.

Friedman, Milton and Kuznets, S. (1945), *Income from Independent Professional Practice*, New York: National Bureau of Economic Research.

Gehrig, Thomas and Jost, Peter J. (1995), "Quacks, Lemons and Self-Regulation: A Welfare Analysis", *Journal of Regulatory Economics*, 7: 309–25.

Glaeser, Edward L. and Shleifer, Andrei (2003), "The Rise of the Regulatory State", *Journal of Economic Literature*, 41(2): 401–25.

Gorton, Gary and Mullineaux, Donald J. (1987), "The Joint Production of Confidence: Endogenous Regulation and Nineteenth Century Commercial Bank Clearinghouses", *Journal of Money, Credit, and Banking*, 19: 457–68.

Grady, Mark and Parisi, Francesco (eds) (2006), *The Law and Economics of Cybersecurity*, New York: Cambridge University Press.

Grajzl, Peter and Murrell, Peter (2007), "Allocating Lawmaking Powers: Self-Regulation vs Government Regulation", *Journal of Comparative Economics*, 35: 520–45.

Gravelle, Hugh (1985), "Economic Analysis of Health Service Professions: A Survey", 20 Social Sciences and Medicine, 1049–61.

Greenlaw, David, Hatzius, Jan, Kashyap, Anil K. and Shin, Hyun Song (2008), "Leveraged Losses: Lessons from the Mortgage Market Meltdown", *Proceedings of the U.S. Monetary Policy Forum, 2008*, Chicago: US Monetary Policy Forum, 7–59.

Greif, Avner (1989), "Reputation and Coalitions in Medieval Trade: Evidence on the Maghribi Traders", *Journal of Economic History*, 49: 857–82.

Hadfield, Gillian (2001), "Privatizing Commercial Law", *Regulation*, 24: 40–45.

Holen, Arlene S. (1965), "Effects of Professional Licensing Arrangements on Interstate Labor Mobility and Resource Allocation", *Journal of Political Economy*, 73: 492–8.

Horowitz, Ira (1980), "The Economic Foundations of Self-Regulation in the Professions", in Blair, Roger D. and Rubin, Stephen (eds), *Regulating the Professions: A Public-Policy Symposium*, Lexington, MA: Lexington Books.

Hutter, B.M. (2001), "Is Enforced Self-Regulation a Form of Risk Taking? The Case of Railway Health and Safety", *International Journal of the Sociology of Law*, 29: 379–400 .

Katz, Avery (1996), "Taking Private Ordering Seriously", *University of Pennsylvania Law Review*, 144: 1754–63.

Kay, John (1988), "The Forms of Regulation", in Seldon, Arthur (ed.), *Financial Regulation – or Over-Regulation*, London: Institute of Economic Affairs, 33–42.

Kessel, Reuben A. (1970), "The A.M.A. and the Supply of Physicians", *Law and Contemporary Problems*, 35: 267–83.

Klein, Daniel B. (ed.) (1997), *Reputation: Studies in the Voluntary Elicitation of Good Conduct*, Ann Arbor, MI: University of Michigan Press.

Kissam, P.C. (1980), "Anti-Trust Law, the First Amendment, and Professional Self-Regulation of Technical Quality", in Blair, Roger D. and Rubin, Stephen (eds), *Regulating the Professions: A Public-Policy Symposium*, Lexington, MA: Lexington Books.

Kleiner, Morris M. (2006), *Licensing Occupations: Ensuring Quality or Restricting Competition?*, Kalamazoo, MI: W.E. Upjohn Institute for Employment Research.

Lees, D.S. (1966), *The Economic Consequences of the Professions*, London: Institute of Economic Affairs.

Lutz, Stefan, Lyon, Thomas P., and Maxwell, John W. (2000), "Quality Leadership when Regulatory Standards are Forthcoming", *Journal of Industrial Economics*, 48(3): 331–48.

Lyon, Thomas P. and Maxwell, John W. (2003), "Self-Regulation, Taxation and Public Voluntary Environmental Agreements", *Journal of Public Economics*, 87: 1453–86.

Lyon, Thomas P. and Maxwell, John W. (2008), "Corporate Social Responsibility and the Environment: A Theoretical Perspective", *Review of Environmental Economics and Policy*, 2(2): 240–60.

Maurizi, Alex R. (1974), "Occupational Licensing and the Public Interest", *Journal of Political Economy*, 82: 399–413.

Maxwell, John W., Lyon, Thomas P. and Hackett, Steven C. (2000), "Self-Regulation and Social Welfare: The Political Economy of Corporate Environmentalism", *Journal of Law and Economics*, 43(2): 583–617.

Mayer, Colin and Neven, David (1991), "European Financial Regulation: A Framework for Policy Analysis", in Giovannini, Alberto and Mayer Colin (eds), *European Financial Integration*, Cambridge: Cambridge University Press.

McEvoy, David M. and Stranlund, John K. (2010), "Costly Enforcement of Voluntary Environmental Agreements", *Environmental and Resource Economics*, 47: 45–63.

Milgrom, Paul R., North, Douglass, C. and Weingast, Barry R. (1990), "The Role of Institutions in the Revival of Trade: The Law Merchant, Private Judges, and the Champagne Fairs", *Economics and Politics*, 2: 1–23.

Moore, Thomas G. (1961), "The Purpose of Licensing", *Journal of Law and Economics*, 4: 93–117.

Moran, Michael (2003), *The British Regulatory State, High Modernism and Hyper-innovation*, Oxford: Oxford University Press.

Nunez, Javier (2010), "Can Self Regulation Work? A Story of Corruption, Impunity and Cover Up", *Journal of Regulation Economics*, 31: 209–33.

Nyborg, Karine (2000), "Voluntary Agreements and Non-verifiable Emissions", *Environmental and Resource Economics*, 17(2), 125–44.

OECD (Organisation for Economic Co-operation and Development) (2002), *Regulatory Policies in OECD Countries: From Interventionism to Regulatory Governance*, Paris : OECD.

Ogus, Anthony (1995), "Rethinking Self-Regulation", *Oxford Journal of Legal Studies*, 15: 97–108.

Ostry, Sylvia (1978), "Competition Policy and the Self-Regulating Professions", in Slayton, Philip and Trebilcock, Michael J. (eds), *The Professions and Public Policy*, Toronto: University of Toronto Faculty of Law.

Pashigian, B. Peter (1980), "Has Occupational Licensing Reduced Geographical Mobility and Raised Earnings?", in Rottenberg, Simon (ed.), *Occupational Licensure and Regulation*, Washington, DC: American Enterprise Institute.

Paul, Chris W. (1982), "Competition in the Medical Profession: An Application of the Economic Theory of Regulation", *Southern Economic Journal*, 48: 559–69.

Pirrong, Stephen Craig (1995), "The Self Regulation of Commodity Exchanges: The Case of Market Manipulation", *Journal of Law and Economics*, 38: 141–206.

Plott, Charles R. (1965), "Occupational Self-Regulation: A Case-Study of the Oklahoma Dry Cleaners", *Journal of Law and Economics*, 8: 195–222.

Price, Monroe E. and Verhulst, Stefaan G. (2005), *Self-Regulation and the Internet*, The Hague, The Netherlands: Kluwer Law International.

Quinn, John (1982), "Multidisciplinary Legal Services and Preventive Regulation", in Evans, Robert G. and Trebilcock, Michael J. (eds), *Lawyers and the Consumer Interest: Regulating the Market for Legal Services*, London: Butterworths, chapter 11.

Rajan, G. Rhaguram (2005) "Has Financial Development Made the World Riskier?", *The Greenspan Era: Lessons for the Future*, Kansas City: Federal Reserve Bank of Kansas City.

Rees, Joseph (1988), *Reforming the Workplace: A Study of Self-Regulation in Occupational Safety*, Philadelphia, PA: University of Pennsylvania Press.

Reinhardt, Forest L., Stavins, Robert N. and Vietor, Richard, H.K. (2008), "Corporate Social Responsibility through an Economic Lens", *Review of Environmental Economics and Policy*, 2(2): 219–39.

Reinhart, Carmen M. and Rogoff, Kenneth S. (2009), *This Time is Different: Eight Centuries of Financial Folly*, Princeton, NJ: Princeton University Press.

Ronnen, Uri (1991), "Minimum Quality Standards, Fixed Costs, and Competition", *Rand Journal of Economics*, 22: 490–504.

Rothbard, Murray N. (1973), *For a New Liberty*, Basingstoke: Macmillan.

Scarpa, C. (1998), "Minimum Quality Standards with More Than Two Firms", *International Journal of Industrial Organization*, 16(5): 665–76.

Schanze, Erich (1988), "Regulation by Consensus: The Practice of International Mining Agreements", *Journal of Institutional and Theoretical Economics*, 144: 152–71.

Schwartz, Marlene B., Ross, Craig, Harris, Jennifer L., Jernigan, David H., Siegel, Michael, Ostroff, Joshua and Brownell, Kelly D. (2010), "Breakfast Cereal Industry Pledges to Self-Regulate Advertising to Youth: Will they Improve the Marketing Landscape?", *Journal of Public Health Policy*, 31: 59–73.

Segerson, Kathleen and Miceli, Thomas J. (1998), "Voluntary Environmental Agreements: Good or Bad News for Environmental Protection?", *Journal of Environmental Economics and Management* 36 (2): 109–30.

Segerson, Kathleen and Miceli, Thomas J. (1999), "Voluntary Approaches to Environmental Protection: The Role of Legislative Threats", in Carraro, Carlo and Lévêque, Francois (eds), *Voluntary Approaches in Environmental Policy*, Boston and London: Kluwer Academic.

Shaked, Avner and Sutton, John (1981a), "Heterogeneous Consumers and Product Differentiation in a Market for Professional Services", *European Economic Review*, 15: 159–77.

Shaked, Avner and Sutton, John (1981b), "The Self-Regulating Profession", *Review of Economic Studies*, 47: 217–34.

Shepard, Lawrence (1978), "Licensing Restrictions and the Cost of Dental Care", *Journal of Law and Economics*, 21: 187–201.

Smith, Denis and Tombs, Steve (1995), "Beyond Self-Regulation: Towards a Critique of Self-Regulation as a Control Strategy for Hazardous Activities", *Journal of Management Studies*, 32: 619–36.

Stefanadis, Christodoulos (2003), "Self Regulation, Innovation and the Finance Industry", *Journal of Regulation Economics*, 23: 5–25.

Tambini, Damien, Leonardi, Danilo and Marsden, Christopher (2005), *Codifying Cyberspace: Communications Self-Regulation in the Age of Internet Convergence*, Abingdon, UK: Routledge.

Trachtman, Joel (2006), "Global Cyberterrorism, Jurisdiction, and International Organization", in Grady, Mark and Parisi, Francesco (eds) (2006), *The Law and Economics of Cybersecurity*, New York: Cambridge University Press.

Trautwein, Hans-Michael and Rönnau, Andreas (1993), "Selfregulation of the Medical Profession in Germany: A Survey", in Faure, Michael, Finsinger, Jörg, Siegers, Jacques and Van den Bergh, Roger (eds), *Regulation of Professions: A Law and Economics Approach to the Regulation of Attorneys and Physicians in the US, Belgium, Netherlands, Germany and the UK*, Antwerp: Maklu, 249–306.

Trebilcock, Michael J. (1982), "Competitive Advertising", in Evans, Robert G. and Trebilcock, Michael J. (eds), *Lawyers and the Consumer Interest: Regulating the Market for Legal Services*, London: Butterworths, chapter 5.

Trebilcock, Michael J. (1983), "Regulating Service Quality in Professional Markets", in Dewees, Donald N. (ed.), *The Regulation of Quality: Products, Services, Workplaces and the Environment*, London: Butterworths, chapter 4.

Tuohy, Carolyn and Wolfson, Alan (1978), "Self-Regulation: Who Qualifies?", in Slayton, Philip and Trebilcock, Michael J. (eds), *The Professions and Public Policy*, Toronto: University of Toronto Faculty of Law.

Umbeck, John (1981), *A Theory of Property Rights with Applications to the Californian Gold Rush*, Ames, IA: Iowa State University Press.

Van den Bergh, Roger and Faure, Michael G. (1991), "Self Regulation of the Professions in Belgium", *International Review of Law and Economics*, 11: 165–82.

Vickers, John (1991), "Discussion of Mayer and Neven", in Giovannini Alberto and Mayer Colin (eds), *European Financial Integration*, Cambridge: Cambridge University Press.

Weingast, Barry R. (1980), "Physicians, DNA Research Scientists, and the Market for Lemons", in Blair, Roger D. and Rubin, Stephen (eds), *Regulating the Professions: A Public-Policy Symposium*, Lexington, MA: Lexington Books.

White, William D. (1979), "Dynamic Elements of Regulation: The Case of Occupational Licensure", *Research in Law and Economics*, 1: 15–33.

Wilson, R.A. (1987), "Returns to Entering the Medical Profession in the UK", *Journal of Health Economics*, 6: 339–63.

Zamagni, Stefano (2009), "The Lesson and Warning of a Crisis Foretold: A Political Economy Approach", *International Review of Economics*, 56: 315–34.

Other References

Akerlof, George, A. (1970), "The Market for 'Lemons': Qualitative Uncertainty and the Market Mechanism", *Quarterly Journal of Economics*, 84: 488–500.

Arrow, Kenneth (1963), "Uncertainty and the Welfare Economics of Medical Care", *American Economic Review*, 53: 941–73.

Ayres, Ian and Braithwaite, John (1992), *Responsive Regulation: Transcending the Deregulation Debate*, Oxford: Oxford University Press.

Baggott, Rob (1989), "Regulatory Reform in Britain: The Changing Face of Self-Regulation", *Public Administration*, 67: 435–54.

Baggott, Rob and Harrison, Larry (1986), "The Politics of Self-Regulation: The Case of Advertising Control", *Policy and Politics*, 14: 143–60.

Baldwin, Robert (1987), "Health and Safety at Work: Consensus and Self-Regulation", in Baldwin, Robert and McCrudden, Christopher (eds), *Regulation and Public Law*, London: Weidenfeld and Nicholson, chapter 7.

Bardach, Eugene and Kagan, Robert A. (1982), "Mixing Public and Private Regulation", in Graymer, LeRoy and Thompson, Frederick (eds), *Reforming Social Regulation: Alternative Public Policy Strategies*, London: Sage Publications, chapter 10.

Baumol, William, J., Panzar, John C. and Willig, Robert D. (1982), *Contestable Markets and the Theory of Industry Structure*, New York: Harcourt Brace Jovanovich.
Black, Julia (1996), "Constitutionalising Self-Regulation", *Modern Law Review*, 59: 24–55.
Black, Julia (1997), *Rules and Regulators*, Oxford: Clarendon Press.
Bratton, William, Mccahery, Joseph, Picciotti, Sol and Scott, Colin (eds) (1997), *International Regulatory Competition and Coordination: Perspectives on Economic Regulation in Europe and the United States*, Oxford: Clarendon Press.
Cane, Peter (1987), "Self Regulation and Judicial Review", *Civil Justice Quarterly*, 6: 324–47.
Carver, Charles, S. and Scheier, Michael F. (1981), *Attention and Self-Regulation: A Control Theory Approach to Human Behavior*, Berlin: Springer-Verlag.
Coase, Ronald H. (1960), "The Problem of Social Cost", *Journal of Law and Economics*, 3: 1–44.
Dawson, Sheila, Willman, Paul, Clinton, Alan and Bamford, M. (1988), *Safety at Work: The Limits of Self-Regulation*, Cambridge: Cambridge University Press.
Demsetz, Harold (1968), "Why Regulate Utilities?", *Journal of Law and Economics*, 11: 55–65.
Fisher, Andrew (1997), "The Licensing of Taxis and Minicabs", *Consumer Policy Review*, 7: 58–161.
Fishman, James J. (1993), "A Comparison of Enforcement of Securities Law Violations in the UK and US", *Company Lawyer*, 163–72.
Grabosky, Peter and Braithwaite, John (1986), *Of Manners Gentle: Enforcement Strategies of Australian Business Regulatory Agencies*, Oxford: Oxford University Press.
Harden, Ian and Lewis, Norman (1986), *The Noble Lie: The British Constitution and the Rule of Law*, New York: Hutchinson.
Hogan, Daniel B. (1979), *Regulation of Psychotherapists: A Study in the Philosophy and Practice of Professional Regulation*, Cambridge, MA: Ballinger.
Kay, John and Vickers, John (1990), "Regulatory Reform: An Appraisal", in Majone, Giandomenico (ed.), *Deregulation or Re-regulation: Regulatory Reform in Europe and the United States*, London: Frances Pinter.
Latin, Howard (1985), "Ideal versus Real Regulatory Efficiency: Implementation of Uniform Standards and 'Fine-Tuning' Regulatory Reforms", *Stanford Law Review*, 37: 1267–332.
OECD (1985), *Competition Policy and the Professions*, Paris: Organisation for Economic Co-operation and Development.
Office of Fair Trading (1982), *Opticians and Competition*, HMSO.
Page, Alan C. (1986), "Self-Regulation: The Constitutional Dimension", *Modern Law Review*, 49: 141–67.
Page, Alan C. (1987), "Financial Services: The Self-Regulatory Alternative", in Baldwin, Robert and McCrudden, Christopher (eds), *Regulation and Public Law*, London: Weidenfeld and Nicholson, chapter 13.
Quirk, Paul J. (1981), *Industry Influence in Federal Regulatory Agencies*, Princeton, NJ: Princeton University Press.
Schmitter, Philippe C. (1985), "Neo-Corporatism and the State", in Grant, Wyn (ed.), *The Political Economy of Corporatism*, London: Macmillan, 32–62.
Schwartz, Alan and Wilde, Louis L. (1979), "Intervening in Markets on the Basis of Imperfect Information: A Legal and Economic Analysis", *University of Pennsylvania Law Review*, 127: 630–82.
Tollison, Robert D. (1982), "Rent Seeking: A Survey", *Kyklos*, 35: 575–602.
Tullock, Gordon (1967), "The Welfare Costs of Tariffs, Monopolies and Theft", *Western Economic Journal*, 5: 224–232.
Waterson, Michael (1988), *Regulation of the Firm and Natural Monopoly*, Oxford: Basil Blackwell.

PART IV

INTERNATIONAL LAW

14 International law as a source of law

Paul B. Stephan

1. Introduction

The nature of international law as a legal system, and thus as a source of law, is controversial. At the conceptual level, the objection to characterizing international law as law is that it lacks a rule of recognition, i.e. there exists no agreement about the mechanism for determining which propositions of international law have the character of a legally binding obligation (Hart 1994: 213–37). At the practical level, the objection is the absence of a centralized enforcement authority (Scott and Stephan 2006: 5). Advocates of international law respond that substantial social conventions have emerged that constitute a rule of recognition, even if disagreement survives around the edges of the concept. They further assert that international law employs a range of enforcement mechanisms of varying degrees of centralization, including reputational effects, retaliation, and reciprocal rewards as well as some direct enforcement (Dunoff and Trachtman 1999; Guzman 2008; Scott and Stephan 2006; Sykes 2007; Trachtman 2008).

A functional approach to the problem of recognizing international law as a source of law can clarify both the analytic and evidential issues. Focusing on the characteristics and competence of the particular institution that might apply international law enables the identification of instances where international law operates as a significant constraint on state actors, although within limited domains. This approach requires distinguishing among several institutional settings. Treaty-based international institutions, whether an organ of the United Nations, the Dispute Settlement Body of the World Trade Organization (WTO), a tribunal constituted under a bilateral investment treaty and the Washington Convention on the Settlement of Investment Disputes between States and Nationals of Other States, or some other body, operate on the basis of particular treaties, general principles about the application and interpretation of treaties, and their own traditions as embraced or tolerated by affected parties. National tribunals will look to their particular constitutions, legal traditions, and their past practices as means of determining both what they will recognize as international law and when to apply those rules to disputes within their competence. National bureaucracies responsible for repeated interactions with their counterparts in other states (militaries constituting an important example, but also ministries of finance, foreign relations, environmental protection, and the like) will look to their constituting authority (typically domestic statutes) and their past practices to determine what rules of international law they will recognize and apply. Finally, private actors, principally academics and advocates for particular interests, will construct and invoke international law to advance their causes. There is no reason to believe that the patterns of selection, interpretation and application of international law will converge across these functional groups, and much evidence to suggest that they diverge profoundly (Stephan 2010).

Scholars trained in economics find the functional approach sketched above congenial. It is only the last decade, however, that has seen much use of economic analysis to study the problem of legalization of international law. Political scientists to some extent have preceded economists in this endeavor. Their work combines rational-choice concepts drawn largely from economic theory with sociological insights that to some extent rest on assumptions and methodologies that oppose economic analysis (Keohane, Moravcsik and Slaughter 2001). Earlier studies of the problem, by contrast, rested entirely on a mix of sociology and moral theory (Chayes and Chayes 1995; Franck 1995).

2. Definition of International Law

As a formal matter, international law derives from two processes, treaty-making and custom. Each of these mechanisms presents many difficult and controversial problems. With respect to treaties, there are persistent issues of interpretation and scope, as well as technical questions such as whether a treaty is in force and the means by which it can (as well as if it can) be suspended or terminated. Custom is said to result from state practice based on *opinio juris*, that is, a belief that the practice reflects a legal obligation rather than only a policy preference. There is no consensus, however, on what counts as state practice or how to determine the existence of *opinio juris*. International law specialists also debate whether there exist alternative sources of international law based on convergences in state practice that do not rise to the level of custom.

2.1 Treaties

Treaties are express agreements among states that create legal obligations. The creation of treaties involves three steps: (1) *making* the treaty by representatives of the states that intend to become parties: (2) *confirmation* of the treaty by competent lawmakers in those states; and (3) *ratification* of the treaty by representatives of the state parties. The second step presents only questions of domestic law. In the United States, for example, the Constitution specifies that two-thirds of the Senate must consent to a treaty.[1] Whether a treaty has

---

[1] The US judiciary, however, does not dictate which international agreements constitute treaties subject to this requirement. Scholars have analyzed the strategic opportunities this rule presents to the Executive (Hathaway 2008).

been made and ratified so as to give rise to legal obligations turns first on non-treaty international law, which is to say customary international law (CIL). As a secondary matter, however, a particular institutional actor (international tribunal, domestic court, domestic bureaucracy, or private actor) might look to domestic law as well to determine whether it will recognize a treaty as in force. Again looking to a US illustration, the Supreme Court has indicated that it will defer to the Executive in determining whether a treaty has entered into or remains in force.[2] The Executive may derive the rules that it applies in such cases through the basis of bureaucratic interactions with other states, especially those among foreign ministries. But the US judiciary normally will not conduct an independent examination as to either the derivation or the application of those rules in cases where the Executive reaches a conclusion.

Application of treaties in force requires determinations of the meaning of the rules contained in a treaty (interpretation) and the extent of the treaty's domain (scope). International tribunals, domestic courts, domestic bureaucracies, and private actors have occasion to make such determinations, which each does based on its perception of the state of CIL, as well as its prior history in addressing such questions. There exist no formal mechanisms to induce the various actors that might apply treaties to conform to each other's determinations, and substantial evidence indicating that these determinations vary based on the actor involved as well as on context and interests (Stephan 2009). US courts assert that they give substantial deference to treaty interpretations proposed by the Executive, but they do not invariably follow them.[3]

States can affect *ex ante* determinations as to a treaty's interpretation and scope through formal reservations, understanding and declarations (RUDs) made at the time of a treaty's ratification. Some treaties provide expressly for such measures, but others do not. Two controversial issues follow: when are RUDs effective in the absence of treaty language providing for them? If a party has made an invalid RUD, is the legal consequence nonapplication of the treaty to that party, or instead application of the treaty in full without taking the invalid RUD into account?[4]

---

2 *Charlton v Kelly*, 229 US 447, 474–5 (1913); *Terlinden v Ames*, 184 US 270, 285 (1902). This issue is distinct from the question of whether the President may unilaterally terminate a treaty. See *Goldwater v Carter*, 444 US 996 (1979) (considering but not deciding the issue).

3 E.g., *Chan v Korean Airlines*, 490 US 122 (1989).

4 A related but distinct issue is whether a treaty maker has, as a matter of domestic law, the capacity to make an RUD that will bind a domestic court. Compare *Sosa v Alvarez-Machain*, 542 US 692, 734 (2004) (treating reservation as legally binding on domestic court), with *Igartua-de la Rosa v United States*, 417 F.3d 145, 186–9 (1st Cir. 2005) (Howard, J., dissenting) (arguing that US treaty makers lack constitutional authority to impose RUDs that would limit judicial power).

Some scholars have used economic arguments to support a liberal approach to RUDs. They argue that giving effect to RUDs in most cases where a treaty does not expressly prohibit them allows more states to take part in treaty regimes by overcoming barriers to ratification that would otherwise exist (Bradley and Goldsmith 2000). Others maintain both that RUDs create negative externalities by undermining regimes as a whole, and that refusing to give effect to an RUD while regarding a state as still bound by the unmodified treaty will not have a significant affect on treaty ratification (Goodman 2002). The latter argument rests fundamentally on claims about the socialization process and not on rational-actor models (Goodman and Jinks 2004). Yet another line of analysis argues that the threat of retaliatory and symmetrical RUDs deters states from invoking this mechanism as often as a simple rational-actor model might predict (Parisi 2009; Fon and Parisi 2008).

2.2 *Custom*

Perhaps the greatest controversies in the field involve the practicality and the legitimacy of looking to custom as a source of binding international law. Traditional doctrine asserts that consistent state practice reflecting a sense of legal obligation can produce a binding norm of international law, even with respect to states that did not participate in the formation of the custom. The issue becomes especially fraught when a national legal system incorporates CIL into national law. In hierarchical national legal systems, such as that of the United States, there arise subsidiary but important questions such as (1) does CIL partake in the nature of federal law and thus pre-empt inconsistent state law? (2) does CIL limit the discretion of Congress to enact inconsistent statutes? (3) does CIL that arises after enactment of a congressional statute supersede that statute? and (4) do members of the Executive branch have the authority to act inconsistently with CIL (Bradley and Goldsmith 1997)?

Drawing on game theory, Goldsmith and Posner have attacked the premise that states frequently act out of a sense of legal obligation rather than out of self-interest. They argue that most instances where states exhibit behavioral regularities reflect common interest. They offer as an example the nineteenth-century custom of naval vessels during times of war not to interfere with peaceful fishing by their adversary's subjects. Interdiction of nonthreatening fishermen, they argued, diverts resources from combat for no appreciable gain. In instances where interests diverge, the possibility of working out a stable solution to a multiple-play, multiple-player game is small (Goldsmith and Posner 1999; 2005: 23–78).

Norman and Trachtman challenged Goldsmith and Posner's game-theory analysis. They argued that, under certain realistic assumptions, a stable solution to a multi-player, multiple-iteration prisoners' dilemma game could arise. This solution in turn would represent a custom based on obligation rather than interest (Norman and Trachtman 2005; Trachtman 2008). Guzman offered a different challenge to Goldsmith and Posner. He maintained that states have an interest in a reputation for law-abiding behavior, and that this interest bridges the gap between rational-actor models of state behavior and the legal-obligation component of CIL (Guzman 2002, 2008). Scholars in turn criticized Guzman's account of state reputational interests. They observe that states have an interest in being seen as cooperative and other-regarding, but that it is incorrect to identify this interest with a reputation for law-abiding behavior. Much that international law permits is uncooperative, and much cooperative behavior is not required by international law (Downs and Jones 2002; Brewster 2009).

More generally, scholars have sought to ground theories of CIL in law-and-economics accounts of spontaneous law and informal norm enforcement (Parisi 2000; Fon and Parisi 2006, 2009; Swaine 2002; Verdier 2002). The parallels are obvious and the insights fruitful, but more work needs to be done on specifying (1) the mechanisms that lead states, as distinguished from individuals, to make particular choices, and (2) the relevant characteristics of the international community, as distinguished from communities populated by individuals (Dunoff and Trachtman 1999; Posner and Sykes 2007; Scott and Stephan 2006: 43–58). In particular, one can model state behavior as a two-level game in which domestic and state-to-state interactions proceed with each in mind (Putnam 1988). Individual behavior does not lend itself easily to this model. In other words, a successful theory of CIL needs a convincing theory of state decisionmaking with respect to international relations that takes into account the disaggregated interests of domestic actors. Accounts of custom within communities made up of individuals do not do this.

2.3 Other Sources

There also is a debate over the existence of sources of international law other than treaties and custom. Many treaties constituting international tribunals, most prominently the Statute of the International Court of Justice, authorize the tribunal to invoke "the general principles of law recognized by civilized nations" as well as "judicial decisions and the teachings of the most highly qualified publicists of the various nations, as subsidiary means for the determination of rules of law."[5] Prominent British treatises have argued from the fact that international tribunals can apply these rules that international law comprises these "general principles" as well as the "best practices" of national courts and the teachings of publicists (Brownlie 2003: 15–18; Jennings and Watts 1992: 36–40). Some international law professors in particular have found the reference to the "teachings of the most highly qualified publicists" as especially

---

5 Statute of the International Court of Justice, Art. 38(1)(c), (d).

compelling and have sought to persuade other actors that their writings should be seen as a source of binding international law.[6]

A more careful analysis, however, leads only to the conclusion that international tribunals, including ad hoc bodies set up to address particular disputes, generally have been provided with terms of reference that allow them to refer to those principles of national law that they find attractive. The two leading British treatises contain no examples of invocations of this principle that do not involve international tribunals. There is no basis to infer that this practice also authorizes national courts or national bureaucracies to find in general principles of national law a rule of decision that their own national law does not contain. Private actors, of course, are free to do what they wish but remain subject to reputational constraints.

The argument for allowing international tribunals to invoke sources other than treaties and CIL rests on the assertion that their mission is to resolve disputes, not to contribute to the development of a general body of law that binds other tribunals, much less other actors. There is no rule of recognition, comparable to the common law concept of precedent, that obliges a particular international tribunal to apply the same rules and to use the same reasoning as earlier tribunals, except in the relatively unusual case where the tribunal has a permanent charter and stable membership (such as the International Court of Justice). Under conditions of one-off dispute settlement, giving a tribunal a relatively free rein to choose from among potential legal rules complements its function to reach a reasonable settlement. The absence of precedential effect minimizes the risk that the decision made will generate negative effects on subsequent behavior (Benvenisti 2004). By contrast, scholars have argued that delegating comparable discretion to permanent international bodies presents serious agency problems (Stephan 2002).

One pathway to the "domestification" of foreign law, specifically the general principles recognized by "civilized nations," involves characterizing these principles as international law, and thus as a component of national law.[7] Most

---

6 At least one US court has met this argument with indignation:

> This notion – that professors of international law enjoy a special competence to prescribe the nature of customary international law wholly unmoored from legitimating territorial or national responsibilities, the interests and practices of States, or (in countries such as ours) the processes of democratic consent – may not be unique, but it is certainly without merit. (*United States v Yousef*, 327 F.3d 56, 102 (2d Cir. 2003))

7 An alternative mechanism has been to interpret particular provisions of domestic law as inviting incorporation of foreign standards. The US Supreme Court, for example, on occasion has looked to foreign practice as a guide to determine what constitutes "evolving standards of decency," which some members see as a component of the Eighth Amendment's prohibition of "cruel and unusual punishment." Other Justices criticize this practice. For the latest instance of this practice, see *Graham v Florida*, 130 S. Ct. 2011. (2010).

observers concede that the process of selecting principles of law found in domestic legal systems for elevation into international law involves subjective judgments and under-examined normative preferences. Some have argued that the practice of showing solidarity with other national legal systems strengthens the role of national courts, independent of the content of the rules over which they show solidarity. This safety-in-numbers argument in turn has been criticized on the grounds that judicial authority does not function as an end in itself and that some forms of judicial solidarity can be pernicious. For a review of the literature, see Stephan (2006).

In addition, the foreign solidarity argument is in tension with, if not directly opposed to, a conventional model found in the law-and-economics literature that portrays the judiciary as an agent of lawmakers (Posner 1982; Landes and Posner 1975). The capacity to pick and choose among foreign laws and juristic opinions to find rules to apply amounts to an unlimited power to act as the rule-applier wishes, thereby breaking the bond between agent and principal. Granting domestic judges the authority to invoke foreign law when they find it more appealing than domestic law entails a significant departure from traditional explanations of the judicial function. Justification of this step rests more on normative moral arguments than on positive economic analysis.

3. Uses of International Law

Recognition of a rule as belonging to the body of international law is only the first step in treating international law as a source of law. A competent body must then determine that it may apply that rule. This second step necessarily requires analysis of the applying body's authority.

Not all bodies have the authority to invoke all possible rules. Limitations such as standing requirements and choice of remedies effectively constrain which actors can invoke international law on whose behalf (Sykes 2005). Official institutions, whether international or domestic, have terms of reference that specify what they have the legal capacity to do. In some instances official authority is delegated to private actors, most frequently through the mechanism of arbitration. When exercising delegated authority, private actors work within the constraints of the delegation. In those instances where private actors function on their own account, they do not face formal constraints on their competence, but their determinations have consequences only to the extent that other actors choose to approve and follow their position. The pressure to win approval in turn acts as a constraint on what private actors can do.

3.1 International Institutions

Many different kinds of international institutions have dispute-resolution authority that requires them to announce and apply rules of decision. For purposes of analysis, one can separate these institutions into five categories

– (1) nonjudicial institutions empowered to take actions that states by treaty are obligated to implement; (2) institutions that have the authority to identify lawbreakers and hence to "name and shame"; (3) institutions that may advance or withhold resources to states or private persons on the basis of legal determinations; (4) formal dispute resolution tribunals with settled jurisdiction and membership; and (5) ad hoc tribunals that acquire jurisdiction after a dispute has arisen. There are differences in the way institutions in each category invoke and apply international law.

3.1.1 Nonjudicial bodies with authority to bind states The best example of a nonjudicial institution with authority to make decisions that by treaty bind states is the UN Security Council. Decisions of the Council, which typically deal with economic and military sanctions imposed on states that threaten international peace and security, are mandatory, in the sense that membership in the United Nations carries with it a treaty commitment to comply with those decisions.[8] The European Commission (EC) and the European Parliament (EP) also fit into this category, as do comparable bodies in other regional organizations.

Because decisions of the Security Council are not subject to review by other organs of the United Nations and the five permanent members have a common interest in maintaining that body's authority, the Security Council has a tendency to make, rather than follow, international law.[9] By contrast, institutions that face judicial review within their own treaty regime, as do the EC and the EP with respect to the European Court of Justice, face stronger limitations and tend to articulate more fully the legal basis for their actions.

3.1.2 Nonjudicial bodies with authority to impose reputational sanctions A number of treaties creating substantive obligations in areas such as human rights and combatting corruption set up committees comprising representatives of the state parties. Typically these bodies review the performance of parties, and in some cases can entertain complaints by private persons. They issue reports, which can have reputational consequences (Helfer and Slaughter 2005: 924–8). There exist no other formal enforcement mechanisms that these bodies can

[8] That a treaty obligation binds a state does not necessarily mean that, as a matter of domestic law, a national authority may implement a decision of the Security Council in advance of instructions from its parliament. See, e.g., *Kadi v Council* (Joined Cases C-402/05 and C-415/05), 2008 ECR I-6351 (refusing to enforce Security Council decision because of inconsistency with European law). Cf. *Medllín v Texas*, 552 U.S. 491 (2008) (regarding capacity of Security Council to enforce decisions of International Court of Justice as undercutting argument that those decisions operate directly in US law in the absence of congressional authorization).

[9] E.g., UN Sec. Counc. Res. 1757, S/RES/1757 (2007) (ordering treaty with Lebanon to enter into force in spite of Lebanon's failure to ratify).

employ, and correspondingly there are no formal means to obtain review of the their decisions. Casual empiricism suggests that some committee reports contain strong, if not unprecedented, claims about rules of international law, typically in a manner that promotes bootstrapping of jurisdiction.[10] The phenomenon has not been studied systematically, however.

Very little empirical work has been done on the effectiveness of name-and-shame international institutions. One study reported that a statistically significant negative correlation existed between a state's decision to join treaties that contain these mechanisms and the state's adherence to treaty standards, as measured by nongovernmental monitors (Hathaway 2002). This study provides some evidence to support the hypothesis that these councils are ineffective as a means of influencing state behavior. Critics of the study respond that it failed to follow state behavior along a sufficiently lengthy time horizon and therefore does not exclude the possibility that the combination of treaty adherence and council supervision produces cultural changes that eventually influence state behavior (Goodman and Jinks 2003).

3.1.3 Nonjudicial bodies with authority to extend or withhold resources Some international institutions control valuable resources that states wish to obtain. Important examples are the various international financial institutions, including the International Bank for Reconstruction and Development (the World Bank) and the International Monetary Fund (IMF). These bodies make their decisions largely on the basis of business and policy criteria, but on occasion they also make determinations about the legality of a state's actions. Both the World Bank and the IMF, for example, will consider whether a state has complied with various international obligations, such as anti-corruption measures or environmental commitments, as a factor in their extension of financial resources (Stephan 1996–7). The Financial Action Task Force (FATF), a working group associated with the Organisation for Economic Co-operation and Development (OECD), determines whether states maintain sufficient safeguards against money laundering. A negative determination puts private banks on notice that a transfer of money to or from banks in the sanctioned country entails heightened risk of (national) prosecution for money laundering and thus induces a boycott of those banks.

A study of IMF regulation of national currency controls argues that that institution seldom exercises its authority to make legal determinations directly

---

10 E.g., General Comment No. 24, Issues Relating to Reservations made upon ratification of accession to the Covenant or the Optional Protocols thereto, or in relation to Declarations under Article 41 of the Covenant, CCPR/C/21/Rev.1/Add.6 (1994) (official document of Human Rights Committee maintaining that state consent was irrelevant to coverage of major human rights obligations).

(Simmons 2000). Instead, it relies on private capital markets to discipline state actors. IMF influence on state behavior operates indirectly through the tendency of private banks to respond to signals that it issues. A similar mechanism explains the influence of the FATF on state behavior. This limited evidence, when compared with the record of "name-and-shame" councils discussed above, is consistent with a conjecture that signals backed up by potential threats to withhold material resources induce a greater state response than do less tangible reputational threats.

A somewhat different but analogous instance of a resource-controlling international institution involves the Internet Corporation for Assigned Names and Numbers (ICANN). This entity, a nonprofit corporation established under US law with the blessing of the US government and, implicitly, the international community, controls the assignment of internet domain names. It exercises a dispute resolution function with respect to a species of trademark law, namely the ownership of domain names. Arbitration under ICANN auspices results in determinations that this body then applies through the effective sanction of refusing to recognize a disallowed name. Because ICANN controls the technical process that matches domain name with numeric addresses of internet sites, the sanction is immediate and absolute. Interested persons can relitigate their ownership claims in national courts, which have no obligation to respect the ICANN determinations. National litigation, however, involves considerably greater costs than does ICANN arbitration. Accordingly, ICANN exercises significant authority over economically significant ownership rights with only limited state supervision (Goldsmith and Wu (2006) at 168–71).

3.1.4 Formal and ongoing international tribunals Formal international dispute-settlement tribunals have received considerable attention in recent years. These bodies are defined by their receipt of jurisdiction *ex ante* to consider particular categories of cases, as well as their stable structure and membership. Examples include the International Court of Justice, the Dispute Settlement Body of the WTO, the Tribunal for the Law of the Sea, and the International Criminal Court, as well as regional tribunals such as the European Court of Justice in Luxembourg (the court for the European Community) and the European Court of Human Rights in Strasbourg (the court for the Council of Europe, that is the parties to the European Convention on Human Rights).

The number of such tribunals has grown in the last two decades, leading some scholars to infer that they constitute successful substitutes for diplomatic resolution of international disputes (Helfer and Slaughter 2005). More skeptical observers identify potential mission creep as an agency cost that may lead states to decrease resort to some tribunals (Stephan 2002). The evidence is anecdotal rather than systematic, but does suggest that international tribunals that are perceived as idiosyncratic and self-aggrandizing lose business, largely through states withdrawing acceptance of their jurisdiction (Posner 2009; Posner and Yoo 2005; Posner and Figueiredo 2005; Scott and Stephan 2006). The phenomenon is too recent, and the data set too small, to make conclusive assessments at this time.

Several scholars have documented the existence of autonomy among tribunals. Although a few tribunals have a two-stage structure analogous to the dyad of a first-instance court and an appellate court, no tribunals are constrained by any formal obligation to adopt the jurisprudence of any other. As a matter of practice, substantial divergences have arisen in the interpretation of the same substantive provisions of international law by different international tribunals (Brown 2007; Posner 2009; Stephan 2010). This practice provides weak evidence for the proposition that tribunals act in a way that reflects the particular contexts in which they operate and that a strong incentive to develop universal and general principles of international law across tribunals seems not to apply.

3.1.5 Ad hoc international tribunals Ad hoc tribunals are those given terms of reference for settling a controversy that has already arisen. Both states and private actors invoke this mechanism. In some instances states and private actors make an *ex ante* commitment to use this mechanism but do not specify the members of the tribunal or its precise terms of reference until a specific controversy occurs. On other occasions, disputants will agree to use this mechanism in the absence of any prior commitment. Some formal and ongoing international tribunals, such as the International Court of Justice and the Permanent Court of International Arbitration, accept cases on an ad hoc basis. The Dispute Settlement Body of the WTO combines ad hoc tribunals, used for the first-instance consideration of a case, with a permanent tribunal that exercises appellate review.

Resort to ad hoc tribunals to address private international commercial disputes has grown significantly over the last two decades (Wood 2007). These bodies do not have to answer to any permanent international body for their actions. Constraints on their activity come in two forms. First, their awards are not self-executing, but rather depend on states to give them effect. Second, the disputants control selection of the members of the tribunal. There is substantial evidence that private parties take into account the records and reputations of potential arbiters. Arbiters in turn give some consideration to the fact that their awards will have value to parties only if states will give effect to them. For two particular categories of ad hoc dispute settlement – international commercial disputes and disputes between foreign investors and a host state – treaties oblige most states to honor these awards, but contain exceptions in instances of tribunal misconduct or overreaching, including the granting of awards that violate fundamental state interests. Arbiters thus have an incentive to thread a line between pleasing the disputants and not antagonizing enforcing states by deviating too greatly from enforcing states' laws and policy (Posner 1999).

Ad hoc tribunals that hear disputes between states face more complex incentives. Selection to these tribunals involves complex networks of relationships, complicated by the possibility that government officials selecting tribunal members might someday become candidates for such appointments themselves. Unlike private arbitration, there is a greater possibility that the tribunal might award something more or other than a claim to money compensation. For example, the ad hoc tribunal operating under the auspices of the London Court of International Arbitration that resolved a long-term trade dispute between Canada and the United States required Canada to collect additional charges from lumber exporters.[11] Actions of this sort require greater cooperation from the losing state than does an order to pay money, and to that extent constrains the arbiters' discretion to invoke new or surprising rules attributable to international law. Some research on ad hoc state-to-state tribunals indicates that this device enjoys growing popularity precisely because of such constraints (Posner and Yoo 2005).

3.2 National Courts

National courts have treated international law as a source of law since time immemorial, but practice varies across states. The extent to which national courts invoke international law as well as the particular rules they choose depend on several variables, including relevant instructions from the respective national parliament to invoke international law, the particular policy area and its domestic context, the constitutional structure of the domestic court and its relationship with the domestic executive and parliamentary branches, and the international position of the state in question. The normative aspirations of the judges of these courts also have an obvious influence on these questions, although these do not readily lend themselves to economic analysis.

When judges act as agents of national lawmakers to implement instructions to apply international law, they must develop a methodology to determine the content of international law. In areas such as property boundary disputes and rules of contract, which often have the nature of a coordination problem rather than a prisoners' dilemma, a court might take a liberal view as to what constitutes applicable international rules. In other areas, however, the risk of foreign retaliation might be greater and a court correspondingly might demand clearer proof that an international rule exists before applying it pursuant to a

[11] *United States v Canada*, LCIA, Case No. 7941, Award on Remedies, February 23, 2009.

general legislative instruction. The behavior of the US Supreme Court is broadly consistent with this pattern.[12]

Early work explored the incentives that domestic judges face in deciding whether to derive rules of decision from international law. One model contrasted the possibility that judges might act as norm entrepreneurs with an alternative conception of judges as agents of a state engaged in playing a tit-for-tat game styled on the classic prisoners' dilemma (Stephan 1990). Judges who seek to function as norm entrepreneurs will invoke international law for one of two reasons. First, the judges may wish not simply to affect policy outcomes in their own jurisdiction, but to influence outcomes in other states. Second, the judges might not have available a domestic law that corresponds to their preferred outcome. In this latter case, the judges also need to construct a rule of hierarchy that allows a rule derived from international law to override domestic rules. Judges in federalist systems can elevate rules of international law by aligning them with national rules that trump subnational ones. Judges also can invoke the last-in-time convention to treat an international rule as overruling an earlier national rule.

The question of why judges might want to become international norm entrepreneurs is not well addressed by the economics literature. Sociological explanations focus on the existence of judicial networks, through which peers influence each other across borders (Slaughter 2004). Judges indeed might find offers of international travel and invitations to international meetings to be a valuable fringe benefit, given the strong restrictions most judges face on alternative sources of income. There is anecdotal evidence that national judges may take ambitious positions on the invocation of international law as a means of deflecting national limits on their behavior and expanding post-judicial career opportunities.[13] No systematic evidence exists indicating that such behavior occurs on a widespread basis, however.

Putting doctrinal and legitimacy concerns to the side, the principal economically based objection to judicial international norm entrepreneurship is its downstream effect on judicial practice. Lack of clarity about when judges will go outside domestic law and the mechanisms for locating international rules within a domestic legal hierarchy raise agency costs associated with

---

[12] Compare *Sosa v Alvarez-Machain*, 542 US 692 (2004) (setting high standard for rules applicable under the so-called Alien Tort Statute), and *Banco Nacional de Cuba v Sabbatino*, 376 US 398 (1964) (refusing to recognize the CIL of international investor protection), with *United States v California*, 381 US 139 (1965) (offshore boundaries). For a survey of the post-war practice of the Court, see Stephan (2011).

[13] A colorful example is Baltasar Garzón Real, who obtained a position with the International Criminal Court after Spain suspended him from his judicial position due to alleged misconduct based on his exertion of jurisdiction over controversial international law claims in apparent violation of national legislation.

the judiciary (Scott and Stephan 2006: 198–203). These costs in turn make international cooperation more costly by limiting the ability of representatives of national governments to specify the terms of their international commitments. Government representatives will find it more difficult to control the downstream consequences of an agreement if they cannot effectively constrain how their courts will implement it. Expansion of international norm entrepreneurial activity by domestic judges thus may impede state-to-state cooperation, including the development of international law based on international agreements.

Reviews of the application of international law by national courts indicate systematic variation in the rules invoked. These studies indicate that, rather than seeking to develop general and universal rules, national courts develop semi-autonomous international law regimes that respond to both the particular geopolitical context of the country in which they operate and their constitutional status within that country's legal regime (Bradford and Posner 2010). Benvenisti (2008) documents the way in which national courts invoke international law to protect their governments from international pressure. Stephan (2009) describes how the content of international law invoked at the national level corresponds to geopolitical power relations.

3.3 National Bureaucracies

A great deal of state-to-state international interactions takes place through government bureaucracies with little or no supervision by domestic courts or international tribunals. Military bureaucracies, for example, develop handbooks on the laws of war, negotiate and implement arms control treaties, and impose discipline over soldiers, thereby developing and using international humanitarian law (also called the law of war, or *jus in bello* and *jus ad bellum*). Lawyers from foreign offices, competition authorities, financial regulators, environmental regulators, and other bureaucratic formations also meet regularly to work on various cooperative projects. Claims about international law suffuse this work, most of which are never tested outside of the bureaucracies themselves.

Over the last 15 years, a vast literature has emerged on international regulatory networks. It studies the mechanisms of cooperation among bureaucrats and the extent to which these interactions enable them to achieve independence from national constraints in the pursuit of multinational cooperative activity (Chayes and Chayes 1995; Slaughter 2004). This work largely focuses on processes of acculturation that stem from and further facilities cooperative conduct, including the development of rules that the actors regard as binding even when short-term national interests push in the opposite direction. Critics argue that these accounts are more aspirational than empirical and that the claim that international regulatory networks have a significant impact on the development of rules and policy remains unproved (Verdier 2009). Other research documents the extent to which international bureaucratic interactions correspond to conventional rational-actor models without any need to impute a heightened preference for cooperation to the actors (Licht 1999).

Complex issues arise when advocates seek to persuade official actors to recognize international law developed by bureaucratic actors as providing a binding rule of decision. International tribunals, both permanent and ad hoc, work within particular terms of reference. The doctrinal device available to these bodies for refusing to apply a bureaucratically derived rule is to characterize it as *lex specialis* and therefore not available as general CIL. National courts also filter these arguments through their particular constitutional constraints and traditions.

3.4 Private Actors

Private actors function as norm entrepreneurs regarding international law. Some serve as advocates for private disputants, some perform functions that complement (and perhaps even supersede) the "name-and-shame" function of international institutions, and some advance particular claims about international law through scholarship. Each of these activities has an impact on the development and application of international law, but only to the extent that these advocates can influence other actors exercising the authority to apply international law in a consequential manner.

Measuring the influence of private actors over persons possessing the authority to apply international law presents significant methodological challenges. No systematic study of the problem exists. One concept that has some salience is tournament theory, which studies competitive processes that result in the selection of winners and losers (Baker, Choi and Gulati 2006). Competition among private advocates for influence in the recognition of international law, as measured by adoption of positions advocated as well as the consequences of the adoption, is relatively easy to model and could be measured indirectly through observable data such as citations, positive outcomes in dispute resolution, and appointments to formal bodies. At present, however, no one has undertaken this task.

Bibliography

Baker, Scott, Choi, Stephen J., and Gulati, Mitu (2006), "The Rat Race as an Information-Forcing Device," **81** *Indiana Law Journal* 53–82.

Benvenisti, Eyal (2008), "Reclaiming Democracy: The Strategic Uses of Foreign and International Law by Foreign Courts," **102** *American Journal of International Law* 241–74.

Benvenisti, Eyal (2004), "Customary International Law as a Judicial Tool for Promoting Efficiency," in Benvenisti, Eyal and Hirsch, Moshe (eds.), *The Impact of International Law on International Cooperation – Theoretical Perspectives*, New York, NY: Cambridge University Press, 85–116.

Bradford, Anu and Posner, Eric A. (2011), "Universal Exceptionalism in International Law," **52** *Harvard International Law Journal* 1–54.

Bradley, Curtis A. and Goldsmith, Jack L. (2000), "Treaties, Human Rights, and Conditional Consent," **149** *University of Pennsylvania Law Review* 399–468.

Bradley, Curtis A. and Goldsmith, Jack L. (1997), "Customary International Law as Federal Common Law: A Critique of the Modern Position," **110** *Harvard Law Review* 815–76.
Brewster, Rachel (2009), "Unpacking the State's Reputation," **50** *Harvard Journal of International Law* 271–321.
Brown, Chester (2007), *A Common Law of International Adjudication*, New York, NY: Oxford University Press.
Brownlie, Ian (2003), *Principles of Public International Law*, 6th ed., New York, NY: Oxford University Press.
Chayes, Abram and Chayes, Antonia Handler (1995), *The New Sovereignty: Compliance with International Regulatory Agreements*, Cambridge, MA: Harvard University Press.
Downs, George W. and Jones, Michael A. (2002), "Reputation, Compliance, and International Law," **31** *Journal of Legal Studies* S95–114.
Dunoff, Jeffrey L. and Trachtman, Joel P. (1999), "Economic Analysis of International Law," **24** *Yale Journal of International Law* 1–59.
Fon, Vincy and Parisi, Francesco (2009), "Stability and Change in International Customary Law," **17** *Supreme Court Economic Review* 279–309.
Fon, Vincy and Parisi, Francesco (2008), "The Hidden Bias of the Vienna Convention on the Law of Treaties," **4** *Review of Law and Economics* 383–406.
Fon, Vincy and Parisi, Francesco (2006), "International Customary Law and Articulation Theories: An Economic Analysis", **2** *Brigham Young University International Law & Management Review* 201–32.
Franck, Thomas M. (1995), *Fairness in International Law and Institutions*, New York, NY: Oxford University Press.
Goldsmith, Jack L. and Posner, Eric A. (2005), *The Limits of International Law*, New York, NY: Oxford University Press.
Goldsmith, Jack L. and Posner, Eric A. (1999), "A Theory of Customary International Law," **66** *University of Chicago Law Rev*iew 1113–77.
Goldsmith, Jack L. and Wu, Tim (2006), *Who Controls the Internet? Illusions of a Borderless World*, New York, NY: Oxford University Press.
Goodman, Ryan (2002), "Human Rights Treaties, Invalid Reservations, and State Consent", **96** *American Journal of International Law* 531–60.
Goodman, Ryan and Jinks, Derek (2004), "How to Influence States: Socialization and International Human Rights Law," **54** *Duke Law Journal* 621–703.
Goodman, Ryan and Jinks, Derek (2003), "Measuring the Effects of Human Rights Treaties," **14** *European Journal of International Law* 171–200.
Guzman, Andrew T. (2008), *How International Law Works – A Rational Choice Theory*, New York, NY: Oxford University Press.
Guzman, Andrew T. (2002), "A Compliance-Based Theory of International Law," **90** *California Law Review* 1823–87.
Hart, H.L.A. (1994), *The Concept of Law – Second Edition*, New York, NY: Oxford University Press.
Hathaway, Oona A. (2008), "Treaties' End: The Past, Present, and Future of International Lawmaking in the United States," **117** *Yale Law Journal* 1236–373.
Hathaway, Oona A. (2002), "Do Human Rights Treaties Make a Difference?" **111** *Yale Law Journal* 1935–2042.
Helfer, Laurence R. and Slaughter, Anne-Marie (2005), "Why States Create International Tribunals: A Response to Professors Posner and Yoo," **93** *California Law Review* 901–56.
Jennings, Robert and Watts, Arthur (1992), **1** *Oppenheim's International Law*, 9th edition, Harlow, England: Longman Group UK Limited.
Keohane, Robert O., Moravcsik, Andrew, and Slaughter, Anne-Marie (2001), "Legalized Dispute Resolution: Interstate and Transnational," in Goldstein, Judith L., Kahler, Miles, Keohane, Robert O. and Slaughter Anne-Marie (eds.), *Legalization and World Politics*, Cambridge, MA: MIT Press, 73–104.
Landes, William M. and Posner, Richard A. (1975), "The Independent Judiciary in an Interest-Group Perspective," **18** *Journal of Law & Economics* 875–901.
Licht, Amir N. (1999), "Games Commissions Play: 2x2 Games of International Securities Regulation," **24** *Yale Journal of International Law* 61–128.

Norman, George and Trachtman, Joel (2005), "The Customary International Law Game," **99** *American Journal of International Law* 541–80.
Parisi, Francesco (2009), "The Economics of Treaty Ratification," **5** *Journal of Law Economics and Policy* 209–24.
Parisi, Francesco (2000), "Spontaneous Emergence of Law: Customary Law," in Bouckaert, Boudewijn and De Geest, Gerrit (eds.), **5** *Encyclopedia of Law and Economics*, Cheltenham, UK, Edward Elgar, 603–30.
Posner, Eric A. (2009), *The Perils of Global Legalism*, Chicago, IL: Chicago University Press.
Posner, Eric A. (1999), "Arbitration and the Harmonization of International Commercial Law – A Defense of *Mitsubishi*," **39** *Virginia Journal of International Law* 647–70.
Posner, Eric A. and Figueiredo, Miguel F.P. (2005), "Is the International Court of Justice Biased?" **34** *Journal of Legal Studies* 599–630.
Posner, Eric A. and Sykes, Alan O. (2007), "An Economic Analysis of State and Individual Responsibility under International Law", **9** *American Law & Economics Review* 72–129.
Posner, Eric A. and Yoo, John C. (2005), "A Theory of International Adjudication," **93** *California Law Review* 1–74.
Posner, Richard A. (1982), "Economics, Politics, and the Reading of Statutes and the Constitution," **49** *University of Chicago Law Review* 263–91.
Putnam, Robert D. (1988), "Diplomacy and Domestic Politics: The Logic of Two-Level Games," **42** *International Organization* 427–60.
Scott, Robert E, and Stephan, Paul B. (2006), *The Limits of Leviathan – Contract Theory and the Enforcement of International Law*, New York, NY: Cambridge University Press.
Simmons, Beth A. (2000), "Money and the Law: Why Comply with the Public International Law of Money?" **25** *Yale Journal of International Law* 323–62.
Slaughter, Anne-Marie (2004), *A New World Order*, Princeton, NJ: Princeton University Press.
Stephan, Paul B. (2010), "Disaggregating Customary International Law," **21** *Duke Journal of Comparative & International Law* 191–205.
Stephan, Paul B. (2011), "Treaties in the Supreme Court: 1946–2000," in Sloss, David L., Ramsey, Michael D. and Dodge, William S. (eds.), *International Law in the U.S. Supreme Court: Continuity and Change*, New York, NY: Cambridge University Press, 317–52.
Stephan, Paul B. (2009), "Symmetry and Selectivity: What Happens in International Law When the World Changes," **10** *Chicago Journal of International Law* 91–123.
Stephan, Paul B. (2006), "Process Values, International Law, and Justice," **23** *Social Philosophy and Policy* 131–52.
Stephan, Paul B. (2002), "Courts, Tribunals and Legal Unification – The Agency Problem," **3** *Chicago Journal of International Law* 333–52.
Stephan, Paul B. (1996–97), "Accountability and International Lawmaking: Rules, Rents and Legitimacy," **17** *Northwestern Journal of International Law and Business* 681–735.
Stephan, Paul B. (1990), "International Law in the Supreme Court," **1990** *Supreme Court Review* 133–61.
Swaine, Edward T. (2002), "Rational Custom," **52** *Duke Law Journal* 559–627.
Sykes, Alan O. (2007), "International Law," in Polinsky, A. Mitchell and Shavell, Steven (eds.), **1** *Handbook of Law and Economics*, Amsterdam, Netherlands: Elsevier, 757–826.
Sykes, Alan O. (2005), "Public versus Private Enforcement of International Economic Law: Standing and Remedy," **34** *Journal of Legal Studies* 631–66.
Trachtman, Joel P. (2008), *The Economic Structure of International Law*, Cambridge, MA: Harvard University Press.
Verdier, Pierre-Hughes (2009), "Transnational Regulatory Networks and Their Limits," **34** *Yale Journal of International Law* 113–172.
Verdier, Pierre-Hughes (2002), "Cooperative States: International Relations, State Responsibility and the Problem of Custom," **42** *Virginia Journal of International Law* 839–67.
Wood, Diane P. (2007), "Private Dispute Resolution in International Economic Law," in Guzman, Andrew T. and Sykes, Alan O. (eds.), *Research Handbook in International Economic Law*, Cheltenham, UK, and Northampton, MA, USA: Edward Elgar, 575–97.

15 International treaties

Vincy Fon[*]

1. Introduction

This chapter concerns itself with legal agreements which are treaties. A treaty is a formal agreement between multiple states, recognizing specific rights and obligations laid out within the context of the treaty; it is meant to define the relationship between the parties. More specifically, this chapter examines the formation of and reservations to modern treaties which are governed by the Articles established in the Vienna Convention on the Law of Treaties.

Human history has seen a long line of treaties. The oldest known written treaty, the Kadesh Peace Treaty, was established about 16 years after the battle in 1274 BC between the Hittites and the Egyptians. Over the last three millennia, untold numbers of treaties were formulated to consolidate cooperation, to resolve conflicts, to seal promises, and to coerce compliance across countries. The need for international agreements has increased substantially in the last few decades, as the world grew more integrated and interactions between states became ubiquitous and increasingly unavoidable. Witness the over 500 major multilateral instruments deposited with the Secretary-General of the United Nations (as of 1 January 2009) and over 158,000 treaties and related subsequent actions recorded in the United Nations Treaty Series (December 1946–December 2006) (United Nations Treaty Collection, Overview section). As treaties multiplied, it was recognized that codification of an overarching set of principles and rules to govern the conclusion, application, and interpretation of treaties was needed. Subsequently, international effort began in 1949, and the Vienna Convention on the Law of Treaties (hereinafter the Vienna Convention on Treaties) was signed May 23, 1969 and entered into force in January 1980. This convention is generally accepted as the authoritative codification of treaty law by the international community.

Recently, law and economics scholars have studied different forces that lead to the formation of international agreements. In general, international agreements can be sorted into different categories. Chief among these categories are treaties, customary international law, and non-legal international agreements. A treaty is an international agreement that is binding under international law.

* I would like to thank Dan Milkove for his helpful comments.

Customary international law encompasses consistent practices regularly adopted by states due to a sense of legal obligation. The third category of instruments of international cooperation consists of non-legal agreements between states, such as administrative agreements, letters of intent, memoranda of understanding, joint declarations, and statements or declarations of principles. Even a handshake between heads of states can be construed as a non-legal agreement. We will delve briefly into how treaties distinguish themselves from customary international law and non-legal international agreements.

Section 2 tallies potential drivers for international cooperative behavior, such as the need for coordination and the existence of transnational externalities. Although instruments other than treaties can specify international agreements, the discussion of factors that bring about international agreements will be framed in terms of treaties, as treaties are the center of attention. While many factors that lead to treaties could also lead to customary international law, Section 3 discusses differences between treaties and customary international law and contemplates the strength of treaties over customary international law. Likewise, Section 4 compares non-legal international agreements and treaties. It suggests reasons why treaties may be the preferred instrument adopted by states to form agreements. Section 5 discusses the modalities of formation of treaties, analyzes the state's incentive problem in deciding whether to be a founding negotiating state or an acceding state, and underscores the relationship between the acceding protocol of the treaty and the treaty content.

Next we turn to the issue of reservations to a treaty. Section 6 discusses the ability of an applicant state to express reservations while becoming a party of the treaty, and the legal effects of reservations and of objections to reservations, according to the procedures set forth by the Vienna Convention on Treaties. It shows different needs for reservations and how successfully the Vienna Convention fulfills those competing needs. Section 7 examines the benefits and costs of being a reserving state versus a non-reserving state, to better understand whether the Vienna Convention on Treaties is truly neutral toward both kinds of states. Section 8 summarizes research discussed in previous sections.

A. FORMATION OF INTERNATIONAL TREATIES

2. Factors Conducive to Treaties and Other International Cooperation

Preamble

Traditional international legal scholars have highlighted morality and legality to explain the existence of treaties and customary international law. Goldsmith and Posner (1999, 2005) adopted a different avenue of research by using rational choice theory in general and game theory in particular to analyze why international treaties and customary international law arise. Other law and economics researchers extended and expanded the economic forces conducive to international cooperation. These factors, along with some non-economic factors, are discussed below. Before that, it is important to discuss the basic assumptions behind the rational choice theory of international cooperation and the characteristics of game-theoretical research.

The fundamental assumption behind the rational choice approach is the existence of a preference of the state. That a state is motivated by its own well-defined self-interest is both questionable and defensible, but it is taken here as a given. Further, it is assumed that a state only cares about its own interests and not the welfare of other nations. The preference of the state then provides a clear picture of the benefits and costs of international cooperation. Other practical constraints, such as the value of resources and technological know-how, determine the pecuniary portion of the costs of fulfilling an international obligation. Along this line, the cost of consenting to be bound by a treaty depends not only on the costs of compliance but also on the likelihood of those costs being realized (Hathaway, 2003). Lastly, the transaction costs, including negotiation costs, of international agreements need to be considered as well (Fon and Parisi, 2007). The transaction costs ought to be broad enough to include the monetary costs of reaching the agreements and the political costs of accepting and maintaining the agreements (Sykes, 2007). Thus, when states gain more than they lose through cooperation, they contemplate treaties. With benefits exceeding costs, nations are motivated to pursue their own interests while accounting for other states' behavior and responses. Taking into account other nations' reactions given one's own action is the strategic framework that game theory employs and that many researchers use to understand international agreements.

Taking nations as strategic players who would sign a treaty when the net private benefits from treaty participation are positive, the following considerations may influence the formation of treaties. Although many of these considerations may serve equally well to promote customary international law, the forces conducive to international cooperation will be framed and discussed in terms of treaties. The driving forces toward international cooperation include: coincidence of interest, coercion, cooperation, coordination, externalities, public goods, institutional designs, and morality-induced private gains.

Coincidence of Interest

When the interests of states align themselves and the same action is the best option available for each state regardless of the choices made by other states, states would find themselves adopting the same action, or cooperating, whether or not there is a treaty. Given that each nation would engage in the same action, there is no apparent reason for nations to form a treaty. However, it is possible that treaties may strengthen the cooperative relation between states even though there is a coincidence of interest. There may be underlying motives that inspire nations to come to an explicit legal agreement. One example is the Treaty of Moscow, signed in May 2002, in which Russia and the United States agreed to reduce their nuclear warheads to a certain level by 2012 (Goldsmith and Posner, 2005, p. 89). Although each nation finds the reduction of its nuclear arsenal to be its best option, without a treaty each country may be tempted to reduce its warheads more slowly to maintain its nuclear advantage, knowing that the other state will reduce its nuclear stockpile. A treaty increases the sense of security for both nations and the likelihood that the other party will do the right thing.

Coercion

A powerful state or a group of powerful states with similar interests may force other states to engage in acts that they would not adopt absent pressure from the powerful, such as agreeing to a treaty (Goldsmith and Posner, 2005). Coercion exists when the powerful state's net gain depends on the weaker state's action and when the stronger state can punish the weaker state for a deviation that does not suit the powerful state. This is especially true if the cost of punishment incurred by the coercing state is relatively small and thus the threat of punishment is credible, and the punishment imposed on the coerced state is harsh. However, similar to coincidence of interests, coercion does not necessarily imply that a treaty is necessary, although a treaty may bring other advantages. When a treaty is formed and compliance with treaty obligations is practiced, the coerced state can have peace of mind, having fully understood all the demands from the coercing state, and is freed from other harassment or punishment. Meanwhile, when the rights and expectations are clearly specified and accepted, the coercing state can expect less resistance from the coerced and perhaps receive more respect in the international arena.

Dynamic Cooperation

Sometimes, two states find themselves in a Prisoner's Dilemma situation in which both gain if they cooperate, but individually each has the incentive not to cooperate. When this situation is repeated over time, game theorists have shown that parties will find it beneficial to cooperate repeatedly under some circumstances. Specifically, suppose that the following conditions hold: the parties clearly understand what counts as cooperation and as cheating; they care enough about the future (discount rates are sufficiently low); the situation repeats itself indefinitely and the states expect it never to end; and gains from defection are not too high relative to gains from cooperation. Then incentives to cheat in the short run can be overcome, and a strategy of cooperating indefinitely unless the other party defects will bring about indefinite cooperation. Goldsmith and Posner (1999, 2005) maintain that this situation provides solid ground for the states to enter into a bilateral treaty. Sandler (2008) extended the potential cooperative nature through indefinitely repeated situations beyond the Prisoner's Dilemma, expanded the grounds that would foster dynamic cooperation, and provided a foundation for multilateral treaties.

Coordination

The case of coordination is similar to the case of coincidence of interest in that the interests of the states converge. The difference is that, unlike coincidence of interest, under coordination each state's best action depends on the action of the other state as well. Typically, with the convergence and interdependence of interests of the states, there is more than one collaborative solution and the problem is one of coordination. The use of treaty as an instrument of agreement will bring focus to the collaborative solution acceptable to all states involved. As Goldsmith and Posner (2005) point out, there may be difficulties coordinating multiple states, and thus bilateral treaties are more likely. Sandler (2008) extended the arguments to show that multilateral treaties are quite possible for states that are similar (homogeneous). However, a minimal number of collaborating states are often required for a treaty to have an impact (e.g. eliminating terrorist safe havens), and the probabilities of states' adherence to the treaty terms are highly influential toward the success or failure of multilateral treaties. Specifically, the smaller the minimal number of collaborating nations that is required and the more likely it is states believe that other states will adhere to their treaty obligations, the likelier it is that coordination will prove successful and lead to a treaty.

Transnational Externalities

In an increasingly globalized world, actions of one state can create transnational external effects beyond their borders. This engenders a need for states to cooperate in order to find ways to internalize these externalities. International agreements could enable states to adopt actions that bring the equilibrium with externalities closer to the Pareto frontier (Sykes, 2007). That is, if gains are to be had by some states without hurting other states' welfare, international agreements induced by externalities could bring about these superior outcomes. Externalities provide an opportunity for states to cooperate and improve their welfare as long as transaction costs to reach international agreements are sufficiently low. As an example, when individual countries unilaterally impose tariffs on their imports, they alter the terms of trade to their advantage. These unilateral trade policies impose externalities on other states: the costs of these trade interventions are borne by exporting states. These externalities created by unilateral action of individual states then become engines of international cooperative trade policy. International agreements could diminish the terms of trade externalities across countries, while reducing tariffs and improving states' welfare in the process.

Transnational Public Goods
In an international context, a public good is one where the consumption of a good by one state cannot diminish the consumption of the same good by another state (non-rivalry), and no state can be excluded from the benefit (or cost) of the good (non-excludability). The existence of a public good provides important incentives for states to form treaties (Sandler, 2008). While a transnational public good (or public bad) creates spillover benefits (or costs) for other countries, international treaties can help bring about joint efforts that produce benefits (or curtail costs and damages). The North Atlantic Treaty Organization, an alliance to provide common defense, is an international cooperative example of a transnational public good, and the Helsinki Protocol on sulfur emissions to control pollutants is an example of a transnational public bad.

Institutional Design
A treaty can be framed to motivate nations to come to an agreement and to fulfill obligations without the need for enforcement. When designed properly, the treaty innovation can create the right incentive for states to commit to the treaty. By using principles that enhance self-enforcing behavior in which adherence to treaty terms is in the states' interests, treaties become an important instrument for guaranteeing international cooperation (Sandler, 2008). Special innovation in the design of treaty rules can often convert reluctant states into willing participants. One example of special institutional innovation involves international joint peacekeeping, in which leadership has been borne by those countries closest to the conflict, as in the case of the United States for Haiti. Another example concerns international cooperative effort to fight diseases and pests, where a minimum threshold of effort must be reached to be effective. A properly designed treaty might result in rich countries and neighboring states of the problematic areas as the main contributors. In our third example, the International Monetary Fund (IMF) provides incentives for generosity; countries with higher cost shares ("quotas") are rewarded with more votes in IMF decisions. Further, a treaty can also be designed to reallocate jurisdiction (Trachtman, 2008). For example, the European Union (EU) was established to trade jurisdiction from Member States of the EU to the EU Commission.

Morality, Conformity, and Other Factors
Rational choice theory can be augmented by morality, legality, justice, and conformity, the important promoters for international cooperation highlighted by traditional international legal scholars. Including morality- and conformity-induced private gains in the strategic framework strengthens the rational choice analysis of the formation of international agreements. For example, if citizens of a nation perceive that membership in a club of states who value clean air has many social, moral, and economic benefits, it would increase and fortify

the state's interest in joining an environmental treaty (Sandler, 2008). It is quite possible that the Montreal Protocol on Substances that Deplete the Ozone Layer grew from a few nations to most nations because of the increasing recognition of the importance of all these forces in countries around the world.

Besides the many forces already discussed, other factors can enhance the likelihood of treaty formation. One factor that can sway treaty participation and commitment is the manner in which individual states' contributions determine the overall level of public good consumption. In the case of weakest-link public goods, the least stringent efforts to monitor a deadly disease such as bird flu can determine the safety of all at-risk nations (Sandler, 2008). In order to compensate for the potential lack of effort, perhaps due to financial constraints of some nations, the rich countries may decide to shore up the weakest link by providing income transfers or to simply pick up the missing contributions. Treaties then become the instrument to formalize the shoring-up process. Further, economies of scale to pursue common goals and network effects can also be important promoters of international cooperation (Fon and Parisi, 2007).

Using treaties as signaling devices (Martin, 2005) is the last driver that we shall mention. Choosing to sign a treaty over more informal means of agreement may signal the degree of commitment of states to the cause, both to their domestic constituents and worldwide, especially if the cost of non-compliance is large and severe. Before the Treaty of Moscow was made, President Bush proposed a handshake with President Putin to seal the deal on nuclear warheads reduction. Putin and the US Congress objected, insisting on having the treaty ratified. Thus, key parties in the two treaty signatories wanted to highlight the importance of the roles they play, as well as to strengthen and signal their strong commitment to the legalized treaty (Goldsmith and Posner, 2005). This last example brings out the issue of treaties versus other instruments such as non-legal international agreements and customary international law. To these comparisons we now turn.

3. Customary International Law and Treaties

Treaties and customary international law (henceforth called CIL) are both instruments of international cooperation. As characterized in Restatement (Third) of the Foreign Relations Law of the United States, 1987, §102(2), CIL "results from a general and consistent practice of states followed by them from a sense of legal obligation." That is, CIL is conventionally characterized by a regular, widespread, and convergent state practice and a belief that the practice has taken on the role of a legal obligation. The latter requirement, the recognition and acceptance that adherence to the widespread practice is an international obligation, is known as *opinio juris*, the central concept in CIL.

Rather than the doctrine of *opinio juris* recognized under CIL, the doctrine of *pacta sunt servanda* holds under treaties. As specified in Article 26 of the

Vienna Convention on Treaties, the *pacta sunt servanda* states that "Every treaty in force is binding upon the parties to it and must be performed by them in good faith." Thus, every treaty party has an absolute obligation to comply with the treaty terms. Clearly, the *pacta sunt servanda* doctrine imposes a more forceful and definitive requirement on treaty signatories, whereas the *opinio juris* doctrine only provides guidance to a CIL practitioner state that believes the practice in question has reached the status of a legal obligation. No clear and solid guidelines determine when a common regular practice of states has been adopted widely enough to reach this legal status.

Why then should rational states follow CIL practices? Other than the sense and recognition of legal obligations, the economic drivers conducive to treaties enumerated in the previous section (coincidence of interest, coercion, cooperation, and coordination) could also lead to CIL (Goldsmith and Posner, 1999 and 2005; and Sykes, 2007). Convergence in state practice takes place because of the self interest of states, and self interest could give rise to continued adherence to CIL practices over time. Further, concern for reputation may be at work here (Guzman, 2002 and 2008). States may continue to cooperate on some issues to develop or maintain a good reputation for future negotiations; and reputational considerations may sustain regular state practices over time. Thus, not only do nations believe in their own legal obligations over some regular state practices, they feel that other nations should commit to their legal obligations as well. Defecting from CIL obligations will then lessen the reputation of a state.

CIL is and will remain an important part of international law. Many fundamental principles of international law are governed by CIL (for example, territorial sovereignty, diplomatic immunity, and sovereign equality). The strength of CIL is that it does not require large transaction costs for negotiation, administration, enforcement, and institutional innovations. Behavioral regularities that have become CIL can be sustained by the states' sense of legal obligations and the desire to maintain their reputations, without incurring monitoring and enforcement expenses. Even in areas where treaties are abundant, CIL may provide interpretive presumptions, extend treaty norms beyond a group of signatories, and induce efforts to expand treaty regimes (Goldsmith and Posner, 2005). Generally, states may avoid an obligation by objecting at the early stage of an emerging practice, but once they have demonstrated their agreement through conforming behavior, deviation is no longer possible. Not surprisingly, CIL works better and is more useful when states have homogeneous preferences and similar constraints (Fon and Parisi, 2009b).

While CIL offers considerable strength for international cooperation, this strength can turn into weakness under different circumstances; treaties then become the more desirable instrument for international agreements. As intimated earlier, it is generally difficult to decide whether a certain regular practice of states has been consistent and should be considered a legal obligation. Further, a sense of legitimacy, conformity, and justice may be fleeting. States can and often do change their views on the content of CIL, even in a short period of time. The uncertainty of the status of CIL then makes the use of treaties, where every obligation is spelled out, more attractive.

Goldsmith and Posner (2005) presented various case studies to document how CIL rules are often violated when it is in the interest of a state to deviate. A salient example is provided by the frequency with which rogue states violate the rules of diplomatic immunity. Because of the short time horizon and high discount rate for future welfare, rulers of rogue states value short-term gains much more than long-terms benefits. Thus, we observed the Iran hostage crisis, the 1967 attack on the British embassy by followers of the Chinese Cultural Revolution, and the 1958 Iraqi military coup that burned the British embassy. Goldsmith and Posner also pointed out that states tend to limit CIL to practices that are acceptable to them from their normative perspective, while besmirching CIL practices incompatible with their normative or cultural beliefs.

Various other reasons make treaties the more appropriate instrument for international agreements. Sykes (2007) reminded us that although reputation considerations may help maintain CIL practices, they may not be practical in many settings. Current events, domestic or international, may make the benefit of maintaining a reputation for compliance insignificant, especially when the CIL practice lacks wide support for being considered a legal obligation. Complicated problems encompassing a broad array of issues which require much negotiation, monitoring, and enforcement among many nations also tip the scale to make treaties more valuable. Externalities are yet another factor that can be handled more easily under treaty negotiation than under CIL. Likewise, Sandler (2008) reasoned that treaties can deal with the public goods cooperation problem better because institutional designs can be adopted to take care of special public goods production problems. Finally, treaties can provide a better infrastructure, well-recognized signatories, and clearly defined obligations.

All these pros and cons of employing treaties or CIL as instruments of international agreements make both instruments indispensable. Both treaties and CIL, and also non-legal international pledges, reside in the muddy grounds of international diplomacy. It is interesting to note that in spite of the importance of the Vienna Convention on Treaties and the fact that the United States is a signatory to many treaties, as of 2010, the United States never ratified the Vienna Convention. In responding negatively to the question whether the United States is a party to the Vienna Convention, the Treaty Affairs, Frequently Asked Questions section in the US Department of State website states, "The United States considers many of the provisions of the Vienna Convention on the Law of Treaties to constitute customary international law on the law of treaties." The ground is very muddy indeed.

4. Non-Legal International Agreements and Treaties

Other than treaties and CIL, states often use non-legal agreements as instruments for international cooperation. Although some scholars apply the term "soft law" to treaties with weak obligations, "soft law" often represents non-legal agreements between states. Likewise, other scholars prefer the term "pledges" to mean non-legal agreements. In this section, pledges and non-legal agreements mean the same thing. Sometimes, it is difficult to decipher whether an unfamiliar international agreement is a treaty or a pledge. For example, the 2001 Convention on International Interests in Mobile Equipment is a treaty, while the 1988 Basle Capital Accord, the agreement to promote international convergence of capital measurement and capital standards, is considered a pledge.

Why do states use non-legal international agreements? Two prominent explanations – flexibility and domestic law and politics issues – have been advanced in the literature (Guzman, 2005). States use non-legal agreements instead of treaties because non-legal agreements are less binding on states and they give states more flexibility. If necessary, states can more easily deviate from the terms, renege, or renegotiate the terms of agreements. The domestic processes for approving international agreements matter quite a bit. For example, in the United States, a treaty requires a two-thirds super-majority vote in the Senate but no consideration from the House, a congressional-executive agreement requires a simple majority vote in both the Senate and the House and approval by the President, and a sole executive agreement only requires consent from the President. Since a small minority of senators can prevent a super-majority consent, treaties in the United States are politically vulnerable, more cumbersome, and often embed less reliable legal commitments than the alternatives. Although seemingly less dignified than treaties, congressional-executive agreements and sole executive agreements have been on the rise in the United States. Thus, Hathaway (2008) advocates replacing most treaties by congressional-executive agreements in the United States.

Other important considerations in the choice between treaties and non-legal agreements, such as form and substance, may elevate treaties to be the preferred instrument of agreement (Raustiala, 2005). Two features of agreements relate to form: legality and structure. Legality refers to the choice between the accord being legally binding or non-binding, and structure concerns the specific provisions for monitoring and sanctioning non-compliance. The other important consideration of agreements relates to substance, which addresses the issues of substantive provisions and their deviations from the status quo. These features are not unrelated and there are trade-offs among them. The choice between treaties and pledges depends on the trade-off between form and substance. For example, if compliance with pledges is highly problematic, then legality needs to be the salient feature of the agreement and treaties are preferred. When states are uncertain of the distribution of future cooperative benefits, they tend to prefer substance over form, and pledges are the preferred instrument of their agreements. Similarly, when states do not understand the underlying problems well, they cannot estimate compliance costs for the legal obligations (Abbott and Snidal, 2000). In these cases, pledges are preferred, allowing states to take more risk under uncertainty.

As in the case of treaties versus CIL, treaties are not always superior to pledges. However, a treaty generally embeds a higher level of commitment and increases the credibility of commitment relative to pledges. Treaties may be employed to reveal information about a state's strong and lasting commitment to the agreement. Treaties should be formed if states want to stress their intent to have binding agreements, thereby inducing more impact on other states' behavior. Formal treaties are subject to the default rules of the Vienna Convention on Treaties, reducing uncertainty on interpretations of agreement terms. Lastly, treaties are more likely than non-legal international agreements to enjoy higher levels of domestic support and to withstand shocks in political arenas, and are more durable following changes in administrations (Guzman, 2005; Goldsmith and Posner, 2005; and Sykes, 2007).

5. Modalities of Treaty Formation

When a group of states considers it beneficial to form a treaty and start the process of drafting the treaty, besides agreeing on the treaty content, the states must choose from among the alternative modalities with which they can organize their treaty. Specifically, the negotiating states – those states which take part in drawing up and adopting the treaty text – need to decide whether and in what manner membership of the treaty can be expanded. Article 15 of the Vienna Convention on the Law of Treaties states that, "The consent of a State to be bound by a treaty is expressed by accession when: (a) the treaty provides that such consent may be expressed by that State by means of accession; (b) it is otherwise established that the negotiating States were agreed that such consent may be expressed by that State by means of accession; or (c) all the parties have subsequently agreed that such consent may be expressed by that State by means of accession." This Article implicitly requires prior or subsequent consent by the signatory states for an applicant state's accession to an existing treaty, and explicitly lists the three modalities that govern the manner in which a state may subsequently join the treaty agreement.

Fon and Parisi (2007) denote the three approaches specified in the Vienna Convention on Treaties as open, semi-open, and closed treaties, and analyze the different structures and incentive issues confronting states. In open treaties, the negotiating states agree to leave the treaty open for accession. Semi-open treaties accept acceding states through approval by a majority of the existing member states. Closed treaties require unanimous consent of parties to the treaty – states which have consented to be bound by the treaty and for which the treaty is in force.

Open treaties do not require affirmative action by the original negotiating states. Any state is welcome to express its consent to be bound by the treaty by accession. By formulating the conditions and prerequisites for accession, the negotiating states avoid the necessity to formally renegotiate the treaty, while permitting expansion to states with similar preferences that are more likely to accede to the treaty. Open accession clauses are common in multilateral treaties, particularly those intending to promote cooperation and foster dispute resolution across states. The Vienna Convention on Diplomatic Relations (1961) is an example.

Closed treaties disallow automatic accession; acceptance of a new member to a closed treaty requires unanimous approval by the current party states. A closed treaty typically focuses on narrow issues and provides exclusivity. For example, in an effort to limit the number of states that hold special privileges with regard to nuclear weapons, the Treaty on the Non-Proliferation of Nuclear Weapons, signed in 1968, extended the special privileges only to states that manufactured nuclear explosive weapons prior to 1967. Most bilateral treaties, especially bilateral investment treaties, are closed since they concern a specific relationship between two states.

The intermediate case of semi-open treaties consists of treaties in which acceptance of a new member requires majority approval of the signatory states. Semi-open treaties leave greater political discretion to current member states. At the same time, expansion of treaty participation means that the treaty content can be modified by a majority of the member states, brought about by accession of new states. The revised treaty content may differ in important ways from the treaty content with which the original negotiating states agreed to be bound. This creates a risk for the treaty's negotiating states. The 1974 Agreement on an International Energy Program, which promotes secure acquisition of oil, is an example of a semi-open treaty. In order to maintain a balance of power among the original negotiating states, the treaty requires an acceding state to gain approval of a majority of the Governing Board, which is composed of representatives from the founding states.

States can become part of an international treaty in two ways: as a founding negotiating member of a treaty or by acceding to an existing treaty. In light of the possibility of joining an existing treaty through accession, a state should consider the benefits and costs of being a founding member versus being an acceding state. A founding member of the treaty can strongly influence treaty content and set rules to control accession. But the negotiating and drafting costs can be substantial and have to be paid upfront, while benefits will be delayed. If being an acceding member of the treaty is possible, the costs of acceding to an existing treaty are typically lower, costs of compliance with treaty terms are less risky, and benefits are more immediate. However, while an acceding state can make reservations to certain treaty obligations in the process of ratification, thereby altering the effect of the treaty through its interaction with states who accept the reservations, its impact on treaty content is limited. The next two sections will turn to this issue.

In their study, Fon and Parisi unveil an important relationship between the formation of the treaty and its substantive content. When a treaty is left open and accession of other states is expected, treaty content is set not only according to existing interests of the negotiating states, but also on the basis of their expectation of treaty enlargement. Hence treaty content may differ from that which would be chosen under other treaty forms or if no expansion was expected. Lastly, it is observed that homogeneous states are most likely to form an international treaty to cooperate; they surmise that the treaty would likely be open or semi-open. Any state willing to join the open treaty and accept the treaty content as specified is likely to be similar to the founding negotiating states. Likewise, acceptance by a majority of signatory states of the accession of a new state to a semi-open treaty means that similar interests in all these states will be served. In the heterogeneous case with strong and weak states, the treaty is likely to be closed, since the more powerful states would refuse to give away advantageous stakes from the negotiation.

The default rule dictates that a treaty is closed for accession, unless specified otherwise (Bishop, 1971, p. 119). Since 1966, the International Law Commission has unsuccessfully advocated changing the default rule to make all multilateral treaties open for accession unless otherwise stated. The prevailing default rule favoring closed-form treaties may be justified. States face incentive problems when confronted with treaty participation. Since treaty negotiation is costly, leaving all multilateral treaties open for accession by default could undermine states' incentives to invest in the initial negotiation and drafting of treaty agreements. Further, treaties with open accession clauses cannot ensure that the rights and obligations of the negotiating states remain undisturbed (Fon and Parisi, 2007; Stark, 1989, pp. 458–9).

B. TREATY RESERVATIONS

6. Reservations

Under the CIL of sovereign equality, no state can be forced to consent to be bound by any specific treaty term, let alone the entire treaty. When widespread participation in a treaty is considered a high priority, there is a need to reconcile minor disagreements. In order to promote greater international cooperation, meet the need for greater flexibility brought about by the increasing number of multilateral treaties, and accommodate differences in opinions and interests concerning a treaty, the Vienna Convention on Treaties allows an applicant state to make reservations against some treaty provisions when signing, ratifying, or acceding to the treaty, unless specified otherwise. In particular, a state that expresses its consent to be bound by the treaty in general is free to make reservations on selected provisions of the treaty, as long as the reservations are not prohibited by the treaty and are not incompatible with the object and purpose of the treaty (Article 19).

If the provisions for which a reservation is made are deemed essential for the application of the entire treaty to uphold the object and purpose of the treaty, Article 20(2) requires unanimous acceptance of the reservation by all parties to the treaty. Otherwise, individual treaty participants decide whether the reservation is acceptable. Hence, while a state can propose a reservation to a treaty, the reservation must meet with the approval of another non-reserving state for the relevant provisions to apply between the two states. If a non-reserving state accepts, or at least raises no objection to, the reserving state's reservation, the relevant treaty provisions are modified for both of them under Article 21. However, the reservation does not modify the relevant treaty provisions for other parties to the treaty *inter se*. If a non-reserving state objects to the reservation within 12 months, then the provisions to which the reservation relates do not apply between the two states.

Thus, in order to promote international cooperation, to ease frictions arising from some treaty provisions, and to advance consensual relations between parties to a treaty, reservations are used to inject greater flexibility into treaties. This is necessary; otherwise, a state in favor of the treaty content in general but finding some specific treaty terms unacceptable will have no course of action other than not participating in the treaty. The Vienna Convention on Treaties provides an intermediate ground that allows states to include reservations along with their acceptance of other treaty obligations. However, if the unilateral reservations from states are not constrained, the essence and cohesiveness of multilateral treaties may be corroded and the net benefits of treaty participation for signatory states may be reduced. To this end, a reservation must be acceptable to the non-reserving state before the provisions can be legally modified. A treaty modified by the reservation enters into force only between the reserving state and those states that do not object to the reservation. Conversely, states that object to the reservation and the reserving state are not bound by the reserving provisions in their mutual relations. Further, other parties to the treaty remain bound to the original treaty provisions in their relations with one another.

International law lacks an overarching enforcer of the rules. To infuse multilateral treaties with flexibility, reservations are allowed when states agree to accept the treaty obligations. To ensure integrity of treaties, reservations must be accepted, explicitly or tacitly, before the relevant treaty provisions come into force between the reserving and non-reserving states. The Vienna Convention on Treaties achieves these goals through the principle of reciprocal reservations. If a state introduces a reservation, the treaty relation between the state and a non-reserving state is modified according to the scope of the reservation: the exception or limitation claimed by the reserving state applies equally to both states. This effectively introduces an identical reservation against the reserving state.

Parisi and Ševcenko (2003) investigate the tension between treaty flexibility and integrity and illustrate that the principle of reciprocity, or the matching-reservation constraint, may ease the tension. A state seeking to exempt itself from a treaty obligation must permit other nations to escape the same burden. Thus, when states are homogeneous with symmetric incentives, they have no reason to attach merely *strategic* reservations to the treaty during negotiations. States know that the matching-reservations mechanism will make their sought-after advantage automatically available to others. A strategic reservation matched by others may occasion mutual losses for all states involved. States then refrain from introducing strategic unilateral reservations to maximize their expected returns from the treaty relationship; optimal treaty obligations are likely included in the original treaty agreement. That is, in settings where states have symmetric incentives, the matching-reservations constraint set forth by Article 21 leads to socially optimal levels of treaty ratification and participation.

When states face asymmetric incentives, however, recent game-theoretic models raise doubt about the effectiveness of matching constraints, such as those set forth by Article 21 (Fon and Parisi, 2003). Matching constraints positively influence cooperation behavior, but with heterogeneous parties they cannot generate a global optimum unless additional benefits to cooperation are very high. Thus, when asymmetric states have different benefits and compliance costs from the treaty, the dominant ratification strategy is to attach unilateral reservations that preserve national interests in spite of the matching reservations. Rules introduced by the Vienna Convention cannot discourage all reservations; erosion of the original treaty content may be inevitable, unless negotiating states preclude reservations in the treaty (Fon and Parisi, 2009a).

Fon and Parisi (2008) argue that due to the reciprocity principle, reservations under the Vienna Convention on Treaties create a bias when states are not homogeneous. Specifically, consider a state that is relatively high-cost and low-benefit in terms of issues covered in the treaty. If such a state wishes to avoid application or to reduce the content of a treaty, it can do so via unilateral reservations. But no similar opportunity is afforded to states that desire to add provisions or to increase treaty obligations. Thus, given the opportunity to introduce reservations, Article 21 tilts the balance in favor of high-cost, low-benefit states that can take advantage of the reciprocity mechanism. States with a comparative disadvantage in treaty implementation have a systematic advantage under the Vienna Convention on Treaties. This bias, introduced by the reciprocity principle in treaty reservations, has potential distributive effects among different groups of states.

7. Reserving versus Non-Reserving States

The Vienna Convention on Treaties seemingly endows equal rights to reserving and non-reserving states. If one state is given the right to formulate a reservation, then the other party ought to have the right to object to the reservation. Article 21 ensures such a balance. Does this mean that the reservation paradigm under the Vienna Convention on Treaties is truly impartial in its treatment toward reserving and non-reserving states?

There is some disagreement on the answer to the question, although it is widely considered that reserving states are favored. For example, Greig (1994) criticizes the Vienna Convention on Treaties for providing an unacceptable advantage to reserving states. Klabbers (2000) advances that whether or not a state accepts the other state's reservation, the reserving state generally gets what it wants. Fon and Parisi (2008) bring out the fact that the Vienna Convention on Treaties favors states with comparative disadvantages in treaty implementation that would turn into reserving states. Meanwhile, Swaine (2006) disagrees that the Vienna Convention on Treaties disfavors the non-reserving states. Helfer (2006) extends Swaine's thesis, providing more reasons why non-reserving states may not be disadvantaged after all. The researchers stress that, while there are gains to making reservations, a reserving state must bear some costs as well. Further, benefits can be derived by non-reserving states. Consequently, the Vienna Convention on Treaties may plausibly serve the interests of non-reserving states more than reserving states.

It is recognized that the Vienna Convention on Treaties carries various ambiguities. For example, a reservation can be made only if it is not incompatible with the treaty's object and purpose. But it is not clear how, when, and in what way the incompatibility kicks in. If a non-reserving state is uncertain whether the reservation is considered compatible with the treaty's object and purpose, it may fail to raise its objection within the required 12 month period. In general, any limbo resulting from uncertainty over the reservation process benefits the reserving state. To better understand the controversy, it is also important to consider the incentive problem facing a reserving state. After all, it is the pursuit of the state's interest that inspires the state to consider participating in a treaty while making reservations that incur unacceptable costs. As discussed in the last section, reserving states also have strategic benefits (Parisi and Ševcenko, 2003; Fon and Parisi, 2008; Fon and Parisi, 2009a).

Swaine (2006) highlights the informational value generated from negotiating, concluding, and administering treaties. In fact, many treaties are oriented toward information production, especially if more worthy and demanding goals are beyond reach. Human rights treaties are a good example. In the international arena, states often hide their motives. But information is useful because it may help influence future behavior, build consensuses, and form other treaties. Sometimes information on other states is very difficult to generate; states do not wish to disclose embarrassing information about themselves, create disagreements, however minor, with other states, or risk retaliation. That is to say, making a reservation has an informational cost. Making a reservation to a treaty signals that the state is willing to cooperate, but only on its own terms and according to its own schedule. Helfer (2006) further points out that the informational signal is stronger the earlier the state makes the reservation, although reputation costs to early reserving states can be substantial. But information goes both ways. Reserving states may learn something from the reactions of other states. Further, non-reserving states may withhold their objections to early reservations for fear that doing so may cause other states not to ratify or to participate in the treaty. These are among the important benefits and costs that a potential reserving state must juggle before making a decision.

It is universally agreed that the international reservations regime contributes to broader participation: reservations lead to more states agreeing to be bound by a treaty. Treaty participants, including non-reserving states, may gain from broader participation whether they accept or object to specific reservations. With more participants to the treaty, each party state may acquire positive externalities and other benefits, such as lower compliance costs occasioned by the additional participation of the reserving states. Besides the benefits of breadth (more participation), the international reservations regime can also increase the depth of treaty participation. Given the opportunity to make reservations and to be exempt from certain provisions, treaty terms may be more demanding and therefore generate more benefits for participating states, even after some reservations are made and accepted. These benefits are available to all treaty participants, reserving and non-reserving states alike.

Non-reserving states can gain from information: the informational costs from reservations incurred by a reserving state also represent informational benefits to non-reserving states. Since the act of reserving reveals valuable information about a state's reputation and its propensity to comply, non-reserving states gain knowledge about the risks and benefits of contracting with reserving states. Non-reserving states can build on this information, reserve their judgment as to whether and how the reservations should be objected, and try to find ways to shift risks in their favor.

The number of reservations attached to international treaties is considered relatively low despite the rules governing reservations set forth in the Vienna Convention on Treaties. For example, Gamble (1980) found no reservations in 85 percent of all multilateral treaties that allowed reservations; only 61 treaties had more than three reservations. Given the competing benefits and costs of reserving, perhaps this is not as surprising as it may first sound.

8. Conclusion

In their pursuit of self-interest, states often need to interact with other states. International law and economics scholars reveal many factors that may secure the formation of treaties and other international agreements. Among the important factors are coincidences of interest, coercion, repeated cooperation over time, coordination to align states' actions, external effects induced by one state's action on other states, the transnational public goods problem which may require joint effort to produce benefits or to curtail costs affecting multiple states, and the treaty design, which if framed properly can create the right incentives for states to cooperate.

In the international arena, while agreements can function as treaties, customary international law, and other informal agreements, treaties are sometimes preferred over other instruments. Relative to customary international law, which are behavioral regularities that states consider they have a legal obligation to adhere to, treaties are more desirable when, for example, there is uncertainty over the legality of the states' practices, where lengthy negotiations are involved, externality problems are prevalent, or a more organized infrastructure for interstate agreements is required. Relative to informal international agreements, sometimes referred to as pledges, treaties are superior when, for example, there is little uncertainty relating to the benefits and compliance costs of the agreement, when states want to signal their strong commitment and increase their credibility, or domestic constituents need to be placated through more formal agreements.

According to the Vienna Convention on the Law of Treaties, there are three modalities in which treaties can be formed. Negotiating states may agree to leave the treaty open for accession, acceptance of a new party to the treaty is made possible through approval by a majority of existing member states, or acceptance of a new party requires the unanimous consent of the parties to the treaty. Each protocol has its own strength; in general, the form of the treaty and the substantive content are related. For example, if unanimous approval of accession is required from existing parties, treaty obligations may be made more stringent, making it more manageable to keep treaty obligations intact to achieve the object and goal of the treaty.

To facilitate broad participation in international treaties, the Vienna Convention on Treaties extends the possibility of reservation to treaty provisions to a state during its signing of or accession to the treaty. While the acceding state may propose a reservation to the treaty, the Vienna Convention dictates that a non-reserving state must accept the reservation, or else the two states are not bound by the provisions related to the reservation. Thus, the reservations regime under the Vienna Convention attempts to balance the need to respect the conditional consent of reserving states and to honor the unqualified consent of the treaty by the non-reserving states; it bridges the gap between the differing desires of heterogeneous states and the need for consensus.

Unfortunately, much ambiguity remains in the legal reservations regime under the Vienna Convention. It is arguable that the uncertainties induced by the ambiguities, the possible strategic moves, and the freedom to make reservations mean that the Vienna Convention favors the reserving states. But the information content generated by the reservation process may be invaluable to non-reserving states as well. Much controversy remains concerning which parties the Vienna Convention favors.

Even with millennia of bargaining experience to establish interstate agreements, states still often find it difficult to come to an agreement. It is not surprising that many states attempt to bargain around the Vienna Convention on Treaties. For example, an unforeseen increase in compliance costs may inspire a state to denounce the treaty and to re-accede the same treaty with reservations. As Helfer (2008) notes, grounding treaties on formal consent has many advantages. But consent has significant costs as well, including the inability to ensure that all states affected by the transnational problem join treaties that endeavor to alleviate those problems. In light of the many problems addressed, additional analyses of treaties are warranted and much needed.

Bibliography

Abbott, Kenneth W. and Snidal, Duncan (2000), "Hard and Soft Law in International Governance," **54** *International Organization*, 421–56.

Bilder, Richard B. (1981), *Managing the Risks of International Agreement*, Madison, WI: The University of Wisconsin Press.

Bishop, W.W., Jr. (1971), *International Law: Cases and Materials* (3rd ed.), St Paul, MN: West Publishing Co.

Brownlie, Ian (2008), *Principles of Public International Law* (7th ed.), New York: Oxford University Press.

Fon, Vincy and Parisi, Francesco (2003), "Reciprocity-Induced Cooperation," **159** *Journal of Institutional and Theoretical Economics*, 76–92.

Fon, Vincy and Parisi, Francesco (2006), "International Customary Law and Articulation Theories: An Economic Analysis," **2** *International Law and Management Review*, 201–32.

Fon, Vincy and Parisi, Francesco (2007), "The Formation of International Treaties," **3** *Review of Law and Economics*, 37–60.

Fon, Vincy and Parisi, Francesco (2008), "The Hidden Bias of the Vienna Convention on the International Law of Treaties," **4** *Review of Law and Economics*, 383–406.

Fon, Vincy and Parisi, Francesco (2009a), "The Economics of Treaty Ratification," **5** *Journal of Law, Economics, and Policy*, 209–24.

Fon, Vincy and Parisi, Francesco (2009b), "Stability and Change in International Customary Law," **17** *Supreme Court Economic Review*, 279–309.

Gamble, John K, (1980), "Reservations to Multilateral Treaties: A Macroscopic View of State Practice," **74** *American Journal of International Law*, 372–94.

Goldsmith, Jack L. and Posner, Eric A. (1999), "A Theory of Customary International Law," **66** *University of Chicago Law Review*, 1133–77.

Goldsmith, Jack L. and Posner, Eric A. (2005), *The Limits of International Law*, New York: Oxford University Press.

Greig, D.W. (1994), "Reciprocity, Proportionality, and the Law of Treaties," **34** *Virginia Journal of International Law*, 295–403.

Guzman, Andrew T. (2002), "A Compliance-Based Theory of International Law," **90** *California Law Review*, 1823–87.
Guzman, Andrew T. (2005), "The Design of International Agreements," **16** *European Journal of International Law*, 579–612.
Guzman, Andrew T. (2008), *How International Law Works: A Rational Choice Theory*, New York: Oxford University Press.
Hathaway, Oona A. (2003), "The Cost of Commitment," **55** *Stanford Law Review*, 1821–62.
Hathaway, Oona A. (2008), "Treaties' End: The Past, Present, and Future of International Lawmaking in the United States," **117** *Yale Law Journal*, 1236–372.
Helfer, Laurence R. (2006), "Not Fully Committed? Reservations, Risk and Treaty Design," **31** *Yale Journal of International Law*, 367–82.
Helfer, Laurence R. (2008), "Nonconsensual International Lawmaking," **1** *University of Illinois Law Review*, 71–125.
Horn, Frank (1988), *Reservations and Interpretive Declarations to Multilateral Treaties*, Amsterdam: North Holland.
Klabbers, Jan (2000), "Accepting the Unacceptable? A New Nordic Approach to Reservations to Multilateral Treaties," **69** *Nordic Journal of International Law*, 179–93.
Koremenos, Barbara (2005), "Contracting Around International Uncertainty," **99** *American Political Science Review*, 549–65.
Martin, Lisa L. (2004), "Self-Binding (How US Benefited from Multilateralism)," *Harvard Magazine*, September–October.
Martin, Lisa L. (2005), "The President and International Commitments: Treaties as Signaling Devices," **35** *Presidential Studies Quarterly*, 440–65.
Parisi, Francesco (1998), '*Opinio Iuris* Revisited: A Law and Economics Perspective,' **4** *International Legal Theory*, 21–2.
Parisi, Francesco and Fon, Vincy (2008), *The Economics of Lawmaking*, New York: Oxford University Press.
Parisi, Francesco and Ghei, Nita (2003), "The Role of Reciprocity in International Law," **36** *Cornell International Law Journal*, 93–123.
Parisi, Francesco and Ševcenko, Catherine (2003), "Treaty Reservations and the Economics of Article 21 of the Vienna Convention," **21** *Berkeley Journal of International Law*, 100–26.
Piper, Catherine L. (1985) "Reservations to Multilateral Treaties: The Goal of Universality," **71** *Iowa Law Review*, 295–322.
Raustiala, Kal (2005), "Form and Substance in International Agreements," **99** *American Journal of International Law*, 581–614.
Rose-Ackerman, Susan and Tobin, Jennifer (2005), "Foreign Direct Investment and the Business Environment in Developing Countries: The Impact of Bilateral Investment Treaties," Yale Law & Economics Research Paper No. 293.
Sandler, Todd (2004), *Global Collective Action*, New York: Cambridge University Press.
Sandler, Todd, (2008), "Treaties: Strategic Considerations," **1** *University of Illinois Law Review*, 155–79.
Sinclair, Ian (1984), *The Vienna Convention on the Law of Treaties* (2nd ed.), Manchester, UK: Manchester University Press.
Stark, J.G. (1989), *Introduction to International Law* (10th ed.), Waltham, MA: Butterworth-Heinemann.
Swaine, Edward T. (2006), "Reserving," **31** *Yale Journal of International Law*, 307–66.
Sykes, Alan O. (1991), "Protectionism as a 'Safeguard': A Positive Analysis of the GATT 'Escape Clause' with Normative Speculations," **58** *University of Chicago Law Review*, 255–305.
Sykes, Alan O. (2007), "International Law," in Polinsky, A. Mitchell and Shavell, Steven (eds), *Handbook of Law and Economics*, vol. 1, Amsterdam; North-Holland, 757–822.
Trachtman, Joel P. (2008), *The Economic Structure of International Law*, Cambridge, MA: Harvard University Press.
Tyagi, Yogesh (2000), "The Conflict of Law and Policy on Reservations to Human Rights Treaties," **71** *British Yearbook of International Law* 181, 220–1.
van Aaken, Anne (2006), "To Do Away with International Law? Some Limits to the 'The Limits of International Law," **17** *European Journal of International Law*, 289–308.

Other References

1974 Agreement on an International Energy Program, available at: <http://untreaty.un.org/English/UNEP/energy_program_english.pdf>.

Basle Committee on Banking Supervision, International Convergence of Capital Measurement and Capital Standards (Basle Capital Accord), available at: <http://www.bis.org/publ/bcbs04a.htm>

Convention on International Interests in Mobile Equipment, International Institute for the Unification of Private Law, available at: <http://www.icao.int/icao/en/leb/capetown-conv.pdf >.

Draft Articles on the Law of Treaties, International Law Commission, available at: <http://untreaty.un.org/ilc/texts/instruments/english/commentaries/1_1_1966.pdf>.

Restatement (Third) of the Foreign Relations Law of the United States (1987), American Law Institute.

Treaty on the Non-Proliferation of Nuclear Weapons, available at: <http://www.iaea.org/Publications/Documents/Infcircs/Others/infcirc140.pdf>.

United Nations Treaty Collection, Overview, available at: <http://treaties.un.org/Home.aspx>.

US Department of State, Frequently Asked Questions on Vienna Convention on the Law of Treaties, available at: <http://www.state.gov/s/l/treaty/faqs/70139.htm>.

Vienna Convention on Diplomatic Relations (1961), available at: <http://untreaty.un.org/ilc/texts/instruments/english/conventions/9_1_1961.pdf>.

Vienna Convention on the Law of Treaties, available at: <http://untreaty.un.org/ilc/texts/instruments/english/conventions/1_1_1969.pdf>.

16 Customary international law

Jef De Mot, Vincy Fon and Francesco Parisi*

1. Introduction

Given the absence of a world legislature and the cost of forming and ratifying multilateral treaties, customary law has played a fundamental role in governing relationships among sovereign states in both historical and modern settings. Despite some assertions of its diminishing importance (see e.g. van Hoof, 1983), today customary international law is playing an increasingly prominent role in the international legal system (see e.g. Jiménez de Aréchaga, 1978; Lepard, 2010). For example, the customary law of human rights has flourished, many crimes under international law are defined primarily by customary law and customary international law plays an increasing role in the protection of the environment (see Lepard, 2010). In this chapter, we focus on contributions that consider the process of formation and evolution of customary international law. This process differs from the process of formation and evolution of other sources of law. Rather than through political deliberation or adjudication, the rules of customary international law emerge gradually through states' independent and spontaneous adherence to certain behavioral standards.

This chapter is structured as follows. In Section 2, we give a brief overview of the relatively few principles that govern the formation of customary international law. We discuss the two formative elements for an enforceable custom to emerge. We also discuss the persistent-objector and subsequent-objector doctrines, which allow states to avoid the binding force of customary international law. Section 3 contrasts traditional theories of customary international law with basic insights from the law and economics approach. Most notably, law and economics scholars have criticized traditional theories with respect to the reason why states adhere to international custom. Section 4 provides a basic model of customary international law formation, and discusses the impact of the number of states and of uncertainty and time lags in the process of emergence and recognition of custom. Section 5 considers a variation in the process of custom formation in which custom emerges when states undertake action consistent with the expression of a belief contained in their prior or concurrent articulations.

* University of Ghent, Postdoctoral Researcher, Research Foundation – Flanders (FWO).

Section 6 looks at the effects of the persistent-objector and subsequent-objector doctrines on the formation and evolution of customary international law. Section 7 concludes.

2. Basic Principles

2.1 Two Formative Elements

When the resolution of a dispute requires the application of customary international law, an international tribunal verifies the presence of two formative elements of a custom: (1) a quantitative element consisting of a general or emerging practice; and (2) a qualitative element reflected in the belief that the norm generates a desired social outcome. Only when both elements are present does the international practice gain the status of a customary international law that is binding on participating states. The quantitative element concerns both the length of time and the universality of the emerging practice. The longer the formative stage of a custom, the less likely it is for the custom to effectively provide a valuable substitute for formal law or treaty agreements or to adapt to changing circumstances over time. There is no universal minimum duration for the emergence of customary rules. These rules have evolved from both immemorial practice and single acts. However, French jurisprudence has traditionally required the passage of 40 years for the emergence of an international custom; German doctrine has generally required 30 years (Tunkin, 1961; Mateesco, 1947). With respect to the condition of universality, international legal theory is ambivalent as to whether unanimous consent by all participants is required before binding customary law is formed. Charney (1985), for example, dismisses the requirement of unanimous consent, suggesting that the system of international relations is analogous to a world of individuals in the state of nature. Well-accepted restatements of international law refer to consistency and generality rather than universality (D'Amato 1971; Brownlie 1990). The consistency requirement is not met when it is impossible to identify a general practice because of fluctuations in behavior. More recent cases in international law restate the universality requirement in terms of increasing and widespread acceptance, allowing special consideration for emerging general norms that are expected to become widespread over time. The second, qualitative element of a customary rule is generally identified by the phrase *opinio iuris ac necessitatis*, which describes a widespread belief in the desirability of the norm and the general conviction that the practice represents an essential norm of social conduct. Those who follow the custom should do so believing that it represents a necessary and obligatory convention (Kelsen 1939 and 1945; D'Amato 1971; Walden 1977).

There is a great deal of disagreement among scholars over the rules of customary international law (Lepard, 2010). D'Amato (1971) has lamented the lack of a consistent theory of custom. According to Kelly (2000), customary law no longer has any authority or legitimacy and should be eliminated as a source of international law, due to the pervasive subjectivity involved in determining customary international law. Bederman (2010) wonders why, after nearly half a millennium of debate, we are no closer to conclusive answers as to what makes a binding custom among nations. Lepard (2010) advocates a new definition: "A customary international law norm arises when states generally believe that it is desirable now or in the future to have an authoritative legal principle or rule prescribing, permitting, or prohibiting certain conduct." This belief constitutes *opinio iuris*, and is sufficient to create a customary law norm. It is not necessary to satisfy a separate "consistent state practice" requirement in every case. State practice is just one source of evidence that states believe that a particular authoritative principle or rule is desirable now or in the near future. Note, however, that, according to many practicing international lawyers, the tendency has been, in order to prove whether something is a rule of customary international law, simply to show that a certain practice is really followed by states and to forget about the motives for the norm's observance (Bederman, 2010). Some scholars have suggested that one needs to make a distinction between the traditional formulation of custom and modern custom (for a discussion, see Bederman, 2010). Traditional custom is "identified through an inductive process in which general custom is derived from specific instances of state practice.... *Opinio iuris* is a secondary consideration invoked to distinguish between legal and nonlegal obligations". On the other hand, modern custom, which has arisen particularly with the human rights revolution after the Second World War, is "derived by a deductive process that begins with general statements of rules rather than particular instances of practice. This approach emphasizes *opinio iuris* rather than state practice because it relies primarily on statements rather than actions.

2.2 The Persistent Objector Doctrine

Some states have argued that if they persistently object to an emerging rule of customary law, if and when a rule is formed, it cannot be applied to them. These claims led to the gradual recognition of a principle known as the persistent-objector doctrine, allowing states to opt out of a new and otherwise universal rule of customary international law by remaining opposed to the practice (Brownlie, 1990; Kontou, 1994; Stein, 1985; and Wolfke, 1993). Objection to an emerging custom may be full or partial. Full objection signifies that the state neither accepts nor wishes to become bound by any part of the emerging custom. A partial objection implies acceptance of some part of the custom. Partial objection is generally found when states object by articulating or implementing a different rule which they consider preferable to the emerging custom. Full persistent objection leads to a complete exemption from the emerging custom, while partial objection leads to a partial exemption. Once the custom solidifies, the portion of the custom that was not opposed binds the partial persistent objector. Some well-known cases decided by the International Court of Justice have confirmed the persistent objector doctrine. For example, in *United Kingdom v Norway*, the court ruled that, because the government of Norway had consistently opposed the territorial fishing zone regime, Norway was a persistent objector and therefore not bound by such customs.[1]

To successfully invoke the doctrine, states must satisfy two elements. First, the objecting state must make its objections widely known before the practice solidifies into a binding rule of custom. The state must clearly object to the law from the moment of its conception or from the moment the state learns about any relevant practice or declaration that may lead to the establishment of a custom. The objection may be expressed in the form of statements, votes, or protests, or may be implied by "abstaining from practice or adhering to a different practice" (Viller, 1985). Second, a state's objection to a practice must be consistent. The state must clearly object to the law from the beginning, and continue to do so throughout its formation and after its acceptance as international custom (Loschin, 1996). A state may not adhere to a practice on some occasions and object to the practice on other occasions. A consistency requirement allows other states to rely on the position of the objecting state, and prevents the objecting state from benefiting from ambiguities in its own course of action. Furthermore, a state may not invoke the persistent-objector doctrine if the customary law has achieved the status of *jus cogens* or imperative law, since these rules serve the most fundamental interests of the international community and should be obeyed by all states without exception (Loschin, 1996).

The influence of the persistent-objector doctrine was traditionally quite limited (Stein, 1985). However, the greater accessibility and verifiability of general customary law has given the doctrine momentum (Loschin, 1996). Although the doctrine's popularity has increased, acceptance of the doctrine is not unanimous in the international community. Some authors argue that it is of negligible importance, while others claim it does not exist. D'Amato (1971), for example, argues that the cases of the International Court of Justice speak to special or regional custom rather than to general custom. Generally, the wide-ranging literature spawned by the doctrine leaves the impression that commentators have not sufficiently explained the rationale for this exception (see Lepard, 2010). Building further on his new definition of customary international law (see Section 2.1), Lepard (2010) suggests that persistent objection "should not be allowed to customary norms that states generally

---

[1] *Fisheries case (United Kingdom v Norway)*, 1951 ICJ 116, 124–31. Another case is the *asylum case (Colombia v. Peru)*, 1950 ICJ 266, 272–8.

believe further such important values that they should bind all states, even states that have persistently objected to them".

2.3. The Subsequent Objector Doctrine

According to traditional international law, states can object to a norm of customary international law only during its emergence. A state cannot unilaterally depart from a customary rule once it has become bound by it (Wolfke, 1993). This traditional approach may lead to excessive rigidity of customary international law when the needs of the international community change over time. International law practice has gradually developed some doctrines to avoid unnecessary inflexibility. One such doctrine is based on the principle of *rebus sic stantibus*, often referred to as the law of changed circumstances. It allows states to depart from international law in the face of fundamental changes in the state of affairs that led to the original legal obligation (Kontou, 1994; Shaw, 2008). Several types of changes cannot be covered by this principle. For example, changes to individual states' costs and benefits are not covered, due to their limited verifiability. Likewise, states cannot invoke changes in internal laws or policies as a justification for a unilateral departure from customary international law. However, departures from customary law that are not supported by the *rebus sic stantibus* principle could in theory be accommodated by a subsequent-objector doctrine (Brownlie, 1990, 2008). The subsequent-objector doctrine, which is not generally recognized (see e.g. Bradley and Gulati, 2009), specifies that, in the face of a unilateral departure from an existing custom, a subsequent objector can gain an exemption from a rule of customary law only if, and to the extent that, its departure from the custom is not opposed by other states. Since the reactions of the other states may differ from one another, this doctrine may fragment a previously uniform rule of custom into a network of bilateral relations. The relationship between a subsequent objector and a fully acquiescing state is governed by a bilateral obligation consistent with the norm advocated by the objector state. The relationship between a subsequent objector and an opposing state remains governed by the pre-existing custom. When the departure is only partially opposed, the content of the rule governing the bilateral relation between the departing state and the (partially) objecting state changes according to the extent of the latter state's acquiescence.

3. Law and Economics versus Traditional Theories

The traditional formulation of *opinio iuris ac necessitatis* is problematic because of its circularity. It is quite difficult to conceptualize that law can be born of a practice which is already believed to be required by law. Some scholars have questioned the notion of *opinio iuris* and the resulting circular explanation of the binding nature of customary law, providing a more complex formulation of the factors that lead states to adhere to international custom. According to

Goldsmith and Posner (1999 and 2005), customary law is a relevant source of international law to the extent that it creates state reliance. The reasons for state compliance with custom, however, should be found elsewhere. Goldsmith and Posner explain compliance with custom by considering a number of factors that are consistent with their view of states' interest-oriented behavior. The first is coincidence of interest, whereby all states behave identically because it is in their unilateral interest, regardless of the choices made by other states. They offer ambassadorial immunity as a possible illustration. States may protect the ambassadors of other states given that they perform a valuable function in facilitating communication with other governments. A second explanation is coercion. They provide as an example the custom of "free ships, free goods," whereby all property on neutral ships is immune from seizure. Weak states may respect the principle for fear of retaliation by powerful states. Another reason for states' compliance with custom is that a common practice may represent the solution to an iterated Prisoner's Dilemma. They again offer ambassadorial immunity as a possible example. An exchange of ambassadors can be viewed as an exchange of hostages. A final reason for convergence is that a custom may provide a focal point for a coordination problem. They provide the three-mile limit for territorial waters as an example. For security and other reasons, nations have an interest in claiming dominion over coastal waters, but the exact limit is to a certain degree a matter of indifference. The three mile limit functions as a focal point that is acceptable to all states.

In summary, Goldsmith and Posner argue that convergence in customary practices occurs for reasons of pure self-interest and that continued adherence to such practices happens not because of any sense of legal obligation, but because the self-interested reasons remain in place. To support their claim that customary law per se has no influence on state behavior, they argue that rules of customary law are often violated when states have an interest in deviating, and that rogue states, which may have shorter time horizons and higher discount rates, are more likely to deviate than other states. Sykes (2007), however, notes that detractors of the traditional view cannot prove the nonexistence of *opinio juris* merely by pointing to self-interested deviations from custom. It could just be that the force of *opinio juris* is limited. In such a case, when a state's narrow self-interest is sufficiently strong, these counter-incentives could override the force of *opinio juris* and the same observations that Goldsmith and Posner catalogue would be observed.

4. Customary International Law Formation

Parisi and Fon (2009, pp. 137–56) present a model of the process of custom formation. In its simplest version (for extensions, see further), two states are faced with a voluntary participation problem in the absence of an existing custom. For example, one state is facing an emergency, and the other state faces the decision of whether to voluntarily rescue the other and how much effort to spend in doing so. Voluntary participation in a new practice (e.g. rescue) imposes costs on one state, while conferring benefits on another. The states are engaged in repeat interaction. After the initial time period, the states alternate roles (until infinity). Their future roles (e.g. as rescuers or rescued) are only known on a probabilistic basis. In each period, there is a probability that a given state will be the beneficiary of other states' activities and a probability that the state will continue to be on the giving side. The practice is assumed to be socially desirable (e.g. the total benefits of rescue outweigh the total costs). The socially desirable practices are followed, subject to reciprocity. Whatever the level of effort chosen by the state, it can expect that the effort will be reciprocated when it needs to be rescued. Compliance is sustained by reputational constraints. Thus two main factors influence a state's choice to engage in a given action: the immediate costs and benefits of the action (circumstantial interest) and the interest that it may have in establishing a customary rule which would bind it for the future (normative interest). The process of formation of customary law described above poses a cooperation problem. At each moment in time, the circumstantial interest of one state (e.g. the costs of the rescuer) is in conflict with the commonly shared normative interests of all the states (e.g. that a customary practice of rescue is socially desirable). Parisi and Fon show that the acting state's participation constraint is less likely to be satisfied and that the state's effort level in the formative stage of the customary rule will be lower when (a) the cost of the activity is higher, (b) the benefit from cooperation is smaller, (c) the probability of being on the benefiting side in future time periods is lower and (d) a state's discount rate is higher. These results are fairly intuitive, because participation in an emerging custom (or increased effort) imposes a present cost in exchange for the expectation of a future benefit whose (present) value is reduced by higher discount rates, by a lower probability of being on the benefiting side, and by a smaller benefit from cooperation. Parisi and Fon also compare the privately optimal conduct with the socially optimal level of effort, finding that the optima will coincide only in limited instances. Intuitively, this can be explained in terms of externalities. The privately optimal conduct could be lower than the socially optimal level of effort because the first-mover (here, the rescuer) internalizes only part of the social benefit of his action (e.g. the creation of a desirable rescue custom). The opposite can also be true, since the first-mover does not bear the full cost of his action (the other state may be called upon to rescue the first-mover at a later stage).

As a first extension, Parisi and Fon examine the case of multilateral custom. Unlike in the previously described case of bilateral custom, states are not always involved in one role or the other (e.g. as victims or rescuers) in the case of multilateral custom. Formally, it is assumed that participants in a customary practice are randomly drawn from a larger population. At any time, a positive number of non-participants observe others' activities without participating. When the probability of a state's involvement decreases, it becomes less likely that the state will take part in the customary practice and the effort expended by the state decreases. These results are related to the fact that the choice of initial participation imposes a present and sure cost on the states, while the probability of future involvement with the emerging custom and the resulting net benefits may decrease with the number of participants. These results are consistent with the empirical findings of sociologists and anthropologists that close-knit environments and small communities of players provide the most fertile environments for the emergence of efficient custom (Ulmann-Margalit, 1977; Parisi, 1998; Ellickson, 2001). This result also supports Goldsmith and Posner's (1999 and 2000) skepticism about reciprocity explanations of international cooperation involving more than two states.

Another extension concerns uncertainty in the formation of custom. In real-life settings, initial participants in a customary practice have no guarantee that their initial effort will be met with reciprocity. For example, a potential rescuer has no perfect assurance that his effort will be met with like behavior when fortunes (and roles) are reversed. As intuition suggests, states that have higher expectations that their behavior will successfully consolidate into a binding custom are more likely to participate in the practice, and their initial actions will be performed with more effort.

A final extension considers the effect of time lags on the process of emergence and recognition of custom. Time lags and delays affect the time in which the initial participants are able to capture the benefit of the custom when roles are reversed. The delays can be determined by the type of practice, such as events of rare occurrence (e.g. a rescue in outer space or on the high seas), or action in the legal system (e.g. some legal systems require a long-standing practice of 20 or 30 years before the usage is recognized and enforced as a binding customary rule). The authors find that when states have a positive time preference, delays have negative participation and effort effects on the initial participants. These results suggest that customary settings that entail infrequent states' actions should require a lower number of observations, and thus a shorter waiting period, before the practice is allowed to solidify into a binding rule. Otherwise, states would heavily discount the benefits of future applications of the custom.

5. Articulation Theories

As discussed above, states' actions can form international customs. Statements and expressions of belief, however, can also play a role in custom formation. Theories under which statements and expressions of belief play a role in custom formation are called articulation theories. D'Amato (1971) considers articulation a formative element in customary international law. In D'Amato, this element operates in conjunction with state practice and abstention. According to articulation theories, states' statements and expressions of belief should be attentively considered in the process of ascertaining the qualitative element of *opinio iuris*. States can signal which rules they intend to follow by articulating norms that they would agree to be bound by. Articulation lends tangibility and objectivity to the otherwise subjective and intangible element of *opinio iuris*, allowing belief to be expressed before or in conjunction with customary action. These theories suggest that greater weight should be given to beliefs that have been expressed prior to the emergence of a conflict in order to avoid the effect of biased articulations.

Fon and Parisi (2006) examine whether an alternative, hypothetical process in which articulation determines the content of emerging customs can mitigate the shortcomings of the traditional approach. Their model of custom formation considers a setting similar to the model described in the previous section. The major difference is that states are allowed to choose a rule by means of articulation in the initial period. The endorsement of a hypothetical rule by means of articulation requires no practice or effort expenditure. For example, states are allowed to express their beliefs on the norm of rescue before their respective roles are unveiled and before any state needs rescue. The future horizon for the states is unchanged (role reversal etc.). The most interesting differences can be summarized as follows. First, the participation constraint is more easily satisfied in the articulation case than in the traditional customary law case. Allowing potential participants to announce ex ante their participation in the emerging custom and to articulate the level of effort that they consider appropriate and desirable for such activity facilitates the formation of customary law. Second, under articulation theory, the states' discount rate has no effect on the optimal level of effort. Articulation processes, unlike traditional processes of custom formation, eliminate incentives to understate the states' true normative interests by letting states commit to a customary rule before their specific circumstantial interests are unveiled. Third, the optimal effort that states would rationally choose under articulation is greater than the effort that those same states would choose under traditional customary law processes. Note, however, that homogeneous states or unbiased role reversibility are important prerequisites of processes of custom formation even under articulation theories. In our rescue example, the two states will face incentives to articulate efficient rescue rules only when the probability of being rescued equals the probability of becoming a rescuer in the future. This is so because the states will assign equal weights to the expected costs and benefits of future rescue missions. This is not the case when states face asymmetric probabilities of being rescuers or victims. With asymmetry, the private and social incentives diverge and the resulting articulations will be affected by the diverging interests of the states. In general, the lack of alignment between private and social incentives is due to the fact that a privately optimal effort level is obtained by balancing the expected private marginal cost and benefits. Such privately optimal balancing takes into account the individual probabilities of receiving a benefit or being burdened by a cost. For a social optimum, no such discounting should be made. The social marginal cost and marginal benefit for the states should be balanced, but the distribution of probabilities between states would not enter the calculation for a social optimum, because the ex post distribution of costs and burdens between the states becomes irrelevant when all values are aggregated in the social function. Thus, the private optimum and the social optimum will coincide only when the probabilities are uniform for all players.

The same extensions are considered as in the traditional customary law case. With respect to multilateral custom, an increase in the number of potential participants under articulation also renders participation less likely, but has no impact on the optimal level of effort expended by a state. This is a substantial improvement over traditional customary law processes that, as seen above, are affected by pervasive strategic problems in multilateral settings. The effect of uncertainty in the formation of custom is the same as in the traditional customary law case: an increase in the probability that others will reciprocate has a positive impact on the willingness of a state to advocate customary norms by means of articulation and increases the state's willingness to expend effort. Finally, the presence of time lags negatively affects the participation choice under articulation theories as well as traditional processes of custom formation. The longer the delay before any enforcement of the articulated rule takes place, the less likely that the state will actively engage in the articulation process. However, this delay has no effect on the qualitative standards advocated by the states and the resulting rules of custom. These results can be explained by considering that delays in the implementation of the rule decrease the present-discounted value of the future payoff, thereby weakening the incentives to participate in the articulation venture. On the other hand, delays in future events do not alter the balance between expected benefit and expected cost in the future. Consequently, if the participation constraint is fulfilled, the state has no reason to alter its choice of optimal effort no matter how long the delay. Also in this case, articulation processes of custom formation improve upon traditional processes with respect to states' incentives and the resulting qualitative content of the emerging custom.

6. The Effects of the Persistent-Objector and Subsequent-Objector Doctrines

6.1. *The Persistent-Objector Doctrine*

Fon and Parisi (2009) analyze the impact of the persistent-objector doctrine on the process of custom formation when heterogeneous states are involved. In the initial time period, a number of heterogeneous states need to decide whether to participate in a customary rule and to choose levels of effort. There is no initial cost of custom compliance because the persistent-objector doctrine requires the objection to be "consistent" (i.e. states' objections should be formulated ex ante). Once the custom is established, in later periods each state confronts a certain probability that it may receive a benefit from other states' compliance with the custom, and a certain probability that the state may be called upon to fulfill obligations created by the custom. Due to the fact that states are heterogeneous – and may face different probabilities, costs, benefits, and participation constraints – the interests of states may diverge. This implies that states may have different views on the desirability and content of the custom. The persistent-objector doctrine provides a mechanism through which the different actions and objections of the states are brought together to generate a rule of custom. Persistent objectors may opt out in part or in full from customary obligations. Objection is partial when a state is willing to join the custom, but prefers a level of effort lower than that required by the emerging custom. When a state chooses not to participate in the emerging custom, that state faces the cost of its own effort each time it seeks to obtain a benefit for itself ("self-help"). For example, imagine an emerging customary rule which imposes a duty on coastal states to rescue foreign vessels within a certain range from the state's coastline. Rejection of the custom implies that the state faces the burden of rescuing its own ships, even when they are far from the state's own coastline. In the face of a persistent objection, other states take advantage of the reciprocal effects of a unilateral objection, allowing them to adopt the same customary level against the objecting state. Logically, a state will choose to participate in the custom when the best obtainable payoff under the custom is higher than the payoff under self-help. The most important findings can be summarized as follows. First, different categories of states may choose to opt out of an emerging custom. Full objection is a rational strategy not only for states that consider the emerging custom excessively burdensome, but also for states that like the custom but want more of it. Some states agree with the spirit of the custom but are not satisfied with the emerging rule because they would like a custom with a greater level of obligation. Some of these states may be better off opting for a no-custom regime and addressing the issue on their own. The payoff in a no-custom regime represents the opportunity cost of custom participation. This opportunity cost will likely be larger for stronger states that face a lower cost of self-help, and which may have greater opportunities to stand alone and generate benefits for themselves in the absence of international cooperation. For those states, customary cooperation is less indispensable than for other states that have less opportunity to address the underlying need by acting on their own. Given the lower payoff obtainable in a no-custom regime, weaker states facing higher costs may be more willing to go along with an emerging custom that does not correspond to their ideal levels. Second, the likelihood of participation in a less than ideal custom depends on the ratio of the probability of being on the receiving side versus the probability of being on the giving side of the customary relationship in future time periods. States that are more likely to benefit from the custom than to be burdened by it are more likely to participate in the custom, even though the custom does not correspond to their ideal optimum.

6.2. The Subsequent Objector Doctrine

Unlike persistent objectors, who raise objections prior to facing a compliance problem with an emerging custom, subsequent objectors manifest their objections by departing from an already binding rule of customary law. Given an existing rule of customary law, a state may become a subsequent objector for many reasons (see Fon and Parisi, 2009). Some reasons are merely strategic: a state may object to an existing rule of customary law to avoid the cost of fulfilling its obligations under that rule. Other subsequent objections are driven by changes in the costs and benefits of the custom. To understand how other states react to a subsequent objector's departure from existing custom, it is useful to separate states into three groups. The first group consists of first-party states that have reasons to become subsequent objector states. The second group of states comprises second-party states that would benefit from the subsequent objector's fulfillment of the customary obligation. Finally, third-party states neither expend effort to fulfill the customary obligation nor receive any direct benefit from the subsequent objector's compliance in the current period. Fon and Parisi consider three types of cases. In the first case, the probabilities, benefits and costs associated with expected long-term participation in the custom do not change for any state. A first-party state may still become a subsequent objector for strategic and myopic reasons. In one period, the first-party state is faced with taking its turn to fulfill its obligations under customary law. The need to incur the immediate cost of compliance with the custom may induce the first-party state to invoke a partial erosion of the pre-existing customary rule. Second-party and third-party states, however, will always oppose such strategic attempts to depart. The third-party state continues to find the existing custom obligation privately optimal. Nothing changes for a third-party state. A second-party state, on the other hand, prefers an even larger level of effort than existing customary law requires. Although the circumstances of the second-party state do not change, this state derives an immediate benefit from the subsequent objector's fulfillment of the customary obligation in the current period.

In the second case, exogenous factors that affect the behavior of states may change, but changes are uniform for all states. Suppose the cost of performing increases for all states. In such cases, there is a *partial* convergence of interests between the subsequent objector and the third-party state. The subsequent objector's departure from the current custom is motivated by an attempt to reduce the burden of immediate compliance and to minimize the impact of higher compliance costs in the future. The third-party state shares the motive to reduce the future effect of higher compliance costs. Thus, the subsequent objector has incentives to depart more extensively from the existing custom than the third-party state would likely permit. For the second-party state, the net effect of an exogenous change in costs depends on whether the presence of an immediate benefit for the second-party state is offset by the increase in future performance cost. If the immediate benefit dominates, the second-party state is either content with the current customary rule or prefers a level of custom higher than the current level. The second-party state opposes any departure by the subsequent objector from the current custom, and the relationship between the two states remains governed by the existing customary rule. If the impact induced by the increase in future performance cost dominates, the second-party state's private optimum falls below the existing customary law. Still, the second-party state's private optimum exceeds the level preferred by the subsequent objector. In this case, a partial convergence between the interests of the subsequent objector state and the second-party state takes place. The second-party state foregoes part of the immediate benefit from the custom by providing partial acquiescence. The custom governing the relationship between the two states changes from existing customary law to the level desired by the second-party state. This analysis reveals a potential factor of inertia in the process of custom formation. When exogenous changes affect the states' ideal levels of customary law, opposition from second-party states may hinder the adaptation of customary law to such changes in circumstances. Second-party states may oppose the subsequent objector's departure not so much because they value the current custom, but because they are attracted by the immediate benefit from custom compliance. This further justifies the workings of the subsequent-objector doctrine, allowing the bilateral obligations of first- and third-party states to adapt to changed circumstances in spite of second-party states' opposition.

The third case is characterized by asymmetric exogenous changes for the states involved. We consider the case in which the subsequent objector chooses a level of departure effort below the existing customary law effort, either for strategic reasons or for reasons induced by environmental changes. Given that the problems confronting a second-party state and a third-party state are similar except for the extra immediate benefit factor enjoyed by the second-party state, we discuss only the problem confronting the third-party state. If the exogenous changes in the third-party state are such that its new optimal level of effort is greater than the existing customary law effort, the third-party state would like to raise the content of the custom obligation to its privately optimal value. But this is not an option for the third-party state. Consequently, the third-party state does not acquiesce. Next, consider the case in which the exogenous changes in the third-party state induce an effort level less than the existing customary law level. Clearly, there is no reason for the third-party state to acquiesce in any change in current custom that brings the level of customary obligation below its privately optimal value. Thus, when the subsequent objector's desired level is larger than the third-party state's optimal value, the third-party state provides full acquiescence. The subsequent objector's desired level becomes the content of the bilateral custom that governs the relationship between the first-party state and the third-party state. In the opposite case, the third-party state is only willing to provide partial acquiescence. The third-party state's privately optimal value characterizes the bilateral custom between the third-party state and the subsequent objector.

6.3. Change and Stability in Customary Law

Both the persistent- and subsequent-objector doctrines assure that any new rule of customary law or any change to existing customary law affects only those states for which the new rule or the change in existing rule constitutes a Pareto improvement. A state facing a net prejudice from a newly emerging custom can opt out of that rule by persistently objecting. Likewise, any state facing a prejudice from a departure from an existing custom can oppose the departure and enforce the current rule. There are, however, limits to custom formation when heterogeneous states are involved. Through the application of the persistent-objector doctrine, high-cost states effectively constrain the emergence of new custom in their relationships with other states. The resulting level of custom formation may be suboptimal compared to the alternative scenario in which high-cost and low-cost states effectively bargain with one another for the choice of a value-maximizing customary effort. The subsequent-objector doctrine creates the opposite problem. By allowing the acquiescences of other states to serve as constraints, this doctrine may lead excessive customary obligations to outlive the circumstances that justified their emergence. In the presence of heterogeneous states, the persistent- and subsequent-objector doctrines allocate control of the resulting level of customary law among different states. By doing so, these doctrines promote stability in customary relations, but may fail to induce first-best social optima obtainable via compromise solutions. These results are consistent with the traditional wisdom that custom is an effective source of international law when homogeneous states are involved, but that alternative sources, such as treaty law, may be better instruments for the pursuit of first-best outcomes when heterogeneous parties are involved.

7. Concluding Remarks

Most of the economically inspired literature on customary international law is quite recent, and there is room for exponential growth in this field of academic research. For instance, theoretical extensions could investigate the influence of reputational costs on the formation of customary norms. Objector states may face reputational costs when objecting to customary law, and second- and third-party states may also face reputational costs when opposing another state's departure from an existing custom. The practice of customary law is heavily affected by considerations of diplomatic and political expediency, and such costs may create frictions and biases in the process of custom formation that are worthy of consideration. Further, if reputational costs differ from state to state, this may create a systematic advantage for states that place less weight on reputation. The process of custom formation is further affected by free-riding and opportunistic behavior by second- and third-party states, none of which fully internalize the benefit of monitoring other states' compliance with custom. When states face a private cost in opposing departures from customary law and generate a public benefit for the international community, a public good problem may arise. As a result, states may fail to oppose other states' departures more often than is desirable for the world community as a whole. Future research should verify the relevance of this analysis for understanding other social and legal settings where social norms or customary rules are created through the spontaneous interaction of parties in society.

Bibliography

Akehurst, M. (1974–5). "Custom as a Source of International Law". *British Yearbook of International Law* 47:1–53.

Bederman, David J. (2010). *Custom as a Source of Law*. New York: Cambridge University Press.

Binmore, K. and Samuelson, L. (1994). "An Economist's Perspective on the Evolution of Norms". *Journal of Institutional and Theoretical Economics* 150: 45–63.

Bradley, Curtis A. and Gulati, G. Mitu (2009). "Withdrawing from International Custom". *Yale Law Journal* 120: 202–75.

Brownlie, I. (1990). *Principles of Public International Law*. 4th edition. Oxford: Clarendon Press.

Brownlie, I. (2008). *Principles of Public International Law*. 7th edition. Oxford: Clarendon Press.

Charney, J.I. (1985). "The Persistent Objector Rule and the Development of Customary International Law". *British Yearbook of International Law* 56: 1–24.

Cooter, R.D. (1994). "Structural Adjudication and the New Law Merchant: A Model of Decentralized Law". *International Review of Law & Economics* 14: 215–27.

D'Amato, A. (1971). *The Concept of Custom in International Law*. Ithaca, NY: Cornell University Press.

Ellickson, R.C. (2001). "The Market for Social Norms". *American Law and Economics Review* 3: 1–49.

Fon, V. and Parisi, F. (2003). "Reciprocity-Induced Cooperation". *Journal of Institutional and Theoretical Economics* 159: 1–17.

Fon, Vincy and Parisi, Francesco (2006). "International Customary Law and Articulation Theories: An Economic Analysis". *International Law and Management Review* 2: 201–32.

Fon, Vincy and Parisi, Francesco (2009). "Stability and Change in International Customary Law". *Supreme Court Economic Review* 17: 279–309.

Goldsmith, Jack L. and Posner, Eric A. (1999). "A Theory of Customary International Law". *University of Chicago Law Review* 66: 1113–77.

Goldsmith, Jack L. and Posner, Eric A. (2000). "Understanding the Resemblance between Modern and Traditional Customary International Law". *Virginia Journal of International Law* 40: 639–63.

Goldsmith, Jack L. and Posner, Eric A. (2005). *The Limits of International Law*. New York: Oxford University Press.

Jiménez de Aréchaga, Eduardo (1978). "International Law in the Past Third of a Century". *Recueil des cours* 159: 1–344.

Kearney and Dalton (1970). "The Treaty on Treaties". *American Journal of International Law* 64: 495–561.
Kelly, J.M. (1992). *A Short History of Western Legal Theory*. Oxford: Clarendon Press.
Kelly, J. Patrick (2000). "The Twilight of Customary International Law". *Virginia Journal of International Law* 40: 449–543.
Kelsen, H. (1939). "Théorie du Droit International Coutumier". *Revue Internationale de la Théorie du Droit* (New Series) 1: 263–4.
Kelsen, H. (1945). *General Theory of Law and the State*. Cambridge, MA: Harvard University Press.
Kontou, Nancy (1994). *The Termination and Revision of Treaties in the Light of New Customary International Law*. Oxford: Clarendon Press.
Lepard, Brian D. (2010). *Customary International Law: A New Theory with Practical Applications*. New York: Cambridge University Press.
Loschin, L. (1996). "The Persistent Objector and Customary Human Rights Law: A Proposed Analytical Framework". *UC Davis Journal of International Law & Policy* 2: 147–71.
Mateesco, N.M. (1947). *La Coutume dans les Cycles Juridiques Internationaux*. Paris: Editions A. Pedone.
McClane, B. (1989). "How Late in the Emergence of a Norm of Customary International Law May a Persistent Objector Object?" *ILSA Journal of International and Comparative Law* 13: 1–26.
Parisi, F. (1995). "Toward a Theory of Spontaneous Law". *Constitutional Political Economy* 6: 211–31.
Parisi, F. (1998). "Customary Law". *The New Palgrave Dictionary of Economics and the Law*. Basingstoke: Macmillan, 572–8.
Parisi, F. and Fon, V. (2009). *The Economics of Lawmaking*. New York: Oxford University Press.
Posner, E. (1996). "Law, Economics, and Inefficient Norms". *University of Pennsylvania Law Review* 144: 1697–744.
Shaw, Malcolm N. (2008). *International Law*. 6th edition. Cambridge: Cambridge University Press.
Stein, T.L. (1985). "The Approach of the Different Drummer: The Principle of the Persistent Objector in International Law". *Harvard International Law Journal* 26: 457–82.
Sykes, Alan O. (2007). "International Law", in Polinsky, M. and Shavell, S. (eds.), *Handbook of Law and Economics*. Amsterdam: Elsevier.
Tunkin, G.I. (1961). "Remarks on the Juridical Nature of Customary Norms in International Law". *California Law Review* 49: 419–30.
Ullmann-Margalit, E. (1977). *The Emergence of Norms*. Oxford: Clarendon Press.
van Hoof, G.J.H. (1983). *Rethinking the Sources of International Law*. Deventer: Kluwer Law and Taxation Publishers.
Viller, M.E. (1985). *Customary International Law and Treaties*. Dordrecht, The Netherlands: Martinus Nijhoff Publishers.
Walden, R.M. (1977). "The Subjective Element in the Formation of Customary International Law". *Israel Law Review* 12: 344–64.
Wolfke, K. (1993). *Custom in Present International Law*. 2nd edition. Netherlands: Kluwer Academic Publishers.

17 International organization: institutions and order in world politics

Alexander Thompson and Duncan Snidal[*]

1. Introduction

The modern history of international organization (IO) reflects an uneven development of both the practice and concept that go under that name. The term is used in differing ways and we apply it to both IO conceived as formal organizations and in a more general sense of order creation. Furthermore, international organization includes not only interstate arrangements but, increasingly, arrangements among non-governmental and transnational actors. Thus, the landscape of international organizations (IOs) includes both intergovernmental organizations (IGOs) and international non-governmental organizations (INGOs). International organization is clearly a very broad concept, which has evolved with the practice of various forms of international governance. Our main task here is to chart the theoretical development of understanding about IO. We emphasize approaches that are most relevant to international law and economics, while noting important contributions and challenges posed by alternative perspectives.

After a descriptive summary of the history and evolution of IOs, we discuss three general conceptions of IO: as formal organization, as international ordering principle and as international regime. We then review the theoretical literature on IO, addressing such topics as regime theory, institutional variation and design, compliance and effectiveness, and the role of non-state actors in global governance. We conclude by noting that there is substantial overlap in the interests of political scientists, law scholars and economists when it comes to the study of IO, a confluence that is leading to productive intellectual debates.

A. A BRIEF HISTORY OF INTERNATIONAL ORGANIZATION

2. The Rise of Intergovernmental Organizations

Beginning with the Peace of Westphalia in 1648, the principle of national sovereignty placed the states of Europe on an equal legal footing and established

[*] We thank two anonymous reviewers for valuable comments.

the norms of territorial integrity and non-interference in the domestic affairs of other states. Westphalian sovereignty helped to order political life at the international level, though in a highly decentralized and limited way (Falk, 1969; Krasner, 1999), and was critical to the subsequent development of international organization. However, it was not until the nineteenth century that formal intergovernmental organizations (IGOs) began to appear in significant numbers. Prior to that, there was insufficient contact between states, few problems arising from interdependence among them, and little perceived need for institutionalized mechanisms to manage international relations (Claude, 1964).

The first serious attempt at international organization among states came with the Congress of Vienna (1814–15), which established a new diplomatic order whereby representatives of states met at regular intervals – not just in the aftermath of war – to discuss political issues. The resulting "Congress system" was a more systematic and institutionalized approach to managing issues of war and peace, which some view as a fundamental turning point in the conduct of international relations (Schroeder, 1994).

The Congress system gave way to the more informal Concert of Europe, "A looser association of the Great Powers . . . limited to dealing with problems as they arose, not seeking to anticipate them or to iron them out of existence" (Hinsley, 1963, p.213). This featured sporadic gatherings throughout the century, mostly in response to wars: Paris in 1856, Vienna in 1864, Prague in 1866, Frankfurt in 1871, Berlin in 1878, Berlin in 1884–5, and The Hague in 1899 and 1907. These last two conferences went so far as to establish panels of arbitrators to settle international disputes and produced a Convention for the Pacific Settlement of International Disputes. These are the earliest examples of formal organizations designed to manage security issues. The result of the Concert was, indeed, quite a long period of relatively peaceful interstate relations among the great powers of Europe.

Many of the most dramatic developments in international organization during the nineteenth century grew from the increased geographic scope of economic activity, which created new interdependencies among states. To facilitate international trade and regulate traffic, the states of the Rhine established the Central Commission for the Navigation of the Rhine in 1815, and commissions were subsequently established for the Danube (1856) and Elbe (1821) rivers. The Zollverein, a customs union of Germanic states established in 1834, was the first effort at international economic integration and governance in Europe. A related set of IOs, the Public International Unions, were concerned primarily with technical matters and with establishing standards. They included the International Telegraphic Union (1865), the General (later Universal) Postal Union (1874), the International Union of Railway Freight Transportation (1890), and the International Bureau of Weights and Measures (1875). Some of these organizations had elaborate institutional frameworks, including permanent bureaus that represented forerunners of secretariats (Archer, 1983, p. 12).

Parallel to these developments in IGOs was a rise in non-governmental and transnational actors as important participants in global governance. Notable groups created in the nineteenth century were the International Committee of the Red Cross, the international labor movement in Europe, and transatlantic advocacy networks focused on the abolition of slavery and women's suffrage (Boli and Thomas, 1999; Keck and Sikkink, 1998, chapter 2; Reinalda, 2009, chapters 4–5). In some cases, these groups provided services (such as the Red Cross's efforts to aid civilians and prisoners during times of war), but arguably their most important role was to raise awareness of issues and pressure governments to accept new norms governing them.

The periods following the two world wars saw the greatest proliferation of institutions. Diplomats met in 1919 at the Versailles Peace Conference to create a global security IGO in the League of Nations. This was the first attempt at collective security – that is, an institution operating on the principle that an attack against one state is considered an attack against all (Claude, 1962; Kupchan and Kupchan, 1991; Miller, 1999). The League Covenant established the Permanent Court of International Justice, the first universal forum of its kind and predecessor to today's International Court of Justice. Versailles was also the first instance of widespread participation by non-governmental actors in a large interstate conference; two products were the establishment of the International Labor Organization and a more formal partnership between states and the Red Cross. This marked the beginning of a trend toward increased participation by non-governmental organizations (NGOs) in global governance throughout the twentieth century (Skjelsbaek, 1971).

Though President Woodrow Wilson was its chief proponent, the United States never joined the League (the Senate failed to ratify the Covenant) and it never lived up to its promise of preventing war. Nevertheless, as the first attempt to forge a security order based on a formal IGO with universal membership, the League of Nations left an important legacy.

3. Post-World War II International Organizations

The architects of the postwar system established an ambitious framework of international law and institutions. Though the number of formal IGOs increased from about 50 to 80 during the interwar period, they flourished in the decades following World War II and numbered over 200 by the 1970s (Wallace and Singer, 1970; Jacobson, 1984).

The most important of these organizations is the United Nations (UN). The UN Charter was finalized and signed at the United Nations Conference on International Organization, which took place in San Francisco in 1945. The UN is comprised of six principal organs – the General Assembly, the Security

Council, the Economic and Social Council, the Secretariat, the Trusteeship Council, and the International Court of Justice – and dozens of programs, commissions and specialized agencies, which have proliferated over the years to address specific issues (Yoder, 1989; Mingst and Karns, 2007; Schachter and Joyner, 1995). Unlike the League, which focused almost exclusively on security issues, the UN is designed to address a range of social, economic and political issues.

One set of organizations, known as the Bretton Woods institutions, was created following World War II for the purpose of promoting economic stability and development. The International Monetary Fund was charged with lending money to address temporary balance-of-payments difficulties and to maintain stable exchange rates, though its role has expanded to include longer-term debt and other structural problems and intervention following financial crises. The World Bank's initial task was to facilitate postwar reconstruction in Europe. Its focus quickly shifted to lending for major economic development projects, usually in cases where governments cannot secure loans from private banks. The General Agreement on Tariffs and Trade (GATT) was established to maintain open trade based on the principle of non-discrimination. It was replaced in 1995 by the more encompassing and centralized – for instance, it contains strengthened dispute settlement procedures – World Trade Organization (WTO).

Alongside these global institutions, an important development in the postwar period has been the rise of regional institutions (Fawcett and Hurrell, 1995; Taylor, 1993; Nye, 1968). Some perform a range of functions within a given geographical area, such as the Organization of American States, the Organization of Central American States, the Arab League, the African Union, and the Association of South East Asian Nations. Others are specifically security related, such as the North Atlantic Treaty Organization, the Organization for Security and Cooperation in Europe, and the now-defunct Warsaw Treaty Organization. The largest number are economic, including the European Free Trade Association, the North American Free Trade Agreement, the Southern Cone Common Market, the Andean Common Market, and the Asia-Pacific Economic Cooperation forum. In fact, many of these regional arrangements combine economic, political and security goals, and they have been credited with simultaneously promoting economic exchange and regional stability (Haftel, 2007).

Of these regional arrangements, the European Union is by far the most institutionalized, with rules and formal organizations governing economic relations (Armstrong and Bulmer, 1998; Eichengreen and Frieden, 1994; Kenen, 1995), human rights (Voeten, 2008; Moravcsik, 2000), legal dispute resolution (Alter, 2001; Burley and Mattli, 1993; Garrett, 1995), and, increasingly, security cooperation (Jones, 2007; Kupchan, 1997). To a greater degree than any other IGO, the EU represents a "pooling of sovereignty" (Moravcsik, 1998) and some argue that it is an example of true supranational governance (Sandholtz and Stone Sweet, 1998).

4. Recent Trends

As globalization intensifies the level of interaction and interdependence across national boundaries, international organization is becoming more complicated in terms of the number of actors and institutions involved and the range of issues addressed. While states are still the most important actors, political scientists and legal scholars describe an increasingly complex network of public and private entities that supply governance functions.

Following an exponential growth rate in the decades following World War II, the number of IGOs exceeded 300 by the early 1990s, but has leveled off since then (Pevehouse, Nordstrom and Warnke, 2004). IGOs also sometimes become inactive; more than one-third of those in existence in 1981 were defunct by 1992, including many in Eastern Europe and the developing world. Nevertheless, the number of regional IGOs continues to rise, especially in the Americas, Europe and Africa, a trend driven largely by the increased regionalization of the world economy (Mansfield and Milner, 1999). Overall, it is the rich countries of Western Europe that participate most in IGOs, as reflected in their high number of memberships. This has led to concerns over a "growing polarization between powerful countries – dominated by the literate, wealthy, and democratic – that establish and control IGOs and countries whose populations and governments are badly off and increasingly disengaged from international organizations" (Shanks, Jacobson and Kaplan, 1996, p.594).

The UN and its various agencies have become more active since the end of the Cold War. Demand for an expanded range of UN services in the area of international security has produced a much more active Security Council and an increase in the number and complexity of peacekeeping operations (Roberts, 1993; Malone, 2004; Price and Zacher, 2004). This replaces the gridlock of the Cold War, during which the two opposing blocs often failed to agree on how to address security issues. The UN and related organizations have also become more active in settling international disputes and monitoring compliance with international law, through a variety of new organizations (e.g., the International Criminal Court, the International Tribunal for the Law of the Sea, the WTO's dispute settlement mechanism, and the Human Rights Council) and increased activity by older ones (e.g. the International Center for Settlement of Investment Disputes and the Security Council).

Today, IGOs range in size from small consultative organizations such as the Northwest Atlantic Fisheries Organization to very substantial bureaucracies like the World Bank or EU with elaborate administrative structures, large budgets, many employees and extensive operational capacities. While IGOs were traditionally established by treaty, a majority are now "emanations", that is, organizations created by other organizations. A striking feature of the landscape of IGOs is the degree of overlap in terms of functions, membership and rules, producing a complex – and sometimes confusing – network of institutions (Alter and Meunier, 2009).

Parallel to the growth in governmental organizations has been a continued proliferation of international non-governmental organizations (INGOs). From 176 in 1909, there were 1,255 INGOs in 1960 and are now more than 5,500 (UIA, 1997/98, Table 2, Appendix 3). Non-governmental organizations pressure governments for change, but also work with them to manage a variety of issues, including the environment, human rights, and international regulation in various settings (Raustiala, 1997; Rosenau and Czempiel, 1992; Keck and Sikkink, 1998; Abbott and Snidal, 2010). They also work with and through IGOs, including the UN, the World Bank and the WTO (Weiss and Gordenker, 1996; Charnovitz, 1996). Today's world is thus one of "transnational" relations and governance, where governmental actors at various levels interact with their counterparts abroad, but also with IGOs and private actors, to manage international issues (Hall and Biersteker, 2002; Slaughter, 2004; Keohane and Nye, 1972; Risse-Kappen, 1995).

As this historical summary makes clear, international organization has generally been a response to or manifestation of deeper changes in international relations, not a driver of these changes.

B. CONCEPTUAL APPROACHES TO IO

The theory and practice of IO have developed together in the modern era, and especially in the post-World War II period. One consequence of this progressive development is substantial ambiguity in what we mean by "international organization", since the practice and concept have co-evolved over time. A compensating virtue is that we have developed a richness of different possibilities for organizing international behavior and for thinking about it. It is useful to distinguish three different conceptions of the term.

5. IO as Formal Organizations

The most familiar and straightforward definition of international organization is as formal organizations, usually among states or with states selecting representatives. As noted above, the Congress of Vienna (1815) established the Rhine Commission as the first formal IGO, but not until the last third of the nineteenth century did IGOs begin to proliferate rapidly to facilitate expanding commercial and other forms of interdependence among European states. In the current period, formal IGOs are exemplified by the United Nations and its agencies, as well as a host of functional and regional organizations.

The study of formal organizations took off in the early twentieth century, especially as the débâcle of World War I led to the creation of the League of Nations. The interwar analysis was heavily descriptive and normative and focused on the legal and organizational structure of emerging or proposed institutions (Yalem, 1966). It suffered from a relative neglect of the actual incentives of states, including their reluctance to transfer sovereignty to federal or supranational organizations. This led to its being labeled as "idealistic" in distinction to the "realist" account of international life as being fundamentally driven by the harsh realities of power politics (Carr, 1939; Morgenthau, 1948). Realism continues to view power, not institutions, as the key organizing principle of international affairs, and is skeptical of any significant role for formal organizations.

Despite the failure of the League, the concern for international organizations carried through World War II, although it was significantly changed by David Mitrany's ([1943] 1966) "functionalist" theory. Technological advancements and the desire to promote welfare concerns were seen as creating a need for interstate cooperation that required both international governmental organizations and non-governmental organizations to manage the necessary technical cooperation. The theory further emphasized the important role of professionals within those formal organizations in effecting international cooperation. "Neofunctionalism" extended this argument by suggesting that successful collaboration in one area would increase the benefits of cooperation in related areas, and generate joint pressure from domestic interest groups and international officials to extend the realm of cooperation (Haas, 1964; Lindberg and Scheingold 1971; Nye, 1971; Groom and Taylor, 1975). This "spillover" would then provide the motor for broad international – and especially regional – integration, as exemplified by the development of the European Community. Although this body of literature had a limited impact in the end (see Haas, 1975), it represented an important move away from description towards a theoretical analysis whose ideas continue to be echoed in contemporary discussions.

While these theories argued that formal IGOs could perform functions that would lead them to acquire authority, subsequent theory focused on how increasing interdependence was eroding state sovereignty. This trend has not been monotonic, as illustrated by high levels of pre-World War I economic interdependence that declined precipitously in the interwar period and were only surpassed well after World War II. Nevertheless, long-term and increasing interactions among states in all fields of activity – including health, technology, security, environment, culture and economics – mean that even the most powerful states are sensitive to events elsewhere and cannot always achieve goals by themselves. Small states that are dependent on larger states have even stronger reasons to seek support from such organizations. Moreover, this interdependence takes increasingly complex forms, including the increase in the number of significant transnational actors such as multinational corporations and environmental groups (Keohane and Nye, 1972, 1977). These changes have increased opportunities for formal international organizations, but have not necessarily increased the willingness of states to transfer political authority to them.

Indeed, formal international organizations had come to be viewed unfavorably from both practical and theoretical standpoints until quite recently. From a practical perspective, IGOs have not always lived up to the high expectations they have raised. This was true with the League of Nations in the 1930s and with the UN by the 1970s, when the General Assembly and various UN agencies seemed to have become little more than forums for ideological debate (between North and South and between East and West). Developing countries in particular have felt that the Bretton Woods institutions are biased against them (Wilkinson, 2000; Stiglitz, 2002) and have created alternative institutions such as the UN Conference on Trade and Development to further their interests, but with mixed success. In the 1980s, the UN system faced open hostility from the United States, its most powerful member. Similarly, the high expectations for the European Community appeared to have stalled in this period – both within Europe itself and with regard to transferring the regional community model elsewhere.

Nevertheless, formal IOs continued to play an important role throughout the postwar period (Karns and Mingst, 1990). Economic organizations were instrumental in the performance of the global economy, while NATO was the most institutionalized, and probably the most successful, alliance. In the post-Cold War years, formal organizations have experienced somewhat of a renewal. There has been an effort to make better use of existing organizations, as the United States did with the UN during the Gulf War, to change organizations such as NATO to address a different set of problems, and to expand the purview of organizations such as the World Bank and IMF to address new issues, including the environment. Skepticism regarding the effectiveness of formal IGOs is neither over nor unwarranted, but there is continued interest in pursuing the possibility of improved governance through IGOs.

The theoretical literature is experiencing a similar sharp turnaround from the preceding decades, where, in the words of one commentator, there had been a "steady disengagement of international organization scholars from the study of [formal] organizations, to the point that today one must question whether such a field even exists any longer except in name" (Rochester, 1986). This new attention to formal IOs should not be understood as a continuation of the earlier tradition, however, but as a reconstitution of a substantive interest, now on stronger theoretical footings. On the one hand, the new literature is decidedly non-idealist and questions of enforcement of agreements and incentives to obey institutions are key concerns of its proponents. On the other hand, the literature is theoretical as it seeks to move well beyond the institutional-descriptive accounts that dominated much of the earlier literature (Abbott and Snidal, 1998; Hawkins et al., 2006; Barnett and Finnemore, 2004).

Legal scholarship, especially the doctrinal analysis of the rules and outputs of formal IOs, has continued to provide a rich description of the institutional forms and details of IOs. Although traditionally a-theoretical (see Virally, 1972, for a partial exception), its implicit emphasis on problem-solving states is highly amenable to rationalist theoretical development. This work examines how similar problems are addressed under different IO arrangements (Amerasinghe, 1996; Dupuy, 1988; Kirgis, 1993) and the best is comparative (Schermers and Blokker, 1995). An especially promising recent development, discussed below, is the reuniting of the legal concern with detailed arrangements and more theoretical developments in economics (Trachtman, 1997) and international relations (Abbott, 1992; Slaughter, Tulumello and Wood, 1998; Guzman, 2008).

Finally, the emphasis on formal organizations represents a very narrow view of the forms of, and possibilities for, international governance. Indeed, the failure of the "classic" IO model to live up to an exaggerated promise of managing international affairs in a relatively depoliticized and expert manner has led to its disrepute in many quarters. Improved understandings of governance suggest that formal organizations are only one among numerous institutional possibilities. This is reflected in practice in the expanding use of informal arrangements such as G-groups (the Group of 77 and Group of 8, for example) to address international problems and in an emerging theoretically oriented study of informal institutions.

6. IO as Ordering Principle

If formal organization provides a narrow view of international organization, the most expansive definitions of international organization are framed in terms of broad ordering principles of the international system. We focus on two here: the realist conception of self-help in anarchy and the English School view of a "society". We do not consider other ordering principles such as Marxist theories of imperialism (Lenin, [1917] 1939) or of a "world capitalist system" (Wallerstein, 1979), although the economic logic they describe certainly constitutes an alternative international ordering principle. The two we do consider play a central role in debates regarding the nature of international organization and pose major alternatives to regime theory, which we consider below.

Self-Help in Anarchy

The traditional realist view centers on sovereign territorial states in a state of anarchy, with Thomas Hobbes' "state of nature" as the relevant metaphor. Anarchy is defined primarily in terms of the absence of central authority, not necessarily in terms of chaos or war (Milner, 1991, offers a valuable discussion of different meanings of anarchy). However, the realist view does imply that international politics is inherently competitive and conflictual, that survival is the primary goal of states, and that relative power is of central importance. Waltz (1959, 1979), the most influential contemporary realist commentator on anarchy, emphasizes that the fundamental difference between domestic and international politics is that the former is hierarchic while the latter is irreducibly anarchic. This creates some irony with respect to realist reliance on Hobbes as their intellectual forebear since they part ways with him on his central conclusion that actors in a dire state of anarchy would choose a Leviathan, and thus transform anarchy into hierarchy. The best explanation for states' failure to do so is that international anarchy is not as brutish as Hobbes' vision of domestic anarchy (Beitz, 1979).

Nevertheless, given the absence of central authority, the key realist ordering principle is self-help: states must take care of themselves (Waltz, 1979; Glaser, 2010). Security is seen as the overwhelmingly central problem and balance of power provides the unique source of international order. Thus a central focus of realist theory is the relation between the distribution of power and international outcomes, including but not restricted to war – although there are sharp debates over the precise impact of different power distributions (Kaplan, 1957; Gilpin, 1981; Waltz, 1979). Power and security considerations are further seen as the deep source of states' attitudes towards, and arrangements for, other (secondary) issues such as economics, human rights or environment. Thus lower-order institutions – including formal organizations and regimes – are seen as largely epiphenomenal, with the organization of the system explained largely by the balancing of power among states (Mearsheimer, 1994–5; Wight, 1973).

International Society and Norms

A very different tradition in the international relations field, inspired by Hugo Grotius ([1625] 1925), focuses on the system of states as an "international society" that contains persistent elements of order (Bull, 1977; Wight, 1977). According to Bull (1977, p. 13), the most prominent member of this English school, "states form a society in the sense that they conceive themselves to be bound by a common set of rules in their relations with one another, and share in the working of common institutions". This framework of rules and institutions guides state behavior in patterned ways.

Social constructivist scholars of international relations make related arguments regarding international norms, which operate as a social structure. States, embedded in a dense network of social relations that shape their judgments, define their interests according to "internationally shared norms and values that structure and give meaning to international political life" (Finnemore, 1996, p. 3; see also Katzenstein, 1996; Tannenwald, 2007). Shared norms of what constitutes legitimate behavior may lead states to act according to more cooperative and multilateralist principles (Ruggie, 1993a; Finnemore, 2004;

Hurd, 2007). The simple notion of anarchy thus cannot capture the richness and order of the international system.

Scholars working in this area critique the rationalist underpinnings of regime theory and other institutionalists (see below) for failing to capture many of the dynamics of international cooperation and organization. States abide by rules and norms, even when it is not in their material interest, because they have a long-term interest in the maintenance of a "law-impregnated international community" and share a sense of "moral community" (Hurrell, 1993). Some of this work has attempted to integrate regime theory into the study of international society, arguing, for example, that functional theories of regimes are largely accurate but that international society is a precondition for their development (Buzan, 1993). Hurrell (1993) suggests that the field of international law can provide a bridge for understanding the interaction between normative structure and self-interested cooperation. This recognition that regime theory and the notion of a norm-laden international society are not mutually exclusive offers a promising path for future work in the study of IO and cooperation more generally.

7. IO as Regimes

Between the narrow understanding of formal organizations and the extremely broad understanding of ordering principles lies the now somewhat dated concept of "international regime". Regime theory is premised on the twin observations that international politics is highly interdependent (Keohane and Nye, 1977), thus implying mutual interests in cooperation, and that "international behavior is institutionalized" in a variety of ways (Ruggie, 1975, p. 559). There is agreement over these empirical phenomena, but the approach includes a diverse set of theoretical and methodological orientations. There has been wide adherence to a "standard" definition of regimes as "sets of implicit or explicit principles, norms, rules and decision-making procedures around which actors' expectations converge in a given area of international relations" (Krasner, 1983, p. 2). This very broad conception of regimes includes the endpoints as well as the vast middle ground between formal organizations and broader ordering principles in international relations.

The definition of regime has been criticized as being expansive to the point of vagueness (Strange, 1982). An unfortunate consequence is that an inordinate amount of effort has been expended in arguing about whether or not there is an effective regime in a particular area. The corresponding virtue is that this broad definition allows for a broader view of governance possibilities than is suggested by the narrower concern with formal institutions. The various categories in the definition also point towards a greater level of specificity than is often achieved by more ethereal discussions of ordering principles. Finally, the breadth of the definition leaves room for a plurality of approaches – liberal as well as realist, rationalist as well as constructivist. This has provided some unity to the field despite the diversity of approaches sometimes employed.

Much of the early regimes literature focused on explaining why states create international regimes and demonstrating that they "matter", that is, that they influence state behavior in a meaningful way. From the beginning, however, regime theorists were addressing issues such as why regimes change or evolve (Lipson, 1982) and how to measure a regime's effectiveness (Haas, Keohane and Levy, 1993; Bernauer, 1995). Regime theory has been applied to a wide variety of issue areas, including international security (Jervis, 1982; McCalla, 1996), trade (Finlayson and Zacher, 1981; Aggarwal, 1985; Yarbrough and Yarbrough, 1987), finance (Cohen, 1982; Lipson, 1985), human rights (Donnelly, 1986), telecommunications (Cowhey, 1990; Zacher, 1996; Sandholtz, 1993), and the environment (Young, 1989; Young and Osherenko, 1993; Haas, Keohane and Levy, 1993). International legal scholars have increasingly used regime theory to better understand issues such as international trade law, arms control agreements, and the law of treaties (Abbott, 1985; Smith, 1991; Setear, 1996; see also Aceves, 1997).

Scholars in the regime tradition have increasingly moved towards alternative terminology, including *institutions*, *multilateralism*, and *governance systems*, to describe phenomena of international organization that exist between formal organizations and broader elements of order in the international system (Ruggie, 1993a; Haas, Keohane and Levy, 1993; Young, 1989, 1997).

C. CONTEMPORARY THEORETICAL APPROACHES TO IO

8. Rationalist Regime Theory

The most substantial vein of regime theory relies on rational choice understandings of state behavior, where states were initially viewed as unified, self-interested actors (Keohane, 1984; Hasenclever, Mayer and Rittberger, 1997). We emphasize rationalist approaches because they are closest to the law and economics tradition.

Rationalist regime theory was a natural outgrowth of the increasing propensity among international relations scholars, beginning in the 1970s, to theorize international cooperation problems as analogous to "market failure". They used a public choice approach to problems such as public goods provision and externalities at the international level (Russett and Sullivan, 1971; Ruggie, 1972; Snidal, 1979; Fratianni and Pattison, 1982) and applied Coase's theory of property rights and bargaining to the process of international organization (Conybeare, 1980). But the most important move in the literature emerged from the "folk theorem" of economics and its result that decentralized cooperation can be an equilibrium outcome when a circumstance is repeated through time. This provided a response to the realist claim that the lack of centralized authority in anarchy prevents international cooperation. Indeed, by taking a Hobbesian specification of anarchy as akin to a prisoner's dilemma (Taylor, 1976), international relations theorists began to develop a theoretical argument that cooperation was not only possible in realist anarchy, it was in some sense likely (Axelrod, 1984). Thus the title of Oye's (1986) *Cooperation under Anarchy* reflected the emerging synthesis in the literature that international order did not require centralized institutions (see also Keohane and Ostrom, 1995).

The seminal work for the study of rationalist regime theory is Robert Keohane's *After Hegemony* (1984), which draws on rational choice logic and microeconomic theories to explain the continuing strength of international institutions. "Political market failure" is a central notion in Keohane's analysis: "Like imperfect markets, world politics is characterized by institutional deficiencies that inhibit mutually advantageous cooperation" (1984, p.85). While bargaining could in principle correct these failures (Coase, 1960), Keohane argues that the underlying conditions for Coasean logic to operate – well-defined property rights, perfect information, and zero transactions costs – do not naturally exist in the international system. Regimes serve to fill in these gaps. They also bring states together in a common forum, ensuring that they will interact repeatedly over time and thereby enhancing reputational incentives to comply and cooperate.

Rationalist regime theory and cooperation theory have been challenged in several important ways, especially as to whether their underlying assumptions truly apply in international relations. Possibly states, or their leaders, are not properly characterized as rational agents with the capacities or inclinations necessary to maintain decentralized cooperation. An alternative, realist critique is that states seek power and relative rather than absolute gains, limiting cooperation in international affairs (Grieco, 1988; Mearsheimer, 2001), but this argument has been countered by analyses demonstrating that these limits are not great (Snidal, 1991; Powell, 1991). A more important limitation of early regime theory is that it did not address the substantial variation we see across institutions at the international level. It helps us understand the rise of international organization but not its form.

9. Institutional Variation and Design

More recently, many international relations and legal scholars have focused on the design of IGOs and international agreements. These writers go beyond explaining the general demand for international regimes (Keohane, 1982, 1984) to provide explanations for why institutions vary and for their particular design features. They use the detailed study of institutions to draw broad theoretical implications about international cooperation in a manner consistent with the goals of rationalist regime theory.

The earliest studies on variation and design looked at broad-gauge differences across institutions and sought to explain these as a function of the strategic problem facing states. Using insights from game theory, for example, Snidal (1985) and Stein (1982) argued that states facing prisoner's dilemma-type problems should create more robust institutions, with monitoring and enforcement, whereas coordination problems require only minimal institutionalization since they have self-enforcing equilibria. Other scholars were drawn to the related question of why some agreements and organizations are stronger or more formalized than others, and sought to identify the tradeoffs presented by these design choices (Lipson, 1991; Kahler, 1996; Martin, 1992).

Related to these theoretical developments was the introduction of the new economics of organization (NEO) – or transaction cost economics – into the study of international organization. In the early 1990s, economists began to notice "striking parallels between the central questions of NEO and those of international relations" (Yarbrough and Yarbrough, 1990). An important aspect of this NEO wave is an attempt to theorize the organizational design of international institutions rather than treating them as black boxes. The assumption is that states create institutions with the governance structures intended to be the most effective, resulting in a variety of institutional forms. Yarbrough and Yarbrough (1992) use an NEO approach to explain why international trade liberalization has taken unilateral, bilateral, minilateral and multilateral forms over time. Lake (1996) builds on NEO to present a theory of contracting whereby organizational choice in security relations – which varies on a continuum from anarchic alliances to hierarchic empires – is determined by considerations of transaction costs and the risk of opportunism. Other political scientists have explained the institution of state sovereignty through this lens (Spruyt, 1994; Cooley and Spruyt, 2009). International lawyers have similarly applied transaction costs economics to explain variation in legal institutions (Aceves, 1996; Trachtman, 1997).

The more recent rational design literature draws on a number of independent variables (factors that shape institutional design) to explain outcomes (institutional design features). For example, the most comprehensive treatment seeks to explain the scope, centralization, decisionmaking rules, and flexibility of institutions as a function of distribution and enforcement problems, the number and asymmetry of actors involved, and uncertainty (Koremenos, Lipson and Snidal, 2004). In studies of economic, environmental, and security arrangements, institutional flexibility – in the form of escape clauses, adaptable rules, and duration provisions – is attributed to various types of uncertainty (Koremenos, 2001; Rosendorff, 2005; Thompson, 2010; Downs and Rocke, 1995). The legal literature has built on this to examine the design of international agreements, with special attention to features such as exit clauses, reservations, dispute resolution and monitoring (Helfer, 2005; Guzman, 2005; Swaine, 2006). One interesting finding in this literature is that states are willing to create institutions that are quite independent if doing so helps them achieve joint gains more efficiently over the long term (Abbott and Snidal, 1998; Haftel and Thompson, 2006; Garrett and Weingast, 1993), although they also take measures to protect themselves in case of breach. What unites these works is an attempt to explain institutional outcomes as a result of rational choices by states to solve specific cooperation problems.

An important branch of the design literature, and one that unites political scientists and legal scholars, explores variation in the "legalization" of international institutions. Goldstein et al. (2001) define legalization as a form of institutionalization characterized by three dimensions: obligation (binding rules), precision (specific rules), and delegation (reliance on third parties to implement rules, create rules or resolve disputes). As Abbott and Snidal (2000) note, "hard" law is not inherently superior to softer forms; the choice between them depends on what types of problems states are seeking to address. For example, harder forms of law are more effective when it comes to deterring violations, but they may also deter participation in the first place, creating an incentive for softer forms (von Stein, 2008). Thus soft law may be a stepping stone on the way to hard law, but it can also be a rational institutional outcome in its own right. Pollack and Shaffer (2009) provide an important extension and application that looks at the interaction of hard and soft law regimes.

10. Compliance and Effectiveness

One critique of rational design theory is that it assumes states will choose efficient institutional solutions without exploring whether in fact such institutions are more effective (Wendt, 2001). Contemporary scholars of IO have spent considerable energy addressing the question of why some agreements and IGOs are more effective than others, including the related question of why some elicit higher rates of compliance.

The question of why states comply or fail to comply with international rules has sparked debate in the fields of international law and international relations. The answer has important implications for whether and how international institutions matter. The literature is divided between norm-based and instrumentalist models (Hathaway, 2005; Keohane, 1997). For legal scholars who focus on the normative characteristics of law, states feel an internalized obligation to comply with international rules which exert an independent "compliance pull" (Franck, 1990). This view resonates with constructivist scholars who stress the importance of international norms in shaping state behavior and interests (Katzenstein, 1996; Finnemore, 1996).

Instrumentalists view the compliance decision as one based on calculations of self-interest. Pessimists in this tradition argue that states create institutions to reflect their interests and thus little change in behavior is required for compliance

(Downs, Rocke and Barsoom, 1996). The realist variant of this logic denies that international law and institutions have any independent effect on the actions of states; compliance occurs either when it is costless or when powerful states promote it (Mearsheimer 1994–5; Goldsmith and Posner, 2005). Other instrumentalists are more optimistic, however, stressing the incentives to comply that result from concerns over reputation and reciprocity (Guzman, 2008; Simmons, 2000) – although Brewster (2009) offers a useful critique. Finally, others show how power and the use of law are inextricably intertwined through their institutional setting (Steinberg, 2002).

The "managerial school" of compliance begins from the premise that compliance with international agreements is generally high, and that violations are the result of legal ambiguities, inadvertence, or the incapacity of states to comply rather than calculated "cheating" (Chayes and Chayes, 1993, 1995). Moreover, the incidence of this non-compliance is partly a function of how the relevant international institutions are designed, implying that one pathway to higher rates of compliance lies in improved institutional design (Mitchell, 1994a, 1994b; Sand, 1990). The resulting arguments are thus prescriptive as well as descriptive.

Compliance should not be conflated with effectiveness, defined as the real-world impact of an agreement or institution on the problem it is intended to address. Even high rates of compliance will not produce positive outcomes if the rules themselves are not well suited to the task. A substantial literature on "regime effectiveness" explores these issues both theoretically and empirically, with an emphasis on environmental issues (Young, 1999; Miles et al., 2002; Helm and Sprinz, 2000). Many IGOs have been subject to systematic assessments of their effectiveness, including the IMF (Vreeland, 2003), the World Bank (Flores and Nooruddin, 2009), and the UN in its peacekeeping role (Fortna, 2008), and there is increased interest in studying the performance of IGOs (Gutner and Thompson, 2010). These studies pose various methodological problems, as it is often difficult to discern the causal impact of a particular organization or set of rules in a context where many political and economic factors are at play.

11. Actors beyond the State

While much of the theoretical literature treats states as the main actors in IO, there is increasing recognition that a state-centric model is outmoded. Scholars now focus considerable attention on a wide range of actors, both private and public, that operate across national boundaries.

Building from past work on 'transnational relations' (Keohane and Nye, 1972), the literature on globalization stresses the large and growing number of non-state actors in the international system, such as firms, private associations, and religious groups (Cerny, 1990; Krugman, 1995; Risse-Kappen, 1995; Gupta, 1997). The fact that economic and other transactions increasingly take place without regard to national boundaries has important implications for international politics. One conclusion drawn by globalization theorists is that the traditional state has become structurally inappropriate as a political unit, leading some to consider whether globalization has gone too far (Rodrik, 1997). In terms of international organization, Philip Cerny argues that the "residual state" will no longer be the most important entity driving collective action in the international system and will not be able to provide global public goods, such as the regulation of the world market (Cerny, 1995; see also McGrew and Lewis, 1992; Ruggie, 1993b; Strange, 1996).

The result of globalization may be increased reliance on private sources of governance that are more flexible and appropriate, such as interfirm alliances (Dunning, 1997), international NGOs (Boli and Thomas, 1999), and looser networks of activists (Keck and Sikkink, 1998). The complexity of contemporary governance also creates a more important role for governmental actors below the level of the state, as regulators seek to solve technical problems of a transnational nature (Slaughter, 2004). One possibility is that governmental and non-governmental actors will increasingly have to work together to solve important political problems, in the form of public-private partnerships (Abbott and Snidal, 2010; Andonova, 2010).

International relations scholars are also increasingly comfortable with the idea of treating IGOs themselves as actors. Rationalists usually think of this in terms of delegation, where states (as principals) have incentives to delegate tasks to IGOs (as agents) if the latter can perform them more efficiently (Hawkins et al., 2006; Bradley and Kelley, 2008). IGO bureaucracies are now important players in some areas of global governance (Biermann and Siebenhüner, 2009). Once this delegation takes place, however, there are limits to the ability of states to control their IGO agents, and indeed the latter may seek to carve out more autonomy over time. Important examples come from courts and the behavior of international judges (Alter, 2008; Voeten, 2008; Posner and de Figueiredo, 2005; Burley and Mattli, 1993). Scholars working in the sociological tradition have outlined various sources of IGO autonomy and explored some of the problems that can result when the staff develop their own goals and culture (Barnett and Finnemore, 2004). The issue of delegation and IGO autonomy has arguably become more acute with the increase, noted above, in emanations, and scholars debate the consequences for democratic principles of having substantial authority delegated to the international level (Keohane, Macedo and Moravcsik, 2009).

While there is widespread agreement that the state is now joined by a host of other actors in supplying global governance, there is no consensus on what this means for the future of the state. Globalization has resulted in transfers of authority (Kahler and Lake, 2003), to be sure, but there is no clear successor to the state in the foreseeable future.

D. CONCLUSION

Theorists and practitioners have employed a number of differing conceptions of "international organization". These conceptions can usefully be thought of as falling into three categories: IO as formal organization, IO as ordering principle in the international system, and IO as regime. All three have informed a vibrant literature on the sources and effects of international institutions and global governance.

Political scientists who study IO have begun in recent years to return to the study of formal organizations, though this time they have done so with explicitly theoretical intentions (Snidal, 1997). At the same time, international legal scholars have sought to meet international relations theorists halfway. The result is a self-conscious effort from both sides to integrate the two fields (Abbott, 1989; Burley, 1993; Keohane, 1997). In his treatment of the negotiations on dispute resolution in the Uruguay Round of GATT, for example, Abbott (1992, p. 112) recognizes that "meaningful analysis of matters like these requires a theoretical framework". Burley (1993, p. 222; Slaughter, Tulumello and Wood, 1998) offers an historical account of the interaction of the law and international relations literatures and suggests some "components of an institutionalist interdisciplinary dialogue". This "dual agenda" includes the study of organizational design, compliance, and international ethics, and suggests that the future of IO scholarship will be more interdisciplinary than ever before.

Indeed, common concerns and methodology among political scientists, legal scholars and economists increasingly characterize the IO literature. More than ever, international legal scholars are using modes of analysis drawn from political science and economics to understand international organizations and law (Trachtman, 2008; Guzman, 2008; Bhandari and Sykes, 1997; Mock, 1992; Shell, 1995; Aceves, 1996; Chang, 1995; Colombatto and Macey, 1996; Setear 1996). This interdisciplinary movement is clearly evident in substantive work on compliance with international rules and on dispute settlement. Scholars from various traditions have come together to understand why nations comply with international law and institutional rules (Mitchell, 1994a; Keohane, 1992; Downs, Rocke and Barsoom, 1996; Cameron, Werksman and Roderick, 1996; Chayes and Chayes, 1995; Franck, 1990, 1995; Koh, 1997), as well as the development of supranational adjudication in international organizations (Alter, 2001; Helfer and Slaughter, 1997; Horlick and DeBusk, 1993; Hudec, 1990; Jackson, 1994; Kovenoch and Thursby, 1992; Pescatore, 1993; Yarbrough and Yarbrough, 1997). Through this intellectual interaction, the study of international organization, like the practice of international governance itself, is becoming more energized and, one hopes, more sophisticated.

As far as the practice of IO is concerned, the future is likely to be much more complicated than the past in terms of the complexity of the issues to be addressed and the variety of actors, both public and private, that will supply governance functions. Contemplating this question, one group of scholars asks provocatively "who governs the globe?" (Avant, Finnemore and Sell, 2010). While states will be the most important actors for the foreseeable future, they will continue to face challengers and partners from above and below.

Bibliography

Abbott, Kenneth W. (1985), "The Trading Nation's Dilemma: The Functions of the Law of International Trade", 26 *Harvard International Law Journal*, 501–32.

Abbott, Kenneth W. (1989), "Modern International Relations Theory: A Prospectus for International Lawyers", 14(2) *Yale Journal of International Law*, 335–411.

Abbott, Kenneth W. (1992), "The Uruguay Round and Dispute Resolution: Building a Private-Interests System of Justice", 1 *Columbia Business Law Review*, 111–49.

Abbott, Kenneth W. and Snidal, Duncan (1998), "Why States Act through Formal International Organizations", 41(1) *Journal of Conflict Resolution*, 3–32.

Abbott, Kenneth W. and Snidal, Duncan (2000), "Hard and Soft Law in International Governance", *International Organization*, 421–56.

Abbott, Kenneth W. and Snidal, Duncan (2010), "International Regulation without International Government: Improving International Organization Performance Through Orchestration", *Review of International Organizations*: 315–44.

Aceves, William J. (1996), "The Economic Analysis of International Law: Transaction Cost Economics and the Concept of State Practice", 17 *University of Pennsylvania Journal of International Economic Law*, 995–1068.

Aceves, William J. (1997), "Institutionalist Theory and International Legal Scholarship", 12 *American University Journal of International Law and Policy*, 227–66.

Aggarwal, Vinod (1985), *Liberal Protectionism: The International Politics of Organized Textile Trade*, Berkeley, CA: University of California Press.

Alter, Karen J. (2001), *Establishing the Supremacy of European Law: The Making of an International Rule of Law in Europe*, Oxford: Oxford University Press.

Alter, Karen J. (2008), "Agents or Trustees? International Courts in their Political Context", 14 *European Journal of International Relations*, 33–63.

Alter, Karen J. and Meuner, Sophie (2009), "The Politics of International Regime Complexity", *Perspectives on Politics*, 13–24.

Amerasinghe, Chittharanjan (1996), *Principles of International Law of International Organizations*, Cambridge: Cambridge University Press.

Andonova, Liliana B. (2010), "Public-Private Partnerships for the Earth: Politics and Patterns of Hybrid Authority", 10 *Global Environmental Politics*, 25–53.

Archer, Clive (1983), *International Organizations*, Winchester: Allen and Unwin.

Arend, Anthony Clark (1998), "Do Legal Rules Matter? International Law and International Politics", 38 *Virginia Journal of International Law*, 107–53.

Armstrong, Kenneth and Bulmer, Simon (1998), *The Governance of the Single European Market*, New York: St Martin's Press.

Avant, Deborah D., Finnemore, Martha and Sell, Susan K. (eds) (2010), *Who Governs the Globe?*, New York: Cambridge University Press.

Axelrod, R. (1984), *The Evolution of Cooperation*, New York: Basic Books.

Barnett, Michael and Finnemore, Martha (2004), *Rules for the World: International Organizations in World Politics*, Ithaca, NY: Cornell University Press.

Beitz, Charles R. (1979), *Political Theory and International Politics*, Princeton, NJ: Princeton University Press.

Bernauer, Thomas (1995), "The Effect of International Environmental Institutions: How We Might Learn More", 49 *International Organization*, 351–77.

Bhandari, Jagdeep S. and Sykes, Alan O. (eds) (1997), *Economic Dimensions in International Law: Comparative and Empirical Perspectives*, Cambridge: Cambridge University Press.

Biermann, Frank and Siebenhüner, Bernd (eds) (2009), *Managers of Global Change: The Influence of International Environmental Bureaucracies*, Cambridge, MA: MIT Press.
Biersteker, Thomas and Weber, Cynthia (eds) (1996), *State Sovereignty as Social Construct*, New York: Cambridge University Press.
Black, Cyril E. and Falk, Richard A. (eds) (1969), *The Future of the International Legal Order, Vol. 1 Trends and Patterns*, Princeton, NJ: Princeton University Press.
Boli, John and George M. Thomas (eds.) (1999), *Constructing World Culture: International Non-governmental Organizations since 1875*, Stanford, CA: Stanford University Press.
Bradley, Curtis A. and Kelley, Judith G. (2008), "The Concept of International Delegation", 71 *Law and Contemporary Problems*, 1–36.
Brewster, Rachel (2009), "Unpacking the State's Reputation", 50 *Harvard International Law Journal*, 231–69.
Bull, Hedley (1977), *The Anarchical Society: A Study of Order in World Politics*, New York: Columbia University Press.
Burley, Anne-Marie (1993), "International Law and International Relations Theory: A Dual Agenda", 87 *American Journal of International Law*, 205–39.
Burley, Anne-Marie and Mattli, Walter (1993), "Europe before the Court: A Political Theory of Legal Integration", 47 *International Organization*, 41–76.
Buzan, Barry (1993), "From International System to International Society: Structural Realism and Regime Theory Meet the English School", 47 *International Organization*, 327–52.
Cameron, James, Werksman, Jacob and Roderick, Peter (eds) (1996), *Improving Compliance with International Environmental Law*, London: Earthscan Publications.
Carr, Edward H. (1939), *The Twenty Years' Crisis, 1919–1939*, London and New Jersey: Zed Books.
Cerny, Philip (1990), *The Changing Architecture of Politics: Structure, Agency, and the Future of the State*, London: Sage.
Cerny, Philip (1995), "Globalization and the Changing Logic of Collective Action", 49 *International Organization*, 595–625.
Chang, Howard F. (1995), "An Economic Analysis of Trade Measures to Protect the Global Environment", 83 *Georgetown Law Journal*, 2131–213.
Charnovitz, Steve (1996), "Participation of Nongovernmental Organizations in the World Trade Organization", 17 *University of Pennsylvania Journal of International Business Law*, 331–58.
Chayes, Abram and Chayes, Antonio Handler (1993), "On Compliance", 47(2) *International Organization*, 175–206.
Chayes, Abram and Chayes, Antonio Handler (1995), *The New Sovereignty: Compliance with International Regulatory Agreements*, Cambridge, MA: Harvard University Press.
Claude, I.L. (1962), *Power and International Relations*, New York: Random House.
Claude, I.L. (1964), *Swords into Plowshares*, 3rd edn, London: University of London Press.
Coase, Ronald H. (1960), "The Problem of Social Cost", 3 *Journal of Law and Economics*, 1–44.
Cohen, Benjamin (1982), "Balance-of-Payments Financing: Evolution of a Regime", 36(2) *International Organization*, 457–78.
Colombatto, Enrico and Macey, Jonathan R. (1996), "A Public Choice Model of International Economic Cooperation and the Decline of the Nation State", 18 *Cardozo Law Review*, 925–56.
Conybeare, John (1980), "International Organization. and the Theory of Property Rights", 34 *International Organization*, 307–34.
Cooley, Alexander and Spruyt, Hendrik (2009), *Contracting States: Sovereign Transfers in International Relations*, Princeton, NJ: Princeton University Press.
Cowhey, P. (1990), "The International Telecommunications Regime: The Political Roots of International Regimes for High Technology", 44 *International Organization*, 169–99.
Cox, Robert W. (1996), *Approaches to World Order*, Cambridge: Cambridge University Press.
Cox, Robert W. and Jacobson, Harold K. (1974), *The Anatomy of Influence: Decision Making in International Organization*, New Haven, CT: Yale University Press.
Donnelly, Jack (1986), "International Human Rights: a Regime Analysis", 40 *International Organization*, 599–642.
Downs, George and Rocke, David (1995), *Optimal Imperfection? Domestic Uncertainty and Institutions in International Relations*, Princeton, NJ: Princeton University Press.

Downs, George, Rocke, David and Barsoom, Peter (1996), "Is the Good News about Compliance Good News about Cooperation?", 50 *International Organization*, 379–406.

Dunning, John H. (1997), *Alliance Capitalism and Global Business*, New York, NY: Routledge.

Dupuy, Rene Jean (ed.) (1988), *A Handbook on International Organisations*, Hingham, MA: Kluwer.

Eichengreen, Barry and Frieden, Jeffry (1994), *The Political Economy of European Monetary Unification*, Boulder, CO: Westview Press.

Falk, Richard A. (1969), "The Interplay of Westphalia and Charter Conceptions of International Legal Order", in Black, Cyril E. and Falk, Richard A. (eds), *The Future of the International Legal Order, Vol. 1 Trends and Patterns*, Princeton, NJ: Princeton University Press, 32–72.

Fawcett, Louise and Andrew Hurrell (eds) (1995), *Regionalism in World Politics*, New York: Oxford University Press.

Fearon, James (1998), "Bargaining, Enforcement, and International Cooperation", 52 *International Organization*, 269–305.

Feld, Werner J. and Jordan, Robert S. (1988), *International Organizations: A Comparative Approach*, 2nd edn, New York: Praeger.

Finlayson, Jock and Zacher, Mark (1981), "The GATT and the Regulation of Trade Barriers: Regime Dynamics and Functions", 35(4) *International Organization*, 561–602.

Finnemore, Martha (1996), *National Interests in International Society*, Ithaca, NY: Cornell University Press.

Finnemore, Martha (2004), *The Purpose of Intervention: Changing Beliefs about the Use of Force*, Ithaca, NY: Cornell University Press.

Flores, Thomas E. and Nooruddin, Irfan (2009), "Financing the Peace: Evaluation World Bank Post-Conflict Assistance Programs", *Review of International Organizations*, 1–27.

Fortna, Virginia Page (2008), *Does Peacekeeping Work? Shaping Belligerents' Choices after Civil War*, Princeton, NJ: Princeton University Press.

Franck, Thomas M. (1990), *The Power of Legitimacy among Nations*, Oxford: Oxford University Press.

Franck, Thomas M. (1995), *Fairness in International Law and Institutions*, Oxford: Oxford University Press.

Fratianni, Michele and Pattison, John (1982), "The Economics of International Organizations", 35 *Kyklos*, 244–62.

Garrett, Geoffrey (1992), "International Cooperation and Institutional Choice: The European Community's Internal Market", 46(2) *International Organization*, 533–60.

Garrett, Geoffrey (1995), "The Politics of Legal Integration in the European Union", 46 *International Organization*, 533–60.

Garrett, Geoffrey and Weingast, B. (1993), "Ideas, Interests, and Institutions: Constructing the European Community's Internal Market", in Goldstein, J. and Keohane, R. (eds), *Ideas and Foreign Policy: Beliefs, Institutions, and Political Change*, Ithaca, NY: Cornell University Press, 173–206.

Gilpin, Robert (1981), *War and Change in International Politics*, Cambridge: Cambridge University Press.

Glaser, Charles (1994–5), "Realists as Optimists: Cooperation as Self-Help", 19 *International Security*, 50–90.

Glaser, Charles (2010), *Rational Theory of International Politics: The Logic of Competition and Cooperation*, Princeton, NJ: Princeton University Press.

Goldsmith, Jack and Posner, Eric A. (2005), *The Limits of International Law*, New York: Oxford University Press.

Goldstein, Judith, L. Kahler, Miles, Keohane, Robert O. and Slaughter, Anne-Marie (eds) (2001), *Legalization and World Politics*, Cambridge, MA: MIT Press.

Gowa, Joanne (1994), *Allies, Adversaries, and International Trade*, Princeton, NJ: Princeton University Press.

Grieco, Joseph (1988), "Anarchy and the Limits of Cooperation: A Realist Critique of the Newest Liberal Institutionalism", 42 *International Organization*, 485–507.

Groom, A.J.R. and Taylor, Paul G. (1975), *Functionalism: Theory and Practice in International Relations*, London: University of London Press.

Grotius, Hugo ([1625] 1925), *De Jure Belli ac Pacis*, trans. Francis W. Kelsey, Oxford: Clarendon.

Gruber, Lloyd (2000), *Ruling the World: Power Politics and the Rise of Supranational Institutions*, Princeton, NJ: Princeton University Press.

Gupta, S. (ed.) (1997), *The Political Economy of Globalization*, Boston, MA: Kluwer.

Gutner, Tamar and Thompson, Alexander (2010), "The Politics of IO Performance: A Framework", *Review of International Organizations*, 227–48.

Guzman, Andrew T. (2005), "The Design of International Agreements", 16 *European Journal of International Law*, 579–612.

Guzman, Andrew T. (2008), *How International Law Works: A Rational Choice Theory*, New York: Oxford University Press.

Haas, Ernst B. (1961), "International Integration: The European and the Universal Process", 15 *International Organization*, 366–397.

Haas, Ernst B. (1964), *Beyond the Nation-State: Functionalism and International Organization*, Stanford, CA: Stanford University Press.

Haas, Ernst B. (1975), *The Obsolescence of Regional Integration Theory*, Berkeley, MA: University of California Press.

Haas, Peter, Keohane, Robert O. and Levy, Marc A. (1993), *Institutions for the Earth: Sources of Effective International Environmental Protection*, Cambridge, MA: MIT Press.

Haftel, Yoram Z. (2007), "Designing for Peace: Regional Integration Arrangements, Institutional Variation, and Militarized Interstate Disputes", *International Organization*, 217–37.

Haftel, Yoram Z. and Thompson, Alexander (2006), "The Independence of International Organizations: Concept and Applications", *Journal of Conflict Resolution*, 253–75.

Hall, Rodney Bruce and Biersteker, Thomas J. (eds) (2002), *The Emergence of Private Authority in Global Governance*, New York: Cambridge University Press.

Hasenclever, Andreas, Mayer, Peter and Rittberger, Volker (1997), *Theories of International Regimes*, Cambridge: Cambridge University Press.

Hathaway, Oona A. (2005), "Between Power and Principle: An Integrated Theory of International Law", *University of Chicago Law Review*, 469–536.

Hawkins, Darren G., Lake, David A. Nielson, Daniel L. and Tierney, Michael J. (eds) (2006), *Delegation and Agency in International Organizations*, New York: Cambridge University Press.

Helfer, Laurence R. (2005), "Exiting Treaties", 91 *Virginia Law Review*, 1579–648.

Helfer, Laurence and Slaughter, Anne Marie (1997), "Toward a Theory of Effective Supranational Adjudication", 107 *Yale Law Journal*, 273–391.

Helm, Carsten and Sprinz, Detlef (2000), "Measuring the Effectiveness of International Environmental Regimes", *Journal of Conflict Resolution*, 630–52.

Hinsley, Francis H. (1963), *Power and the Pursuit of Peace: Theory and Practice in the History of Relations between States*, Cambridge: Cambridge University Press.

Horlick, Gary and DeBusk, Amanda (1993), "Dispute Resolution under NAFTA: Building on the U.S.-Canada FTA, GATT and ICSID", 27 *Journal of World Trade*, 21–41.

Hudec, Robert E. (1990), "Dispute Settlement", in Schott, Jeffrey (ed.), *Completing the Uruguay Round*, Washington, DC: Institute for International Economics, 180–204.

Hurd, Ian (2007), *After Anarchy: Legitimacy and Power in the United Nations Security Council*, Princeton, NJ: Princeton University Press.

Hurrell, Andrew (1993), "International Society and the Study of Regimes: A Reflective Approach", in Rittberger, Volker (ed.), *Regime Theory and International Relations*, Oxford: Oxford University Press, 49–72.

Jackson, John (1994), "The World Trade Organization, Dispute Settlement, and Codes of Conduct", in Collins, Susan and Bosworth, Barry (eds), *The New GATT*, Washington, DC: Brookings Institution.

Jacobson, H.K. (1984), *Networks of Interdependence: International Organizations and the Global Political System*, 2nd edn, New York: Alfred A. Knopf.

Jervis, Robert (1982), "Security Regimes", 36(2) *International Organization*, 357–78.

Jones, Seth G. (2007), *The Rise of European Security Cooperation*, New York: Cambridge University Press.

Kahler, Miles (1996), *International Institutions and the Political Economy of Integration*, Washington, DC: Brookings Institution.

Kahler, Miles and Lake, David A. (eds) (2003), *Governance in a Global Economy: Political Authority in Transition*, Princeton, NJ: Princeton University Press.

Kaplan, Morton (1957), *System and Process in International Politics*, New York: Wiley.

Karns, Margaret and Mingst, Karen (1990), *The United States and Multilateral Institutions*, Boston, MA: Unwin Hyman.

Katzenstein, Peter (ed.) (1996), *The Culture of National Security*, New York: Columbia University Press.

Keck, Margaret E. and Sikkink, Kathryn (1998), *Activists beyond Borders: Advocacy Networks in International Politics*, Ithaca, NY: Cornell University Press.

Kenen, Peter (1995), *Economic and Monetary Union in Europe: Moving beyond Maastricht*, Cambridge: Cambridge University Press.

Keohane, Robert O. (1982), "The Demand for International Regimes", 36(2) *International Organization*, 325–56.

Keohane, Robert O. (1984), *After Hegemony: Cooperation and Discord in the World Political Economy*, Princeton, NJ: Princeton University Press.

Keohane, Robert O. (1992), "Compliance with International Commitments: Politics within a Framework of Law", 86 *American Society of International Law Proceedings*, 176–80.

Keohane, Robert O. (1997), "International Relations and International Law: Two Optics", 38 *Harvard International Law Journal*, 487–502.

Keohane, Robert O., Macedo, Stephen and Moravcsik, Andrew (2009), "Democracy-Enhancing Multilateralism", 63 *International Organization*, 1–31.

Keohane, Robert O. and Nye, Joseph (eds) (1972), *Transnational Relations and World Politics*, Cambridge, MA: Harvard University Press.

Keohane, Robert O. and Nye, Joseph (1977), *Power and Interdependence: World Politics in Transition*, Boston, MA: Little Brown.

Keohane, Robert O. and Ostrom, Elinor (eds) (1995), *Local Commons and Global Interdependence: Heterogeneity and Cooperation in Two Domains*, Thousand Oaks, CA: Sage.

Kirgis, Frederic L. Jr. (1993), *International Organizations in their Legal Setting*, 2nd edn, St Paul, MN: West Publishing Company.

Koh, Harold (1997), "Why Do Nations Obey Inernational Law?", 106 *Yale Law Journal*, 2598–659.

Koremenos, Barbara (2001), "Loosening the Ties that Bind: A Learning Model of Agreement Flexibility", *International Organization*, 289–325.

Koremenos Barbara, Lipson, Charles and Snidal, Duncan (eds) (2004), *The Rational Design of International Institutions*, New York: Cambridge University Press.

Koskenniemi, Martti (1996), "The Place of Law in Collective Security", 17 *Michigan Journal of International Law*, 455–90.

Kovenoch, Dan and Thursby, Marie (1992), "GATT, Dispute Settlement and Cooperation", 4 *Economics and Politics*, 151–70.

Krasner, Stephen (1983), *International Regimes*, Ithaca, NY: Cornell University Press.

Krasner, Stephen (1985), *Structural Conflict: The Third World against Global Liberalism*, Berkeley, CA: University of California Press.

Krasner, Stephen (1999), *Sovereignty: Organized Hypocrisy*, Princeton, NJ: Princeton University Press.

Kratochwil, Friedrich and Ruggie, John G. (1986), "International Organization: A State of the Art on an Art of the State", 40(4) *International Organization*, 753–76.

Krugman, Paul R. (1995), "Growing World Trade: Causes and Consequences", *Brookings Papers on Economic Activity*, 327–77.

Kupchan, Charles (1997), "Regionalizing Europe's Security: The Case for a New Mitteleuropa", in Mansfield, Edward and Milner, Helen V. (eds), *The Political Economy of Regionalism*, New York: Columbia University Press, 209–39.

Kupchan, Charles and Kupchan, Clifford (1991), "Concerts, Collective Security, and the Future of Europe", 16(1) *International Security*, 151–98.

Lake, David (1996), "Anarchy, Hierarchy, and the Variety of International Relations", 50(1) *International Organization*, 1–34.

Lenin, Vladimir I. ([1917] 1939), *Imperialism: The Highest Stage of Capitalism*, New York: International Publisher.

Lindberg, Leon N. and Scheingold, Stuart (1971), *Regional Integration: Theory and Research*, Cambridge, MA: Harvard University Press.

Lipson, Charles (1982), "The Transformation of Trade: The Sources and Effects of Regime Change", 36 *International Organization*, 417–55.

Lipson, Charles (1985), *Standing Guard: Protecting Foreign Capital in the Nineteenth and Twentieth Centuries*, Berkeley, CA: University of California Press.

Lipson, Charles (1991), "Why Are Some International Agreements Informal?", 45 *International Organization*, 495–538.

Malone, David M. (ed.) (2004), *The UN Security Council: From the Cold War to the 21st Century*, Boulder, CO: Lynne Rienner.

Mansfield, Edward and Milner, Helen V. (eds) (1997), *The Political Economy of Regionalism*, New York: Columbia University Press.

Mansfield, Edward and Milner, Helen V. (1999), "The New Wave of Regionalism", *International Organization,* 589–627.

Martin, Lisa L. (1992), "Interests, Power, and Multilateralism", *International Organization,* 765–92.

McCalla, Robert B. (1996), "NATO's Persistence after the Cold War", 50 *International Organization*, 445–75.

McGrew, Anthony and Lewis, Paul (1992), *Global Politics: Globalization and the Nation-State*, Cambridge, MA: Blackwell.

Mearsheimer, John (1994–5), "The False Promise of International Institutions", 19 *International Security*, 5–49.

Mearsheimer, John (2001), *The Tragedy of Great Power Politics*, New York: W.W. Norton.

Miles, Edward L., Underdal, Arild, Andresen, Steinar, Wettestad, Jørgen, Skjaerseth, Jon Birger and Carlin, Elaine M. (2002), *Environmental Regime Effectiveness*, Cambridge, MA: MIT Press.

Miller, Lynn H. (1999), "The Idea and Reality of Collective Security", 5(3) *Global Governance*, 303–32

Milner, Helen V. (1991), "The Assumption of Anarchy in International Relations Theory", 17 *Review of International Studies*, 67–85.

Milner, Helen V. (1997), *Interests, Institutions and Information*, Princeton, NJ: Princeton University Press.

Mingst, Karen A. and Margaret P. Karns (2007), *The United Nations in the 21st Century*, 3rd edn, Boulder, CO: Westview Press.

Mitchell, Ronald B. (1994a), *Intentional Oil Pollution at Sea: Environmental Policy and Treaty Compliance*, Cambridge, MA: MIT Press.

Mitchell, Ronald B. (1994b), "Regime Design Matters: Intentional Oil Pollution and Treaty Compliance", 48 *International Organization*, 425–58.

Mitrany, David ([1943] 1966), *A Working Peace System: An Argument for the Functional Development of International Organization*, Chicago: Quadrangle Press.

Mock, William B.T. (1992), "Game Theory, Signalling, and International Legal Relations", 26 *George Washington Journal of International Law and Economics*, 33–60.

Moravcsik, Andrew (1998), *The Choice for Europe: Social Purpose and State Power from Messina to Maastricht*, Ithace, NY: Cornell University Press.

Moravcsik, Andrew (2000), "The Origins of Human Rights Regimes: Democratic Delegation in Postwar Europe", *International Organization*, 217–52.

Morgenthau, Hans (1948), *Politics Among Nations*, New York: Alfred A. Knopf.

Morrow, James (1994), "Modeling the Forms of International Cooperation: Distribution versus Information", 48 *International Organization*, 387–424.

Nugent, Neill (1994), *The Government and Politics of the European Union*, Durham, NC: Duke University Press.

Nye, Joseph (ed.) (1968), *International Regionalism*, Boston, MA: Little Brown.
Nye, Joseph (1971), *Peace in Parts: Integration and Conflict in Regional Organization*, Boston, MA: Little Brown.
Oye, Kenneth A. (ed.) (1986), *Cooperation under Anarchy*, Princeton, NJ: Princeton University Press.
Pescatore, Pierre (1993), "The GATT Dispute Settlement Mechanism", 27 *Journal of World Trade*, 5–20.
Peterson, M.J. (1986), *The General Assembly in World Politics*, Boston, MA: Unwin Hyman.
Pevehouse, Jon C., Nordstrom, Timothy and Warnke, Kevin (2004), "The Correlates of War 2 International Governmental Organizations Data Version 2.0", *Conflict Management and Peace Science*, 101–19.
Pollack, Mark A. and Shaffer, Gregory C. (2009), *When Cooperation Fails: The International Law and Politics of Genetically Modified Foods*, New York: Oxford University Press.
Posner, Eric A. and de Figueiredo, Miguel (2005), "Is the International Court of Justice Biased?", 34 *Journal of Legal Studies*, 599–630.
Powell, Robert (1991), "Absolute and Relative Gains in International Relations Theory", 85 *American Political Science Review*, 1303–20.
Price, Richard M. and Zacher, Mark W. (eds) (2004), *The United Nations and Global Security*, New York: Palgrave Macmillan.
Putman, Robert (1988), "Diplomacy and Domestic Politics: The Logic of Two-Level Games", 42 *International Organization*, 427–60.
Raustiala, Kal (1997), "States, NGOs and International Environmental Institutions", *International Studies Quarterly*, 719–40.
Reinalda, Bob (2009), *Routledge History of International Organizations*, New York: Routledge.
Risse-Kappen, Thomas (1995), *Bringing Transnational Relations Back In: Non-State Actors, Domestic Structures and International Institutions*, Cambridge: Cambridge University Press.
Roberts, Adam (1993), "The United Nations and International Security", 35(2) *Survival*, 3–30.
Rochester, J. Martin (1986), "The Rise and Fall of International Organization as a Field of Study", 40(4) *International Organization*, 777–813.
Rodrik, Dani (1997), *Has Globalization Gone Too Far?*, Washington, DC: Institute for International Economics.
Rodrik, Dani, Obstfeld, Maurice, Feenstra, Robert and Williamson, Jeffrey (1998), "Symposium on Globalization in Perspective", 12(4) *Journal of Economic Perspectives*, 3–72.
Rosendorff, Peter B. (2005), "Stability and Rigidity: Politics and Design of the WTO"s Dispute Settlement Procedure", *American Political Science Review*, 389–99.
Rosenau, James N. and Czempiel, Ernst-Otto (1992), *Governance without Government: Order and Change in World Politics*, Cambridge, Ontario: Collier-MacMillan.
Ruggie, John G. (1972), "Collective Goods and Future International Collaboration", 66 *American Political Science Review*, 874–93.
Ruggie, John G. (1975), "International Responses to Technology: Concepts and Trends", 29 *International Organization*, 557–83.
Ruggie, John G. (1993a), *Multilateralism Matters: The Theory and Praxis of an Institutional Form*, New York: Columbia University Press.
Ruggie, John G. (1993b), "Territoriality and Beyond: Problematizing Modernity in International Relations", 47 *International Organization*, 139–74.
Russett, Bruce M. and Sullivan, John D. (1971), "Collective Goods and International Organizations", 25 *International Organization*, 845–65.
Sand, Peter H. (1990), *Lessons Learned in Global Environmental Governance*, Washington, DC: World Resources Institute.
Sandholtz, Wayne (1993), "Institutions and Collective Action: the New Telecommunications in Western Europe", 45 *World Politics*, 242–70.
Sandholtz, Wayne and Stone Sweet, Alex (eds) (1998), *European Integration and Supranational Governance*, New York: Oxford University Press.
Schachter, Oscar and Joyner, Christopher (eds) (1995), *United Nations Legal Order*, 2 vols, Cambridge: Cambridge University Press.

Schermers, Henry and Blokker, Niels (1995), *International Institutional Law: Unity within Diversity*, 3rd edn, The Hague: Mouton.
Schroeder, Paul W. (1994), *The Transformation of European Politics, 1763–1848*, Oxford: Clarendon.
Setear, John K. (1996), "An Iterative Perspective on Treaties: A Synthesis of International Relations Theory and International Law", 37 *Harvard International Law Journal*, 139–229.
Shanks, Cheryl, Jacobson, H.K. and Kaplan, Jeffrey H. (1996), "Inertia and Change in the Constellation of International Governmental Organizations, 1981–1992", 50(4) *International Organization*, 593–627.
Shell, Richard G. (1995), "Trade Legalism and International Relations Theory: An Analysis of the World Trade Organization", 44 *Duke Law Journal*, 829–927.
Shermers, Henry and Blokker, Niels (1995), *International Institutional Law: Unity within Diversity*, 3rd edn, The Hague: Nijhoff.
Simmons, Beth (2000), "International Law and State Behavior: Commitment and Compliance in International Monetary Affairs", *American Political Science Review*, 819–35.
Skjelsbaek, Kjell (1971), "The Growth of International Nongovernmental Organizations in the Twentieth Century", 25 *International Organization*, 420–442.
Slaughter, Anne-Marie (2004), *A New World Order*, Princeton: NJ, Princeton University Press.
Slaughter, Anne-Marie, Tulumello, Andrew and Wood, Stepan (1998), "International Law and International Relations Theory: A New Generation of Interdisciplinary Scholarship", 92(3) *American Journal of International Law*, 367–97.
Smith, Edwin M. (1991), "Understanding Dynamic Obligations: Arms Control Agreements", 64 *Southern California Law Review*, 1549–606.
Snidal, Duncan (1979), "Public Goods, Property Rights, and Political Organization", 23(4) *International Studies Quarterly*, 532–66.
Snidal, Duncan (1985), "Coordination versus Prisoners' Dilemma: Implications for International Cooperation and Regimes", 79 *American Political Science Review*, 923–43.
Snidal, Duncan (1991), "Relative Gains and the Pattern of International Cooperation", 85 *American Political Science Review*, 701–26.
Snidal, Duncan (1997), "International Political Economy Approaches to International Institutions", in Bhandari, Jagdeep S. and Sykes, Alan O. (eds), *Economic Dimensions in International Law: Comparative and Empirical Perspectives*, Cambridge: Cambridge University Press, 477–512.
Spruyt, Hendrik (1994), "Institutional Selection in International Relations: State Anarchy as Order", 48 *International Organization*, 527–57.
Staiger, Robert (1995), "International Rules and Institutions for Trade Policy", in Jones, Ronald and Kenen, Peter (eds), *Handbook of International Economics*, Vol. 2, Amsterdam: North-Holland.
Stein, Arthur (1982), "Coordination and Collaboration Regimes in an Anarchic World", 36 *International Organization*, 299–324.
Steinberg, Richard H. (2002), "In the Shadow of Law or Power? Consensus-Based Bargaining and Outcomes in the GATT/WTO", 56 *International Organization*, 339–74.
Stiglitz, Joseph E. (2002), *Globalization and its Discontents*, New York: W.W. Norton.
Strange, Susan (1982), "Cave! Hic dragones: A Critique of Regime Analysis", 36(2) *International Organization*, 479–98.
Strange, Susan (1996), *The Retreat of the State*, Cambridge: Cambridge University Press.
Streit, Manfred E. and Voigt, Stefan (1996), "Toward Ever Closer Union – Or Ever Larger? Or Both? Entry to the European Union from the Perspective of Constitutional Economics", 16 *International Review of Law and Economics*, 385–8.
Swaine, Edward T. (2006), "Reserving", 31 *Yale Journal of International Law*, 307–66.
Sykes, Alan O. (1990), "Mandatory Retaliation for Breach of Trade Agreements: Some Thoughts on the Strategic Design of Section 301", 8 *Boston University International Law Journal*, 301–31.
Tannenwald, Nina (2007), *The Nuclear Taboo*, New York: Cambridge University Press.
Taylor, Michael (1976), *Anarchy and Cooperation*, London: Wiley.
Taylor, Paul G. (1993), *International Organization in the Modern World: The Regional and Global Process*, New York: Pinter Publishers.

Thakur, Ramesh (2006), *The United Nations, Peace and Security*, New York: Cambridge University Press.

Thompson, Alexander (2006), "Coercion through IOs: The Security Council and the Logic of Information Transmission", *International Organization*, 1–34.

Thompson, Alexander (2010), "Rational Design in Motion: Uncertainty and Flexibility in the Global Climate Regime", *European Journal of International Relations*, 269–96.

Trachtman, Joel P. (1997), "The Theory of the Firm and the Theory of International Economic Organization: Toward Comparative Institutional Analysis", *Northwestern Journal of International Law & Business*, 470–555.

Trachtman, Joel P. (2008), *The Economic Structure of International Law*, Cambridge, MA: Harvard University Press.

Union of International Associations (UIA) (various dates), *Yearbook of International Organizations 1997/1998*, Munich: K.G. Saur.

Virally, Michel (1972), *L'Organisation Mondiale (Global Organization)*, Paris: Armand Collin.

Voeten, Erik (2008), "The Impartiality of International Judges: Evidence from the European Court of Human Rights", *American Political Science Review*, 417–33.

von Stein, Jana (2008), "The International Law and Politics of Climate Change: Ratification of the United Nations Framework Convention and the Kyoto Protocol", *Journal of Conflict Resolution*, 243–68.

Vreeland, James Raymond (2003), *The IMF and Economic Development*, New York: Cambridge University Press.

Wallace, Michael D. and Singer, David J. (1970), "Intergovernmental Organization in the International System: A Quantitative Assessment", 24 *International Organization*, 239–287.

Wallerstein, Immanuel (1979), *The Capitalist World Economy*, Cambridge: Cambridge University Press.

Waltz, Kenneth N. (1959), *Man, State and War*, New York: Columbia University Press.

Waltz, Kenneth N. (1979), *Theory of International Politics*, Reading, MA: Addison-Wesley.

Weaver, Catherine (2008), *The Hypocrisy Trap: The World Bank and the Poverty of Reform*, Princeton, NJ: Princeton University Press.

Weiss, Thomas G. and Gordenker, Leon (1996), *NGOs, the UN, and Global Governance*, Boulder, CO: Lynne Rienner.

Wendt, Alexander (2001), "Driving with the Rearview Mirror: On the Rational Science of Institutional Design", *International Organization*, 1019–49.

Wight, Martin (1973), "The Balance of Power and International Order", in Alan, James (ed.), *The Bases of International Order*, Oxford: Oxford University Press, 85–115.

Wight, Martin (1977), *Systems of States*, Leicester: Leicester University Press.

Wilkinson, Rorden (2000), *Multilateralism and the World Trade Organization*, New York: Routledge.

Willets, Peter (1982), *Pressure Groups in the Global System: The Transnational Relations of Issue-Oriented Non-Governmental Organizations*, New York: St Martin"s Press.

Wittman, Donald A. (1991), "Nations and States: Mergers and Acquisitions; Dissolutions and Divorce", 81 *American Economic Review: Papers and Proceedings*, 126–9.

Woolf, Leonard (1916), *International Government*, 2nd edn, London: Allen and Unwin.

Yalem, Ronald J. (1966), "The Study of International Organization, 1920–65: A Survey of the Literature", 10 *Background*, 1–56.

Yarbrough, Beth V. and Yarbrough, Robert M. (1987), "Institutions for the Governance of Opportunism in International Trade", 3 *Journal of Law, Economics, and Organization*, 129–33.

Yarbrough, Beth V. and Yarbrough, Robert M. (1990), "International Institutions and the New Economics of Organization", 44(2) *International Organization*, 235–59.

Yarbrough, Beth V. and Yarbrough, Robert M. (1992), *Cooperation and Governance in International Trade*, Princeton, NJ: Princeton University Press.

Yarbrough, Beth V. and Yarbrough, Robert M. (1997), "Dispute Settlement in International Trade: Regionalism and Procedural Coordination", in Mansfield, Edward and Milner, Helen V. (eds), *The Political Economy of Regionalism*, New York: Columbia University Press, 134–63.

Yoder, Amos (1989), *The Evolution of the United Nations System*, New York: Crane Russak.

Young, Oran R. (1989), *International Cooperation: Building Regimes for Natural Resources and the Environment*, Ithaca, NY: Cornell University Press.

Young, Oran R. (ed.) (1997), *Global Governance: Drawing Insights from the Environmental Experience*, Cambridge, MA: MIT Press.

Young, Oran R. 1999. *The Effectiveness of International Environmental Regimes: Causal Connections and Behavioral Mechanisms*. Cambridge, MA: MIT Press.

Young, Oran R. and Osherenko, Gail (1993), *Polar Politics: Creating International Environmental Regimes*, Ithaca, NY: Cornell University Press.

Zacher, Mark with Sutton, Brent (1996), *Governing Global Networks: International Regimes for Transportation and Communications*, Cambridge: Cambridge University Press.

PART V

FEDERALISM, LEGAL HARMONIZATION AND DEVELOPMENT

18 Federalism

Robert P. Inman and Daniel L. Rubinfeld

1. Introduction

Federalism is today a topic of intense intellectual debate in many countries throughout the world. In Europe, the former Soviet Union, South Africa and elsewhere, the view that good government will involve a blending of local and central governmental decision-making is now well accepted. With a topic such as federalism that has been so widely debated from so many perspectives, it would be impossible to provide a comprehensive review of the literature. Rather, we provide a particular perspective, one that balances the twin goals of political participation and economic welfare. A carefully specified theory of federalism has many useful applications: to government expenditure policy (Martinez-Vasquez 1994), to tax policy (Inman and Rubinfeld 1996), to deficit policies (Inman 1990), or to regulatory policy (Rose-Ackerman and Mashaw 1984).

Confederations of small governments have been praised by many – from Plato and Aristotle, through Rousseau, Montesquieu, Smith, and Mills, to contemporary federalist legal and economic scholars – as that political institution most likely to encourage a trio of social virtues: political participation, protection of the sovereign rights of citizens, and economic efficiency.[1] Other scholars have been more skeptical. *The Federalist Papers* (particularly at No. 47), the intellectual blueprint for the US Constitution, raises serious doubts about the virtues of loose confederations of small governments. Leading contemporary social scientists from political science (Robert Dahl and William Riker) and economics (Joseph Schumpeter and Paul Samuelson) have lent theoretical support to the Federalists' concerns.[2] Like the Federalists, these scholars have argued that a strong, democratically elected central government is generally the more effective means to ensure political participation, protection of the rights of citizens, and more efficient and equitable resource allocations.

1 On participation and the virtues of small governments, see Pateman (1970: 46, 110, 111), and Frug (1980). On economic efficiency and the positive role of small governments, see Smith (1776) and Tiebout (1956).

2 On small governments and their consequences for meaningful political participation, Schumpeter (1943), Dahl (1956), and Dahl and Tufte (1973). On the potential inability of small governments to protect group rights, see Riker (1964). For a discussion of why small governments might be economically inefficient, see Samuelson (1954).

Which level of government is best suited to make public policies, given that we want those policies to be democratically decided, respectful of personal rights, and economically efficient? A considered answer – whether for Europe's new Economic Union, the new South African Constitution, or to the regulation of anticompetitive firm behavior within the United States or the Economic Union – requires a careful balancing of the benefits and costs of decentralized and centralized political structures. To fashion such a balance, it is essential that we first review the potential virtues of each federalist structure.

We begin by defining what is meant by decentralized and centralized federalist structures. In this chapter, governments will be defined as "decentralized and state" or "centralized and national" according to the combination of two constitutional decisions. The first decision – called the *partition decision* – divides the single national citizenry into states. Following the partition decision, there will be a group of separate state governments and one central government to which each state will send (for simplicity) one representative to a central legislature, the single policy-making body of the central government. Policy decisions made by state governments will be decided by their separate legislatures.[3]

Courts and legislatures are concerned with the second constitutional decision – the *assignment decision* – which allocates final political responsibility for choices over a social or economic policy to either the legislature of the central government or to the legislatures of each of the separate states. If the assignment decision allocates ultimate responsibility for a social or economic policy to the states (or their localities), then we describe policy-making for this class of government decisions as "state" or "decentralized." In contrast, if the assignment decision gives final responsibility for a social or economic policy to the central government, then we describe policy-making for these assigned responsibilities as "national" or "centralized." Together, these two constitutional decisions define the essential federalist – decentralized or centralized – structure of the government. We realize, of course, that federalist structures may have decentralized and centralized components, as, for example, when the central government mandates the form and function of certain decentralized government activities.

The much-debated virtues of these decentralized or centralized governmental structures include democratic political participation and enhanced economic efficiency. Which federalist structure or combination of structures favors which virtues given the realities of the political and economic marketplace? We review

---

3 Adding another legislative chamber or an executive with a veto to our analysis will only improve the ability of federalist systems to meet the participation, sovereignty, and efficiency objectives. For an analysis of the effects of bicameral legislatures on government performance, see Levmore (1992). For an analysis of the effects of a president with veto powers on government performance, see Fitts and Inman (1992).

the arguments and the contemporary evidence in Section A (participation) and B (economic efficiency) below. Not surprisingly, neither a centralized nor a decentralized structure maximizes public participation and economic efficiency all the time. Which structure is preferred turns on a balancing of these values. In Section C we discuss briefly how a society might set that balance.

A. POLITICAL PARTICIPATION

2. The Benefits of Participation

Political participation is defined as "actions through which ordinary citizens of a political system influence or attempt to influence (political) outcomes" (Nagel 1980: 1). Actions include voting, debating, marching, picketing, contributing, and passive and armed resistance. The aim of these actions is to influence the direction of government policy. Active citizens may be successful in moving public policies closer to their preferred outcomes because of their participation. In this case, citizens are said to have influence. Or active citizens may be unsuccessful, their political actions having no effect on policy outcomes. In this case, the citizens have attempted, but failed, to influence political outcomes.

The benefits to citizens of their own, and others' participation, can be divided into three categories: instrumental or utilitarian, developmental or educative, and intrinsic or consumptive. In the utilitarian view, perhaps argued most directly in the work of Bentham and James Mill, political participation serves a specific function; to ensure that government maximizes aggregated citizen utility or welfare. In democratic societies, political participation is the necessary check on abuses of citizen welfare by ill-informed or even greedy elected officials. Political participation guarantees that abusive elected officials will be exposed and defeated at the next election. For the utilitarians, political participation's value is fundamentally instrumental; it plays, in the words of Carole Pateman (1970), a "protective function" for the public welfare.

For Jean-Jacques Rousseau and John Stuart Mill, political participation was instrumental to another, perhaps more important, end: it protected citizen liberties. While both Rousseau and Mill acknowledged the instrumental value of participation in protecting private economic interests and ensuring good (efficient) government, they extended the argument of the utilitarians to include participation's protective value for personal freedom as well. Participation ensures that no one individual or group is master over any other – "The rights and interests of every or any person are only secure from being disregarded, when the person interested is himself able, and habitually disposed, to stand up for them" (Mill 1960: 186).[4]

[4] See Pateman (1970), Chapter 2, particularly at 26–7, for a summary of the arguments of J.S. Mill and J. Rousseau in favor of political participation.

For many scholars, however, participation does much more than just protect private economic interests and personal liberties. Aristotle, Rousseau, J.S. Mill, de Tocqueville, and contemporary commentators such as Dewey and Pateman view citizen political participation as serving an important educative function as well. By participating in the political process, the individual learns that his private interests are intimately linked to the interests of others. This knowledge leads to a willingness to compromise, to put private interests aside and to call upon values of justice and common good when making public choices. There may be beneficial spillovers to private decision-making, too. Having recognized and accepted the validity of others' interests in the public arena, we may be more accepting of those interests in our private dealings. Simply put, we may be different people – more tolerant, less selfish – after political participation.

Finally, political participation may provide direct consumptive benefits to those who participate. From those who simply like to hear the sound of their own voice or revel in controlling others, to those who take genuine satisfaction in having contributed to a cause they feel is worthy, the act of political participation offers many a personal consumption benefit. How else might we explain widespread voting in national elections?[5] While perhaps not the most compelling argument for increased political participation, it should not be ignored.

3. Metrics of Political Participation

If political participation is an activity to be valued, how do we know if there is more or less of it within society? The instrumental, or influence, effects of individual political participation can be measured by a metric of political *power*. At one extreme, the individual fully controls the outcome, while at the other the individual has no influence over the outcome. If one person controls the outcome, then, of course, all others must be powerless.[6] The participatory, or "actions", effects of political participation can be measured by a metric of political *effort*. One plausible effort metric would be the hours, or the hourly equivalent of dollar contributions, given by the individual to political activity.

Whether an individual engages in political activity and whether those activities translate into political influence depends on the individual's personal desires to participate and to have power, and on how society's political environment translates individual participatory activity into influence. Important attributes of the political environment will include the political institutions that define voting rights, freedom of expression, and access to elected officials and the

---

5 Ordeshook and Riker (1973), Chapter 3.

6 See Nagel (1975) for a detailed discussion.

legislature. Also important is the number of citizens who can participate in public decision-making.

As a theoretical matter, one would expect that participation would be higher in local politics simply because the benefits of influence are greater the fewer the number of disparate constituents. However, individual political effort is not so easily predicted. When participatory effort is more productive in producing political influence, as it is likely to be in small democratic states, individuals might actually participate for fewer hours, choosing to allocate some of their increased "political productivity" into other, non-political activities. Ultimately, how political institutions and the population of the nation and its states affect political influence and political effort is an empirical question. Certainly the early (Aristotle, Rousseau, J.S. Mill) and contemporary (Pateman, Frug) advocates of participatory politics see the small, democratic state as most conducive to high values of influence and effort for the average citizen.

4. Measuring Participation

How will the two constitutional decisions central to setting the federalist structure – the partition decision and the assignment decision – affect the level of political participation in a society? The answer is ultimately empirical: how do political influence and participatory effort change as political decision-making moves from large central governments to smaller, decentralized states and local polities? Participation theorists have not hesitated to make predictions, typically arguing that a federalist system with a large number of small states with substantial policy responsibilities will increase the political influence of each citizen and generate increased political effort as well. There is little doubt that this is true for political influence, especially in societies with strong guarantees of equal political rights. Less certain, however, is the relationship between political effort and the size of states with decision-making power; it is not difficult to present arguments that effort may rise, fall, or even remain unchanged as federalist systems become more decentralized.

The empirical evidence on how political influence and participatory effort change as the governmental structure becomes decentralized is sparse, but what is available generally supports the prediction that both influence and effort will rise as the size of government declines. Within-country comparisons of political influence and effort across small and large governments seem the most appropriate testing ground of the participation hypothesis.[7] First, citizens surveyed in five countries (United States, Britain, West Germany, Italy, and Mexico) all reported making greater effort to understand, and having more

---

7 See Dahl and Tufte (1973: 44–53) for a review and critique of the cross-national evidence on size and participation.

success in understanding, local rather than national political issues. In the surveyed countries, citizen efforts to influence government were also typically two to three times higher for local than for national governments. In supporting evidence, a detailed survey of political participation across Swedish cities found average citizens in small communities were more aware of local politics than their counterparts in middle size cities and both knew more basic local political facts than large city residents. Second, political effectiveness or influence – at least as perceived by citizens – also seems to increase as governments get smaller in size. Again, the five-nation survey finds that citizens feel much more influential at the local than at the national level; typically, half of the citizens in the surveyed countries felt they had no influence over national policies, while only 25 to 30 percent felt powerless at the local level. A more detailed analysis of the US subsample showed a significant positive correlation between an index of political powerlessness and size of government (Finifter 1970: 389–410). Indirect evidence from the Swedish study also implies that citizen influence declines as governments get larger; the gap between the percentage of citizens and the percentage of elected officials who would support a tax increase increases as communities get larger. Finally, evidence from the United States, the Netherlands, and Switzerland all show that politics in larger communities, states, and cantons are increasingly dominated by organized interest groups or political parties. While such groups make participation easier for some citizens, they may also make it more difficult for others. If so, then Rousseau's concern that participation becomes more unequal as governments get larger is confirmed.

Any final conclusions regarding the effects of institutional decentralization on participatory effort and political influence must await more complete empirical analyses. Nonetheless, theoretical argument and the current empirical evidence lead us to the tentative conclusion that smaller governments, and thus more decentralized federalist structures, are likely to encourage the valued goal of greater political participation.

B. FEDERALISM AND ECONOMIC EFFICIENCY

5. The Pros and Cons of Decentralization

Using the economic efficiency criterion to choose the appropriate federalist structure is a complex endeavor involving a comparison of the economic benefits and costs of assigning responsibility to each level of government: in the US, to the national or central level, the state level, or the local government level. In a federal system, there are two important dimensions to economic efficiency. First, *inter*jurisdictional efficiency involves the appropriate allocation of individuals and other resources, such as capital, *among* the different jurisdictions. Interjurisdictional efficiency is achieved when the public activities of these interacting governments satisfy the collective demands of individuals living in different jurisdictions at a minimum economic cost.[8] Second, *intra*jurisdictional efficiency requires a choice of public activities which satisfies the collective demand *within* a given jurisdiction, measured as the willingness to pay for those activities for all individuals within the jurisdiction, and again does so at minimum costs.

In our complex federal system, both interjurisdictional and intrajurisdictional inefficiencies can arise, the former because of *spillovers*, the decisions and actions of individuals within one jurisdiction can have effects on individuals located in other jurisdictions that are not accurately reflected in the marketplace, and the latter because the political process may not generate outcomes within a jurisdiction which maximize the well-being of its residents, i.e. create *political inefficiencies*. In a broad sense, the choice of the appropriate jurisdiction to be responsible for a government activity involves a trade-off – the larger the jurisdiction the less likely that there will be spillovers from one jurisdiction to the next, but the more likely that the political process will lead to a misallocation of resources within jurisdictions.

A decentralized system of governments is ideal from the point of view of intrajurisdictional efficiency, since assigning economic responsibility to the smaller and more homogeneous of the jurisdictions increases the likelihood that services provided and regulations promulgated will be consistent with the desires of each and every member of the population. In other words, in a decentralized system of governments, local tastes for public goods are likely to be less disparate than national tastes. The resulting reduction in the inefficiency of providing public goods (since citizens with similar tastes would prefer to consume the same level of public goods) has been characterized as the *decentralization theorem* by Wallace Oates (1972).

Unfortunately, decentralization has its disadvantages, due primarily to the spillovers that are likely to arise when jurisdiction size is small. A less decentralized system with larger jurisdictions can minimize the spillovers involved, while at the same time taking advantage of the lower cost of promulgating and enforcing certain regulations or dispensing the benefits of public programs, and the lower cost of obtaining and using information.

Our analysis of the political economy of federalism begins with a critique of the arguments for a strongly decentralized system. While we agree that a focus on the presence of substantial spillovers is appropriate, we stress the fact that

---

8 A full analysis would also include the economic costs of politically deciding what those policies should be and ensuring that the politically decided policies are what the government actually provides. These latter costs have been identified elsewhere as the transactions costs of government. They include the costs of selecting legislators, the decision-making costs of setting a policy, and the monitoring costs of ensuring that the policy is put in place; see Breton and Scott (1978).

decentralization will not guarantee an optimal public sector mix even when no spillovers are present. We believe that a complete theory of federalism cannot rely solely on the "Tiebout Model", an ideal model of a fiscal competition between many independent local governments. Appropriately specified, Tiebout's decentralized (1965) model of governmental competition is formally analogous to the purely competitive market model with complete information used to study market competition between private firms. In the Tiebout model, government policies are determined by *market*, or economic, exchange alone. Unfortunately, the assumptions needed to ensure that governmental competition is fully analogous to efficient private market competition are very strong, and may not hold in realistic public economies.[9]

A more appropriate analytic framework – based upon political models of state government decision-making and interstate bargaining – yields, we feel, more appropriate conclusions as to the likely economic performance of decentralized public environments. In the section that follows, we study how such systems are likely to work. We conclude that when viewed as a *political* rather than market process, decentralized federalism may be economically inefficient. This conclusion suggests the need to consider a more centralized environment, using the central, or national, government to set policy. To be consistent, however, the analysis of central government performance must use the same political model that found inefficiencies at the decentralized level. This we do by explaining how central government regulatory policies also might be inefficient – indeed, potentially worse, for political reasons, than the inefficient state and local policies which the central policies had hoped to correct.

6. The Tiebout Approach

According to one view, the world of decentralized, competitive governments will allow for a national regulatory marketplace, in which individuals move among local jurisdictions or states to select the regulatory combination that they most desire. Just as a private marketplace forces suppliers to produce their goods at the lowest cost, and to provide the goods most desired by consumers, so too will the pressure of taxpayers shopping, through exit and relocation, force governments to be efficient in their provision of public goods and public goods and services.

According to this view, public activities should be decentralized, except when there are significant economic spillovers from the regulating jurisdiction to its neighbors. When spillovers result, decentralized governments may ignore important economic costs or benefits which will lead them to over-, or under-, provide the activity. In these instances, central government review is appropriate.

We must be clear, however, about the assumptions built into the Tiebout model of decentralized governments on which this model relies. Each household

---

9 See, for example, Rubinfeld (1987).

and business is highly mobile and chooses to reside in the jurisdiction that offers the tax-expenditure-regulation package that it most prefers. As typically specified, five conditions define the competitive Tiebout public economy:

1. Publicly provided goods, services, and regulatory activities are provided at minimum average cost;[10]
2. There is a perfectly elastic supply of political jurisdictions, each capable of replicating all attractive economic features of its competitors;[11]
3. Mobility of households and businesses among jurisdictions is costless;
4. Households and businesses are fully informed about the fiscal and regulatory policies of each jurisdiction;[12] and,
5. There are no interjurisdictional externalities or spillovers.[13]

7. Critiquing Tiebout

While a useful starting point, the Tiebout model does not provide a complete theory of federalism. The assumptions 1 through 5 may arguably apply to a

---

[10] If assumption 1 holds, there is an efficient population size which minimizes the average cost per household of providing that government activity. This rules out using Tiebout competition to allocate "pure public" goods, those goods where additional users of the government's facility do not reduce the consumption benefits enjoyed by previous users. Typical examples of a pure public good include defense, television or radio signals, and new knowledge. Goods which can be allocated by the Tiebout competitive process are those goods where more users reduce, proportionally, the benefits enjoyed by current users. Rather than *pure* public goods, these goods are *congested* public goods. Education, highways, police protection, and parks are examples. The efficient scale of operation for such goods must be sufficiently small (e.g. 15,000 in population) so that each household can find a suitable jurisdiction in which to reside. Existing evidence suggests that this constraint can be met for many government services; see, for example, Ladd and Yinger (1989: 83, 85).

[11] This assumption ensures that efficient alternatives exist; this is the task of public sector entrepreneur-politicians who run against, and defeat, inefficient incumbents; competitive political entrepreneurs play a role analogous to take-over "artists" in the private market. Or public sector entrepreneurs can appear as enterprising real estate developers who build new jurisdictions – analogous to "new entrants" in a private market – to draw away dissatisfied residents from inefficient governments. See Epple and Zelenitz (1981).

[12] Assumptions 3 and 4 ensure that when possible inefficiencies arise, households and businesses can move to otherwise similar jurisdictions without those inefficiencies.

[13] Assumption 5 ensures that all public regulatory activities can be provided within these efficient jurisdictions – larger governments or intergovernmental cooperation is not required. In the end, a regulated economy satisfying assumptions 1 to 5, and organized as a fully decentralized network of competing jurisdictions, will maximize economic efficiency. Citizens and businesses can consume their preferred levels of the public regulatory activity with a minimum expenditure of production and transactions costs.

local public activity such as rent control, which is imposed in California in only a relatively few cities, thereby leaving most households the opportunity to move to non-rent control jurisdictions as they see fit. However, the assumptions are less likely to hold for more centralized activities, where choices are more limited and moving is more costly.

If assumptions 2 through 5 do not hold, we must rethink the optimality of complete decentralization. The model of perfectly competitive *private* markets has long been an appealing paradigm for economists, in part because some real world markets do actually seem to operate in that manner, and in part because if they do, the efficiency consequences seem clear. Neither of these reasons applies without qualification to the Tiebout framework for competitive *governments*, however.

Consider assumption 2, that there is a perfectly elastic supply of political jurisdictions. The model of perfectly competitive markets yields an efficient allocation of resources in part because firms are free to make the efficient choices of inputs and outputs, and in part because entry into and exit from an industry are free. In the Tiebout model, competitive governments fill the role of firms. But governments may be constrained by internal politics when making their input and output choices, and free entry of new governments is by no means assured in actual public goods economies.[14] For example, an entrepreneur cannot simply invest his capital to build a new city.

If assumption 2 does not hold, four potentially adverse consequences for economic efficiency are likely to arise. First, with a limited supply of jurisdictions, each government is likely to contain citizens with different views of what constitutes the government's best policy. If so, local politics becomes important. If local decisions are made by majority rule, the outcome will not necessarily be economically efficient (see Bergstrom, Rubinfeld, Roberts, and Shapiro 1988). Second, when the economy can no longer replicate attractive local jurisdictions, economic rents can be earned. The presence of these publicly created rents associated with the desirability of some locations over others can in turn create a tension between the fiscal entrepreneurs who wish to develop new communities and the owners of the desirable locations. As a result, there is no guarantee that the market for land and for other scarce resources will be economically efficient.

Third, when private sector job opportunities are not identical in all locations, productive private sector employment may be sacrificed as labor is attracted

---

[14] See generally, Epple and Zelenitz (1981), arguing that limited entry permits competitive governments to maximize public "monopoly profits" from the provision of public goods and public regulations and the level and allocation of those profits will be determined politically within the jurisdiction.

to less efficient locations for fiscal reasons. The consequence is a less efficient private economy.[15]

Fourth, once the supply of jurisdictions is fixed, the analogy of the decentralized model of federalism to anonymous free market competition is no longer valid. Each local government may be aware of the potential effect of its action on other jurisdictions. It will then act strategically in making its decisions on the basis of its best guess as to how other jurisdictions will respond. In this framework the actions of each local jurisdiction, even if small, can have a substantial effect on the welfare of the rest of the decentralized world. Essentially, a self-interested decision by those in power in one jurisdiction can result in a series of distortions that arise throughout the affected network of other jurisdictions. For example, a decision by one jurisdiction to offer a tax break to attract new business could lead to a competition in which many jurisdictions offer a variety of business tax benefits.

While it is difficult to predict the exact consequence of the rather complex behavioral patterns that can arise when these strategic interactions are taken into account, it seems clear that an efficient outcome is unlikely to arise. States may, for example, underprovide welfare services, or more generally may underprovide public services in which they have particular production advantages and therefore should provide in abundance.[16] This could occur because a state realizes that by providing a high level of welfare benefits it is likely to attract new low-income residents from nearby states, thus adding substantially to its cost of providing such benefits. States might also provide substantial tax benefits to attract business, or at least to avoid losing business to other competing states, and in the process undertax business capital and overtax the residential base.[17]

An equivalent phenomenon can occur with respect to regulatory policies. States might relax their environmental controls to encourage business migration, or simply to forestall the loss of business because other states had or were about to relax their environmental regulations.[18] Note that the competitive process which leads to a uniformity of regulation among states is not consistent with the advantages of the diversity associated with the Tiebout model, nor is it

---

15 See Buchanan and Goetz (1972) for the initial presentation of this argument and the summaries in Boadway and Flatters (1982) and Wildasin (1986).

16 See Gramlich and Laren (1984) on welfare competition among states, and Pestieau (1977).

17 See, for example, Break (1967: 23–4). See also Oates (1972: 142–3). For a review of the more recent literature, see Inman and Rubinfeld (1996).

18 This argument has been developed by Cumberland (1981). See also Fischel (1975: 119), and more generally, Oates and Schwab (1986).

likely to be efficient. The result could be a "race to the bottom" resulting in an equilibrium in which environmental regulations are "undersupplied."[19]

Assumption 3, that citizens and businesses are costlessly mobile between political jurisdictions is also problematic. The assumption applies best to suburban jurisdictions among which individuals and firms have a good deal of mobility. When the number of cities and towns within a metropolitan area is substantial, families and firms have significant choice in their provision of public goods and public regulations. Empirical evidence supporting the Tiebout hypothesis has focused entirely on this local public sector.[20] Activities of local governments in metropolitan areas – save those with significant spillovers – are likely to meet the competitive test (see Courant and Rubinfeld 1981). Yet much economic activity occurs at the state level, where assumption 3 is unlikely to hold. Studies of migration show that most household moves are within metropolitan areas, not between states. Those who do move between states are typically job motivated, and are not primarily seeking a more attractive public service/public regulation environment.[21] If assumption 3 does not apply, then the model cannot guarantee overall (i.e. market plus public sector) efficiency.

Assumption 4, that households and businesses are fully informed, presents another problem for the Tiebout argument. Households and firms must have reasonably accurate information about the tax, spending, and regulatory policies of the communities in which they will reside. Yet, it is often difficult for individuals and firms to ascertain the implications of regulations within their own jurisdiction, let alone make a reasonable judgment about the public activities that will exist in other jurisdictions at a future point in time after which they have relocated.[22] When we view the location decision as involving

---

[19] The uniformity of occupational regulation is described in Stigler (1971: 130). For a more general argument that the regulatory actions of individual states may not result in an optimal federal system, given the incentives that determine political choice, see Rose-Ackerman (1981). See also, Revesz (1992).

[20] For studies of household relocation, see Gramlich and Rubinfeld (1982), who used survey data for Michigan and concluded that their results were "reasonably consistent with a Tiebout interpretation: in large metropolitan areas there is quite extensive grouping; in smaller areas, there is some grouping" (at 554–5). Oates (1972: 162–79) studied the metropolitan New Jersey region, using tests of the capitalization of public goods differentials into property values, and concluded that public goods preferences could explain migration among neighboring cities and towns. For evidence that businesses are sensitive to local taxes and services when relocating within a metropolitan area, see Bartik (1988) and McConnell and Schwab (1990), suggesting that environmental regulations are not an important factor affecting business location decisions.

[21] Easterbrook (1983: 35 n. 28). See also the detailed evidence on interstate and interregional location of households reviewed in Greenwood (1986).

[22] Stigler (1971: 130), has argued, "(t)he voter's expenditure to learn the merits of individual policy proposals and to express his preferences . . . are determined by expected

a choice of public sector packages, and we take into account the fact that other jurisdictions are likely to be changing those packages over time, the informational demands that must be satisfied for the competitive system of governments to work effectively seem very great.

When assumption 4 no longer holds, i.e. when there is incomplete information about the costs and levels of regulatory activity, an important principal–agent problem arises. Households and firms have two options: go it alone and risk being exploited by better informed fiscal entrepreneurs and local factors of production, or hire an agent to protect household and firm interests. Complications arise when information about agent performance is costly and some deceitful agents survive, or when the expertise provided by agents to households and firms cannot itself be kept private.[23] In both instances, there will emerge externalities in the market for agents that can cause an inefficient level of information to be provided about the fiscal performance of the Tiebout communities.[24]

The final assumption, requiring no spillovers, is an important real-world violation of the Tiebout framework that may require central government intervention. A spillover or externality arises when the activities of a jurisdiction affect directly the well-being of an individual or firm in another jurisdiction and the decision-making of the first jurisdiction does not take these effects on others into account.[25] One occurs when a spillover offers a positive benefit to a neighboring community, for example, through the regulation of socially damaging air pollution emitted by a locally valuable firm. When such positive spillovers exist, state and local governments may provide too little of the activity.

---

costs and returns" and that, in the case of regulatory policy, this cost-benefit calculus dissuades voters from discovering very much.

[23] To the extent the market for "agents" works perfectly – all inefficient or exploitive providers are exposed, and only truthful agents survive – the final outcome will still be efficient, but some fiscal surplus will be allocated to the agents as payment for services performed. Such payments can be made as a contingent fee conditional on the performance of the agent in managing the purchase of the public good, or as a competitively determined lump-sum payment to a previously identified – by reputation or certification – "truthful" agent.

[24] When information about agent performance or abilities is available at no cost, then agent efforts can be fully monitored (avoiding all problems of moral hazard) and agent abilities will be fully known (avoiding all problems of adverse selection). The agent market can then work perfectly. When information about agents is costly, however, there is no guarantee that the efficient agent market will arise; see Holmstrom (1985). Similarly, when the information provided by the agents to households cannot be kept private, then there will be externality-caused inefficiency in the information market.

[25] For a discussion of public goods externalities, see Williams (1966) and Brainard and Dolbear (1967) among others. This literature is critically reviewed and extended by Pauly (1970). For a discussion of tax externalities see the survey in Inman and Rubinfeld (*Journal of Public Economy* 1996).

The converse case provides a third example. Here a socially productive firm produces only local pollution, for example, a garbage or nuclear waste site. The incentive is for the local community to impose stringent regulations on such a firm so as to force its relocation onto a neighboring community. A negative regulatory externality results. If the neighboring communities respond with similar regulations, the firm may have no place to go, even though it is in the interests of all jurisdictions to have the firm locate in at least one locality. With negative spillovers, there may be too much state and local activity.[26] The general point is clear: when assumption 5 is violated, there is no guarantee that decentralized competition will produce an efficient allocation of public and private resources.

Our review of the assumptions of the Tiebout framework leads us to conclude that the analogy between the model of competitive governments and the model of competitive markets is not sufficiently strong to serve as the basis of a theory of federalism. If we are to have a compelling efficiency basis for drawing the lines between decentralized and centralized governmental policy, it must be found in an analysis based upon paradigms other than Tiebout's model of public sector competition. Our discussion in the next two subsections seeks to provide that paradigm.

8. The Politics of State Legislative Policy

Economic efficiency demands that state public activities be efficient both with respect to the preferences of residents of the state (*intra*jurisdictional efficiency) and with respect to the preferences of residents outside the state (*inter*jurisdictional efficiency). Separate political institutions exist through which each dimension of efficiency might be achieved. State legislatures and their appointed state agencies are the means through which residents within a state might hope to obtain intrajurisdictional efficiency. Interstate cooperative agreements struck between residents, or their elected agents, of neighboring states are the means to interjurisdictional efficiency. We consider the potential of each, beginning with an analysis of state legislative processes.

When elected representatives join together in a state legislature, they are free to fashion coalitions and set regulatory policies as they wish, subject only to

---

[26] For an illustration of this point with respect to the regulation of solid wastes, see David and Lester (1989). In these circumstances, a federal or state set of uniform standards may be preferred by all. In fact, uniform national regulation not only can take advantage of economies of scale in administration, it can also produce scale economies of production and distribution for firms, while at the same time reducing their location costs; see Rose-Ackerman (1994). Augmentation of national standards by states or localities can be allowed, but only if the additional regulations do not generate spillovers by benefiting local households and businesses at the expenses of non-residents.

the constraint that decisions receive the approval of a majority of legislators. Majority-rule legislatures making decisions over multiple public policies must resolve a fundamental structural defect: the propensity of the majority-rule process to cycle from one policy outcome to another.[27] When no winning coalition is capable of holding its majority against small policy variations offered by a losing minority, then either no decision will be made or final policy outcomes will be random and uncertain.

If legislatures are to reach decisions, additional legislative institutions must be discovered for overcoming this inherent instability of the majority-rule process. Two institutional approaches are commonly used by legislatures. The first assigns agenda-setting powers to a small subset of members, say the speaker of the house or a key legislative committee. Other members in the legislature then simply vote – up or down – on the items in the approved agenda. Most likely, policies will be approved by a bare majority – a minimal winning coalition – in this strong agenda-setter legislature.[28] A second strategy shares agenda-setting powers among all members, giving each legislator a right to select his most preferred policy in that policy area most germane to the legislator's constituents. This second approach to legislative decision-making involves each legislator deferring to the preferred policies of all other legislators, provided the other legislators defer to the legislator's own policy requests. The guiding principle here is a norm of deference – "You scratch my back, I'll scratch yours" – and it typically results in legislative proposals which are approved unanimously. For this reason such legislatures are often called "universalistic."[29]

---

[27] This fundamental observation regarding majority rule processes has been well recognized at least since the work of M. de Condorcet in the "Essai sur l'Application de L'Analyse à la Probabilité des Decisions Rendues à la Pluraliste des Voix" (1785) and is known popularly as the paradox of voting: even though majority rule leads a legislature to vote for policy A over policy B, and for policy B over policy C, it is certainly possible, and often likely, that policy C will defeat policy A. Kenneth Arrow (1963) proves that this paradox of voting is a symptom of a more fundamental problem with all democratic processes: there is no guarantee that such processes can find a best outcome or are immune to manipulation. Thus, the design of political institutions will almost inevitably be a search among the second-best. For a survey of this literature in the context of the new political economy, see Inman (1987).

[28] For articulation of the general theory of how this process overcomes cycling, see Baron and Ferejohn (1989). For a careful description of what legislative institutions are used to assign agenda control, see Shepsle (1979). There is an extensive literature which tests for the direct influence of agenda-setters – typically congressional committees – on policy outcomes; see Krehbiel (1992) for a critical but balanced review.

[29] The guiding theory can be found in Weingast (1979) and Niou and Ordeshook (1985). The theory has been developed for, and its applications must be limited to, understanding how legislative bodies allocate government projects and government regulations – what has been called *distributive* politics; see Lowi (1969). A norm of deference is not an appropriate model for predicting how legislatures will decide

A single legislator uncertain as to whether she will be one of the lucky winners in the bare majority legislature will typically favor the more open rules of the universalistic legislature. Intuitively, the universalistic legislature is preferred because under universalism activities that benefit the legislator's district are nearly certain to be chosen, and a substantial portion of the costs will be borne by other districts.[30]

Universalistic state legislatures operating under a norm of deference run a significant risk that their public activities will be economically inefficient, however. Consider, for example, the typical case of a state regulation which raises industry prices within a state, effectively reducing output below competitive levels. Those who benefit from such a regulation are state residents who own capital and other "specialized" factors of production employed in the regulated industry. Those who lose are the state's consumers who buy the output of the regulated industry and the state's taxpayers who pay for the regulatory bureaucracy.

Assume further that the industry would be competitive, pricing at marginal cost, if unregulated, but would act as a profit-maximizing cartel if regulated. The cartel would choose to maximize its profits by raising its price above the competitive level, and by reducing its output. Three conclusions follow from this framework. First, industry producers within the state prefer to be at a regulated output near the cartel profit-maximizing level, because, as regulation nears this level, industry profits, the "marginal benefits" of regulation to the interest groups that own the specialized inputs that gain from regulation, are maximized. Second, state consumers of industry output prefer the competitive output, for, at zero industry regulation, the tax costs and lost consumer benefits from regulation – the "marginal costs" of regulation – are minimized. Finally, any regulation of a competitive industry is inefficient from the perspective of *all* state residents, because the additional cost to state taxpayers and consumers everywhere is greater than the additional benefit to state producers.

How then will a universalistic state legislature set government policy for the state? Under the norm of deference, each elected state representative is allowed to propose a state policy which maximizes the returns to his constituents. Consider how one legislator (perhaps with a group of other legislators

---

*re*distributive policies such as welfare or progressive taxation, politics where one group of constituents must lose to another. Details regarding the legislative institutions needed to enforce the norm of deference can be found in Weingast and Marshall (1988) for the details of how such a legislative norm of deference might be enforced.

30 If benefits exceed average project costs in a majority of districts – a likely case – then a legislature run by a norm of deference will be the preferred legislative institution. Barry Weingast (1979) and Emerson Niou and Peter Ordeshook (1985) prove exactly when this outcome holds. See also Schwartz (1989) or Inman and Fitts (1990), both of whom extend the analysis to legislative projects of variable size. The conclusion that legislators prefer universalism to bare-majority rule extends to this more general case.

representing similar districts) might view an activity when all of the benefits, but only a small fraction of the state's costs, are felt within the district(s). In this case, constituents would internalize all of the marginal benefits, while constituents will take into account only a small fraction of the marginal costs. For the affected legislator(s), the preferred activity would be a higher than efficient output. But not all legislators will propose inefficient activities. Only those legislators from districts whose local economy has concentrated benefits will find the activity to be in their interests. When they do, state politics will generate an *intra*jurisdictional inefficiency.

States with strong political parties capable of disciplining party members or states with strong governors capable of mobilizing broad-based citizen support may be able to control these intrajurisdictional inefficiencies of universalistic legislatures, but not perfectly. Consider first the ability of strong political parties to control policy. By definition, strong parties form a stable legislative majority. Members who might be tempted to deviate from the party's platform can be disciplined so that deviations will not occur. Government policy will therefore be the policy which is in the interests of the stable, majority party. In this stylized framework, only those producers in legislative districts belonging to the majority party will be favored. Minority party districts will receive no benefits.

When proposing an activity for their constituents, representatives in the majority party will be required by the party to consider the effects of their proposed activity on constituents in all districts controlled by the party. From the perspective of the majority party, therefore, an activity in one district will still provide benefits to party constituents, but will now impose only a fraction (perhaps slightly greater than 50 percent) of the total cost of the activity on party members.

From the majority party's perspective, the preferred activity level in a party-controlled district will be an efficient level, where *party* marginal benefits equal *party* marginal costs. Because the party-preferred level internalizes the costs to party members, the inefficiency must be less than the inefficiency created by the universalistic legislature. The loss of intrajurisdictional efficiency declines accordingly. Put simply, by internalizing more of the costs of government activity, strong political parties can improve the efficiency performance of state regulations.[31]

---

[31] For empirical evidence that strong political parties may have controlled legislative inefficiencies, see Inman and Fitts (1990: 111–15). Political parties may even promote full economic efficiency. This limiting case occurs if the political party controls all representatives in the legislature. Here there is an incentive for all districts to elect a representative to the stable majority party, since this is their only way to join the controlling coalition and to receive constituent benefits. With a single stable majority party, therefore, there is strong pressure towards full economic efficiency. Donald Wittman makes this argument in "Why Democracies Produce Efficient Results" (1989).

So too can strong governors. Michael Fitts and Robert Inman present an analysis of executive leadership in economic policy where the executive who has access to needed political resources – appointment powers, control over appropriated budgets, and an executive veto – and with the appropriate political incentive – running in a national or state-wide election – will seek efficient economic reform. Using appointment powers and discretionary executive authority over policies and the budget, the governor can fashion a reform coalition in which each member district agrees to sacrifice its inefficient policy for a compensating *executive-controlled* substitute policy. Facing a universalistic legislature, executive-led reform will improve economic efficiency for all state residents. A successful reform package must share the benefits of this reduced inefficiency with residents in the original district and the rest of the state's taxpayers and consumers. On balance, reform makes all residents in the state better off, thereby increasing the governor's chances of re-election. But only strong governors, those with sufficient executive-controlled resources to pay compensation to those districts made worse off, can hope to achieve reform. Even then reform will typically fall short of full efficiency.

We conclude that state politics will often encourage inefficient governmental activities for state residents, and that these *intra*jurisdictional inefficiencies are likely to be greatest in those states with weak political parties and weak executives. Importantly, these intrajurisdictional inefficiencies occur even when there are no spillovers to citizens outside the state. Matters are even worse, however, when there are spillovers, for here even strong political parties and strong governors will find it politically useful to support the (now nationally) inefficient activity. The case of activities with out-of-state spillovers involves *inter*jurisdictional inefficiency.

As with the case of intrajurisdictional inefficiency, the marginal benefits continue to reflect the benefits to residents within the state. The marginal costs, however, now encompass the national marginal costs to the residents of the state (state marginal costs *plus* the marginal costs of lost consumer benefits to out-of-state residents). These national marginal costs are greater than the state-wide marginal costs discussed previously because they reflect the additional lost consumer surplus suffered by out-of-state residents. Government policy remains a political decision within the state, however, set by the balancing of state constituents' marginal benefits and costs.

Large interjurisdictional inefficiencies can remain even when strong parties and strong governors successfully control their own state's intrajurisdictional inefficiencies. Even though the inefficient regulation declines with a strong party (or strong governor), significant interjurisdictional inefficiencies may remain. Even a fully efficient state government setting policy efficiently within the state could impose large interjurisdictional inefficiencies on out-of-state citizens; the "state" of OPEC is a prominent example.

9. Coasian Interjurisdictional Bargains

Might we imagine a political response from neighboring states to correct these interjurisdictional spillovers? Economists have designed systems of grants (matching and non-matching, specific and general) as well as tax and subsidy arrangements which can greatly increase the efficiency of a decentralized system. However, a more distinctive approach, which we pursue in depth here, is the facilitation of interstate agreements, or Coasian bargains, to remove interjurisdictional inefficiencies. The bargain would require the out-of-state residents to "compensate" the producers from the regulating state for the profits they lose when the inefficient regulation is removed. As Coase and others have pointed out, there are sufficient benefits to in-state and out-of-state consumers and taxpayers harmed by the activity that compensation can be paid to the state-created cartel, with the out-of-state residents remaining better off.

In practice, such compensation would be paid through an interstate agreement with neighboring states paying compensation to the regulating state, with the resulting compensation then passed on by that state's governor or legislature to within-state producers. But we expect such a Coasian bargain between out-of-state consumers and within-state producers will be hard to effect. Successful Coasian bargains require five assumptions to be met:

1. There are no, or very small, resource costs associated with the bargaining process;
2. Preferences over bargaining outcomes and the resources of households are common knowledge;
3. Bargaining agents perfectly represent the economic interests of their constituents;
4. All bargaining agreements are costlessly enforceable; and
5. The parties can agree to a division of the bargaining surplus.

Only when assumptions 1 through 5 hold will interjurisdictional efficiency be achieved. How likely are these assumptions to be valid?

On its face, assumption 1 seems defensible. The institutions for bargaining – elected state officials – are already in place, and the marginal costs of applying these institutions to one additional political agreement are likely to be very small, but only to a point. Legislatures do not solve all problems in every year. The legislative agenda is limited, and at some point it simply does not pay to bring additional policies to the floor for consideration. Those policies which will be excluded are likely to be the marginal problems, those which have only a small effect on the economic well-being of voters.

Even if 1 holds, assumptions 2 to 5 may fail. If the preferences of the participants to the bargain are not common knowledge (2 no longer holds), then there may be a strategic advantage to concealing costs and benefits, demanding greater compensation from the agreement if you represent the "winning" state or offering less compensation if you represent one of the "losing" states. If both parties adopt the "conceal" position, however, no agreement may be forthcoming.

In choosing their bargaining strategy, jurisdictions must assess the extent to which other parties are likely to make concessions. In game-theoretic terms, the parties try to assess the threat points of the other parties – the minimum offer that they are willing to accept in order to accept a negotiating offer. In addition, they try to estimate the extent to which the other party will be willing to make concessions prior to reaching their threat point. If the parties make poor estimates of each other's threat point, or miscalculate the chances that the other party will accept a compromise offer, they may take a hard line in the bargaining process. Clearly, therefore, Coasian bargainers will not be immune to possibilities for strategic behavior when they negotiate, and to the extent that they succumb, Coasian bargaining may break down.[32] Such attempts at free-riding behavior are likely to undo a Coasian bargain when preferences are not common knowledge and the number of states with affected consumers is large.[33]

Even if consumer preferences and industry profits are common knowledge, there is no guarantee that state elected officials will choose to make the constituents of the Coasian bargain better off (3 no longer holds). While the favored industry is well represented in its state (why else would there be regulation?), consumers of the product may not be so fortunate in their states. They may be in a minority in a majority-rule state. In contrast to private market agreements, here the affected parties are heard only if generally elected representatives choose to make their case.

Assumption 4 is perhaps the least problematic of the five Coasian assumptions. *If* states do reach an agreement and sign an interstate compact, typically the agreement is legally enforceable.[34] Enforcement difficulties arise only when important contingencies which might affect the agreement cannot be foreseen in advance. For example, if a future event occurs which alters the benefits and

---

32 See Polinsky (1980); Crawford (1982); and Kreps and Wilson (1982).

33 For the first treatment of the effects of group size on voluntary agreements see Olsen (1965). The effect of group size and other variables on bargaining has been studied extensively through the use of experiments. See, for example, Hoffman and Spitzer (1982). See also Bagnoli and McKee (1991).

34 See Ellickson (1979). Ellickson discusses the idea of creating a series of public property rights and duties to encourage bargaining solutions to environmental spillovers. Note that monitoring costs, a serious problem in many contracts, are not likely to be a problem here. States which have agreed to curtail their monopoly overcharge regulation will know if they have been paid compensation. Consumer states which pay compensation will be able to observe if the regulating state has re-introduced regulation. For a discussion of importance of monitoring costs to contract enforcement, see Williamson (1985).

costs of a particular policy, then the state choosing the activity may decide to break the previous interstate agreement.

Arguably the most important and perhaps least appreciated source of bargaining failure is the loss of assumption 5. Even if 1 through 4 hold, the parties may not be able to agree as to how the economic surplus generated by the bargaining process can be divided. Each Coasian bargain does two things: it establishes an efficient exchange, thereby creating economic surplus, *and* it distributes that surplus among the bargaining parties. Proponents of Coase emphasize the first outcome and have largely ignored the important difficulties of the second. Yet it is well known that the division of any economic pie is a bargaining problem which may have no solution.[35] The often observed result in "divide-the-pie" games that bargaining breaks down because the proposed division is not "fair" illustrates the point. In such situations, one state rejects an economically beneficial offer from another state because the proposed offer violates the first state's exogenous, and no doubt politically motivated, sense of economic fairness.

What is seen as an exogenous norm of fairness in a one-time game may be a rational endogenously chosen strategy in a repeated political game. For example, a governor seeking re-election cannot appear "weak" when bargaining with another state. If the money involved in a regulatory agreement is modest relative to the overall state budget – as it is likely to be – then the political symbolism of the "share" from the divide-the-pie game may be far more important for re-election prospects than the actual dollars involved. If so, and if both governors must demand more than 50%, then agreement will not be possible.[36] Strategic interplay becomes even more complicated, and agreement less likely, as the number of bargaining states increases beyond two.[37]

We conclude that economically inefficient policies are likely at the state and local level. Our analysis of state and local political institutions reveals strong political pressures towards favoring narrow, geographically concentrated interests at the expense of more diffused interests. While strong political parties and powerful governors have a political incentive to internalize the costs, even in these states some inefficiencies will remain for residents.[38]

---

35 When redistribution games might have equilibrium outcomes is an important topic of recent economic research; see Rubinstein (1982) and more recently Binmore, Rubinstein and Wolinsky (1986).

36 For evidence from the experimental literature that a sense of fairness is crucial to the ability of parties to reach agreement, see Roth (1985).

37 This is true even if preferences are fully known and the free-rider problem is not at issue; see Haller (1986).

38 For evidence that state regulations are politically motivated, and in particular, are more likely for geographically concentrated industries and occupations, see Stigler (1971).

These intrajurisdictional regulatory inefficiencies are compounded when the effects of government activity spill over onto consumers in other states. In these instances, even strong political parties and governors have a political incentive to choose activities. The hope that voluntary interstate compacts might control these interjurisdictional inefficiencies seems to us to be very optimistic. The assumptions required for such Coasian agreements are very demanding and unlikely to hold in practice. This seems particularly so when the efficiency costs on any one individual are small, costs are not common knowledge and are diffused over groups in many states, the affected individuals are themselves a minority within a state, and state politicians treat the division of proceeds from the bargain as a signal of their political "toughness."[39] When any one of the assumptions 1 to 5 fails to hold, Coasian agreements will not arise and state-created interjurisdictional regulatory inefficiencies will remain.

10. The Politics of Central Government Legislative Policy

Within federalist public economies, whenever state and local governments are economically inefficient, it is appropriate to ask whether the central government might do a better job.[40] But the comparison must be a consistent one, allowing for potential political inefficiencies at both the state and federal levels of government. Deciding whether to centralize regulatory policy at the national level first requires an analysis of how the national legislature will set such policies.

The effects of state regulatory policies on industries and consumers outlined previously generalizes to central government regulatory policy-making as well. In this instance, industries are concentrated in particular congressional districts or states: tobacco in North Carolina, defense production in Washington and California, automobiles in Michigan. Like their counterparts in state government, congressional legislators have an incentive to look for central government activities which will benefit households and firms located in their districts. However, such national activities will have significant costs for US taxpayers, costs which may exceed the benefits.

Whether such economically inefficient activities will be legislated in the central authority depends upon the institutions of legislative decision-making. If the legislature is "universalistic," then we can expect it to favor inefficient activities.[41] As with state legislatures, reform of policy-making will require

---

[39] For evidence of the difficulties states have in fashioning Coasian agreements, even when the number of states is few, see Kolstad and Wolak (1983), and Coates and Munger (1995).

[40] See, for example, Oates (1972), particularly at chapters 1 and 2.

[41] For evidence that US congressional institutions have supported a universalistic legislative process, see Weingast and Marshall (1988). See also Silberman and Durden's study of labor market regulations (Silberman and Durden 1976) and Kalt and Zupan's study of environmental regulations (Kalt and Zupan 1984).

strong presidential leadership and/or political parties capable of controlling the inefficient policy demands of members.

Given that state and central legislatures face the same political pressures to choose inefficient activities, and neither seems, at the moment at least, institutionally well equipped to resist those pressures, we conclude that neither states nor the central government can be preferred unambiguously as the appropriate domain for choosing economic activities. The current evidence shows economic inefficiencies arising from choices at both levels of government.

All this said, there remains a final argument, a variant of Justice Brandeis' famous plea for "states as laboratories," which we feel tries to tip the balance in favor of decentralizing policy for economic efficiency. Here the laboratory is the state legislature and the experiment is the political ability of a state's governor or a strong political party to control the legislature's excesses. Under our analysis, those states with strong governors or strong political parties will typically have more efficient policies. If so, they become models of "good government" which other states might copy. Recent research by Timothy Besley and Anne Case (1995) suggests that residents do use the economic performance of neighboring states as a "yardstick" against which to measure the performance of their own political process, typically the governor. Governors who fail to control legislative inefficiencies face a significantly lower chance of re-election. Only the decentralization of regulatory policy to the states will give this process of political "yardstick" competition a chance to promote efficiency.

C. BALANCING PARTICIPATION AND EFFICIENCY IN A FEDERALIST SYSTEM

11. Conclusion

We have concluded to this point that political arguments and the current evidence on participation appear to support the use of small decentralized governments to maximize citizen political participation. However, a more centralized alternative can be supported by economic arguments and evidence concerning the economic efficiency of governmental activity. As a result, trade-offs between the potentially competing values of political participation and economic efficiency may be required when evaluating the optimality of a federalist structure.

How are such choices to be made? The analyses in Sections A and B can be used to clarify the potential trade-off between the federalist values of political participation and economic efficiency. Consider how economic efficiency, measured in the dollars of economic output, is likely to change as the public sector becomes more decentralized through the assignment of responsibility to more and more, and thus smaller and smaller, governments. Economic benefits rise as responsibility for policy moves from a single central government to the assignment of responsibility to lower-level governments, but only to a point. Efficiency improves because decentralization limits the reach of inefficient government activities; rather than the country as a whole bearing the burden of inefficiency, only residents within a state are so burdened. Further, interstate political competition may point the way to more *intra*jurisdictionally efficient policies. But as we decentralize, we also increase the likelihood of *inter*jurisdictional inefficiencies – that is, spillovers. Moving initially from a centralized structure, the gains from intrajurisdictional efficiencies exceed any losses from interjurisdictional inefficiencies. Eventually, however, inefficient spillovers come to dominate, and the overall performance of the economy declines.

There is a similar relationship between decentralization and the extent of political participation. Consistent with our theoretical and empirical analysis of Section 2, greater decentralization is likely to increase political participation, though perhaps at a decreasing rate.

Combining our efficiency and participation analysis, we conclude that political participation rises with increased decentralization, but economic efficiency first rises and then falls. It is when efficiency declines that we face a trade-off. Increasing decentralization initially allows both efficiency and participation to increase, but beyond a point more political participation through decentralization must mean less economic efficiency.

The choice of an "optimal" level of decentralization ultimately depends upon the relative importance one places upon the competing federalist values of economic efficiency and political participation; alternative weightings for the values of efficiency and participation will dictate different federalist structures. For example, if efficiency is weighted more highly than participation, the optimal federalist structure will move away from a fully decentralized system so as to increase efficiency and reduce participation. We look forward, with anticipation, to seeing how these federalism issues will be resolved in the emerging constitutions throughout the world.

Bibliography

Arrow, A. Kenneth (1963), *Social Choice and Individual Values*, New York: Wiley.

Bagnoli, Mark and McKee, Michael (1991), "Voluntary Contribution Games: Efficient Provision of Public Goods", **29** *Economic Inquiry,* 351–66.

Baron, David and Ferejohn, John (1989), "Bargaining in Legislatures", **83** *American Political Science Review,* 1182–206.

Bartik, Timothy (1988), "The Effects of Environmental Regulation on Business Location in the United States", **19** *Growth & Change,* 22–44.

Bergstrom, Theodore, Rubinfeld, Daniel, Roberts, Judy and Shapiro, Perry (1988), "A Test for Efficiency in the Supply of Public Education", **35** *Journal of Public Economy,* 289–307.

Besley, Timothy and Case, Anne (1995), "Incumbent Behavior: Vote-Seeking, Tax-setting, and Yardstick Competition", **85** *American Economic Review,* 25–45.

Binmore, Kenneth, Rubinstein, Ariel and Wolinsky, Asher (1986), "The Nash Bargaining Solution in Economic Modelling", **17** *Rand Journal of Economics,* 176–88 .

Boadway, Robin and Flatters, Frank (1982), "Efficiency and Equalization Payments in a Federal System of Government", **15** *Canadian Journal of Economics*, 613–33.

Brainard, William C. and Dolbear, F. Trenery (1967), "The Possibility of Oversupply of Local Public Goods", **75** *Journal of Political Economy,* 86–90.

Break, George (1967), *Intergovernmental Fiscal Relations in the United States*, Washington DC: Brookings Institute, 23–4.

Breton, Albert and Scott, Anthony (1978), *The Economic Constitution of Federal States,* Toronto: University of Toronto Press.

Buchanan, James M. and Goetz, Charles (1972), "Efficiency Limits of Fiscal Mobility: An Assessment of the Tiebout Model", **1** *Journal of Public Economy,* 25–43.

Coase, Ronald (1960), "The Problem of Social Costs", *Journal of Law and Economics,* 1–44.

Coates, Dennis and Munger, Michael (1995), "Strategizing in Small Group Decision-Making: Host State Identification for Radioactive Waste Disposal Among Eight Southern States", **82** *Public Choice,* 1–15.

Cooter, Robert (1982), "The Cost of Coase", **11** *Journal of Legal Studies,* 1–34.

Courant, Paul and Rubinfeld, Daniel (1981), "On the Welfare Effects of Tax Limitation", **16** *Journal of Public Economy,* 289–316.

Crawford, Vincent (1982), "A Theory of Disagreement in Bargaining", **50** *Econometrica,* 607–37.

Cumberland, John (1981), "Efficiency and Equity in Interregional Environmental Management", **2** *Review of Regional Studies*, 1–9.

Dahl, Robert (1956), *A Preface to Democratic Theory*, Chicago: University of Chicago Press.

Dahl, Robert and Tufte, Edward (1973), *Size and Democracy,* Stanford CA: Stanford University Press.

David, Charles E. and Lester, James P. (1989), "Federalism and Environmental Policy" in Lester, James P. (ed)., *Environmental Politics and Policy: Theories and Evidence,* Durham, NC: Duke University Press, 57–9.

de Condorcet, M. (1785), "Essai sur l'Application de L'Analyse à la Probabilité des Decisions Rendues à la Pluraliste des Voix", Paris.

Easterbrook, Frank (1983), "Antitrust and the Economics of Federalism", **26** *Journal of Law & Economics,* 23–50.

Ellickson, Robert (1979), "Public Property Rights: Vicarious Intergovernmental Rights and Liabilities as a Technique for Correcting Intergovernmental Spillovers", in Rubinfeld, Daniel (ed.), *Essays on the Law and Economics of Local Governments*, Washington, DC: Urban Institute.

Epple, Dennis and Zelenitz, Alan (1981), "The Implications of Competition Among Jurisdictions: Does Tiebout Need Politics?", **89** *Journal of Public Economy*, 1197–217.

Finifter, Ada W. (1970), "Dimensions of Political Alienation", **30** *American Political Science Review*, 389–410.

Fischel, William (1975), "Fiscal and Environmental Considerations in the Location of Firms in Suburban Communities" in Mills, Edwin and Oates, Wallace (eds.), *Fiscal Zoning and Land Use Controls*, Lexington, MA: Lexington Books, 119–74.

Fitts, Michael and Inman, Robert P. (1992), "Controlling Congress: Presidential Influence in Domestic Fiscal Policy", **80** *Georgetown Law Journal,* 1737–85.

Frug, Gerald (1980), "The City as a Legal Concept", **93** *Harvard Law Review,* 1059–159.

Gramlich, Edward M. and Laren, Deborah S. (1984), "Migration and Income Redistribution Responsibilities", **19** *Journal of Human Resources,* 489–511.

Gramlich, Edward M. and Rubinfeld, Daniel L. (1982), "Micro Estimates of Public Spending Demand Functions and Tests of the Tiebout and Median Voter Hypotheses", **90** *Journal of Political Economy,* 536–60.

Greenwood, Michael J. (1986), "The Factor Market Consequences of U.S. Immigration", **24** *Journal of Economic Literature,* 1738–72.

Haller, Hans (1986), "Noncooperative Bargaining of N 3 Players", **22** *Economic Letters,* 11–13.

Hoffman, Elizabeth and Spitzer, Matthew L. (1982), "The Coase Theorem: Some Experimental Tests", **25** *Journal of Law & Economics,* 73–98.

Holmstrom, Bengt (1985), "The Provision of Services in a Market Economy" in Inman, Robert (ed.), *Managing the Service Economy: Prospects and Problems*, New York: Cambridge University Press. 183–213.

Inman, Robert (1987), "Markets, Government, and the New Political Economy", in Alan Auerbach and Feldstein, Martin (eds.), *Handbook of Public Economics*, Vol. II, Cambridge, MA: MIT Press.

Inman, Robert P. (1990), "Public Debts and Fiscal Politics: How to Decide", **80** *American Economic Review*, 81–5.

Inman, Robert and Fitts, Michael (1990), "Political Institutions and Fiscal Policy: Evidence from the U.S. Historical Record", **6** (Special Issue) *Journal of Law, Economics and Organization*, 79–132.

Inman, Robert P. and Rubinfeld, Daniel L. (1996), "Designing Tax Policies in Federalist Economies: An Overview", **60** *Journal of Public Economics*, 307–34.

Kalt, Joseph and Zupan, Mark (1984), "Capture and Ideology in the Economic Theory of Politics", **74** *American Economic Review*, 279–300.

Kolstad, Charles and Wolak, Frank (1983), "Competition in Interregional Taxation: The Case of Western Coal", **91** *Journal of Political Economy*, 443–59.

Krehbiel, Keith (1992), *Information and Legislative Organization*, Ann Arbor, MI: The University of Michigan Press.

Kreps, David and Wilson, Robert (1982), "Reputation and Imperfect Information", *Journal of Economic Theory*, 253–79.

Ladd, Helen F. and Yinger, John (1989), *America's Ailing Cities*, Baltimore, MD: Johns Hopkins University Press.

Levmore, Saul (1992), "Bicameralism: When are Two Decisions Better than One", **12** *International Review of Law & Economics*, 145–62.

Lowi, Theodore J. (1969), *The End of Liberalism*, New York: Norton.

Martinez-Vasquez, J. (1994), "The Challenge of Expenditure-Assignment Reform in Russia", **12** *Environment and Planet*, 277–91.

McConnell, Kenneth and Schwab, Robert (1990), "The Impact of Environmental Regulation on Industry Location Decisions: The Motor Vehicle Industry", **66** *Land and Economics*, 67–81.

Mill, John Stuart (1960), "Representative Government", *Three Essays*, Oxford: Oxford University Press.

Nagel, Jack (1975), *The Descriptive Analysis of Power*, New Haven, CT: Yale University Press.

Nagel, Jack (1980), *Participation*, Englewood Cliffs, NJ: Prentice Hall.

Niou, Emerson and Peter Ordeshook (1985), "Universalism in Congress", **29** *American Journal of Political Science*, 246–58.

Oates, Wallace E. (1972), *Fiscal Federalism*, London: Harcourt Brace Jovanovich.

Oates, Wallace E. and Schwab, Robert M. (1986), "Economic Competition among Jurisdictions: Efficiency Enhancing or Distortion Inducing?", **35** *Journal of Public Economics*, 333–54.

Olsen, Mancur (1965), *The Logic of Collective Action*, Cambridge, MA: Harvard University Press.

Ordeshook, Peter and Riker, William (1973), *An Introduction to Positive Political Theory*, Englewood Cliffs, NJ: Prentice-Hall.

Pateman, Carole (1970), *Participation and Democratic Theory*, New York: Cambridge University Press.

Pauly, Martin (1970), "Optimality, `Public' Goods, and Local Governments: A General Theoretical Analysis", **78** *Journal of Political Economy*, 572–86.

Pestieau, Pierre (1977), "The Optimality Limits of the Tiebout Model", in Oates, Wallace (ed.), *The Politics of Fiscal Federalism*, Lexington, MA: Heath-Lexington Press.

Polinsky, A. Mitchell (1980), "Resolving Nuisance Disputes: The Simple Economics of Injunctive and Damage Remedies", **32** *Stanford Law Review*, 1075–112.

Revesz, Richard (1992), "Rehabilitating Interstate Competition: Rethinking the 'Race-to-the-Bottom' Rationale for Federal Environmental Regulation", **67** *New York University Law Review*, 1210–55.

Riker, William (1964), *Federalism: Origins, Operation, Significance*, Boston, MA: Little, Brown, and Co.

Rose-Ackerman, Susan (1981), "Does Federalism Matter? Political Choice in a Federal Republic", **89** *Journal of Political Economy*, 152–65.

Rose-Ackerman, Susan (1994), "Environmental Policy and Federal Structure: A Comparison of the United States and Germany", **47** *Vanderbilt Law Review*, 1587–622.

Rose-Ackerman, Susan and Mashaw, Jerry (1984), "Federalism and Regulation", in Eads, George C. and Fix, Michael (eds.), *The Reagan Regulatory Strategy: An Assessment*, Washington, DC: Urban Institute Press, 111–52.

Roth, Alvin (1985), "Towards a Focal Point Theory of Bargaining", in Roth, A. E. (ed.), *Game Theoretic Models of Bargaining*, New York: Cambridge University Press.

Rubinfeld, Daniel L. (1987), "The Economics of the Local Public Sector", in Auerbach, Alan and Feldstein, Martin (eds.), *Handbook of Public Economics,* Volume II, Amsterdam: North-Holland, 571–645.

Rubinstein, Ariel (1982), "Perfect Equilibrium in a Bargaining Model", **50** *Econometrica,* 97–110.

Samuelson, Paul (1954), "The Pure Theory of Public Expenditure", **36** *Review of Economics and Statistics,* 386–9.

Schumpeter, Joseph (1943), *Capitalism, Socialism, and Democracy*, New York: Harper and Row.

Schwartz, Thomas (1989), "Representation as Agency and Pork Barrel Paradox", Mimeo, UCLA.

Silberman, Jonathan and Garey Durden (1976), "Determining Legislative Preferences on Minimum Wage: An Economic Approach", **84** *Journal of Political Economy*, 317–29.

Shepsle, Kenneth (1979), "Institutional Arrangements and Equilibrium in Multidimensional Voting Models", **28** *American Journal of Political Science,* 27–59.

Smith, Adam (1776), *An Inquiry into the Nature and Causes of the Wealth of Nations*, London: Methuen & Co.

Stigler, George (1971), "The Theory of Economic Regulation", **2** *Bell Journal of Economics and Managment Science,* 3–21.

Tiebout, Charles (1956), "A Pure Theory of Local Expenditures", **64** *Journal of Political Economy*, 416–24.

Weingast, Barry (1979), "A Rational Choice Perspective on Congressional Norms", **23** *American Journal of Political Science,* 245–62.

Weingast, Barry R. and Marshall, William (1988), "The Industrial Organization of Congress", **96** *Journal of Political Economy,* 132–63.

Wildasin, David E. (1986), *Urban Public Finance*, Chicago: Adademic Publishers, Harcourt Press.

Williams, Alan (1966), "The Optimal Provision of Public Goods in a System of Local Governments", **74** *Journal of Political Economy*, 18–33.

Williamson, Oliver E. (1985), *The Economic Institutions of Capitalism*, New York: The Free Press.

Wittman, Donald (1989), "Why Democracies Produce Efficient Results", **97** *Journal of Political Economy,* 1395–424.

19 Legal harmonization

Enrico Baffi and Paolo Santella

Legal harmonization is a process that aligns legal rules either within a federal framework (that is, in the presence of a superior, rule-making entity with respect to the federated entities), through the adoption of regulatory models agreed at a multilateral level (such as conventions adopted within the OECD or UN) or through the unilateral adoption of a foreign sovereign state's legal system by a different sovereign state.

The economics of legal harmonization can be considered as a complement to the economics of federalism. Legal harmonization should be applied when a regulatory solution reached through the competition of political units is not optimal or when the economies of scale and scope, externalities and the provision of public goods prevent a decentralized approach to regulation. However, this interpretation denies the autonomy of legal harmonization from the economics of federalism. Two reasons justify why there should be a second definition for legal harmonization.

First, federalism consists of the distribution of legislative and judicial powers between local and central authorities. Legal harmonization consists not only of federal level harmonization, but also of sovereign state harmonization. Unilateral adoption by a sovereign state of the legal system of another sovereign state is defined as "legal transplantation". Legal transplantation reduces or potentially eliminates differences between legal systems through the unilateral non-cooperative effort of one system. The wholesale transplantation of the 1900 German Civil Code to Japan is an example of the unilateral adoption of legal rules belonging to another system.

Second, the research subjects of the two areas are different from an economic point of view. The economics of federalism focuses on those goods and services that are offered in sub-optimal quantity within a federal context, such as public goods, goods with externalities and markets with economies of scale and scope. The literature on legal harmonization consists mainly of the study of contract and corporate law.

Federalism and legal harmonization use the same theoretical model. This model is based on the subsidiarity principle, which states that the federal solution (harmonization) is accepted whenever the initiative from local authorities is inefficient. For instance, since 2004 the European Commission is required to accompany every legislative proposal (directive or regulation) with a study that shows that the objective pursued may not be adequately obtained at a decentralized level.

Although legal harmonization may be studied without reference to the efficiency of its solutions, the economics of legal harmonization aims at verifying whether harmonization produces efficient results. Ribstein and Kobayashi (1997) list the benefits from harmonization and transplantation, specifically stating that a more uniform legal regime decreases litigation and information costs because it is easier to ascertain each state's laws. Harmonization also reduces externality problems from state laws, such as local laws that favor domestic consumers and investors, while hurting foreign producers and issuers.

Scholars of legal harmonization tend to conclude that harmonization promotes efficiency. However, this conclusion appears to be valid only for contract law, while corporate law and securities law have arguments in favor of competition among jurisdictions.

Finally, while there is a tendency to study legal harmonization with reference to a specific subject, a small group of scholars have adopted a global approach to legal harmonization (Parisi and Carbonara 2007, 2009).

Legal Harmonization in General

Generally, harmonization of standards produces two negative effects that cannot be eliminated. First, harmonization restricts the possibility of an exit strategy, because there are fewer possibilities for leaving the current legal order for another if legal orders are harmonized (Ribstein and Kobayashi (2006) themselves acknowledge this). Second, harmonization drives interest groups to ask for the introduction of mandatory rules to benefit themselves, which creates inefficiencies (Ribstein and Kobayashi 2006). Mandatory rules are less detrimental when there is competition among the legal orders, because subjects can evade the mandatory rules by changing legal orders (the exit strategy).

Alesina, Angeloni and Etro (2005) state that the benefits of centralization consist in the possibility of exploiting economies of scale through the central allocation of policy responsibility. Their paper characterizes the costs of harmonization as principally deriving from the heterogeneity of preferences across regions. Balancing the benefits and costs of harmonization, the optimal degree of harmonization should ensure that all the functions where economies of scale are predominant should be held at the central level and all the functions with high heterogeneity of preferences should be left at local level. This point is illustrated in a related paper (Alesina, Angeloni and Schuknecht 2005), where the authors provide empirical evidence of the expansion of the policy-making role of the European Union between 1971 and 2000. They find that the European Union's process of allocation of powers is far from optimal. Substantial harmonization has occurred in areas where heterogeneity of preferences is predominant (such as social protection or agricultural policy), but other areas with strong economies of scale have remained in the local domain (such as defense and environmental protection).

By studying the effects of the harmonization of contract law, Parisi and Carbonara (2009) depart from a position where harmonization is usually efficient and arrive at two important conclusions. First, they affirm that when switching costs are exogenous, a cooperative solution leads to greater harmonization compared with non-cooperative solutions. Second, they reveal that the equilibrium that is reached by means of cooperative solutions is a Nash equilibrium that does not allow for total elimination of the legal distance among legal orders.

The most surprising solution results when considering the hypothesis that switching costs are endogenous. In that case, when considering an operation in two steps, of which the first is characterized by the preparation of the agreement, a state can act to bind itself so that it will not be able to change the standards of its legal order for reasons such as the constitutional relevance of a legal principle or a public commitment by stubborn politicians not to change a specific feature of their national legislation. (These actions can be considered to be "hand-tying actions", in the sense that the cost of introducing a change to the legal order is greater than the benefits of harmonization.) In doing so, a state places the full burden of harmonization on the other state. According to Parisi and Carbonara, this result is worse than the result that would come from harmonization that is not guided by possible international agreements, because states would autonomously move toward a certain level of harmonization without following strategic behavior.

The position of Parisi and Carbonara does not always appear to be justified. Even in the case of a two-stage process, that is, when two states adopt measures for harmonization and then move on to stipulate the agreement, a country might autonomously bind itself without the sure prospect of a treaty, hoping that this would drive the other nation to bring its law into conformity.

Parisi and Carbonara's idea of self-binding behavior is based on the strategic nature of a country's efforts to reduce legal differences with other countries. Such efforts are strategic substitutes, which means that the marginal benefit from increasing one country's effort reduces another country's effort. This leads each state to decrease its efforts when the other country increases its efforts.

The dynamic occurrence of legal harmonization among several countries depends on various factors, among which is the original choice of law regime. Imagine a case in which countries have introduced binding standards, in which the standards of the A states are more efficient than the standards of the B states. You might suppose that the B states would conform to the A states' standards, but this is not necessarily true. The result would depend on the percentage of states that originally adopt the two standards. If the inefficient B states constitute such a majority that they can take advantage of externality networks in conforming and the switching costs are not high, then it will be the efficient A states that conform to the standards of the less efficient B states.

Under the opposite hypothesis, that the number of A states is larger than the number of B states, and if the switching costs are not too high, it might be convenient for the B states to conform to the law of the A states. This would lead to state laws that are harmonized and efficient. The same line of reasoning may be followed if there is a single A state that is sufficiently large to make it convenient for the B states to conform to the laws of the single A state.

The final hypothesis is that interstate exchanges cannot take place so no country changes its own law.

Normally, liberal choice is considered the best choice of law regime to produce efficient laws. Liberal choice means a regime in which the parties choose or lay down their preferred law. In reality, this conclusion does not always seem to be correct. Imagine that a state C has adopted the standards of the B states, while its businesses have chosen the law of the A states. There are few incentives for state C to adopt the rules of the A states, because its businesses can resolve the inefficiency problem by opting out of the inefficient law altogether. Parisi and Carbonara (2009) also consider a third model of a choice of law regime, which they define as semi-restrictive, according to which businesses and individuals must adopt the national law if they belong to the same state, while they are free to choose the law that is most suitable to their interests if they belong to different states. Even in that case the solution depends on the initial situation, on the switching costs and on the benefits of a particular law. In one or more states, an inefficient law might prevail.

For the majority of scholars, harmonization of standards is believed to be the necessary consequence of competition among states. This is especially valid in the fields of contract and corporate law. There are often insufficient incentives for a country to change its own laws, since the businesses in the liberal choice of law regime choose their own law. However, under some hypotheses, the incentives for changing the law do exist. There are authors who recognize a race to the bottom, meaning a downward harmonization toward inefficient rules, in the competition among legal orders to attract businesses or legal parties. Other authors recognize a race to the top, that is, a race that leads to the harmonization of efficient standards. This theme has mainly been dealt with in regard to corporate law. That does not mean that competition necessarily leads to harmonization. It is possible that a federated state will make no changes following a state laying down new standards (Parisi and Carbonara 2007).

Finally, scholars of public choice have pointed out that it is necessary to keep in mind the effects that interest groups have on the creation of standards. Therefore, a regime of liberal choice of law may reduce the incentive to introduce laws favorable to interest groups that formerly benefited, for example, from inefficient rules in a regime of restrictive choice of law (Ribstein and Kobayashi 1997).

The model of Parisi and Carbonara can be useful for understanding the results obtained from Alesina's et al. analyses. They provide a model that shows which sectors are subject to inefficient legal harmonization: those selected by the group of B states (or by one large B state). This choice conditions the A states to conform and accept the harmonization of one inefficient sector (for example, agriculture).

There is another possibility, which may not have been considered by Parisi and Carbonara in their work. This is an "exchange" between A and B states, in which the former proposes to the latter the harmonization of some sectors with the laws of A in exchange for the harmonization of other sectors with the laws of B. The same line of reasoning can be applied to the choice not to harmonize in order to maintain a competition among legal orders. The A states could be interested in maintaining competition between legal orders for some sectors (for example, taxation), and they might obtain this concession from the B states in exchange for accepting the latter's priority of maintaining competition among the legal orders of other sectors (for example, defense).

Corporate Law, Legal Harmonization or Competition?

Since the 1960s, the question addressed in relation to legal harmonization or competition has been whether it is preferable to allow each state to be free to lay down its own corporate law, or if the central government should dictate a law that is effective for all states.

The idea of a race, either upwards or downwards, is reflected in the American reality in which Delaware changed its law in such a way as to induce businesses to incorporate there. By doing this, Delaware, one of the smallest states in the United States, obtained fees for incorporation which guarantee 25% of its state revenue. At times, other states have followed Delaware's actions, even if, adopting the liberal choice of law regime, it is not necessary to modify the law but to leave businesses free to adopt the law they prefer. On the other hand, for larger states like California, legal incorporation fees are a tiny part of its revenue, and therefore such states may not have had a strong incentive to corner such legal fees. But Delaware was interested in the fees and produced new legislation according to the needs of businesses. Was this process a race that pushed toward efficient laws (a race to the top), or did it drag the laws toward inefficient solutions that were to the exclusive advantage of managers (a race to the bottom)?

In the 1970s, Cary held that the race was downwards because states forced themselves to make laws to protect board directors (Cary 1974). In reality, this question should be examined with reference to two distinct periods. In the first period, the business goes public. In the second period, the established business carries out extraordinary operations like mergers and acquisitions to bring about the transfer of its headquarters to another state.

In the initial stage, the issuer has an interest in maximizing the value of the securities it issues – that is, the value of the firm – and will look for a law that lays down efficient standards that do not produce deadweight loss. In this way, the state's race to offer the best law will be directed at providing legislation to ensure the issuer's incorporation there. But during the lifetime of the firm, other choices must be made. For a series of reasons, these choices are taken by managers without being influenced by stockholders in an efficient way. Will these choices be carried out in order to maximize the value of the firm or to guarantee privileges for the directors? In the period between the 1970s and 1980s, there was a wave of takeovers to which states reacted by introducing anti-takeover standards. More specifically, directors defended themselves by introducing standards that, in various ways, blocked takeovers or made them extremely difficult. The aim was essentially to protect company workers present in each state because of the fear that a successful takeover would cause mass layoffs. Not even Delaware was immune from this trend, even if it reacted later and more gently compared with other states. This result reinforced the opinion of those who envisioned a race to the bottom among states in corporate law. However, there was also proof that companies were not interested in these changes and actually sought to avoid laws that exclusively protected incumbent managers. The loss in value of listed companies because of these laws may have been severe. Therefore, when Pennsylvania issued anti-takeover statutes that blocked takeovers in a nearly total manner, many companies abandoned Pennsylvania and reincorporated in other states that were less restrictive with regard to takeovers (Romano 1993).

According to Winter (1977), companies continuously seek efficient laws because they must accumulate capital, and if the company is under a legal framework that penalizes investors, the investor will be willing to pay less for its bonds and stocks. The cost of capital for these companies will increase to such an extent that such companies will find themselves in a disadvantaged position compared with those companies that have an efficient organization and a lower cost of capital.

However, such conclusions do not always apply, and even Roberta Romano (1993), who supports the usefulness of competition among states, hypothesizes that in some specific cases harmonization by the federal government may be necessary. In the last few years, the federal government intervened to carry out a partial harmonization of corporate law with the Sarbanes-Oxley Act. Some authors believe Sarbanes-Oxley to be a downward harmonizing intervention (Easterbrook 2009). But other law and economics scholars maintain that mandatory rules are necessary, given existing distortions in the charter amendment process and in decisions to move the registered office, because directors are able to introduce rules in charters that benefit themselves to the detriment of owners (Bebchuk 2005).

Legal Harmonization in the EU

The organization of the European states known as the European Union (EU) developed from the idea of some politicians to ensure that citizens of Europe had access to four freedoms: the free movement of goods, individuals, services and capital.

It should be said that the bulk of legislative provisions (directives and regulations) adopted within the EU are such as to configure a process of legal harmonization. Besides, this process is not limited to contract and company law (the two fields most often investigated by the economics of legal harmonization), but also includes many other fields, such as: telecommunications, air transportation, medical standards, and others. EU law today is the most important case of legal harmonization in a (sort of) federal context. It impacts many new fields compared with the two that are mainly examined in the literature of legal harmonization.

The four fundamental freedoms of the EU pose a problem as to whether competition or harmonization among states is preferable.

The free movement of individuals poses a problem that is widely discussed: for contract law, is it preferable to proceed with harmonization rather than with competition among Member States?

Many scholars have stated that, in the field of contract law, harmonization is socially efficient because it eliminates the costs of studying different laws and excludes a conflict of laws. This facilitates the free movement of individuals because they can stipulate contracts without committing the error of believing the contract is governed by a different state's laws. The EU has issued some regulatory acts to harmonize contract law. The EU has harmonized parts of contract law in which a party is a consumer (for example, Directive 93/13 EEC). An important step toward partial harmonization took place with a regulation that was intended to harmonize international contract law (Regulation (EC) 44/2001). Nevertheless, it can be argued that the laws of the various Member States concerning contract law remain different (Bussani and Werro 2009).

The free circulation of goods developed through an unforeseeable step by the European Court of Justice. The EU tended to prefer a harmonization of the standards that regulate the characteristics of the goods that can circulate within EU territory. In 1979, with the *Cassis de Dijon* verdict (case 120/78), the Court affirmed that goods can circulate across the EU on condition that they respect the legislation of the Member State where they were produced. This verdict left space for competition among Member States to attract producers to their country. A race to the bottom could have occurred, that is, a race by Member States to pass progressively inferior requirements for goods produced in their country. But that did not happen. One explanation is that products are also sold to citizens of the country where they are produced, and therefore the legislators preferred not to reduce the requirements too greatly in order not to harm their own citizens.

After the *Cassis de Dijon* verdict, the EU headed in a direction that targeted (so-called) "harmonized competition": the EU laid down certain ground rules that goods must satisfy in order to circulate in the European market, leaving Member States with the ability to introduce further requirements, allowing for de facto regulatory competition.

In the context of corporate law, European legal harmonization was carried out to integrate the incomplete provisions of the Treaty of Rome regarding the subject of freedom of establishment of companies. Although the Treaty recognized freedom of establishment for companies as well as for people, it did not define the concept of a company. As a result, there was no clear definition of whether company mobility – one of the consequences of the freedom of establishment – referred to the possibility of moving a registered office independently of the actual headquarters. Moreover, the lack of a definition did not permit cross-border mergers. These problems created the need for legal harmonization. Faced with the possibility of introducing rules that could bring about competition among Member States in the field of company law, until the mid-1980s the European Union instead focused on achieving a harmonization that would exclude such competition. This process of harmonization halted due to the impossibility of identifying a common European model for the mandatory participation of workers in the management of companies and for discipline of groups (Santella 2010).

Later developments have produced, among other things, the introduction of cross-border mergers and in general they have created a legal situation that is characterized by a partial harmonization supported by the freedom of competition among Member States, which we define as harmonized competition. The European Court of Justice also contributed to this result: since the 1999 *Centros* verdict (Case C-212/97) for companies of initial formation the Court recognized the right to locate the registered office in a different Member State than the actual headquarters. It is difficult to formulate a judgment in terms of the efficiency of the choices carried out by the European Union. It could be that the competition introduced among states in company law is for the most part efficient, as has been seen with regard to American law. But more likely, the directives and regulations that make up European company law must be evaluated individually, since they probably contain both efficient and inefficient provisions.

The discipline of financial services is also an integral part of the freedom of movement of capital. A first wave of legislation in the 1970s and 1980s introduced minimum harmonization in some financial services, leaving ample space for

Member States to adapt EU legislation to national specificities (European Commission 1999). The impetus for further integration in the direction of the completion of a single market for financial services in the EU came through a series of directives and regulations adopted following the Financial Services Action Plan of 1999. This aimed to tackle three strategic objectives: (i) a single market for wholesale financial services; (ii) open and secure retail markets; and (iii) advanced prudential rules and supervision. The issue of harmonized competition was also dealt with in the adoption of an Action Plan through a new institutional arrangement (the so-called Lamfalussy Procedure) to coordinate the design and implementation of some of the directives within the Action Plan, with the aim of restricting, but not eliminating, Member States' discretion (Maes 2007). The financial crisis of 2008 has elicited a general revision of the entire legislative framework concerning financial services. These changes are aimed at introducing more harmonization through (i) the redrafting of the existing legislation with less discretion for EU Member States; (ii) expanding the regulatory perimeter to include new areas of the EU financial market (i.e. hedge funds, short selling, and the post-trading infrastructure) and (iii) the introduction of new agencies in charge of providing a more uniform approach to the enforcement of EU financial legislation (European Commission 2009).

Bibliography

Alesina, A. and Angeloni, I. and Etro, F. (2005), "International Unions, *American Economic Review*, 95(3), 602–15.

Alesina, A. and Angeloni, I. and Schuknecht, L. (2005), "What does the European Union Do?", *Public Choice*, 123(3), 275–319.

Bebchuk, L.A. (1989), "Limiting Contractual Freedom in Corporate Law: The Desirable Constraints on Charter Amendments", *Harvard Law Review*, 102. 1820–60.

Bebchuk, L.A. (2005), "The Case for Increasing Shareholder Power", *Harvard Law Review*, 118, 833–914.

Bussani, M. and Werro, F. (2009), *European Private Law: A Handbook*, vol. I, Brussels: Bruylant.

Cary, l.W. (1974), "Federalism and Corporate Law: Reflection upon Delaware", *Yale Law Journal*, 83, 663–705.

Easterbrook, F.H. (2009), "The Race for the Bottom in Corporate Governance", *Virginia Law Review*, 95, 685–706.

European Commission, "Implementing the Framework for Financial Markets: Action Plan 1999", available at: http://ec.europa.eu/internal_market/finances/docs/actionplan/index/action_en.pdf.

European Commission, "Report of the High-Level Group Chaired by Jacques de Larosière 2009", available at: http://ec.europa.eu/internal_market/finances/docs/de_larosiere_report_en.pdf

Maes, I. (2007), *Half a Century of European Financial Integration: From the Rome Treaty to the 21st Century*, Brussels: Mercatorfonds.

Parisi, F. and Carbonara, E. (2007), "The Paradox of Legal Harmonization", *Public Choice*, 132, 367–400.

Parisi, F. and Carbonara, E. (2009), "Choice of Law and Legal Evolution: Rethinking the Market for Legal Rules", *Public Choice*, 139(3) 461–92, available at SSRN: http://ssrn.com/abstract=1011376.

Ribstein, L.E. and Kobayashi, B.H. (1997), "Federalism, Efficiency and Competition", available at SSRN: http://ssrn.com/abstract=110071 or doi:10.2139/ssrn.110071.

Ribstein, L.E. and Kobayashi, B.H. (2006), "The Economics of Federalism", University of Illinois Law & Economics Research Paper No. LE06–001; George Mason Law & Economics Research Paper No. 06–15. Available at SSRN: http://ssrn.com/abstract=875626.

Romano, R. (1993), *The Genius of American Corporate Law*, AEI Studies in Regulation and Federalism, Washington, DC: AEI Press.

Santella, P. (2010), "Perspectives of European Corporate Law" (Prospettive Del Diritto Societario europeo) (in Italian), available at SSRN: http://abstract/1621809.

Winter R. (1977), "State Law, Shareholder Protection, and the Theory of the Corporation", Journal of Legal Studies, 6, 251–92.

Cases

Judgment of the Court of 20 February 1979, Case 120/78, *Rewe-Zentral AG* v *Bundesmonopolverwaltung für Branntwein* (*Cassis de Dijon*), European Court Reports 1979 p. 649.

Judgment of the Court of 9 March 1999, Case C-212/97, *Centros Ltd v Erhvervs- og Selskabsstyrelsen,* European Court reports 1999, p. I-01459.

20 Forum shopping and the evolution of rules of choice of law

Nita Ghei

1. Introduction

In a perfect world, the outcome of litigation would be entirely independent of the choice of forum, and the outcome would be the same, no matter where the suits were brought. In the world as it exists, with a variety of legal regimes, jurisdictions that overlap, and interests that might conflict, the choice of forum can sometimes be a matter of life and death (Ghei and Parisi 2004).[1] The fact that the choice of forum can be outcome-determinative is intuitively troubling, particularly in that this offers an opportunity for forum shopping, with all the accompanying possibilities of efficiencies. However, this can also offer an opportunity for forum selection, which might enhance efficiency, as will be discussed later.

A variety of theoretical approaches have been suggested to correct this perceived problem, and, in reality, a complex jurisprudence exists to deal with issues when more than one sovereign's law might possibly apply to the litigation at hand. While in many situations this might be a matter of two or more sovereign nations, the United States is peculiar in its federal structure, in that the various states retain considerable sovereignty. Consequently, conflicts law has emerged from the common law, and has evolved over time, to correct some of the more significant problems of moral hazard (Shavell 1979), with the additional bound imposed by constitutional restrictions on personal jurisdiction (McDougall, Felix and Whitten 2004).

2. A Brief History

The conflict of laws developed on the Continent in Europe, and in England, under the influence of concepts of international law, which consequently

[1] Among other examples, Ghei and Parisi (2004) discuss the widely publicized case of the "Beltway Snipers" from 2002. John Allen Muhammed and John Lee Malvo were alleged to have committed murders in the state of Maryland, the District of Columbia, and the Commonwealth of Virginia. They were eventually tried in Virginia, where the death penalty was a possibility for Muhammed, as an adult. He was executed in 2009. At the time Muhammed and Malvo were charged, Maryland had a moratorium on the death penalty, a factor that played into the decision to choose Virginia as the forum, though Maryland had, arguably, at least as strong an interest in prosecuting the case, in view of the fact that several of the murders took place within its boundaries.

influenced American conflicts law, even though it largely deals with interstate matters (McDougal, Felix and Whitten 2001).

The earliest developments of conflicts law, for modern purposes, originate in the "rediscovery" of Roman law in the Middle Ages in Italy. Scholars in Italy began to study Roman law as the universal law, and started with the assumption that multistate issues required a choice among competing local laws. "A Glossator called Magister Aldricus, . . . believed to be the founder of our discipline gave a simple answer: he favored application of that law which is better and more useful" (Juenger 1993). Medieval jurists also experimented with multilateralism, and other approaches, which modern courts have developed more fully.

History intervened, however (McDougal et al. 2004). With the coming of the Industrial Revolution, and the rise of capitalism, along with increased explorations, mercantile and maritime law regulated an increasing share of litigation. The rise of nation states, and concentration of power into sovereign authority, resulted in conflicts law largely explained by the doctrine of territoriality in conflicts, dominated by the influential seventeenth century Dutch scholar Ulrich Huber, who relied on international law principles, particularly comity.

English common law courts, on the other hand, remained relatively isolated. The common law was uniform. The English courts did not entertain suits having to do with matters of maritime or mercantile law, nor did they entertain foreign suits. As such, the English common law did not need to develop until the middle of the nineteenth century, when the countries in continental Europe had long had well-developed rules for conflicts (Sack 1956).

This late-developed English law was imported into the American colonies, and augmented by case law, but was also heavily influenced by Joseph Story (starting with the first edition in 1834). The first modern treatment of conflicts in the United States was given by Joseph Beale as the Reporter of the first Restatement of Conflict of Laws (Leflar 1981). The Restatement (First), as is discussed in more detail in the next section, emphasized "vested rights" rather than comity, and consequently favored a territorial approach to conflicts of laws. This was, over the second half of the twentieth century, replaced by a multitude of more flexible approaches in the majority of the states, while the United States Supreme Court developed its own jurisprudence for choice of law for federal courts sitting in diversity[2] (Roosevelt 2010).

3. Approaches to Conflicts

Modern approaches to conflicts of laws largely reflect these origins in their effort to address three main issues: adjudicatory jurisdiction; substantive

2 Allowing federal courts to sit in diversity cases, and act as state courts, is an effective check to the adverse selection/ moral hazard forum shopping problem within the United States dual sovereign federal system, as is discussed below.

competence and choice of governing law; and recognition of judgments (Parisi and O'Hara 2002). The goals of the rules of conflicts, traditionally, were uniformity, predictability and avoidance of forum shopping, though Brainerd Currie (1963) de-emphasized them in his interest analysis approach, changing the focus to other values, including the interests of the state. Nonetheless, a legal system is considered a success to the extent that it achieves uniform and predictable outcomes. The gold standard for a conflicts regime remains the "mirror image test" (Ghei and Parisi 2004): the same set of facts should result in the application of the same substantive law, no matter the forum where the suit is filed, eliminating the incentive to forum shop.

Approaches to conflicts can be divided into three broad categories, all of which largely seek a balance between the goals of uniformity, predictability and avoidance of forum shopping. The first, and simplest, is a unilateral approach, exemplified by *lex fori*, where the law of the forum is always applied, as was the custom in England several centuries ago. The second is a multilateral approach, where the court attempts to balance the interests of the jurisdictions involved. Most conflicts regimes fall within this category. Rules-based regimes, such as of the civil law countries; Rome I and Rome II of the European Union; and the Restatement (First) are multilateral in their approach. So too are standards-based regimes such as Currie's interest analysis and the multifactor tests of Restatement (Second). The third is a substantive approach, which tries to apply the best law to the fact pattern. Leflar's "better rule of law" approach best exemplifies this category (Cox 2001) (though the Glossator Magister Aldricus foreshadowed him).

None of these approaches is perfect in avoiding forum shopping, but each has its own advantages in its applications.

3.1 Unilateral Approach

The unilateral approach has the advantages of clarity, predictability and economy. The rule is simple to understand. It creates valuable precedent, which is a public good, and thus increases social welfare (Mueller 2003). Knowledge of applicability of forum law removes one source of uncertainty in structuring transactions. As long as there is an exit option, a *lex fori* approach forces a jurisdiction to internalize the costs of bad laws, and promotes competition among jurisdictions to improve laws – a matter of some importance in a federal system that exists in the United States. On the other hand, it can allow interest groups to organize and lobby the legislature for laws to favor them (Olson 1971), such as, for example, the plaintiff trail bar lobby for plaintiff-favoring law, which in turn would mean that certain tort suits could be filed in those jurisdictions with the knowledge that the forum law would be applied. This suggests the counter-intuitive conclusion that uncertainty about which forum's law will apply might actually reduce forum shopping.

3.2 Multilateral Approach

Under a multilateral approach, the court tries to balance the interests of the sovereigns impacted by the litigation. This can be done either by bright-line rules, or through the use of a standards-based regime.

The European Union, through Rome I and Rome II, favors the use of a rules-based regime, which is not surprising, given that, historically, civil law jurisdictions favor such an approach. The purpose of the Convention on the Law Applicable to Contractual Obligations (Rome I), effective in 1991, was to establish uniform rule concerning choice of law in contract among EU member states (Zhang 2009). In 2007, the EU promulgated the Regulation on the Law Applicable to Non-Contractual Obligations (Rome II), to cover conflicts of laws in certain other situations within the EU. In the United States, the Restatement (First) of Conflicts was also a rules-based approach.[3] It was based on a vested-rights theory, with territoriality as a guiding principle (Brilmayer and Goldsmith 2002).

In theory, a rules-based approach should work well. The court is not supposed to consider the forum interests in making the determination as to which substantive law applies. As long as the rules are applied consistently, the same fact patterns should result in the application of the same substantive law. The result should be the same outcome always, and in theory, should eliminate forum shopping. *In theory*, a rules-based multilateral approach is highly successful in terms of the "mirror image test."

The problem is, of course, that rules are not followed consistently. Under the Restatement (First), courts often used the public policy exception to avoid applying the clear rule.[4] Matters were made even less clear when the suit could be characterized as either tort or contract. The problem was further compounded when courts engaged in *dépeçage*, or *renvoi*.[5] The use of escape devices

---

[3] The Restatement (First) is now a minority view in the United States (Symeonides 2001).

[4] See e.g., *Paul v Nat'l Life*, 352 S.E.2d 550 (W. Va. 1986). Two West Virginia residents drove into Indiana, where they were involved in a one-car accident, resulting in their deaths. The estate of the passenger sued the estate of the driver for wrongful death. Indiana had a guest statute which granted immunity to the defendant. The West Virginia trial court applied Indiana law, as being consistent with Restatement (First) rules, that is, the law of the place of the tort applies. On appeal, Judge Neely used the public policy exception to reverse the trial court's decision, holding that West Virginia law should apply. The Restatement (First)'s rule of place of injury for tort was circumvented by this decision, even as the judge explicitly stated his preference for the rules-based approach of the Restatement (First) to other approaches to conflicts.

[5] Nor is the problem limited to the United States, or to the Restatement (First). The Supreme Court of England, in November 2010, handed down a judgment in *Dallah Real Estate and Tourism Holding Co. v The Ministry of Religious Affairs, Gov't of Pakistan*, [2010] UKSC 46. It was a case of enforcement of judgment of an arbrital award made

reduces the probability of uniform outcomes, and correspondingly increases the incentive to forum-shop.

Standards-based regimes, on the other hand, accept the increased probability of forum shopping, and decreased clarity and predictability, as a trade-off for the objective of furthering state interests. In a standards-based approach, such as the Restatement (Second) and Currie's interest analysis, the court undertakes multistep analysis, and not surprisingly, the result is a multifactor test, with no clear a priori rules. In addition to the lack of clarity and predictability, the focus on state interests makes these approaches particularly vulnerable to special interest lobbying at the legislative level (Olson 1971; Mueller 2003).

3.2.1 Substantive approach In this approach, the court is freed from considering the interest of any particular sovereign, and focuses on choosing the best applicable law. This is Leflar's "better law approach" and should spur a race to the top. It is costly, however, and can be accomplished efficiently only if the judge is fully knowledgeable in all foreign law. Furthermore, it is irrelevant when the parties have made a choice of law *ex ante*, as in a contract. It is likely to work best in mass litigation situations, which span multiple jurisdictions.

Thus, no approach is free of the possibility of forum shopping, and no approach entirely passes the mirror image test.

4. Moral Hazard and Forum Shopping[6]

The possibility of forum shopping, and the moral hazard associated with it, arises only in the presence of uncertainty. In litigation, there are two sources of uncertainty: the choice of opposing party, and the choice of forum. In terms of game theory, this is a sequential game. At step one, either defendant chooses plaintiff or plaintiff chooses defendant. A third option is that neither party exerts full control – as in a contract claim, which begins with a consensual transaction. To the extent that there is private information, and one party is exerting control, there will be some degree of adverse selection (Akerloff 1970; Gale 2001).

At step 2, typically, the plaintiff has the choice of forum, since the plaintiff files the suit. If the same substantive law applies, there is no strategic advantage for choice of forum. Choice of forum matters only if there is non-zero, positive

---

in France. In an interesting point about conflicts, the issue was which law governed the validity of an arbitration agreement. English law provides, in the absence of the choice by the parties, that it is the law of the country where the agreement was made – France, in this case. The French *Cour de Cassation*, however, has held that transnational law governs arbitration agreements made in France, not French local law. The Law Lords chose to not *renvoi*, and apply French law to the case – surely not the result to be expected in a rules-based regime.

6 This section draws heavily upon Ghei and Parisi (2004).

probability that the outcome will vary depending on the choice of forum. In that case, the plaintiff will choose the forum most likely to yield a favorable outcome (O'Hara and Ribstein 2001). However, the defendant can choose to remove the suit to another forum, if possible.

The situation, of course, is not always quite so clear cut, with the declaratory judgment action being the classic example. The declaratory judgment action is an interesting variation of an intentional tort (Moore 2001). The "natural" plaintiff is the holder of the patent, but, in a declaratory judgment action, the infringer, the "natural" defendant, becomes the plaintiff. In this case, the plaintiff controls the choice of both defendant and forum, because the potential infringer can choose the patent to infringe on, and the location where to conduct the infringing activity (the potential forum). The potential infringer can, in effect, *ex ante* strategically forum shop for a jurisdiction that offers relatively low protection for patent rights. The result is inefficient for society as a whole as patent rights receive sub-optimal protection.

The situation, however, could be mitigated, if the strategic control is divided. Thus: defendant picks plaintiff (as in an intentional tort), but the plaintiff picks the forum. If the choice of the forum is the plaintiff's, it is likely to be one that favors the plaintiff. This will act as a deterrent to the defendant from undertaking actions resulting in litigation.

Much of conflicts law, in conjunction with venue and transfer statutes, and, in the United States, constitutional restrictions on personal jurisdiction, create precisely this countervailing power. A striking example of this is the possibility of removing suits from state to federal courts under diversity jurisdiction. As long as the parties are from different states (that is, they are diverse), the defendant can ask to remove the suit to federal court. In such cases, the federal court will apply the state court's law, but presumably, be free from local biases the removing party is concerned about.

5. Evolution of Rules in Conflicts and Efficiency

American conflicts law in particular, has been widely criticized and is seen as being in need of sweeping reform. In the case of American conflicts law, the proposals have included national legislation (Whitten 2001); a new Restatement (Symeonides 2000); and somewhat less radical modification using efficiency as a guideline (O'Hara and Ribstein 2001). The first is unlikely to happen, the second would still depend on the adoption by the courts for its effectiveness, and, arguably, the third is in the process of adoption.

The law is not immutable. This is particularly true for a common law system like that of the United States. Conflicts laws issues are not decided wholly separately from substantive claims, just as judges in the common law system do not decide cases deductively (Sterk 1994). Conflicts rules, however, have evolved, as have rules about personal jurisdiction, in ways that work surprisingly well to limit the worst excesses of forum shopping, but allow ex ante forum selection that could be efficiency enhancing.

The most striking example is that of contracts. Rome I, in the EU, granted vast party autonomy for contract. Under the Restatement (First), however, enforcement of a choice of law made by contracting parties was generally disfavored as being "private law." With the rule being that the place of contract applied. Restatement (Second) explicitly provided for honoring the voluntary choice of law by contracting parties. The modern rule is to honor the *ex ante* choice of law, even in the minority of states that otherwise adhere to Restatement (First) conflicts rules. This is both efficient and just. The term is bargained for before the contract is signed; it can be safely assumed that it is welfare enhancing for all contracting parties. The explicit choice eliminates uncertainty, and an issue for litigation, and therefore increases judicial economy as well.[7] This is more correctly classified under *ex ante* forum selection, and is clearly efficiency enhancing.

Just as clear is the rule that has to with real property. The *situs* rule clearly attaches to all claims based on real property, including those of land use, title, ownership in interest, testamentary disposition or intestate succession. This clear *ex ante* rule is essential for efficiency due to the immovable nature of real property, and the very strong regulatory interest the state has in it. The unambiguous *situs* rule clarifies property rights, and makes transfers easier. It also eliminates strategic forum shopping. It is clearly welfare enhancing, and it is unsurprising that it has survived unchanged through time.

Most of the concern about conflicts law and confusion in conflicts law, quite correctly, arises from claims based on torts. This is the area where the possibility for strategic, illegitimate forum shopping is the greatest. The relationship between the tort-feasor and the victim is essentially non-consensual. In an intentional tort, the tort-feasor chooses the victim; that is, the defendant chooses the plaintiff. In an unintentional tort, the tort-feasor acts in such a way as to increase the risk of a class of persons becoming victims. Allowing the plaintiff to choose the forum is a way to offset the adverse selection problem.

The Restatement (First) rule was the place of the wrong applied. The problem with this in the case of intentional torts is that it gave the control of forum to the tort-feasor (which would be particularly problematic in cases such as the declaratory judgment discussed earlier). While the rule was not quite so egregious for unintentional torts, it did violate expectations that would otherwise be justified, because it barred the separation of conduction regulation rules from

---

[7] The United States Supreme Court has upheld a choice of law clause even when it was that of neither party. See *The Bremen v Zapata Off-Shore Co.*, 407 US 1 (1972) (upholding choice of law of a third country).

loss regulation rules.[8] It was therefore not surprising that courts often used escape devices to circumvent this strict *lex locus delicti* rule, in effect, vitiating the benefits of a rules-based regime. The result has been a move to multifactor tests, which are admittedly vague. On the other hand, the Restatement (Second) test list includes the consideration of the plaintiff's domicile, which immediately reduces the strategic advantage in forum selection held by a defendant in an intentional tort claim.

O'Hara and Ribstein (2001) advocate a place of injury rule for non-market torts, and a place of sale rule for product liability cases, where there is no explicit choice of law clause. They advocate enforcing choice of law clauses to the extent that they exist for market-based torts. The United States Supreme Court would seem to agree. In *Carnival Cruise Lines, Inc v Shute*, 499 US 585 (1991), the Court upheld the choice of forum clause listed in a cruise ticket, even though the term had not been bargained for. Goldman (1992) criticized the decision, and the "Chicago School model" on the notion that it rested on perfect information and the idea that some consumers would bargain for the clause. The effect of enforcing the choice of law clause, however, is to eliminate a source of uncertainty for the party who will be the repeat player in the market, and faces a high probability of being a litigant. It also eliminates a source of *ex post* strategic forum shopping.

The final check on the forum shopping problem is personal jurisdiction, in the American system. As conflicts law has evolved to increase the availability of forums available to litigants, personal jurisdiction doctrine has evolved to limit strategic forum shopping. *Erie R.R. v Tomkins*, 304 US 64 (1938) ended the possibility of shopping between federal and state courts. Personal jurisdiction now requires the "purposeful availment" test of *McGee v Int'l Life Ins. Co.*, 355 US 220 (1957),[9] which is a far cry from the tag jurisdiction of *Pennoyer v Neff* 95 U.S. 714 (1877).[10]

6. Forum Selection or Forum Shopping

Forum selection is a multidimensional activity, and is an integral part of the legal process in a world with multiple jurisdictions and legal regimes. It will,

---

8 Thus, in *Alabama Great South. R.R. v Carroll*, 97, Ala. 126 (1892), both the plaintiff employee and the defendant employer were Alabama residents. The injury took place in Mississippi, even though the negligent conduct occurred in Alabama. The court held that Mississippi law applied, and denied the plaintiff certain damages, which he would have been entitled to under Alabama law.

9 Which has three parts, all of which need to be satisfied for personal jurisdiction: state interest, forum not unduly inconvenient, and purposeful availment of the forum.

10 Holding that physical presence in a state is sufficient for asserting *in personam* jurisdiction.

inevitably be a strategic choice. Some of it could be efficiency enhancing, while much of it, as has been discussed, will not.

The most egregious forum shopping, perhaps, is due to statutes of limitations. These are considered a procedural rule; the choice of forum determines which one applies. It is essentially arbitrary in nature, yet can determine whether a suit is heard or not. There are good reasons to have statutes of limitations, including repose and certainty, and states have good public policy reasons to have varying durations. There is no simple or fair way to eliminate this problem. It may well be that the cost of eliminating the problem might exceed the benefits, and one of the costs of living with multiple regimes that cannot be eliminated.

Lastly, there are efficiency-enhancing reasons to select a forum, even *ex post*. One might be speed of adjudication, which could reduce the deadweight losses associated with litigation. Another might be the expertise of the judges in a specialized area, such as Delaware for corporate law. In such cases, forum selection is efficiency enhancing, not a zero-sum, or a negative-sum game of forum shopping.

Nonetheless, as long as the world has multiple jurisdictions, with multiple legal regimes, it is impossible to eliminate forum shopping. The courts, as in the United States, have evolved a system, which seems chaotic on the surface, and is certainly by no means perfect, but seems to limit the worst excesses of strategic forum shopping surprisingly well.

References

Akerloff, George (1970), "The Market for Lemons", *Quarterly Journal of Economics*, 84: 488–500.

Brilmayer, Lea and Jack L. Goldsmith (2002), *Conflict of Laws: Cases and Materials*, New York: Aspen.

Cox, Stanley E. (2001). "Substantive, Multilateral and Unilateral Choice of Law Approaches", *Willamette Law Review*, 37: 171–207.

Currie, Brainerd (1963), "Survival of Actions: Adjudication versus Automation in the Conflict of Laws", in *Selected Essays in the Conflict of Laws*, Durham, NC: Duke University Press.

Gale, Douglas (2001), "Signaling in Markets with Two-Sided Adverse Selection", *Economic Theory*, 18: 391–414.

Ghei, Nita, and Francesco Parisi (2004), "Adverse Selection and Moral Hazard in Forum Shopping: Conflicts Law as Spontaneous Order", *Cardozo Law Review*, 25: 1367–92.

Goldman, Lee (1992), "Public Policy: My Way or the Highway: The Law and Economics of Choice of Forum Clauses in Consumer Form Contracts", *Northwestern Law Review*, 86: 700–41.

Juenger, Friedrich K. (1993), *Choice of Law and Multistate Justice*, Dordrecht, Netherlands: Martinus Nijhoff Publishers.

Leflar, Robert A. (1981), "The Nature of Conflicts Law", *Columbia Law Review*, 81: 1080–95.

McDougal III, Luther L., Robert L. Felix, and Ralph Y. Whitten (2004), *American Conflicts Law: Cases and Materials*, 4th ed. Danvers, MA: Lexis Nexis, Matthew-Bender & Co.

McDougal III, Luther L., Robert L. Felix, and Ralph Y. Whitten (2001), *American Conflicts Law*, 5th ed. Transnational.

Moore, Kimberly A. (2001), "Forum Shopping in Patent Cases: Does Geographic Choice Affect Innovation?", *North Carolina Law Review*, 79: 889–938.

Mueller, Dennis (2003), *Public Choice III*, New York: Cambridge University Press.

O'Hara, Erin A. and Larry. E. Ribstein (2001), "From Politics to Efficiency in Choice of Law", *University of Chicago Law Review*, 67: 1151–232.

Olson, Mancur (1971), *The Logic of Collective Action*, Cambridge, MA: Harvard University Press.
Parisi, Francesco, and Erin A. O'Hara (2002), "Conflict of Laws", *New Palgrave Dictionary of Law and Economics*, vol. 1 New York: Palgrave Macmillan.
Roosevelt III, Kermit (2010), "Choice of Law in Federal Courts: From Erie and Klaxon to CAFA and Shady Grove", Public Law and Legal Theory Research Paper Series, Research Paper No. 10–28, University of Pennsylvania Law School.
Sack, Alexander N. (1937), "Conflict of Laws in the History of English Law", in *Law: A Century of Progress 1835–1935*, Vol. 3, re-printed in *AALS Reading on Conflicts of Laws*, vol. 1 (1956).
Shavell, Steven (1979), "On Moral Hazard and Insurance", *Quarterly Journal of Economics*, 93: 541–62.
Sterk, Stewart E (1994), "The Marginal Relevance of Choice of Law Theory", *University of Pennsylvania Law Review*, 124: 949–1031.
Story, Joseph, (1834), *Commentaries on the Conflict of Laws*, 1st ed., Clark, NJ: Lawbook Exchange.
Symeonides, Symeon C. (2001), "Choice of Law in the American Courts in 2000: As the Century Turns", *American Journal of Comparative Law*, 49: 1–47.
Symeonides, Symeon C. (2000), "The Need for a Third Conflicts Restatement (And a Proposal for Torts Conflicts)", *Indiana Law Journal*, 75: 437–74.
Whitten, Ralph U. (2001), "Curing the Deficiencies of the Conflicts Revolution: A Proposal for National Legislation on Choice of Law, Jurisdiction, and Judgments", *Willamette Law Review*, 37: 259–97.
Zhang, Mo (2009), "Party Autonomy in Non-Contractual Obligations: Rome II and Its Impact on Choice of Law", *Seton Hall Law Review*, 39: 861–917.

21 The law and economics of regulatory competition

Jonathan Klick

Introduction

Regulations[1] exist for many reasons. They may exist to correct for market failures arising from externalities. They may exist to reduce transactions costs or informational asymmetries. They may also exist to constrain behavior to bring it into accord with the normative preferences of the median voter or some other politically powerful entity in the jurisdiction. However, regulations may also serve as rent-seeking vehicles for politicians and other actors in the jurisdiction.

Regulatory competition, whereby different jurisdictions compete for residents or other mobile resources on the basis of the regulations they offer, is often characterized as leading to a race to the top or a race to the bottom. That is, depending on who is doing the characterizing and what the regulatory status quo is, increasing the amount of inter-jurisdictional competition is predicted to lead to systematically better or worse regulatory outcomes.

For example, environmentalists predict that state competition on environmental standards will lead to a race to the bottom as jurisdictions compete for the

1 For the purposes of this chapter, regulations are viewed as being separate from laws that are enforced primarily through litigation. Of course, at a high enough level of abstraction, all laws serve to regulate behavior to some degree or to create a starting point for contractual bargaining. While some of the law and economics literature distinguishes the two by suggesting that regulation constrains behavior ex ante, while litigation operates ex post, this distinction does not matter analytically since regulations will be enforced via fines or some other penalty after the action takes place, and the expectation of litigation and a resulting judgment will surely impact behavior ex ante. Perhaps a more useful distinction arises from the notion that litigation, at least in traditional common law systems, can only result in a judgment if actual harm occurs, while many regulations can lead to a punishment once the prohibited action occurs, even if it results in no harm. If individuals make decisions probabilistically, this makes no analytical difference in most contexts, except with respect to those regulations that proscribe activities that do not lead to harm. Further, under the plausible assumption that many regulatory infractions will go undiscovered or unpunished in cases where no harm occurs, or as legal systems consider liability for activities that merely increase risk or allow for punitive damages, the small distinction becomes even smaller. With that in mind, it is not surprising that much of what is contained in this chapter also applies to jurisdictional competition based on laws that are enforced through litigation or even through private arbitration (see, for example, Benson 1990).

tax base that comes with industrial development. In their eyes, regulatory harmonization (at least at a high enough level of environmental protection) or federalization, a kind of mandatory harmonization, is to be preferred to regulatory competition.

Others might counter that regulatory competition has the potential to improve environmental quality even in the case where states are primarily motivated by the tax bases that come with businesses. That is, firms wish to maximize profits of which regulatory compliance costs are only one element. Another element is labor costs. If employees or potential employees value environmental amenities, a firm located in a high pollution area will need to pay compensating wage differentials that may be larger than regulatory compliance costs, inducing firms to gravitate to jurisdictions with more rigorous environmental regulations. Further, compared to a federalized system, under these assumptions, jurisdictions might even choose a higher environmental standard than is possible under harmonization, and the potential for experimentation that is available in a non-harmonized system may lead to innovations that both improve environmental conditions and lower compliance costs. Such innovation may be retarded in a federalized system that provides little incentive for experimentation, if it allows it at all.

Beyond simplistic discussions of race to the top/bottom, which are generally framed by commentators or activists who view policy success or failure in single dimensional terms, different jurisdictions may simply value trade-offs differently. Residents of California may be willing to sacrifice most other values for marginal improvements in environmental quality, while residents of New Jersey are not. In this context, increasingly rigorous environmental standards are not necessarily a good thing; much depends on the preferences of the individuals in the jurisdiction. Given the potential for preference heterogeneity, harmonization has the potential to lower welfare, even if it raises regulatory strictness on average, relative to a system of jurisdictional competition.

On the other hand, if there are regulatory spillovers, such as air pollution impacting neighboring jurisdictions, the desirability of regulatory competition declines.[2] Trading off the gains to customizing regulation in line with the

---

2 While virtually all analysts would include so-called "real" externalities as a problem with regulatory competition (with jurisdiction-specific regulations limiting activities that generate negative inter-jurisdictional externalities being set too low, while leaving them set too high in instances where the inter-jurisdictional externality is positive), it is not clear how pecuniary and fiscal externalities should be treated. While standard public finance analysis suggests that these should be ignored (see, for example, Holcombe and Sobel 2001 and Browning 1999), it is not at all clear that this is generally true, depending on whether normative principles beyond efficiency affect the decision rule. Even if efficiency is the only relevant criterion, however, which individuals' utilities "matter" or how they should be weighted will often affect whether pecuniary or fiscal externalities are relevant. For

preferences of the residents of a jurisdiction against inter-jurisdictional externalities is of central importance in evaluating the choice between regulatory harmonization and competition. On top of this analysis, questions of administrative costs arise, since a given regulatory area may exhibit economies or diseconomies of scale in theory. The total cost of processing evidence regarding best practices and scientific knowledge could be reduced by centralization, particularly if there is a relatively low level of human capital available in most jurisdictions. However, centralized decision makers may face a high cost of determining individual preferences, may be harder to incentivize, and may be less likely to innovate than their counterparts in a decentralized, competitive system. Along similar lines, political economy forces may affect the optimal degree of regulatory centralization.

This chapter provides an analytical framework for the optimal degree of regulatory competition, including discussions of the relevant factors considered, drawn from the law and economics literature on regulation and the public finance literature on fiscal federalism. Special problems that arise when multiple regulatory decision makers share regulatory competence are discussed, including vertical (and hierarchical) state and federal interactions and co-equal horizontal interactions among multiple state or local regulatory decision makers. The chapter then includes a brief section on the scholarly value of decentralization in the new empirical law and economics/legal studies movement which relies on policy variation to draw causal inferences about the effects of various regulatory provisions.

Analytical Framework

A useful starting point is Shavell's (1984a, 1984b) model of the choice between using ex post litigation or ex ante regulation to induce individuals undertaking risky activities to internalize the expected external costs those activities create.[3]

---

example, imagine two contiguous jurisdictions that exist in the same nation, A and B, both of which border the foreign jurisdiction C. While existing law allows free movement of citizens between A and B, it does not allow free movement between C and any jurisdiction in the nation. However, for various reasons, enforcement of the national law depends on the regulatory enforcement of individual jurisdictions. If A prefers to allocate its scarce budget to activities other than immigration enforcement, while B focuses its budget on enforcement, (illegal) immigration of C's residents into A may induce A's residents to relocate to B for a host of reasons, including increasing home prices due to increased demand and declining wages due to increased labor supply in A, leading to price effects in B as well. The respective policy decisions of A and B generate pecuniary (and likely fiscal) externalities for each other. If the welfare of C's residents is considered in the decision rule, optimality may require B to reduce its enforcement, while if only A's and B's residents are counted, optimality may require A to increase its regulatory enforcement.

[3] Interestingly, Helland and Klick (2007) show empirically that, contra Shavell's model, regulation and litigation tend not to be substitutes on the margin. Instead, they show that states with higher levels of regulation tend to have higher levels of litigation

As suggested above, this distinction is somewhat illusory analytically since regulations are enforced through ex post punishments such as fines while the expectation of facing litigation and a potential judgment will affect behavior ex ante. Perhaps a better way to state the distinction involves whether or not the cost imposed on the individual undertaking the risk is or is not conditioned on actual harm occurring. In the regulatory context, as it is generally conceived, the punishment is conditioned on the regulated act. That is, if I pollute beyond the regulated threshold, I pay a fine even if the pollution does not harm anyone, whereas under common law systems, damages will almost always be a necessary element of a successful civil claim.

With this distinction in mind, Shavell suggests that the optimal system will generally be a mixture of regulation and litigation. The relative weights on each mechanism will depend on a number of factors. For our purposes, the most important of these factors is heterogeneity in terms of both the cost of the expected harm arising from the activity and in terms of the cost of precaution, which may include the opportunity cost involved in refraining from the activity as well as the costs of any available additional safety measure that either the risk taker or the potential victim can invest in.

Heterogeneity matters in this context because the greater the heterogeneity, the greater the social cost generated by the "one size fits all" regulation. If the cost of harm and precaution were uniform, it would be socially wasteful to engage in the process involved in litigation, saving both parties and the state administrative costs and opportunity costs. In fact, there would be savings because human capital could be re-allocated away from litigation altogether since a regulation could be announced, dictating which activities are prohibited and what precautions are required, and violators would be penalized accordingly,[4] significantly reducing the need for lawyers and judges.[5]

In addition to the administrative and opportunity cost savings of regulation, Shavell points out that regulation will mitigate the problem of judgment-proof defendants who will not be deterred by litigation.[6] It seems likely that the

too. Of course, Shavell's model is a normative one, so Helland and Klick's empirical results do nothing to invalidate it, but they do suggest that the current systems in place in the US diverge from the theoretically optimal system in important ways.

4 This abstracts away the possibility that enforcement costs might be higher than the costs of litigation. It also ignores the reality that regulatory enforcement, in many cases, involves something that approximates litigation anyway.

5 In fact, some fields of litigation have been turned into essentially regulatory or administrative practices in many states, such as the field of workers' compensation.

6 Shavell asserts that regulatory authorities could stop individuals from taking risks if they had insufficient funds to cover the required precautions or could stop the individual from the activity altogether if the expected harm was very high, by incarcerating the individual. Presumably there are many cases where the regulatory authority does not detect individuals engaging in the prohibited activity before the fact, as well as instances

costs associated with harms and precautions will be geographically clustered, implying that relative to a national regime of regulation, regulation at lower jurisdictions might have a larger domain where it dominates litigation. That is, if things like wages and property values (i.e. the sorts of things that generate the cost of damages or precautions) exhibit lower variance at the state (or local) level than they do at the national level, federalized regulations, taking the costs of harm and precaution at their national average, will generate more losses in the Shavell framework than a system that tailors the regulations to state or local means. This implies that the optimal federalized system will rely more heavily on litigation, with its attendant higher costs, than a system that is able to set different regulatory standards in each jurisdiction. On the margin, the preference for multi-jurisdictional regulations will be affected by the presence of inter-jurisdictional externalities and any economies of scale that might exist, but the insight about heterogeneity provides a basis for favoring regulatory competition.

In terms of integrating this heterogeneity issue with concerns about inter-jurisdictional externalities, the field of fiscal federalism in public finance economics provides a number of insights. Although fiscal federalism is an under-appreciated topic in the law and economics literature, its framework for analyzing the provision of public goods can easily be adapted to the question of regulatory harmonization versus competition.

Tiebout's (1956) famous model for the provision of public goods provides a point of departure. Tiebout's article responds to Samuelson's (1954) model of public good provision, which suggests that the free-rider problem leads individuals to understate their preference for public goods in the hope that others will pay for the public good, and since public goods exhibit a lack of excludability, the free rider will get the benefit of the public good without paying for it. However, since everyone has the same incentive, Samuelson and others suggested, public goods will be under-supplied by the market, requiring government intervention to achieve efficient provision. Tiebout points out that if local governments provide public goods, individuals can sort themselves into communities based on their favored level of public good provision and tax bill. Individuals effectively reveal their true preference for the public good by voting with their feet. Oates (1969) provides evidence that the public good and tax mix is capitalized into local home prices, with high public good, low tax communities exhibiting systematically higher values, all other things equal. Fischel (2002) suggests that Oates' empirical support provided significantly higher visibility for the Tiebout hypothesis as it suggested that individuals do indeed vote with their feet, generating competitive pressures across local communities.

---

where the regulatory authority is not permitted to use police powers, in which case this benefit of regulation is reduced, as Shavell admits (Shavell 1984a, fn. 7).

Buchanan and Goetz (1972) were among the first to point out that Tiebout's model fails to limit the free-rider problem on its own, since individuals can still move into jurisdictions providing high levels of public goods without paying for them due to the excludability problem. If property rights allow a mechanism of exclusion from the local jurisdiction, Buchanan's (1965) earlier theory of club goods would seemingly be applicable, and Hamilton (1976) suggested that this exclusion occurs through local land use or zoning regulations. This insight somewhat resolves the puzzle as to why Oates' (1969) results hold despite Buchanan and Goetz's critique which otherwise suggests that free riders should cause instability in the Tiebout sorting mechanism, dissipating any value arising from popular public good mixes.

This literature suggests that competition among jurisdictions is not merely theoretical speculation among economists. Subsequent empirical testing (see, for example, Dee 2000) continues to provide support for the proposition that migration patterns respond to the bundle of services offered by local jurisdictions. In principle, there is no reason why regulatory offerings do not constitute part of that bundle. Indeed, Fischel (1978, 1985) among others suggests that regulations are a necessary condition for stability in the Tiebout sorting mechanism.

While jurisdictional competition allows individuals to sort according to their heterogeneous preferences, whether this sorting is efficient requires an accounting of inter-jurisdictional externalities. Tiebout ruled out the possibility of such spillovers in his model, but real life is not so well behaved.

Fiscal federalism, an area of public finance finding its origins in Musgrave (1959) and Oates (1972), provides a decentralization theorem which is described by Oates (1999) as suggesting that, in the absence of economies of scale or inter-jurisdictional externalities, localized public good provision can always provide at least as high, and typically higher, welfare levels than if a uniform level of public goods is provided across jurisdictions. Oates suggests that, while in theory, a unified government could provide different levels of public goods to different sub-national locations, information problems and political constraints limit the feasibility of moving beyond one size fits all national public good provision. Nothing in these models precludes applying them to the provision of regulations as well.

Given this presumption in favor of the efficiency of local provision of regulations, any attempt to harmonize or federalize must rely on arguments regarding economies of scale, inter-jurisdictional externalities, or some political economy problem that makes it more likely that higher-level government decision makers face better incentives than do local decision makers.

Economies of scale might arise for a number of reasons. In instances where scientific or expert knowledge, as opposed to local preference, is determinative on a regulatory issue, having a single decision maker may be preferable to having multiple jurisdictions discover and process the relevant information.

This may be especially true if there is relatively little human capital available, making it difficult for local decision makers to draw relevant conclusions. However, in practice, this factor is probably not as important as it would otherwise appear.

First, in such a situation, the federal government could serve merely as a clearinghouse of such information, providing guidance and advice to local jurisdictions without mandating any particular approach. This advisory role would allow the benefits of centralization without creating the potential for mistakes in categorizing an issue as one where local preference does not matter when, in fact, it does. Second, there are relatively few areas where scientific certainty is high enough to offset the loss of policy experimentation that is likely to accompany centralization. While there are some theoretical arguments that sub-national jurisdictions will experiment too little (see, for example, Strumpf 2002, which argues that since innovation is itself a public good, local jurisdictions will engage in too little experimentation relative to a national government with a more encompassing interest), there are relatively few examples, at least in the US context, where the federal government has in fact engaged in experimentation whereby different regulatory regimes are operated simultaneously. States and local governments, on the other hand, regularly try different regulatory approaches when allowed to do so.

Inter-jurisdictional externalities, however, do represent a serious and frequent source of concern with respect to regulatory decentralization. Local residents and decision makers have no incentive to consider the costs or benefits their regulations impose on other jurisdictions. Further, because inter-jurisdictional bargaining is likely to be difficult, it is unlikely that Coasian bargaining will undo the effects of even very inefficient policy choices.[7]

Klick and Sitkoff (2008) provide a salient example of the potential for local regulation to lead to very large efficiency losses. Because of a peculiar corporate structure, the Hershey Company (makers of Hershey's Chocolate and Reese's Peanut Butter Cups) is controlled by a charitable trust run for the benefit of the Milton Hershey School in Central Pennsylvania. Under Pennsylvania law (as in most states), charitable trusts are monitored by the state attorney general. For diversification purposes, the trust was interested in selling its control interest

---

[7] In addition to the usual transaction costs arguments for why bargaining does not occur (which are presumably more acute in the inter-governmental context given the political economy and agency cost problems that plague public decision makers, if for no other reason than that public decisions will involve more individuals, each with his own interests that may not line up with efficiency concerns), in the US context at least, states are not permitted to enter into agreements under Article I, Section 10, Clause 3 of the US Constitution (the so-called compact clause) without the approval of the federal government.

in the firm, and this move would have had the salutary effect of improving the performance of the firm.[8] However, there was a strong possibility that a new owner would have moved most of Hershey's operations out of Pennsylvania due to its relatively high costs of operation. The state attorney general, who happened to be running for governor at the time, opposed the sale despite the fact that it was necessary to diversify the trust's investment portfolio,[9] and the sale would have generated a very large premium over the market value of the stock holding. Although the attorney general did the "right" (or at least the politically expedient) thing with respect to the interests of the town of Hershey, and Pennsylvania residents more generally, his actions leading the trust to drop the sale, generated a loss in wealth of the order of $3 billion.[10] Fundamentally, because most of these losses accrued to individuals living outside of Pennsylvania (or to non-voting future trust beneficiaries), the attorney general externalized the costs of his regulatory decision in this case. Although not as colorful as the Hershey example, instances of cost externalization via local regulation abound across virtually every substantive area of law.[11]

This concern over inter-jurisdictional externalities motivates federal pre-emption doctrine. Epstein and Greve (2007), relying on traditional legal analysis as well as the data collected in Greve and Klick (2006), suggest that there is no other way to make sense of the constitutional law cases examining pre-emption. For example, if pre-emption doctrine were simply an issue of federal power versus states' rights, it is difficult to square the voting patterns observed in recent Supreme Court terms on preemption cases with the patterns observed in other states' rights issues.

---

[8] Essentially, because the trust controlled the firm but the trustees had no incentive to ensure that the firm was run efficiently, the market for corporate control was non-functional with respect to Hershey, leading to significant agency costs within the firm. Evidence of this was provided when the sale was announced, at which time the class of firm shares that would not have been involved in any sale (i.e. the publicly traded shares that had effectively zero voting rights) appreciated significantly. Further evidence was provided when the sale was dropped, leading to a corresponding decline in the value of the publicly traded shares.

[9] Of a corpus exceeding $8 billion, more than half was held in Hershey stock.

[10] Although Klick and Sitkoff (2008) cannot directly judge the loss that would have accrued to Hershey (or Pennsylvania) residents if the sale had occurred, they present calculations suggesting that the loss in firm value represented more than $60,000 for each resident of Hershey. While it is impossible to know for sure, it seems unlikely that this amount is less than the value the average resident places on living in Hershey with the company still there as compared to living in Hershey after the company departs (adjusted for the probability of relocation) or as compared to living somewhere else.

[11] Moncrieff (2009) even suggests inter-jurisdictional externalities arise in medical malpractice law, which has traditionally been viewed as a very local area of substantive law.

The extent of these externalities is a central concern in determining the value of regulatory competition. However, while it is generally assumed that local decision makers respond to the preferences of their constituents, leading to generally good outcomes except in the case of cost externalization, Glaeser and Shleifer (2005) provide a model and some historical evidence suggesting this assumption need not hold. Specifically, they show how sometimes it may be in a decision maker's best interests to undertake policies which actually drive residents away, leaving behind the core supporters of the decision makers currently in power. By doing so, these decision makers may be able to consolidate their power and remove the possibility of political challenges. Such a view stands in contrast to the sentiment expressed in Fischel (2000) which suggests that by chasing votes, residents, and tax base, local regulatory authorities will generally reach locally desirable outcomes. While certainly not the dominant model of the political economy of local regulatory decisions, the Glaeser and Shleifer argument does underscore the need to examine the incentives decision makers face before blindly assuming that local regulatory decisions will at least benefit local residents.

The analytical framework for judging the value of regulatory competition then is relatively straightforward. Heterogeneity in preferences and costs lead to a presumption in favor of local determination of regulatory standards even judged solely on efficiency grounds. This presumption could be overturned, however, if there are economies of scale in regulatory analyses or enforcement, inter-jurisdictional externalities, or if local decision makers face relatively bad incentives as compared to national decision makers.

Other Structural Issues

Although public finance scholars have investigated the peculiar analytical issues that arise from the interplay of various levels of government making decisions about public good provision and the taxes required to pay for that provision, relatively little of this work has made its way into the field of law and economics. Further, virtually none of it has been extrapolated to cover regulatory decisions per se.

Parisi, Schulz and Klick (2006) represents an exception to this dearth of analytical work on structural problems involved in the interaction of regulatory authorities. Specifically, they consider situations where multiple jurisdictions share regulatory authority. Such a situation could arise when multiple states all regulate access to a resource or when multiple regulatory agencies have jurisdiction over some activity.[12] While they model these situations as being

12 Examples of these overlapping jurisdictions abound. One illustration is the authority the National Park Service and the Fish and Wildlife Service share over fish and animal herds that move across federal lands and waterways and, if the relevant fauna

pure rent-seeking games, nothing changes if this assumption is relaxed such that regulatory authorities balance both socially valuable objectives with some non-trivial rent-seeking aspect, such as expanding the bureau's budget either to gain financially or to reduce the effort each regulatory employee must expend.

The model differentiates regulatory activities along two dimensions. First is the question of whether the authorities have the power to stop an activity, leaving the individual undertaking the activity free to proceed unless the regulator(s) intervenes, or whether the regulation is set up to require approval such that the individual cannot proceed without first securing approval. They refer to these as negative and positive authority respectively. Second, they distinguish between situations where the multiple regulatory actions serve as substitutes or complements. In a substitute arrangement, any regulatory act is sufficient such that, in the case of positive authority, an individual need only secure approval from a single regulator, whereas in negative authority, every regulator holds veto power over the activity. Complementary regulatory powers, on the other hand, require an individual to secure approval from all relevant regulators in the case of positive authority, whereas complements in the negative authority context imply that all regulators must restrict the activity for the individual to be prohibited from proceeding.

They solve for a game wherein all of the regulators act simultaneously. Relative to a unified (federalized or harmonized) regulator, they show the following:

Table 21.1 Interaction of regulatory authorities

	Regulatory Substitutes	Regulatory Complements
Positive Authority	Activity over-permitted	Activity under-permitted
Negative Authority	Activity over-restricted	Activity under-restricted

The welfare implications of these results depend on the assumption about the desirability of the underlying activity,[13] but the conclusions relative to a unified regulator have a fairly simple intuition. When regulators' interests are

also moves across non-federal lands, state authorities will claim jurisdiction as well. Authority over building projects is often shared too, with some projects falling under the jurisdiction of the Environmental Protection Agency, state-level counterparts, as well as local building commissions.

[13] Parisi et al. (2006, Table 2) provide welfare implications in the various arrangements of regulatory substitutes and complements and positive and negative authority for cases where the regulators are assumed to be rent seekers, shirkers, and where regulatory benevolence is assumed.

not unified, they ignore the effect their actions have on the ability of the other regulators to extract rents.

Klick and Parisi (2005) also provide analysis of a similar situation when regulators act sequentially in the case of regulatory complements.[14] Specifically, they investigate a situation where a single higher level of the government (e.g. federal) makes regulatory decisions and then lower levels (e.g. states) subsequently make decisions. In the sequential Stackelberg game, Klick and Parisi show that the joint level of restriction in the positive authority complementary competence exceeds the level that would be chosen by a unified regulator. Once again, the intuition is that each rent-seeking regulator ignores part of the deadweight loss created by its rent seeking, effectively externalizing some of this cost onto the other regulators. However, in the sequential game modification, an interesting insight arises. Namely, while the first mover, say the federal government, would benefit from some coordination among the lower-level regulators (e.g. the states) since that coordination would lower overall rent seeking (leaving more rents for the federal regulator), the first-mover regulator would be worse off if that coordination changed the game into a simultaneous game where the unified lower regulators no longer need to act as a second mover. Thus, Klick and Parisi argue that this provides some insight into how the compact clause of the US Constitution has been interpreted.[15]

On the whole, however, the structural questions regarding how different regulators interact, both positively and normatively, have been largely uninvestigated in the law and economics literature, at least in a formal systematic way. Adapting the theoretical public finance literature on this topic in the tax context to the regulation context probably represents some low hanging fruit since these structural issues come up repeatedly in more traditional legal scholarship without much analytical structure.

Learning from Regulatory Competition

It has already been suggested that an additional value of regulatory competition arises from the experimentation that is more likely to occur in a decentralized system as opposed to a system with forced harmonization or federalization. The value of this innovation should not be discounted.

---

14 Technically, Klick and Parisi (2005) frame their discussion in terms of multiple authorities sharing a tax base, but it is trivial to adapt the model to any regulatory setting in which the regulators have some rent-seeking objective.

15 Specifically, although the clause itself disallows compacts without prior federal approval, the courts have interpreted the clause to allow compacts unless the federal government intervenes or unless the compact would constitute a threat to the supremacy of federal power. This is consistent with the federal regulator benefiting from some, but not too much, coordination among the states.

From a scholarship perspective, regulatory competition also offers greater opportunities to engage in empirical research as compared to a system that is federalized. Since regulations change the implicit relative prices of activities, they can be used to identify the effect of these price changes on behavior. This is important from a policy evaluation perspective, but also from a more basic inquiry about the determinants of behavior.

In order to isolate causal effects in this context, however, it is necessary to have policy variation that is separate from idiosyncratic effects peculiar to a jurisdiction and separate from general, potentially non-linear, temporal trends. While a regulatory change has the potential to identify effects separate from jurisdictional idiosyncratic effects, if the change occurs everywhere at once, it will not be possible to net out the temporal effects. That is, while state and local regulatory changes leave open the possibility of using non-changing jurisdictions as a counterfactual comparison, federal-level changes do not leave a counterfactual.[16]

It is interesting to note that, while there has been an explosion of empirical work across most areas of law in the past decade, including torts, property, contracts, health, insurance, crime and a host of other topics, areas of purely federal law have seen very little inferential work.[17] Areas like intellectual property[18] and immigration law have been notable during the past decade because the empirical revolution has left them mostly untouched.

Conclusion

While discussions of regulatory competition are often reduced to predictions of races to the top or races to the bottom, detailed welfare analyses are more useful than position papers. More or more stringent regulation is not necessarily a good thing, just as less stringent regulation is not unconditionally good either.

Careful analysis of the value of regulatory competition starts with a recognition of the benefits of jurisdictional customization and its ability to incorporate heterogeneous preferences and costs. This flexibility is almost certainly lost in

---

16 While, in theory, researchers could use other countries as the counterfactual comparison, this approach will not generate much confidence given the other dissimilarities that exist across countries (e.g. different macroeconomic conditions, different languages and cultures, etc.). While New York and New Jersey are relatively comparable, the US and Mexico are not. This is a general empirical problem.

17 While some descriptive work exists in the purely federal areas, much of it involves describing and categorizing case law, which, while valuable, is not very helpful for understanding the effects of law on behavior, much less for understanding deeper questions about how people respond to incentives.

18 Abrams (2009) is a notable exception here. Instead of using legal differences across jurisdictions, he uses differential effects of intellectual property law on types of innovations treated differently by the law but that are otherwise comparable.

a harmonized or federalized system of regulation. Thus, all other things equal, regulatory decentralization is a good thing.

However, all other things are not necessarily equal. Federalization, in some circumstances, offers the potential for economies of scale in information collection and processing. Further, and perhaps more important, federalization may be necessary to constrain the tendency of local decision makers to externalize the costs of their activities to other jurisdictions. These inter-jurisdictional externalities represent the strongest argument against jurisdictional competition. Additionally, while we generally assume that local decision makers have an incentive to maximize the welfare of their constituents, this need not always be the case, so it is important to consider the actual incentives these decision makers face.[19]

Lastly, it is important to consider the value of experimentation and innovation. Using the states (or local jurisdictions) as regulatory laboratories holds out the hope of generating information in terms of the effectiveness of various regulatory provisions and the costs of implementation. We learn significantly less about regulatory efficacy and efficiency in federalized systems. Further, in the right institutional context, state and local decision makers will have not only the opportunity but also the incentive to innovate as they compete over voters, residents and tax bases.

Although the law and economics literature could benefit from additional systematic study of the theoretical underpinnings of regulatory competition, the basic framework is fairly straightforward and easily applied across legal areas. What is less well understood are the empirical parameters regarding the size of inter-jurisdictional externalities in different legal contexts, the rate of regulatory innovation in different legal areas, and the potential for regulatory economies of scale. This is where the focus of research should be going forward in the area of regulatory competition.

References

Abrams, David (2009). "Did TRIPS Spur Innovation? An Analysis of Patent Duration and Incentives to Innovate". *University of Pennsylvania Law Review*, 157(6): 1613–47.

Benson, Bruce (1990). *The Enterprise of Law: Justice Without the State*, San Francisco: Pacific Research Institute.

Browning, Edgar (1999). "The Myth of Fiscal Externalities". *Public Finance Review*, 27(1): 3–18.

Buchanan, James (1965). "An Economic Theory of Clubs". *Economica*, 32(125): 1–14.

Buchanan, James, and Charles Goetz (1972). "Efficiency Limits on Fiscal Mobility: An Assessment of the Tiebout Model". *Journal of Public Economics*, 1(1): 25–43.

Dee, Thomas (2000). "The Capitalization of Education Finance Reforms". *Journal of Law and Economics*, 43(1): 185–214.

[19] This goes for the incentives faced by the federal decision makers too. While the incentives may be poorly aligned at both levels of government, the relevant question has to do with which level has the relatively better incentives to improve welfare, and which level of government has better incentives to fix a regulatory mistake made in the past.

Epstein, Richard, and Michael Greve, eds. (2007). *Federal Preemption: States' Powers, National Interests*. Washington, DC: AEI Press.
Fischel, William (1978). "A Property Rights Approach to Municipal Zoning". *Land Economics*, 54(1): 64–81.
Fischel, William (1985). *The Economics of Zoning Laws: A Property Rights Approach to American Land Use Controls*. Baltimore, MD: Johns Hopkins University Press.
Fischel, William (2000). *The Homevoter Hypothesis: How Home Values Influence Local Government Taxation, School Finance, and Land-Use Policies*. Cambridge, MA: Harvard University Press.
Fischel, William (2002). "Public Goods and Property Rights: Of Coase, Tiebout, and Just Compensation", in Terry Anderson and Fred McChesney, eds, *Property Rights: Cooperation, Conflict, and Law*. Princeton, NJ: Princeton University Press.
Glaeser, Edward, and Andrei Shleifer (2005). "The Curley Effect: The Economics of Shaping the Electorate". *Journal of Law, Economics, and Organization*, 21(1): 1–19.
Greve, Michael, and Jonathan Klick (2006). "Preemption in the Rehnquist Court: A Preliminary Empirical Analysis", *Supreme Court Economic Review*, 14: 43–94.
Hamilton, Bruce (1976). "Capitalization of Intrajurisdictional Differences in Local Tax Prices". *American Economic Review*, 66(5): 743–53.
Helland, Eric, and Jonathan Klick (2007). "The Tradeoff between Regulation and Litigation: Evidence from Insurance Class Actions". *Journal of Tort Law*, 1(3): Article 2.
Holcombe, Randall, and Russell Sobel (2001). "Public Policy toward Pecuniary Externalities". *Public Finance Review*, 29(4): 304–25.
Klick, Jonathan, and Francesco Parisi (2005). "Intra-jurisdictional Tax Competition". *Constitutional Political Economy*, 16(4): 387–95.
Klick, Jonathan, and Robert Sitkoff (2008). "Agency Costs, Charitable Trusts, and Corporate Control: Evidence From Hershey's Kiss-Off". *Columbia Law Review*, 108(4): 749–838.
Moncrieff, Abigail (2009). "Federalization Snowballs: The Need for National Action in Medical Malpractice Reform". *Columbia Law Review*, 109(4): 844–92.
Musgrave, Richard (1959). *The Theory of Public Finance*. New York: McGraw-Hill.
Oates, Wallace (1969). "The Effects of Property Taxes and Local Public Spending on Property Values: An Empirical Study of Tax Capitalization and the Tiebout Hypothesis". *Journal of Political Economy*, 77(6): 957–71.
Oates, Wallace (1972). *Fiscal Federalism*. New York: Harcourt Brace Jovanovich.
Oates, Wallace (1999). "An Essay on Fiscal Federalism". *Journal of Economic Perspectives*, 37(3): 1120–49.
Parisi, Francesco, Norbert Schulz and Jonathan Klick (2006). "The Two Dimensions of Regulatory Competition". *International Review of Law and Economics*, 26(1): 56–66.
Samuelson, Paul (1954). "The Pure Theory of Public Expenditure". *Review of Economics and Statistics*, 36(4): 387–9.
Shavell, Steven (1984a). "Liability for Harm versus Regulation of Safety". *Journal of Legal Studies*, 13(2): 357–74.
Shavell, Steven (1984b). "A Model of the Optimal Use of Liability and Safety Regulation". *RAND Journal of Economics*, 15(2): 271–80.
Strumpf, Koleman (2002). "Does Government Decentralization Increase Policy Innovation?", *Journal of Public Economic Theory*, 4(2): 207–41.
Tiebout, Charles (1956). "A Pure Theory of Local Expenditures". *Journal of Political Economy*, 64(5): 416–24.

22 Growth-oriented legal reforms

Robert Cooter and Hans-Bernd Schäfer

1. Introduction

This chapter deals with the obstacles pertaining to growth-oriented institutional reforms and policies in developing countries and with methods to overcome them.

Economic growth is crucially dependent on institutions, which protect private investors, their property, their contracts and their firms. This is now a widely held consensus among economists (Rodrick, Easterly, Hall, Bardhan), even though the institutional forms which cause this protection may differ from country to country.[1]

Makers of wealth must be given chances and should keep most of their profits. Otherwise growth cannot occur. The maker of wealth must be protected against private and public predators. This protection can be achieved by the rule of law but some countries such as China and Vietnam have successfully used other means of credibly protecting private investors.

At first sight, the implications of this insight for modernizing institutions and the law seem to be clear: since the 1990s Western countries and development agencies have poured hundreds of millions of dollars into rule of law projects.[2] Are they likely to succeed? If one sees the problems of legal and institutional reform exclusively at the implementation level, failure is likely to be around the corner. This view implicitly assumes that poor countries have a weak legal and institutional system because they do not know better and that legal reforms just bridge a know-how gap between rich and poor countries. Or it implicitly assumes that legal reforms are difficult, because the problem of sharing the costs of reform (the free-rider problem) cannot be solved. A know-how gap and a free-rider problem might exist, but both problems cannot explain why legal or other institutional reforms are not carried through or fail in many countries. Often reforms are not in the interest of those who have the power to initiate or block them (Dixit, Acemoglu, Eggertsson).[3] Then a country cannot develop the institutions for efficient markets and remains being caught in poverty.

1 Rodrik et al. (2004); Rodrik (2006); Alesina et al. (1999); Hall and Jones (1999); Bardhan (2004).

2 Daniels and Trebilcock (2004).

3 This was an error of the law and development movement in the 1970s. See Trubek and Galanter (1974), Dixit (1987), Acemoglu (2003) and Eggertsson (2005).

We deal with the impediments of reform and show that not all wealth-increasing reforms are feasible. Given that a reform does not benefit everyone and bears losses to some, such a reform will not be implemented, if the potential losers are veto players in the political game. This problem cannot be easily overcome through political and institutional negotiations which compensate losers. There is no easy political Coasian bargaining, which guarantees the viability of any wealth-increasing reform. This might be especially difficult in countries with extreme wealth concentration (Alesina, Rodrick, Persson, Tabellini).[4] Moreover, we show that the amount of information about future positions determines who perceives himself as a winner or a loser and consequently who supports or blocks a reform. We also show that a reform can still fail if it makes everybody better off, because problems of coordination, the free-rider problem (splitting the costs) and the bargaining problem (splitting the benefits) can arise.

Another problem pertaining to legal reforms for economic growth arises independently of the above problems of motivation and coordination. To introduce the rule of law is a deep reform. It takes decades and its beneficial effects show up with a time lag. A legal reform agenda, which aims at creating economic growth quickly through comprehensive legal reform, might be overly ambitious and might destabilize a government if results do not surface quickly. To initiate growth, correct phasing of reforms and the development of intermediate institutions to protect property and contracts are therefore important.

2. Pareto-Improving Reforms, Cost-Benefit Reforms and Cost-Benefit Detriments

2.1 Three Types of Reform

Many reforms cut into existing wealth and power positions even if they increase total wealth. Using terminology from welfare economics,[5] we can differentiate between wealth-increasing reforms, Pareto gains without losers and cost-benefit gains. A cost-benefit gain benefits the winners more than it harms the losers. When the winners are more powerful and outnumber the losers, a cost-benefit improvement generates more support than opposition.[6]

We will distinguish three types of legal reforms, using examples from privatization in Russia after 1990. When communism collapsed, ownership of

---

4 Alesina and Rodrick (1994); Persson and Tabellini (1994); Coase (1960).

5 Dixit (1987); Acemoglu and Robinson (2000); Eggertsson (2005).

6 As Machiavelli reminds us in *The Prince* (1513), chapter VI, "the reformer has enemies in all those who profit by the old order, and only lukewarm defenders in all those who would profit by the new" (in modo che tu hai inimici tutti quelli che hai offesi in occupare quello principato, e non ti puoi mantenere amici quelli che vi ti hanno messo, per non li potere satisfare in quel modo che si erano presupposto e per non potere tu usare contro di loro medicine forti, sendo loro obligato), available at http://www.liberliber.it/biblioteca/m/machiavelli/il_principe/html/princi_a.htm.

most state enterprises passed into private hands.[7] Konstantin Magin divided the complicated process of privatization into stages.[8] In the first stage, from roughly 1990 to 1994, managers became owners by grabbing state assets, especially in small firms.[9] Restaurants, clothiers, grocers, and other small state businesses were given away or sold cheaply to their managers. Approximately 14,000 Russian enterprises of medium size or larger (at least 50 employees), and many more small firms, passed from state to private ownership.[10]

After privatization, competition among small businesses benefited consumers through lower prices and higher quality. The new owner-managers of these small businesses increased efficiency and profited personally. In reorganizing these businesses, some employees were promoted and others were fired. On average, the privatization of small firms in Russia was beneficial to far more people than it caused harm, and this process generated more political support than opposition.

The story is different when we turn from small to large enterprises. Similar to other centrally planned economies, Russia created industrial giants. State ministries controlled unprofitable conglomerates making steel, automobiles, refrigerators, ships, etc. After the collapse of communism during the 1990s, the industrial ministries sought vast state subsidies to keep these conglomerates operating. The Russian state subsidized them by printing money, not by collecting taxes, which caused hyper-inflation in 1994–5.

Despite resistance from the industrial ministries, managers and reformers in government privatized many large enterprises.[11] In Magin's second stage, the state created private companies from large enterprises and distributed stock options to employees and other citizens ("voucher privatization"). The privatization process, however, included fraud, intimidation and political chicanery. Against the background of ineffective laws, insiders were able to expropriate the holdings of outsiders.[12] Foreseeing this result, outsiders who owned a few vouchers in large firms sold them to insiders at trivial prices.

---

7 Paul Stephan argues that Gorbachev abandoned central planning with the aim of supporting the Communist Party's power by taxing a market economy, but he could not retain political control for the Communist Party as the economy privatized. See Stephan (1996, 1993).

8 Magin (2003).

9 This is called "spontaneous nomenklatura privatization".

10 Andrei Shleifer and Daniel Treisman, *Without a Map, Political Tactics and Economic Reform in Russia*, MIT Press, 2001, page 9. This figure covers the years 1991 to 1995, whereas Magin's characterizes the first state of privatization as the years 1990–1994.

11 See Shleifer and Treisman (2001: 13).

12 The "control premium" – the difference in the price per share when someone buys a few shares of stock, and the price per share when someone buys a controlling block of shares increases with the number of unresolved corporate governance problems of public companies.

What began as dispersed ownership of options ended in concentrated ownership of stock.[13]

Many scholars believed that rapid privatization of socialist firms and dispersed ownership of shares would stimulate legal reform in order to protect property rights. They were wrong. Former managers and tycoons with access to finance bought under-priced firms and took control. Their political influence was so great that protecting property rights seemed unnecessary to them. Instead, they blocked the development of laws for capital markets, as well as laws against self-dealing and stripping a firm of its assets. The private owners of large enterprises, who were known as the "oligarchs," preferred to manipulate politics and demanded property rights only after the Russian state regained power and used it against some of them.[14]

The economic effects of privatizing large enterprises were mixed. Some industries modernized, ended dependence on subsidies and sold goods at competitive prices. In other industries, closing unprofitable plants caused local unemployment which harmed entire communities, and buyers faced high prices from private firms with monopoly power. Privatizing large enterprises benefited many Russians and harmed others. The process generated controversy and disagreement, not consensus.

Magin's next stage, 1998–2001, represents the response to this controversy and disagreement. In this period, Boris Yeltsin yielded the presidency of Russia to Vladimir Putin, who vigorously re-asserted central authority and brought the oligarchs under government control.[15] With more centralized power, the government slowed runaway inflation by resisting the demands of industries for state subsidies.

In this stage, however, politicization replaced privatization as the dynamic of change for large enterprises. Successful operation of large enterprises now required the protection and participation of politicians. Unrealistic tax laws in Russia created tax liabilities on paper that few firms could pay. Given this fact, politicians were able to threaten the owners of firms with prosecution for tax evasion, fraud and other crimes. To settle their tax arrears and avoid criminal prosecution, politicians sometimes required an owner to transfer his firm or its

---

13 Magin (2003) describes several causes of concentrations. The banks that organized auctioning of shares were also buyers, so they manipulated the process to direct shares to themselves or to associated companies. Inflation pauperized workers and caused them to sell their shares to wealthy people. Inflation also caused the state to borrow money from 1995 to 1998. The lenders were the oligarchs who got shares as collateral. When the state defaulted, the oligarchs kept the shares.

14 Hoff and Stiglitz (2002).

15 Some oligarchs were expropriated under threat of imprisonment. Others were bought, notably by giving them the privilege of buying high yielding government bonds. See Shleifer and Treisman (2001: 13).

assets to another firm controlled by politicians.[16] Politicization disrupts property law and capital markets – why buy what you can take? Politicization also deflects wealth-seeking towards influence, not production. On balance, politicizing firms harms the economy as a whole and benefits some politicians and their friends.

In discussing Russia's recent history, we distinguish between privatizing small firms, privatizing large enterprises, and politicizing large firms. Concepts from welfare economics explain the essential difference in these three examples.[17] In the first example of privatizing small firms, many gain and a few lose. Following this logic to its conclusion leads to changes that benefit some people without harming *anyone*. A "Pareto gain" – to use the technical term for this concept – has winners and no losers.[18] Some legal reforms approximate Pareto gains, such as privatizing small enterprises in Russia.[19]

The second example, privatizing large enterprises, has many winners and many losers. Judging on the basis of evidence from around the world, the firms in most industries will ultimately perform better under private ownership than under state control. Almost everywhere, the economy has benefited from private ownership in such industries as steel, automobiles, refrigerators and ships. When a legal change benefits the winners more than it harms the losers, the change is a net gain by the standard of cost-benefit analysis.[20]

In the third example of politicizing large firms, a few politicians gain a lot and the economy as a whole suffers. When the sum of the costs exceeds the sum of the benefits, the change is a net loss by the cost-benefit standard.[21]

Table 22.1 depicts the three types of Russian legal reforms: Pareto gains, net gains, and net losses. Here we relate these to the political support and opposition provoked by them. Most people favor reforms when they expect to gain from them, and, conversely, they oppose reforms when they expect to lose. Because few lose from reforms that approximate Pareto gains, such reforms provoke the smallest number of opponents and can often proceed by consensus, an example of which is the privatization of small Russian firms. By contrast,

16 Frydman et al. (1996a), Frydman et al. (1996b).

17 Dixit (1987); Acemoglu and Robinson (2000).

18 Vilfredo Pareto, a 19th century Swiss economist, first recognized the centrality of these changes to economic analysis.

19 The paradigm in economic theory for Pareto gains is exchange in free markets. In the absence of coercion or misinformation, exchange creates a surplus that the parties share to their mutual benefit.

20 The paradigm for a net gain is state provision of a local public good such as a road. Commuters ideally gain from driving on a road much more than taxpayers lose from paying for it. Those taxpayers lose who pay for the road, but do not use it, such as pedestrians who do not drive. There is a net gain for society, but some individuals lose.

21 The paradigm for a net loss is a cartel. The members of the cartel gain less in monopoly profits than consumers lose from higher prices.

reforms with net gains divide people into winners and losers, and the former usually outnumber the latter, as, for example, with privatizing large Russian firms. A majority usually (but not always) favors reforms with net gains. Finally, when legal changes cause net losses, the losers usually outnumber the winners, as with politicizing large Russian firms. A minority usually (but not always) favors legal changes with net losses.

Table 22.1 *Welfare and politics*

Name	Economics	Politics
Pareto gain	All win	Consensus
Net gain	More win than lose	Majority
Net loss	More lose than win	Minority

3. Pareto Reform, Information and Identity

The boundary between Pareto-improving and cost-benefit gains is not as clear and fixed as might appear at first glance. It depends on the level of information in society. If all members of a society are perfectly informed about their own position and how the reforms affect them, the set of Pareto-improving reforms is small compared to cost-benefit reforms. If, however, all members of the society act behind a veil of ignorance, reforms which are in line with general notions of efficiency, equity and fairness become possible. Behind the veil of ignorance the gains and losses from a reform are randomly distributed among the members of society. Consequently, any wealth-increasing reform becomes Pareto improving ex ante and can in principle generate unanimous consent. To illustrate: in the USA and the EU, almost all citizens are sometimes pedestrians and sometimes car drivers. Assume that the most efficient new traffic regulation or safety standard can save the lives of 1000 car drivers and only 100 pedestrians, whereas the second-best regulation would save the lives of 300 pedestrians and 300 car drivers. There is little doubt that almost all US and EU citizens would prefer the first regulation, since they are behind a veil of ignorance and therefore prefer the regulation which saves the highest number of lives. In a country like India, however, poor people are always pedestrians and never car drivers. They cannot profit from a regulation which saves the lives of car drivers. Therefore while a new safety regulation might be uncontroversial in the USA or the EU, where it leads to an ex ante Pareto gain, the same reform proposal might lead to political strife in a country such as India, where it leads only to a cost-benefit gain. And the second reform might be politically preferred even though it saves fewer lives.

Provided that all citizens act behind a veil of ignorance for all wealth-increasing reforms, all those reforms become Pareto gains. Such situations seldom arise. But deep crisis can create a situation of general uncertainty about future status and wealth and can wipe out interest groups. Such constitutional moments[22] in the history of nations can allow far-reaching constitutional reform. Full information and the veil of ignorance are endpoints on a scale of possible information distributions, when deciding whether a reform is of the Pareto-improving or cost-benefit type. Usually, there is some asymmetric information in society, marking an interim stage between full information and the veil of ignorance. Some players are better informed than others about what the consequence of reform might be for them. The more members of society shift from full information to the veil of ignorance, the larger is the set of Pareto-improving reforms and the easier it is to introduce far-reaching wealth-increasing institutional changes.

Politics must not wait for a constitutional moment. A "veil of ignorance" descends when political randomizing obscures the identity of future winners and losers. Growth with random winners and losers is similar to a game where two players each pay a dollar to draw straws and the winner gets five dollars. The game creates an *expected* gain for everyone in the statistical sense,[23] or an "expected Pareto gain." To overcome opposition, include more classes of people in the innovation game by opening competition. Politics too can diffuse the costs of growth. When many people each bear a small proportion of the costs of growth, their opposition will probably remain passive, like urban taxpayers subsidizing farmers. Passing costs onto taxpayers or consumers pacifies opponents by diffusing the costs.[24]

These policies often combine and interact. Thus, joining the World Trade Organization requires a country to lower its tariffs, which stimulates the economy as a whole and depresses some industries. To overcome opposition, the government may retrain impacted workers (buyoff), pay for retraining with taxes (dispersed costs) and increase uncertainty by lowering many tariffs all at once (randomize).

---

22 The term "Constitutional Moment" is borrowed from Bruce Ackerman. He, however, uses it in a different way, as a revolutionary and mass supported, but consensual, way of changing the constitution, such as during the birth of the the USA, in contrast to constitutional change by elite political management, such as via the treaties of Rome to Lisbon in modern Europe. See Ackerman (1992).

23 In statistical terms, each player expects to win 1.5, so playing the game makes everyone better off ex ante than not playing the game. Ex post, however, one person wins 4 and the other loses 1.

24 Note that diffuse costs pacify opponents, and diffuse benefits pacify proponents. When diffuse benefits pacify proponents, we have a "free rider problem": everyone waits for someone else to take the initiative of enacting the growth-promoting reform.

Table 22.2 Circumventing opposition to growth-promoting reforms

Policy	Consequence
buy-off/Pareto gain	convert opponents to supporters
randomize/expected Pareto gain	convert opponents to supporters
concentrate benefits and diffuse costs	activate supporters and pacify opponents

4. Inequality, Power and Rights Protection

Some authors have argued that differentials in economic inequality can explain differentials in long-term economic growth, for instance the different economic performance of North and South America.[25] Others have argued that it is not inequality of wealth but political inequality that causes such differentials. However, there seems to be an emerging consensus that economic inequality leads to political inequality and that political inequality leads to institutions which protect existing wealth but are not conducive to economic growth.[26]

The fathers of the American constitution did everything they could to protect private property through constitutional safeguards and the division of political power. They understood that wealth owners had to be protected by a strong legal and constitutional asset shield. In the United States, many people who were engaged in the drafting of the constitution were wealthy. George Washington and Thomas Jefferson were millionaires. But none of them was so wealthy as to be able to transform wealth directly into political power. They knew that their property had to be protected by constitutional safeguards and constrained government. But they were not interested in protecting the wealth of particular individuals or families. They protected any property, but not the wealth of a particular group.

In other colonies, where European immigrants settled in large numbers, they set up institutions of property rights protection and contract enforcement that maximized their own wealth and that of their children. Colonies with few settlers were more interested in a strong and exploitative government, which maximized their wealth in the short run.[27]

Many countries with private ownership are different from the USA in the sense that the richest people are so rich that they can transform their wealth into political power and monopoly positions and need no constitutional safeguards to protect it. After the collapse of communism, Russia privatized 14,000 medium

25 Engerman et al. (1997).
26 Acemoglu and Robinson (2000).
27 Acemoglu et al. (2001).

and large enterprises. It was widely believed that rapid privatization of socialist firms would cause pressure for legal reform and better protection of property rights. It was expected that privatization would cause corporate governance problems. This would lead to a vast number of minority holders who would ask for better corporate governance rules and in general for better protection of property. This did not happen. Former managers and tycoons with access to finance bought under-priced firms and took control. These oligarchs became so rich, and there were so few of them, that they could map their wealth directly into political power to protect it. They could influence politics to such an extent that protection of property rights did not seem necessary for them. They even blocked the development of capital market law and securities law, as well as laws against self-dealing and asset stripping.[28] They did not want strong securities and exchange control and they did not get it. The oligarchs preferred to manipulate politics and demanded property rights only after the Russian state regained power and used it against some of them.

We can observe oligarchic structures in the economies of many developing countries. Claessens et al.'s (2002)[29] findings regarding ownership of corporate assets by the 15 richest families in selected Asian countries is shown in Table 22.3.

Table 22.3 Ownership of company assets by the 15 richest families in selected Asian countries (1996)

Country	Ownership of company assets (%)
Indonesia	61.7
The Philippines	55.1
Thailand	53.3
Korea	38.4
Singapore	29.9
Hong Kong	34.4
Malaysia	28.3
Taiwan	20.1
Japan	2.8

Note: This compares with 2–3% ownership of company assets by the 15 richest families in the USA.

Source: Claessens et al. (2000).

28 Hoff and Stiglitz (2002).
29 Claessens et al. (2000).

This leads to a more general observation. If a small group of families owns the land and the capital stock of a country, this group is not interested in the legal protection of property rights. Wealth translates directly into power. Such groups can sometimes better serve their interests if they coordinate their mutual problems outside the law and manipulate politics rather than submit to the rule of law. They are not interested in constraining government discretion by the strong rule of law. Even a law which effectively protects their property is less valuable for them than direct protection through a discretionary state working in their interests. Property law protects each and every property. It does not protect monopoly positions. It provides chances for small properties to get bigger. It does not protect large properties against risk and it undermines the position of oligarchs and monopolists.

If oligarchs are interested in laws at all, they take an interest in the legal protection of their monopoly positions, not in the legal protection of those who might destroy them. Therefore a fundamental difference exists between laws that protect property and laws that protect wealth. Economic theory tells us that private cartels are inherently unstable, as it always pays to defect. They become more stable if they are supported and enforced by law. Import restrictions, import duties, licensing laws and unfair trade practice laws are the kinds of law demanded by oligarchs. Such legal norms can cement monopolies and stabilize cartels. The legal system they represent is a rule *by* law rather than the rule *of* law. In an oligarchic society with monopolistic firms the commitment problem can render it impossible to introduce a growth-oriented rule of law in exchange for side payments, even if the gains might be gigantic.

In more general terms, it seems that oligarchic societies, in which a small minority owns the majority of land and capital, have great difficulties in establishing legal rules which trigger entrepreneurial innovations outside the dominant industries. Empirically negative correlations between growth and inequality in cross-country studies have been found by Alesina and Rodrick (1994), Persson and Tabellini (1994) and Perotti (1996).[30]

Extreme inequality leads to concentration of political power and blocks a rule of law conducive to growth. A symmetric pattern emerges in societies with extreme equality.

Extreme equality of wealth is by definition not compatible with the protection of property rights. Whenever a property right leads to its owner having more than average wealth, equality requires the dilution of such wealth by taxes and wealth-sharing rules. This destroys the profitability of new ideas.

The establishment of constrained government and the rule of law is therefore not a know-how problem. And there is no guarantee that a political system can

30 Alesina and Rodrick (1994); Persson and Tabellini (1994); Perotti (1996).

change the institutions to promote growth, however large the overall benefits might be.

If small groups benefit greatly from lawlessness and large groups benefit from the rule of law, but with a smaller gain per capita, this adds to the collective choice problem inherent in any provision of public goods. The potential winners have less incentive to organize than the potential losers.

Table 22.4 Power, politics, and law

Power	Politics	Law
extreme inequality	oligarchy	power and no law
moderate inequality	majority	law and rights
Strict equality	minority	law and no rights

5. Logic of Reform in China

Now we turn to some important historical examples of overcoming opposition to growth-promoting reforms. Chinese reforms generated economic growth rates of 9% per year for more than 25 years, reduced absolute poverty from 25% to less than 5% of the population, and increased life expectancy from 64 to over 70 years.[31] China proceeded by "dual track development," which means adopting a different approach for the traditional socialist sector of heavy industry and for the free sector of light industry. The socialist sector mostly continued under state planning in its traditional way. As socialist industries stagnated, workers, directors and party members kept their jobs. Meanwhile China unleashed the free sector, especially in light industries. The free sector escaped bureaucratic controls and retained most of its profits. Under the dual track system, the socialist sector remains shielded from competition and declines gradually, while the free sector grows quickly, raises national income, and creates better jobs for the young and adventurous.

The dual track system can be viewed as a political deal between the socialist and free sectors to share the benefits of growth. Instead of abruptly privatizing the socialist sector, the state gradually shrinks its employment while sustaining wages. Meanwhile, incomes increase rapidly for entrepreneurs and successful employees in the free sector. The party and the state bureaucracy allow people to keep most of the wealth that they make – the burden from taxes and corruption is modest. Party chairman Deng Xiao Ping promoted reforms with the slogan: "For everyone to get rich, some must get rich first." This aphorism suggests

[31] Qian (2001).

that reforms will benefit everyone at uneven rates. Everyone gets a little richer and inequality increases as entrepreneurs in the free sector get a lot richer first.

Communist and state officials support the free sector because they benefit from its growth. In the free sector, individuals often share ownership of firms with local and regional governments. Entrepreneurs thus include private people and some officials in the Communist Party and the state. People who acquire political power in the Communist Party and the state also have opportunities to acquire wealth.

Like China, Pareto growth was the development strategy adopted in Japan, the Republic of Korea, Taiwan, Hong Kong and Singapore. As they opened their markets to domestic and international competition in the 1950s, these countries developed instruments to share the surplus and diffuse the costs, so almost everyone gained. The instruments were in part public services such as schools, hospitals and rural infrastructure, and in part, they were legal forms, such as land reform and judicial independence. Also these countries protected new wealth from confiscation and predation. These policies encouraged economic transformation without legal or political disruption. The result approximates a Pareto gain with an unequal distribution of the surplus.[32]

It should also be noted that many people in East Asia were able to start new businesses and rise in the social hierarchy. Open competition among entrepreneurs, which requires a legal framework that protects economic liberty, naturally randomizes the winners and losers from growth. China offers its people an economic lottery with good odds on winning, so they are eager to play. Growth-promoting reforms spread a veil of ignorance over future winners and losers.[33]

6. The Loser's Dilemma in Economic Growth

We explained how the Chinese government successfully used three strategies to overcome opposition to growth-promoting reforms. Why isn't every country like China? Why do governments reject growth-promoting reforms with Pareto

---

[32] In the language of Campos and Root (1996: 175), these countries made "credible commitments" to property owners that secured "the political foundation of economic rights." Campos and Root stress the advantages of policies that not only cause Pareto gains, but also convince the public of the state's commitment to such policies. Their account of Asia's success is very similar to ours.

[33] The "veil of ignorance" is the famous phrase used by John Rawls in his magisterial book, *A Theory of Justice* (1971). Rawls connects ignorance with fairness, because people are more nearly impartial about a law when they do not know who will win and lose. Ackerman suggests that the veil of ignorance can descend historically when a society faces a large constitutional crisis and everyone is uncertain about the future. This is one kind of "constitutional moment." See Ackerman (1992).

gains or expected Pareto gains?[34] Reforms usually require a political bargain with an inherent obstacle that we will explain by the "dictator's dilemma."

General Augusto Pinochet staged a military coup against the government of Chile in 1973. After ruling the country as dictator for more than a decade, he eventually returned political offices to civilians in a process ending with his resignation as head of state in 1990. He remained head of the army until he stepped down from that position in 1998. In 2004 he was arrested and charged with various crimes. He died in 2006 before most criminal charges were resolved by courts. This story depicts a dilemma: an aging dictator wants to resign from power, and his countrymen agree, but he fears prosecution for crimes. The dictator's dilemma is that his only effective guarantee against prosecution is to retain the power that he wants to relinquish.

The dictator's dilemma exemplifies a general problem of trust in politics. The proponents of growth-promoting legal reforms may want to buy off the opposition, but the reformers may be unable to commit legally to providing the losers with subsidies, retraining, tax breaks, protection against competition, etc. They cannot commit because the law preserves their right to change their minds later. A future government can legally repeal almost any policy or law made by the current government.[35] The many who benefit from growth may want to buy off the few who oppose it, but the political bargain is not legally enforceable. The *loser's dilemma in economic growth* is that growth erodes the political power that guarantees his share in the gains.

A historical example from India illustrates this problem. Before independence, India contained many states where maharajas ruled and owned much of the land. Abolishing these states had many advantages for India, including removing local impediments to development. Societies in which a small minority owns most of the land and capital often have difficulties establishing legal rules that broadly trigger entrepreneurial innovations broadly. As compensation for the transfer of their states into the Union of India and their loss of tax income in 1947, the maharajas were granted a subsidy called the "Privy Purse." However, the subsidy was revoked in 1975.[36] In general, political commitment is especially problematic when the bargain extends for years, as with the Privy

---

[34] Economists sometimes summarize these facts by saying "There is no political Coase Theorem." The Coase Theorem is the proposition that people can always achieve the surplus from bargains when transaction costs are not too high. This proposition is more true of individual choices than of collective choices. Coase (1960).

[35] A legislature sometimes enacts a statute forbidding its repeal by a future legislature, but most constitutions give the legislature broad powers that effectively preclude such "entrenchment."

[36] The government tried to abolish the privy purse by an executive order, which the Supreme Court ruled unconstitutional in 1971. Parliament subsequently abolished it by an amendment of the Indian constitution in 1975 (Sorabjee 2006).

Purse. "Grandfather clauses" that preserve minority privileges look worse to the majority as memory fades of the bargain that created them.

7. Calming Disagreements about Redistribution

Like the double-trust dilemma of innovation, the dictator's dilemma is a problem of trust with no perfect solution.[37] The best solution aligns the interests of the reformers and the groups harmed by growth-promoting reforms. To align interests, the parties bargain and make agreements, but they are seldom legally enforceable. Political deals often need to encompass groups with a history of confrontation, not cooperation. The dictator's dilemma is more severe than the innovator's dilemma because politics involves more confrontation and less cooperation than business.[38] To avoid prosecution, Pinochet needed political cooperation from families whose members he had imprisoned.

Trust has no magic solution, but a general strategy for building it in business also applies to politics. Two executives begin discussing the promising and dangerous possibility of merging their companies. They agree to meet for lunch each Tuesday to discuss the matter. Should they take turns to pay the bill for lunch, or should each buy his own lunch? Behavior at lunch may reveal something about their traits that helps to predict behavior in a merger. By taking turns to pay, they will be able to see whether the other party orders inexpensive wine when he pays and expensive wine when the other party pays. After a lot of lunches, they may start to trust each other. The general strategy for building trust is to break reliance down into many small steps and spread them over time.

People concentrate on making wealth when they believe that they will be able to keep most of it. Security in property builds gradually over years, like building trust over many lunches. To illustrate, in common law countries like Canada and India, judges create fundamental property law through the gradual accretion of precedents. Over time, the common law creates a baseline of secure property rights. Security of property requires the calming of redistributive disputes. Calm descends when most people accept the broad division of wealth that property law yields. Once citizens feel secure against others taking their property, they can accept moderately adverse redistributions of wealth by taxes, government expenditures, statutes and regulations. In general, introducing the rule of law into a society is a deep reform which takes decades. Conversely, a political agenda that

---

37 The dictator's dilemma is a single-trust problem: The dictator gives up power first and trusts the civilian government not to prosecute him. In contrast, innovation is a double-trust problem.

38 In terms of game theory, politics has relatively more zero-sum games (redistribution), and business has more positive-sum games (production). The political philosopher Carl Schmitt famously defined the political as the sphere of conflict in which people confront each other as enemies.

goes too fast might destroy the trust necessary to secure property, and the reform might collapse like a sprinter on the starting blocks who leans too far forward.

We began by contrasting examples of gradual reforms in China and abrupt reforms in Russia. A similar historical case contrasts agricultural reform in France in the late 18th century and Prussia in the early 19th century. The French national assembly abolished the feudal system in a sweeping reform in 1789. By abolishing feudal obligations, the peasants ceased to be serfs. In addition, the reforms redistributed aristocratic lands among the peasants, which impoverished aristocrats. (Besides losing their wealth, many lost their heads.) The reforms created the framework for markets in land and also disrupted property rights and unleashed redistributive disputes. Production grew in the long run, but slowly. In 1851, agricultural productivity per worker in France still amounted to only 44% of the British level.[39]

Prussia, in contrast, wanted modernization without revolution, so it crafted reforms that benefited both peasants and aristocrats. Under the feudal system, serfs kept part of the harvest and gave the rest to their lords. Furthermore, each side was tied to the other by feudal bonds that restricted freedom of contract. To modernize the system, reforms from 1807 to 1822 applied a simple formula: the peasants had to buy themselves out of serfdom by transferring up to half of the land to the lords. Both sides were freed from feudal restrictions, including compulsory labor. Like France, Prussian land reform created a framework for markets in agricultural land and labor, but, unlike France, Prussian reforms enlisted the support of landlords and peasants by benefiting both. As a result, the transition was relatively smooth and production rose. Two widely used measures of productivity, production per worker and production per unit of arable farm land, increased by 60% and 44% respectively over the relevant period between 1800 and 1850. In contrast, during the four previous centuries, agricultural productivity had barely advanced.[40]

The rule of law comes partly from constitutions that distribute power to offices and rights to citizens. For example, the constitution of the United States played this role to calm the uncertainties created by the American Revolution. Many of the statesmen who created the USA's constitution were wealthy, but no one was rich enough to transform his wealth directly into political power. They secured their property through the division of political power and constitutional rights.[41] As constitutional protection proved effective, redistributive disputes calmed down and economic growth soared.

---

39 Clark (1991).

40 Figures taken from Helling (1966: 134 and 139). The latter figure refers to cereal products only for the whole of Germany. It remains, however, debatable how much of these productivity gains can be attributed to the reforms.

41 See Federalist Papers 10 and 51.

Iceland in the 17th and 18th centuries is a case where vested interests blocked economic reform, with tragic consequences described by Eggertsson.[42] From the late Middle Ages to the 19th century, laws required all laborers and servants to live and work on farms. They could not leave the farms and work in the fishing industry. This law kept agricultural wages low, which benefited the small number of people who owned land – in 1700 around 80 individuals owned 50% of the total arable land. People were forbidden to become fishermen even in years of famine when they suffered from hunger while local waters teemed with fish. Shifting labor to more productive uses could, in principle, have benefited workers and landlords, but, instead of finding a way to share the gains, the landlords opposed change. A similar story is told about the Caribbean plantation islands in the 18th century, where an oligarchy of landowners resisted new opportunities and technologies. In general, oligarchic societies in which a small minority owns most of the land and capital have difficulty establishing legal rules that trigger entrepreneurial innovations outside of the dominant industries that they control.

8. Conclusions

The many who win from economic growth can overcome the few who lose, and economic analysis shows how. Three principles provide a guide to activating support and pacifying opposition to pro-growth reforms. First, a more comprehensive political bargain that uses subsidies, taxes, and privileges turns losers from economic growth into winners (Pareto gain), which turns opponents into supporters. Second, short of turning losers into winners, a more comprehensive bargain spreads the losses, which pacifies opponents. Third, more open competition among entrepreneurs gives more people the possibility of winning the innovation lottery (expected Pareto gain), which turns opponents into supporters. Conversely, concentrating the losses from economic growth on a small group of people activates their opposition and, if they are powerful, they may frustrate policies that benefit the nation. In principle, giving them more of the gains from economic growth can buy them off or pacify them, but doing so requires guaranteeing a share of the gains from growth. Guarantees are difficult since every policy or law can be repealed or amended. In politics, credible guarantees mostly depend on the recipient's power against the guarantor, which poses a dilemma. Since power accompanies wealth in politics, economic growth that realigns wealth also redistributes power. The loser's dilemma is that economic growth erodes the power that guarantees his share in the gains. While this dilemma has no perfect solution, something can be done. Doing something requires evolving institutions, not just enacting laws. Laws

---

42 Eggertsson (2005) chapter 7.

and social norms must be braided into institutions that strengthen each other like the strands in a rope. Trust develops from a history of cooperation, like taking turns to buy lunch. If not cooperation, then a history of fair competition can develop trust, like tennis players refereeing their own games. By solving trust problems, law helps to end the poverty of nations through economic innovation and political reforms.

References

Acemoglu, D. (2003), "Why Not a Political Coase Theorem? Social Conflict, Commitment, and Politics", *Journal of Comparative Economics*, 31(2003), 620–52

Acemoglu, D., S. Johnson and J.A. Robinson (2001), "The Colonial Origins of Comparative Development: An Empirical Investigation", *American Economic Review*, 91(5), 1369–401.

Acemoglu, D. and J.A. Robinson (2000), "Political Losers as a Barrier to Economic Development," *American Economic Review*, 90, 126–30.

Acemoglu, D. and J.A. Robinson (2006) "Persistence of Power, Elites and Institutions," NBER Working Paper No. 12108.

Ackerman, B. (1992), *The Future of Liberal Revolution*, New Haven, CT: Yale University Press.

Alesina, A., R. Baqir and W. Easterly (1999), "Public Goods and Ethnic Divisions", *Quarterly Journal of Economics*, 114(4), 1243–84.

Alesina, A. and D. Rodrik (1994), "Distributive Politics and Economic Growth", *Quarterly Journal of Economics*, 109(2), May.

Bardhan, P. (1999), "Understanding Underdevelopment: Challenges for Institutional Development from the Point of View of Poor Countries", *Journal of Institutional and Theoretical Economics*, 156, 216–45.

Bardhan, P. (2004), *Scarcity, Conflicts and Cooperation: Essays in Political and Institutional Economics of Development*, Cambridge, MA: MIT Press.

Bleiber, H. (1993), "Die Preußischen Agrarreformen, in der Geschichtsschreibung der DDR". in B. Sösemann (ed.), *Gemeingeist und Bürgersinn, die Preußischen Reformen*, Berlin: Duncker and Humblot, pp. 109–25.

Campos, J.E. and H. Root (1996), *The Key to the Asian Miracle, Making Shared Growth Credible*, Washington, DC: Brookings Institution Press.

Claessens, S., S. Djankov and L. Lang (2000), "The separation of Ownership and Control in East Asian Corporations", *Journal of Financial Economics*, 58, 81–112.

Clark, G. (1991), "Labour Productivity in English Agriculture 1300–1860", in B.M.S. Campbell and M. Overton, *Agricultural Productivity in the European Past*, Manchester: Manchester University Press, 211–35

Coase, R. (1960), "The Problem of Social Cost", *Journal of Law and Economics*, 3, 1–44.

Daniels, R.J. and M.J. Trebilcock (2004), "The Political Economy of Rule of Law Reform in Developing Countries", Manuscript.

Dixit, A. (1987), "On Pareto-Improving Distributions of Aggregate Economic Gains", *Journal of Economic Theory*, 41(1) 133–53.

Eggertsson, T. (2005), *Imperfect Institutions, Possibilities and Limits of Reform*, Ann Arbor, MI: University of Michigan Press, 99–127.

Engerman, S.L. and K.L. Sokoloff (1997), "Factor Endowments, Institutions, and Differential Growth Paths among New World Economies," in Stephen Haber, ed., *How Latin America Fell Behind*, Stanford, CA: Stanford University Press.

Frydman, R., K. Pistor and A. Rapaczynski (1996a), "Investing in Insider-Dominated Firms: A Study of Russian Voucher Privatization Funds", in Frydman et al. (eds.), *Corporate Governance in Central Europe and Russia, Vol. 1: Banks, Funds, and Foreign Investors*, Central European University Press.

Frydman, R., K. Pistor and A. Rapaczynski (1996b), "Exit and Voice after Mass Privatization: The Case of Russia", *European Economic Review*, 40(3–5), April, 581–8.

Hall, R.E. and C.I. Jones (1999), "Why Do Some Countries Produce So Much More Output per Worker than Others?" *Quarterly Journal of Economics*, 114(1), 83–116.

Helling, G. (1996), "Die Entwicklung der Agrarproduktivität in der deutschen Landwirtschaft im 19. Jahrhundert", *Jahrbuch für Wirtschaftsgeschichte*, 1, 129–41.

Hoff, K. and J. Stiglitz (2002), "After the Big Bang? Obstacles to the Emergence of the Rule of Law in Post-Communist Societies," National Bureau of Economic Research Working Paper 9282.

Human Development Report (1983–2008), New York: Human Development Report Office, United Nations Development Programme.

Machiavelli, N. *The Prince* (1513), chapter VI, available at http://www.liberliber.it/biblioteca/m/machiavelli/il_principe/html/princi_a.htm.

Magin, Konstantin (2003), "Corruption in Russia in the 1990s: A Time Bomb or a Necessity of Business?" Ph.D dissertation, Department of Economics, University of California at Berkeley.

Perotti, R. (1996), "Growth, Income Distribution and Democracy: What the Data Say", *Journal of Economic Growth*, 1(2), 149–87.

Persson, Torsten and Guido Tabellini (1994), "Is Inequality Harmful for Growth?", *American Economic Review*, 84(3), June, 600–21.

Qian, Yingyi (2001), "How Reform Worked in China", UC Berkeley, Discussion Paper, 2001, 1–63.

Rawls, J. (1971), "A Theory of Justice", Cambridge, MA: Belknap Press of Harvard University Press.

Rodrik, D., (2006), "Goodbye Washington Consensus, Hello Washington Confusion? A Review of the World Bank's Economic Growth in the 1990s: Learning from a Decade of Reform", *Journal of Economic Literature*, 44(4), December, 973–87.

Rodrik, D., A. Subramanian and F. Trebbi (2004), "Institutions Rule: The Primacy of Institutions over Geography and Integration in Economic Development", *Journal of Economic Growth*, 9, 131–65.

Shleifer, A. and D. Treisman (2001), *Without a Map: Political Tactics and Economic Reform in Russia*, Cambridge, MA: MIT Press.

Sorabjee, S.J. (2006), "Palkhivala and the Constitution of India", in M.G.N. Kuma (ed.), *Nani Plakhivala A Role Model for India*, Delhi: Universal Law Publ. Co., pp. 46–61.

Stephan, P. (1993a), "The Fall – Understanding the Collapse of the Soviet System," *Suffolk University Law Review*, 29(1996): 17–49.

Stephan, P. (1993b), "Privatization after Perestroika: The Impact of State Structure," *Whittier Law Review*, 14, 403–26.

Trubek, D.M. and M. Galanter (1974), "Scholars in Self-Estrangement: Some Reflections on the Crisis in Law and Development," *Wisconsin Law Review*, 1062–101.

Vogel, B. (1980), "Introduction", in B. Vogel, (ed.) *Preussische Reformen 1807–1820*, Königstein/Ts: Verlagsgruppe Athenäum, Hain, Scriptor, Hanstein. pp. 1–29.

Williamson, J. (1993) "Democracy and the 'Washington Consensus'", *World Development*, 21(8), 1329–36.

World Resources Institute (2010), Rule of Law Index, available at http://earthtrends.wri.org/searchable_db/index.

Index